Melancholy, Love, and Time

Melancholy, Love, and Time

Boundaries of the Self in Ancient Literature

Peter Toohey

THE UNIVERSITY OF MICHIGAN PRESS
Ann Arbor

Published in the United States of America by
The University of Michigan Press
Manufactured in the United States of America
∞ Printed on acid-free paper
2007 2006 2005 2004 4 3 2 1

A CIP catalog record for this book is available from the British Library.

Library of Congress Cataloging-in-Publication Data

Toohey, Peter, 1951–
Melancholy, love, and time : boundaries of the self in ancient literature / Peter Toohey.
p. cm.
Includes bibliographical references and index.
ISBN 0-472-11302-X (cloth : alk. paper)
1. Classical literature—History and criticism. 2. Psychology in literature. 3. Alienation (Social psychology) in literature. 4. Mythology, Classical, in literature. 5. Depression, Mental, in literature. 6. Melancholy in literature. 7. Love in literature. 8. Time in literature. 9. Self in literature. I. Title.
PA3015.P78 T66 2004
880′.09—dc22 2003016901

ACKNOWLEDGMENTS: I would like to acknowledge the following institutions and organizations for granting me permission to reprint the various figures in this book: for the Eumenides Painter's "The Purification of Orestes" (fig. 1), Art Resource N.Y.; for "Greek Mourning" (fig. 3), the British Museum; for Exekias's "The Suicide of Ajax" (fig. 7), the Château-Musée of Boulogne-sur-Mer, and for his "Achilles and Ajax" (fig. 8), Photo Vatican Museums; for "Zeus malinconico" (fig. 6) and for the Pompeian wall painting of Narcissus (fig. 9), the Ministero per i beni e le attività culturali, soprintendenza per i beni archaeologici delle province di Napoli e Caserta; for Giorgio de Chirico's *The Melancholy of a Beautiful Day* (fig. 13), the Royal Museum of Fine Arts, Brussels, Belgium, and for his remaining paintings (figs. 10 and 12–17), the Estate of Giorgio de Chirico / SIAE (Rome) / SODRAC (Montréal) 2002; for Arnold Böcklin's *Odysseus and Calypso* (fig. 11), the Öffentliche Kunstsammlung Basel, Kunstmuseum (photo credit: Öffentliche Kunstsammlung Basel, Martin Bühler).

For Mollie

Contents

Figures

Introduction

Methinks he is either melancholick, or one of those academick asses

—ROBERT BURTON, *Philosophaster*

The expostulation by Burton that serves as the epigraph for this introduction has often been leveled at me because of my interest in the subject of melancholy and boredom. It has been sometimes assumed that I am subject to the emotions myself or that I am the victim of a misplaced and pedantic obscurantism. I hope this book will demonstrate that neither assumption is necessarily correct.

My main concern is to demonstrate that there took place in the first and second centuries of our era (and to a lesser extent in the early Hellenistic period) a shift in the presentation of the self and of self-consciousness in certain key works of the literature of antiquity. There is—or was—a marked change in the mode by which such affective states as melancholia, love, lovesickness, and boredom and such affective registers as time (I mean this seriously) and even leisure (my topics for this book) are presented.[1] Increasingly, I will argue, they become a locus through which the self and self-consciousness gain vivid representation. There is, it appears to me, a thickening or a deepening of the manner by which these emotions and, flowing from this, the self are represented. The presentation, not just of self, but also of self-consciousness, is far more detailed and far more evident in these periods than it is in earlier literature.[2] This is a sense of self (or self-consciousness or self-definition, but not self-knowledge in the Socratic sense) as constituted by inwardness. It is built upon an opposition of "inside-outside," a partitioning off of the self from the world about us. (And so it is with the various emotions and psychological registers upon which I shall focus.) "Thoughts, ideas, or feelings . . . [are] 'within' us, while the objects in the world which these mental states bear on are 'without,'" states Charles Taylor in a different context (1992, 111–12). He continues to observe that "[human] capacities or potentialities [are] 'inner,' awaiting the development which will manifest them or realize them in a public world." So it is in this period, but at a cost.

We tend to associate such a presentation of self with recent, post-Enlightenment literary and social experience (e.g., Porter 1997; Mascuch 1997). Part of the purpose of this book (as was the case for Golden and Toohey 1997) is to demonstrate the comparability of this novel experience between its ancient and modern literary representations. To this end I have adduced a number of parallels between the later ancient and modern depiction of emotions such as those already noted—melancholia, boredom, lovesickness, suicidal urges, and the experience of time. The modern parallels for these emotions and for the presentation of self through them are drawn from a promiscuous body of material: novels, nonfiction books, newspapers, art, and ethnological reports. I have used a very broad range of evidence both modern and ancient: Greek and Roman prose and verse authors, Greek and Roman painting, modern prose and painting, and modern newspapers, magazines, and television. As Robert Burton might have objected, the resultant effect may seem at times to produce a "rhapsody of rags gathered together from several dunghills." Notwithstanding such colorful objections, the citation of such material seemed to me to be the best way to go about demonstrating sameness. The range of evidence is justified because I am trying to demonstrate the similarities between the ancient and modern depictions of the various registers of the sentiments or sentimental registers surveyed in this book. In this way I intend to illustrate that these conditions were not recent inventions of periods such as the Enlightenment. How better can one illustrate parallel responses to similar stimuli than by appeal to a wide range of modern parallels?

To insist upon this sameness as it relates to the emergence and maintenance of human affectivities and psychological registers, as they are depicted in ancient and modern cultural and literary experience, is to insist these are not specific cultural or social artifacts. At any rate, I have demonstrated the common traits that are shared and exhibited by melancholia, boredom, lovesickness, monkish acedia, the perception and experiencing of time and leisure, and even the drive to do away with oneself. I have also looked briefly at a variety of contagious emotional states, such as the use of the evil eye, "boning," and assault by voodoo. In doing so I have attempted to show how they fit within a single experiential template. Still other matters, such as literacy, utopianism, and notions of the Golden Age, are mentioned in passing. My conclusions are that the emotional conditioning to be associated with these topics and registers exhibits a sameness as it relates one to another and through time. The responses embodied in these topics and registers are shared and even predictable. They are capable of being mapped through time, almost in a structuralist fashion.

Despite this commonality, a degree of periodization is possible for the charting of the currency of the different forms taken by these conditions. I indicated the existence of this periodization at the very outset of this introduction. Where such a periodization of the representation of emotions and of the self is possible, this seems to exist only in the simplest of senses. Thus, through time we see a simple alternation—or better perhaps, an evolutive progress—between apparent polar opposites: a movement from or between activity and passivity, body and mind (interiority), complicity and estrangement, assertion and yielding, complicity and isolation, participation and withdrawal, public and private, the mark and the sign, surface and depth, lack of control and control, and so forth. It will be my suggestion that this evolutive movement is evident in each of the affective registers treated or mentioned within this book. Thus they relate to the mapping of the self. In fact, the relations between these emotional states and their seemingly oscillating movements can almost be mapped. It is, then, partly through the movement from one set of these qualities to the other that I will attempt to establish an approximate periodization for the literary representation (the discursive representation) of emotions and of the self within the periods of the ancient world surveyed in this book.

In this book, as I have stated, I argue that there took place in the first and second centuries of our era (and to a lesser extent during the Hellenistic period) a shift in the presentation of the self in a number of key works of antiquity. This claim raises the issue of the recurrent problem, for historians of psychology and psychiatry, of whether an emotional state or sentiment is more prominently mentioned and discussed and defined in a particular era and whether this emotional state or sentiment is in fact more prevalent in that era.

To a large extent, my evidence is inconclusive. Most of the ancient witnesses that I will present are derived from literary texts. The evidence is essentially linguistic and therefore skewed by a variety of historical constraints: by genre, above all, but also by the period in which the form was used and by its host language's current linguistic resources, by the decorum of the language form itself, and even by the style of the language itself (Greek or Latin) in its regional and periodical base, not to mention the constraints under which individual authors composed. I have attempted to find both diachronically and synchronically parallel passages and utterances. The evidence that I present therefore tells us more, strictly speaking, about language (or discourse) than about real life. To be honest, I think that I must at least initially remain with that position, that I am in the first instance producing a conclusion that relates primarily to language or discourse. Having said this, however, my suspicion is that the increased frequency of usage in various periods points to a greater prevalence in real life.

How can this be justified? In chapter 1, I will argue that melancholia was understood in most popular ancient literature as an angry illness. This was largely the case until the middle of the first century of our era. At that point popular literature began to take an interest in melancholia of a depressive form (a type that had been long acknowledged by medical writers). This is what we understand by the term *melancholia*. Does this suddenly increased interest in depressive melancholy point to an increased prevalence of the condition in real life? Conclusions become more possible if we survey other affective conditions. The registering of the response to erotic infatuation, which I will survey in chapter 2, follows a historical trajectory seeming to match that of melancholia. In popular literature down until the middle of the first century of our era, frustrated erotic infatuation produces an active or violent reaction, that which we could term mania. Subsequently the reaction privileged in popular literature is a depressive one, of the passive and fretful character that we associate with lovesickness. Boredom, the subject of my third chapter, appears to evince a close relationship to the pattern for which I argue in the first two chapters. As a passive, named, and "spiritualized" condition, it gains real prominence in the middle of the first century of our era.

The change taking place here is probably not so much to be related to melancholia, lovesickness, or boredom proper but, rather, as I have indicated at the beginning of the introduction, to a shift in the presentation of the self and self-consciousness in a number of key works of ancient literature. There was a thickening or deepening of the manner by which the emotions I have mentioned were described, and with this came a far greater stress on interiority and passivity.[3]

My fourth chapter looks at the famous disease of monks' acedia, a form sometimes of melancholia, sometimes of boredom. Its symptoms match those outlined in chapters 1 and 3. Two aspects are of special interest in the case of acedia. First is the viral-like manner by which this illness was transmitted. One could literally catch this illness that closely resembled melancholia or boredom. Second, this illness has sufficient historical testimony to allow us to recognize that we are here dealing not with discourse but with real life. So what does this infection tell us about melancholia, lovesickness, and boredom? First, the striking resemblance between acedia and these conditions demonstrates the possibility and likelihood of a viral fashion of transmission for the conditions surveyed in chapters 1 through 3 and, relatedly, for this new mode of understanding the self. Second, the historical veracity of the existence of acedia, its transcendence of mere discourse, suggests to me that the same could be said for the new forms of melancholia, lovesickness, and boredom. We can, therefore, answer tentatively the historical question posed earlier in this introduction. In the case of the sentiments highlighted in chapters 1 through 3, their prominent mention should be equated with their prominent appearance in real life.

The affective registers surveyed in chapters 5 through 7 reinforce the conclusions that I have just put forward. Self and self-awareness seem to be registered in much the same way in reflections on suicide, time, and passing time (leisure) as in the cases of melancholia, lovesickness, and boredom. New modes of registering and reflecting on suicide, time, and leisure became prominent, I will argue, in the first century of our era. These reflect upon the presentation of self and, in its attendant vocabulary, are reliant on a language that underscores individual passivity and interiority. I have no doubt that we are here dealing with more than just discourse. The variety of the modes by which this new manner of representing the self is evident suggests to me that real life is at issue here.

Having said all of this, perhaps now I might be allowed one caveat. My periodization and my analysis aim to highlight tendencies, not rock-graven truths. Exceptions may always be found to the patterns and mappings and stratigraphies proposed here. These exceptions cannot be said to invalidate discursive realities.[4] I should also note, furthermore, that my approach to history is open-ended, even experimental. I would not wish to see what is an essentially heuristic and analytic distinction (a model more than a set of rules) transformed into an ill-founded historical dogma. Criticisms that treat my suggestions as such will miss the point.[5]

It is with some hesitation that I use the ugly, amorphous, and modish term *self* within the argument of this book.[6] I can think of no other adequate term. What makes this so difficult is that the "self" is so much a subject of debate in philosophical and political theory and in psychoanalytical circles (Alford 1991; Taylor 1992; Kohut 1971, 1977, 1985).

The debate can be as bewildering as it can be wearying. Definitions can veer wildly between two ends of a spectrum. At the one end is the apparently reasonable assumption that the self is a form of individual consciousness that uses "categories such as resemblance, succession, and causation, that provide the hidden thread holding discrete experience together" (Alford 1991, 4); at the other is Lacan's belief (1977) that "what we take to be the self is actually a symptom of our inability to accept our inauthenticity" (Alford 1991, 4). These two poles are mediated by a concept of the "social self,"[7] one that is constructed by "(1) how we imagine we appear to the other; (2) how we imagine the other judges us; and (3) pride or mortification as a consequence of number 2" (Alford 1991, 6; see too Baumeister 1986).

There are complications. The understanding of "self" will vary, depending on whether one is attempting to register and generalize upon one's own sense of self or that of another.[8] Registering that of another is perhaps easier: one looks in another person for a certain habitual style, attitude, "voice," or emotional response—character in short.[9] Registering one's own sense of self is more tricky. I suppose that the simplest way to think of this is to say that such a sense of identity (or self, or style, or voice, or character) is built on memory and the continuity it implies for potentially discrete experience.

What is memory? It, too, depends on your beliefs. In the most plain of understandings, it is consciously remembering the past and, from construing this, establishing a personal, mental continuity that holds "discrete experience together." A Freudian would want to add subconscious memory to this suggestion; a Marxist, historical and social forces; a Pythagorean, the inherited soul; a Foucaldian, discourse. All of these, if they have any phenomenological validity, may modify conscious recollection and, with this, the construction of self.

Were we, however, to focus further on this simple sense of personal self, that built on conscious memory, experience would suggest that it is not something that can survive the vicissitudes of memory. Illness, alcohol, strokes, senility, Alzheimer's disease, trauma, severe depression, drinking at the river Lethe, and many other comparable events both actual and metaphorical can destroy memory. Does this take the self with it? I would say yes. My mother, for example, had for my family and me the traces of her "self" or character after she had fallen victim to multiple infarct dementia. From my mother's point of view, however, she clearly had no sense of self as she swiftly lost her ability to recognize us and to recall her past. It had vanished as her brain came sadly to resemble Swiss cheese.[10]

The "self" that I want to look at in this book is a very simple thing.[11] It is a personal self and relates to our perception of ourselves as autonomous beings, as creatures set apart from others and from the physical world.[12] This sense of separateness is not something that all creatures possess. Small children do not seem to possess this. Freud, Piaget, and even Lacan have described this childish condition more or less concretely.[13] Many people (and I count myself among them) can recall the astonishing childhood insight that they were not part and parcel of the world around, that they had a separate existence. The very old can gradually lose this sense of separateness. Many animals, householders such as dogs and cats, can have little sense of this at all. Watch them.

Mental disease can create havoc with this human sense of separateness, by blurring dangerously the *boundaries of the self.* I could best explain what I mean by this blurring of boundaries by reference to mania and depression, on which two topics I focus much in this book. In the former state the individual easily loses a sense of himself or herself as an entity separate from the world about. There is a sort of a catastrophic communion between the individual and the world. The boundaries of the self expand outward and can become wholly blurred. We could compare the condition of the opposite pole, depression.

Here the individual becomes so drawn in on himself or herself that the outside world begins to cease to exist as a separate entity. Thus ensues a type of autistic state. The boundaries are set dangerously high but are no less blurred.

One should not confuse this form of self-awareness with the type of moral or philosophical self-knowledge urged upon us by the precept "Know thyself" or by Greek admonitions concerning the worth of the unexamined life. Nor should my use of the term *self* be confused with that relating to the *representation* of the self—in the autobiographical mode by which we represent ourselves and our apparent identity to the world (our race, gender, sexuality; our personality or "voice" or character—the normally visible *signs* of who we are) (see Mascuch 1997; Porter 1997). That "self" resembles our particular personal "signature." Scholars such as Haijo Westra (2001) or Brian Stock (1994; see too Cary 2000) suggest that the appearance of this kind of self is very late in ancient literature. They associate this with Augustine's *Confessions.* Literature to that point was dominated by topic, by a presentation of self that was conditioned more by generic constraint and even discourse than by a desire for autobiographical verisimilitude.

The "self" with which I am concerned is far less specific. I am using the term, rather, in the sense of "self-consciousness," as a sense of oneself as a sentient being, separate from those about. Such a sense of self is built on a realization that what matters is within us. It is built finally on a sense of alienation from others and from the world. Such a sense of self is not shared by all creatures. As I have noted, observe your dog or cat (on most occasions), or your very young,[14] or many of your very old.

When such a registering of self is apparent in literary texts, it is built upon an opposition of "inside-outside," a partitioning off of the self from the world about. We could speculate that the sense of self evident in such texts may evince a standing outside oneself, a concern almost to watch, to weigh up, and to react to one's emotional and physical state almost as if it were another. Such a representation of self may involve the highlighting of an individual's inner mental processes. It may involve not just a partitioning between the inner self and the outer world but also a partitioning between the body (approximating the outer world) and the self (approximating the inner world). It is as if the subject stands at a remove from his or her emotional reactions. The subject watches his or her reactions and may feel powerless in their face. There emerges a disjunction between the body and a person's consciousness of it. It is for this reason that I have made so much of Hostius Quadra in my final chapter in this book.

The sense of self I will discuss herein is built on, as I have stated, boundaries. These boundaries between the self and others and the world are not achieved with ease. Throughout one's life, they require constant renegotiation and recalibration.[15] In the first part of this book, I will demonstrate how in ancient literary experience, these boundaries could be blurred or even destroyed or could seem not to exist at all. I will illustrate the suffering that can result from the blurring of these boundaries. (So in the first four chapters of this book, I will illustrate how a variety of psychological conditions—melancholia, boredom, lovesickness, and acedia—can lead to the breakdown of the self and can lead an individual even to death.) In the second half of this book, I will illustrate how these boundaries, when threatened, can be remapped, renegotiated, and reformulated. (So, by examining some ancient experiences of suicide, time, and leisure, I will illustrate how the self can be shored up against disintegration, how it can, in the face of psychological trauma, be reformulated.) I will suggest that this process of renegotiation takes place through a self-assertion based especially upon an acceptance of alienation and estrangement. The psychological reintegration of the self is achieved through an acceptance of estrangement, or to put it another way, an acceptance of the slippery relationship between a person's "inner" and "outer" (almost words and things). This is not, I must admit, a very postmodern conclusion to reach. As good a critic of classical literature as David Wiles (1997, 14) maintains, following Lacan and others, that the self is fragmented and, in this sense, unstable. I agree with the latter definition, though not perhaps in the way meant by such Lacanians. As to the former, the protagonists I study in this book establish, almost by subterfuge, rock-solid psyches, mostly, I should emphasize, by complaining about their psychic fragility. Wiles also suggests that the self is "compounded of a series of discursive networks."[16] That this cannot be the case (and I really do wish it were the case) is illustrated again and again by the experiential sameness of reactions produced by Australian Aboriginals and in the lovesickness of Sappho, Charicleia, and Chaereas. It is illustrated above all by acedia, as I survey it in chapter 4. What can I say? The ego is autonomous and highly developed. The self is the product of pain and alienation and a product of total otherness from family, from community, and, paradoxically, even from the self itself. It is defined by the chasm, enforced on a child at a very young age, between the individual and the world about. The sense of self, at least the sense of self exhibited by the characters analyzed in this book, is permanent and durable and is formulated from a basic set of constraints. It makes itself felt in a standard set of modalities. There is, I will show, neither anything terribly new nor anything terribly fragmented about the self.

One of the more unexpected conclusions of this mode of argument is that a measure of depression is as inevitable as it is good for you. That may sound like an offensive conclusion to the many sufferers of this condition. Yet the advantages provided by the self-awareness bestowed by a modicum of depression will become apparent. At least in the realms surveyed within this book, especially in chapters 5 through 7, it seems to provide a measure of protection against the sickness brought on by the blurring of the boundaries of the self. I have argued in chapter 8 that self-awareness is built on a sense of distance from oneself, on a capacity to observe oneself. This is a type of alienation that is tantamount to mild depression (can it be any other way?). I suggest in that chapter, furthermore, that should the distance become too great, the risk run represents a type of psychological disintegration to be associated with depression. Should the gulf become too narrow, even negligible, the risk run is that of mania and autism. Self-awareness, a concomitant of mild melancholy, seems, then, to guard against the dangers of suffering major reactive depression or mania (or to put it in other words, destructive inaction versus unthinking and destructive reaction). Self-awareness, I am saying, rests on the erection of boundaries between the self and others, between the self and the physical world. The alienation resulting from this is viscerally painful, but it does highlight the need for psychological and attitudinal vigilance. Instinct, thus, is controlled only by these boundaries, I believe.[17]

I have, like any number of Australians before me, been forced to work for a considerable time in geographical isolation. It follows that this is a more personal book than it might have been otherwise. It also follows that I have fewer deep personal and institutional obligations than might be expected. It is, therefore, with all the more feeling that I must acknowledge those who have helped me. My particular thanks are owed to Professors Mark Golden, David Konstan, Elaine Fantham, and Emanuele Narducci and to Mr. Peter Dale, who between them read most of an earlier draft of the manuscript. Peter Dale allowed me to print his translations of the poetry of Gioacchino Belli. I owe especial thanks to my daughter, Kate, for alerting me to the Eumenides Painter's Orestes, for stressing to me the importance of the paintings of Giorgio de Chirico, and for collaborating with me on the appendix related to his paintings. I also thank Professor Ian Worthington, Dr. Alan Treloar, Professor David Rankin, Dr. Hanne Sigismund Nielsen, Dr. John Dearin, Professor Martin Kilmer, Dr. Tom Hillard, Professor David Sansone, Dr. Suzanne McAlister, Dr. Françoise Wemelsfelder, and Dr. John Vallance. My former colleagues Rob Baker, Minor Markle, Roger Pitcher, Iain Spence, and Greg Stanton listened to me talk about this topic for a number of years. I extend to them my gratitude for their patience and help. Brennan Wales helped me, again and again, with Italian. Various people have provided me with reading material or answered specific queries: Dr. Joan Booth, Professor Beryl Rawson, Professor Herwig Maehler, Professor Sandra Citroni Marchetti, Professor Mario Citroni, Professor Martin Cropp,

Dr. Moren Spliid, Dr. John Papadopoulos and Ms. Carrie Tovar, Dr. Jacque Clarke, Dr. Athanasios Koukopoulos, Professor Andreas Marneros, and Dr. Haijo Westra. My former colleague Dr. Ann Ghandar introduced me to, and loaned me a copy of her thesis on, Robert Burton (Bright 1970). My former student Jennifer Kenyeres generously checked many of the references for me. Some of the material in this book has appeared in rather different forms in *Illinois Classical Studies, Glotta,* and *Maia* and in several books. I have also had the good fortune of being able to try out some of my ideas on a larger, "popular" reading audience. Many thanks to the *Bulletin,* the *Age Monthly Review,* the *Canberra Times,* the *Sydney Morning Herald,* the *Australian,* and their various section editors: James Hall, the late Robert Haupt, Chris McGillion, Peter Fray, Jim Buckell, and especially Amanda Wilson.

A group of retirees from the Armidale chapter of the University of the Third Age (U3A), with whom I read the *Odyssey* in the winter of 1996, convinced me that purposelessness in literature is what really matters. I extend my gratitude to that group. It would be churlish of me if I were not to offer thanks as well to the many doubters and detractors whose reservations or outright hostility have spurred me on—in particular I would like to single out the stimulus provided me in Australia by that "wise" and "senior" individual who characterized my work with velvet animus as being the product of "that safe Australian." I hope that this "safeness" mitigates somewhat the considerable amount of unruly speculation within this book. Other audiences have assisted me in a more positive fashion with their comments at the University of New England, the University of Sydney (I especially thank Frances Muecke), the University of Winnipeg, the University of Florence (I especially thank again Emanuele Narducci), the University of Western Australia (at the Twenty-Sixth Congress of the Australian Universities Language and Literature Association in February 1991), and the University of Calgary (at the annual meeting of the Classical Association of Canada in 1994 and again in March 1999) and in Rome at a November 1999 conference of the psychiatric group devoted particularly to manic depression, the Aretaeus Society (I thank again Dr. Athanasios Koukopoulos). I began this book at the University of New England in Australia and finished it at the University of Calgary in Canada. I thank both institutions for the financial and emotional assistance they provided. I would especially like to register my gratitude to the University of Calgary for providing me with what has amounted to much more than refuge. I would also like to acknowledge the Australian Research Council, the Australian Taxation Department, the largesse of the Province of Alberta, and the austere physical support of the Lancing Naval Old Comrades Club (for that now long demolished caravan). From the University of Michigan Press, I would like to thank

Collin Ganio, who commissioned this book. It has not been possible to include, with any sort of system, bibliographical material appearing later than mid-2001. In most instances translations in this book are my own. Longer prose versions are taken or lightly adapted from the relevant Loeb volume.

Once again I'd like to acknowledge Kate, Matt, and Phyl. It was in the company of the late Bert Warr that I began first to think about this material. Thanks, Bert. My book is dedicated to Mollie, who started it.

PART I

Blurring the Boundaries of the Self

1

Sorrow without Cause

Periodizing Melancholia and Depression

> Borage and Hellebore fill two scenes
> Sovereign plants to purge the veins
> Of melancholy, and cheer the heart
> Of those black fumes which make it smart . . .
>
> —ROBERT BURTON, *The Anatomy of Melancholy*

If we did not know that it was Orestes and had not noticed that he had a sword in his hand, then we would say that the male seated in the center of the representation in figure 1 was bored. That is the usual first reaction to the painting of Orestes by the Eumenides Painter on this fourth-century B.C.E. red-figure Apulian vase from the Louvre.[1]

It is the faces. Start with Orestes. Look at his heavy, half-closed eyes and at the dissatisfied, tired, even unhappy expression on his face.[2] Notice the slight drooping forward of his head. Look, too, at the pensive and indecisive way that his right index finger seems to scratch at his chin, and notice how his body is slumped slightly in lassitude (and is supported, almost, by his left hand). Compare the other expressions, those on the faces of Apollo and Artemis (to Orestes' left). Apollo's head droops at an angle comparable to that of Orestes; his eyes seem half-closed (with the same tired line beneath the eye as has Orestes). Most striking of all, his mouth is turned down in precisely the same doleful manner as is that of Orestes. Exactly the same points could be made of the expression of Apollo's sister, Artemis, as she strides onto the scene carrying her hunting weapons. Her mouth mirrors those of Apollo and Orestes. Her head droops slightly.

Boredom is out of the question. The rite being enacted in this picture would hardly allow that emotion. The rite is one of religious purification. It is explained to us by Aeschylus in the *Eumenides* at verses 42–43 and 448–52. There we learn that before the scene depicted on this pot takes place, Orestes has fled

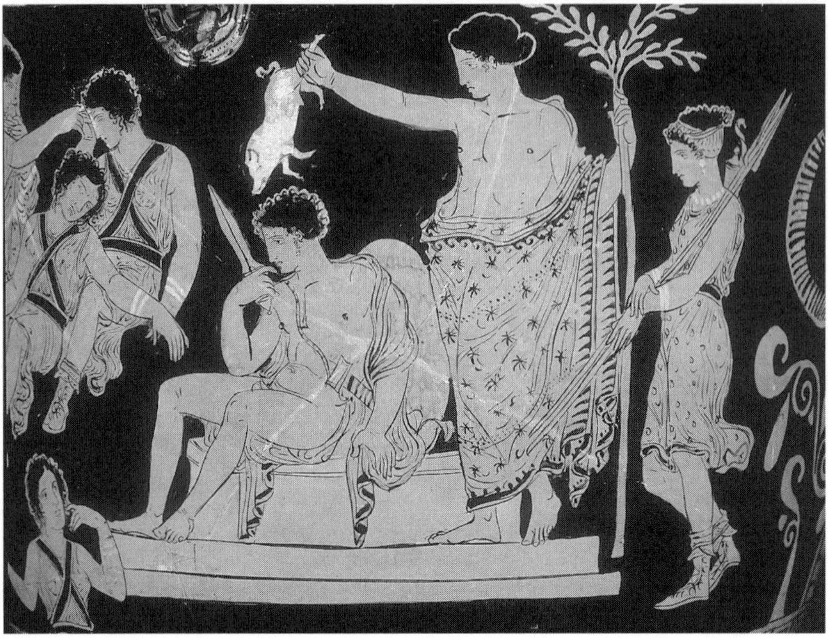

FIG. 1. "The Purification of Orestes" (first quarter of the fourth century B.C.E.). Attributed to the Eumenides Painter. Detail of a red-figure bell krater from Apulia. 48.5 cm. Inv: CP 710. (Photo: Hervé Lewandowski. Copyright Réunion des Musées Nationaux / Art Resource, N.Y.)

Argos. There he had killed his mother, Clytaemnestra, and her lover, Aegisthus, for their parts in the murder of his father, Agamemnon. Orestes had fled north to Apollo's shrine at Delphi, where the god would attempt to purify him of matricide. This is what we are about to witness, and this is how we should understand the scene. The blood of the piglet (once its throat has been cut, perhaps by the sword Orestes holds drawn) is intended to wash away the pollution of the matricide. Once this has been accomplished, the Furies, who rest traditionally asleep to Orestes' right, will stop their hounding.

Look at these Furies. Three of them are visible in this reproduction. One sleeps in what is almost a deathlike pose.[3] The Fury supporting her, however, is awake and, most unexpectedly, exhibits a facial expression which closely resembles that of Orestes, Apollo, and Artemis.[4] There is the same angle of droop of the head, the same half-closed eyes, and the same downturn of the mouth. The posture of the Fury in the bottom left of the picture is also noteworthy.[5] Observe that her right arm seems to support her head. It is positioned in a mode to match that of Orestes. Her face, almost fully turned to us, does not allow an easy registering of her emotional state. The posture of the arm suggests, however, that this Fury is subject to an emotion which matches those of Orestes, Apollo, and Artemis.[6]

What, then, is the emotion depicted on the faces of these individuals? Just as surely as it is not boredom, it is not a serious solemnity designed for a religious occasion. It is far too oppressive and oppressed for this. Depression or, to put it more formally, melancholia seems a better diagnosis. But it is a melancholia or depression of a seemingly unusual type. Nowadays we tend to associate this state with a general slowing down of bodily and mental processes, with what is usually termed a psychomotor retardation. It is treated accordingly with chemical stimulants (Koukopoulos and Koukopoulos 1999). That understanding can hardly be what is called for here.

Orestes' face and much of his posture exhibit a patina of motor retardation. But there are clear signs of mental activity—of agitation. There is the sword in his right hand: that Orestes intends it for some form of violent use is apparent by the apprehensive index finger on his right hand. That the sword points in the general direction of the Furies suggests that it is intended for use against them,[7] rather than as a symbol of his act of matricide (Shapiro 1994; Sommerstein 1989; Podlecki 1989), as a symbol of suicidal thoughts (see Euripides *Iphigeneia in Tauris* 974), or simply as a means for slitting the piglet's throat. It was probably wrong, furthermore, to describe Orestes' general posture as one suggesting lassitude. In the upper torso and stomach regions is a tautness, a tension, that contrasts with the doleful, slow facial set. The tension—even contradiction—between bodily posture and facial expression is evident elsewhere in this remarkable picture.

As I have already indicated, Artemis's face projects melancholy and lassitude. Her face contrasts, however, with the vigor of her body. She is striding toward Orestes—or at least toward Apollo. Not only is her right foot poised to swing firmly forward, but her haste has flattened her raiment against her legs and lower belly. Her garment billows backward in the draft created by her haste. The contrast between her hunting weapons and her facial expression is also startling. As for Apollo, the motion implied by the position of his left foot is far less hasteful, but it does speak of motion, movement, and perhaps an agitation belied by facial features. The Furies, too, capture this duality, this agitated melancholy, in the most alarming of manners. The two seated Furies are at rest. One sleeps. But we know (from Aeschylus and other sources) that these Furies will soon stir to create their mayhem and agitation. Their melancholy is offset by that of which we know they are capable. One final observation on this theme of agitation and fear needs to be made. The gleaming ball that decorates the picture just above and to the left of the piglet (which in its shape seems to mirror that of the navel stone behind Orestes) creates, with its swirling patterns (best viewed in color), the most unsettling of effects. It seems almost to mirror the conflict so animating this picture—between vigor and calm, between agitation and melancholy, between fear and stillness.

The question needs to be put again: what emotion is given form by these individuals, especially Orestes, on this pot? It is best described as an agitated form of melancholy, as an agitated depression. It is a state in which motor retardation, at least in the case of Orestes and the Furies, seems to betray considerable inner agitation and turmoil. The simultaneity of these apparently contrasting emotions requires emphasis here, for the condition should not be likened to bipolar depression, where mania *alternates* with depression. In the Eumenides Painter's rendition, the mania—or flight of thought, or anxiety—represents the internal state. Externally, the victim, Orestes, appears to suffer from extreme motor retardation.[8]

Assistance with the conceptualization of Orestes' psychological state may well be had by comparing a graphic (and moving) photograph (fig. 2) of one of the patients of one of the great figures of the diagnosis and treatment of mania and depression, Emil Kraepelin. Kraepelin (1921, 106) designates this person as suffering from "manic stupor," a condition not unlike "depression with flight of ideas." In such cases, "the patients are usually quite inaccessible, do not trouble themselves about their surroundings, give no answer, at most speak in a low voice straight in front . . . occasionally [there are] isolated *delusions* of changing content and utterance . . . they [may] become lively, give utterance to loud and violent abuse, make a pert, telling remark amidst almost unrestrained laughter, jump out of bed, throw food around the room . . ." Kraepelin seems to diagnose in such cases a contemporaneity, rather than an alternation of mania and stupor. So, in the photograph of Kraepelin's patient, corporeal rigidity and a downcast facial expression barely mask an inner agitation that is apparent in the tension in the shoulders and hands, in the hostility of expression, and in the bizarre headdress of twigs and torn-off leaves.[9] The parallels to the combination of oppression and tension in the Eumenides Painter's Orestes is striking.[10]

One final point will assume more significance as we proceed. The scene represented on this red-figure vase painting is a famous one within a very famous mythological sequence. For this reason its depiction is quite that which would be expected. The scene is important in another, less expected way. The purification represents the point at which we (and the painter) might expect Orestes to be cured of his melancholia and insanity. These have been caused by the

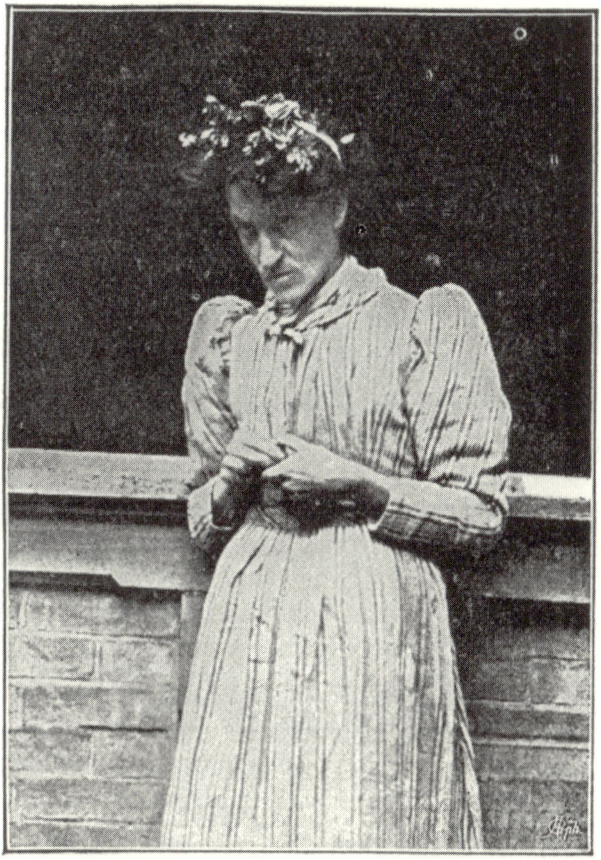

FIG. 2. Emil Kraepelin's patient exhibiting stuporous mania (ca. 1890s). (Reprinted from Emil Kraepelin, *Manic-Depressive Insanity and Paranoia,* trans. R. Mary Barclay and ed. George M. Robertson [Edinburgh: Livingstone, 1921], 107.)

guilt attached to his crime of matricide. The purification, like psychopharmacological therapy, will remove these.

Orestes is mad. That is the verdict of most ancient writers. They no doubt reflect the same tradition that underlies the agitated melancholy inspiring the depiction of this red-figure vase from the Louvre. Orestes' madness is given several names. Varro (first century B.C.E.) wrote a tract about him that termed the condition *insania,* a violent form of madness (Aulus Gellius 13.4.1). Some commentators suggest that Orestes was the victim of melancholia. This is the verdict of Cicero writing in the *Tusculans* (3.5) in approximately the same period, and by implication, it is that of Persius working a century later. Whether the verdict is that Orestes is insane or melancholic, however, the symptoms most stressed by these writers focus on Orestes' violence, on his delusory and angry fits, and on his extreme agitation. This is a psychological state mirrored by the violence, anger, and agitation of the Furies themselves. It is as if the Furies corporealize the inner agitation of Orestes. In these figures, depression is not at issue.

It is fascinating that the ambivalence, the unexpectedness, and the sophistication of the representation of the madness of Orestes on the Eumenides Painter's vase does not have its reflection within the contemporary Greek literary tradition. I suppose that it is simpler to represent Orestes' complex madness visually than it is in words. This thinning deserves illustration, for contemporary verbal representations of Orestes' madness involve a simplification of his mental state. This is nowhere more visible than in Euripides' remarkable and melodramatic play the *Orestes,* which was composed about fifty years before the Louvre pot. It dramatizes many of the events associated with this purification.[11] These take place before Orestes has taken flight to Delphi, where the purification will take place.

A comparison of the Eumenides Painter's depiction of Orestes and Euripides' literary portrait of Orestes is instructive. It demonstrates the literary and discursive tradition's indifference toward (or we could say, its difficulties with) this emotion. In the remainder of this chapter, I intend to trace the long course that it took for this literary tradition to "catch up" with the insights exemplified by the Eumenides Painter's Orestes. Not until this happens does this condition seem comfortably to assume its place within what we might call the popular imagination.

Euripides' play begins with Orestes mad and being nursed by his sister, Electra. They are still in Argos, the scene of the matricide. The Argives, hostile to the crime, look set to condemn the brother and sister to death. Menelaus, Orestes' uncle who is returning from Troy to Sparta with Helen, is of no help. So mad Orestes and Electra, urged on by Orestes' grim friend Pylades, plan to kill Helen and to seize Menelaus's daughter Hermione as a hostage. Helen is mysteriously whisked away. They look set to slaughter Hermione unless Menelaus steps in to save their lives from the Argives. Then appears the god Apollo to impose a settlement: Orestes will be brought to trial at Athens and, after being freed, will marry Hermione and become regent of Argos. The purification is not mentioned.

Euripides' *Orestes* provides a sobering illustration of the inability or unwillingness of the literary tradition to represent melancholia in a truly complex manner. In Euripides' melodrama, although the sequence of the emotion of madness is vividly detailed, the illness has little of the ambivalence of the Eumenides Painter's depiction. Orestes' illness is "bipolar" in Euripides' play, in the sense that, according to Electra, it seems to oscillate between the poles of mad insanity and clearheadedness. So, speaking of the illness, she tells Orestes—and us too (vv. 253–54):

> Alas, brother, your gaze is disordered
> And suddenly you become wild, when just now you were sane.[12]

A more detailed description of Orestes' madness is provided in verses 34–45, where we learn more about his periods of comparative sanity.

> Since then, wasted by his wild illness,
> This wretched Orestes, collapsed on his bed,
> Lies still, yet his mother's blood drives him on
> With its Furies. I hesitate to call the goddesses
> Kindly Ones. They drive him out of his wits with fear.
> This is the sixth day since, of murder,
> Our dead mother's body has been purified by fire.
> In this time he's taken no food to his mouth.
> Nor has he washed. Beneath his blanket,
> Hidden away, whenever his body is freed of the illness,
> He recovers his wits and weeps. Then from bed
> He leaps up quickly, like a colt freed from the yoke.

There is no evidence here of manic behavior alternating with profound depression and psychomotor retardation. Rather, a periodic delusory vision startles Orestes from his wits with fear (vv. 36–38), and in a manic fashion, he leaps up in reaction and rushes about like "a colt freed from the yoke" (v. 45).[13] Fear produces the violent reaction. The passing of this terrifying vision seems to leave Orestes in a completely exhausted state (vv. 35, 43), so much so that he loses his desire for food (v. 41) and for maintaining personal hygiene (v. 42). This exhausted state in between the fits ought not necessarily to be linked with a polar depression. Exhaustion may resemble depression, but it is not at all the same thing.[14] Even Orestes' weeping (v. 44) may be more innocent than it sounds (i.e., no symptom of an enervating sorrow): it might as well result from humiliation and frustration. This sequence and display of emotions has led at least one critic (Pigeaud 1981, 413) to diagnose Orestes' condition as epileptic. Certainly the violence of his fits might be confused with this, and certainly his exhaustion after the attack may resemble that of an epileptic.[15] Whether his condition is epilepsy, madness, or melancholy matters little. What is important is that this condition is not bipolar.

The play offers many other descriptions of Orestes' sickness (termed a *nosos* at vv. 34, 43, 211, 232, and elsewhere). These seem to relate to three discrete phases of his illness—the fit itself, the period immediately after the fit, and a later period when Orestes has somewhat recovered. Orestes' condition is brought about by the gods (v. 31) and is best characterized as a mad fit or frenzy: at verses 227–28 it is a *nosos manias*, a "mad illness"; at verse 37 (and passim) it is a *mania*, a "frenzy." It can be a *lyssa*, a "mad rage" (vv. 224, 793, 325–26; at v. 845 it is a *theomanês lyssa*, a "mad rage brought on by the gods") or even the type of crazed frenzy that can be brought on by a gadfly bite (v. 791). These various descriptions best characterize the fit itself (vv. 44–45, 135, 227–28, 253–54), which can cause Orestes to rave, pant, and gasp (vv. 227–29) and to become prone to acts of violence (v. 268 ff.). These fits, as we have seen, are brought on by a delusion that is god-sent.[16] Orestes imagines that he is actually seeing the Furies (others cannot see them) and that his sister Electra is a Fury. His delusion leads to ludicrous and melodramatic acts of violence (v. 268 ff.)

What happens after the fits? Euripides' play is quite detailed on this matter too. Orestes' hair is damp or matted (vv. 223–25, 387), he has foam in his eyes and on his lips (v. 220), and he tends to remain dirty and unwashed (vv. 42, 226). He is amnesiac (vv. 215 f., 277 f.). At times like this his exhaustion is such that he barely seems to breathe (v. 84), his vision becomes blurred (v. 224), and he loses his appetite (vv. 34, 41, 189) and wastes away (v. 34). His desire for movement is severely limited (vv. 42–43), and he seems close to death (vv. 200, 336) or even corpselike (vv. 82–83, 200). Sleep provides the only relief (vv. 211–15).

The fits cause lingering problems for Orestes. His recovery may appear to be fairly complete (or to be forgotten?) by the end of the play, when he attacks Helen and abducts Hermione. Orestes remains, however, prey to a persistent exhaustion (vv. 91, 228, 800), to a weakness (vv. 800, 888), and to a sense of helplessness (v. 235). He shows signs of listlessness (v. 232), grief (v. 398), and regret (v. 402). He even warns Pylades to be careful not to catch his illness by contagion (v. 793). At verse 415, he is warned by Menelaus against suicide (an option he rejects outright). But, and we must recognize this, Orestes becomes clearheaded and well enough by the end of the play to be able to hatch and carry out extravagant schemes against Helen and her daughter.

Violent, delusory fits, followed by utter physical and mental exhaustion, followed by a slow recovery to a relatively normal level of activity—this is the sequence, the narrative sequence, pursued by Euripides for Orestes. If we were to ask what single activity is common to Orestes in most phases of the play, it is violence and anger. The fits manifest themselves in this manner. Orestes' apparently sane conduct at the end of the play could also be characterized thus.

To compare the Apulian red-figure Orestes from the Louvre and Euripides' Orestes is to compare two radically different figures. One is solemn, melancholy, and subject to an agitated depression; the other is violent, angry, and, when not totally exhausted, prone to crazed and dangerous fits. The difference between the two could be described as one between action (Euripides' Orestes) and affect (the Eumenides Painter's Orestes). Euripides aims to convey the results of an extreme mental state as it effects other individuals and their community, while the Apulian red-figure vase aims to convey an emotional state or psychological mood. In the most general of senses, Euripides' version concerns itself with activity, the body, complicity, the mark, a lack of control, and the male. The Eumenides Painter's Orestes concerns itself with passivity, the mind (and interiority), estrangement, the private, the sign, control, and the female.

Both characters, paradoxically, represent the melancholic. Euripides' character does so by the assertion of Cicero in the *Tusculans*. The Eumenides Painter's Orestes does so by the very assertion of our own eyes and common sense. What links both figures is that they are prey to an extreme agitation and an awful fear (even terror) that play havoc with their lives. But the agitation and fear of Euripides' Orestes and his violent melancholia is driven from without—from the gods and the Furies. The fearful agitation of the Eumenides Painter's Orestes is driven from within—the Furies cannot have caused this, because they share the same facial expression. This agitation provides the real link between these two characters and their melancholia. Perhaps the two apparently incompatible visions of Orestes may represent two poles of a constant experience.

Why does each author choose to highlight a specific mode of melancholy—the one typified by depression and apparent inactivity, the other by violent fits? The answer resides in the aspect of Orestes' symptoms that an author, a genre, a tradition, or an era may choose, or may have the ability, to highlight. Euripides' tradition, by focusing on the outer, visible results that Orestes' illness brings to the community, must highlight its violence.[17] The locus of attention must become the fits, because it is these that will cause so much trouble for the Argive community. The exhausted, seemingly depressive phase of Orestes' illness is of little relevance, for during this period Orestes' insanity is of scant importance for his community. It is little wonder, therefore, that, while the exhausted phase is exploited for its picturesque and melodramatic contribution to the play, its exact nature becomes blurred and is subservient to the more dynamic, violent phase. In modern terms, we would, and I must stress this, diagnose Orestes as a manic-depressive type. Yet the ancient tradition, because of its concern with action and with the outer, can only underplay the puzzling, little understood, depressed phase of Orestes' illness. The Eumenides Painter's Orestes, however, chooses mood and the inner. The decorum of the vase and of the heroic would hardly allow the depiction of fits, of matted hair, of foam on the lips and in the eyes, of a contorted visage. A hero huddled under his blanket would be visually dreary, not to say bizarre. Decorum and an interest in affect, therefore, privileges depression. If you doubt this, consider how less striking the representation on this pot would have been without the psychological component, without its emphasis on affect.

There is another, important factor that conditions the characterization of the Euripidean Orestes: Euripides is writing narrative. This (with its words in writing) entails and implies a sequentialization of the descriptions of Orestes' psychic conditions. Narrative, whether it is telling a story or describing a sickness, follows a *sequence* of events. The narrative of the story of Euripides' play follows a simple pattern: alienation for Orestes from the city of Argos; a crisis resulting in his being condemned to death and, as a reaction, in the assaults on Helen and Hermione; then reintegration through Apollo's imposed solution. The narrative of Orestes' illness follows, storylike, a comparable route. The illness is brought on by an initial "alienating" offense (matricide), is followed by crisis (the violent fits), and is completed by reintegration (of sorts: the lulls of complete exhaustion following the fits). Unlike the Eumenides Painter's version, the violence of the fits does not exist simultaneously with the low-spirited reaction of the periods subsequent to the fits.

It is much easier to render things sequentially when using words, especially when writing in a medium where wordage is limited.[18] It is certainly easier to *understand* things that are rendered sequentially, and words themselves (literacy itself) rely for their effect on the sequential exposition of a particular phenomenon. There is no doubt, too, that *conceptualization* (verbalization, that is) of a particular experience can be more difficult than the *visualization* of the same experience. The result of narrative, words, and sequentialization is a thinning, a type of a failure to represent the complexity of certain inner experiences. I think that this is true in the case of Euripides' version of the emotion of insanity, at least as it relates to Orestes. Perhaps from a desire to make the insanity comprehensible and communicable, or perhaps from too great an enthusiasm for melodrama in this instance, Euripides sequentializes and so flattens the complexity. This tendency persists in many of the outstanding descriptions of melancholy and depression in the ancient world. Perhaps this sequentialization is why a depiction of the complex emotion of the Eumenides Painter's Orestes comes so late in ancient literature.

There may be another reason for Euripides' thinning of Orestes' emotion. It is easiest to understand melancholia when it has a cause. That of Orestes has an obvious one, the killing of his mother. The divine punishment that followed in the form of his delusion (i.e., the pursuit of the Furies) provides, simply, an enactment of the extreme grief that will beset the matricide. Euripides understood this causation and has Orestes state, of the origin of his illness, that it came from the Furies, or the "Frenzies, avengers for my mother's death" (v. 400). In two very famous lines of the play, Euripides goes one step further and seems to allude, as cause for Orestes' violent melancholy, to something that resembles "conscience" *(synesis)* or at least "understanding" (vv. 395–96; Menelaus questions, Orestes replies).

> "What is it you suffer? What disease is destroying you?"
> "It is conscience/understanding *[synesis]*—that I know I've done
> terrible things."

Whatever the term *synesis* is actually intended to convey, it does illustrate that, as far as Euripides and Orestes are concerned, the manic illness has a precise cause.

The situation is reversed in the case of the Eumenides Painter's Orestes. The viewer may choose to interpret, and to provide an explanation for, Orestes' downheartedness. The picture may *imply* that the Furies, the embodiment of the psychic punishment due to the matricide, corporealize and cause Orestes' illness; that the purificatory ceremony depicted by the vase is aimed at removing Orestes' matricidal guilt and that it will, it is hoped, allay the hostility of the Furies; that this will remove the delusions which cause Orestes' manic fits; that the ceremony aims to counteract the cause of Orestes' *nosos.* But the picture does not *tell* us any of this, not in a way that the sequential rendering of Euripides' play can. It cannot be sufficiently emphasized that the picture itself provides no explanation, no etiology for Orestes' state of mind. It depicts for us a slice of time. It aims not at explanation but at the conveying of affect. That is the initial and the lasting impression it creates. It presents to us a vision of sorrow without cause.

There are three traditions relating to melancholia. There is that of the despondent, dejected, and, we would say, depressed individual, such as the Eumenides Painter's Orestes. (I mean those described outside the scientific literature.) There existed a popular tradition viewing melancholia as a condition that made individuals behave like the Euripidean Orestes. There also existed, independently of these, a medical tradition that ascribed melancholia to those individuals who exhibited despondency, fear, delusion, and a persistent, debilitating sorrow[19] that was without a clear cause. (I will discuss this medical tradition in the next section of this chapter.) We will find that, eventually, the first and the third of these traditions intersect. The despondent individual of popular literature came to be described in a manner that reflected the terminology of the doctors. It is at this point that there seems to emerge in nonscientific literature that most modern of characters, the individual suffering persistent sorrow without cause. This condition could best be described as a type of existential melancholia. There are hints of this first state of mind in Apollonius of Rhodes's epic on the Argonauts, in Cicero's *Tusculans*, and in Horace, but its heyday does not come until the time of Seneca. Depressive melancholy was welcomed gradually into nonscientific literature. With Seneca we sense a pervasive feeling of depressive melancholy. This emotional register emerges, furthermore, at precisely the same time as the doctors begin more vigorously to discuss depressive melancholy.

But before proceeding to outline this emotion, I need to mention one more preliminary matter. "Depression," as a concept and as an illness, is often said best to be associated with industrialized societies and nation-states. It is sometimes argued that depression belongs to the modern world, that it is built upon such psychological registers as alienation, helplessness, anomie, and reification. It is a passive, "depressive" (what other word can I use?) condition, one firmly based on the economic and labor conditions that have evolved since the Industrial Revolution and, before that, the Enlightenment.[20] Ruth Padel's splendid *Whom Gods Destroy* (1995) has added fuel to this fire. Her analysis of madness in classical Greek literature stresses its violence.[21] Melancholics, preeminently mad, are a very angry cohort. According to Padel, they remained that way, in the literary sphere at any rate, until the Enlightenment; only since the early eighteenth century have they become "depressive."[22]

In the pages that follow, I will challenge this understanding. Such a challenge is a crucial part of my argument. Despite a postmodern interest in fragmented personality (cf. Wiles 1997, 6), depression is a condition that in so many ways is at the heart of modern self-perception and self-characterization. It is so easily seen as being uniquely modern, as a product of modern sociological pressures. Certainly much of the recent work in cultural history and cultural studies conspires to place such an affective register within a very recent temporal band. This is to misrepresent. As the Eumenides Painter's Orestes demonstrates, depressive melancholia existed from early in antiquity. It emerges as a literary entity late within classical antiquity. This chapter will show when and how, but not why.

Let us begin not with representations of melancholy but with the concept itself. The earliest medical uses of the term *melancholia* eschew psychological characterization. By the late fourth century B.C.E., however, the term begins, in medical circles, to be associated with the depressive. Nonmedical usage, though, associates the term with violence and anger. The distinction seems to mirror precisely that gulf between the Eumenides Painter's (depressive) Orestes and the Euripidean (violent and angry) Orestes.

The earliest medical descriptions of melancholia are found scattered among the texts of the Hippocratic corpus. In its first and infrequent appearances, melancholia seems to be linked with a physiological condition rather than with a psychological type; in its first appearances, that is, melancholia has none of the psychological implications and resonances that it possesses for us moderns. Melancholia referred to the presence within the human body of the substance termed black bile (or Greek *melaina cholê*). Black bile, occupying scant place in the speculation of the earliest Greek medical texts (Flashar 1966, 21 ff.), is a normal physical constituent of the human physiology (like blood or bone or hair), rather than an illness (but note Flashar 1966, 22). Gradually, as humoral medicine took hold, a typical physiology for the preponderance of black bile came into being (a melancholic physiology), and even more gradually, there came into being a matching psychology for the preponderance of black bile (a "melancholic" temperament) (Flashar 1966, 24 ff.). Such typicalities become apparent when black bile, or melancholy, comes to be the dominating humoral component within the human body. Such a picture is apparent, for example, in the Hippocratic text *On The Nature of Man* (usually dated to approximately 400 B.C.E.; see Flashar 1966, 39). Here black bile, rather than being just another corporeal component of the human body (like flesh or bone), comes to play a key role in human health. Although black bile characterizes, in *On The Nature of Man,* primarily the physiology of specific human beings (cf. Flashar 1966, 39 ff.; Pigeaud 1981, 123),[23] its temperamental implications become quickly apparent.

According to *On the Nature of Man* 3–7, there were four humors (blood, yellow bile, black bile, and phlegm) with which were associated four different sorts of physiology. Physiological disorder could be pinned down to the preponderance of one or another of these humors within a particular individual (Flashar 1966, 39 ff.). I suppose it is inevitable that temperament may to some degree come to be classified accordingly. It is easy to guess how this may have happened. The four humors and their related physiological types gained their particular characters by being associated with a season (spring, summer, autumn, and winter) and with a set of opposites (blood with warm and moist, yellow bile with warm and dry, black bile with cold and dry, phlegm with cold and moist).[24] Good health was the product of a proper mix *(eucrasia)* of these humors, while bad health was the product of an ill mix *(dyscrasia)*. I suppose that in the part-practical, part-speculative minds of these earlier medical practitioners, it was an easy step from such physiological generalities to temperament. So, in this view, the individual in whom black bile preponderates will be associated with coldness and dryness, with autumn, and with blackness (a color that always had its psychological basis; see Flashar 1966, 37).[25] Autumn can signify age (the years between twenty-five and forty-five) as easily as a season (it signifies both in the Hippocratic treatise *On the Nature of Man*). Physiological typicalities thus haltingly give rise to psychological or temperamental typicalities. The individual in whom the black bile predominates comes increasingly to be seen as "melancholic," a temperament that was, if we follow the implications of *On the Nature of Man,* essentially depressive.

During the fourth century B.C.E., there seems to have developed a shift in the conception of melancholia. Melancholia seems to have taken on an almost pathological significance, as well as implying a particular type of depressive temperament.[26] Melancholia became a disease as well as a character trait and was produced by an excess of black bile. This was typified by coldness and dryness and was dangerously common in autumn.[27] This conception seems to have based itself on popular traditions, which associated melancholia with madness and mania (the Euripidean tradition signifies both) and on the speculation of those Hippocratic texts that linked melancholia with depressive illnesses (rather than temperaments), such as exhibiting an "aversion to food, despondency, sleeplessness, irritability, restlessness." The same writers also note that "fear or depression that is prolonged means melancholia."[28] Typical of this tradition may be *Problema* 30.1, written in the late fourth century B.C.E. In this epochal essay, composed by either Aristotle or his pupil Theophrastus, there developed a concept of melancholia that became influential for millennia.[29] *Problema* 30.1 (for the text and translation see Klibansky, Panofsky, and Saxl 1964, 18–29) addresses this problem: why is there a correlation between political, philosophical, and artistic ability and a temperament that is inclined to melancholia?[30] The author of the *Problema* answers that those gifted in these areas have a permanent excess of black bile in their nature; these abilities are linked, that is, to a pathological constitution whose characteristics are driven by an excess of black bile. Thus those who display these abilities are subject to the various illnesses associated with black bile's superfluity.

The vital aspect of the formulation of black bile and its workings provided in *Problema* 30.1 are constituted in three ways. First, a superfluity of black bile (melancholia) is envisaged to be a key contributor to human excellence generally. The *Problema* ushers in what is an almost romantic conception of black bile and its affective influence (Flashar 1966, 62). Second, and what matters particularly for this discussion, the author of the *Problema* also believes that an excess of the humor black bile can cause severe depression. Third, and paradoxically, this humor can cause mania. How does this apparently dual (or bipolar) nature of black bile come about? The author of the *Problema* conceives of black bile as a mixture of hot and cold. Melancholics fall into two broad groups, those in whom the black bile becomes very hot and those in whom the black bile becomes very cold. Put coarsely, this means that where the black bile is hot, one would expect what we term the *manic phase* of melancholia;[31] where the black bile is cold, one would expect the *depressed phase*. The melancholia of the *Problema* is, to use modern terms, bipolar, although this bipolarity need not be found in the individual.[32] The *Problema*, therefore, provides a remarkable solution to the puzzle provided by the two Orestes with whom this chapter began. Both are melancholic, it has been noted, but both seem to reside at the opposite ends of an experiential spectrum. What can link these two ends is black bile *(melaina cholê)* and whether it is cold (the Eumenides Painter's Orestes) or hot (the Euripidean Orestes).

There is something drearily oversystematic and overclever about the formulation of *Problema* 30.1. It is as if the author of this essay faced the problem of the apparent identity, yet difference, of characters such as the two Orestes, then posited a simple humoral link between the two. The variable in the link is temperature. What especially unsettles in the formulation of the *Problema* is the vigor with which this writer embraces sequentialization, narrative, and metaphor as solutions for what is little more than a semantic puzzle. At any rate, the sequentialization can best be emphasized by quoting the *Problema*.

> [B]lack bile, being cold by nature . . . can induce paralysis or torpor or depression or anxiety . . . but if it is overheated it produces cheerfulness, bursting into song, and ecstasies and the eruption of sores and the like . . . those who possess much hot bile are elated and brilliant or erotic or easily moved to anger and desire . . . If it [sc., black bile] is unduly cold . . . it produces irrational despondency . . . those who become despondent as the heat in them dies down are inclined to hang themselves . . . Most of those men in whom the heat is extinguished suddenly make away with themselves unexpectedly, to the astonishment of all, since they have given no previous sign of any such intention.

The sequence is very easy to explain and to understand. Either by nature or circumstances, we guess, an individual's excess of black bile may overheat. This heat, if you are given to trusting simple metaphors (compare the English "boiling with rage" or "burning with fury"), produces the anger. But note that the preponderant bile must be black, for when cooled, it must have characteristics capable of producing depression. Black bile is the only one able to do this. (Again metaphor is crucial. Most cultures and languages link downheartedness with "black.") Cool, surely, hot bile must, so leaving an excess of the now depressive material. The *Problema*'s notion of suicide is linked with this cooling process. It is less inspired than predictable (remember Menelaus's warning to the melancholic Orestes in *Orestes* 415: "Don't speak of death. That is not clever"), and it serves to accommodate a popular prejudice (which I will address in chapter 5) that depression easily leads to suicide.[33]

This sequence produces a very appealing and easily recognizable narrative pattern. Where Euripides followed a narrative mode of alienation, crisis, and reconciliation, the author of the *Problema* opts for the enormously exciting, melodramatic, and sequential pattern of bipolar *alternation:* the hero's violent, manic crisis is followed not by exhaustion but by a deep and despairing depression. The narrative model must have been Ajax from Sophocles' play of the same name.[34]

The interpretation offered to us by *Problema* 30.1 homogenizes the experiences of the two Orestes. It does this, no doubt, to provide a systematized understanding of their comparably linked conditions. We are justified in suspecting that such homogenization thins lived experience and belies experiential variety. (The glamorization of melancholia by linking it with genius is in itself a meretricious formulation.)[35] This desiccation of experiential complexity is nowhere more apparent than when we contrast the bipolar narrative of the *Problema* with the complex and ambivalent representation of agitated depression in the Eumenides Painter's Orestes.

A measure of the oversystematizing nature of the *Problema* can be drawn from a comparison of subsequent medical discussions of melancholia. Whether humoral (i.e., based on the four humors of Hippocratic medicine) or not, their main focus does not reflect the bipolarity of the *Problema*. Rather, it is usually on the depressive side of the illness, with, naturally, an apparent and occasional awareness of the agitation that depression may often mask. For example, Rufus of Ephesus, a Greek doctor who worked during the second century of our era and who is held by some to have been a key figure in the formulation of future notions of melancholia (ranking in antiquity as third in importance as a medical writer after Galen and Hippocrates),[36] composed a treatise on melancholy.[37] Although he does stress the potential for mania in melancholia, his main emphasis is on its depressive aspects. Rufus firmly believes that the source of the trouble is an excess of black bile (collecting in the region of the hypochondria). For him, melancholics were often gloomy, sad, and fearful. The chief signs of their illness were fear, doubting, and a single delusional idea. Interestingly Rufus may have linked too much intellectual activity with melancholia. This notion modifies the glamorizing stance of *Problema* 30.1.[38]

Even where the humoral basis for medicine was abandoned, melancholia was still a depressive illness, and the speculation of the *Problema* can be seen as out of step. The Roman author Celsus (active during the first century C.E.) provides an account of melancholia (for a translation see Spencer 1935–38) that, while not relying upon a theory that saw health as the product of a balance between four humors, maintains that melancholia is the product of an excess of black bile. He epitomizes the condition thus: "but if despondency *[tristitia]* is prolonged with long-standing fear and wakefulness, the disease of black bile supervenes" (2.7.19–20; cf. 3.18.17). He does not appear to have associated mania with melancholia in the manner of *Problema* 30.1. Celsus, furthermore, appears to have been little concerned with the etiology of the disease. His interest was in its treatment.[39] The same point could be made of Soranus of Ephesus,[40] who worked in Alexandria during the Trajanic and Hadrianic periods and whose writings on melancholia survive in the Latin compendium of Caelius Aurelianus. He neither associates melancholia primarily with mania nor accepts a humoralist basis for its etiology. He believed that the disease was so named because the patient vomits black bile.[41] Soranus characterized a melancholic as exhibiting "mental anguish and distress, dejection, silence, animosity towards members of the household, sometimes a desire to live and at other times a longing for death, suspicion . . . that a plot is being hatched against him, weeping without reason, meaningless muttering and . . . occasional joviality" (trans. Jackson [1986, 34], quoting Drabkin [1950, 561]).

Aretaeus of Cappadocia may have a floruit between 50 and 150 C.E.[42] He has recently been recognized as a key figure in the history of the understanding of melancholia (Koukopoulos and Koukopoulos 1999; Marneros and Angst 2000 [cf. Angst and Marneros 2001; Marneros 2001a, 2001b]). He provides one of the most noteworthy, but exceptional, challenges for the pattern that I am arguing about. Aretaeus, while focusing primarily on the depressive side of melancholia and while appearing to have accepted the role attributed to black bile in the causation of melancholia, does seem to have understood melancholia as part of a bipolar condition. So, like the writer of the *Problema*, he allows a manic side to melancholia and attributes this to the changeability of the disease. As Marneros and Angst (2000) note: "Aretaeus was very careful in his description of diseases . . . In his "On the Aetiology and Symptomatology of Chronic Diseases" and "The Treatment of Chronic Diseases" he described . . . mental disorders. [He] . . . addresses melancholia . . . [and] . . . mania." Marneros (1999) convincingly notes the manner by which Aretaeus links melancholia and mania together as a single experiential continuum (e.g., he quotes Aretaeus as stating, "in most of them [sc., melancholics] the sadness became better after a various length of time and changed into happiness; the patients then developed mania").[43] Marneros and Angst (Marneros and Angst 2000) summarize Aretaeus's position on melancholia as follows (note also their criticism of Ackerknecht 1959 and Fisher-Homberger 1968):[44]

a. Melancholia and mania have the same etiology, namely, disturbances of the function of the brain and some other organs.
b. Mania is a worsening of melancholia.
c. Mania is the phenomenological counterpart of melancholia.
d. His concepts of melancholia and mania were broader than the modern concepts: depression, psychotic depression, schizoaffective disorders, mixed states, schizophrenia with affective symptomatology, and some organic psychoses were involved.
e. He differentiated between melancholia, which is a biologically caused disease, and reactive depression, a psychologically caused state.

If Aretaeus raises doubts as to the universality among the *medici* (medical doctors) for seeing melancholia as depressive, Galen should set this to rest. Galen, as is well known, followed the Hippocratic system and seems to have formularized many of the aspects of the *medici*'s beliefs.[45] He was a humoralist and paired the four humors with the dyadic qualities mentioned earlier; illness was a result of an imbalance of the humors. He characterized individuals according to the dominance of one or another of the humors: the sanguine, choleric, melancholic, and phlegmatic personalities matched blood, yellow bile, black bile, and phlegm. In his scheme of things, there were three types of melancholia:[46] the first is primarily a disease of the brain; in the second, the entire mass of the blood is infected, with a resultant darkening of the skin; in the third—melancholic hypochondria—the disease was located in the upper abdominal area (the hypochondria) and resulted in indigestion and flatulence (this is also Rufus's preferred mode of melancholy). Here is Galen's description of the manifestations of melancholy (trans. Jackson [1986, 42], quoting Siegel [1976, 93]).

> Therefore, it seems correct that *Hippocrates* classified all their symptoms into two groups: fear and despondency. Because of this despondency patients hate everyone whom they see, are constantly sullen and terrified, like children or uneducated adults in deepest darkness. As external darkness renders almost all

> persons fearful, with the exception of a few naturally audacious ones or those who were specially trained, thus the colour of the black humour induces fear when its darkness throws a shadow over the area of thought [in the brain].

Galen may play variations on the formulation of the *Problema*. The change that he makes, however, relates to bipolarity: melancholia is essentially a depressive illness (Siegel 1976, 93).

Depression may have been synonymous with melancholia for most medical practitioners, but that, as I have indicated, was not the case for the literary and popular imagination. Popular imagining seems to have viewed the melancholic as a kind of Euripidean Orestes. It is this tradition that the systematizing author of the *Problema* was attempting to accommodate when he spoke of the mania produced by the overheating of the black bile. This tradition associated madness and violence, that is, mania with melancholia. A popular consistency in the interpretation of melancholia as mania stretches from the fifth century B.C.E. until at least the second century C.E.[47] Such an interpretation runs increasingly in the face of contemporary medical theory. In the fifth and fourth centuries B.C.E., for example, popular melancholia stood at the antipodes to medical opinions (and thus to popular twentieth-century opinion). It was violent and angry, mad, not the depressive condition of the Hippocratic texts. So we find the verb *melancholan* (a derivative of *melancholia*) meaning simply "to be mad," rather than "to be melancholy." It is "a coarse synonym for *mainomai*," a verb that implies rage and anger as well as madness (Padel 1995, 48). An instance of this use occurs in Aristophanes' *Birds* (staged in 414 B.C.E.), where the verb *melancholan*[48] is "spoken by a 'fool' bird salesman" (Padel 1995, 48) and indicates, precisely, madness and anger.[49] Later, during the fourth century, we hear in Menander's *Epitrepontes* 878 ff.:[50]

> This fellow is going mad *[hypomaineth']*, by Apollo, he is mad *[mainetai]*,
> He has truly gone mad *[memanêt']*, he is mad *[mainetai]*, by the gods.
> The master, Charisius, I mean. The black
> Bile *[cholê melaina]* has struck him, or something like that.
> What else would you guess has happened to him?

This popular interpretation of melancholia as mania had a long life indeed (Padel 1995, 48 ff.; cf. Flashar 1966). As late as 44 B.C.E., we find Cicero linking melancholia with mania. His views deserve quoting in full. At *Tusculan*

Disputations 3.5, Cicero is discussing the various terms used in Latin and Greek for insanity and, in passing, offers a definition for melancholia.

> Now I cannot readily give the origin of the Greek term *mania;* the meaning it actually implies is marked with better discrimination by us than by the Greeks, for we make the distinction between "unsoundness of mind" *[insania],* which from its association with folly *[stultitia]* has a wider connotation, and "frenzy" *[furor].* The Greeks wish to make the distinction but fall short of success in the term they employ: what we call frenzy *[furor]* they call melancholia, just as if the truth were that the mind is influenced by black bile *[atra bili]* only, and not in many instances, by the stronger power of wrath or fear or pain, in the sense in which we speak of the frenzy of Athamas, Alcmaeon, Ajax, and Orestes.

What matters is the correlation between the Greek term *melancholia* and the Roman term *furor.* For Cicero, the Greek word means either frenzy (*furor* embraces both anger and violence) or the sort of folly *(stultitia)* that he associates with *insania.* It is notable that Cicero does not associate melancholia with *tristitia* ("despondency" or "depression"). The definition offered by the *Problema* and those offered by later *medici,* as we have seen, paid very serious attention to the importance of depression in melancholia. Was Cicero ignorant of the medical discussions? The characterization of Athamas, Alcmaeon, Ajax, and Orestes as *melancholici*—or in Roman terminology, *furiosi*—is indicative. These were characters whose melancholia was preeminently violent.[51] It appears that Cicero preferred the popular, commonsense interpretation of melancholy.

It is surely this popular conception that exerts its influence on the bipolar *Problema.* Here the illustrative stress is essentially on manic melancholia, on the tradition epitomized by the Euripidean Orestes. As I have stated earlier, there can be little doubt that Orestes and, especially, Ajax were manic-depressives.[52] Yet the literary tradition at this phase of antiquity, because of its concern with action and its results and thus with the outer, cannot easily conceptualize or describe such inner experiences of the depressive phase of bipolar melancholia. Perhaps we should go back three centuries from Cicero and reevaluate the melancholic characterizations of the *Problema.* Heracles provides a good starting point. This is what the *Problema* has to say of him (trans. Klibansky, Panofsky, and Saxl 1964, 18).

> Why is it that all those who have become prominent in philosophy or politics or poetry or the arts are clearly melancholics, and some of them to such an extent as to be affected by diseases caused by the black bile? An example from heroic mythology is Heracles. For he apparently had this constitution, and

therefore epileptic afflictions were called after him "the sacred disease" by the ancients. His mad fit in the incident with the children points to this, as well as the eruption of sores which happened before his disappearance on Mt. Oeta; for this is with many people a symptom of black bile.

To understand what the *Problema* is getting at, we need to turn to Euripides' play *Heracles* (it matters little that melancholy is accorded apparently scant importance in Euripides' version).[53] Although it was composed well in advance of the *Problema* (up to a century), it provides an accurate indication, if not of the medical basis of what the pseudo-Aristotle must have meant, at least of the symptomatology upon which his deductions were based.

In this play, Heracles' family (his wife, Megara, and his three sons) are facing death at the hands of the Theban regent, the usurper Lycus. Heracles is absent and cannot protect them. He is performing his labor in the underworld of bringing back the dog Cerberus to the daylight. Heracles does return to Thebes in the nick of time, however. It is at this point that his tragedy begins to unfold. As he performed, in company with his family, propitiatory sacrifices to Zeus, his old enemy Hera, Zeus's wife, drove him mad. In his delusion he mistook his wife and family for members of the clan of his adversary Eurystheus. He slaughtered them in his mad frenzy. Hera's revenge was complete only when Heracles, now bound for self-protection to a pillar, woke to sanity to face the awful consequences of his madness.

Is this frenzy evidence of melancholia? The *Problema* certainly thought so. This must be based upon the vivid symptoms of the Euripidean madness itself (see vv. 930–1008, 867–70): Heracles exhibits rolling and bloodshot eyes, foam at the lips, and, along with his terrible violence, an utter delusion. Theodoru (1993, 34) has usefully listed the symptoms exhibited by Heracles in Euripides' play. The following occur during his attack:

1. silence (v. 930)
2. head thrown back, tossing (v. 867)
3. rolling of the eyes (vv. 868, 932)
4. heavy, irregular, and hot breathing (v. 869)
5. bloodshot eyes (v. 933)
6. foaming (v. 934)
7. making loud animal sounds (v. 870)
8. wild, insane laughter (v. 935)

Theodoru also notes that after the attack, Heracles "is confused (cf. 1094 ff.) and amnesiac (1105–8), his breathing still hot and irregular (1092 f.)". It is striking that much of this description has parallels in the melancholic behavior of Euripides' Orestes. To suggest, as many commentators would, that Euripides' portrait of Heracles is "conventionalized and indistinguishable from the frenzy occasioned by physical pain" is to misread the tradition and, above all, to ignore the reality of the delusion.[54] This is melancholy in the popular (nonmedical) sense as it is exploited in Euripides' *Orestes.* The melancholia of Euripides' Heracles that the *Problema* attributes to the same hero is synonymous with a madness that exhibits itself as anger, violence, and destruction—in other words, mania. There is nothing in either Heracles of the Hippocratic depressive illness, even when he awakes to discover that he has murdered his wife and children (that is mere exhaustion). His madness has its literary origin in the manic phase of melancholia attributed by the *Problema* to the exhalations of hot black bile. Heracles' melancholy, thus, is of a very specific kind that, outside the *Problema,* does not receive widespread description in the medical tradition.[55] But it is quite standard in the popular tradition associated with melancholia. Were we to look at later versions of the legend, such as that by Seneca, we would find two things: (1) that later writers understood his condition as melancholy; (2) that things have not greatly changed from Euripides.[56] Virgil was certainly aware of the tradition of *Hercules melancholicus.* In *Aeneid* 8.219–20, Virgil attributes manic melancholy to the hero: "here in truth did burn with the madness *[furor]* of melancholy *[atrum fel]* the pain of Hercules" (Hercules is setting angrily off in pursuit of Cacus). That, at any rate, is how the *atrum fel* ("melancholy" or "black bile") is usually interpreted.

The *Problema* provides other examples of melancholy that reflect this same popular Orestean tradition. They are worth examining as further evidence of this tradition. Given the extraordinary influence that the *Problema* has exerted in Western thought, it deserves further attention. My point, and this is a novel one, is that the bipolarity of the *Problema* is a chimera. Close examination of its illustrative heroes indicates that it is mania, not depression, that characterizes them. They remain, therefore, examples of the popular tradition that I have associated with Euripides' Orestes.

Lysander (d. 395 B.C.E.), the Spartan general who sealed Athens's fate in the Peloponnesian War (431–404 B.C.E.), backs up this claim. The discussion of the pseudo-Aristotelian *Problema* tags him as melancholic. The following delineation occurs at the end of the passage cited earlier concerning Heracles (trans. Klibansky, Panofsky, and Saxl 1964, 18).

> His [Heracles'] mad fit in the incident with the children points to this [his melancholia], as well as the eruption of sores which happened before his disappearance on Mount Oeta; for this is with many people a symptom of the

> black bile. Lysander the Lacedaemonian too suffered from such sores before his death.

Nearly five hundred years after the *Problema,* Plutarch (ca. 50–120 C.E.), in the most useful source for Lysander's life, repeats the claim that the Laconian general was a melancholic.[57] First, he states (*Lysander* 2),

> And Aristotle, when he sets forth that great natures, like those of Socrates and Plato and Heracles, have a tendency to melancholy, writes also that Lysander, not immediately, but when well on in years, was a prey to melancholy.

Later, and without absolute consistency, Plutarch adds (*Lysander* 28),

> Since he was now of an altogether harsh disposition, owing to the melancholy that persisted into his old age, he stirred up the ephors and persuaded them to fit out an expedition against the Thebans [in which, in 395 B.C.E., he perished].

At no point, however, does Plutarch mention the sores, nor does he catalog other symptoms typically associated with the illness. How is Plutarch's notion of Lysandrian melancholy to be understood? The second of the two passages is quite precise. Plutarch states of Lysander that he was *chalepos ôn orgên dia tên melancholian* (literally, "being harsh as regards his anger because of his melancholy"). The melancholy manifests itself, in other words, as *orgê,* or anger. For Plutarch, therefore, melancholy seems to be inextricably associated with violent anger (or mania). It is striking that Lysander is subject to this emotion in more than one place in Plutarch's life.[58] How did melancholia bring about Lysander's *orgê*? The black bile must have overheated and set the general's mind afire. Plutarch, it seems to me, provides a gloss on the *Problema.* His narrative suggests that Lysander may be sited, therefore, firmly within the tradition exemplified by Euripides' Orestes.

The *Problema* continues to discuss two further victims of the exhalations of hot bile, Ajax and Bellerophon.[59] We might do well to survey these too. The *Problema* states (trans. Klibansky, Panofsky, and Saxl 1964, 18 f.):

> There are also the stories of Ajax and Bellerophon: the one went completely out of his mind, while the other sought out desert places for his habitation; wherefore Homer says [*Iliad* 6.200–203]:
>
> And since of all the gods he was hated
> Verily over the Aleian plain he would wander
> Eating his own heart out *[hon thumon katedôn],* avoiding the pathway
> of mortals.

Let us look at Bellerophon first. His is a fascinating case for the light that it casts upon the preferences of the *Problema* and for popular Euripidean attitudes toward melancholia.

Bellerophon's wandering and the grief associated with it were brought on by the enmity of the gods. The Homeric scholia linked with this passage suggest that the divine hostility manifested itself in the killing of Bellerophon's children, Isandros and Laodamia (see too Clerici 1996, 330 n. 124). Bellerophon's grief, therefore, was the manifestation of his state of mourning for the children. Such an understanding is reinforced—should we doubt it—by Cicero in *Tusculans* 3.63. Immediately after quoting *Iliad* 6.201–2, Cicero mentions Niobe and Hecuba. They, too, mourned excessively because of the loss of children. In Niobe's case the loss of children was the product of divine enmity. There is an unstated parallel, then, between Bellerophon and Niobe.

The author of the *Problema* reflects a tradition that saw Bellerophon's grief as being so severe as to cross the bounds from acceptable grief into melancholy. Over six hundred years later, Rutilius Namatianus, in his travel poem *De reditu suo* (1.439 ff.), reflects this tradition. He states that Bellerophon was melancholic. But in what way was he melancholic? Rutilius is a little more detailed on this matter than either Homer or the *Problema*. I quote the passage that relates to Bellerophon (we will see it again in the discussion of acedia in chapter 4).

> In our crossing of the ocean Capraria reared up next.
> The island is polluted by a plenitude of men who flee the light.
> They call themselves *monachi* [monks], using the Greek term,
> Because they want to live alone, without a witness
> . . . .
> Perhaps they seek their cells *[ergastula]* as punishment for their actions.
> Perhaps their mournful guts *[tristia viscera]* are swollen with black gall *[nigro felle]*.
> Homer attributed the condition of a superfluity of the bile *[bilis]*
> To Bellerophon's anxieties *[Bellerophonteis sollicitudinibus]*.
> For, after the blows of cruel sorrow, the human race
> Is said to have displeased the young man.

There can be little doubt that Rutilius saw Bellerophon's condition, like that of the monks, as driven by a deep depression, a *tristitia*, a depression that could be attributed to *nigrum fel*, to black bile, the cause of melancholia. There is no question here of mania, or violence, or fits. Rutilius's Bellerophon more resembles the Eumenides Painter's Orestes. Had we any further doubt on this matter, we could turn to the discussion of *Iliad* 6.200–203 provided by (pseudo-)Galen (*Introductio seu medicus* 14.740.16).

> The cause of melancholy is black bile, a colder and gloomy humor. Therefore such people [sc., melancholics] are gloomy and downcast. They are suspicious of everything and rejoice in solitude, as did Bellerophon, as Homer explains.

Galen's Bellerophon is melancholic in the depressive sense. There is no reason why this should not have been the case for Homer's Bellerophon as well.

The *Problema*, erroneously, interprets Bellerophon as exhibiting melancholia, a form of bipolar melancholy, of anger and depression. The author of the *Problema* muddles. Bellerophon shows no bipolarity. He shows no mania, only depression. He ill fits, therefore, a context that demands bipolarity but in fact illustrates the deleterious effects of melancholic mania. One can see why. Nearly all of this writer's illustrations are manic, angry, or violent individuals. It appears, then, that his main intention is to link firmly, through the notion of bipolarity, the two traditions of the popular and medical. It is as if he has determined that depressive melancholics are outstanding and that he would like to extend the mode of understanding to the manic as well. The *Problema*'s real interest, then, is in manic behavior, and it invents an intellectual system to anchor this popular type to the medical form. We have been fooled ever since.

This reference to Bellerophon allows us to draw some conclusions of a more general nature. The first is this. Depressive melancholy, as the Eumenides Painter's Orestes demonstrates and as Bellerophon himself demonstrates, was always on the cards. So, too, must have been bipolar depression. Orestes, Heracles, and Lysander may exemplify it. Yet the nonmedical literary tradition exhibits little interest in depression. As we have just seen with Bellerophon, a writer such as that of the *Problema* attempts to "regularize" depressive melancholia by systematizing it within his bipolar grid. Depression, I might also add, is no cultural construct. It is a persistent cultural entity that, not unexpectedly, certain eras find difficult to accommodate conceptually. In Greek of the period we have been discussing, the literary focus is on the surface of things, on the manifest, and on how the individual relates to the community. There is little interest in affect. Current "discourse," in the Foucaldian sense, shapes not reality but how reality is constructed within literary texts.[60]

The author of the *Problema* seems to believe that the Sophoclean character Ajax, the protagonist of the play of the same name (dating from pre-441 B.C.E.) gives a very clear indication of "bipolar" melancholy. Let me, as a final illustration, recapitulate the story of Ajax and of Sophocles' play. Ajax, we learn in this play, had been denied the dead Achilles' arms by the Greek leaders at Troy, despite his universally being acknowledged as the leading living warrior. The arms were given instead by Agamemnon and Achilles to the canny Odysseus. Enraged at his defeat and full of a desire for vengeance, Ajax set out at night to kill Agamemnon, Menelaus, and Odysseus. He would have murdered them had Athena not deluded him into mistaking some plundered cattle for his quarries. Ajax, in his delusion, whipped and tortured the cattle, believing them to be his human opponents. After his eventual return to sanity, the ignominy and the humiliation of his actions drove Ajax to plan and carry through a shamed and solitary suicide. (I will come back to Ajax in chapter 5.)

Why did Ajax do it? Sophocles no doubt has his ideas, but the opinions of the *Problema* are what matter here.[61] Fortunately the *Problema* does provide some useful information on the apparently bipolar nature of melancholy. I have quoted the relevant passage already, but for the sake of clarity, I repeat its substance here (trans. Klibansky, Panofsky, and Saxl 1964, 23 ff.).

> [B]lack bile, being cold by nature, . . . can induce paralysis or torpor or depression or anxiety . . . but if it is overheated it produces . . . [individuals who are] easily moved to anger and desire . . . those who become despondent as the heat in them [sc., of the black bile] dies down are inclined to hang themselves . . . Most of those men in whom the heat is extinguished suddenly make away with themselves unexpectedly, to the astonishment of all, since they have given no previous sign of any such intention.

How can this interpretation be applied to Ajax? If, following the *Problema,* it is correct to view Ajax as melancholic, then his initial fit of madness (Sophocles *Ajax* 91–133) must be interpreted as the result of the overheating of the naturally cold black bile. Thus he becomes "easily moved to anger." After the act of frenzy and the mistaken slaughter of the cattle, Ajax's putatively atrabilious temperament begins quickly to cool. The result of this sudden extinguishing is a profound despondency (*Ajax* 645 ff.), which leads him to take his life, "to the astonishment of all, since [he has] given no previous sign of any such intention." It seems likely that this is how the *Problema* might have interpreted Ajax's actions as they are recorded for us by Sophocles and others.

As a rider to this, I would like to refer to one recent and well-known interpretation of Ajax's characterization in Sophocles' play, a psychological analysis based upon modern criteria. Collinge,[62] with implicit approval by Stanford (1963, 237), argues first "that Sophocles was more truly medical, more seriously and instinctively a devotee of the craft than any other literary figure of the fifth and fourth centuries except (if we can call him literary) Aristotle."[63] Collinge and Stanford continue to list the frequency of medical terms in Sophocles' *Ajax* and, further, to argue that Sophocles' play has detailed most of the symptoms of what would now be termed manic depression. Stanford (1963, 237) summarizes as follows:

> Sophocles has produced most of the symptoms of the manic-depressive syndrome in his portrait of Ajax: first (in the depressive phase) sadness, "psychomotor retardation in the forms of difficulty of thinking . . . and of sitting in the same position for a long time . . . fleeting delusions of persecution . . . and of mockery . . . The manic phase shows the opposite qualities: elation . . . brutal violence . . . persistent hallucinations . . . delusions of grandeur . . . irritability if thwarted or opposed . . . Collinge . . . concludes: "Sophocles has, maybe instinctively or because he has observed people's behaviour with a clinical eye, put a traditional phenomenon, Ajax mad, into the correct and consistent framework of a well-observed psychosis."

In a sense, Collinge has brought the *Problema* up to date. But, we may well ask, with how much justification? There can be little doubt that Ajax's mentality as it is described during the assault on the cattle is rendered in a manner that makes him seem very like Euripides' Orestes and Heracles. There is all of the sudden violence (vv. 218–20) and anger; there is the delusion (vv. 91–133). The attack Ajax suffers is said to be an illness, a *nosos* (vv. 271, 452, and passim) or a *mania* (vv. 216, 257–61, 292 ff.), and is linked with mad violence, *lyssa* (v. 452). While suffering this, Ajax can be said to be "out of his wits" *[aphrôn]* (cf. v. 355).

Subsequent to this attack, however, Ajax does not exhibit signs of deep depression. He is exhausted, almost dumb (v. 323), disgusted with himself, ashamed, and bewildered. He does not eat (v. 323), though it cannot be long since he has. These are all the expected reactions of someone who has fallen victim to such a manic attack as has Ajax. As we have seen in the cases of Orestes and Heracles, they do not amount to depression. Ajax's suicide is sometimes said to be evidence of depression. There is little in the play (as opposed to the life situation it exploits) to indicate that this is the case. The more common critical mode of reaction to the suicide of Ajax is one of admiration (cf. vv. 479–80) and to state, with Stanford (1963, 290), that it is a measure of Ajax's heroic character. His suicide becomes, as I will argue more generally in chapter 6, a mode of self-authentification.

The treatment of Ajax by the *Problema* is in many ways as instructive as is that of Bellerophon, who, essentially depressive, was rendered manic. This displays the basic bias of the *Problema,* which was to make the manic strangely respectable by association with the depressive. If the chance was missed with Bellerophon, in Ajax's case it was quite different. There was no question of him being essentially manic, but bipolarity rendered him depressive as well. As we have just seen, this entails a considerable misrepresentation of the tradition.

The (as I have said, meretricious) attempt of the *Problema* to unite the medical and the popular traditions of melancholia is intriguing. The text has no sense of or feeling for the depressive. History did not allow it this insight. Its attempts to include this are fraught with the same problems we encountered in Euripides' *Orestes:* narrative privileged and affectivity thinned.[64]

If I have dwelt overlong on the *Problema,* it is because of the enormous influence that this text has exerted in Western literature. It is vital to understand, however, that this canonical text is quite deceptive and in fact masks the reality of the ancient understanding of melancholy. Despite the homogenizing attempts of *Problema* 30.1, the distinction between depressive and manic melancholia persisted. One tradition (that of the Eumenides Painter) was essentially medical, the other (that of Euripides' Orestes) popular. By and large, as the *Problema* overwhelmingly demonstrates, the popular interest was in the manic form.[65] Depressive melancholia was periodically acknowledged, but its time had not come. This simple, though astounding, fact has been little understood. The discursive tradition, then, with which depressive melancholy had to contend was one taken up with the outer, the surface, the mark, and the body as it is perceived in society. The passivity of depressive melancholia—for this period a mere epiphenomenon of mania[66]—has little to offer such a tradition.

Depressive melancholics (those resembling the Eumenides Painter's Orestes) were depicted in ancient literature. It would be astounding if they were not. Yet the frequency with which they appear is not marked, nor are their appearances to be noted in all eras. This stands to reason. Much of ancient literature focuses on social or physical matters (the polis, the state, the universe itself, individual *aretê* or *virtus*). Nor was there, in all periods, a literary valuation of that self-consciousness and inwardness required for depressive conditions to come into textual prominence.[67] Genre itself could conspire against the depiction of the inner experience: there is no doubt that the Athenian stage was not the ideal place for the dramatization of neurotic symptomatology. Nor was there the sort of conceptual armament that medical thought increasingly offered. As I attempt to trace the appearances of depressive melancholia in popular literature, I will note how, at first, it is registered but not conceptualized. As time passes, the importance of the emotion gradually becomes apparent. It seems that as the mind, or at least the inward life, becomes separated from the body, there follows an increased consciousness of a restless, depressive mentality. Conceptualization of this emotion is the result of the eventual importation of medical descriptors into the popular or "literary" rendering of the depressed individual. The importation of medical terminology produces a verbal representation that finally matches the sophistication of the Eumenides Painter's Orestes. With the importation of this vocabulary, we begin to witness the "popular" depiction of depressive melancholy—of sorrow without cause.

Times and traditions do change. Jason, the Hellenistic hero of the poem on the voyage of the *Argo* by Apollonius of Rhodes (born ca. 295 B.C.E.), provides one of the earliest and most instructive examples of just how. The romantic hero of Apollonius's neo-epic the *Argonautica* (on which see Toohey 1992c) is not characterized by ancient writers as a melancholic. His problems were not attributed to the heavy and lugubrious effects of the black bile. Some modern writers, however, have accused him of a propensity for melancholia.[68] There can be little wonder at this, for Jason's strength of purpose and his usual reaction to adversity during his expedition to gain the Golden Fleece is often emotional, even tearful.[69] At any rate, his "melancholia" contrasts markedly with the type to which Heracles, Lysander, or Ajax were said to be prone.[70] Jason's melancholia is depressive, not manic. This propensity distinguishes him from his companion voyagers, the Argonauts, and at the same time makes him one of the more singular protagonists of ancient epic.

Does Jason exhibit any of the symptoms normally associated with the illness? Soranus of Ephesus, though postdating Apollonius Rhodius by nearly four hundred years, produced a description of melancholia—typical of the tradition—that may assist in an analysis of Jason. Soranus characterized a melancholic as exhibiting "mental anguish and distress, dejection, silence, animosity towards members of the household, sometimes a desire to live and at other times a longing for death, suspicion . . . that a plot is being hatched against him, weeping without reason, meaningless muttering and . . . occasional joviality" (trans. Jackson [1950, 561]).

There are character traits in Jason that, if they do not indicate outright melancholy, may have made Soranus raise an eyebrow. There is in many speeches in the *Argonautica* an insistence on the mental anguish and distress that Jason suffers. At *Argonautica* 1.460–61 Jason is depicted brooding over the enormity of the impending tasks (he is *amêchanos* and *katêphioônti eoikôs*, "hapless" and "downcast").[71] At 2.410, after Phineus's painful predictions, Jason is *amêchaneôn kakotêti* [utterly resourceless because of his woeful circumstances]. At 2.622–23 Jason extravagantly states, to Tiphys, that he is grieving and that he is "distraught in wretched and helpless ruin"; a few lines later he is "wrapped in excessive fear and cares unbearable" (2.627–28). Soon afterward (2.631–33) Jason protests to Tiphys that rather than sleeping, he groans throughout the night, worrying for the future. Shortly after the death of Tiphys, Jason is again reduced to a state of helplessness (at 2.885 he is *amêchaneôn*, and at 2.888 he and his companions are "vexed at heart" [*aschaloôsin*]).[72] On their home voyage, Jason and the Argonauts are forcibly beached on the Libyan coast. Jason's reaction is despair (*aniazonti*, 4.1347). Then nymphs appear to provide assistance. Apollonius describes his hero's reaction to their appearance as not merely amazed but "distraught" or "grief-stricken" [*atyzomenon*] (4.1316–18) and stricken by utter helplessness (*amêchanié*, 4.1318). The whole passage (4.1313–18) runs as follows:

> [The nymphs] gathered beside Jason,
> And with their hands gently drew the mantle from his head.
> But he turned his eyes away in the other direction
> Out of awe for these deities; for he alone could see them,
> And, to him in his grief-stricken state [*atyzomenon*], they spoke soothing words:
> "Poor wretch, why so stricken by absolute helplessness?"[73]

Such anxieties and dejections, while uncommon in any Homeric hero but a mourning one,[74] are in Jason's case excessive, even for a Hellenistic hero. Jason's passivity, pliability, helplessness, and grief are as remarkable as they are unexpected in a warrior. His attitude, were we to attempt to envisage it expressed live on a human face, might well match that of the Eumenides Painter's Orestes or that of Kraepelin's stuporous maniac. Do such character traits point to a depressive nature?[75] They undoubtedly do, but not to one that we could judge so in the strictly medical sense. At this point, at least, Jason's problems are attitudinal and are comprehensible given the situations in which he finds himself. Yet his reactions are not those one would expect of a Homeric hero.[76]

There are other qualities in Jason at which Soranus might have balked and that might lead us back to the Eumenides Painter. There were Jason's silences. At 1.1286–1289, after the disappearance of Heracles, Jason's reaction is remarkable.

> But Jason, amazed and utterly helpless [*amêchaniêsi atychtheis*],
> Said never a word, one way or the other, but sat there
> Bowed under his heavy load of ruin, in silence,
> Eating out his heart [*thymon edôn*].

Jason's silence, stillness, and dejection are as remarkable as they are unpredictable—in what we assume is a heroic man of action. Of especial noteworthiness in this context is the description of Jason "eating out his heart." This is the same description (but in Greek with the prefix *kata* dropped) given by Homer to the depressive Bellerophon and singled out as applicable to a depressive melancholic by *Problema* 30.1 and, most significantly, Galen (*Introductio seu medicus* 14.741.6, cited earlier in this chapter) in their discussions of Bellerophon. If ever we needed confirmation of Jason's status as a melancholic, this is provided by the relative uncommon phrase *thymon edôn*, "eating out his heart." This phrase indicates definitively that in the eyes of some ancients, even if they lived after him, his attitudes were to be associated with those suffering from a medical form of melancholia.

Jason is silent elsewhere. For example, after Aeetes assigns Jason his tasks (3.422–25), the reaction is comparable.[77] Jason is also given to tears. He weeps at 1.534–35 as he leaves his homeland and at 4.1703–4 when he and his companions are trapped in darkness on the Cretan sea. Notice, furthermore, that Jason is seldom jovial. Rare instances occur at 1.1104 (when Mopsus interprets a favorable omen for him), at 3.1148 (after meeting Medea and declaring his love), and at 4.93 (again in reaction to Medea). Soranus would have had few reservations in diagnosing that Jason was, strictly speaking, classifiable as a melancholic. Galen, if his notes on Bellerophon are anything to go by, would have felt the same way.

It is the very absence of a clear-cut concept of melancholia which so fascinates in descriptions of emotional states resembling those that we would associate with depression and melancholia. Jason is clearly of a melancholic disposition, and he is evidently depressed. A Greek doctor such as Galen would have had no hesitation in diagnosing him as such. Yet it is evident that while Apollonius may be able to "see" his dour hero for what he is, he lacks the psychological vocabulary (something that only the doctors could provide) to say what he is. Jason's depression, however, is extraordinarily interesting in another way. It is quite clear that Jason has good grounds for feeling miserable—things seldom go his way, at least not without considerable help from others. His persistently depressive response to adversity suggests a disposition that is prone to melancholia. We might say that—whether or not he is certifiable as a melancholic—he has the signs of an individual who is prone to sorrow without cause.

There are, not surprisingly, few texts in ancient literature that focus on psychological states like those exhibited by Apollonius's tearful hero Jason.[78] There are even fewer that concentrate on abnormal psychological dispositions. One comes with considerable excitement, therefore, to Cicero's *Tusculan Disputations*, a text composed in 44 B.C.E., in the year before Cicero's death. The *Tusculan Disputations*, taking their name from Cicero's villa at Tusculum, are written in the form of dialogues, but with a rather more continuous exposition than actual dialogue. This is Cicero in lecturing mode. The lecturer's target is those types of aberrant psychological register that may render one incapable of living the happy life *(vivere beate)*. So, in the first of the five books of the *Tusculans,* Cicero discusses fear of death. Such an emotion, if it becomes all-pervasive, may render one absolutely incapable of living happily. In the second book, Cicero advises his general reader on the need for endurance of pain, while in the third, of especial importance for this discussion of psychological aberrance, he instructs on the control of such distressing emotions as grief, jealousy, lament, and mourning. In the fourth book, he continues to examine distressful mental conditions: immoderate delight, lust, and fear, all conditions that, like those of book 3, may be controlled by the exercise of will. The final book argues that for the conduct of a happy life, inner virtue is a prerequisite.

It is the third book that is of importance for this discussion.[79] Here, as I have indicated, Cicero provides for us a detailed discussion of psychological distress, something he terms *aegritudo animi.* What does he mean by this phrase (which I have translated as "psychological distress")? To answer this it may help to look through some of the key elements of the argument of *Tusculans* 3. This will help us home in on precisely what Cicero means. Cicero begins with the propositions that the wise man is susceptible to psychological distress but that such distress is disorder of the soul and, therefore, an unsoundness of mind (3.7). (His conclusion will be that psychological distress is not natural but voluntary and is due to mistaken opinion [3.81–84]; we can therefore control it by the exercise of moral, philosophical fortitude.) There is in our nature weakness, Cicero asserts, which philosophy must remove (3.12, 13) and from which the wise man (the one who is steeped in philosophy) is thus free (3.15, 20, 21). The cause of psychological distress and all other psychological disorders (there are three others: immoderate delight, desire, and fear; psychological distress is worst [3.26, 27]) is opinion and judgment—anticipation of distress, we might paraphrase, or an overvaluation of its virulence. Psychological distress cannot be relieved by diverting one's attention (3.32, 33), for distress comes from the unexpected (3.28–31, 52–54). Time may bring alleviation, Cicero points out, but reflection and reason are the true remedies (3.55–59). The cause of psychological distress lies, as he has stated, in opinion and judgment (3.61). This may even lead people to think it right to feel distress (3.62–65). Distress can be got rid of, Cicero asserts (3.66). It is useless. Those who suffer most bear it most easily (3.67). Wise men are not distressed at their shortcomings (3.68, 69). Distress must not be yielded to as natural (3.70–74).

What does Cicero mean by this condition that he describes as *aegritudo animi*? He states that it encompasses almost any form of emotion where "psychological distress of the soul *[aegritudo animi]* closely resembles the conditions of bodies not in a healthy state," adding, "thus that distress in the soul *[aegritudo animi]* has a name that in meaning is not distinct from the meaning of pain" (3.23). Cicero attempts therefore to bring a medical formulation and description to this psychological state. This, as I have repeatedly emphasized, points to the beginnings of the confluence of the two ways of viewing sorrow without cause, as despondency and as medical melancholia. Elsewhere Cicero backs off, noting that *aegritudo animi* "is nothing else than the idea and conviction of an instant and pressing great evil," but adding that "a life spent honorably and brilliantly affords a solace so complete that either no touch of [psychological] distress approaches those who have lived such a life, or else the prick of pain in the soul is only superficial" (3.61). But perhaps the clearest definition is provided by Cicero at *Tusculans* 3.83: "there is one principle in all forms of distress *[aegritudo]*; their names are many. For envy is a form of distress *[aegritudo]*, and rivalry, and jealousy and compassion and trouble, lament, mourning, attacks of suffering, wailing, agitation, grief, vexation, torment, and despondency *[desperare]*. All these the Stoics define, and the terms I have given are used for each manifestation of distress *[aegritudo]*." Two aspects of his description are striking. The first is that, as we may judge from the rest of *Tusculans* 3, these various forms of *aegritudo animi* have an easily identifiable etiology—opposition in one's endeavors or in love, the death of a friend, disappointment, pain, and so on.[80] These conditions are not necessarily persistent, nor are they necessarily debilitating. They all have, furthermore, identifiable causes. Melancholia has no need of such simplistic causes. The second aspect is that many of the descriptive terms used for *aegritudo animi* could as easily be used for depressive melancholia (so "attacks of suffering, wailing, agitation, grief, vexation, torment, and despondency" *[lamentari, sollicitari, dolere, in molestia esse, adflictari, desperare]*).[81] What should we conclude from all of this? Cicero's "psychological distress" is not depressive melancholia. But it does exhibit some of the hallmarks.

What so fascinates in Cicero's discussion is what is not said. When one reads of *aegritudo animi*, when one reads Cicero's sensitive comments on *maeror* and *luctus* ("grief" and "mourning"), one easily assumes that it is depression that is being referred to—*angoscia esistenziale*, as Emanuele Narducci (in Clerici 1996, 32) puts it.[82] The best evidence we have for associating Cicero's *aegritudo animi* with a depressive disposition is the stress laid upon mourning within *Tusculans* 3: the link between mourning and melancholia has been made canonical by Freud.[83] There are, furthermore, other places in Cicero's work where mourning and melancholia seem to be confused.[84] So it is that one wrongly assumes Cicero is pointing toward depressive melancholy (the emotion, at any rate, of which the doctors were conscious). Cicero does not at any point refer to this condition. Why? I suppose it is because he did not want to: he may have viewed depression as trivial by comparison with those other states he had examined.[85]

But things are surely more complex than this. Part of the reason must also be that Cicero has no verbal or conceptual register for noting the existence of depressive melancholy (melancholia, as he tells us at *Tusculans* 3.5, is a violent disease, a mania). For that we can only blame history. It had not yet undergone the circumstances necessary for the problematization of the emotion.

There are unexpected spin-offs from Apollonius's and Cicero's silences. The absence of terminology for depressive melancholy in their works may help us to periodize the unfolding of depressive melancholia within ancient culture. It is quite clear from Cicero's *Tusculans* that the time had not quite come for the conceptual or textual "discovery" of this condition in nonscientific literature. Yet the lineaments of the emotion are present—a metaphorical vocabulary, a metaphorical symptomatology. All that is needed is for Cicero to determine that *luctus*, *maeror*, or *tristitia* need have no clearly identifiable etiology. Cicero was not just the product of his conceptual era. His thinking, like that of Seneca and other Stoics, was dogged by a pernicious desire to seek the easy etiology and the easy cure for psychological distress. Willpower and moral behavior become the cause and the cure. Cicero would have seen Orestes' *synesis* as bad conscience. This is a most unfortunate—indeed a most childish—way to judge madness.[86]

The unambiguous signs of the discovery of existential melancholy did not take place until the next century. But things did not stand still in the meantime. Horace, less afraid than Cicero of trivial emotions, several times alluded to a condition that resembles depressive melancholia.[87] I will have more to say on this topic in my discussion of boredom in chapter 3. For now it may suffice to point toward *Epistles* 1.8. In this poem, Horace initially alludes to a restless dissatisfaction that has him oscillating inconstantly between a variety of preferences and experiences. So *Epistles* 1.8.11–12 have Horace describing himself as follows:

> What harms me I follow; I run from what I believe helps.
> At Rome I, fickle *[ventosus]*, love Tibur and at Tibur Rome.

The root of Horace's problem is psychological. In verses 9–10 of the poem, he describes himself as locked into a perverse frame of mind.

> I offend faithful doctors and become angry at friends,
> Because they are anxious to get me away from this melancholy
> *[veternus]*.

I have translated *veternus* as "melancholy." The term in Latin is linked with the word for "aged" *(vetus)* and is no doubt suggestive of the sluggishness and torpor that can be associated with old age.[88] That this may approximate a form of depressive psychology is probable, if not immediately apparent.[89] What is important is that the emotion has been complicated and expanded to the point that it has become almost existential. Medical melancholia, however, is not at issue.[90]

What is wrong with Persius?[91] In his magnificent *Satires* 3 he seems to suffer a strange psychological illness, an unexpected compound of a lethargy and an anger. The illness is not unequivocally named. Perhaps it was too obvious to require naming. Or, more likely, such psychic illnesses (then as now) defy easy designation. It is my contention that what is wrong with Persius is what is wrong with the Eumenides Painter's Orestes.[92] Persius, the author of six difficult satires composed during Nero's reign, marks a new phase in the ancient history of melancholia.[93] In Persius's *Satires* 3 the medical tradition moves into popular literature. Jason's *amêchaniê* and Horace's *veternus* receive a clinical name.

Direct symptoms of Persius's illness (called such at vv. 83 and 88) fall under two headings, of lethargy and of anger.[94] (The parallels between the paradigms offered by the Eumenides Painter's Orestes and the Euripidean Orestes should be apparent at once.) There are a cluster of related or analogized images. Lethargy—even sleepiness (note Persius's yawning at vv. 3 and 54–55)—is linked with ideas of looseness (vv. 58, 85), of cold, and of liquid, of flowing away and dilution, even moistness (vv. 14, 20). It is also linked with paleness (vv. 43, 85, 94, 96) and emaciation (v. 85). Anger is expressed directly or through a series of interlinked images: of heat (v. 108), burning (v. 3) , cooking (vv. 6, 22) and boiling (vv. 37, 116); of swelling (vv. 8, 9, 27), and of fatness and being crammed full (v. 12 and passim); of blackness (v. 13) and poison (v. 37). The condition suffered by Persius seems to involve, thus, a swelling with anger (vv. 12, 13, 85, 116–17) and a dissipation of this into lethargy. The condition can be characterized in different places as exhibiting all of these analogized symptoms. While Persius's emotional state can involve an oscillation between the two states (an apparent bipolarity), it also presents itself as a nearly simultaneous compound of the two conditions.

The author of the poem seems to have decided that what Persius suffers from is a type of madness. His actions are those of a person who is *non sanus* (so he is in v. 118, the very last line of the poem). References to insanity occur elsewhere (vv. 5, 20, 32, 81) or are implied.[95] To judge by the references to medical figures in the poem (v. 80 ff.), it is a form of insanity that would have been understood by a doctor (v. 118). This combination of lethargy and anger (in succession or alternating) can imply both *insania* and melancholy. What is remarkable here is that Persius all but gives the complex illness a name. This is unparalleled in nonmedical literature (and perhaps within—Aretaeus is the main exception). This naming happens three times in the poem. In one instance, Persius's friend admonishes him thus (vv. 117–18):

> You say and do what even
> Orestes would swear are the actions of a madman.

Orestes, as an expert in the matter, certifies the madness of Persius. In part this was because Orestes' *insania* was typified by anger (by *furor*). But Orestes, as we have seen again and again in this chapter, was a victim of melancholia. Roman authors such as Cicero, with whom Persius would have been thoroughly familiar, were clear on the matter.[96] This melancholic tone or strain is highlighted in the lines of the poem immediately preceding those just quoted. The friend attempts here to demonstrate to Persius the extent of his venality. So, when faced with the prospect of gain, this normally healthy man exhibits the bipolar symptoms of a melancholia (an extreme oscillation between anger and fear). These might have been drawn straight from the pages of Aretaeus or the pseudo-Aristotelian *Problema* (30.1). So at *Satires* 3.115–18 we read:

> You shiver, when white fear *[timor albus]* has shaken up corn ears all
> over your limbs.
> Now, as if a torch has been brought near, your blood boils and with
> anger
> Your eyes flash, and you say and do what even
> Mad Orestes would swear are the actions of a madman.

The description and imagery, indicating an alternation between the extremes of psychic "heat" and "cold," are best interpreted by reference to Aretaeus's or the *Problema*'s melancholic alternation between depression (cold) and mania (heat).

A second instance in which Persius's illness acquires a name occurs in verse 8. Its context goes as follows:

> One of the companions speaks. Is it true? "Quickly, let
> Someone come here. Is there no one?" The black bile is swelling.
> "I'm splitting"—you'd say that all the herds of Arcadia were braying.
> Now there's a book and a parchment, two-toned and trimmed,
> In his hand, and paper, and a jointed pen.
> Then we complain, that the thick ink sticks to the pen,
> That the black ink is ruined when water is mixed in.
> We complain because the pen makes two washy drops.
> Poor man, and poorer each day. Has it come
> To this?

It is not just the irresolution that makes this passage so important for the history of the depiction of melancholy. It is that Persius seems to envisage his addressee as a real depressive melancholic. What is most striking in Persius's portrait is that he is so precise in his designation of the condition of his addressee. In verse 8 of the poem, it is said of the sufferer: *turgescit vitrea bilis* [his glasslike bile swells]. One convincing gloss for this passage interprets *vitrea bilis* as an imitation, via Horace's *Odes* 3.13.1 *(splendidior vitro)*, of Horace's *Satires* 2.3.141, which contains the expression *splendida bilis* (Harvey 1981, 80). Horace's expression has been convincingly explicated by Kiessling-Heinze as *melaina cholê* (the black bile that provides the term *melancholy*). If this understanding of the echoes inherent in *vitrea bilis* is correct, then it indicates that Persius is unequivocally suffering from a medical form of melancholia (see too Squillante 1995, 26). That is why I have translated this line as "the black bile is swelling."

Other aspects of this passage assist in reaching this conclusion. These extend beyond the medical. The imagery of the pen and its black ink ("l'encre de la mélancholie,") is striking. The blackness and stickiness (above all the blackness, but also the stickiness, which hints at constipation) project an image that is infused with that of depressive melancholia and that, given its application to writing, seems to characterize the act of literary composition itself. There is also the imagery of swelling and splitting. This picks up the analogies made for the author's anger and even, as I have described it, his agitation and flight of ideas. The combination of depression and anger echoes the central polarity of the poem, between lethargy and anger.

Persius's illness exhibits an affective ambivalence that matches that of the Eumenides Painter's Orestes. He seems to combine the latent agitation of Orestes (this "splitting" and anger) with the apparent despondency (evident above all in the metaphor of black ink and earlier in the yawning). (The anger [*furor* or *mania*] matches that, it also deserves stating, of the Euripidean Orestes.) The image of Persius catches, furthermore, the bipolarity of fear and anger mentioned at the close of the poem.

A third "naming" of Persius's illness occurs in verse 63 of this satire, when hellebore is suggested as a cure for those whose skin swells.

> When the diseased skin swells already, you would see
> People demanding hellebore in vain.

The illness requiring cure here is usually said to be dropsy. This is because of the swelling alluded to in the next line. In this poem, however, swelling has been associated with anger (see the references to swelling at vv. 8, 9, 27, and 39). This swelling is a collateral condition of the author's lethargy.[97] Elsewhere in my discussion of the poem, I have associated swelling and lethargy with melancholia and bipolarity. I see no reason not to do so here. Hellebore is termed in Latin *elleborum* or *veratrum*. It existed in a white form, *elleborum album* or *veratrum album*, and a black form, *elleborum orientale* or *veratrum orientale*. Popular usage does not seem to have distinguished these.[98] White or black, it is a powerful emetic and was a useful treatment for anything involving the retention of fluid (such as dropsy) or the stool (constipation—this condition picks up all the imagery in the poem of being crammed) or bile (such as melancholia). It did this by purging the body of hard-to-budge fluids.[99] So hellebore was the standard emetic treatment for melancholy (cf. Celsus 3.18.17 and the epigraph to the present chapter). That the addressee should call for such an emetic treatment points to his suffering from melancholia (see Gildersleeve 1979, 132).[100] It reemphasizes the remarkable union in this poem between the lay and the medical traditions.

Support for this contention also comes from an unexpected quarter. In *Satires* 3.88–107, Persius's interlocutor imagines an individual who, already seriously ill and under treatment from a doctor, takes the first opportunity to be again out and about, to frequent the houses of the wealthy, to bathe, and to drink. The overindulgence while the man is ill brings on his death. This vivid passage offers an allegory linking the behavior of this ill man and those spiritual degenerates who, like Persius, would ignore philosophy. The passage runs as follows (the translation is adapted from Conington 1893):

> "Examine me. There's a strange palpitation in my chest. My throat is
> Bad, and foul breath is rising from it. Please, examine me."
> Suppose a patient were to say this to his physician, and were to be
> told to rest,
> And then when the third night found the current of his veins steady,
> Were to ask from a great house for some mellow Surrentine for his
> moderately thirsty bottle
> before bathing. "Sir, you look pale," "O, it's of no consequence."
> "You had better attend to it, though,
> Whatever it is; your skin is getting quietly bloated and quite yellow."
> "I tell you, you're paler than I am; don't come the guardian over me;
> I've buried *him* long ago, and now I've got you in my way." "Go on,
> I'm dumb."
> So our hero goes to his bath, with his stomach distended with eating
> and looking white,
> And a vapour of sulphurous properties slowly oozing from his throat;
> But a shivering comes on while he drinks, and makes him drop his hot
> tumbler

From his fingers; his teeth are exposed and chatter;
The rich dainties dribble back again from his dropping jaws.
So it's trumpets and tapers; and, laid out
On a high bed and daubed with gluey balm,
He turns up his heels stark and stiff towards the door;
And citizens of twenty-four hours' standing in their caps of liberty
carry him to the grave.

Aspects of the symptoms of this ill man continue the pattern of imagery evident in the poem thus far: the ill man is pale (v. 94), and his skin is swollen (*turgidus*, v. 98; *cutis aegra tumebit*, v. 63). His lips are slackened (*laxis labris*, v. 102) in the way that Persius's jaw is (*laxumque caput*, v. 58). The man's symptoms match to some degree those of Persius. But of most significance is that the ill man has a remission of his sickness on the third day of its course, then on the fourth day a relapse. His death on that day exhibits symptoms of fever (vv. 101–2).

What is wrong with this individual? The best guess is that he is suffering a four-day fever, that is, quartan fever (Conington 1893, 68; Gildersleeve 1979, 138). Quartan fever would account for the symptoms, the third-day remission when the patient goes out on the town, and the fourth-day relapse—hence the name "quartan" fever (see Celsus 3.3 on some of these details).[101]

Quartan fever is relevant for the context of this poem in two ways. First, and this is something that I will illustrate at greater length in the next chapter but that I must firmly emphasize here, quartan fever is associated with melancholy (see the Hippocratic treatise *On the Nature of Man* 15).[102] Second, quartan fever, the illness probably in question here, exhibits the alternation between hot and cold that Persius suffers (see vv. 108–9 for this alternation in the case of this illness) and that the melancholic Orestes seems to have.

Other passages within Persius's poem reinforce these conclusions. Not only is the addressee aimless, but he also displays a seeming psychomotor retardation and despondency that matches that of the Eumenides Painter's Orestes. In the following passage (*Satires* 3.58–62) the addressee's aimlessness and despondency (so the lolling and yawning) is emphasized.

Are you still snoring—with your head lolling on a drooping neck?
He's yawning off yesterday with his jaws dangling all over the place.
Is there anything that you aim at, against which you direct your bow?
Or are you chasing crows with the first missiles you can get hold of,
Content where your feet lead and living for the moment.

What intrigues in Persius's depiction of his melancholic state is that his portrait more or less explicitly names the condition from which his addressee suffers. Depressive melancholia, of an essentially existential sort, now is labeled using the terms of medicine. So we could take Persius's portrait as representing the end point of a progression that we have begun with Jason. Jason suffered from a depressive condition for which Apollonius's conceptual apparatus lacked a proper term. With Cicero and with Horace the progression toward interiority becomes more intense. Cicero does not seem to conceive that *aegritudo animi* could actually lack a proper etiology, let alone the simplistic cure of willpower. Horace is more sophisticated. But vocabulary again lets him down. To designate symptoms and to name the condition, he is forced to use metaphor. While Seneca's depiction of this depressive condition is undoubtedly the most detailed in terms of symptomatology, he still lacks a clear name. It is left to Persius to make the remarkably modern, almost too familiar union between depression and melancholy.

What is equally striking in this diagnosis provided by Persius is that its essentially bipolar analysis of melancholia occurs at approximately the same time as does that of Aretaeus of Cappadocia (whose views I have already outlined). It appears that in this period a new mode of interpreting human psychology was taking root.

It is possible to draw some conclusions from all of this material. I have examined three ways of looking at melancholia: that of the despondent, dejected, depressed individual typified by the Eumenides Painter's Orestes; the popular mode, which, like Euripides in his Orestes, saw the condition as essentially manic; and a medical tradition that saw melancholia as an essentially depressive and debilitating illness. As we have just observed, late in antiquity the first and third conditions intersected. The concepts of medicine animated the Eumenides Painter's tradition to produce what might best be termed an existential melancholia. This can best be seen, as the first and last sections of this chapter demonstrated, in the remarkable portrait of the existential melancholy provided by Persius's *Satires* 3. For the sake of clarity, we should repace the major conclusions from the various sections of this chapter.

The earliest views of melancholia link it simply to a physiology conditioned by the predominance of black bile, one of the four humors. This physiology, however, soon became associated with temperament or psychology. It seems that, during the fourth century, this new melancholic temperament and pathology were distinguished. While a melancholy temperament may have involved nothing more than a certain sluggishness, a temporary or even persistent overabundance of black bile could produce a pathological condition characterized by despondency, fear, and delusion. Things changed irrevocably at the end of the fourth century with the appearance of the pseudo-Aristotelian *Problema* (30.1). The *Problema* associates melancholia with exceptional people. It also allows that melancholy can display itself as either mania or depression, depending on whether the bile has heated or cooled. Much subsequent medical thought turned its back on the manic side of melancholy (with the noteworthy exception of Aretaeus). Whether subsequent medical writers were humoralists or not, they associated melancholy with depression—it was a disease exhibiting despondency, fear, and delusion.

The popular view of melancholia is, with few exceptions, remarkably consistent. Whether it is Euripides, Cicero, Menander, or Plutarch, they saw melancholia as a preeminently violent and angry condition. To judge from Aristophanes and Cicero, this was the way Greeks, at any rate, used the word *melancholia*. If pressed to offer a physiological basis for this interpretation, I suppose they might have had recourse to the lore of the *Problema*, on the basis of which they could have attributed the mania to an overheating of the black bile.

The bifurcation between medical and lay perceptions seems to have deprived the literary individual of a word to describe sorrow without cause. But this is not to say that there was no consciousness of the condition.[103] It has been suggested that Jason, for example, and the addressee of Persius's *Satires* 3 exhibit a despondency so pervasive as rightly to be termed melancholy. Apollonius's Jason suffered from a depressive condition that is not named: Apollonius's conceptual apparatus lacked a proper term. With Cicero and with Horace the progression toward a depressive interiority becomes more intense. Cicero does not seem to conceive that *aegritudo animi* could actually lack a proper etiology, let alone the simplistic cure of willpower. Horace is more sophisticated. But vocabulary again lets him down. To designate symptoms and to name the condition, he is forced to use metaphor.

There are, as I have indicated, unexpected spin-offs from Apollonius's and Cicero's silences. The absence of terminology for depression and melancholy in their works may help us to periodize the unfolding of depressive melancholia within ancient culture. It is quite clear from Cicero's *Tusculans* that the time had not come for the conceptual or textual "discovery" of this condition. And yet the lineaments of the emotion are present—a metaphorical vocabulary, a metaphorical symptomatology. All that is needed is for Cicero to determine that *luctus*, *maeror*, or *tristitia* need have no clearly identifiable etiology to become sorrow without cause. What fascinates in Persius's epochal depiction of his melancholia is that his portrait more or less explicitly names the condition from which he suffers. (Depressive—or existential—melancholia in a literary text is now labeled using the terms of medicine.) Persius's portrait is very important in another way. His melancholia exhibits "mixed" symptoms. His depressive symptoms are over- and underlaid with traces of mania. His is an agitated melancholy that has a striking parallel in the remarkable painting of Orestes held in the Louvre. It also has a remarkable textual parallel in the diagnosis of melancholia that is provided by Aretaeus of Cappadocia.

The periodization that I am attempting to highlight should be apparent. The major change—admittedly the end point of a gradual progression—takes place during the first century of our era. This major change is the emergence—or better, the conceptualization in popular literature—of a form of depressive melancholy and, in Persius's case, of mixed-state melancholy. (It is significant that the beginning point of the process of discovery is in the Alexandrian period.) That melancholy to which I am referring is identifiably modern. It is the type of emotion so often claimed as having been invented with the Enlightenment.

The change that I have attempted to highlight may be characterized through a simple set of contrasts. We witness in this evolutionary shift a movement from activity to passivity, from body to mind (and interiority), from complicity to estrangement, from public to private, from the mark to the sign, and, paradoxically and above all, from lack of control to control. This last shift deserves emphasis, for our depressive melancholic observes a type of control in his or her private relations that the manic figure finds impossible. Thus the final change (and this is something that will become more clear as we progress) is that depressive melancholia, pointing to an increased interiority, is accompanied by a greater self-consciousness, or, to put it another way, self-awareness.

Inevitably one asks why these changes occurred. The reasons for the shift in perception are beyond the scope of this inquiry. Obvious causes are, from the literary and generic point of view, an increased interest in psychological or empathetic narrative and a focus directed more on motives than on actions; from the point of view of society, there is an increase in urbanization and, with this (in some centers at any rate), a societal situation in which the traditional ruling and intellectual elites were excluded from political decision making (there must follow inevitably a heightened sense of powerlessness).[104] But these pressures can provide only a partial answer, for medical literature exhibits some concern, at any rate, for depressive melancholia from early on—certainly from before the urbanization of the third century B.C.E. and the first century C.E. What one can say with confidence is that disturbing conditions such as melancholia appear most to flourish in eras and in social matrices where individual, private freedoms are encouraged but where public freedom (I mean the freedom to participate in the ruling of the polis or of the state) is firmly—even vigorously—curtailed.

The extent to which this effects public mentality and its private expression throughout various literary and scientific genres is difficult to pin down. What we may say is that there is, first in the early Hellenistic period and then later under the early Roman Empire, both in the literature and in the life experience rendered, an increasing problematization of will (or volition) or of control. Fueled as much by philosophies like Stoicism as by social conditions in which individuals were conscious of limited political freedoms, this concern is inevitably accompanied by an inward-lookingness, by an "interiority," which seems to fuel concern for the boundaries of self and of self-consciousness. I am not saying that this problematization engenders the sorts of conditions in which sorrow without cause can take root. Rather, it seems to highlight and perhaps to foster the constellation of affective conditions of which melancholia forms such a critical part.

There are, finally, a number of immediate payoffs that this focus on melancholia can provide. The first is that it offers us some idea of the early history of an illness that still is at the very heart of the psychiatric and psychological enterprise. It indicates, furthermore, the experiential sameness of the illness through time. So it underlines the mistake made by those who would locate the origins of this illness in the Enlightenment. The second point relates to the periodization of mania and depression. One's instinct—affirmed by the great German psychiatrist Kraepelin—that earlier societies privilege mania while later ones privilege depression is borne out in the literature of Greco-Roman antiquity.[105] A registering of complex mixed states, though evident in art, comes late. As Orestes and Persius demonstrate, this was understood, if not necessarily conceptualized, in all periods.[106] There is, it seems, a lag between the conceptualization apparent in various media. Visual art had the tools to represent melancholia of the depressive (and of the mixed) sort far earlier than did written media. (This probably holds true for the representations of many other emotions in ancient literature.) Related to this is my third point: above all, ancient literary texts understood melancholia as a manic or violent illness; depression was most commonly registered as a mere epiphenomenon. Contexts in which depression are highlighted, therefore, are particularly deserving of attention. My final points relate to the presentation of self-consciousness—of an awareness of oneself as a sentient being, separate from those about, whose "identity" is predicated on such a self-awareness—in ancient literature. This is intimately related to the emergence of depressive melancholia. This stands to reason, because the ailment highlights the interior, psychic, spiritual state of the sufferer—their interiority, as it might be termed. Linked to this is a fascinating type—even genre—within ancient writing, which might be termed "the literature of the self."[107] Above all, this comprises those texts that highlight the emergence of depressive melancholia as a subject requiring careful attention.

2

Medea's Lovesickness
Eros and Melancholia

> I come at last to that heroical love, which is proper to men and women, is a frequent cause of melancholy, and deserves much rather to be called burning lust, than by such an honourable title.
>
> —ROBERT BURTON, *The Anatomy of Melancholy*

> "Here comes the downpour, here the lightning and the cursed hail,
> the roar of thunder and the croaking of frogs."
> Thus speaking with each rapid breath, the slender maid,
> already close to death, enflames
> the fire which love has spread throughout her limbs.
>
> —SRÌ HARSA-DEVA (trans. Ingalls [1965, 232])

Erotic infatuation is violent. Love comes unexpectedly and overwhelms its victim. Its attack brings speechlessness, swooning, silence, blushing, insomnia, the sweats, and weeping.[1] It vanquishes the strongest of wills. When eros remains unconsummated (whether intentionally or merely through circumstance), there is persuasion,[2] then, if that is unsuccessful, rape.[3] Sometimes neither persuasion nor rape are useful. The very old must endure their lack of consummation, as must lovers permanently separated, through death, distance, conclusive rejection, physical infirmity, or gender.[4] This enforced endurance may lead to acts of violence, anger, and crime, especially crime if it is a woman who is subject to the frustration.[5] Or it may lead to a melancholic lovesickness—anorexia and eventual death.[6]

Violence remains the most common reaction to erotic frustration.[7] Valerius Flaccus's description of Medea's lovesickness, completed by 92 or 93 C.E., is typical of this tradition. Medea was a young, barbarian princess from Colchis in what is now Georgia. When the young Greek adventurer Jason first arrived in Colchis in pursuit of the Golden Fleece, Medea had no inkling of the emotional turmoil that the force of erotic passion would create in her life. It led her to abandon her family, to murder her brother and, later, her own children, and to take up a vagrant life on the Greek mainland. Erotic infatuation was connived at by Jason's divine patron, Juno, who intended Medea's assistance for her favorite. Without Medea's help, Juno believed, Jason would fail in his mission for the fleece, and her divine plan would be awry. So Juno gave Medea a girdle that would inflame passion (*Argonautica* 6.467 ff.), and when this was not sufficient for the task, she had Venus herself visit Medea, disguised as her aunt Circe (*Argonautica* 7.193 ff.). The overwhelming power of erotic infatuation was guaranteed by supernatural agents.

Once Medea had been infected (erotic infatuation is compared to a sickness by Valerius),[8] she underwent the symptoms that were typical of the erotic tradition. Medea was on fire and could not take her eyes off Jason. She was subject to *furor.* She blushed. She experienced *languor.* She suffered insomnia and inconstancy of purpose. Had Jason proposed then and there and had this been accepted by Medea's father, Aeetes, all would have been well. Consummation would have provided the cure for the sickness. But love was frustrated by her father's intransigent opposition to Jason's quest. Aeetes had no intention of letting the fleece go to a Greek stranger. Marriage, therefore, was out of the question.

Medea's erotic frustration intensified and gave way to mania and violence. She raged angrily like a bacchante (*Argonautica* 7.300–22). Elsewhere we read of more disquieting symptoms. Medea has become like the crazed Orestes of Euripides' play of the same name. This was, I should emphasize, the melancholic mythological hero with whom the last chapter began. Here is how Valerius, describing Medea, makes the connection with Orestes and continues—but in an amatory context—this tradition (*Argonautica* 7.144–52).

> Fresh fear broke her sleep,
> And she sat bolt-up in bed. She recognized her servants and her
> Loved home, she who just now rushed through Thessaly's cities.
> She is like mad Orestes who, in his blind terrors, snatched up
> A sword and struck at the phantom squadrons of his cruel mother.
> Snakes and the wild, terror-inducing whip made him quake in fear.
> He thought that he was again thick in the bloodshed of that
> Impure Spartan woman, and that then, tired, returning from the goddess's
> Counterfeit slaughter, he'd collapsed on the breast of his unhappy sister.

Poor Medea. She is constrained by the respect and love for her family that a liaison with Jason would mean abandoning. She is constrained, too, by her father's hostility toward Jason. This would render any illicit liaison extremely dangerous. So it is that her erotic frustration boils over.

In the passage I have just quoted, Medea's symptoms are provided with the most remarkable of depictions. That comparison with Orestes demands especial attention, in three ways. First, Orestes was mad, subject to mania and violence, at least in the Euripidean version. So, too, this simile suggests, is Medea. Second, Orestes was diagnosed as a melancholic. The comparison may suggest that Medea was too. Third, implicit in this portrait of Medea is the linking of melancholia, lovesickness, and violence. This last point is crucial, for it represents a view that we do not share. Love, lovesickness, and depression enjoy in our era a banal symbiosis that was not necessarily reflected in antiquity. Love was not always associated with lovesickness.[9] Nor was lovesickness necessarily associated with melancholia. Nor was it necessarily depressive.

The focus of this chapter will be on the tenuous relationship between these three conditions, but especially on lovesickness[10] and melancholy.[11] Five conclusions will be offered. First, the depressed, fretting, passive, and physically ill lover (sometimes termed the love melancholic), though present in ancient literature, is more a cliché of medieval and modern literary experience. The dominant reaction to frustrated love in ancient literature was manic and frequently violent. Second, lovesickness, in its literary depictions, mirrors the distinctions that the ancient medical writers posited for melancholia itself: there was a depressive type and there was a manic type. Third, the depressive variety of lovesickness, though always on the cards (just like depressive melancholia), becomes more frequent late in antiquity, above all during the first century of our era. Fourth, these dominant traditions of amatory mania and depression find exact parallels in those associated with melancholia proper and depression. Fifth—and this conclusion can only be foreshadowed here—these manic and depressive reactions to the trauma of erotic infatuation are means by which individuals attempt to restore the integrity of the self.

Although the doctors may have thought lovesickness a depressive condition, that is not the way it is depicted in the majority of ancient literary texts. Lovesickness, displayed in a violent or manic fashion, receives descriptions in almost all of the periods of ancient literature. The popular prejudice for mania seems to match that which we observed for melancholia in the last chapter. This type of reaction to erotic trauma, I am suggesting, matches closely that of the Euripidean Orestes of the last chapter. Mania, then, is the dominant amatory cliché for the representation of erotic frustration. One of the best—and most representative—descriptions of the experience may be found in Apollonius Rhodius's version of the love of Medea for Jason (composed about 250 B.C.E.; that should not be confused with the version composed by Valerius Flaccus in 92 or 93 C.E.). Let us therefore stay with this barbarian heroine for a little longer. We will find that the symptomatology of Apollonius's portrait is explicit, consistent, and far more lavish in its detail than that of Valerius Flaccus. The initial attack of love produces a violent, physical reaction. Subsequent frustrations recapitulate, though in a more pronounced manner, this emotional reaction. The descriptions, as we will see in the next section, match those used of melancholy but lack the precision of humoral diagnosis. The two Medeas, it will also be apparent, though separated in compositional time by three and a half centuries, offer an experiential continuum. This affective continuum provides us with a version of lovesickness (or love melancholy) that, like the dominant form of melancholia, was predicated on violence and activity; that is, erotic infatuation was "conceptualized" in much of antiquity in a way that matches the conceptualization of melancholia. In the pages to follow, but beginning with the representative Medeas, I will attempt to demonstrate this.

Medea's infection is precipitated by Hera.[12] Wishing to help Jason succeed in gaining the fleece from King Aeetes, she persuaded Aphrodite to have Eros make Medea fall in love with Jason (*Argonautica* 3.36–110). When Eros wounds Medea (3.284–98), the subjection to love is sudden and complete.

> He [Eros] shot at Medea. Speechlessness *[amphasiê]* overcame her.
> And back from the high-roofed hall he
> Sped laughing, and the shaft burnt in the girl,
> Deep below her breast, like fire *[phlogi eikelon]*. Continuously
> She cast bright glances at the son of Aeson. In her turmoil
> Her clever wits left her breast. No memory
> Did she sustain. Her heart was flooded with a sweet agony *[aniê]*.
> As a woman heaps kindling on a smouldering log
> (A working woman for whom spinning is a livelihood)
> To spread light through her home in the dark,
> While she works nearby, and as, kindled from a little brand,
> The great blaze reduces the kindling to ashes,
> So, coiled within her [Medea's] breast, stealthily smouldered
> Woeful love *[oulos erôs]*. Her soft cheeks turned
> To white then to red in the whirl of her mind *[akêdeiêisi nooio]*.

The description of Medea's reaction, though incomplete, gives a fair idea of the violence of her response. The imagery bears this out: Eros's shaft is "like fire," and Medea's heart is full of "agony"; the shaft causes, furthermore, forgetfulness, mental turmoil *(akêdeiê)*, and pallor alternating with red-colored flushing.[13]

Once Medea's condition has been established, it is not allowed to run its course. Her love is frustrated in two ways. First, loyalty and fear of her father, Aeetes, restrain her from succumbing to the emotion. Second, Jason's own fecklessness threatens to prevent her love from reaching its obvious conclusion. In response to both frustrations, Medea's reaction is violent. *Argonautica* 3.444–71 shows how she is affected by loyalty and fear. She is racked by contradictory emotions: she cannot remove Jason's image from her imagination (3.453–58); she fears for his safety (3.459–60) but mourns him as if he were already dead (3.460–61); she hopes that he will escape unharmed (3.464–68) but that he will know of her sympathy if he does perish (3.468–70). These contradictions seem to be the result of the illicit nature of Medea's passion: love impels her to hope for Jason's success, but this, she knows, will be at the expense of her father. Medea's "lovesickness" results in part from a conflict between *aidôs* (a sense of shame) and *himeros* (desire) (3.653). The former dictates loyalty; the latter dictates that she follow her longing for Jason. This ambivalence is especially evident in the dream sequence at 3.616–32[14] and in her actions (3.645–68) after the first monologue (3.636–44). She hesitates to leave her room but hangs on its exit. She casts herself writhing onto her bed. She weeps. Finally her aunt Chalciope hurries to her (3.670 ff.). She manages to disguise her willingness to assist Jason as concern for Chalciope's sons who are now in the company of the Argonauts (3.681 ff.). There follows the description of another bout of anguish. The symptoms of her condition are becoming more and more explicit (3.755–65).

> Quickly did her heart within her breast throb. 755
> . . . .
> A tear of pity ran from her eyes, and within, unceasingly, 761[15]
> Pain wore her away burning through the skin along the nerve 762
> Endings right up to the muscles of the neck beneath the head, 763
> Where pain is the most severe whenever grief *[anias]* 764
> Is cast by the tireless loves *[akamatoi erôtes]* into one's mind
> *[prapides]*. 765

Despite this physical anguish, Medea does not take to bed and begin to fade away. She makes her decision. *Erretô aidôs* [Let shame perish], she states (3.785). She will betray her parents. Medea herself gives a name to the condition: it is *atê*, a violent delusion.

In *Argonautica* 4 there is no longer a conflict between shame and desire. Medea has abandoned Colchis.[16] Her passion is frustrated now by the fecklessness of Jason, who seems likely to give in to the threats of the pursuing Colchians. Near the beginning of this book, Medea's lovesickness is described with real precision: her eyes are filled with fire, and her ears ring; she clutches at her throat, pulls at her hair, groans, is suicidal (4.16–23). These physical woes seem the product partly of frustrated love, partly of fear.[17] Later, when the Colchians manage to cut off the *Argo*'s party (4.303–38), Jason, sensing their situation is hopeless, strikes a deal *(synthesiê)* with the Colchians. They will keep the fleece but leave Medea on a nearby island with its priests of Artemis. Judges can later arbitrate her future (4.339–49). Medea's reaction to this treachery is not to swoon, take to bed, begin a wasting illness, or even contemplate suicide; rather, it is to threaten violence. She wrathfully argues that Jason is under oath to protect her (4.358–59, 388). If abandoned, she threatens, she will curse him. Jason at once backtracks and hatches a plan to murder the leader of the Colchians, Medea's brother, Apsyrtus (4.395–20). There follows a most extraordinary personal intrusion into the narrative (4.445–51).[18]

> Wretched Love, great woe and great object of hatred for humans,
> Because of you destructive strife, groaning, and wailing,
> and countless other pains pierce us.
> Against the sons of our enemies arm yourself and rouse your spirit
> And cast hateful madness *[stygerê atê]* into Medea's heart.
> For how, then, with awful death did she overcome
> Apsyrtus in his hot pursuit? That is the next part of my song.

Medea's lovesickness then reaches its apogee of violence. The bloody murder of her brother, Apsyrtus, follows. In the thrall of passion, Medea, it seems, will go to any length.

I have dwelt at such length on these versions of the Medea story because they provide such detailed (and moving) instances of the realization of the violent power of frustrated passion. Medea's lovesickness—and there can be no other word for it (she is still a virgin, and a young one at that)—leads her to remarkable acts of violence. In Apollonius's reading of the emotion of lovesickness, the onset of love and, later, its frustration—the lover's trauma—can lead to violent physical and emotional disorders. It can lead, furthermore, to acts of violence, even murder. Not only does Apollonius graphically illustrate its effects, but he also editorializes on its dangers.

Love in Apollonius's version of the story of Medea is a typical, if extreme, instance of what seems to have been the prevailing ancient view of the dangers of lovesickness. (Frustrated love—lovesickness, we would say—leads not to a fretting, passive, depressed state of mind but to mania and violence.) Let me offer a few other examples to illustrate and to bolster this contention. The tragic heroine of Virgil's *Aeneid,* Dido, suffers like her model Medea. Her love for Aeneas, like that of Medea for Jason, has been thrust upon her by divine scheming (*Aeneid* 1.657 ff.).[19] Dido's infection is likened to a wound (*Aeneid* 4.1–2, 67), and it burns like fire (4.2, 66). Like anyone who is lovesick, Dido becomes insomniac (4.5) and anxiety-ridden (4.9 ff.). But like Medea, she sees giving in to her passion as a form of betrayal (4.27; cf. 4.172), and giving way to the passion results in exactly this (4.86–89, 193–94). Also like Medea, she is betrayed, in her case by Aeneas. The "betrayal" comes after Jupiter sends Mercury to Aeneas (4.237–78) to warn Aeneas that he must remember his mission and cease from Carthaginian affairs. But before Dido meets Aeneas, she senses that treachery is afoot. Her reaction is not depressive but manic. Dido rages through the city like a bacchante (4.300–303) to meet Aeneas. Dido, her love frustrated and after an unsuccessful attempt at persuading Aeneas to delay sailing (4.416–49), again reacts violently: she sets about planning her own death (4.450–552). Notice that Virgil compares her to Pentheus, an embodiment of violent anger, and (as does Valerius with his Medea) to Orestes, that emblematic figure for melancholia (4.469–73).[20] Elsewhere he stresses her anger.[21] Dido's soliloquy, delivered as she watches the Aeneadae sail away, shows no relaxation of anger (4.590–629): she summons the sun, the gods, and the Furies to avenge her, on Aeneas first, then on all of his descendants. Soon afterward she suicides. Orestes stands out: Virgil's paradigm for madness, this hero recapitulates the Euripidean version of melancholy that was investigated in the last chapter. His invocation emphasizes again the conceptual, discursive, and experiential symmetry that exists between melancholy and lovesickness.

Among Virgil's other love-blighted, if not lovesick, protagonists, such as Corydon (*Eclogues* 2—which is based on Theocritus's *Idylls* 11),[22] Cornelius Gallus (*Eclogues* 10), or Orpheus (*Georgics* 4),[23] only Orpheus gives signs of breaking the violent amatory paradigm and of showing symptoms of real depressive lovesickness (*Georgics* 4.508 ff.).[24]

> Beneath a high cliff near the waters of the lonely Strymon
> He wept . . .
> Like a nightingale lamenting beneath a poplar's shade
> Who laments her young, which a harsh ploughman
> Cannily has taken still unfledged from the nest.

Yet even he meets a most violent end (*Georgics* 4.523–27). Perhaps Virgil's amatory reservations are based on Epicureanism. Lucretius's famous descriptions and rejection of love and its effects (*On the Universe* 4.1037–1287) seem in line with Virgil's view of lovesickness as a dangerous, violent *pestis* (see Beecher and Ciavolella 1990, 52–53).[25] For the Epicurean Lucretius, love is "a disease of the soul that slowly pervades the entire body, just like madness, and that must be eradicated before it completely upsets the physiopsychological balance of the man" (Beecher and Ciavolella 1990, 52). Most important for the present discussion is Lucretius's opinion that the onset and effects of love produce not a state of depressive enfeeblement but madness. Lucretius is to the point: love is a madness (*rabies,* 4.1083) and a dangerous one at that (4.1079–83).

> What they [sc., lovers] have sought, they press close to and make pain
> For the body, and they fasten teeth to lips,
> And kiss vehemently, because their pleasure is not unalloyed,
> For there are secret goads, which compel them to harm the thing
> itself,
> Whatever it is, whence arise those seeds of madness *[rabies].*

His contemporary Cicero does not tell us of lovesickness, but he has his suspicions of love. In the *Tusculan Disputations* (4.75), which I surveyed briefly in connection with melancholia in the last chapter, he notes of love that "of all disturbances of the soul there is assuredly none more violent," adding, "the disorder of the mind in love is in itself abominable." Horace's *Satires* 1.2, another Epicurean diatribe against love (which might as well be designed as advice for Corydon in *Eclogues* 2), reproduces the same vision of love, if not lovesickness, as a type of dangerous mania.[26]

There exist in ancient literature many other examples of manic lovesickness. Here I will confine my survey to just a few. There is, for example, Catullus's Ariadne (whose characterization owes much to Apollonius's Medea). Love-blighted and frustrated in poem 64, she is compared to a bacchante (v. 61), and she eventually works herself into a frenzy and, like Dido or Valerius's Medea, is "maddened" (*furens;* see vv. 124, 154). Scylla, the heroine in the pseudo-Virgilian *Ciris,* owes much to Ariadne. In her mania she will go to any length to consummate her love for Minos. So, too, behaves Medea in Ovid's *Heroides* 12, who is frenzied rather than depressed. Much, much later the Roman emperor Caracalla fell in love with his stepmother, Julia, who, "as if through carelessness, had uncovered the greater part of her body" (*Historia Augusta, Caracalla* 10). He was encouraged by her compliance: "his disordered madness was given strength to carry out the crime, and he contracted the marriage, which . . . he alone should have prohibited." The description and language used of Caracalla's emotions might be compared to those used of a mad *(furiosus)* slave who is said to have attacked Hadrian (*Historia Augusta, Hadrian* 12).

The violence inherent within erotic trauma is particularly emphasized in the writings of one of Virgil's near contemporaries, the Greek Parthenius. He composed for Virgil's friend the elegiac poet Cornelius Gallus (himself a victim of love in *Eclogues* 10) a handbook of sorry tales concerning eros (for the text see Edmonds and Gaselee 1916 and Lightfoot 1999). There are thirty-six erotic stories in Parthenius's collection. Of these, only two (17 and 26) refer to the wasting effects that frustrated love can bring to bear upon an individual. But approximately twelve of these relate tales that highlight the potential and actual violence that can be wrought by frustrated love (cf. Crump [1931] 1997, 108).[27] This is not the place to look at all of these stories in detail. Instead I will cite just two representative tales, the stories of Periander (17) and of Apriate (26) .

Periander, the bloodthirsty tyrant of Corinth, became, at a very young age, the object of his mother's erotic affections. At first she satisfied herself simply with hugging the boy. Later, assuming the cover of another woman and the disguise of night (she would not let Periander see her), she slept with her son, pretending that she was arranging this assignation for another woman. Periander developed for the "woman" a passion equal to that of his mother for him and, eventually, decided that he must learn the identity of the woman with whom he had been sleeping. He pressed his mother to reveal the identity of his paramour.

> But when his mother refused, alleging the shame felt by the woman, he made one of his body-servants conceal a light in the chamber: when she came as usual, and was about to lay herself down, Periander jumped up and revealed the light: he saw that it was his mother he made as if to kill her. However, he was restrained by a heaven-sent apparition, and desisted from his purpose, but from that time on he was a madman, afflicted in brain and heart; he fell into habits of savagery, and slaughtered many of the citizens of Corinth.[28]

The madness to which Periander becomes subject is the product of his frustrated love. We have witnessed this type of emotion before. Notice that this madness manifests itself as violence.[29]

The story concerning Apriate is very brief, but it, too, illustrates well Parthenius's understanding of the effects of frustrated eros.

> Trambelus, the son of Telamon fell in love with a girl named Apriate in Lesbos. He used every effort to gain her: but, as she showed no signs at all of relenting, he determined to win her by strategy and guile. She was walking one day with her attendant handmaids to one of her father's domains which was by the seashore, and there he laid an ambush for her and made her captive; but she struggled with the greatest violence to protect her virginity, and at last Trambelus in fury threw her into the sea, which at that point happened to be deep inshore. Thus did she perish.[30]

All of Parthenius's stories are brief and to the point. Unfortunately they do not usually dwell upon the physiological symptoms of frustrated eros: we see no inner and visceral anguish, such as that suffered by Medea, nor is there reference to madness such as that suffered by Caracalla. Trambelus nevertheless seems to have suffered love very badly—at any rate, he was willing to go to extreme lengths to gain his way with Apriate. We do not know if, in his frustration, he raged like Medea and Dido. But the end product was similarly violent. Frustrated by Apriate's repeated rejections, he became angered and drowned the young woman. This violent outcome was followed by an equally violent coda. When, later, Achilles was ravaging Lesbos, he came into contact with Trambelus, and this cycle of violence continued. Achilles killed Trambelus with a violent wound to the breast.

Not all of Parthenius's tales reproduce or imply the physiological disorders of lovesickness that I have outlined in this chapter. That concerning Periander does. Those tales that do not, like that of Apriate, still seem to participate in and to reproduce an emotional experience of a comparable order. Certainly the violence to which those suffering from frustrated love resort seems to match that with which we have become familiar.

A further pair of illustrations will test these conclusions. These concern the lovesickness of Phaedra as it is depicted by Euripides *(Hippolytus)* and by Seneca *(Phaedra)*.[31] Euripides' heroine (sometimes compared to Dido) is certainly lovesick.[32] She has fallen unexpectedly in love with her stepson, Hippolytus. The infatuation has been caused by Aphrodite, who, angered at Hippolytus's insulting behavior (*Hippolytus* 12 ff.), intends to use Phaedra's love to bring him down. Phaedra's love is frustrated, for the object of her desire is the son of her still living husband, Theseus. What are the symptoms of her lovesickness? Initial impressions suggest a condition that might easily be confused with depressive melancholia. Phaedra has become bedridden (vv. 131–34) and debilitated (vv. 198–202) and seems to be unable to take food (vv. 135–38); she is pallid (vv. 174–75) and inconsistent in her wants (v. 176 ff.). If her symptoms continue she will die (vv. 38–40). But as the drama unfolds, it emerges that these symptoms are feigned (vv. 391 ff., 400–401, 419 ff.). Phaedra, mindful of *aidôs* (v. 385), *timê* (v. 329), *sophrosynê* (v. 399), and *ta esthla* (v. 331), has determined to preserve her honor and to disguise the *erôs* by starving herself to death. It seems, however, that the real symptom of lovesickness, if it is allowed to manifest itself, is mania. Thus at 188–238 Phaedra is caught off guard by the nurse and reacts in a manic fashion (v. 206; note too *emanên* at v. 241). She admits as much to the chorus at verses 243–48, and after the nurse indicates Phaedra's love to Hippolytus (v. 601 ff.), her reaction to the nurse (she does not meet Hippolytus) is angry and violent abuse (v. 682 ff.). Her offstage suicide follows soon after, and soon after that Theseus returns to discover the body and, with it, the note that mendaciously dooms Hippolytus to a most violent death. It is significant that the contents of the letter seem to declare themselves in a most vehement manner (vv. 877–80). What, then, are we to make of Phaedra's early, seemingly depressive symptoms? I suspect that an audience saw Phaedra's illness not as the direct result of lovesickness but merely as indicating a means of attempting a suicide that would guard her honor against the onset of desire. The *modus moriendi* here is the common ancient tactic of *inedia*—starvation.[33]

Seneca's Phaedra also exhibits a form of lovesickness that is best described as manic, rather than depressive. Seneca's depiction of Phaedra's condition, however, is not as carefully constructed as that of Euripides. Seneca is at times more rational: Phaedra's passion, for example, can be explained away as resulting from the neglect (*Phaedra* 91 ff.) of an adulterous husband (vv. 97–98). Seneca's Phaedra also does not make much of an effort to hide her passion from the nurse: at times it is all that she can talk about (vv. 218–221, 225, 241). Seneca does skimp logically. Phaedra's decision to look after her good name (her *fama;* Euripides' Phaedra was concerned with *timê* but also with *aidôs* and *sophrosynê*) seems rather an afterthought (vv. 250–54, 258–60).

What are the symptoms of Phaedra's lovesickness? In the early parts of the play it is a violent madness (a *furor;* see vv. 184–85, 186–87, 268, and especially 339 ff.). Later, after she has determined to guard her *fama,* she begins to suffer a wasting illness (vv. 360–86), which more resembles what we would expect of depressive, rather than manic, lovesickness. It is unclear in Seneca's version whether these symptoms are feigned or whether they are simply the result of a prolonged starvation aimed at suicide. At any rate, the wasting illness does provide her with a chance to be alone with Hippolytus and to declare her love. That she is likely to have been feigning the illness is perhaps confirmed by her reaction to Hippolytus's rejection. Once spurned, she becomes angry (vv. 824–28) and guilefully dooms Hippolytus by claiming (v. 868 ff.) that he had raped her. *Furor* overcomes her in the end as well. After Hippolytus's death is reported, she comes on stage mad (v. 1156) and suicides. In the Senecan portrait of Phaedra's lovesickness, amatory infatuation is persistently, if not unequivocally, manic.

I would like to conclude this section by looking ahead from Seneca by 150 years. This will take us five hundred years from this chapter's chronological starting point, Apollonius's Medea. The affective symptoms of erotic trauma, we will see, change little. My target here is the didactic epic poet (or poets), Oppian. In two bizarre treatises on hunting (one on hunting land animals, a *Cynegetica;* one on hunting sea animals, a *Halieutica*), Oppian betrays a remarkable obsession with violence and eros.[34] I examine here just the *Cynegetica*. Despite an intention to describe the hunter's needs (book 1), the various animals to be pursued (books 2–3), and how to hunt (book 4), Oppian in fact focuses persistently on animal "friendships and their bridal chambers of tearless love upon the hills" and on "the births, that among the wild beasts need no midwifery" (Artemis's instructions at 1.34–40). Eros becomes Oppian's real focus, and it is almost always an eros of a very violent form. So book 1 of the *Cynegetica*, after prefatory remarks (1.1–157), begins its discourse on horses with a warning against the inconveniently lustful and uncontrollable nature of mares (1.158–65).

> As for horses, let them bring to the hunt proud
> Stallions, not only because mares are inferior in speed
> For accomplishing long courses in the woods,
> But also because it is necessary to avoid the passion
> Of the swift-footed horses and to keep mares far away,
> In case, in their amorous desire, they neigh
> And, hearing this, the wild beasts incontinently take to chilly flight—
> Fawns and swift gazelles and timid hare.

The subsequent list of horse breeds (1.166–367) is punctuated at 1.236–38 with a remarkable utterance—"above others, again, horses honor nature, and it is utterly unheard of that they should indulge unlawful passion, but they remain unstained of pollution and cherish chaste desire"—and with an even more striking narrative panel demonstrating how horses abhor incest (1.239–70). Oppian concludes with a description of genetic manipulation (1.331–67). The catalog to follow, of the various breeds of dogs (1.368 ff.), is interrupted at 1.376–92 by the *philotêsia erga* [erotic doings] of spring—most of which are of a manic variety. Verses 1.376–92 represent such a remarkable passage that it deserves quoting in full.

> If you should desire to mix two breeds,
> Then first of all mate two dogs in spring,
> For in spring chiefly the works of love possess the hearts
> Of wild beasts and dogs and deadly sea snakes
> And the fowls of the air and the finny creatures of the sea.
> In spring the serpent, foul with angry venom,
> Comes to the shore to meet his sea bride.
> In spring all the deep sea rings with love
> And the calm sea foams with fishes mating.
> In spring the male pigeon pursues the female.
> Horses assail the pasturing mares

And bulls lust after the cows of the field.
In spring the rams of crooked horn mount the ewes
And fiery wild boars mate with the sows—
And the he-goats with the shaggy females.
Yes, and mortals also in spring are prone to desire,
For in spring the spell of love is heavy on all.

Oppian's enthusiasms do not change in *Cynegetica* 2. He describes the violent mating habits of bulls (2.43–175) and presents a fascinating panel on Syrian bulls, the hero and athletic prototype Heracles, and the lustful and violent river Orontes (2.109–58). Many other creatures are subject, like Orontes, to a woeful eros. Certainly stags (2.160–295), fighting cocks and brilliantly colored birds (2.189–90), the gazelle (2.315–325), and the lascivious partridge are. But wild goats and sheep are not (2.326–444). Oppian is very fond of goats. They are especially good to their families and care well for their aged (2.343–76). Approval for animals who will look after their young is repeated at the end of this book when Oppian comes to discuss apes (2.605–11). They have twins but love one and, in cruel thrall to eros, let the other perish.

I pass over the triple breeds of apes, those wicked mimics.
For who would not loathe such a race, ugly to look on,
Weak, loathsome, evil of aspect, crafty of counsel.
These, though they give birth to evil-looking twins,
Do not divide love equally between them,
But they love one and hate and become angered at the other,
And he perishes in the very arms of his parents.

Bad animals who do not care for their young are usually obsessed by physical, carnal love. Thus bears (3.139–82) will induce the early births of their offsprings so that they can return to mating. Sexual jealousy leads the male wild ass to murder its own male offspring (3.183–250). Wild boars are utterly lustful (3.364–90). Ostriches exemplify the same failing (3.480–503) as do hares (3.504–25). Of the last group, Oppian comments, "the shameless female never forgets her lust but fulfills all her desire, and not even in the throes of birth does she refuse to mate." Violence and eros are thus closely intertwined in Oppian's amatory universe.

Ancient medicine has very little to say of lovesickness. What is said (confined to Aretaeus, Galen, Oribasius, Caelius Aurelianus, and Paul of Aegina) interprets lovesickness as a depressive illness that matches depressive melancholia in symptoms, but not in etiology (for surveys see Beecher and Ciavolella 1990; Jackson 1986; Wack 1990). This medical tradition stands in stark contrast to the popular one. Just as we have seen with melancholia, the diagnosis of the doctors was depression, whereas the popular diagnosis was mania.

Aretaeus of Cappadocia (ca. 150 C.E.), for whom melancholy was perhaps a bipolar condition, seems to see love melancholy as a depressive, rather than a manic, illness (Marneros and Angst 2000). The following passage (Aretaeus 3.5, trans. Adams [1856, 300]) illustrates how lovesickness could easily be confused with melancholy.

> A story is told, that a certain person, incurably affected, fell in love with a girl; and when the physicians could bring him no relief, love cured him. But I think that he was originally in love, and that he was dejected and spiritless *[katêphen de kai dusthumon]* from being unsuccessful with the girl, and appeared to the common people to be melancholic. He then did not know that it was love; but when he imparted the love to the girl, he ceased from his dejection, and dispelled his passion and sorrow; and with joy he woke from his lowness of spirits, and he became restored to understanding, love being his physician.

This passage, which appears in Aretaeus's chapter on melancholia, is advice for doctors. Its obvious intent is to caution physicians against a too hasty diagnosis of melancholia. The symptoms may resemble those of the illness of melancholia, Aretaeus is saying, but the actual illness may be other. The problem in this case is that lovesickness (which makes a person "dejected and spiritless") is outwardly identical to depressive melancholia. At any rate, the truth of Aretaeus's diagnosis was demonstrated by the man's cure. This took place when he declared his love to his beloved. Aretaeus's distinction may seem to us to be hairsplitting. He was, however, a humoralist and attributed melancholia to a superfluity of black bile. The sufferer in this instance was the victim not of an excess of black bile but of a psychological disturbance.

This passage, or at least the diagnosis, is echoed later in the century by Galen (as we shall see in a moment) and is eventually picked up in the "popular" literature. As we will see in the next section of this chapter, the descriptions of depressive lovesickness (which mirror the discursive chronology of depressive melancholy) invariably produced symptoms that mirror those of the medical descriptions of melancholia. But it was some time before this medical confusion was reflected and acknowledged in popular literature. This takes place (as I will demonstrate in the next section of this chapter) in Heliodorus's novel the *Aethiopica*.[35] The conflation of the popular and medical traditions of love melancholy offers an analogue to that conflation of the popular and medical traditions concerning depressive melancholia that was evident in Persius's *Satires* 3.

Galen (ca. 130–200 C.E.) was, like Aretaeus, also a humoralist. One finds in Galen, therefore, the same careful distinction between melancholia and lovesickness. In a detailed passage that seems to echo Aretaeus, Galen describes lovers as sometimes "emaciated, pale, sleepless, and even feverish."[36] In one instance he discusses his treatment of a woman who exhibited symptoms of sleeplessness at night and restlessness during the day, taciturnity, and, when Galen consulted her, a reaction as follows: "she turned her face away, threw her clothes over her body and hid herself away completely" (quoted by Beecher and Ciavolella 1990, 51). Galen diagnosed, "Either she was tormented by melancholy, or she was grieving over some cause she did not want to confess." Subsequently he discovered love was the problem. He discovered that her pulse rate rose when mention of the stage dancer Pylades was made. Although easily confused with depressive melancholia, the real origin of the woman's condition—and love melancholy generally—is psychological rather than physical (i.e., it is not brought on by an excess of black bile).[37] Two other writers are of significance in this matter. Oribasius (326–403 C.E.) and Paul of Aegina (fl. ca. 640 C.E.) present in their discussions what seems to be a shared view of lovesickness. Oribasius, the physician to the emperor Julian, treated lovesickness as a distinct illness and attributed to it symptoms such as sadness, insomnia, hollow eyes, and an inability to cry; sufferers, he noted, "appeared to be filled with voluptuousness; and their eyelids, the only part of the body not weakened, were continuously blinking."[38] For Paul of Aegina, the lovesick were "desponding and sleepless." He describes them in "On Lovesick Persons" in terms very similar to those used by Oribasius.[39]

Caelius Aurelianus (fifth century C.E.), who translated the Trajanic medical writer Soranus of Ephesus,[40] believed that lovesickness manifests many of the symptoms of depressive melancholy: "unhappiness, mental anxiety, tossing in sleep, frequent blinking of the eyes, and disturbances of the pulse." He wrote, "it manifests itself now in anger, now in merriment, now in sadness or futility, and now, as some relate, in an overpowering fear of things which are quite harmless." Wack (1990, 11–12), whose translation I am quoting, links the preceding reference to anger with Caelius's statements elsewhere correlating melancholia with anger (on which topic see the next section of this chapter). Although not humoralists,[41] it may be possible that Caelius and Soranus were conscious of a tradition of manic lovesickness.

The description of lovesickness in all of these writers presents a condition that, while not technically melancholia, shows the outward signs of the illness in its depressive phase. Aretaeus and Galen are at pains to point this out. (Caelius's comments on anger may offer the only modification.) Centuries later, Avicenna (980–1037 C.E.) makes the very same point (Jackson 1986, 354–55). The link, therefore, between lovesickness, depression, and melancholia is a vital one. Lovesickness, according to the major surviving medical view, was a condition typified by sadness, insomnia, despondency, dejection, physical debility, and blinking. Aretaeus and Galen seem to have thought of the condition not (unlike melancholia) as a specific illness but, rather, as a vague psychological disturbance presumably best cured by therapeutic intercourse (on which topic see Allen 2000). Oribasius and Paul of Aegina conceived of lovesickness as an actual illness, but not one based upon an excess of the black bile.

As we saw was the case with the medical understanding of melancholia, the medical understanding of lovesickness as a depressive condition seems eventually to have been absorbed into the popular tradition. Increasingly, erotic trauma, manifest as lovesickness, was registered in poetry and in nontechnical prose as generally, though not exclusively, a passive affair. In the next section of this chapter, I will offer a brief overview of this process. The history of the coming together of these two traditions will be seen to climax with a depiction of lovesickness given by the Greek novelist Heliodorus. His narrative version of lovesickness matches that of his near medical contemporaries Aretaeus and Galen. The chronology of this "passivizing" of erotic infatuation and trauma, therefore, matches precisely that of melancholia.

The most famous ancient description of lovesickness, and the one with which I would like to begin my survey of the depictions of depressive lovesickness, is Sappho's incomplete *phainetai moi* ode (31 Campbell). This poem (translated by Catullus as his poem 51) aims to convey the experience of thwarted sexual desire. Here is the poem.

> He seems to me like the gods,
> that man who, opposite you, can
> sit nearby and listen to your
>   sweet voice
>
> And to your lovely laughter. This
> sets the heart in my breast aflutter.
> For when I look at you for a moment, it's
>   not possible for me to speak,

But my tongue has snapped, a light
fire runs straightway beneath my flesh,
I see nothing with my eyes, my
ears hum,
Sweat pours from me, and trembling
takes hold of me. I am whiter
than grass, and I'm little
short of dying.

But all must be endured for even a poor man . . .

What is happening in this poem is not totally clear.[42] But it is plain that our speaker is watching another woman and a man seated together. The sight of that other woman speaking and laughing with this man induces the extreme symptoms described in stanzas three and four: speechlessness (v. 9), a burning sensation on the skin (vv. 9–10), loss of vision (v. 11), ringing in the ears (vv. 11–12), cold sweat (v. 13), trembling (vv. 13–14), pallor (vv. 14–15), and a near-death experience (vv. 15–16). These are symptoms that we will meet again and again in the course of this book.[43] They are always symptomatic of severe psychological frustration and are very often, but not exclusively, to be linked with eros.[44] What causes the frustration in this instance seems at first sight to be jealousy.[45] But that, as many critics have argued, is no certain thing. It might as easily be the attractiveness of the woman and the inattentiveness of the man that causes this reaction, just as easily as it could be jealousy engendered by the attentiveness of the man. What matters, however, is that desire and the speaker's remarkable symptoms are linked. What we can say with certainty is that a panic attack of the gravity of that suffered by the speaker of this poem requires a correspondingly grave etiology. In a triangular situation such as this (a triangular situation inevitably hints at the amatory), in which the language describing the perception of the other woman and the other man is emotionally charged (so, "like the gods," "sweet voice," and "lovely laughter"), it defies common sense to exclude erotic frustration. In such a situation an etiology is the only one I can think of that could cause such a powerful response. In the next chapter we will see reactions like those of the speaker of this poem as associated with a death threatening experience. The causative emotion here must be, to repeat, of the utmost gravity. It is then, if not jealousy, at least frustrated love. There can be no other way of describing such a condition than as lovesickness.[46]

Was this experience depressive or was it manic? I wish we could say, but Sappho does not tell us. The poem is incomplete, and the outcome of the speaker's emotions are not made plain. We might speculate that the resolution displayed in the final surviving line of the poem suggests that both mania and depression have been surmounted.[47] Or it may be possible that Sappho had no clear understanding of or interest in formulating this issue. The sole piece of evidence from Sappho's poetry that may be relevant to this matter is equally inconclusive. In poem 94, parting from a lover makes the speaker of the poem want to die—a sure form of erotic frustration. Sappho says:

> And honestly I wish I were dead.
> She left me weeping
> Greatly and said this to me:
> "Alas, how terribly we have suffered,
> Sappho; indeed I leave unwillingly."
>
> And I answered her in this way:
> "Go well and remember
> me, for you know how we cared for you.
>
> If not I want to remind you . . .
> . . . .
> . . . and that we fared well."

This lacunose poem carries on to indicate that the "faring well" between Sappho and the other woman should be understood in an erotic sense. We guess at this from verses 21–23.

> And on soft beds
> . . . .
> you would satisfy your desire *[pothos]*.

But the wish for death with which the poem commences, though doubtless genuine, is not hemmed about, at least in the poem as it survives, with the symptoms that we may associate with lovesickness in poem 31. Reluctantly, therefore, we must conclude that poem 94 does not allow us to determine whether Sappho envisaged love as manic or depressive.

Is there anything in contemporary literature that might help us with Sappho's opinions? We could compare, say, Ibycus 286 and 287 (as numbered in Campbell's collection). In Ibycus 286 the onset of love seems especially violent (in 286.10–11 the word *mania* is used, significantly associated with darkness [*eremnos*, v. 10]). In 287 Ibycus trembles at love's coming. Mania is the characterizing quality of erotic frustration and infatuation in these contexts. The onset of love in Archilochus is equally prepossessing.[48] These nearly contemporaneous descriptions do not conclusively help with Sappho. They suggest to me, however, that Sappho had little interest in the depressive emotion that the *medici* later highlight. This conclusion may disappoint Sappho's many modern admirers.[49] To this I can only say that Sappho, just like the men of her time, was subject to the ineluctable material forces of history.[50]

Unambiguous depictions of depressive lovesickness are not common in ancient literature at any time.[51] Perhaps the first are to be found in early Hellenistic literature (the period in which Apollonius imagined his version of Medea). This comes as no surprise, for it is in this period that the descriptions of depressive melancholia first begin to appear. The best is contained in Theocritus's *Idylls* 2. Here Simaetha has fallen in love with handsome, fickle Delphis. The description of her initial infatuation is remarkable. Lovesickness is like a fever, and it causes Simaetha to become frenzied (*emanên,* v. 82; cf. Phaedrus in Euripides *Hippolytus* 241). Yet, as the emotion lays hold of her, she becomes ill and takes to bed (vv. 82–86).

> When I saw him I went into a frenzy, my heart burnt with fire,
> Wretch that I am, and my beauty melted away; no longer for that
> Procession did I give a thought, and how I got home
> I don't know, but a parching illness possessed me,
> And I lay on my bed for ten days and ten nights.

After ten days her skin had become dull and sallow, her hair had begun to fall out, and she had become reduced to skin and bone (vv. 88–90).[52]

> My skin became like cinnamon bark;
> The hair fell from my head; these were left,
> Just skin and bone.

The cure came when the slave girl Thestylis coaxed Delphis to Simaetha's home. Lovemaking provided the remedy. The outlines of the condition of depressive lovesickness are all present in this story: taking to bed; physical debility leading to emaciation and, potentially, death; and a dramatically altered complexion. The cure is sexual congress.[53] Except for the evidence of the cure, Simaetha might have been suffering from a bout of depressive melancholia.

Theocritus's Polyphemus (a model for Corydon in Virgil's *Eclogues* 2) is also lovesick—for Galatea in *Idylls* 11. Theocritus, however, does not detail the physiology of Polyphemus's condition. At verses 10–11 he is said to love "not with apples, or roses, or ringlets but with downright frenzy *[orthais maniais]*." That does not sound depressive. Nor do verses 15–16, where he has "deep beneath his breast an angry wound that the shaft of the mighty Cyprian goddess had planted in his heart." The only hint of a Simaetha-like passivity is suggested in verses 14–15, where he is described thus: "alone on the wrack-strewn shore, [he] would waste away with love as he sang of Galatea." "Wasting" (here the verbal form is *katetaketo*) is typical of the depressive lovesick. (In Ovid's depiction of the lovesick Cyclops, the latter's emotion seems to be violent; see *Metamorphoses* 13.867–69). Curiously the addressee of *Idylls* 11 is a medical man, Nicias. Whether he would be likely to take more of an interest in lovesickness than would nonmedical figures cannot be known. It is striking, however, that Nicias is also the addressee of *Idylls* 13, which concerns the rape by the love-smitten nymphs of Heracles' young lover Hylas. The passions in this poem, however, are manic. Toward the end of this poem, Heracles, bereft of his young lover but still searching for him, is described thus: "so mad a passion on his vitals preyed." Frustrated love causes Aeschinas in *Idylls* 14 to waste, as it does Daphnis at *Idylls* 7.76. This wasting, unfortunately, is accompanied by the description of few other physiological symptoms.[54]

An even more striking depiction of frustrated love than that to be found with Simaetha in *Idylls* 2 is to be seen in Theocritus's *Idylls* 30. In this poem an older man has fallen violently in love with a boy. The love is not reciprocated. The older man, in his passion and frustration and in his doleful realization of the limitations placed upon him by age, is driven eventually to contemplate suicide. What is most striking about this man's affective predicament is that it is likened, as Gow (1952, 2:512) strongly emphasizes, to quartan fever, a condition ostensibly unrelated to love. Here are some of the relevant verses (Theocritus *Idylls* 30.1–6):

> Alas for this grievous and ill-starred passion of mine!
> A quartan passion has held me for two months now
> For a boy of middle beauty, yet clad he is in charm from head
> To foot, and sweet the smile on his cheek.
> Till now some days the woe lies heavy on me, and other days abates,
> But soon no respite will there be—not even enough to compass sleep.

Quartan fever has strong links, in the eyes of ancient medical practitioners at any rate, with black bile and with melancholia. The Hippocratic treatise *On the Nature of Man* (15) points out: "a secondary reason for their [quartan fevers'] chronic character and difficult resolution is that they are caused by black bile; this is the most viscous of the humors in the body and remains the longest. As evidence of this, note the association of quartan fevers with melancholy . . ." In this poem the symptoms of lovesickness, therefore, are closely, if indirectly, to be linked with melancholia. What is most striking in this immediate context is the match established between lovesickness—a dangerous depressive condition that normally required medical attention—and depression. Such an unambiguous linkage is not to be found again until the era of the Greek novel. Perhaps, however, I should qualify my use of the word *unambiguous.* Theocritus's *Idylls* 30 *implies* a link between these conditions. It does not make this link explicit in the manner by which Aretaeus and Galen did and as Heliodorus in the *Aethiopica* will.

There are many other examples of this condition from this period and from later. Unfortunately many of these are teasingly imprecise in their register of symptoms. There is no conjunction between the medical and the popular traditions. These examples, however, allow us to establish the traces of a periodization of lovesickness, a periodization that seems provocatively to match that for melancholy itself. Callimachus's epigram 44 diagnoses lovesickness as the cause of a drinker's sighing and heaving. Asclepiades (*Greek Anthology* 12.135) makes the same diagnosis of one Nicagoras from his tears, his bent head, and his downcast demeanor. In Callimachus's version of the story of the love of Acontius and Cydippe (which occurs within the third book of his four-book poem the *Aetia*) we have an apparent instance of lovesickness, but one that strains the concept of this definition. Acontius, in this version, had fallen in love, at first sight, with Cydippe when he attended the festivals in Delos. Acontius, violently in love with Cydippe, followed her to the temple of Artemis. He inscribed on a quince the words "I swear by the temple of Artemis I will marry Cydippe" and then threw the fruit near the girl. She picked it up and innocently read the words out loud. The oath, uttered inadvertently but nonetheless in the presence of the goddess, bound her to Acontius. Cydippe had been, however, betrothed to another. Each time her marriage date approached, she fell ill with a mysterious sickness: this was visited upon her by the goddess Artemis, who was angered that Cydippe was on the point of breaking her oath. In the meantime Acontius came from his native Chios to Athens, for he had heard of his beloved's illness. His concerns became the talk of the town. The town's people began to suggest that Acontius had cast the evil eye on Cydippe.[55] Resolution was reached only after Cydippe's father consulted the oracle at Delphi and learned of the oath. The god had her way and the young pair were soon after married. The illness disappeared.

What interests is the illnesses Cydippe suffered on each occasion that she was about to marry. Here is how Callimachus describes Cydippe's condition (*Aetia* fr. 75.12–20).[56]

> But in the afternoon an evil pallor came upon her; the disease seized her,
> Which we blame on the wild goats
> And which we falsely call the holy disease.[57] That grievous sickness
> Then wasted the girl even to the Halls of Hades.
> A second time the couches were spread; a second time the maiden

Was sick for seven months with a quartan fever.
A third time they thought of marriage; a third time again
A deadly chill settled on Cydippe.
A fourth time her father could endure it no more.

Cydippe was not ill because of lovesickness. She was ill because of the anger of the goddess Artemis. Yet some of the symptoms of the three stages of her illness do seem to resemble those that might be associated with lovesickness (or, for that matter, melancholia): the wasting, the quartan fever (suffered by the lover of Theocritus's *Idylls* 30), the taking to bed, and, perhaps, the "deadly chill." (Cydippe's symptoms are very like those of Charicleia that I will mention later in this chapter.) For this context, what intrigues most is the subjection of Cydippe to the quartan fever. We have seen just a moment ago how quartan fever is to be associated with black bile and with melancholia and how it may be associated with lovesickness. Callimachus's tale of Acontius and Cydippe, therefore, *explicitly* denies lovesickness to the young woman but *implicitly* imputes it to her. It is furthermore most important for our process of periodization that her sickness has an implicit link with melancholy. The designation used by Callimachus for Cydippe's second bout of illness is that which Theocritus, in his *Idylls* 30, used of the lovesick. It is significant that Ovid, in his version of the affair between Acontius and Cydippe, describes Cydippe's condition in a way that could easily be confused with lovesickness and, obliquely, in a way that might imply melancholy. Ovid has Cydippe describe her condition as follows (*Heroides* 21.17–21):

The weariness hangs about me for reasons
I do not know. Tired, I find no help
From doctors. My limbs are shrunken; I am pale.
See me now, hardly able to write,
Hardly able to lift myself on my arm.

In the amatory poetry of Rome, at least until the time of Ovid, descriptions of lovesickness are not common, nor are they particularly detailed. The poet Aedituus, who survives only in fragments, admits to lovesickness when he complains of the sweats, confusion, silence, and shame.[58]

When, Pamphila, I try to tell you of the pain in my heart,
The words fail on my lips, to say what I want of you.
My breast is damp with sudden sweat. I am confused.
Silent, confused, I am ashamed and tortured.

Horace, a far better represented poet, describes jealousy (a type of lovesickness) in *Odes* 1.13 and speaks of choking, mental distraction, pallor, and tears.

In *Odes* 4.1.33 ff. he speaks of lovesickness proper, alluding to its tears and silences.

> But why, alas, Ligurinus, why
> Does a tear now and then run across my cheeks,
> And why does my eloquent tongue,
> In the midst of speech, fail with scarcely decorous silence.

Propertius's addressee in his elegy 1.5, Gallus (described in verses 13–21), also has a bad case of lovesickness. This is how he is depicted.[59]

> You will often come running, spurned
> To my door, your brave words perish in sobs,
> Your quaking shivers float on grieving tears,
> And fear etches ugly signs in your face,
> And the words you need to complain elude you,
> And you won't know who you are, or where, poor man!

Whether Gallus ends up wasting away, becoming extremely angry, or merely finding another partner, we do not learn.[60] There are other examples in Propertius and in his coeval Tibullus, but these are confined almost in formulaic fashion to the evocation of wasting and pallor.[61] What is persistently striking about these examples is—despite the obvious familiarity that the authors had with the condition—the lack of interest shown in the outcome of the condition and, indeed, the lack of seriousness with which it was taken.

Things do change, and they seem to be changing at about the time of Ovid. With Ovid, lovesickness, of what seems to be a depressive variety, is first consistently acknowledged. A very useful and detailed example of this is to be found at *Ars amatoria* 1.729–36.[62] The passage runs as follows (translation by Green 1982):

> But let every lover be pale: here's the proper complexion
> For lovers; this gambit, please note,
> Has worked on every occasion. Pale was Orion, roaming
> The woodlands, pining for Side; pale
> Daphnis (ah, unkind Naiad!). Look lean and haggard
> As proof of your passion, don't baulk
> At hooding your lustrous curls. Sleepless nights, the pangs and worry
> Of consuming love—these will reduce young men
> To a thin nothing. If you mean to achieve your purpose
> Be an object of pity, so that passersby
> Will say at once, "He's in love."

The lover described here is not just subject to the usual pangs with which have been those to date (insomnia, anxiety, and so forth);[63] this one is really wasting away. There are a number of places within Ovid's books of love poetry, the *Amores*, which allude to lovesickness, though this is more along the lines with which we have become familiar in Propertius and Tibullus.[64] An unambiguous example of wasting lovesickness—lovesickness, that is, of the depressive, melancholic variety—is to be seen in Ovid's story of Echo and Narcissus (*Metamorphoses* 3.339–510).[65] In the Narcissus tale the symptoms given to lovesickness seem closely to equate with those that are associated with depressive melancholia, but the link is not made explicit. In this tale the nymph Echo had fallen in love with the handsome young Narcissus.[66] He fastidiously rejected her love. Echo's reaction to the rejection may be compared to that of Perdica (discussed shortly). She became grief-stricken (3.395) and anxious and insomniac (3.396); she was unwilling or unable to eat (3.397), and her bones became protuberant (as happened to Perdica, though in a slightly different manner). Narcissus was punished (3.406) for his heartless behavior. He caught sight of his own reflection in a pool and fell in love with it (3.407 ff.). Like Echo he became weak (3.469, 488 ff.) and unable to eat (3.437) and gradually starved to death (3.487–90).[67]

> but, as the yellow wax melts
> Before a gentle heat, as hoar frost
> Melts before the warm morning sun, so does he, wasted with love
> *[attenuatus amore]*,
> Pine away, and is slowly consumed by its hidden fire.

He was transformed into the flower bearing his name.[68]

The tradition reaches full bloom in the generation following Ovid. We could say that it is inaugurated by Valerius Maximus (*Facta* 5.7.1), who recounts the famous ancient example of Antiochus, the son of King Seleucus who fell in love with his young stepmother, Stratonice.[69] Antiochus, either unwilling or unable to reveal his passion, fell ill, took to his bed, and began to waste away.[70] The physician Erasistratus, called to attend Antiochus, noticed how, when Stratonice entered the room, his pulse and breathing quickened and he flushed. (This situation resembles those described by Aretaeus and by Galen.) Erasistratus realized that the cause of Antiochus's troubles was frustrated love. King Seleucus so loved his son that, on hearing Erasistratus's diagnosis, he passed on his wife, Stratonice, to Antiochus. That selfless action afforded the cure. There are many variations of this story, within and without medical literature.[71] Plutarch's variant version is undoubtedly the most influential (*Demetrius* 37.2–3). In Plutarch's revisionist account, Antiochus takes to bed and begins deliberately to starve himself as a means of controlling his passion. Antiochus's motives, on Plutarch's reading, are like those of Euripides' Phaedra. His symptoms, however, are those of the lovesick: physical debility, emaciation, a pallid complexion alternating with a flushed one, labored breathing, and a disturbed pulse rate.

Such lovesickness is not confined to the popular Antiochus and Stratonice story. A narrative clone may be found in the Vandal miniature epic poem *Aegritudo Perdicae*.[72] This story concerns a young man, Perdica, who was studying in Athens. Just before leaving for home, he neglected to sacrifice to Venus and Cupid. He was rewarded with a dream image with which he fell in love. The image was of his mother. Lovesickness caused him not only to reject food but also to suffer insomnia, fearfulness, and physical debility. His mother called a doctor, Hippocrates, who, by feeling for Perdica's pulse, discovered that it increased when his mother entered the room. Realizing the cause of the illness, he resigned the case. Despite his mother's ministrations, Perdica become more and more sick: he became pallid, emaciated; his nose, the tendons in his arms, and his ribs became protuberant. In the end he decided to hang himself. Once again lovesickness manifests itself in a depressive manner and in one that is easily confused with melancholia.[73]

Depressive lovesickness figures large in the following, rather different illustration. This one comes from the life of Marcus Aurelius (ruled 161–80 C.E.) in the *Historia Augusta* (*Marcus Antoninus* 19.12) and repeats an alarming story concerning the conception of the brutal emperor Commodus (ruled 177–92 C.E.).[74] It runs as follows:

> Some say, and it seems plausible, that Commodus Antoninus, his son and successor, was not begotten by him, but in adultery; and they embroider this assertion, moreover, with a story current among the people. On a certain occasion, it was said, Faustina, the daughter of Pius and wife of Marcus, saw some gladiators pass by, and was inflamed with love for one of them; and afterwards, when suffering from a long illness [*aegritudo*—Cicero's term for mental anguish], she confessed the passion to her husband. And when Marcus reported this to the Chaldaeans, it was their advice that the gladiator should be killed and that Faustina should bathe in his blood and in this state lie with her husband. When this had been done the passion was allayed, but their son Commodus was born a gladiator, and not really a *princeps*.[75]

If in this version it is not wholly clear whence Faustina's illness derived, my preceding discussion ought to make this plain. Like Antiochus or Perdica, Faustina was so love-struck by the gladiator that she fell ill and took to her bed. Frustrated love has produced a state of physical enfeeblement. We cannot be sure that this was depressive, but the mention of a "long illness" *[longa aegritudo]* (the noun often means "lovesickness") points to this. The cure may seem remarkable. Yet a little thought will indicate that it offers a variation on a standard method of curing lovesickness pointed to by Aretaeus, sexual congress with the beloved. In this instance it is therapeutic intercourse by proxy. Faustina, coated with the blood of the unfortunate gladiator, undergoes with him a type of sexual union through the proxy of the ineffectual Marcus Aurelius.[76]

Even animals could become subject to the debilitating effects of lovesickness. Aulus Gellius, in his *Attic Nights* 6.8, reproduces this story concerning the love of a dolphin and a boy (Oppian *Halieutica* 5.448 ff. tells much the same story). The tale does not attribute melancholia to its lovesick dolphin,[77] but we would not be wrong, I think, to do so. (There is no explicit link between lovesickness and melancholia, I mean.) I will allow this narrative to speak for itself (Loeb translation adapted).

> That dolphins are affectionate and amorous by nature is shown not only by recent history but also by tales of recent date. For in the sea by Puteoli—during the reign of Augustus Caesar, as Apion has written, and some centuries before at Naupactus, as Theophrastus tells us—dolphins are positively known to have been ardently in love. And they did not love those of their own kind but had an extraordinary passion, like that of human beings, for boys of handsome figure, whom they chanced to have seen in boats or in the shallow waters near the shore.[78]
>
> I have appended the words of that learned man Apion, from the fifth book of his *Egyptian History,* in which he tells of an amorous dolphin and a boy who did not reject its advances, of their intimacy and play with each other, of the dolphin carrying the boy and the boy bestriding the fish; and Apion declares that of all this he himself and many others were eyewitnesses. "Now I myself," he writes, "near Dicaearchia saw a dolphin that fell in love with a boy called Hyacinthus. For the fish came with passionate eagerness at his call and, drawing in his fins to avoid wounding the delicate skin of the object of his affection, carried him as if mounted upon a horse for a distance of two hundred stadia. Rome and all Italy turned out to see a fish that was under the sway of Aphrodite." To this he adds a detail that is no less wonderful. "Afterwards," he says, "that same boy who was beloved by the dolphin fell sick and died. But the lover, when he had often come to the familiar shore, and when the boy, who used to await his coming at the edge of the shoal water, was nowhere to be seen, pined away from longing and died. He was found lying on the shore by those who knew the story, and he was buried in the same tomb with his favorite."[79]

Perhaps the most striking examples of lovesickness seeming to ape melancholy are to be found in the ancient novel (cf. Maehler 1990). Chariton (writing maybe in the middle of the first century C.E.), Xenophon of Ephesus (writing in the second century), and Heliodorus (writing in the third or fourth century) provide descriptions of frustrated young lovers that, in their similarities, seem to indicate depressive lovesickness had become a literary topos.[80] A link with melancholia is implicit in the cases of Chariton and Xenophon of Ephesus. In Heliodorus's case, remarkably, the link becomes explicit. Lovesickness is linked with melancholia in a manner that echoes the striking formulation first offered by Aretaeus of Cappadocia.

Let us begin with Chariton. The hero and heroine of his novel, Chaereas and Callirhoe, spot one another at a public festival of Aphrodite and fall in love at once. The effect of love on Chaereas was dreadful: he was too weak to stand and began to waste away; he looked set to die (1.1). The effect on Callirhoe was worse, because, unlike Chaereas, she would not admit her condition to her parents: she lay on her bed, head covered, crying; and when marriage (not, she thought, to Chaereas) was proposed, she became speechless and sightless, and she almost expired (1.1).[81] Chaereas and Callirhoe were saved from death in the nick of time. They married.

Xenophon's description of the love of Habrocomes and Anthia in his *Ephesian Tale* is more detailed. The youngsters fall in love at a festival of Artemis. Habrocomes, in love (1.5), was worn out, insomniac, weary-eyed, of altered complexion; he was moaning, weeping, and praying pitifully; eventually his body wasted away and his mind gave in. Things were no better for Anthia (1.5), whose beauty was quickly fading. Had their parents not consulted the Delphic oracle and settled on marriage (1.6), Habrocomes and Anthia, who lay ill and in critical condition, would certainly have died (1.5). Xenophon's portrait has an approximate parallel in an interesting passage to be found in his near contemporary Apuleius. In his *Metamorphoses* 10 Lucius relates a tale that he had heard of a beautiful young stepmother who had fallen in love with her handsome stepson. Hippolytus-like, he virtuously rejected her overtures. Frustrated love changed to hate, and the stepmother responded by fabricating a charge of fratricide that almost succeeded. But what matters here is the description provided by Apuleius of the young woman's feigned or real love-wracked condition (10.2) (Loeb translation).

> ... her countenance was pale, her eyes sorrowful, her knees weak, her rest disturbed, and she would sigh deeply because of the slowness of her torment; there was no comfort in her, but continual weeping and sobbing; you would have thought that she had some fever,[82] except that she wept unreasonably ...

This could as well be the description of the far more appetizing Habrocomes or Anthia.

Only one of the lovers in Heliodorus's *Aethiopica* shows full-blown signs of depressive lovesickness. This is the fair-skinned Ethiopian Charicleia.[83] Charicleia had seen the young Thessalian Theagenes (3.5) in the Delphic procession of atonement to Neoptolemus. She was at once love-struck (3.5). Calasiris, her subsequent guide, took her languishing in bed, her moist eyes, and her headache (3.7) for the effects of the evil eye (3.7–9) and promised to help cure it.[84] But her condition continued to deteriorate (3.19): "the bloom was fleeing her cheeks, and it was as if the fire in her glance was being extinguished by the water of her tears." Theagenes and Charicleia saw one another a second time when Theagenes ran in the Pythian games (4.3–4). The effect was catastrophic. Charicleia became still worse, and her whole household was reduced to tears (4.5). Calasiris unsuccessfully attempted to cure her with incantations, incense, and laurel (4.5). Charicleia was subsequently examined by a doctor (4.7). Arcesinus, the physician, discovered at once that the root of the problem was love.

> Can you not see that her condition *[pathos]* is of the soul and that the illness *[nosos]* is clearly love? Can you not see the dark rings under her eyes, how restless is her gaze, and how pale is her face—although she does not complain of internal pain? Can you not see that her concentration wanders, that she says the first thing that comes into her head, that she is suffering from an unaccountable insomnia and has suddenly lost her self-confidence? Charicles, you must search for the man to cure her, the only one, the man she loves.

Charicleia's *nosos* is finally cured by union with her beloved, Theagenes.

What especially interests in Heliodorus's description of the effects of lovesickness are the indications that the physician Arcesinus initially took her problem to be a superfluity of the black bile. He tells Charicles (4.7) that he has discovered no excess of humors *(ou gar chymôn tis perittuei)*. The humor in question can only have been black bile, *melaina cholê*. Further indication that Charicleia's lovesickness could be confused with depressive melancholy is suggested by Arcesinus's testing her pulse (4.7).[85] That seemed to give the game away. Arcesinus's pulse test seems to mirror that applied by Galen and that which we have seen in the stories of Antiochus and Stratonice and of Perdica.[86]

Depressive lovesickness becomes, in Heliodorus, depressive melancholy. This admittedly uncommon tradition of depressive lovesickness, which seems to date only from the Hellenistic period, eventually absorbed the conceptual apparatus of the medical tradition, as we have it in Aretaeus and Galen, and produced the version offered by Heliodorus. This is a link that becomes canonical in later Western literature.

Depressive lovesickness, as I hope my brief survey has demonstrated, is not at all common in the literature of the classical world. Its earliest, unambiguous examples come from Theocritus. The majority of ancient examples, however, are to be drawn from the first century of our era and later. Their appearance coincides approximately with the earliest medical discussions of the condition. While Theocritus and Callimachus may demonstrate that depressive lovesickness was a condition from which people must always have suffered, the remaining instances suggest that, as a sociological phenomenon to be taken seriously, depressive lovesickness is "discovered" in the early imperial era. Depressive love melancholy, if I may make this distinction, is something that comes late even within this uncommon tradition.

Depressive lovesickness embodies a kind of affective passivity. A query occasionally raised concerning the passivity of these *inamorati* of the first and second centuries of our era is this: is it really passivity or is it in fact the result of a literature that interests itself in the young and inexperienced and in love relationships that violate societal taboo? The depressed lovers of the Greek novel are usually young and inexperienced. One might easily blame their sense of powerlessness on their age and social station. Had they been older, more experienced, and more capable of attaining their own ends, then might their frustration have manifested itself as anger, rather than melancholy? Is the "discovery" of depressive lovesickness merely the product of a literature that takes more of an interest in the emotions of a more vulnerable class? There are, in the texts mentioned earlier, several instances that vitiate such a supposition. Chariton's Dionysius, Callirhoe's first suitor after her abduction by the pirates, offers one example. He is a full-grown man. Recently widowed, wealthy, friend of kings, and the father of two children, he might have been expected to react to frustration in anger, rather than in the depressed manner he does (Chariton 2.4). Similarly Theocritus's Simaetha seems to be the victim of neither age nor inexperience. Anger, therefore, might be expected to be the reaction to her infatuation with Delphis. It was not. Medea, however, offers an example, especially in Valerius, of an angry reaction to frustrated love. Like Callirhoe or Anthia or Charicleia, she is young and inexperienced. The likelihood of her being able to marry the foreigner Jason is remote. Her response, therefore, might be expected to be one of depression. It was not. Youth and inexperience act as an inaccurate means of predicting the reaction to love's onset and initial frustration. The same point might be made of a love that violates societal taboo. Here I am thinking of Marcus Aurelius's wife, Faustina, or of Perdica or Phaedra, or of Ovid's Byblis (see especially *Metamorphoses* 9.635–40). It could be argued that were their affections expressed openly, they might run the risk of detection and punishment. Hence come their depressive inversions. But let us compare Medea. The taboo against a relationship with Jason is every bit as strong as that, say, against Marcus Antonius's wife (who could, after all, have had a clandestine affair). For Medea, love meant betrayal of her father and her family. She knew this from the beginning. Yet her reaction was not one of powerlessness but, especially in Valerius's version, one of strong anger. What is noteworthy in the stress on passivity in love is, I contend, not its being confined to the young or to taboo breakers but its efflorescence in the first and second centuries of our era.

Love is a very dangerous emotion. When it is blocked it can lead even to death. We can, however, be quite precise in detailing the various symptoms associated with a condition such as lovesickness. When a person becomes subject to lovesickness, then we may expect the sufferer to register an initially overpowering emotion that will induce speechlessness and cause the person to fall to the ground in a black swoon. Soon they are marked by the burning wound of love. Subsequent reactions may involve depression, a sense of mourning, further swooning followed by a deathlike trance, blushing, silence, insomnia, weeping, and even the sweats. If love remains unconsummated, the victim may either sink into a wasting illness, or attempt suicide, or attempt violence on the beloved. The pattern may be replicated if jealousy is involved. The victim becomes depressed, swoons, exhibits a state resembling mourning, and weeps. She or he may subsequently begin to waste away or to contemplate suicide or may embark on acts of considerable violence.[87]

While ancient medical theory seems in practice to recognize only one form of lovesickness, I hope to have demonstrated that, in the literary sources, while typical symptoms of lovesickness are similar, the outcome of lovesickness exhibits two distinct forms, as I have just indicated—the medically recognized depressive form and the more widespread manic form. I would like to reemphasize now the relationship of these two outcomes of lovesickness with ancient concepts of melancholia. Ancient medical theory focused on two forms of melancholia. There was a depressive form, but the more prevalent type was violent and manic. The information on this matter has been examined in the previous chapter. Perhaps it will suffice here to point to the evidence of the pseudo-Aristotelian *Problema* 30.1.[88] The author of the *Problema* maintains that melancholia is the product of a superfluity of black bile. Black bile was a mixture of cold and hot. Melancholics, accordingly, fall into two broad groups, those in whom the black bile becomes very hot and those in whom the black bile becomes very cold. Where the black bile is hot, one would expect what we term the *manic phase* of this condition; where the black bile is cold one would expect the *depressed phase.* Subsequent theorists, whether humoralists or not, associate the illness with one, the other, or both of the two poles, mania or depression. Celsus, Soranus of Ephesus, and Caelius Aurelianus all associate the disease with depression. Aretaeus of Cappadocia and Galen, on the other hand, allow the bipolarity of the *Problema.*

How does this information relate to ancient concepts of lovesickness? The two types of melancholia mentioned in the *Problema* and depicted later in various medical contexts seem to match the two outcomes of lovesickness that I have been attempting to describe. Just as melancholia could be manic or depressive, so could lovesickness. The congruence is remarkable and perhaps tells us something of the popular perceptions of melancholia and lovesickness. This curious congruence, however, may provide an explanation for two other features of ancient lovesickness: (1) the paucity of descriptions of the depressive form of lovesickness and (2) this condition's relatively late appearance within literary texts.

I have argued elsewhere that the depiction of melancholia as a depressive illness rather than as a manic illness is not common in ancient literature and, furthermore, that existing occurrences appear late in the tradition. They seem to begin seriously in both popular literatures at about the time of Seneca. The same tendencies seem to be observable in the ancient descriptions of lovesickness. Medical discussions of lovesickness are all relatively late and describe the condition as depressive and as not unlike melancholia—also treated as a depressive illness. Of the literary descriptions of lovesickness provided here, the examples of manic lovesickness are distributed throughout most periods. The descriptions of depressive lovesickness appear in the early Hellenistic period, then, after a period of quiescence, reappear in earnest with Valerius Maximus—who wrote under the Roman emperor Tiberius (ruled 14–39 C.E.)—and continue sporadically over subsequent centuries. Descriptions of melancholia as a depressive disease seem to begin seriously at approximately the same times as do descriptions of depressive lovesickness. The parallel between melancholia and lovesickness, therefore, allows us to be more precise in categorizing and dating the phases of the ancient perceptions of lovesickness and perhaps of love itself.

There is another important point to be made of the condition, especially as it is suffered by Charicleia, but also as it is suffered by all of those who were subject to the "pulse test." The state in which Charicleia finds herself has its parallel in that suffered by the Eumenides Painter's Orestes and, subsequently, by Persius's addressee in *Satires* 3. In their cases the melancholia represented a mixed state. Externally the victim appeared depressed, stuporous, retarded in a psychomotor sense, but internally there was agitation (hence the descriptor "agitated depression") and flight of ideas. The flight of ideas in Charicleia's instance is evidenced by the racing pulse that is registered by mention of the name of the beloved.

One final line of speculation needs at least to be toyed with at this point. This relates to the curious congruence of a shift in the perception of sexuality (in the sense of the gender of a preferred partner) and the affective mode by which frustration is registered. It has frequently been remarked that in the post-Senecan literary world there is often registered a stronger, more readily marked demarcation of the distinction between heterosexually and homosexually orientated behavior. This is particularly the case in the Greek novel. We have also noted in this chapter a stronger emphasis on affective passivity as the defining reaction to amatory frustration. Can this new literary emphasis on affective passivity be linked with this new stress on a demarcation between heterosexual and homosexual orientations? It is my belief that they can be linked. This is not the place to argue in detail for such a connection. Here perhaps I can remark only two things. First, the apparently amorphous nature of the early classical response, a response based primarily on the exercise of power, rather than on gender preference, matches rather neatly an apparent predisposition to react to frustration with anger. The amorphous matches the uncontrolled. The exercise of power matches a display of anger. From this simple, but striking, equation, a corollary, as it relates to passivity, may follow. This is my second point: emotional withdrawal—that is, passivity—seems to pair with a greater sense of sexual self-definition. There is, at this point in my argumentative narrative, no strong reason why this should be so. But it will become more apparent as things progress. I will argue, repeatedly, that a greater sense of self is the concomitant of the prominence of a variety of passive affectivities. For now, however, let us observe simply that a greater sense of sexual self-definition may well be linked with a heightened experience of emotional passivity.

One final, related point on this matter of passivity deserves to be made. The representation in literature of depressive lovesickness seems to be linked with the "thickening" or "deepening" of the manner by which the self and self-consciousness are portrayed. The representation of passive lovesickness implies in an individual the partitioning off of the self from the world about. The reverse holds true. The active, manic form of lovesickness, no less painful than the depressive or passive form, is predicated on a blurring of the sense of separateness from the world, a blurring of the boundaries of the self.

I have cited the following passage from the great Colombian novelist Gabriel García Márquez elsewhere. It is such a powerful one and is so indicative of the sameness through time of the emotions I am discussing that it deserves quoting again.

> After Florentino Ariza saw her for the first time, his mother knew before he told her because he lost his voice and his appetite and spent the entire night tossing and turning in his bed. But when he began to wait for the answer to his first letter, his anguish was complicated by diarrhoea and green vomit, he became disorientated and suffered from sudden fainting spells, and his mother was terrified because his condition did not resemble the turmoil of love so much as the devastation of cholera. Florentino Ariza's godfather, an old homeopathic practitioner who had been Tránsito Ariza's confident ever since her days as a secret mistress, was also alarmed at first by the patient's condition, because he had a weak pulse, the hoarse breathing, and the pale perspiration of a dying man. But his examination revealed that he had no fever, no pain anywhere, and that his only concrete feeling was an urgent desire to die.

This passage comes from Gabriel García Márquez's *Love in the Time of Cholera.*[89] I have reproduced it to illustrate a simple point. This description of a depressed, fretting, passive, apparently fevered,[90] physically ill lover—almost a cliché of modern literature[91]—might as easily be of an ancient depressive melancholic as of a victim of cholera or lovesickness.[92] The dominant ancient concept, as I hope to have shown, was a violent one. Do we, therefore, see the origins or the "discovery" of Florentino Ariza's hackneyed condition in the literature of the early Hellenistic period and, above all, in the literature of the early empire (with its best parallels in the Greek novel)?[93]

It is remarkable that love melancholy begins to gain real currency at the same time, approximately, as descriptions of depressive melancholy become current. Do such congruences tell us something about the prehistory and even archaeology of affective states? (Certainly they show how closely allied were the emotions of anger, depression, and love.) Do they suggest that there took place in the literature of the first or second century of our era a shift in the perception of the symptoms of such affective states as love, lovesickness, and melancholia?

The answer, I believe, is yes. But we must be particularly careful in three regards: discovery, proximate, and ultimate causes. Paul Veyne was very helpful on these matters. In a controversial article, he argued that such an affective shift, at least as far as love is concerned, is evident in the early empire. He believed that, with the weakening of the extended, aristocratic Roman family system, romantic love, rather than family compulsion, became the means for securing marital obeisance in marriage from women.[94] It would be easy to interpret love melancholy as another aspect of the new stress on romantic love (which seems above all a passive condition: as love itself became romantic, so did lovesickness become depressive).[95] The active, frequently violent emotions of the lovesick are slowly, but never wholly, replaced by the passivity of Antiochus, or of Habrocomes, or of Florentino Ariza.[96]

Veyne's explanation for the affective shift has been—no doubt rightly—rejected.[97] It does little to explain the passivity of males such as Dionysius. Most, however, accept the existence of an affective shift—of a proximate cause. What was its ultimate cause? The interrelation of lovesickness with melancholia and depression seems sufficiently strong as to demand an explanation that provides a cause not just for the affective shift in the perception of frustrated love but also for depression itself. Veyne's exhilarating thesis may tell us something about the emergence of romantic love and even of lovesickness, but it tells us nothing of the interrelated emergence of its congener, depressive melancholy.[98]

The concept of "discovery" is even more problematic. The passage cited from Gabriel García Márquez suggests a continuity between the Greek novel and the contemporary estimation of love. Yet comparative evidence most certainly sets a lie to this.[99] As a conclusion to this chapter, and as a check against heedlessly Eurocentric notions of "discovery," I would like to append some comparative data, drawn from Egyptian and Sanskrit literature. The lesson this comparative data offers, I suppose, relates to the latency of these changes. They occur in a number of societies. They seem dependent on urbanization and, with this, the centralization of societal power.

Depressive lovesickness is one of the hallmarks of a culture that has come to privilege the self. That lovesickness points to a passivity implying the potential for a reciprocity in amatory matters that demands the considerable resources of the self; it fits ill with the traditional, violent, and self-directed exercise of power within erotic matters or, for that matter, in social affairs generally. One might assume—from the many examples provided in this chapter—that depressive lovesickness and the attendant problematization of the self is a particularly Western affair. It is not: such a condition may receive prominence in different sequences in any number of different cultures.[100] Depressive lovesickness is not the property of all of those dead white European males concerning whom I frequently teach. Nor is the privileging of self, that concomitant of depressive lovesickness, the prerogative of ancient Western society. Nor is it the preserve of the world of the Enlightenment. Nor does it come into being as the inexorable product of the alienation of labor and commodification of the individual that purportedly emerges from the Industrial Revolution.[101]

My purpose here is to provide a check on (my own) tendencies toward cultural naïveté and cultural parochialism. The check will be drawn from Egyptian and Sanskrit literatures.[102] I have stressed a sameness between the ancient and the modern worlds in my desire to dethrone, as it were, an easy periodization based on the European Enlightenment and the Industrial Revolution. But to envisage this psychotic sameness between the ancient and modern worlds as the product of a form of continuity is mistaken. That the ancient and the modern worlds can exhibit now similar, now dissimilar responses to emotional trauma is the result not so much of historical connection but of the limited ways humans may respond to psychic frustration and of the limited forms this frustration can take.[103] These simple comparisons should put paid to oversimple notions of "discovery."

To follow are some remarkable examples, in the first instance from ancient Egyptian literature, of individuals suffering from lovesickness. The Egyptian poems I cite all date to the New Kingdom (the Eighteenth through the Twentieth Dynasties, ca. 1550–1080 B.C.E.), a relatively rich, stable, urbanized, and literate period,[104] at least until well into the Twentieth Dynasty. These poems should provide pause for the most hardened of Eurocentricists.[105] Here is the first of the love poems, taken from the *Papyrus Chester Beatty* I (I:1a, a cycle of seven stanzas), as indicated by Lichtheim.[106]

SEVENTH STANZA
Seven days since I saw my sister,
And sickness has invaded me;
I am heavy in all my limbs,
My body has forsaken me.
When the physicians come to me,
My heart rejects their remedies;
The magicians are quite helpless,

My sickness is not discerned.
To tell me "She is here" would revive me!
Her name would make me rise;
Her messenger's coming and going,
That would revive my heart!
My sister is better than all prescriptions,
She does more for me than all medicines;
Her coming and going to me is my amulet,
The sight of her makes me well!
When she opens her eyes my body is young,
Her speaking makes me strong;
Embracing her expels my malady—
Seven days since she went from me!

The speaker of this poem identifies his complaint as a sickness, one that is the result of an amatory frustration caused by the absence of his "sister" ("sister" or "brother" is the usual designation of the beloved in these poems). The physiological symptoms of the illness are a heaviness (v. 3) and a weakness of the body (vv. 5 and 10 indicate that our victim is bedridden).[107] These symptoms may be intended to evoke a condition of senescence, which in its turn may be an indication of the proximity of death (cf. v. 4: "My body has forsaken me"). Such a condition no doubt involves corporeal wasting. Moreover, the proper diagnosis for the illness defies the powers of medical doctors (vv. 5–6, 13–14), just as did the malady of Heliodorus's lovesick Charicleia. That magicians are also needed for a diagnosis (they are quite "helpless" in v. 7) and that a protreptic device (an amulet) may have been part of their prescription (cf. v. 15: "Her coming and going to me is my amulet") may indicate, as was the case for Charicleia, that his condition was variously attributed to the effects of the evil eye. The only possible cure for the illness is that which we have repeatedly observed in Greek and Roman contexts, union with the beloved (cf. vv. 13–14: "My sister is better than all prescriptions, / She does more for me than all medicines"; 18: "Embracing her expels my malady").

The similarity between the situation described in this Egyptian love poem and the many Greek and Roman contexts just surveyed is marked. This is love melancholy, and the condition is depressive. The similarity exists not just in terms of situation and desired outcomes but also in terms of the amatory illness's etiology, physical symptoms, modes of treatment, and ultimate cure. The poem is, furthermore, suggestive of the constraints and self-actualization evident in Greco-Roman conundrums. It certainly casts doubt on the uniqueness of the Greco-Roman and Western experience.

The next piece of evidence is a poem taken from the collection designated *Papyrus Harris 500.*

IIA THE FIRST COLLECTION

6

I shall lie down at home
And pretend to be ill;
Then enter the neighbours to see me,
Then comes my sister with them.
She will make the physicians unneeded,
She understands my illness!

What are we to make of the mendacity of this writer? He understands the condition of lovesickness so well that he is able to fake it. He knows, furthermore, that his condition will be understood not as lovesickness (except, perhaps, by his "sister"—"she understands my illness") but as a malady that will require medical intervention (v. 5). No doubt the symptoms and their concomitants that his bogus malady presents will be identical to those outlined in the previous poem: a debilitating, wasting sickness, requiring medical and magical treatment, which will apparently threaten the sufferer's life if left unchecked. One of the most interesting aspects of this poem is that it exhibits such an intimate—even self-conscious—understanding of the condition ("I shall . . . pretend to be ill"). It is almost as if the writer of this piece were playing with the traditions associated with this kind of experience and its poetry and mocking them. The poet certainly mocks his "sister." The mockery could as easily be directed against the Greco-Roman traditions.

My third poem comes, like the first, from the *Papyrus Chester Beatty I.* The first of the cycle of seven "stanzas," it is less ironic than the previous poem. While it avows the author's being subject to lovesickness, it provides no detail as to the nature of the lovesickness (designated as "sickness") with which the young woman is afflicted. It runs as follows:

FIRST STANZA

My *brother* torments my heart with his voice,
He makes sickness take hold of me;
He is neighbour to my mother's house,
And I cannot go to him!
Mother is right in charging him thus:
"Give up seeing her!"
It pains my heart to think of him,
I am possessed by love of him.
Truly, he is a foolish one,

But I resemble him;
He knows not my wish to embrace him,
Or he would write to my mother.
Rather I am promised to you
By the Gold of women!
Come to me that I see your beauty,
Father, Mother will rejoice!
My people will hail you all together,
They will hail you, O my *brother*!

What can we say of this poem? The young woman designates her condition of frustrated love as a "sickness." In light of all that has gone before, we can easily understand this sickness as the love melancholy at which we have been looking. Doubtless it is a debilitating, life-threatening illness, and doubtless it will be as resistant to medical or magical treatment as were the conditions exhibited by other victims. The only remedy is union with the beloved. This poem may not necessarily highlight the individual subject, the self, but it does highlight, however obliquely, a condition related to the discourse of the self, a condition this book has been at pains to illustrate.

It is useful, when contemplating these poems, to look ahead to the startling reference (quoted in more detail in chapter 3) given by Lévi-Strauss (1963) to the emotional situation of a young Zuni woman, a twelve year old, who "was stricken with a nervous seizure directly after an adolescent boy had seized her hands."[108] The young boy was accused of sorcery and was made subject to a number of ultimately successful tests at the hands of his community. What fascinated Lévi-Strauss was the treatment accorded to the young man. More relevant here are the hints of the symptoms that the young woman experienced. These match those suffered by the Egyptians. The Zuni attributed them not to love but to the effects of sorcery or something akin to the function of the evil eye. That the effects of the evil eye may match those of lovers is something that we have already observed. The corporeal wasting and rapid degeneration is something that lover and ensorcelled suffer alike. So it is that the young woman's condition may match those of the lovers in the Egyptian poems and those of the lovers in the Greek and Roman texts that I have already discussed. Zunis, ancient Egyptians, Greeks, Romans, and García Márquez's Colombians all suffer in the same manner.[109]

My point should be obvious without needing detailed exemplification. The basis for the bizarre alienation and the dramatic confrontation with the self that lovesickness entails (leading either to a destruction of the self or to a reintegration) is not something nurtured by culture (by some Western or post-Enlightenment experience) but is generated, it seems, by the very physiology of the human body, its psyche, and the social conditions it encounters. This reactive form of depression, therefore, is, given the right social conditions, a universal. As for these conditions, what is needed, on the social plane, for such a confrontation is a reasonably complex social organization (or a near-urban society) that allows a reasonable degree of individual privacy, but within what is—at least for the better-off—an authoritarian social setting. The suffering individual, furthermore, must both perceive and represent him or herself as isolated from the community.[110] (Such communities, furthermore, must be subject also to the varying constraints of literacy.)[111] Finally, for others to recognize it, the amatory experience must be something that requires interpretation: its evidentiary basis must be made manifest through signs. That this Egyptian society exhibited these conditions is apparent.

These conclusions can be reemphasized by looking (briefly in this instance) at a series of Sanskrit love poems, provided for us particularly in the collection *Subhasitaratnakosa* (Treasury of well-turned verse).[112] This anthology, put together shortly before 1100 C.E. by the Buddhist scholar identified as Vidyakara, is the product of a historical period that seems to reproduce the preconditions for the type of presentation of self that is highlighted in the present book (for a historical overview see Basham 1967): a complex social structure (evincing that peculiar, but fecund, mix of state authoritarianism and individual freedom) matched by high literacy and, for its beneficiaries, personal wealth.

The *Subhasitaratnakosa* anthology contains verse by over two hundred poets "who lived for the most part from the eighth to the eleventh centuries A.D." (Ingalls 1965, v). Those poems of particular relevance to my theme are found in the "books" entitled "The Lady Parted from Her Lover" and "The Lover Parted from His Mistress." The stylized portrait of the lovesick in these poems exhibits many of the characteristics with which we have become familiar. Some of the characteristics of the lovesick woman are sighing, sleeplessness, a burning fever, carelessness of personal presentation, and a feeling of emptiness. Ingalls notes (1965, 230):

> The sole exertion of which she is capable is an attempt to paint her lover's portrait. For the rest, she leans her cheek on her hand, while the tears stream forth, black with the collyrium of her eyes, destroying the cosmetic designs on her cheeks and falling in heavy showers on her breast.

A few illustrative examples of this remarkable Indian tradition follow. The young woman in the first is in love with King Bhoja.

749. Is she attacked by dropsy? No;
nor by the major elements.
She is not mad, nor is she suffering
from a syndrome of ailments.
Why, then, this weeping, swooning, sighing
and then this smiling face?
How shall I say it, the foe whom she has seen,
who really is no foe, is none other than
His Sacred Majesty, King Bhoja.

(Chittapa)

We may assume either that the young woman is separated from King Bhoja or that her love has so far met with little response.[113] Her reaction to this frustration is a perplexing sickness that is apparently no sickness at all (neither "syndrome of ailments" nor "dropsy").[114] We have observed precisely this form of "sickness" in the case of, for example, Heliodorus's Charicleia.[115] Her symptoms of weeping, swooning, and sighing are things we have met in a number of previous amatory contexts. These, however, were associated with the historically later form of lovesickness, the passive form. It is also noteworthy that the woman's illness, according to Chittapa, could at first sight be confused with madness (v. 3). The form of madness must be depressive, and in Greco-Roman contexts it would be so understood, because of its confusion with depression. What we witness in poems like this one is the poetic presentation of a powerful *inner* experience. It is one that sets the individual apart from the human world about them. The self, thus, is rendered problematic. The reaction in this and in the following instances is a passive one. This highlighting of the self, because of the dangers of madness, runs the risk of the disintegration of the personality.

The theme in the next poem, "sickness without a cure," picks up that of the previous one and also that of many classical contexts.

744. You may as well burn up my couch
though strewn with lotus leaves.
What use these shaken palm fronds
which take the form of heated coals?
Enough; the cream of sandalwood
no less than moonlight burns my eyes.
Dear friends, my sickness is without a cure
like fire that feeds on water.

(Abhinanda)

This poem also echoes the ancient Egyptian poems surveyed in the previous section of this chapter. What is new, however, is the stress on burning. Fire, a cliché of most love literatures, is introduced with some power. That even moonbeams burn the victim of love is a very striking topos. Sappho felt fire running beneath her skin. So, too, did Medea. While Sappho was being ironic, in Medea's case the fire acted as a spur to action. Here, as other poems show, the fire consumes the passive victim and reinforces the sufferer's helplessness. It is a fire, however, that vividly attempts to reflect the inner experience of the speaker and so marks her off from the world about.

The next short poem emphasizes even more than the others the isolating nature of this erotic illness, the depressingly passive mode by which it is registered, and the apparent dangers it poses for survival.

> *751.* You leave not your couch nor care about your health,
> nor tend your hair bound in a disheveled knot.
> At least take care, dear friend, to stay alive.
> I've seen a hundred women separated from their loves
> but never such as you.

This poem is also the first reference (within my citations) to what becomes canonical in the passive experience, wasting (it is reemphasized by the references to health and to the lack of interest in personal care).[116] If the frustrated lover received no help, then he or she eventually perished,[117] either from the wasting illness or by their own hand. It is a theme that seemingly echoes a repeated topos of the Greek novel.[118]

In the following poem, we have the now common motifs of loss of sense, of swooning, and of fire.

> *755.* Grief cuts my heart and cuts it deep
> but cuts it not in two;
> my body, though it stumbles dazed,
> refuses to lose consciousness.
> An inner fire burns my limbs
> without consuming them;
> the hand of fate which strikes so deep,
> alas, strikes not the life.
>
> [Bhavabhuti]

The motif of an illness that is not a real illness is also present. This is indicated by the author's claim that "the hand of fate which strikes so deep, alas, strikes not the life." The poet is playing with the topos here, however. The usual cliché is that lovesickness can kill. Playfully the poet indicates that this is not the case. In so doing he demonstrates that this is a case not of dejection or of melancholy but of love. (This is a type of play that I have already noted in the

Egyptian material.) Once again the powerful presentation of an inner experience, a presentation that highlights the difficulties related to the boundaries of the self, is paramount. It is difficult to resist emphasizing the words "to lose consciousness." The meaning refers to wakefulness. The implication of "consciousness" in English, at any rate, is "self-consciousness." Love melancholy cannot diminish one's sense of self, it could say. The condition bespeaks a heightened awareness of the boundaries of the self.

It appears that the sufferer in the next poem may eventually expire from the lovesickness she is suffering.

> *710.* The passion of my heart is sharp
> and stealing ever on, brings pain;
> burns like a stirred-up fire, smokeless;
> wastes like a mortal fever in every limb.
> My father cannot save me nor my mother
> nor even you, my friend.
>
> [Bhavabhuti]

We know that the remedy is sexual congress with the beloved. The stress on pain, smokeless fire (again an illness that is not an illness), and fever are common to this genre, in whichever of the cultures we have looked at.

One last example of this type follows (there are, however, others that could have been included).[119] This small poem vividly captures the passivity, the debility, and the withdrawal of the sufferer. Thus are highlighted the boundaries of the self. Thus, too, is highlighted the need for reciprocity.

> *715.* This debility of body and lack of all desire,
> this fixing of your eye in trance,[120] and perfect silence:
> this state bespeaks a heart fixed on one single object,
> What is that one, fair lady; brahma or your lover?
>
> (Laksmidhara)

From these poems it is possible to create a composite picture of this Sanskrit lovesickness. We are dealing with an amatory condition fueled by absence and frustration. It may present itself as a sickness of a feverlike variety that requires for its cure medical intervention and interpretation. Its most common symptoms, apart from fever, are paleness, wasting, an obsessive single-mindedness, sleeplessness, sighing, tears, and sorrow. The cure is intimacy with the separated beloved.

Five points have been made in this chapter. I repeat these here for the sake of clarity. First, the depressed, fretting, passive, and physically ill lover (sometimes termed the love melancholic), though present in ancient literature, is more a cliché of medieval and modern literary experience. The dominant reaction to frustrated love in ancient literature was manic and frequently violent. Second, lovesickness, in its literary depictions, mirrors the distinctions that the ancient medical writers posited for melancholia itself: there was a depressive type and there was a manic type. Third, the depressive variety of lovesickness, though always on the cards (just like depressive melancholia) becomes more frequent late in antiquity, above all during the first century of our era. Fourth, these dominant traditions of amatory mania and depression find exact parallels in those associated with melancholia proper and depression. Fifth, these manic and depressive reactions to the trauma of erotic infatuation are means by which individuals attempt to restore the integrity of the self. I would like to expand briefly on this fifth point. It is of particular importance, if not in this local context, at least for the themes of this book as a whole.

In these poems of erotic trauma, it is the written presentation of self and of self-consciousness that is so striking. The poems seem to exemplify a thickening or deepening, in the nonjudgmental sense, of the manner by which the self and self-consciousness are presented. They are, furthermore, built upon an opposition of "inside-outside," a partitioning off of the self from the world about us. Reading from those ancient texts so far surveyed, we may take this speculative vein concerning the self a step further. The sense of self that is evident in these poems demonstrates a standing outside oneself, a concern almost to watch, to weigh up, and to react to one's emotional and physical state almost as if it were other.[121] Such a sense of self involves the extended highlighting of a person's inner mental processes. It involves a partitioning not just between the inner self and the outer world but also between the body (approximating the "outer" world) and the self (approximating the "inner" world). It is as if the subject stands at a remove from his or her emotional reactions. It is as if the subject were alienated from these. The subject watches its reactions and feels powerless in their face. There comes into being a disjunction between the body and a person's (and other persons') consciousness of it.

This developed sense of the self, as we see it through Egyptian and Indian lovesickness, comes at considerable personal risk. Above all, there is associated with it passivity, yielding, withdrawal, isolation, and estrangement. These can lead to the disintegration of the personality. A chain of other qualities may also be present. These conditions are particularly also to be linked with the private; with interiority, the mind, and "depth"; and even, in some cases, with viscera.

Lovesickness must be able to be interpreted (or read) through the *signs* of this illness—it is as if this were a *literate* illness (read as one would a book). Other characteristics follow: the condition is associated primarily with present time (we guess that earlier eras did not suffer it) and with an urban and individualist lifestyle. It is something to be associated with humans, not with animals. The risk of this highlighted sense of self is, through its associated estrangement, the total disintegration of the personality.

We cannot posit sociological causes for the appearance of this type of poetry that privileges the self. But certain aspects seem to be common between the Egyptian, the Sanskrit, and the Greek and Roman poetry. For example, it is undoubtedly true that the widespread social emergence of these conditions is predicated upon a comparably widespread frustration. It is also true to say that the evidential texts discussed in this book are the product of the more privileged members of their particular communities. A heightened form of emotional conflict, brought on by sociological forces, must be the causative agent in this process. It is much easier to posit this than it is to demonstrate it. I have already suggested of Egyptian poetry that the basis for the bizarre alienation and the dramatic confrontation of the self that lovesickness entails is not something nurtured by culture—it is not discovered—but is generated by the very physiology of the human body and psyche. This mode of reactive depression will reappear as social circumstances allow.[122] This may also hold for Sanskrit poetry and for the Greek and Roman experience. What is needed for such a confrontation is the conflict that is generated within a society exhibiting a reasonably complex social organization (or a near-urban society, one with sufficient leisure for the experience of the emotion and for the composition of complex texts meditating upon this—literacy becomes important at this juncture).[123] Such a social organization must allow a reasonable degree of individual privacy, but within what is—at least for the better-off—an authoritarian social setting. Such a situation seems to have existed for the elites in the courtly worlds that produced the Sanskrit poetry that I have just examined and the Greek and Roman literature on which this book has been focused. Such communities, furthermore, must be subject also to the varying constraints of literacy and to the forms of subjective, interpretative experience brought in its train (see Goody 1998). Thus it is that the amatory experience must be something that, for others to recognize it, requires interpretation: its evidentiary basis must be made manifest through signs, through writing.

That we are dealing with a social organization that juxtaposes individual privacy with, at least in the cases of the better-off, a moderately authoritarian social setting goes some distance toward explaining why all of the literatures discussed here seem to cast into such relief problems related to the issue of control. This becomes apparent again and again as we witness the tensions within this form of poetry. Such tension exists between the passivity of the poet and the activity of, say, the absent lover or, in broader contexts, the community; between the yielding nature of the individual and the obdurate carelessness of his or her associates or the community; between the withdrawal, isolation, and even estrangement of individuals and the quotidian competencies by which the beloved, for example, or the larger community surrounded them. Thus, it seems to follow, this literature offers a focus not on the public, the outer life, or even the body but on the private, the inner life, and the mind (interiority). No better example of this last point may be offered than the philosophical writings of Seneca.

That is as far as I think we should attempt to pursue the isolating of social determinants for the conditions that I have singled out. That aspects of such conditions existed in Alexandria of the third century B.C.E., in Rome in Seneca's era (and, as we shall see, within early monastic communities), and within the Indian and Egyptian communities to which I have alluded in this chapter suggests two things. The etiology of the problem goes deeper than, first, a mere isolation of "crisis cultures" (I doubt there was anything crisis-ridden about, e.g., Ptolemaic Alexandria) or, second, overurbanized and overpopulated centers or cultures subject to a particularly rapid rate of change. While these factors are important and may act as contributory agents, there is also the need for the admixture of the other qualities suggested in the previous paragraphs. It may seem to be frustrating to deny the possibility of isolating a cause for such conditions. But I suggest that the first problem is to describe the conditions and to isolate periods in which they seem to have become paramount. There is too little acquiescence in either of these matters for us to allow ourselves *yet* the indulgence of looking for causes—as Veyne (1978) and many others have done. To this point it is description that really matters.[124]

3

Seasickness
Boredom, Nausia, *and the Self*

The image in figure 3, from a Greek pot (termed a white-ground lekythos) of the mid- to late fifth century B.C.E., depicts a person mourning, either over the remains of a friend or, more likely, over the person's own remains.[1] These are contained in the identical pot by the right knee (another lekythos—a mirror of the one we are looking at).[2] I have often showed this picture to people who are unfamiliar with this type of Greek funerary vase. Their almost unvarying response has been to suggest that the face and crossed arms of the person on the lekythos suggest boredom. Most people assume that we are viewing a male in this picture. They have told me that the origin of the boredom is overindulgence: the bulky arms and chest, the heavy neck, and the apparent garland about the neck suggest an enthusiastic devotee of the banquet scene rather than one of the gym. There are other indications to support their guess. That the person's hair is drooping in ringlets and is apparently oiled, that the person is overweight but quite young, that the head drops toward the left shoulder with a look of tired resignation, and that there is an appearance of intelligence indicate to them quite reasonably "a Greek Oscar Wilde suffering from too many parties" and "fed up" accordingly.

Some respondents have pursued this conjecture concerning the young person's emotional state one step further. They have conjectured that the adjective *depressed* might fit the young person's depiction better than does *bored.* They have suggested to me that there is in this facial set (the eyes, the mouth, the manner) more sorrow and dejection than mere boredom. The weight of the shoulders and neck, rather than pointing to a life of youthful dissipation, might as well point to a disconsolate life that is somehow out of kilter with itself.

The reality is in some ways more surprising. The young person is usually identified by scholars to be a young woman.[3] She is mourning. It is not completely clear whether this mourning is for herself or for another person, but the temptation is strong for us to guess that in fact the picture is intended as a postmortem representation. The young woman is mourning her own untimely

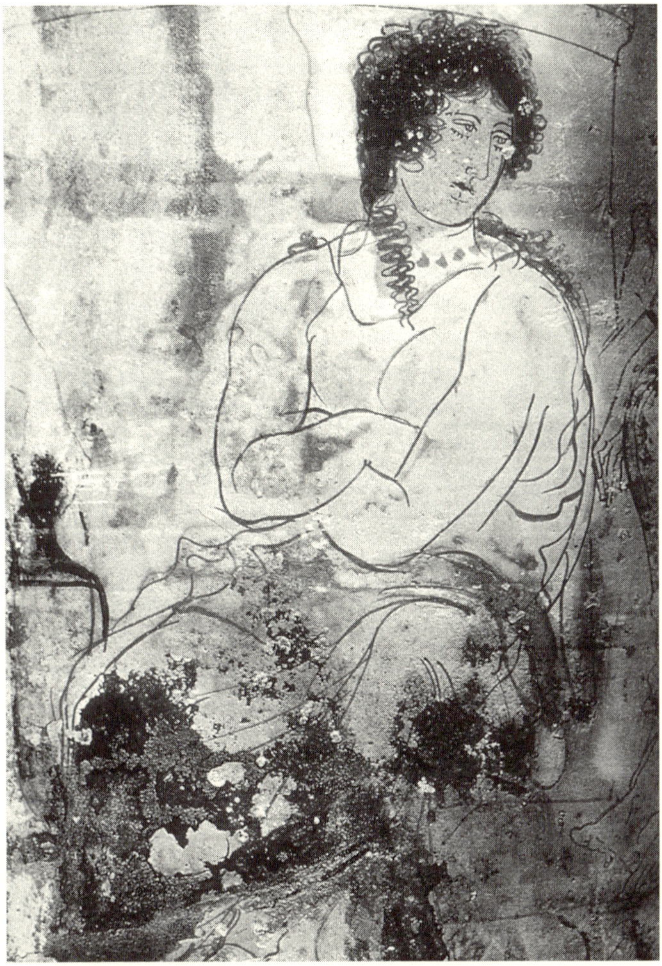

FIG. 3. "Greek Mourning" (fifth century B.C.E.).
(© Copyright The British Museum.)

passing from the banquet of life. The pot on which she is depicted contains her ashes. The pot from which she gazes away with resignation is a replication of this very pot in which her remains are capped. The likeness of the actual lekythos and the figurative lekythos lead most economically to this conclusion.

It is this inevitably implied polyvalence of the young person's emotions that so intrigues. The lekythos provides a remarkable congruence—as far as the intuitive viewer is concerned—between the emotions of boredom, melancholia, and mourning. It illustrates, no doubt, the vase painter's intuitive understanding of the link between these three conditions.

This chapter will attempt to illustrate how the psychological insight concerning the nature of boredom that is evident in this picture eventually became a part of the literary or discursive tradition of antiquity. The gradual "interiorization" of boredom (its generic assumption, we could say, of the status of mourning—even its becoming likened to a sorrow without cause) is part of the theme of the chapter to follow. The link between this and the previous two chapters is through melancholia.[4] Boredom, at least as it was championed throughout the twentieth century, was seen as a cognate form of melancholia. Just as is the case with melancholia, it is sometimes said to have been an invention of the Enlightenment, something that the ancients did not have either the wits or the opportunity to experience. That this is not the case (i.e., that such emotions are not cultural constructs) will be part of the point of this chapter.

The growing link between boredom and melancholia is important in another way.[5] Boredom has been a vital concept for over two thousand years of Western culture—even if sometimes we have had no idea of what we are actually talking about.[6] Ranging from dark age and medieval monastic *acedia*, through the "English disease" of the seventeenth and eighteenth centuries and the French Enlightenment and the *mal de siècle* of nineteenth-century Europe, to the "nausea" and alienation of twentieth-century existentialists, the concept has had a long and powerful history (for surveys see Bouchez 1973; Kuhn 1976; Spacks 1995; Jonard 1998). It is a history of literary and sociological significance (as much felt as written about). Clarification of the prehistory of the emotion is therefore of considerable importance.

In Greek of the archaic, classical, and Hellenistic periods and in Classical Latin, references to boredom are very hard to find. The terms that are used to designate boredom in Greek and Latin are not at all common, they are very vague, and if possessed of an unambiguous sense of "boredom," they tend to come late. In Greek, for example, *alus* is perhaps the best of available terms. It originally meant something like "being other to oneself," thus "distracted" or "grief-stricken." Only in Plutarch's time (the second century C.E.) did it take on an unequivocal sense of "boredom."[7] *Taedium* (literally "tedium") is the best of the Latin terms, but it lacks concision. Its lexical ambit is far wider than that of the English "boredom" (or, for that matter, of such modern-language terms as *l'ennui*, *la noia*, or *Langeweile*).[8] It can mean anything from that weariness brought on by satiety right through to an uncomplicated boredom that too dull a book or concert may engender. When it came to designating boredom, the ancients experienced a shortage of terms (if not necessarily of the emotion itself; all languages have their descriptive blind spots).[9] It follows therefore that descriptions of the condition must be limited in number and in scope.

A typical, random example involves Aristophanes' (ca. 450–385 B.C.E.) old farmer Dicaeopolis, the protagonist in the *Archarnians* (which play dates to 425 B.C.E.), who is depicted at the beginning of this work sitting in the Pnyx, waiting for the Athenian assembly to begin. He has arrived early. The officials and participants are late in arriving. We would expect him to be bored and fed up, and he is. He announces in verses 30–32 of this play:

> I groan, I yawn *[kechêna]*, I stretch, I fart,
> I don't know what to do. I write, I pull at my hair, I figure things out
> As I look to the country, longing for peace . . .

What else can Dicaeopolis be referring to by this yawning, stretching, and farting than boredom? But what is so interesting is that he does not tell us he was bored. Instead he describes what are for us the telltale symptoms of boredom.

Satiety, or "being fed up," is often synonymous with boredom. There are a number of instances where this may be witnessed. Take Euripides' Medea (her play dates approximately to 431 B.C.E.). She seems to think that husbands become "fed up" with their families and then act unfairly. She tells us this in the midst of her great monologue on the role of women in Greek mythical society (*Medea* 244–46).

> A man, whenever he is grieved/fed up/bored *[achthêtai]* with the household,
> Goes out and puts an end to the satiety/boredom *[asê]* of his heart,
> Turning either to a friend or to someone of the same age.

The difficulty that this passage presents to us resides in the imprecision of the language (imprecision, at least, for people asking questions like the ones that I am here). The verb *achthomai* (v. 244) means "weighed down" or "vexed" or "disgusted." The notion of "disgust" links it with satiety and, for some commentators, with boredom. The lexical net for this word is therefore very wide. It seems to imply a whole spectrum of emotions that range from disgust through to boredom. Much the same point can be made of the reference to satiety *(asê)* in the next line. The word indicates "surfeit," hence "disgust." I suppose boredom is not indicated because Euripides does not have a word for it. But, to be clear, he may have thought that he did.

Let us tease out the two words *achthomai* and *asê* a little further. One other intriguing use of *achthomai* is found in *Symposium* 173c of Plato (429–347 B.C.E.). It occurs soon after the beginning of that amatory tract. Apollodorus, one of the dialogue's chief interlocutors, is speaking. After asserting that he knows of nothing that gives him greater pleasure than discussing philosophy, he goes on to say: "as for those of you who are rich and monied, I'm bored *[achthomai]* with you, and I pity your companions, because you think you are doing something when you are not." As eminent a Hellenist as Sir Kenneth Dover (1980, 79) interprets *achthomai* as "bored." One can see why. "Weighed down" or "disgusted" seems too strong for the context. "Bored" or "fed up" seems to catch the tone nicely. Yet that is not quite what Plato says. How could he have when he had no such word? To translate the verb *achthomai* as "bored" requires, therefore, something of a cultural act of faith. Although it would be incredible (and would fly in the face of the picture with which this chapter began) to suggest that Greeks did not feel such an emotion as boredom, it remains to be stated that at this stage in their language, they had no apparent word for the condition.

The ambiguities of *asê* are neatly demonstrated in the poetry of Pindar (518–438 B.C.E.). In Pindar's victory odes (and in oratorical literature) the fear is often expressed that a too lengthy exposition of the achievements of the victor may induce in the audience the emotion of *asê* or, more usually, *koros*. The audience's satiety, Pindar fears, may turn them away from his poetry and from the achievements of his patron, the victor. I think that we in the twentieth century would be more comfortable with a translation of *koros* as "boredom." Pindar's *Pythian Odes* (1.81–83) provides a typical reference to this fear: "if you were to speak to the point, drawing together into a brief space the strands of many things, less blame follows. For irksome satiety *[koros]* blunts swift hopes" (cf. also *Pythian Odes* 8.32; *Nemean Odes* 7.52, 10.20). What is the *koros* referred to here? Is this "satiety" the same thing as "boredom"? Or could it even entail, as Burton maintains (1962, 107; cf. Bundy 1962, 13, 40, 74 ff.), "some sort of offensive action." What Pindar may also be suggesting is the danger that such fulsome praise may rouse the envy of the audience and thus bring hostility against the addressee. In other contexts the result of *koros*, comparably, may be the weakening of the force of the speaker's argument (defense, accusation, request, etc.).[10] Pindar's version of *koros* and *asê*, therefore, leaves us properly as undecided on the link between "satiety" and boredom as does the *Medea*.

One may draw some provisional and simple conclusions from my brief consideration of these terms. Boredom is not easily named. It is most readily alluded to by metaphors. As we have just seen, these relate to digestive disorder (*asê*, *koros*, farting) or to the mildest forms of physical enfeeblement (*achthomai*, at root, probably has this sense).[11] Such metaphors are corporeal; that is, they are easily and publicly visible. They mark the condition. They seem (despite corporeal interiority) to exist on the surface of things.

That is enough of satiety and disgust. I would like now to look at one other topos to illustrate my point. This concerns military service. Unoccupied soldiers, now and in antiquity, are well known for their proneness to boredom. Plutarch (ca. 46–after 120 C.E.) is very useful on this matter. His life of Eumenes (11.3) provides a very neat example. In this passage the effect of the close confinement of the besieged forces is described and Eumenes' attempts to alleviate the feeling of boredom (here designated as *alus*) that was taking hold of his soldiers. The passage warrants quoting in full (Loeb translation modified).

> But most of all detrimental to his besieged forces was their narrow quarters, since their movements were confined to small houses and a place only two furlongs in circumference. Because of this neither men nor horses could get exercise before eating or being fed. Therefore, wishing to remove the boredom *[alus]* of those men who were weakened by inactivity *[apraxia]* and, more than that, to have them somehow or other in training for flight, if opportunity should offer, he assigned the men a house, the largest in the place, fourteen cubits long, as a place to walk, ordering them little by little to increase their pace.

The crucial words are "wishing to remove the boredom *[alus]* of those men who were being weakened by inactivity *[apraxia]*." Activity has been for a very long time a standard, if ineffectual, remedy for boredom—and not just for soldiers. But this is not the real issue. It is that Plutarch, writing late in the first or in the early second centuries of our era, unambiguously designates boredom and, calmly, notes its deleterious, but for us predictable, effect on inactive soldiers. This is an acknowledgment that in the passages previously surveyed, boredom seems not to have been possible because, I have no doubt, of the absence of adequate terms for the word. The change is remarkable, if imperceptible. The emotion of boredom, registered but unnamed in earlier periods, has now assumed a banal lexical life. The strength of the change could be underlined in another way. The earlier terms for boredom, as I have stated, were visible public marks for a condition that, for its designation, required metaphors. The term *alus* (implying literally alienation or otherness—it is linked to the Greek word for other, *allos*) is abstract. It is, if it ever had metaphorical status, a dead metaphor. This is evident from its regularity of usage. It designates an emotion that is hidden, private, and abstract.

Two other passages may reinforce the simple lexical conclusions that I have been emphasizing: *Iliad* 24.403 and Euripides' *Iphigeneia in Aulis* 804–8. These passages were written five hundred or more years before Plutarch. Both passages are instructive in a negative way. They cry out for a clear-cut term like *alus*. Both describe military situations that, on first reading, seem to allude to boredom. (If *Eumenes* is anything to go by, boredom ought to be expected in such situations.) Yet neither context mentions the emotion. In the Homeric passage, Hermes, pretending to be one of Achilles' Myrmidons, is speaking to Priam. He states that the Achaeans will begin fighting the Trojans at dawn. They have become vexed at sitting around waiting *(aschaloôsi gar hoide kathêmenoi)*. Their leaders can no longer restrain them. One might have expected Hermes to express some notion of boredom here. It is implicit, I suppose, in *kathêmenoi* (sitting around). Yet *aschaloôsi* is a precise word. It suggests that the soldiers were not merely bored but vexed—even disgusted—at having to wait. In a comparable passage from Euripides' *Iphigeneia in Aulis,* Achilles has just come on stage and has addressed the chorus. He asks for Agamemnon and seems to complain about the delays he and the soldiers are enduring, bottled up at Aulis.

> For not on equal footing do we remain near the Eurippus.
> Some of us, being unmarried
> And so having left empty homes, here
> Sit by the shore *[thassous' ep'aktais]*; others have wives
> And children.

The key words are *thassous' ep'aktais,* which are occasionally interpreted as referring to the boredom of being bottled up. I am quite sure that the unmarried Greeks were bored. They were probably also frustrated. The passage, with its wide connotative spread, is inconclusive. If, however, we do encounter boredom in this passage, it is of the simple, first type outlined at the beginning of this chapter. The absence of boredom, thus, serves to emphasize the novelty of Plutarch's *Eumenes.*

A little over two hundred years after Euripides composed his *Iphigeneia,* the early Roman poet Ennius (239–169 B.C.E.) put together for the stage his version of the same legend. The play survives only in fragments, but one of those seems to reproduce the sense of frustration—which we would easily interpret as boredom—evident in Homer and Euripides. It is remarkable how the lexical silence and metaphor persist. There is no clear-cut reference to boredom, yet it is certainly implied. The fragment (XCIX, vv. 195–202 in Jocelyn 1967), spoken by a group of soldiers, follows:

> Whoever doesn't know how to use *otium*
> Has more work *[negotium]* than when there is work *[negotium]*
> with/in work/business.
> For a person who has begun a job *[negotium]*,
> Does it, takes pains over it, and takes mental and emotional pleasure
> in it.

When there is a lazy beginning the mind doesn't know what it wants.
This is the same with us. We are not at home and we are not on military service.
We go here, we go there. When we've gone there we want to go away.
The mind wanders indecisively; we only live a sort of a life.[12]

Should we understand *otium* as boredom? The chorus of soldiers may be telling us that *otium* ("ease" or "a lack of things to do") can quickly become "wearying" *(otiosum)* or, as we might say, boring. Thus it is with them. They go here and there (like Lucretius's rich man in the passages to follow) but cannot settle or derive satisfaction from life *(praeterpropter vitam vivitur)*. The fragment is a protest against the indecisiveness produced by a lack of things to do *(otium)* in military life. It is also claiming that when you make a lazy start, you do not know where you are; that if you begin indecisively, things continue that way and a task becomes laborious.[13] But whatever else these soldiers tell us, there is nothing to the boring point, as there is with Plutarch. Ennius, like most of our early witnesses, is silent on this matter.

Taken on their own, the passages and contexts discussed so far can prove nothing. The knowledge, however, that the contemporary term for boredom was either absent or rarely used and that the mental state was rarely described or unambiguously alluded to allows us to note a marked tendency to ignore the emotion. One could conclude that the early Greeks and Romans of these periods, perhaps judging the emotion trivial, did not dignify it with frequent reference.[14] I suppose that is part of it. But as I have indicated in the two preceding chapters, the mode of registering boredom and related conditions (melancholy and love) was historically circumstantiated. The major construction of emotional experience favored emotions that could be registered and seen in a public, "political" sphere. Such an emotion was, for example, anger, a state of mind that manifestly exists on the surface of things and requires a social setting for its causation and manifestation.

If we were to formulate a definition of the boredom that I have just been discussing, it would go something like this:[15] to say that something (a person, an experience, a way of life) is boring can mean, simply, that it is dull and predictable. In such an instance, one's normal expectations, that an experience provide a reasonable amount of varied stimulation, are disappointed. Being shut up indoors for too long can be boring, for example. It is also the case that people can be as "boring" as situations. In people, an excess of long-windedness, for example, or an unwillingness to vary a long practiced routine is often described as "boring." (A "bore" may also be a person who is judged socially inept or socially inferior.) Such situations are not usually long-lived. They are usually related to trivial matters. Animals, as it stands to reason, may experience such situations (Wemelsfelder 1985, 1989). This type of boredom is remedied easily by variety. Boredom becomes more of a problem when it persists and when it is generated by more essential matters. It is one thing to find a concert or a book boring. They can be abandoned. It is another thing altogether to find one's work, one's life partner, or one's whole way of life "boring." Boredom in this case can become pervasive, if not necessarily enervating. It can be remedied: remove the source of entrapment, if this is possible. This type of boredom borders on frustration. The great classical scholar Count Ulrich von Wilamowitz-Moellendorff is said to have angrily thrown boring scholarly books out his study window. His frustration, born of boredom, spilled over into anger. This story may well be apochryphal, but it reflects a real enough emotion.

The sources of boredom are not always easily pinned down. Boredom can appear regularly, as we all know, and it can be as unexpected and as difficult to eradicate as the common cold. Hitherto enjoyable situations or relationships or experiences can suddenly become boring. One can with equal suddenness become bored without a situation or relationship or an apparent experience to generate it.[16] Satiety may be a cause (one is literally "fed up"). The ancient (and modern) disease of *horror loci* (meaning, I suppose, a revulsion toward where one is) provides a famous example of this type. Typically this persistent state of mind is seen in the rich Roman who hurries to his country house only to become bored with this. He then hurries quickly back to his city house, where the same thing happens all over again. It is as if boredom is stalking him. This state of restless dissatisfaction is certainly more serious than that form described previously. This form of boredom, if it is to be associated with humans, is sometimes termed ennui. I suspect that it is suffered more by some sorts of personality than by others (Fenichel 1953; Bernstein 1975). I suspect furthermore that it also has economic or sociological determinants (Lepenies 1992; Deleuze and Guattari 1977). If it can be suffered by an animal, it could exhibit itself as repetitive, neurotic behavior (Wemelsfelder 1985, 1989).

Here is how I would attempt to define this emotion. This form of boredom or ennui is the product of the interaction of three situations: it occurs when a persistent lack of experiential variety combines with a marked restriction in the possibility of exercising conscious choice; these two factors are then embodied within one individual who, paradoxically, enjoys (or experiences) material and physical well-being. This form of boredom, therefore, requires a reasonably advanced economy or at least a stable and adequate one. A wealthy urban-dwelling Roman in the first centuries before or after our era might be in a situation to experience it. A monk in his calm, protected, and secure cell might be expected to be prone to it. So, too, might be a financially secure Canadian or Australian university teacher. In humans the element of conscious choice is crucial for this emotional register. I imagine that, except in the case of extreme confinement, animals do not suffer this.[17] I wonder if Homeric heroes, who often exhibit the volitional control of animals (they so often make their decisions instinctually), were also immune to the condition?

For the first unequivocal description of this form of boredom (of a boredom possessing any psychic complexity), we have to wait for Lucretius (d. ca. 55 B.C.E.).[18] This is contained in his *On the Universe* 3.1053–75, a very famous passage. Its depiction of the anxious, bored lives of the Roman rich[19] was imitated later by Horace and by Seneca. Lucretius's bored individual tires of being at home. He goes out only to return again dissatisfied. He hurries from his city house to his country home to escape the sense of anxiety and ennui. But the same experience awaits him in the country. The key lines are as follows (3.1060–67):

> He often leaves his great home,
> The man whom being at home bores. And he suddenly returns
> Perceiving that being away is indeed no better.
> He rushes with his nags to his country house
> As if he were taking water to a burning house.
> He yawns as soon as he gets home,
> Or he goes heavily to sleep and seeks oblivion,
> Or he even hurries back to the city.

Lucretius seems to blame the unsettled emotions of his wealthy Roman on a fear of death.[20] Presumably Lucretius means that the desire for a change of place of habitation reflects a hope that novelty will assuage or distract his wealthy man from this fear of death. But Lucretius's value system seems underlaid by a dimly sensed realization that not just fear of death but also boredom is at issue. (Were this not the case, there would be no yawning and heavy, oblivion-seeking sleep.) Lucretius strangely seems to place little store in boredom as an emotion capable of motivating conduct such as that of the rich man in this passage: I think that he would prefer his grandee to be driven by something more serious. This passage points to Lucretius's unwillingness to accept that such a banal emotion as boredom could cause such havoc in a life. It may reillustrate my contention that boredom was not an affective condition to be taken very seriously at this time in the ancient world. Notwithstanding that, Lucretius's *On the Universe* 3.1053–75, being such a vivid portrait and one so obviously at odds with authorial ideology, suggests that the emotional state of his wealthy man was not uncommon. Bailey[21] remarks that "boredom and restlessness were a characteristic of Roman life at the end of the Republic and the beginning of the Empire." His observation may well be correct, despite the paucity of contemporary evidence. (I imagine that he was thinking of Horace.) The passage must hint at its prevalence. However, despite the probable frequency of this type of emotion, Roman literature of this and later periods makes few references to it.[22] That in itself is surely significant. The Roman valuation echoes that of the Greeks.

Two further aspects of this passage require emphasis. First, if we are justified in detecting boredom behind these lines, then the boredom matches well the description I have just now suggested, of boredom as the product of the interaction of three situations: it occurs when a persistent lack of experiential variety combines with a marked restriction in the possibility of exercising conscious choice; these two factors are then embodied within one individual who, paradoxically, enjoys (or experiences) material and physical well-being. That our wealthy Roman believed that he suffered from a lack of experiential variety is quite apparent. Perhaps, furthermore, we may speculate that the societal chaos of this period created in the minds of many contemporaries a perception that their ability to choose and to influence current politics had become markedly limited. But that these wealthy individuals experienced material and physical well-being is obvious. My second point is this: the type of boredom that seems, partly, to be implicit in this passage represents a new direction for the representation of the emotion.

The same points may be made of Horace (65–8 B.C.E.), at whom I will look next. What we would describe as a bored restlessness is one of the key characteristics of his *Epistles.* This state of mind becomes extremely helpful when we come to try to sort out Horace's persona and voice and how they provide linking themes for a number of the poems within his first book of *Epistles.* Horace often accuses himself of a type of fickleness—a proneness to boredom, to becoming "fed up"—which we easily recognize and with which we easily empathize. This is not serious enough to be termed melancholia in the medical sense or depression. The symptoms are not quite sufficiently pathological. Save for the fact that Horace's condition seems to represent a permanent personality disorder and not something remediable by variety, we might wish to link it with the simple boredom. The best place to begin to explore this striking state of mind is in *Epistles* 1.11. Bullatius, the addressee of this poem, was traveling abroad and, the poem seems to suggest, was prone to the disorder described in

On the Universe 3.1053–75 (a form of *horror loci*).[23] This poem presents Bullatius's problems as symptomatic of a larger malaise. Verses 25–30 summarize:

> For if logic and prudence, not a locale,
> Commanding the widespread sea, remove cares,
> Climate but not mentality do they change, those who rush across the sea.
> A vigorous lassitude *[strenua inertia]* harries us. In ships and
> Chariots we seek to live well. What you seek is here.
> It is at Ulubrae, if you have a calm mind *[aequus animus]*.

The *strenua inertia*—a synonym for *taedium* (cf. Negri 1988; La Penna 1956)—is certainly a form of boredom (a lassitude, an *inertia*), but one whose consequences are most apparent in the *horror loci* (which produces a vigorous, *strenua* reaction) suffered by Bullatius (but, as the first-person plural verb indicates, the condition is not Bullatius's alone).[24] The solution to the problem is the exercise of *ratio* (logic) and *prudentia* (prudence) and the resultant possession of an *aequus animus* (calm mind). The cure is philosophical. It needs to be stressed that Horace's opinion of *horror loci* seems to differ from that of Lucretius. The incessant desire for change, which this emotion reflects, is symptomatic for Lucretius of a deeper malaise, the fear of death. Novelty distracts one from the fear, while sameness is inclined to encourage it. Horace sees his specialized boredom, *strenua inertia,* as the result of a philosophical pusillanimity. Horace amplifies the symptoms of his condition in *Epistles* 1.8. Here he accuses himself, famously, of being *ventosus.* The word means "windy," but its significance is "fickle" or "easily bored." (It is no admirable condition, as we learn from the use of *ventosus* of the plebs at *Epistles* 1.19.37.) At *Epistles* 1.8.11–12 Horace provides the vigorous self-condemnation that uses the adjective *ventosus.*

> What harms me I follow; I run from what I believe helps.
> At Rome I, "windy"/fickle *[ventosus]*, love Tibur and at Tibur Rome.

In this short poem, however, we come to suspect that Horace's ability to be content with his lot is the result not just of a lack of philosophical conviction but also of his own psychology. More is intended in that than mere autobiography. Horace uses his own poetic persona as an example of the sort of person who is unable to sustain an *aequus animus.* Horace himself (his persona) becomes a lesson to us all: we should avoid the philosophical and psychological conditions that so produce his easily bored nature. Boredom, in this sense, becomes emblematic of why humans so unsuccessfully pursue philosophical solace.

Horace displays his fickleness (his "windy" or easily bored nature) in other ways. He is, ironically, swift to spot the failing in others. So in *Epistles* 1.14 Horace accuses his farm manager (his *vilicus*) of this vice. The *vilicus* longs for the excitements of the city life that he has abandoned for the farm. The dissatisfactions felt by the *vilicus* come in for the same sort of criticisms in *Epistles* 1.12, where Agrippa's procurator, Iccius, feels dissatisfactions with his rustic lot. We might, at this point, look back in time to the slave Davus in Horace's *Satires* 2.7, for he, too, highlights such fickleness. *Satires* 2.7 reports a dialogue between Horace and this slave. Taking advantage of the freedom of speech allowed to slaves during the Saturnalia, Davus upbraids his master for philosophical pusillanimity and accuses him of in fact being the real slave. He argues that Horace is slave to his own lusts, his intrigues, his ambitions, his sensuality, and his fickle nature. The basic notion of the poem is that only the wise man is free: Davus, a slave, is in fact the true free man because he understands this, while Horace, though free, is in reality a slave to his own various and inconstant desires. One of Davus's demonstrations of Horace's lack of freedom hinges upon *horror loci,* as is expressed in verses 28–29.

> At Rome you want the country; in the country the city, you country man,
> You praise Rome to the stars.

Like Lucretius's wealthy man, Horace is unable to find contentment in either the city or the country.

The most strenuous depiction of Horace's emblematic malaise is found in *Epistles* 1.8. This occurs shortly after the characterization, just noted, of Horace as "windy" *(ventosus)*. Here Horace describes his boredom as a kind of illness, a lethargy (something associated with old age), a *veternus* that requires the treatment of doctors. In verses 9–10 of the poem, he describes himself as locked into a perverse frame of mind.

> I offend faithful doctors and become angry at friends,
> Because they are anxious to get me away from this *veternus.*

This *veternus,* as we have come to know it, is not quite a state of melancholia[25] but a playfully exaggerated form of boredom.[26]

Horace's boredom, born perhaps of a fickle nature, is something that is applied fruitfully to poems of a more philosophical cast. Horace's own philosophical beliefs swing wildly between and even within poems. Horace does not make a virtue out of this habit. Instead he allows this to infuse his persona with life and immediacy, because of its understandably human failings. So it is that of himself Horace states (*Epistles* 1.15.42–46):

To be sure, this is me: safe and lowly things I praise
When my means are lacking. I'm strong when it doesn't count.
But when something better or more salubrious happens, it's me who
Claims you're only wise and living well if
Your money is displayed invested in posh villas.

This attitude makes no reference to boredom. But we can see now that just as Horace's easily bored nature causes him to move restlessly between town and country (and to upbraid this behavior in others), just as it can cause him to turn against his loyal friends (*Epistles* 1.8), so does it cause him to swing fickly between the extremes of philosophical belief. At times Horace is the Cyrenaic hedonist, at times the indifferent Stoic sage or the apathetic Epicurean; at times he is the proud and unbending Cynic, at times the accommodating Peripatetic. The unity in all this change is in the fickleness of Horace's character, his easily bored inability to stay with one set of beliefs. What we see here is a philosophical fickleness, a type of philosophical opportunism, it could be said, that is typical of Horace's self-presentation in the *Epistles.* This persona readily matches the psychological fickleness we have seen in *Epistles* 1.8.

Horace has used this strange form of boredom, therefore, not just as an autobiographical self-portrait but as a persuasive tool, designed both to characterize what he sees as a dominant psychology of his age and as a persuasive means to suggest a remedy for this. Such a brilliant use of the persona has little parallel in ancient literature.

The same picture is depicted vividly in *Epistles* 1.1.94–105, where this philosophical fickleness—which we can now see as an intellectualized version of Horace as *ventosus,* as the easily bored Roman—is presented as a type of insanity. Horace is addressing Maecenas.

If a haphazard barber has trimmed my hair and
I meet you, you laugh. If there's a worn shirt
Beneath my neat tunic or if my toga hangs badly,
You laugh. What then, when my views contradict themselves
And scorn what they seek and seek again what they just abandoned,
What if it boils up like a tide and ill fits my whole system of
thinking,
When it pulls down, then rebuilds, when it changes square for
round?
You think I'm mad *[insanire]* in the usual way and don't laugh at me,
And you don't think I need a doctor or a guardian
Court appointed, Maecenas, guardian of my means,
Although you'd be angry at the hangnail
Of one of your dependants, a friend who looks to you in all.

Horace accuses himself here of a remarkable philosophical inconsistency. This is the type of fickleness that I have just noted. Curiously Horace terms it a type of insanity (cf. 101: *insanire*). This is the "windy" Horace of *Epistles* 1.8 again, and I doubt that we would be wrong to connect it, in bipolar fashion, to the *veternus* of that same poem. (It may also pick up the idea of the link between melancholy and boredom to which I have already alluded. *Insanire* makes Horace sound like Orestes.) At any rate, Horace's philosophical opportunism, his doctrinal fickleness, has its psychological parallel in his self-confessed proneness to boredom and in his restless desire for change. Horace is as fickle and as easily bored in philosophical matters as he is in day-to-day life. Philosophy, like his place of habitation or his relations with his friends, is subject to a type of intellectual *horror loci.*

One last observation may be made on this theme of philosophical "boredom." Within Horace's philosophizing is a tension between his attraction to the cynic notions of proud independent *autarkeia* (self-sufficiency) and the philosophical opportunism of the *metriotês* (the mean), the *aequus animus* (a balanced and calm mind) of the Peripatetic, the Epicurean, or the Cyrenaic (La Penna 1995, 243 ff.; Toohey 1997b). Horace is fickly drawn, as I have already suggested, between the realism of the latter and the distasteful idealism of the former. We can see this markedly in *Epistles* 1.1.70–105, a portion of which passage I have just cited. One sees this, too, in the compromised advice *nil admirari* of *Epistles* 1.6. Here the advice to "marvel at nothing" is coupled with the comforting, if hollow, advice—for the dependent such as Horace—that wealth and power count as nothing in comparison to the pursuit of virtue. These are tediously predictable sentiments from one whose station in life denies him such pursuits. Is this philosophical posture, then, that of one who, *ventosus,* is too prone to the habits of which the poet disabuses us? This tension between unrealistic self-sufficiency (to which the poet aspires) and an opportunistic mean (by which compromise the poet must live) becomes a key theme of the *Epistles,* as Antonio La Penna has so brilliantly illustrated (1995, 243 ff.). It exists in an at times uneasy relationship between the dependent Horace and the independent "great" to whom he writes and upon whom he depends. It can, furthermore, mark the relation between poems as well as between sections within single poems. It notably marks the sequence of *Epistles* 1.16, 1.17, and 1.18. Remarkably we hear the advice of 1.17 and 1.18 (both poems on how to cut one's cloth according to the wishes of one's *patronus*) immediately after the sermon on *autarkeia* of 1.16 and its advice to live to oneself and to resist the subtle blandishments of others (can we not read Maecenas, Horace's patron, among these?). It is as if Horace's status as a *cliens,* a client and a dependent, militates against his aspirations to Cynic *autarkeia* (self-sufficiency) and leaves him with a compromised philosophy of the mean, the *aurea mediocritas* (the "golden mean") and the *metriôtês* (the Greek for "mean"). The tension between Horace's status as Maecenas's client, the consequent need for a balanced, calm, and accepting disposition (an *aequus animus*), and Horace's obvious admiration for the *autarkeia* of the Cynic can boil over to produce the tempered impatience of Horace's protestations to Maecenas in *Epistles* 1.7.

All of these poems allow us to draw several useful conclusions concerning Horace, boredom, and the depiction of the self. First, the very absence of a clear-cut term for an emotion that is central to Horace's concerns is significant. It indicates how novel was the emotion, at least how little it had been made the subject of serious literary discourse for ancients of this and preceding periods. This matches the conclusion drawn in the preceding pages of this chapter, that boredom was an ill-defined emotion to this point in the ancient world. Second, boredom, the very key to the distinctive authorial and philosophical psychology displayed in the *Epistles,* is the motif that provides coherence to the displays of the distinctive Horatian persona of many of the poems in the first book of the *Epistles.* It is remarkable, is it not, how Horace has used this emotion to dramatize his compromised philosophical concerns and, at the same time, to produce a persona for himself that, in its thoroughgoing realism, is both strikingly recognizable and strikingly compelling. Just as importantly, Horace allows this persona to catch what must have been the mood of so many of his generation who, because of the dynamics of the politics of the period, had been forced to become what we would call intellectual trimmers (again see La Penna 1995). Third, the type of boredom that we witness here (and in Lucretius) is not quite the all-pervasive and viruslike existential emotion that I will designate as *nausea.* Rather, this affective and intellectual condition occurs because Horace, though subject to a persistent lack of experiential variety and though subject to a marked restriction in the possibility of exercising conscious choice, nonetheless, thanks to Maecenas, enjoys material and psychological well-being in a world that pays at least lip service to intellectual freedom. The resulting disposition, it seems to me, becomes particularly prone to a bored fickleness. Fourth, the *Epistles* aim to produce a type of literature whose force resides in its depiction of a particular, distinctive and isolated individual psychology—this, as I have indicated, is related to boredom. We see this best in the irritable posturing of *Epistles* 1.8. The prominence given to the depiction of the self in this poetry is the product of the experiential conflict that I have already indicated. Horace's focus on this conflict provides a remarkably subtle ancient portrait of the self (bordering on the autobiographical). Fifth, Horace makes it quite clear, like Lucretius, that this experiential (if not philosophical) fickleness is quite widespread.

Horace puns with *nausea* at verse 93 in the first poem of the first book of his *Epistles*. He is attempting to explain the changeability of most people's views and habits. For this reason, he will not go along with all of the opinions that he hears on philosophical matters, and more importantly, he will not reverse his decision to take to writing lyric poetry again. Here is the context in which Horace's *nausea* occurs (*Epistles* 1.1.90–93).

> With what now will I hold Proteus of the changing form?
> What of the poor man? Laugh then: he changes squats, beds,
> Bathhouses, barbers. When he's rented a boat he gets
> As seasick *[nauseat]* as the rich man whom a trireme conveys.

Excessive change, Horace is telling us, is as pointless for the poor man as for the rich man. Both suffer the same outcome. That is demonstrated here by "seasickness" (thus the verb *nauseat* in v. 93): on the sea, rich man and poor man alike suffer seasickness. The poor man's haste for novelty is thus as ineffectual as the rich man's. Know yourself and your limitations, Horace is suggesting, and, poor man or rich man, you may gain a modicum of happiness. Horace knows his limitations. Hence he is unwilling to return to the writing of lyric poetry. *Nauseat,* the verbal form that is used here, literally means "become seasick." That is certainly meaning enough for it here. Yet, as we know from twentieth-century literature, the noun *nausia* (a variant spelling for *nausea*) is associated with boredom. That secondary meaning works quite well in verse 93. So we could translate the lines as "when he's rented a boat he gets / as bored as the rich man whom a trireme conveys." Such a reading for the line works perfectly well (and I am sure Horace intended the double entendre)—unless one jibes at the notion of this poor man boating for recreational purposes.

But let us not dwell on Horace's *nausea*. Let us look instead at another description of the condition, this one penned some eighty years after Horace. It is from Seneca. Its content decries the plight of those who find life repetitive to the point of being meaningless (*Epistulae morales* 24.26).

> [T]he same satiety for doing and seeing and a disdain *[fastdium]*—not bordom *[odium]*—for life assails certain individuals. We are driven into this, philosophy itself forcing us, when we say: "How long the same things? Surely I will yawn,[27] I will sleep, I will eat, I will be thirsty, I will be cold, I will be hot. Is there no end? But do all things go in a circle? Night overcomes day, day night, summer gives way to autumn, winter presses on autumn, which is checked by spring. All things pass that they may return. I do nothing new, I

> see nothing new. Sometimes this makes me seasick *[fit aliquando et huius rei nausia]*. There are many who judge living not painful but empty."

Seneca's *nausia* (his "seasickness" or "biliousness") is certainly a type of boredom. The telltale, if brief, reference to yawning indicates this. The symptoms are a first cousin to those suffered by Aristophanes' Dicaeopolis. This is made quite clear by the stress on tedium and on repetition ("Night overcomes day, day night . . . I see nothing new") and by the emphasis on a kind of sensory entrapment. But the boredom is far more pervasive—even existential—than that of Horace. This *nausia* embodies a satiety with life itself, not just with a specific act. It registers an estimation of the worth of life, one that judges it futile.

Some other points need to be made concerning Seneca's *nausia*. It represents a spiritual condition that has been both corporealized and at the same time represented unequivocally as an illness. This represents a continuation of the Horatian tradition of *Epistles* 1.11. There is, however, no equivocating in Seneca. I suggest that this medicalization of affective states (medicalization requires corporealization) has its precise parallels in that which we saw of melancholia and depression in the instances of Persius's *Satires* 3 (my chapter 1) and Charicleia's lovesickness (chapter 2) and, as we will see (chapter 6), in the corporeal registering of time by Trimalchio as an affective disorder. A final parallel will be provided by Hostius Quadra (a Senecan character) in my last chapter.

The noteworthy frequency with which this heightened emotion of boredom, in all its forms, appears in Seneca's work is remarkable. It points to something of deeper, if of more obvious, significance. This is the persistent inwardness, the introspection, the psychological self-consciousness of Seneca's prose work. Seneca, in his letters, in his philosophical writing, and sometimes in his work on natural history, is relentlessly concerned with his own or other's inner states and the origins and ambit of their emotions. (It is as if, in Seneca, the outside world is there only to reflect, mirror, and comment on his and his associates' mental states.) To a very large extent it is this aspect of his oeuvre, the inner focus, in which he is surely the best successor of Horace, whose focus is on the inner state, the *strenua inertia*, in *Epistles* 1. It is here that Seneca's indisputable greatness (and modernity) resides. There is, in Roman prose, nothing quite as self-absorbed, quite as obsessed with the interior life—and consequently as wearying—as that author whom we encounter in Seneca's writing. His persistent interest in boredom, in all its phases, represents one important aspect of his inward turn. It marks a new point in the registering of this emotion in the ancient world.[28]

The form of boredom that we encounter here is sometimes described as "inner" or "spiritual" or "existential." This is exclusive to humans, in a way that the two previous forms were not. Seneca believed that this form of boredom, this *nausia*, could become a life-threatening condition. This type of emotion is perhaps more familiar from the literature of the nineteenth century, where it was termed the *mal de siècle*. In this period it was also considered life-threatening. (It has had a sort of an afterlife in the conditions suffered by Roquentin in Sartre's *La Nausée* or by Mersault in Camus's *La Peste*, or by Dino, the protagonist of Moravia's *La Noia*.) What makes this form of boredom so different to those described previously is its complex constitution.[29]

In Seneca's writings, as I say, the notion of boredom appears frequently. Its range of connotations is broad and seems to stretch from simple boredom to a type of boredom reflecting that described by Horace in *Epistles* 1.8. Boredom can become so all-pervasive as to sour one's whole approach to life. Similarly broad is Seneca's use of the key term *taedium:* the word can mean anything from "disgust" or "weariness," through simple boredom, to full-blown ennui.[30] Seneca's perception of the emotion represents something new. Simple boredom is often mentioned.[31] Describing a style of speech that is too slow, for example, Seneca suggests that the "boredom" (or "weariness") induced by halting speech causes an audience to lose interest: "for also this paucity and thinness produces a listener who concentrates less because of the boredom *[taedium]* of the stop-start slowness" (*Epistles* 40.3). In a comparable passage (*Epistles* 70), Seneca uses a nautical metaphor. He contrasts the reactions of sailors toward slow versus speedy voyages. Sailors trapped into the first type of passage are wearied by the boredom that is induced in them by windlessness: "for, as you know, the lazy winds sport with and detain and tire one man with their boredom *[taedium]* produced by the slowest calm; another the energetic wind carries along swiftly."

Seneca also describes that *horror loci* that we encountered in Lucretius and Horace. *Epistle* 28.1 devotes itself wholly to this topic (it quotes specifically Horace's *Epistles* 1.11.27 but expands, in Stoic fashion, on its central idea). The opening couple of sentences of the letter are indicative of the theme of the whole: "are you surprised . . . that after such long travel and so many changes of scene you have not been able to shake off the gloom and heaviness *[tristitiam gravitatemque]* of your mind? You need a change of soul rather than a change of climate." The theme is repeated with variations in the *Consolation to Helvia* (12.3.4), where Seneca refers to the extremes to which the rich will go to avoid *taedium*. In this case they vary their bored lives by imitating the poor:

"it isn't the times or a shortage of space that makes them act like the poor; they choose certain days, when boredom *[taedium]* with wealth has got hold of them, on which they eat on the ground and, with the silver and gold plate removed, use pottery."[32] Somewhat the same theme is repeated in *Epistles* 18.7, where the rich are referred to as attempting to escape *taedium* through luxury. So we hear, "you need not think that I mean meals like Timon's, or "paupers' huts," or anything else at which wealth plays because of boredom [*taedium*] with riches."

Boredom (or *taedium* as Seneca usually terms it) can spoil a whole life. The predicament described in *Epistle* 28 was very close to this. The invasive *taedium* outlined in *Epistle* 24 seems stronger again. It can be so powerful as to lead to suicide.[33] We have already noted this in *Epistle* 24.26: observe that in this passage the word *taedium* does not appear.[34] It is replaced by *satietas, fastidium,* and, most remarkably, *nausia*).[35] In that already quoted passage, Seneca's portrait of boredom has taken the pervasive, souring emotion of Lucretius and Horace to its logical extreme. This boredom has become so severe that it influences all portions of life. The victim is left with but one alternative: "there are many who judge life to be not bitter but superfluous," states Seneca (*Epistle* 24.26). The remedy here can only be suicide, that death wish *(libido moriendi, Epistle* 24:25 or *velle mori)* to which, in *Epistle* 77.6, Seneca says the bored person *(fastidiosus)* is subject.

Before leaving Seneca I ought to mention the dialogue *De tranquillitate animi*.[36] It is often and rightly cited in discussions of Seneca's ennui (most recently in Jonard 1998). Written for a young Marcus Annaeus Serenus,[37] Seneca's dialogue begins innocuously with Serenus outlining a condition of irresolution that he terms *fluctuatio animi* (or *bonae mentis infirmitas* or even *nausea*).[38] Its symptoms are a wavering between satisfaction and dissatisfaction with his own possessions (1.4–9), between a desire for public and private life (1.10–12), and, in literary matters, between the high style and the low style (1.13–14). Serenus, who feels himself neither ill nor well, requests Seneca's help. Seneca (2.1–2) replies that Serenus's "illness" is not bad. Rather, it is like the slight fits of fever following a serious illness or the ripples on a tranquil sea. Seneca continues, *quod desideras autem magnum et summum est deoque vicinum, non concuti* [what you desire is a great, noble, and godlike thing: not to be shaken]. The Greek philosopher Democritus, notes Seneca (2.3–5), had a name for this condition of *non concuti,* "not being shaken." This was *euthymia* (see McGann 1969). Seneca calls it *tranquillitas,* "calm." Cicero or Horace (*Epistles* 1.14) might have said that it means possessing an *aequus animus* (a "balanced mind").[39]

The next, key section of *De tranquillitate* (2.6–15) provides a symptomatology, albeit one that goes well beyond the problems suffered by Serenus. A variety of colorful terms describe the illness (most of which do not match the condition of Serenus): nouns or noun phrases such as *adsidua mutatio propositi* [a vigorous changing of one's mind], *cunctatio vitae* [putting one's life on hold], *displicentia sui* or *sibi displicere* [dissatisfaction with oneself], *fastidium [vitae]* [disdain [for life]], *fluctus animi* [spiritual flux], *inertia, levitas* [inconstancy], *marcor* [wasting], *maeror* [grief], *odium vitae* [disdain for life], *oscitatio* [yawning], *residentis animi volutatio et otii sui tristis atque aegra paenitentia* [the vacillation of a mind that never finds rest and the sad and languid endurance of one's leisure], *taedium,* and *tristitia;* of individuals, the adjectives *instabilis* and *mobilis;* and the marvelous adjectival clause *inter destituta vota torpentis animi situs* [the decay of a soul that lies torpid amid abandoned hopes].

Seneca maintains that Serenus's circumstances are representative of a much more widespread malaise. It is, he insists (2.6–9), all the same whether a person is plagued by fickleness, boredom, or shifting purpose (like Serenus) or whether they loll about and yawn. To these four types should be added those who flee *odium vitae* through change or, because of personal *inertia* (Seneca is using Horace's term for ennui), live their lives in the same inadequate circumstances in which they began. The result of all of these conditions is a type of dissatisfaction with oneself *(sibi displicere)*. This ensues from the lack of mental poise, which ensues from not daring to attain what one desires or by desiring more than can be attained. Thence comes a type of existential melancholy and dissatisfaction, a mental state that nowhere finds repose. There is also a sad and languid endurance of one's own leisure (2.10–12). In 2.13–15 Seneca outlines the various antidotes that sufferers have unsuccessfully set to work against this condition: travel to remote places, to seaside resorts, to the city; such dissatisfaction has even led to suicide.

The remaining sections of the *De tranquillitate* (3 ff.) are of less importance. They present a variety of cures for the condition. Seneca recommends, among other things, an involvement in practical affairs, self-understanding, care in the choice of friends, circumspection in the use of wealth, equanimity in the face of fortune, adaptability, an avoidance of misanthropy, and four final pieces of advice: to vary one's company; to use games for relaxation; to get adequate rest; to indulge in mild exercise and wine drinking.[40]

After Seneca, Plutarch provides the most useful set of references for the notion of boredom.[41] To judge from the occurrences of the word *alus* in his work, he preserves part of the range of the meanings evident in Seneca. There are in Plutarch several references to the simple form of boredom.[42] I have already noted, at the beginning of this chapter, the passage from the life of Eumenes: close confinement of besieged forces engendered a boredom *(alus)* that Eumenes felt compelled to remedy. *Alus,* like *taedium,* may also have the sense of "distress" (see *Brutus* 5) or even "depression" (see *Marius* 78). But perhaps the most startling reference to boredom occurs in *Pyrrhus* 13. Pyrrhus, after becoming regent of Epirus and later of Macedonia, withdrew from the latter possession in disappointment at the disloyalty of his subjects. It is in the description of this point of Pyrrhus's life that Plutarch makes his reference to "boredom." The passage deserves quoting in full (Loeb translation adapted).

> [T]hen chance offered Pyrrhus (who had left Macedon for Epirus in exile) the opportunity of being at ease and living in peace, while ruling his own people. But he thought not offering ill to others and not receiving it from others was a sort of nauseous boredom [*alus nautiôdês,* "seasicklike boredom"], just like Achilles could not tolerate ease . . .

Boredom—to the point of nausea or seasickness—did not allow Pyrrhus to enjoy his retirement. He was only content, according to Plutarch, when doing or receiving mischief. To alleviate the boredom, Pyrrhus launched himself on a new round of military activities, at the end of which he lost his life. Boredom and its avoidance are therefore seen as the motivating forces in Pyrrhus's life.[43] Whether or not Plutarch is telling us historical truth is irrelevant—and we have no means of ascertaining the state of Pyrrhus's psychology. What is vital is Plutarch's perception of the emotion. Boredom, like a *mal de siècle,* has become a psychic malady and is seen as capable of devouring a whole life.

For what it is worth, this theme remains a persistent one in Western literature. I here cite a few random examples. Gustave Flaubert, in his letters to Louise Colet, speaks of the "nausea of ennui" (Kuhn 1976). Flaubert's phrase is remarkably close to Plutarch's *alus nautiôdês,* which means literally a "seasicklike [nauseous] boredom" (Toohey 1988). This in turn links with the Senecan estimation of life. The onetime classical scholar Friedrich Nietzsche would have known of the tradition of Senecan nausea. The emotion figures regularly in his work, in the *Genealogy of Morals* (2.24, 3.14), for example, and above all in *Thus Spoke Zarathustra,* where the "dangers of the great nausea and the great pity are among the central motifs" (Kaufmann and Hollingdale 1989, 125). Nausea (estrangement from the human world) is one of the challenges that Zarathustra must overcome. The idea of this nausealike estrangement from the world about (not just from other humans, as it is for Nietzsche) is picked up famously by the French existential philosopher and novelist Sartre. This is central for his novel *Nausea* (1938) and his philosophical tract *Being and Nothingness* (1943). Roquentin, the protagonist of *Nausea,* experiences a revulsion (i.e., a nausea) when confronted by the world of matter and people. The corporeal revulsion, however, is closely linked to an ennui-ridden estrangement that Roquentin had been experiencing since well before his return to France from Southeast Asia. Nausea, in much the same sense, also plays a key role in *Being and Nothingness*, where Sartre (1966, 550) explains it as "the 'taste' of the facticity and contingency of existence." He maintains, "A dull and inescapable nausea perpetually reveals my body to my consciousness."

The century following Plutarch provides further references to boredom, just as we might now expect. There is, for example, Diogenes of Oenoanda (fr. 25 Chilton) referring to the fickle and bored manner in which passersby read his work. Or Aelian (*Varia historia* 14.12) singling out the king of Persia who, to avoid boredom when traveling, kept a knife and a piece of linden wood for whittling (cf. Seneca *Epistles* 16.3). These references describe a form of boredom best understood as belonging to the first or second types. A more alarming form is highlighted by Marcus Aurelius. Farquharson, the editor of Marcus Aurelius, argues for the presence of a reference to ennui, precisely *horror loci*, in *Meditations* 2.7.[44] The passage is as follows:

> Do things from outside break in to distract you? Give yourself a time of quiet to learn some new good thing and cease to wander out of your course. But, when you have done that, be on your guard against a second kind of wandering. For those who are sick to death in life *[kekmêkotes tôi biôi]*, with no mark on which they direct every impulse or in general every imagination, are triflers, not in words only but also in their deeds.

The expression "sick to death in life" may be a very condensed way for describing the aimless life of the overprivileged Roman aristocrat of the type depicted by Lucretius.[45] The vigor of the expression and its doleful context may indicate that we are learning of an emotion more similar to those described by Seneca than to that described by Lucretius.

These increasingly complex forms of boredom come very close to resembling the sorrow without cause, the melancholia, discussed in chapter 1. Can they in fact be distinguished from melancholia (they are not in Lepenies 1992)?[46] Some empirical research has argued that under situations of prolonged and excessive confinement, the emotions of boredom, frustration, and depression form an experiential continuum (Wemelsfelder 1985, 1989). A caged battery hen, for example, will initially exhibit signs of listlessness (boredom?), then anger and even self-directed violence (frustration), then finally a profound psychic dislocation that may exhibit itself in such psychotic (or depressive) behaviors as repetitive, even self-destructive, motor acts and eventually death. To produce the three affective phases of this condition, all that is required is prolonged and harsh confinement. An animal in such a situation will graduate through the three levels. The movement, therefore, from the simple boredom to the more complex "inner" phases is to be expected. Boredom, in its most extreme forms, therefore comes closely to resemble, or even becomes, melancholia.

We should return to the beginning of this chapter and to the white-ground lekythos representing the young person mourning her own death. What it is that I have attempted to demonstrate is that the "themes" of this fifth-century B.C.E. pot—boredom, melancholia, and death—gain their literary representation much later in antiquity. The increasingly complex form of boredom that came to be registered in the literature of Seneca's period reproduces an experience to match that depicted on the lekythos. So it is that Senecan boredom can be characterized in such a manner that it can resemble melancholia, but in such a way also that it is associated with death.

The lag between this artistic representation and the literary representation of this emotion is remarkable. Felt experience, we may deduce, always understood the complex emotions associated with boredom, but early literary experience was not ready or equipped for its representation. The resultant lag has a clear parallel in the manner by which melancholia itself was represented. The insights of the Eumenides Painter's Orestes were just as slow to percolate into popular literary representation.

Several conclusions may be drawn from this brief survey. The first and most obvious is that the ancients were subject to boredom. But qualifications need to be made to this assertion. Greek literature down to the Hellenistic period lacks reference to anything more than the simplest form of boredom. The word *boredom* only seems to appear in the fourth century. Serious or unequivocal consideration of boredom begins in the first century B.C.E. in Rome, but here it is limited to the less complex forms. It is in the first and second centuries C.E. that a pervasive, destructive form of boredom is first referred to. This is apparent initially in Horace's *Epistles*, then in the works of Seneca and Plutarch. Boredom in Seneca can be an emotion that not only effects sporadically but also spreads to influence one's every waking action. It can become a psychic disease. Plutarch, to judge from his life of Pyrrhus, was quite familiar with the concept. In Seneca and Plutarch, therefore, there seems to be the beginnings of the modern concepts of the emotion. Seneca's instance is especially instructive. He represents boredom as a spiritual condition but, at least in the case of his treatment of *nausia,* illustrates for us a condition both corporealized and represented as an illness. This medicalization of boredom, I have suggested, has its parallels in the cases of depression and lovesickness.

I would like to reemphasize this last point, that we can build this periodization of boredom onto the periodizations that have been established in chapters 1 and 2 for melancholia and lovesickness, through the three aspects of spiritualization/interiorization, corporealization, and medicalization. It is striking that these emotions—admittedly linked, but nonetheless distinguishable—gain currency in literature during the same period. As I noted in chapter 2, these peculiar congruences may tell us something about the prehistory of affective states at least as they are given literary representation.

It appears that there took place in the first and second centuries of our era a decisive expansion in the willingness or capacity to depict in literature the interiorized symptoms of such affective states as love, lovesickness, melancholia, and boredom. (In subsequent chapters, I will show that these changes are to be linked with other emotional mutations.) These changes are connected to the written presentation of self and of self-consciousness. It is quite evident that the changes in the presentation of boredom highlight a thickening or deepening, in the nonjudgmental sense, of the manner by which the self and self-consciousness are presented. The presentation of "self" that we witness as achieved through boredom is far more detailed and evident in Horace, for example, than it is in earlier literature. This is a sense of self (or self-consciousness or self-definition—*notitia sui* as Seneca terms it)[47] as constituted by inwardness. It is built upon an opposition of "inside-outside," a partitioning off of the self from the world about us. "Thoughts, ideas, or feelings . . . [are] 'within' us, while the objects in the world which these mental states bear on are 'without,'" states Charles Taylor in a different context (1992, 111–12). He continues: "[human] capacities or potentialities [are] 'inner,' awaiting the development which will manifest them or realize them in a public world. The unconscious is for us within, and we think of the depths of the unsaid, the unsayable, the powerful inchoate feelings and affinities which dispute with us the control of our lives, as inner. We are creatures with inner depths; with partly unexplored and dark interiors." Despite the fact that Taylor is attempting to describe a modern experience, his outline could apply just as well to Horace or to Seneca.

Reading from the ancient texts so far surveyed, we may take things a step further. I would like to link this sense of self with the ability to stand outside oneself, to watch, to weigh up, and to react to one's emotional and physical state almost as if it were other. Anyone who has ever experienced boredom of anything more than the simple frustrated variety will have felt that awful intrusion of the self between, as it were, one's emotional being and the world around, between sensation and volition. The indisputable painfulness of this condition is heightened by an oppressive sense of almost otiose inner self. Boredom, in its more intense phases, is built upon the self's sense of estrangement from the world around it. Perception is therefore directed relentlessly and sharply inward but in a dulled fashion outward.

Such a sense of self involves the extended highlighting of a person's inner mental and emotional processes. It involves not just a partitioning between the inner self and the outer world; it also seems to involve a partitioning between the body (approximating not only the "outer" world but also a person's emotional world) and the self (approximating the "inner," the soul, the animus, the *thymos*, or whatever term is used for it). It is as if the individual stands at a remove from his or her emotional reactions, as if, almost, he or she were alienated from these. The individual watches his or her reactions and feels powerless in their face. There comes into being a disjunction between the body and a person's consciousness of it, between a person's emotions and his or her sense of them. The sense of division is then represented dramatically as, say, the alienation of *veternus* in Horace or the estrangement of *nausia* in Seneca.[48] Such a sense of personal estrangement may lead easily to the disintegration of the personality. Consider again Horace's self-portrait as a victim of the *veternus* or Seneca's portrait of Serenus. Both individuals seem to experience a turning away from friends and even perhaps their community, as well as a turning away from constructive activity. In some cases, Seneca tells us, the estrangement can become so great as to lead people to suicide. We will meet this type of self-destructive disengagement of the personality in the next chapter.

This developed sense of the self, as we see it through "inner" boredom, comes at considerable personal risk. Consider the sorts of characteristics we might associate with these forms of boredom. Above all, there is to be found in *veternus* or *nausia* (or the *situs torpentis animi*), passivity, yielding, withdrawal, isolation, and estrangement. A chain of other qualities may also be associated with boredom of such varieties. Associated as they are with self-consciousness and self-understanding, these conditions are particularly to be linked with the private; with interiority, the mind, "depth"; and even, in some cases, with viscera. These last two qualities may be less apparent than they really are: for Seneca boredom manifests itself *physiologically* as illness, something within the sufferer that disturbs the individual's very constitution. To detect it, one must be able to interpret (or read) the *signs* of this illness—it is as if this were a *literate* illness. Other characteristics follow: the condition is associated primarily with present time (we guess that earlier eras did not suffer it), with an urban and individualist lifestyle. It is something to be associated with humans, not with animals. All of these characteristics, not especially dangerous or life-threatening in isolation, are potentially lethal in combination. Rather like the application of hellebore, in small or controlled doses their combined effect may produce positive results: it can lead to an inchoate or highlighted sense of the self and personal autonomy. But, as easily and as we witness in the instances of Horace and Seneca, it can lead to a personal estrangement that can result in madness (and even death). The risk, then, of this highlighted sense of self, is, through its associated estrangement, the total disintegration of the personality.

Emotional states that can be survived as a child cannot always be survived as an adult. What may be normal in a child may represent a psychosis in an adult.[49] In a child the sense of self is built upon the eventual realization of difference to the world. A rupture between the child and the world about it takes place somewhere between the ages of two and three. Some of us can even remember the trauma.[50] This debilitating moment of cognitive self-awareness, I suspect, is healed by play—in part, because play teaches the child how to master its environment, how to manipulate objects, how to create things; in part, because so much of play is built upon a pleasurable purposelessness, whose essence is constructed on a disjunction between oneself and the world about.[51] Play exploits this disjunction for pleasurable ends and, in so doing, renders it not merely bearable but even to be desired. Learning to negotiate the gulf between the self and the world increasingly comes to be seen as learning to sustain a social personality.

The sense of loss and of mourning that is engendered by this childhood rupture is most usually lost to memory. It is never lost in the analogies of desire. Trauma is what one willingly forgets. So it is that literature is crowded, if not with representations of this rupture, at least with representations of return to the primordial world of the senses, uncomplicated by our subjectivity.[52] Hence we have literatures on mystical afflatus and on the pathologies of crowd identification, the myths of the Golden Age or the Age of Saturn, and texts that evoke the possibilities (however limited their success) of homecoming and the establishment of harmony (the *Aeneid* and Statius's *Thebaid* as much as the *Odyssey* and the *Oresteia*).[53] Probably all creative literature, insofar as it is a revocation of lost time, is rooted in the moment of the subject-object rupture. Creative literature attempts to recapture what was lost by the onset of language itself. So the mystic privileges silence (the disarticulation of language toward the primacy of experience). In literature, we invest words with the weight and presence of what they designate. As symbols, they replace the immediate objects of the lost world of early childhood but are linked to them precisely because of their power to designate. By recovering language from its bored, fallen dullness in the currency of everyday conversation, the writer hopes to restore his or her vanished past to its mint condition.[54]

But I am moving too far from boredom and the concept of the dangers of blurring the boundaries of the self and even the possibility of the disintegration of the self of the personality. What I am suggesting is both simple and straightforward. The pestilential power of psychic or "inner" boredom is so great in its intensity precisely because it recapitulates the childhood experience, masked but not forgotten, of the rupture between the self and the world. When an adult, through personal or social circumstance, must once again confront emotionally this utter disjunction, he or she risks reactivating the trauma and, thus, risks the utter disintegration of the personality.[55]

4

Acedia

Madness and the Epidemiology of Individuality

> . . . pittie the estate of such as grone under the burthen of that heavy crosse, wherein no reason is able to minister consolation, nor the burthen whereof the angels themselves have ability to sustain.
>
> —T. BRIGHT, *A Treatise of Melancholie*

Herbert Basedow was a medical officer who worked among the Aboriginals of central, western, and northwestern Australia toward the end of the nineteenth century. He was also an amateur anthropologist and linguist. He recorded many firsthand descriptions of Australia Aboriginal behavior and customs in the years before their traditional way of life had been chaotically disrupted by imposition of external social demands. The photograph in figure 4, of the Aboriginal pointing the bone, is drawn from one of his long out-of-print books.[1] The Aboriginal is practicing a form of "long-distance sorcery,"[2] a psychic killing known simply as "boning."[3] The following passage describes the process of boning, as well as the effects it produces.[4] It is drawn from Basedow's book *The Australian Aboriginal* (1929, 175–79).

> It is quite as customary among all Australian tribes to bring about the downfall of a rival or enemy by the magic influence of suggestion. This is the wonderfully potent method of "pointing" death at a man, who may or may not be present. The process is usually referred to as "pointing the bone," or simply "boning" . . . Most of the tribes are in possession of different shaped sticks and bones, with which the death pointing is done. These are usually about three or four inches long, pointed at one or both ends, and containing a small bleb of resin at one end, to which a piece of human hair-string is attached. When the instrument is bone it is usually a piece of the dead man's skeleton . . . When a man has been condemned to death, the person or per-

> sons, who are to administer the fatal charm, are nominated. The "pointing" apparatus are produced, and with them the men take up a kneeling position a little distance from the camp. Facing the doomed man's habitation, they lift the bone, or stick, to shoulder height and point it at the victim . . . There is [however] a great number of different methods employed in administering the fatal charm of the pointing-stick, all of which, however, are after much the same principle. A common practice amongst the Aluridja is for the man, about to use the stick, to leave the camp and seclude himself behind a tree or other obstacle. He squats upon the heel of one foot which he has tucked under his body. He points the bone or stick straight at the man who is to die, or, it may be, merely in the direction he imagines he would strike him. Whilst administering the curse, he holds the object in the hand of his outstretched right arm . . . A man who discovers that he is boned is, indeed, a pitiable sight. He stands aghast, with his eyes staring at the treacherous pointer, and with his hands lifted as though to ward off the lethal medium, which he imagines is pouring into his body . . . His cheeks blanch and his eyes become glassy, and the expression of his face becomes horribly distorted, like that of one stricken with palsy. He attempts to shriek, but usually the sound chokes in his throat, and all one might see is froth at his mouth. His body begins to tremble and the muscles twitch involuntarily. He sways backwards and falls to the ground, and for a short time appears to be in a swoon; but soon after he begins to writhe as if in a mortal agony, and, covering his face with his hands, begins to moan. After a while he becomes more composed and crawls to his wurley. From this time onwards he sickens and frets, refusing to eat, and keeping aloof from the daily affairs of the tribe. Unless help is forthcoming in the shape of a counter-charm, administered by the hands of the *"Nangarri"* or medicine-man, his death is only a matter of a comparatively short time. If the coming of the medicine-man is opportune, he might be saved.[5]

The long-distance engendering of psychic and physical pain and illness, such as the severe enfeeblement of the victim of boning, excites endless fascination. Even more fascinating is an examination of just how it is that such transmission is possible. Lévi-Strauss (1963), Showalter (1997), and Hacking (1998) have had very helpful things to say on the topic—Lévi-Strauss on how such deadly transmission becomes possible, Showalter and Hacking on how this can turn into a viruslike phenomenon of epidemic proportions. Their diagnoses will help us better understand the transmission not just of this boning but, more importantly, of the sudden upsurge of the conditions described in the previous three chapters.

In the instance of Basedow's boning, as I have implied, we seem to witness the creation of an emotional and physiological state that matches others that

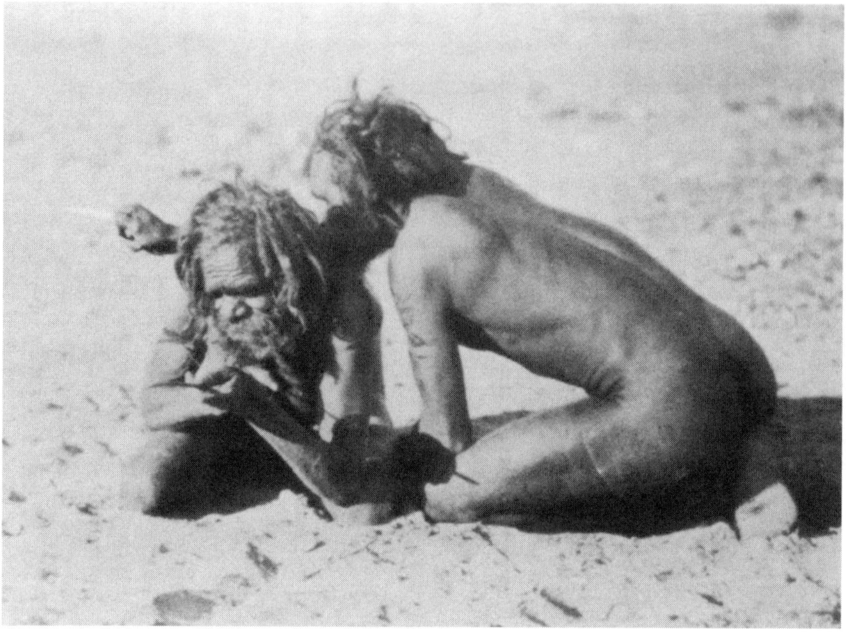

FIG. 4. Basedow's photograph of an Aboriginal "boning" (ca. 1890s). (Reprinted from Herbert Basedow, *The Australian Aboriginal* [reprint, Adelaide: F. W. Preece and Sons, 1925], 177.)

we have seen brought about by more banal means, such as the lovesickness that is discussed in chapter 2. Sappho describes a suffering, of an illness that must owe its origins to love, that is approximately comparable to that of Basedow's victim (so Sappho's speechlessness becomes Basedow's "the sound chokes in his throat," her burning sensation on the skin becomes his "cheeks blanch," her loss of vision becomes his "eyes become glassy," her cold sweat and trembling become his "body begins to tremble and the muscles twitch," and her pallor and near-death experience become his "in a mortal agony"). Heliodorus's Charicleia, to cite a second example, is described as suffering from love in a comparable fashion: suddenly the heroine begins to suffer headaches, she weeps, her gaze is affected, she becomes pallid, and she takes to bed and retreats from her community. Charicleia was definitely suffering from love, but, in the initial confusion created by her sudden illness, the physicians attributed her sickness to the effects of the evil eye (a historically more common variant of boning, I suppose) as well as to a superfluity of black bile.[6] It is almost alarming to imagine that an ancient Greek physician might have understood Basedow's boned Aboriginal as suffering from melancholia.

There are, for the argument of this book, three very useful aspects to Basedow's portrait of boning. The first is, as I have indicated, the set of symptoms experienced by the victim of boning: astonishment, blanched cheeks, glassy eyes, a distorted facial expression, voicelessness, spasms, swooning and collapsing to the ground; then sickening, fretting, the rejection of food and community dealings; and finally imminent death. Incredible as these symptoms may seem, they are real and have often been attested. These symptoms are not far different from those that we have observed in chapter 2 of lovesickness and will observe in chapter 6 concerning suicide (cf. Hawley 1997).[7]

My second point is this: the ability to produce at a distance somatic experience by nonsomatic means is remarkable.[8] But it is something that we have observed, as I have indicated, in Charicleia's illness in Heliodorus's *Aethiopica*. There, however fantastic the diagnosis seemed, medical opinion linked her illness to the effects of another form of long-distance sorcery. Basedow's testimony gives witness to its effective reality. Charicleia fell ill and began to fret away. In fact it was lovesickness. Her physicians, however, initially believed that love was not the root of the problem and that she had been "boned"—she was the victim of the evil eye.[9] Real life-threatening illnesses, as has equally been attested, can be produced by utterly nonsomatic means. When the person who has been boned withdraws from the community, deliberately, it is as if this violent dislocation of the link between reality and its perceived effects (physical illness requires a physical cause; how can the pointing of a mere stick make you die?) destroys the individual's certainty in community and the "reality" that this embodies.[10]

Third, the similarity between the symptoms registered for the victim of boning and those of other psychological affectivities surveyed in this book suggest that there exists an essential sameness—at least on the reactive level—between these various hostile conditions. I am saying that boredom, depression, and lovesickness, a very constellation of affective disorders, may point to a deeper, shared way of responding to psychic trauma. Basedow's boning works—as does the evil eye and lovesickness, no doubt—because of a complicity of belief and a willing suggestibility between perpetrator, victim, and community. When these three coincide (or better, collude), it seems to me, boning, lovesickness, and perhaps even melancholia can flourish. The link between boning and an upsurge in passive depressive conditions is to be found, then, situated between the victim, his victimizer, and his audience.

Many of these themes, and indeed the themes of this book as a whole, reappear in that most famous of all forms of "boredom," acedia, the "bored" (or is it depressive?) condition suffered by monastic incolates during late antiquity and the medieval period.[11] This chapter will attempt to show how the strange virus of acedia, a monastic form of boredom or melancholy, reproduces in its mode of transmission that of boning. The sudden appearance during the fourth century of this enervating spiritual condition evokes abiding fascination. (It may well be that the efficient psychic transmission of affective states, evident in the instances of boning or lovesickness, can account in part for the sudden frequency of depressive conditions such as acedia. It may well be, too, that conditions such as melancholia, lovesickness, and boredom became more frequent during the first century of our era for comparable reasons.) Of all of the forms of melancholy, acedia is without doubt the most famous—and most popular.[12] Its very existence demands comparison with classical antecedents. Surveying acedia, however, means moving away from the temporal parameters favored by this book. Although acedia became prominent in late antiquity—much later than the other affective conditions that I have been examining—it still appears to bear a close resemblance to those conditions already surveyed. It may easily be assimilated with boredom and melancholia.[13]

Acedia represents the dangerous somatization of a dangerous affective state.[14] More was involved than mere somatization. This emotional condition became widespread and even came to represent something of an epidemic. Acedia shows both how and that emotional states may come into being and sweep through a community.[15] The mode by which this variant form of depression or boredom travels closely resembles that by which boning operated. I am not suggesting that monks pointed a biblical bone at one another to induce this enervating condition. I am suggesting, rather, that the conditions that make boning possible also make the transmission of acedia possible:[16] a complicity and willing suggestibility—a complicity of belief—between perpetrator, victim, and community rendered infection possible.[17] There is another point of considerable interest here. The early cenobitic communities that fell prey to acedia housed hermits who placed the ultimate faith in the power of self. The real danger for victims of this illness (as is the case in the instance of boning) lies in their withdrawal from the community and their resultant solitude. (I have noted that, in almost all of the examples of melancholia, or boredom, or lovesickness, death results only when the sufferer becomes convinced of the superfluity of human society.)[18] Perhaps, therefore, we witness in the instance of acedia an "epidemic of individuality."[19] The victim of acedia, just like the victim of boning or of the other conditions mentioned, is forced to confront his or her existence as an independent, self-conscious agent. It takes practice to live with a sense of one's own singularity and uniqueness and difference to the world, with, I am saying, a thoroughgoing sense of self and self-consciousness. This, in different ways, is precisely what we have observed in the previous three chapters.

Why, then, do I make such an issue of the similarities between acedia, and boning, and melancholia? I do so in the first place to illustrate the fact that depression is not a modern illness:[20] it has its analogues in a variety of ancient psychological and psychotic states. The similarities also point to a deep structure, as it were, which offers the reactive basis for a varied group of, for us, key states. I also want to illustrate that these emotions are inextricably tied to a heightened sense of self-consciousness, of independence, of uniqueness, and, I suppose, of psychic isolation. Characters suffering from acedia or boning experience isolation from their community. They experience a dramatic rupture between normal cause and effect, and they are faced with an inability to negotiate between the poles of individual and community. Leisure and play, when these acknowledge their own purposelessness and their own inability to create a fit between the signifier and the signified, may provide the best of remedies.[21]

Acedia is very helpful in other ways, as I have pointed out in the introduction to this book. The similarity of acedia to both boredom and melancholia (as we shall see), its well-documented historical existence, and its capacity for transmission in a viruslike fashion tells us much, I believe, about both the reality and the temporal infectiousness of the sentiments described in chapters 1 through 3. As to the first point, acedia is so well and so frequently documented that we cannot doubt its sudden prevalence and importance in real, not just discursive, life. Its symptomatologic similarity to melancholia and boredom, both of which became discursively more frequent in the first century of our era, suggests to me that I am quite justified in having moved from discursive to real-life speculation in chapters 1 through 3. The mode of transmission for acedia has its analogue in boning. That, in its psychological essence, is a very common mode of transmission that has clear parallels, I will argue, in the instances of not only acedia but also melancholy, lovesickness, and boredom. Acedia, it is my opinion, tells us *how* these conditions became more frequent in real life. (The *why* eludes us.) Acedia, furthermore, gives us clues as to how the emotional registers described in chapters 5 through 7 also became prominent.

In 382 Evagrius (?345–399 C.E.) quit Constantinople for the deserts southwest of Alexandria.[22] Here he joined the hermit colonies gathered at places with such names as Nitria, Scete, and the "Desert of Cells." During the seventeen years that Evagrius passed in these hermetic communities, he developed a formulation of acedia that, to some extent, remains canonical. It is also a formulation that may respond to the conditions of this "Desert of Cells."

For Evagrius acedia represents a "psychic exhaustion and listlessness"

(Wenzel 1967, 5; cf. Driscoll 1989). On the face of things it seems probable that acedia was the product of the extreme monotony, the harshness, and the solitude of anchoritic life (the discussion of acedia in the *Peri tôn oktô logismôn* is quite explicit on this). Consideration of the conditions in which these North African monks lived gives a better idea of the likelihood of this contention. On Mount Nitria, for example, there were nearly five thousand monks. Through the heat, the lack of sleep (acedia was the "demon of noontide"), and the paucity of food, they lived in their separate cells. Their spiritual program lacked elaboration. They practiced a common form of work, probably shared meals, and on Saturday and Sunday shared worship. But apart from work and meals the day was silent, especially in Cellia and Scete (Chadwick 1968, 22–23). There can be little wonder at the fact that they fell into a state that produced symptoms of dejection, restlessness, dislike of the cell, resentment of fellow monks, a desire to quit the cell to seek salvation elsewhere, and even a rejection of the value of anchoritic practices.[23] Wenzel (1967, 5), perhaps the best commentator on Evagrian acedia, observes that "in the end *acêdia* causes the monk either to give in to physical sleep, which proves unrefreshing or actually dangerous, because it opens the door to many other temptations, or to leave his cell and eventually the religious life altogether."

Countermeasures for acedia existed. Endurance, patience, a resolute refusal to quit one's cell, insistent prayer, the reading and recitation of psalms, the remembrance of and meditation on relevant verses from Scripture, keeping to the fore the thought of one's death and heavenly rewards, even the shedding of tears were all felt to be helpful practices. Above all, manual labor was believed to be a most powerful measure against the sin. In spite of the dangers, there were decided benefits to be derived from an onslaught of acedia. The monk who was capable of withstanding it grew immeasurably in strength (qualities are listed in Wenzel 1967, 5 f.).

In its earliest formulations, therefore, acedia gives the appearance of being the disease par excellence of the hermit. The very conditions in which the hermit lived would be conducive to the illness. St. John Chrysostomos (347?–407 C.E.), also a North African, but an erstwhile hermit, provides us with another important outline of the illness. In his *Exhortations to Stagirius*,[24] St. John attempts to assist an anchorite, Stagirius, who suffers a destructive spiritual condition. Although this is termed *athumia*, the condition is usually interpreted as acedia (Klibansky, Panofsky, and Saxl 1964, 75). Stagirius, after his entry into monastic life, began to suffer frightening nightmares, bizarre physical disorders, and a despair that bordered on suicide (*Patrologia Graeca* 47.425–26). What interests most in St. John's discussion is the extremity of the illness. The description of Stagirius suffering a psychotic attack is startling. Stagirius's symptoms were "twisted hands, rolling eyes, a distorted voice, tremors, senselessness, and an awful dream at night—a wild, muddy boar rushed violently to accost him" (*Patrologia Graeca* 47.426; see also Kuhn 1976, 47).[25]

St. John's description modifies the Evagrian portrait in two important ways. First, *athumia,* or acedia, was far more violent than anything described by Evagrius. The second important modification concerns the epidemiology of acedia. The disease is not restricted to the anchoritic community. He compares the attack suffered by Stagirius to attacks suffered by individuals living *delicate* (in Greek they are *truphôntas*—is he attacking homosexuality here?) in the world: "many, while they live in a debauched fashion, are taken by this plague. But after a little time they are freed from the illness, and regain perfect health and marry, and have many children, and enjoy all the benefits of this life" (*Patrologia Graeca* 47.425). The means by which this psychological malady traveled is something that we will come back to. It is transmitted in a manner approximately comparable to that of Basedow's boning. I do not mean, as I have already stated, that anchorites pointed some form of an ecclesiastical bone at one another. Rather, their suggestibility to the illness, their capacity to be infected through what is little other than psychic suggestion, resembles the ease by which Australian Aboriginals seem to have fallen victim to the psychic suggestion of boning. As I say, Stagirius's symptoms may well resemble those of an Aboriginal victim of boning. It is evident, too, that they resemble those of Sappho's victim of love and Heliodorus's Charicleia.

Acedia became the eighth of the vices in the famous list of John Cassian (ca. 360–435 C.E.). Cassian, born in Bethlehem but finally resident in Transalpine Gaul, is the key figure for the Western tradition of acedia.[26] In his work discussing monastic habits, *De institutis cenobiorum,* he stresses its dangers. He links it especially with the hermetic life: it is characterized by laziness and inertia, an unwillingness to pursue spiritual exercises, and a desire to escape present circumstances; by tiredness, hunger, and the slowing of time; by a desire to escape oneself through sleep or company.[27] His cure is labor. That discussion occupies the largest part of *Instituta* 10 (Kuhn 1976, 50–54, provides a useful discussion of Cassian). Cassian's use of the word *acedia* in *Instituta* 10 evinces a shift away from anchoritic dejection or depression to something more closely resembling idleness (*otium* or *otiositas*), even sloth (Wenzel 1967, 22). The reason for this, implies Chadwick and argues Wenzel, is the changed circumstances in the lives of the religious for whom he wrote (Chadwick 1968, 46; Wenzel 1967, 22). Ascetics such as those addressed by Evagrius lived harsh lives, in spite of their community clusters in the North African deserts. Acedia, in their cases, was exacerbated by solitude and deprivation. Cassian created a new milieu. After a period of wandering from Palestine to Constantinople to

Egypt and finally to Marseilles, he established his own cenobitic community. Here the ascetic individualism of the North African hermit was tempered by the demands of a religious community. The individual must contribute to the whole. Idleness, therefore, is a particular danger. Work is of paramount importance—hence the stress of the *Instituta*. "It was basic to the cenobitic life," maintains Wenzel (1967, 22), "that the monastery be a self-sustaining unit for whose support the individual monk had to contribute his share." Laziness endangered its existence.

Cassian's acedia may be described as a type of sloth. Another monkish vice, described in book 9 of the *De institutis cenobiorum*, is *tristitia*. It bears a slight resemblance to Evagrius's and Stagirius's illnesses.[28] Cassian outlines the origins of this state as follows (cap. 13; *Patrologia Latina* 49.360–61): it could arise from past anger, a loss of money, an unspecified disappointment, an unprovoked injury, irrational confusion of the mind, or the sorts of things such as cause one to despair of salvation and life itself (Cassian compares Judas). *Tristitia* can be cured simply by directing one's attention steadfastly on the afterlife. Cassian's category is, however, a jumble. That it was not well thought through is indicated, perhaps, by the brevity of this ninth book. *Tristitia* may signify mental derangement, although Cassian is more concerned with the other categories. These might best be characterized as frustration, although they may represent a frustration that can become so extreme as to be lethal. *Tristitia* may vary from the severity of Stagirius's *athumia* to the triviality of Cassian's *otiositas*.

Rutilius Namatianus was a pagan, a contemporary of Cassian, and also a Gaul (Vessereau and Préchac 1961, vff.). In 417 C.E., seven years after having sacked Rome, Alaric the Visigoth made his famous sea voyage back to a ravaged Gaul. In that year of opportunity, Rutilius sailed home, hoping (no doubt he was bitterly disappointed in this hope) to reestablish himself safely in his Gallic estates. He commemorated his return in a poem—part travelogue, part exhortation to his fellow Romans to overcome their present disasters and to act in the manner that they had when, seven hundred years previously, they had overcome Pyrrhus and Hannibal. He mentions voyaging past a community of monks north of Corsica, near the island of Capraria. He remarks (*De reditu suo* 1.439–52):

> As we crossed the ocean Capraria reared up in front of us.
> The island is polluted by a plenitude of men who flee the light.
> They give themselves the Greek name of *monachi* [monks]
> Because they want to live alone, without a witness.
> They fear the gifts of Fortune and her outrages.
> Who would choose to be miserable to avoid being miserable?

What madness *[rabies]* of a twisted brain is so crazy
As to be unable to tolerate blessings while fearing ills?
Perhaps they seek their cells *[ergastula]* as punishment for their actions?
Perhaps their mournful hearts are swollen with black gall *[nigro felle]*
A superfluity of black bile (*bilis*) was the cause Homer assigned
For the troubles of Bellerophon [*Iliad* 6.200 f.],
For the human race is said to have displeased the young man
After he was made ill by the attacks of cruel depression *[saevi post tela doloris]*.

It is uncertain whether Rutilius is describing a monastic community or a loose confederation of anchorites. He identifies the psychological state of these men as depression or, as he would have termed it, melancholia. The *nigrum fel* to which Rutilius refers is black bile (indicated in the next line also by *bilis*.) This substance was believed in humoralist medicine (into which class falls Galenic medicine) to have been responsible for the condition of melancholia. Bellerophon, whose malaise is compared to that of the *monachi*, suffered from melancholia.[29] For Rutilius, then, these monks were the victims of a clinically defined condition, melancholia. Rutilius's descriptions seem to present us with an acedia whose destructiveness matches the Evagrian or Stagirian type.

St. Jerome (331–419 C.E.) gives further idea of how severe was the malady alluded to by Rutilius. An inhabitant, like Cassian had been, of Bethlehem, Jerome observes among cenobites what can only be termed acedia. He is describing a community that resembles that of Cassian more than that of Evagrius. But the acedia he speaks of matches that of Evagrius or Stagirius. Jerome does not use the circumlocutions of Rutilius. He defines the acedia as melancholia. It is, he avers, best treated by a physician.

> [T]here are those who, because of the humidity of their cells, because of excessive fasting, because of the tedium of solitude *[taedio solitudinis]*, because of excessive reading, and because day and night they talk to themselves, become melancholic *[vertuntur in melancholian]*. They need Hippocratic treatments *[Hippocraticis . . . fomentis]* rather than our advice. (*Epistles* 125.16, *ad rusticum*).[30]

Cassian seems to underestimate the force of acedia. This is surely indicated by the independent testimony of Rutilius and St. Jerome. Is it not unlikely that the acedia within Cassian's two monasteries may compare to that described by Chrysostomos—doubtless the severe melancholia that is discussed repeatedly in medical literature? A recent observation made of Stagirius's illness, termed *athumia* (despondency), may also be made of that described in Cassian's *De institutis cenobiorum* 10.

> [Q]uite apart from the fact that despondency had always been the main symptom of melancholy illness, both the aetiology and semeiology in this case (which gives us a deep insight into early Christian asceticism) agree so completely with the definitions in medical literature on melancholy that Johannes Trithemius was fully justified in rendering the expression *athumia* as it occurs in the epistle to Stagirius by "melancholische Traurigkeit."[31]

Why should Cassian have underestimated the force of the illness? I would guess there is more to the *Instituta* than mere practical advice for monks. Cassian, for personal reasons, may have been keen to advertise the salubricity of his own establishments. But perhaps, too, Cassian was selective in which attacks he sketched. An attack of acedia, that is, may have varied in intensity like many another viral onslaught. Cassian may have been cognizant of—or, more likely, may have chosen to be cognizant of—only the milder forms.

Later witnesses to the *morbus* suggest that this second explanation is probable. Their sketches of the sickness veer wildly between the extremes of the Stagirian and the domesticity of the Cassianic. For example, Abba Isais (d. ca. 480; cf. Bloomfield 1952, 54, 346 n. 87) believed that acedia was the most dangerous of all vices (*Patrologia Graeca* 40.1148). Yet elsewhere he could change his mind and nominate avarice (*Patrologia Graeca* 40.1143; cf. Kuhn 1976, 44). Isais, like Evagrius, lived in the hermetic tradition. The comments of Nilus (d. 450?), an abbot of a monastery near Ankara and a former pupil of St. John Chrysostomos, seem also to reflect both traditions. In one letter, he responds to Polychronius, who requests advice on how to overcome demonic attacks of *akêdia* and *athumia* (*Patrologia Graeca* 79.449: 3.142). But Nilus urges another young man to persist like a soldier, "for even those who have been wounded by the enemy, as long as they will not grow weary [verb *akêdian*] in the hardships of penance . . . will finally triumph" (*Patrologia Graeca* 79.112: 1.67; trans. Wenzel [1967, 10]).[32] Elsewhere he urges persistence and an avoidance of negligence in prayer (*Patrologia Graeca* 79.537: 3.319). The verb used for "negligence" is *akêdian*.

Gregory the Great (540–604 C.E.) dramatically modifies the position of even Isais and Nilus. He may mark a new phase in the history of acedia. In Gregory's scheme of things, to judge from his language, acedia is an unimportant evil—notwithstanding his certain knowledge of it from Cassian. There were now only seven vices likely, *vana gloria* (empty self-aggrandizement), *ira* (anger), *invidia* (envy), *tristitia*, *avaritia*, *gula* (gluttony), and *luxuria*. In the *Morals on the Book of Job*, Gregory seems to have lumped together *tristitia* and acedia to call them the diseases of the solitary (*Moralia* 31.87; Kuhn 1976, 54). Wenzel (1967, 24) argues against simple merging or mere name changing: "it is possible, if Gregory knew Cassian at all, to think of his *tristitia* as a combination of traces from both the *tristitia* and the acedia of the Cassianic-Evagrian scheme of eight vices. The new concept should, however, be considered, not as the result of a simple fusion, following the mathematical rule that two and two make four, but rather a new creation from parts of the old vices."

Gregory offers the impression that acedia, though well known in theory, had as an illness lost its virulence. The disease has reached an epidemiological balance. Commentators subsequent to Gregory bear out this contention. For example, Eutropius, a near contemporary of Gregory, provides a sin sequence that seems to blur the Cassianic and Gregorian tradition. Both *tristitia* and acedia appear. In his *De octo vitiis*, the list is *superbia*, acedia, *vana gloria*, *ira*, *tristitia*, *avaritia*, *gula*, and *luxuria*.[33] Similarly Isidore of Seville (b. ca. 560/70), in the *De differentiis verborum et rerum* (2.40), reverts to the Cassianic octad,[34] though "the inclusion of *invidia* and the merging of *tristitia* and acedia under the former name . . . reveal the Gregorian influence."[35] Johannes Climacus[36] approves of Gregory's list of seven vices, but in all cases bar one, he follows the Cassianic octad (Bloomfield 1952, 76–77).

The descriptions that I have given of acedia seem to fall into two groups. In the first, whose basis may be seen in Evagrius's opinions, but whose most alarming characterization is provided by John Chrysostomos (and echoed by Rutilius Namatianus and St. Jerome), acedia attacks the anchorite in the most frightening of manners. Stagirius's symptoms may represent as extreme a form of this affective condition as we are liable to find: twisted hands, rolling eyes, a problem with speech, physical insensitivity, nightmares, and, subsequently, a sense of despair and a desire for suicide. The second group is typified by the pronouncements of Cassian. His monks, community dwellers rather than solitary anchorites, inhabitants of the more fertile regions of southern France rather than the harsh North African deserts, understood acedia as a form of sloth or laziness. But it was a form of sloth that was invidious to the proper functioning of the monastic community and the spiritual development of a monk. Cassian's less dramatic version of the condition is echoed by later monastic writers such as Abba Isais and, in his very different way, by Gregory the Great.

The first group is of immediate importance for the themes of this book (later we will have cause, however, to look again at the second). Scholars sometimes claim and frequently imply that acedia lacked a parallel within the classical world—as if it sprang to birth fully formed in the deserts of North Africa, rather like Athena from Zeus's head. It is apparent, if we compare the material gathered in previous chapters, that the various aspects of the Stagirian emotion have ample parallels within the literature of classical antiquity. What was new in North Africa was a proper term for this *morbus*. The invention of this label, I suspect, is an indication of the ferocity of the onslaught. It is noteworthy, however, that these monastic circles avoided the classical term *melancholia*, which, as we have seen in Jerome, would have been quite adequate to the purpose. Here are, to be sure, elements of monastic *amour propre* and the *vana gloria* of a desire for exclusivity.

Precedents for the depressive condition suffered by Stagirius or that described by Rutilius Namatianus and St. Jerome have been amply documented by Jackson (1986); Klibansky, Panofsky, and Saxl (1964); and Starobinski (1962). As we have seen in the previous chapters, there is, in the classical period, a reasonably large medical literature on melancholia, depression, and related problems. In the earliest Hippocratic writers,[37] melancholia seems to be linked with "an aversion to food, despondency, sleeplessness, irritability, restlessness." (The Evagrian parallel suggests itself at once.) Sometimes it is also added that "fear or depression that is prolonged means melancholia."[38] These theorists were probably humoralists and believed that melancholy was the result of an excess of black bile (Jackson [1986, 30] cites Jones and Withington [1923–31, 4:3–41] in support of this view). (This is behind the comments of Rutilius Namatianus.) Such an interpretation was followed, with only small modifications, by most of the later medical writers. Celsus interpreted it as such;[39] so did Rufus of Ephesus (who worked during the Trajanic and Hadrianic periods),[40] Aretaeus of Cappadocia (fl. 150 C.E.),[41] and Galen (fl. 161 C.E.).[42] A contemporary of Rufus, Soranus, agreed on the symptomatology but differed on etiology.[43]

An examination of some of the ways in which depression seems to have been depicted in classical texts indicates reasonable similarities between it and some of the versions suffered under the banner of acedia. Compare, for example, the following descriptions of melancholia (the first drawn from Aretaeus of Cappadocia, the second from Soranus) with those of St. John Chrysostomos or Evagrius cited earlier: "in certain of these cases, there is neither flatulence nor black bile, but mere anger and grief, and sad dejection of the mind; and these were called melancholics, because the term *bile* and *anger* are synonymous in import, and likewise *black* with *much* and *furious*";[44] "mental anguish and distress, dejection, silence, animosity towards members of the household, sometimes a desire to live and at other times a longing for death, suspicion . . . that a plot is being hatched against him, weeping without reason, meaningless muttering and . . . occasional joviality" (cf. Drabkin 1950, 561).

Also of considerable significance may be the traditional link between the desert (the haunt of the early anchorite), uninhabited places, and melancholia and madness. This nexus has a distinguished medical parentage. The pseudo-Aristotelian *Problema* (30.1) states:

> There are also the stories of Ajax and Bellerophon: the one went completely out of his mind, while the other sought out desert places *[tas erêmias]* for his habitation; wherefore Homer says [*Iliad* 6.200–203]:
>
> And since of all the gods he was hated
> Verily over the Aleian plain he would wander
> Eating his own heart out, avoiding the pathway of mortals.

Aretaeus of Cappadocia, notes Rosen (1968, 98), makes a similar parallel and links madness with the desert: "Aretaeus speaks of some madmen who 'flee the haunts of men and, going to the wilderness, live by themselves.' Also, in discussing melancholia, he refers to 'avoidance of the haunts of men' as characteristic of those severely afflicted with this condition." It is also doubtless correct to adduce the Gerasene demoniac in the Gospels. According to Luke, the demon who possessed this individual drove him into the desert after he had broken the bonds used to fetter him.[45]

Melancholics of the depressive variety are not uncommon in ancient medical literature. There seems to be every reason to assume that early Christian writers were familiar with the medical traditions[46] and, further, that they consciously or unconsciously utilized them when they attempted to describe or to formulate aspects of acedia. But it is not just a matter of replicating the formulations of classical texts. There is something "canonical" in the description given to Stagirius's illness. I say this because of the close resemblance that his conditions bear to those descriptions of the symptoms of an Aboriginal victim of boning as outlined by Basedow at the beginning of this chapter.

In citing Basedow's description of boning, I singled out three aspects. The first is the set of symptoms experienced by the victim of boning: astonishment, blanched cheeks, glassy eyes, a distorted facial expression, voicelessness, spasms, swooning and collapsing to the ground; then sickening, fretting, the rejection of food and community dealings; and finally imminent death. Consider again the symptoms of Stagirius's illness: twisted hands, rolling eyes, a distorted voice, tremors, senselessness, nightmares, and ultimately a desire to die. Except perhaps for nightmares (Basedow did not ask about this, I imagine), the outward manifestation of boning and of Stagirius's *athumia* or acedia is virtually identical. In both cases, furthermore, death is imminent (Stagirius contemplates suicide; the Aboriginal wills himself to death).

My second point was to highlight the producing of somatic experience by nonsomatic means. This point requires little emphasis—that a psychic condition could be passed like a viral infection, as it were, is perhaps the most remarkable and intriguing aspect of acedia. This psychic condition persistently fascinates—and is the subject of many rationalizing explanations[47]—precisely because it is transmitted in such an improbable manner. It is a manner that closely resembles the transmission of acedia. Acedia, as we will see, seems to have spread, like boning, by psychic contagion.

Third, the similarity between the symptoms registered for the victim of acedia, boning, and those other psychological affectivities surveyed in this book suggests that there exists an essential sameness—at least on the reactive level—between these various hostile conditions. I am saying that boredom, depression, lovesickness, suicide, the registering of time, and the response to leisure[48] may point to a deeper shared way of responding to invasive emotional states. Perhaps the simplest way to illustrate this is through Rutilius Namatianus. As I have already noted, Rutilius understood cenobitic acedia as the product of *nigrum fel*, the black bile, the causative agent of melancholia. Boning, Stagirian acedia, and melancholia may be confused in psychic terms.

I should also add that much of the real damage done by pointing the bone is the result of the individual's withdrawal from the community and fretful pursuit of solitude. The life of the anchorite was built upon what was clearly a very dangerous form of solitude, from which the victim of acedia sought refuge through sleep, company, or escape from the community altogether. Where these remedies were denied, the results must have been disastrous. It is also worthwhile to note that the victim of boning, like those of the other conditions mentioned, is forced—in part through solitude, in part through the individual's perception of the gap between words and deeds, between the subject and the object (how can a yam stick harm you after all?)—to confront his or her existence as an independent, self-conscious agent. That such a confrontation can be disastrous for the individual is one of the themes of this book. Surmounting such a confrontation takes practice and a thoroughgoing acculturation.

There was, however, more to acedia than a destructive melancholia. In the Cassianic scheme of things, it resembles a simple form of boredom. Does Cassian's formulation of acedia as *otiositas* have classical parallels? The most useful of these may be found in the emotion implied by the Greek word *alus*. In its earliest uses (nominal and verbal) it seems to mean "distracted" or "grieved." It can also, in its verbal forms, mean "to wander." To my knowledge, the first unambiguous use of *alus* to suggest "boredom" comes from Plutarch's *Pyrrhus* 13.[49] As I mentioned in the last chapter, Pyrrhus, after becoming regent of Epirus and later of Macedonia, withdrew from the later possession in disappointment at the disloyalty of his subjects. *Alus* or boredom—to the point of nausea—did not allow him to enjoy his retirement. He was only content, according to Plutarch, when doing or receiving mischief. To alleviate the boredom, Pyrrhus launched himself on a new round of military activities, at the end of which he lost his life. This is not quite Cassianic, perhaps, but the restlessness and dissatisfaction may offer some similarity. So, too, may Pyrrhus's cure—activity, the very prescription of Cassian. Comparable references occur in Diogenes of Oenoanda (fr. 25 Chilton), Aelian (*Varia historia* 14.12), and Marcus Aurelius (*Meditations* 2.7). Aelian's anecdote is very apt. It mentions the king of Persia who, to avoid boredom when traveling, kept a knife and a piece of linden wood for whittling.

An important aspect of Cassianic acedia is *horror loci*, a restless dissatisfaction that drives monks from their cells to annoy and to harass (and to pass on the infection to?) others (cf. *Instituta* 10, cap. 2: *qui* [sc., *acedia*] . . . *horrorem loci . . . gignit* [acedia breeds *horror loci*]). There are ample references to this condition (mentioned in chapter 3) in Lucretius's *On the Universe* (3.1060–67) and in Horace's *Satires* (2.7.28–29) and *Epistles* (1.8.12, 1.11.27, and 1.14) (see Kuhn 1976, 23). Horace, however, does not seem to see anything especially sinister in this emotion. Seneca repeats this theme in *Epistles* 28 and at *Consolation to Helvia* 12.3.4. In fact it is Seneca who provides, as with depression, many of the most useful references to this emotion. He could almost be said to have "spiritualized" it. Typical of this tendency are comments such as those at *Epistles* 24.26: of the sufferers, he notes, *multi sunt qui non acerbum iudicent vivere, sed supervacuum* [there are many who judge life to be not bitter but superfluous]. Here boredom, "spiritualized," verges on full-fledged acedia.[50]

Because the intensity of acedia could vary from region to region, from sufferer to sufferer, and from era to era, no single set of symptoms will accurately sum it up. Yet the Evagrian and the Cassianic forms of acedia clearly bear toward one another much more than a mere nominal similarity. They seem to exist as different parts of an emotional continuum. The status of this continuum has been demonstrated with great force in the work of the Dutch researcher into animal behavior Dr. Françoise Wemelsfelder (1985, 1989). Wemelsfelder convincingly explains the interconnections between frustration, boredom, and depression (termed helplessness) in animal behavior. Animals kept in close confinement and in deprived circumstances evince emotional reactions that seem to move on a continuum beginning with frustration, continuing on to what she identifies as boredom, and finally concluding with helplessness (to be linked with depression).

Wemelsfelder outlines frustration in animals in the following manner. If you deprive a chicken of food for twenty-four hours, then place it in a cage in which its food is covered by a see-through container, it will understandably react in a frustrated manner. It will attempt escape, then begin stereotypical back-and-forth pacing. When this fails to produce results (i.e., food), it will indulge in "displacement preening" and, if other chickens are present, become aggressive. Wemelsfelder defines boredom simply as the state arising "because of a general lack of sensory stimulation in the environment" and argues that it "can lead in animals to passivity, redirected behavior, and stereotyped behavior." She further explains, "Dogs who are raised in isolation up to 16 to 32 weeks show whirling, pacing, and bizarre postures." Such stereotypic behavior, Dr. Wemelsfelder suggests, is the initial animal reaction to an unvarying environment. If confinement continues, passivity results: "Tethered sows and fattening pigs spend long periods, up to six hours, of motionless 'sitting,' often with their head hanging down, or pressed against stall divisions." Release from confinement reverses the condition.

Dogs, Wemelsfelder illustrates, may be reduced to a state of helplessness (which we may read as depression) by the repeated application of electric shocks. Unlike those dogs who have received avoidable shocks, these dogs sit passively and take their maltreatment, "having learned, apparently, that irrespective of any response they may give, the unpleasant event will follow." Depression, Wemelsfelder generalizes, "may arise because the environment cannot be controlled in its adverse aspects by the animal." An animal in such a situation, she notes, can react by performing "self-mutilation, or it can become passive, sometimes maintaining motionlessness, so-called 'drowsy' postures for a long time."

The human analogy in all of this seems inevitable: acedia, which may present itself as either boredom or depression (depending largely on the era and the locale), may best be described on this sliding scale that could register anything from a harmless, though debilitating, frustration, through oppressive boredom, to an acute, delusory melancholia. If we were to place this scale in context, then we would say that first there was the Evagrian condition—a specific, perhaps mildly depressive illness brought on by an excess of solitude and physical deprivation. This malaise seems not unlike an acute form of frustration (cf. Cassian's *tristitia*). Second, there was the state of what we might term malicious boredom. This is represented by the Cassianic conception of *otiositas*.

Third, there was the formulation of St. John Chrysostomos,[51] Rutilius Namatianus, and St. Jerome. Acedia here was linked with the clinically defined notion of severe melancholia. At any rate, acedia represents a psychic continuum encompassing the conditions that we would describe as frustration, boredom, and depression. It also appears probable that Cassian was correct in maintaining that the solitary lifestyle of the hermit exacerbated the malady. This is a point made also by Wenzel, who suggests that the physical conditions of the sufferers may have some importance in regulating the severity of the malady.[52] This was certainly a crucial factor in the unfortunate experiences of Wemelsfelder's animals.

The preceding animal analogy should not be pressed too far. The type of illness that we are looking at here, while no doubt exacerbated by physical hardship, could be and was communicated psychically—by long distance. The inadequacy of a "deprivation model" or a trauma model based on laboratory animals is indicated by the statements of Chrysostomos that the condition was not confined to the monastic world. This point, that monks alone were not predisposed to this illness, is of crucial importance. St. John Chrysostomos states in an aside that acedia is a condition also suffered by those living outside monasteries, but for them it was less dangerous.[53] Thus, because the malady suffered by Stagirius has its parallel even in the comfortable world beyond the cave or the monastery, we cannot attribute his *athumia* or acedia to physical deprivation alone.

It is very helpful, I think, to draw a parallel between the prevalence of acedia and that of a modern-day virus.[54] Acedia, rather like influenza or even AIDS, seems to have presented itself with the vehemence of an epidemic. John Chrysostomos calls it a plague (a *loimos* or *pestis*) and a poison (a *loimos* or *pestis* and an *ios* or *virus*) (*Patrologia Graeca* 47.491) and compares it to a fever (*puretos* or *febris*) (*Patrologia Graeca* 47.489).[55] As we can speculate from St. John Chrysostomos and from Gregory the Great, the *morbus* seems to have had an outbreak, a period of intense infectiousness, then an increasingly dormant period. Acedia varied in intensity. It could range from a severe clinical depression to a milder form that more resembled simple boredom. Given that acedia affected lay and religious, hermit and monk alike, it is hard not to conclude that acedia represented a hysterical pandemic. The viral analogy[56] of St. John Chrysostomos is a useful one.[57] It makes it comprehensible that the force of the attack, like that of many diseases, could vary in intensity (Evagrian acedia blurs into a clinical melancholia; Rutilius's melancholia blurs into Cassian's *otiositas*) and that the disease had periods when it was dormant (the Gregorian era) and periods when it was widespread (Chrysostomos's era).

How was the virus spread? Here I would turn back again to Basedow and to his description of boning. That the illness was transmitted by psychic suggestion is beyond doubt.[58] I am not suggesting for a moment that the incolates of Nitria or Scete "boned" one another; rather, I argue that the same sort of suggestibility that allowed boning to succeed among Australian Aboriginals assisted acedia, mutatis mutandis, in just the same manner. Parallels such as that from Basedow make the transmission, if not easily understood, at least far more comprehensible. Just as boning requires the complicity or willing suggestibility of the victim, the victimizer, and the community (if the sorcery is to work), there can be no doubt that acedia requires a similar complicity between victim and community as well. How this transmission originates is probably irrelevant. What matters is that the victim (as well as the victimizer and the community) believes that infection is inevitable.

At the very outset of this chapter, I mentioned that the precise nature of this mode of transmission (as much for acedia as for boning) has been made more clear by Lévi-Strauss (1963), Showalter (1997), and Hacking (1998). Let us begin therefore with the anthropologist Lévi-Strauss and with an essay of his on sorcery (1963). It concerns a twelve-year-old Zuni girl who "was stricken with a nervous seizure directly after an adolescent boy had seized her hands." The boy was subsequently accused of sorcery and brought to "trial" by his community. His fate need not concern us here (he was eventually released), nor need that of the girl (she was cured). What is important is the manner—psychic suggestion—by which the Zuni girl fell ill. I imagine that it can have been no different for Stagirius and, furthermore, that the dramatic descriptions preserved by Chrysostomos represent the opening phase of the course of the illness.

One final and related query that we ought to put is this: can and how does acedia (or boning, or lovesickness, or any other related condition) actually kill?[59] Once again Lévi-Strauss is very helpful. For an explanation of the psychophysiological mechanisms behind such deaths, he refers to the work of Cannon (1942; cf. Reid 1983, xix). I here reproduce Lévi-Strauss's eloquent description (1963, 167–8).

> An individual who is aware that he is the object of sorcery is thoroughly convinced that he is doomed according to the most solemn traditions of his group. His friends and relatives share this certainty. From then on the community withdraws. Standing aloof from the accursed, it treats him not only as though he were already dead but as though he were a source of danger to the

entire group. On every occasion and by every action, the social body suggests death to the unfortunate victim, who no longer hopes to escape what he considers to be his ineluctable fate. Shortly thereafter, sacred rites are held to dispatch him to the realm of shadows. First brutally torn from all of his family and social ties and excluded from all functions and activities through which he experienced self-awareness, then banished by the same forces from the world of the living, the victim yields to the combined effect of intense terror, the sudden withdrawal of the multiple reference systems provided by the support of the group, and, finally, to the group's decisive reversal in proclaiming him—once a living man, with rights and obligations—dead and an object of fear, ritual, and taboo. Physical integrity cannot withstand the dissolution of the social personality.[60]

How are these complex phenomena expressed on the physiological level? Cannon showed that fear, like rage, is associated with a particularly intense activity of the sympathetic nervous system. This activity is normally useful, involving organic modifications which enable the individual to adapt himself to a new situation. But if the individual cannot avail himself of any instinctive or acquired response to an extraordinary situation (or to one to which he conceives of as such), the activity of the central nervous system becomes intensified and disorganized; it may sometimes, within a few hours, lead to a decrease in the volume of blood and a concomitant drop in blood pressure, which result in irreparable damage to the circulatory organs. The rejection of food and drink, frequent among patients in the throes of extreme anxiety, precipitates this process; dehydration acts as a stimulus to the sympathetic nervous system, and the decrease in blood volume is accentuated by the growing permeability of the capillary vessels. These hypotheses were confirmed by the study of several cases of trauma resulting from bombings, battle shock, and even surgical operations; death results, yet the autopsy reveals no lesions.

In the last few years, such hysterical conditions have received excellent discussion by Showalter (1997) and Hacking (1998). Both authors have proposed models that, they hope, pin down the conditions under which these forms of psychic illness can flourish and be transmitted assuming viral proportions such as acedia seems to have achieved. While their conclusions are hardly conclusive, they do introduce into the discussion a level of theoretical sophistication that is very helpful. Hacking's analysis, the more provocative of the two, focuses on a condition termed fugue (or *dromomania,* or ambulatory somnambulism, or even pathological tourism), which is characterized by "aimless wandering driven by irresistible impulses." This "pathological tourism," Hacking argues, had its heyday in France during the twenty-five years—from 1886 to

1909—when it became epidemic. It has not been replicated. Hacking believes that such short-lived psychic epidemics are reserved for "transient mental illnesses" (surely an apt description for acedia). By that he means a mental illness that appears at a certain time only later to disappear. The parallel between fugue and acedia (both are apparently illnesses that in their outward manifestations are "constructed" by their societies) is striking.

Hacking's argument deserves repacing. It begins with the most famous *dromomaniac* in medical history, a French gas fitter named Jean-Albert Dadas (1860–92) who came from the homeland of pathological tourism, Bordeaux. In 1886 Albert was admitted to the Saint-André Hospital there, exhausted and bewildered, after one of his journeys. He was treated, then written up in the medical thesis (entitled "Les aliénés voyageurs") of a mature-aged student, Philippe Tissié (1852–1935). Albert's amnesiac travels were nothing short of astonishing. His greatest began after he deserted the French army near Mons in 1881. He headed east through Prague, Berlin (he was attacked savagely by a dog while begging in East Prussia but could remember nothing of it), Posen, then Moscow. His timing was dreadful. The czar had just been assassinated, on March 13. The nihilists were to blame. Albert was taken for one and jailed. Luckily for Jean-Albert, three months later the prisoners were split into three groups. The first was to be hung, the second to be sent to Siberia, and the third to be marched from Moscow into exile in Turkey. Albert, along with his nihilists and a band of alarmingly promiscuous Gypsies, was placed in the third group and was marched by sword-wielding Cossack guards to the border nearest Constantinople. There the sympathetic French consul funded Dadas's repatriation, at least as far as Vienna, where he took up gas fitting again. He was still amnesiac.

Tissié's thesis either triggered or coincided with an epidemic in fugue. Large numbers of cases were reported in France, Italy, then Germany. Hacking believes (and this intersects with the concerns of this chapter) that Tissié's thesis, because it provided a proper medical classification for pathological tourism, gave it respectability. It also made the illness visible. But medical respectability and visibility were not all that was needed. The illness had to be romantic. It had to tap into contemporary enthusiasms and concerns. In the late nineteenth century, France was obsessed, Hacking suggests, with locomotion. Tourism (this was Baedeker's era) was at a high. So was anxiety over vagrants. Fugue, in its bizarre, romantic way, mirrored both. Hacking also believes that an illness like fugue can become epidemic if it provides an escape. Fugue victims were mostly working-class males. As a real *sickness,* fugue provided them with an irreproachable means for getting time off work.

If the fugue epidemic seems to have been triggered by Tissié's thesis, it was stopped by another medical event, the French psychiatric conference in Nantes in 1909. At that gathering, academics began to overintellectualize the illness. Fugue fragmented into six or seven forms. It lost its status as an independent disorder and became a symptom of deeper mental troubles (schizophrenia, melancholia, hysteria). Without medical authority, the epidemic began to fade. I suppose that there were other reasons as well. With World War I approaching, pathological tourism was becoming more difficult. Had Albert attempted fugue in 1914, he would have found borders closed.[61]

Hacking (1998) produces a formula for the sudden appearances of such epidemics. He believes that for a shadow syndrome to reach epidemic proportions, there must exist what he calls an "ecological niche"; circumstances, that is, need to be just right—as they were for fugue from 1886 to 1909. Four elements are crucial: there must be professionals to *classify* the disease and to make it *visible*, and the disease must possess *romantic allure* as well as providing *escape*.

Can these four elements be seen in the acedia epidemic that we have been viewing in this chapter? Can we isolate an "ecological niche" that makes possible the growth of acedia? There certainly existed a group of individuals capable of talking up such an illness. Evagrius, St. John Chrysostomos, and Cassian, among others, all act as "professionals" who, through their writing, made monastic communities receptive to this sort of illness. In their writings, they both *classify* the illness and, through this, make it eminently *visible*. That acedia could provide an *escape* (the fourth prerequisite for an ecological niche), is apparent in a number of ways. Consider Rutilius Namatianus's complaints. Rutilius, himself escaping from a crippled Rome, chastises the monks for a form of "escape" from the real world that in fact mirrors his own. Or consider Evagrius's anchorites. His writings, both condemning and offering a solution to acedia, suggest that there may well have been attempts to legitimize the condition (through the removal of volitional control over the illness). Stagirius's illness itself seems to have been viewed as an escape ploy.

Did acedia possess a *romantic allure*? Think again of Rutilius's poem. Insofar as it offers a means of withdrawal, it mirrors the very forces that may have made the anchoritic life attractive. The anchoritic life no doubt drew much of its appeal from its offering a safe alternative to the dangers of the threatened (and threatening) city life of the period. The romantic estrangement of the anchoritic life has its own reflex in the withdrawal from this by individuals such as Stagirius.

The last point requiring statement is that overanalysis drove acedia underground as readily as it did fugue at the conference in Nantes. The confusing discussions concerning the seven (or was it eight?) vices exemplified by Cassian point to this. Cassian's very analysis obscures the visibility of the malady.

The claim that it went underground is crucial. I do not think that acedia—or fugue, for that matter—was invented or that it disappeared. I can think of examples for fugue—before Dadas (or Forrest Gump)—from Greek mythology (Bellerophon) or the New Testament (the Gerasene demoniac in Luke). Ben Shephard, an English writer working on war-related post-traumatic stress disorders, lately cited in the *Times Literary Supplement* still other examples from the trenches of World War I. I have often wondered if many of these faces on missing-person posters are not amnesiac fugue victims who, unlike Jean-Albert Dadas (and Forrest Gump), never made it home. Fugue lives on (like the quiescent Repetitive Strain Injury), but (unlike indigenous suicides) not in epidemic proportions. Epidemics come and go, depending on whether the circumstances are right or wrong. But the illnesses linger on, living shadow lives and making do with just a few nameless victims. When the "ecological niche" is right again, the epidemic takes off. As Hacking himself points out, the saber-toothed tiger is said to have evolved (reaching epidemic proportions) and then disappeared on five separate occasions.

It seems likely to me that the apparently increased frequency of melancholia, passive lovesickness, and boredom during the first century of our era may have been spread in a manner comparable to that suggested here for those various hysterical illnesses, including acedia. Communities and sufferers become complicit in their belief in the existence and the importance of these affective conditions and so encourage one another. Experts, such as Seneca and Persius, and romantic novelists, such as Chariton and Heliodorus, talked them up, classified them, and provided them with allure. Their romantic appeal is also, I think, obvious. These hysterical conditions are often associated with younger, more attractive, and more sympathetic individuals. Thus was created a niche for their transmission. If that, then, gives us some clue as to the *how*, is the *why* really as elusive as I have suggested earlier? I suspect that this is the case. The deprivation model of Wemelsfelder offers an attractive how. The difficulty it presents resides in making precise for the ancient world the nature of the deprivation.

Depending on the era, depending on the sufferer, depending on his or her health, acedia could vary in intensity. It could resemble a mild form of frustration, a deeper form of boredom, or a psychotic type of depression. The virus-like hysterical illness affected religious people and laypeople alike. Its severity, however, seems to have been predicated upon historical, geographical, and physiological peculiarities. The variety of the forms that acedia could take, furthermore, allows a more satisfactory examination of its antecedents. The depressive manifestations of the illness and those manifestations exhibiting symptoms of boredom appear to have ample parallels in the literature of pagan antiquity. There was, then, little that was new in acedia, except perhaps the name itself. Its formulation may be the result of the severity of the epidemic in the fourth century.

The similarity of acedia to the other conditions examined in this book may allow us to speculate a little more on the age and types of the persons liable to be infected and a little more on the nature of the infection. Stagirius was young. Youth and old age, as *Problema* 30.1 tells us, are prone to psychic disturbance. Both ages, perhaps because of their marginalization within the society of median-aged adults, suffer a form of psychic isolation. But young people seem particularly prone, if we are to judge from the experiences of lovesickness, suicide, or the depression suffered by Seneca's Annaeus Serenus. If this age factor is allied, as it was in cenobitic communities, with harsh living conditions (extreme heat, lack of bodily comforts, little food, solitude, celibacy), then the type of breakdown that acedia represented is probably to be expected. That such conditions spread rapidly is also comprehensible. Other individuals who were in this "at-risk" category would be liable to develop the illness by imitation, albeit without any necessary conscious intention to do so. (The alarming "epidemic" of the suicides of young Aboriginal men in Australian jails might well be compared.)[62]

Nietzsche sometimes spoke of the self-assertive arrogance of the anchorite. The anchorite's life, in some ways, is the ultimate exemplification of deliberate, self-conscious assertions of the primacy of the individual will, hence the self. It displays this especially in its pursuit of personal salvation through the solitary life of the abnegation of the body and the privileging of the mind's ability to contemplate God and Christ. Perhaps acedia should be viewed within this individualist and self-assertive enterprise. The destructive element in boning and in sorcery generally seems to subsist in that phase where the victim withdraws from the community and where he or she is anathematized by the community. It is in that phase, during which the individual frets over the death complicit in the sorcerer's imprecations, that the individual, deprived of community support, is thrown back onto the inadequate resources of a self that has been formed in a society that is less than individualist. In my opinion the difficulty faced alike by anchorite and, especially, by the victim of acedia is a form of psychic isolation, even a form of "alienation from the self" or at least from the socially constructed self to which they had become habituated. Psychic isolation is tolerable when an individual has a strongly developed sense of self-consciousness and a firm individualist ego. In the communities surveyed in this chapter, both of these qualities seem to have been absent.

There remains one aspect of the problem that I have avoided. What is the social etiology of acedia? Why did it take its particular forms when it did? No satisfactory answer can be provided for this query. It may not be unreasonable, however, to offer at least some speculation. There is clear enough evidence for claiming that the emotions of frustration, boredom, and depression result from circumstances of confinement (Wemelsfelder 1989, 1985). That such circumstances manifest themselves in the anchoritic and cenobitic world is obvious, notwithstanding the fact that the confinement was freely chosen: it cannot have been easy, for example, to abandon Rutilius's island of Capraria. I have suggested, at the conclusion of chapter 1, that psychotic conditions such as melancholia appear most to flourish in eras and in social matrices where individual, private freedoms are encouraged but where public freedom is firmly, even vigorously curtailed. The same point, perhaps not unsurprisingly, could be made of acedia. As I have indicated, it occurs in social conditions that are based on and that highlight individual choice and freedom. Paradoxically the world so freely chosen by these anchorites was one of extreme constraint.

But such an explanation, though useful for the religious, is less so in the example of the lay victim. My suggestion in this case is based upon a not entirely subjective observation that, in the classical period, boredom and depression, the congeners of acedia, seem particularly prevalent in the post-Senecan lay world. The "confinement" of that world is less physical (although we ought not ignore the dramatic increase in urbanization within the period) than emotional (for the traditional elite in the early empire, options, traditional certainties, and even physical freedoms were severely curtailed). Perhaps it was so for the layperson in the late fourth and early fifth centuries. Was "confinement," of an emotional variety, ascendant in this era? The experience of Rome in 410 offers one corroboration. The rapid spread of Christianity itself may offer another. But whatever else we claim, social conditions within the cities must have replicated—physically, psychically, or in both respects—the sort of emotional trauma suffered by Basedow's victim of boning.

As a concluding example, I offer one not entirely frivolous instance of a communicable and dangerous affective condition—a hysteria no less than acedia or lovesickness or passive melancholia. This is known as calenture. It is defined as an irresistible impulse to jump from a ship into the sea. It afflicts sailors (rather than fishermen, e.g.) and can be accompanied by a mild fever and hallucinations (Illman 1991). Some have blamed calenture for the death by drowning off the Canary Islands in 1991 of the publishing tycoon Robert Maxwell. Illman's report (1991) states:

> sailors in the 18th and 19th centuries had to be restrained to guard against "the furious intensity of this delirious state," the French doctor J. P. Falret wrote in 1839. A vessel en route to Rio de Janeiro in 1829 was reported to have lost 100 of its crew of 600 by calenture.

More recent studies have claimed that "no fewer than 50 per cent of the persons interviewed [concerning calenture] had experienced an impulse to jump off the ship."

The resemblance, in the broadest outline, between acedia and this hysterical affliction of calenture should be apparent. Both are psychosomatic. Both are extremely dangerous and are caught and spread in a mode resembling that of viruses. Both are, potentially at least, life-threatening; and, again potentially, both may be accompanied by hallucinations. Both are transmitted, we can assume, by example and by anecdote. Both conditions seem to be triggered, however, by specific living conditions. In fact living conditions may offer the most striking parallel between the two infections. The "working" lives of sailors and anchorites are subject to a combination of constraint (the monastic cell may be likened to a ship on a voyage) and freedom (monks and sailors *choose* their association). It is difficult, furthermore, not to interpret calenture, as we have done for acedia, as an assertion of the self against the frustrations and constraints of a particularly circumscribed form of freedom. We can link calenture with boning (the topic with which I began this chapter), though less apparently, perhaps, than with acedia. What we may now be in a position to say, because of the apparent similarities between boning, calenture, and acedia, is that the efficacy of boning may be dependent on the same psychological pressures as acedia and calenture. We could take the speculation one step further. It may be that the efficient psychic transmission of affective states that is evident in acedia, boning, fugue, or calenture may account in part for the sudden—it appears to me—and apparent frequency (but not for the etiology) of depressive melancholia, lovesickness, and boredom in the first century of this era.

PART II

Remapping the Boundaries of the Self

After a harsh and unpleasing discourse of melancholy, which hath hitherto molested your patience and tired the author, give him leave . . . to recreate himself in this kind after his laborious studies . . .

—ROBERT BURTON, *The Anatomy of Melancholy*

5

The Myth of Suicide
Volitional Independence and Problematized Control in the First Century C.E.

Estragon: Let's hang ourselves immediately!
Vladimir: From a bough? *(They go towards the tree.)* I wouldn't trust it.
Estragon: We can always try.
Vladimir: Go ahead.
Estragon: After you.
Vladimir: No, you first.
Estragon: Why me?

—SAMUEL BECKETT, *Waiting for Godot*

"I'll neck myself, and you'll lose your job."

—TATZ (1997)

The presence of an affective disorder, especially manic-depressive illness, is the single most important risk factor for actual completed suicide.

—GOODWIN and JAMISON (1990, 7)

People do not kill themselves because they are depressed or lovesick or bored or in pain—that is, not unless they are characters in fiction. They kill themselves because they are ill, with manic depression, for example, or schizophrenia. Their deaths are usually swift, private, and accomplished without much warning. People also kill themselves when they are under the influence of drugs or alcohol. But that is a different matter. Judgment then has been irreparably impaired.

People who are depressed, lovesick, bored, or in pain often attempt to kill themselves.[1] The lack of success and the often quite public nature of their death attempts point to a motive that has little to do with an attempt to gain relief from pain. Such attempts speak to an implied audience. The suicide attempt in such cases represents a dialogue with friends, family, associates. The suicide attempt enacts a message for the audience that is not a plea for help or understanding. Rather, it represents a form of self-assertion, an insistence on the volitional integrity of the actor (look at Beckett's Estragon and Vladimir). The suicide attempt is, paradoxically, life-affirming. It insists on the primacy and importance—even the inviolability—of the self. It is an attempt to reformulate the self.[2] Perhaps that is why such actions so frequently fail.

It is for this reason that I assert that suicide is a myth. The very word *suicide* is a distraction. It masks the reality of genuine illness—manic depression, say, or schizophrenia. Or the word masks the paradoxical reality of this life-affirming assertion, this attempt at the reformulation of the self.

Late in the fifth century B.C.E., in the Sicilian city of Syracuse, Chaereas kicked his beautiful, young, and pregnant wife in the belly. He thought she had been unfaithful. He was wrong. He was wrong, too, when he thought that she had perished from the blow. Alive but comatose, poor Callirhoe was entombed in an expensive crypt by her grieving father, Hermocrates, the ruler of Syracuse. She awoke within that tomb. Luckily for her and the baby, she was rescued. But, alas, it was not at the hands of her beloved, intemperate, and jealous young husband, nor was it at the hands of her solicitous father. Instead she was saved by Theron, an unscrupulous leader of a pirate band, who was supplementing his living with tomb robbery. Theron and his crew rescued Callirhoe not out of kindness but in the expectation of extracting a large ransom from wealthy Hermocrates. They did so in vain, for as soon as guilt-stricken Chaereas and Hermocrates learned of Callirhoe's survival and abduction, Hermocrates furnished a trireme to be captained by Chaereas across the Ionian Sea in pursuit of Hermocrates' unfortunate daughter and the pirates.

Chaereas's departure was not easy. Chariton describes it for us in section 3.5 of his novel *Chaereas and Callirhoe* (whence I derive this little tale). Not only was a ship not immediately available, but it was the wrong time of year for sailing. Chaereas's difficulties did not end here. The eventual launching of the trireme was hindered by the clamor of a large crowd of Syracusans—"not only men, but also women and children"—and "there simultaneously occurred tears and prayers, moaning and encouragement, terror and courage, resignation and hope." Many of the Syracusans, in fear for their relatives on the ship, wanted the rescue voyage delayed, despite the obvious dangers for Callirhoe. Chief among these were Chaereas's parents.[3] Ariston, his old and sick father, begged that the launch be delayed until he had time to die "in Chaereas's arms." His mother, dreading familial solitude, asked to accompany the sailors. Let them throw her overboard if she proved a burden, she implored. She then bared her breasts and besought Chaereas to respect the solace they had offered him as a baby.

Faced with this alarming dilemma (should he give up the search for his Callirhoe or should he risk hurting his parents?), Chaereas struck upon a remarkable solution.[4] In full view of the crew and the assembled Syracusans, he threw himself from the war ship and into the sea, *apothanein thelôn* [wanting to die]. This was, by any standards, a remarkable and decisive solution to the dilemma. Chaereas's friends fished him from the water, his parents (no doubt embarrassed) clammed up, and the voyage took place. Chaereas's solution is more than remarkable. It is wholly typical of this romantic hero's response to bafflement and frustration (emotions that, as you might expect, usually relate to Callirhoe). Often in Chariton's novel, when Chaereas suffers marked frustration, he attempts suicide, or prays for death, or goes out of his way to court destruction. Two aspects of Chaereas's suicide attempt single themselves out. First, it reflects a startling helplessness. This is an emotion that troubles, in varying degrees, all of the major male characters of this Greek novel. Second, Chaereas's suicides are usually very public affairs. In this instance his attempt is performed in front of a gathering that engrossed the majority of Syracuse's citizens.

The suicide attempt is bogus, but the helplessness behind it is quite apparent. Chaereas, in this very famous passage, is faced with an intolerable situation in which strong counterclaims are made. Family loyalty demands that he stay in Syracuse. Amatory loyalty (and moral responsibility) demands that he leave Syracuse in search of Callirhoe. It is clear to any reader of the novel that Chaereas will go. But how, in this romantic context, can he do this with the full acquiescence of his parents and the other viewers? With comic brio Chaereas hits instinctively on his remarkable solution. By acting out a suicide attempt, he demonstrates to his parents that his emotional condition is of a far more serious nature than theirs. Chaereas is so devoted to Callirhoe, he attempts to demonstrate to them, that life without her would lead to his demise. This attitude is to be expected (and to be accepted) of real heroes. Chaereas, to gain parental approval, must demonstrate his bona fides. He does so in the time-honored tradition (which I have surveyed already in chapter 2) of matching disunion with death. It would be far too grandiose to claim that life without Callirhoe for Chaereas would lead to the disintegration of his social personality. But, according to the traditions of love literature, something of this order is likely. If Chaereas is to affirm the integrity of his social self, he must resolve the dilemma by, as it were, buying off his parents. The theatrical, but ultimately bogus, suicide attempt does just this. The phony nature of Chaereas's dive, however, does nothing to diminish the veracity of the helplessness and bafflement that to that point he had suffered. But the point remains. Chaereas's suicide attempt is a life-affirming, if risky, action. It affirms and gains public support for his intention. To put it in a grandiose way: it offers a means for the shoring up, even the reconstruction, of the social personality that was under threat from the irreconcilable claims of parents and Callirhoe.

Perhaps real-life suicide attempts are always theatrical. By that I mean that perhaps they always presuppose an audience, even if that audience is not at hand. (The note, the prospect of postmortem discovery, and the announcement of the death to the near and dear are all based on the expectation of an audience, however eventual. Suicides rarely arrange their deaths in such a manner that their bodies simply disappear.) But in real life, as writers such as Jamison (1999, 200; cf. Kraepelin 1921, 78) demonstrate, suicide, when successful, comes swiftly, unexpectedly, and in solitude. It is, furthermore, more likely to be the product of mental illness (manic-depressive illness or schizophrenia) than of anything else. Chaereas, I am saying, does not fit the bill. Frustrated love seldom leads to successful suicide, except perhaps in poetry or the novel. If it does in real life, then the amatory complications mask or are driven by psychosis.

In this chapter I will argue that we witness in Chariton's suicides not so much the reflex reactions of frustrated lovers as we do the reflections of a literary experience of helplessness and passivity. At first sight these suicides (and their apparent helplessness) may seem to match well those various passive affectivities shown, in the preceding and following discussions, to have become prominent in the first century of our era: boredom, depression, depressive lovesickness, interiority, and an oppressing sense of the dominating linearity of time itself. Things are not as simple as this. Suicide provokes interest beyond this totally predictable aspect of mere helplessness and passivity. Most of the suicides that will be cataloged in this chapter and, indeed, most of the discussions of suicide to which I will refer are theatrical (Griffin 1976, 65; Leigh 1997) and unsuccessful.[5] Here suicide is an action to be performed either in front of others or with an expectation of their subsequent viewing and reaction. Often the audience will rescue the sufferer from his or her intended action. We have just observed this in Chaereas's throwing himself from the trireme in front of the assembled Syracusan population. Without an audience, Chaereas's suicide would have no meaning. My point is that while the suicide participant may appear to be driven by helplessness, the suicide itself, as it is being discussed, formulated, and occasionally acted upon, is above all an act of self-affirmation. It affirms the autonomy of the self. It represents an action that, in its end, displays qualities that are the direct opposite of passivity.[6] Suicide therefore becomes a means for the reconstruction and recalibrating of the self and of the social personality, when this comes under threat.[7] It is of profound relevance to this claim that modern literature suggests that depressives, those sad and passive playthings of fate, do not have a high representation among successful or attempted suicides.

Let us return to Chariton and examine in more detail the numerous suicides and suicide attempts within *Chaereas and Callirhoe.* There are more than twenty suicide attempts within this novel (and only one that is successful, at 7.5.14).[8] Chariton's heroes attempt suicide for a variety of reasons. They can be driven apparently by love, unexpected or shocking news, jealousy, guilt, grief, or despair. They can even be motivated by a sense of honor. These suicides regularly betray the registers of frustration, bafflement, passivity, and helplessness. But the common theme in all of them is a self-display and an affirmation of the self.

Let us look at a few typical instances. These concern love. Chaereas, Dionysius, Mithridates, and Artaxerxes endure what might best be described as frustrated love. In the instances of Chaereas and Dionysius, it can make them suicidal. In the instances of Mithridates and Artaxerxes, it does not lead to attempted suicide, but it does cause them to exhibit symptoms of a mental state that can in this novel be associated with either death or suicide.[9] Suicide, whether love is involved or not, often acts as a constituent within an almost formulaic chain of events. If it is lovesickness with which we are dealing, then we may expect the sufferer to register an initially overpowering emotion that will induce speechlessness (the hero becomes *achanês* or *aphthônos*) and cause the person to fall to the ground in a black swoon.[10] Soon they are marked by the burning wound of love.[11] Subsequent reactions may involve depression, a sense of mourning, further swooning followed by a deathlike trance, blushing, silence, insomnia, weeping, and even the sweats.[12] If love remains unconsummated the victim will either sink into a wasting illness or attempt suicide.[13] (Dionysius and Chaereas try to kill themselves by starvation. Chaereas contemplates hanging himself and cutting his throat.) But it is not just love that can cause this lugubrious chain of events. The pattern may be replicated if lovesickness's congener, jealousy, is involved.[14] When Chaereas is falsely informed of Callirhoe's unfaithfulness, he is initially speechless, just as if he were love-struck. Then he becomes depressed, swoons, exhibits a state resembling mourning, and weeps. Chaereas even contemplates suicide, a resolution that is displaced by his sense of anger (1.4.5–8). It is anger that causes him to assault Callirhoe (1.4.10). Discrete elements of this suicidal schema may be found elsewhere, although they do not culminate in suicide, anorexia, or violence. Unexpected events or shocking news may provoke in Chaereas, Dionysius, or Mithridates the very emotions that resemble those attributed to the lovers Chaereas and Callirhoe when they first caught sight of one another. So it is that unexpected events or shocking news causes our heroes to fall, to experience a black swoon and depression, or to exhibit a trancelike state that resembles death (3.1.3 offers a very good example: "At this unexpected news Dionysius was paralyzed; a mist covered his eyes and, completely losing consciousness, he looked just like a dead man").[15] Dionysius's condition resembles, in its symptoms, a number of those that we have witnessed previously. I would here single out again Basedow's descriptions of boning (discussed at the beginning of chapter 4). Figure 5 is a photograph that Basedow claims represents an Australian Aboriginal who has just been "boned." Could we speculate that this is what Dionysus (or Stagirius or the Zuni girl or Sappho or any one of a number of others) might have looked like soon after the attack?

But to return to the schema that I have suggested is exemplified by Dionysius: attempted suicide, or at least a wish for suicide, may appear without these schematic accoutrements, notably in the instances of guilt, grief, or despair. Very occasionally suicide may actually seem to be the right thing to do. This is usually the case when it is Callirhoe who is tempted.

Suicide, comfortably playing a smaller part in a larger affective chain of events, seems, on the surface of things, to mirror the schema that I have noted in earlier chapters in the discussions of boredom and depression. Let us look back then to the constellation of symptoms exhibited by boredom and depression (and forward to the way time was registered) and attempt to see how these are linked to suicide. We have already observed that ancient authors perceive a continuum between melancholy and boredom and suicide. This is no less true for Chariton than it is for Seneca. Do the stages of development that these states exhibit reflect the schema into which I have suggested that suicide may fall? In Chariton, depression and even boredom can be confused with the contributory factors leading to suicide or its partner anorexia. Leisure, so often linked with grievous boredom and melancholia, is behind the Great King of Persia's infatuation with Callirhoe. Artaxerxes' desire, Chariton tells us, is the product of his idleness (his *argia;* see 6.9.4).[16] The term Chariton uses for idleness is easily to be associated with boredom. Artaxerxes' subsequent symptoms—excessive silence (always to be associated with depression), insomnia, weeping, and hints of an attitude resembling that of a person who is mourning—match those

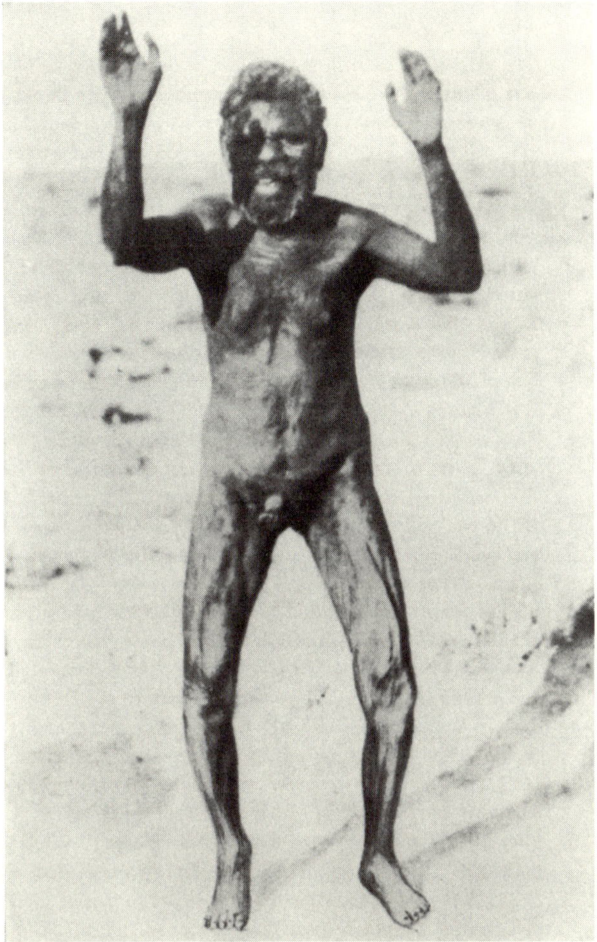

FIG. 5. Basedow's photograph of a victim of "boning" (ca. 1890s). (Reprinted from Herbert Basedow, *The Australian Aboriginal* [reprint, Adelaide: F. W. Preece and Sons, 1925], 193.)

symptoms that we have noted earlier of sufferers especially of melancholia. Mithridates offers us another useful parallel. Significantly he is described in 4.2.8 of Chariton's novel by the present participle *aluôn*. Best translated here as "depressed," that word in its nominal form, *alus*, is the Greek word for boredom and, sometimes, depression.[17] The satrap's silences and weeping do nothing to allay our suspicions that the template upon which his symptoms have been outlined is as applicable to one suffering depression as to one on track for suicide. Perhaps I am here belaboring the obvious, for the conceptual link

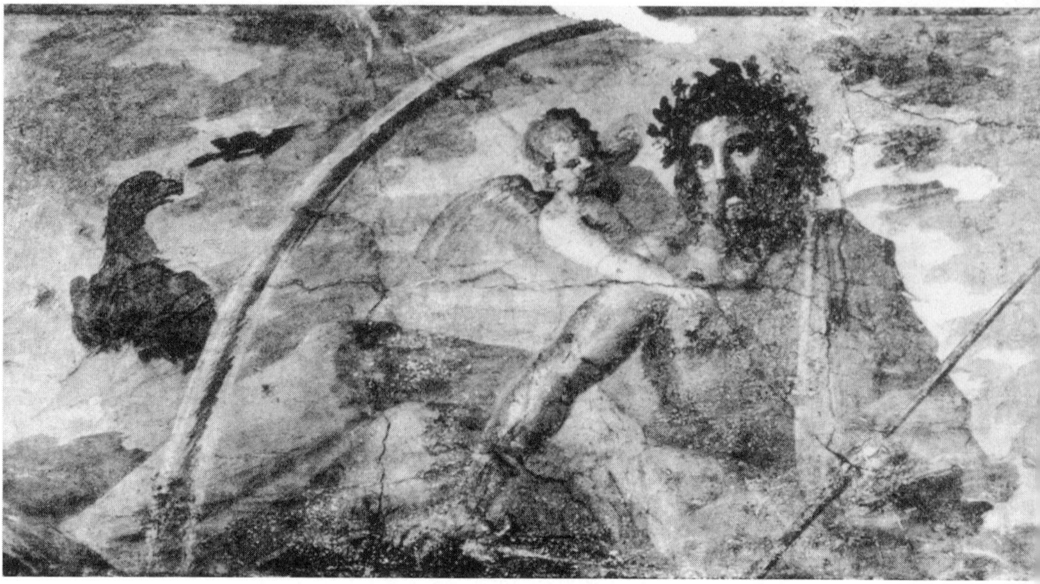

FIG. 6. "Zeus malinconico" (first century C.E.).
(Courtesy of Museo Nazionale di Napoli.)

between boredom, depression, and suicide is an easy one. Yet the similarity of the terms used to describe them is provoking.

A further illustration of this simple point relates to the Greek term *achlus*. The word may designate the black swoon that afflicts, so often and under such different circumstances, Chaereas, Callirhoe, and Dionysius.[18] It is a term often used of those who are love-struck (see Archilochus 112.2; Hunter 1989, 175). But it is also one to be linked, through the Homeric contexts in which Chariton embeds it, to mourning, a preeminently depressive condition. Elsewhere I have argued that it may even act as a synonym, in Apollonius of Rhodes's epic at any rate, for depression itself (Toohey 1992a). This curious conceptual congruity could be pursued to more obvious lengths. We have seen in earlier chapters, for example, how Seneca links boredom with suicide, how depression could lead to self-destruction, and how lovesickness, from which all of the main players of Chariton's *Chaereas and Callirhoe* periodically suffer, could easily be confused in medical circles with melancholia.

But, as I have stated, all of this is on the surface of things. Suicide need not follow the chain of symptoms that I have just described. To demonstrate this, I would like to draw attention back to chapter 2 and to Sappho's *Phainetai moi* ode (31 Campbell). In that poem, we have a charting of the physical reactions of the poem's speaker as she watches another woman and man seated together.

The sight of that other woman speaking and laughing with this man induces extreme emotional—presumably erotic—symptoms: speechlessness (v. 9), a burning sensation on the skin (vv. 9–10), loss of vision (v. 11), ringing in the ears (vv. 11–12), cold sweat (v. 13), trembling (vv. 13–14), pallor (vv. 14–15), and a near-death experience (vv. 15–16). These are symptoms that, as we have just seen (in chapter 4 in the case of boning), are always indicative of extreme psychological frustration. They become, for obvious physiological reasons, canonical in the description of frustrated love.[19] But, and this is my point, what is missing is suicide. Sappho suffers considerably, but no mention is made of death or of nooses. Another striking parallel (but not connected to love) was provided for us in Basedow's description of boning (quoted at the beginning of chapter 4). The symptoms experienced by the victim of boning were astonishment, blanched cheeks, glassy eyes, a distorted facial expression, voicelessness, spasms, swooning and collapsing to the ground; then sickening, fretting, the rejection of food and community dealings; and finally imminent death. The symptoms here match very closely those of Sappho or of Chariton's benighted heroes. Basedow's Australian Aboriginal does not, however, take his own life. Death results, if not quite from wasting, at least from a rapid physiological breakdown.[20] The symptoms highlighted by Chariton, by Sappho, and, remarkably, by Basedow exhibit powerful similarities and help us place the reactions that may precede suicide in Chariton's romance within a larger discursive—and physiological—context. This instructive parallel tells us, however, that these symptoms do not invariably lead to suicide. That is a choice made by Chariton for his characters.

An instructive example of how it is that suicide, or attempted suicide, may supervene on amatory frustration in Chariton's novel is provided at that point where Dionysius decides that he can tolerate his lovesickness for Callirhoe no longer (3.1.1–3) (Loeb translation).

> Frustrated in his love for Callirhoe, Dionysius could endure no longer: he had resolved on suicide by starvation and was drawing up his will with directions for his burial. In it he begged Callirhoe to visit him even if dead. But Plangon was seeking an interview with her master and had been turned away by his attendant, whose orders were to admit no one. Dionysius heard them arguing at the door and asked who was making the uproar. When the attendant told him that it was Plangon, he replied, "This is a bad time for her to come," having no further desire to see anyone who would remind him of his passion, "but call her in anyway!" So she opened the door and said, "Sir, why are you breaking your heart as though all were lost? Callirhoe invites you to marry her. Put on your best clothes, offer sacrifice, and welcome the bride you love!"

As you can see, Dionysius is determined to do himself in. But notice how public an affair his starvation is to be. He is probably on his own, or perhaps in the company of a secretary (will making is no solitary task), but his actions are taking place in the midst of a large and presumably busy palace. His attendant assists. Plangon, to judge from her initial comments, seems to understand what Dionysius is doing. Notice, too, that when Plangon arrives, Dionysius makes little attempt to turn her away, despite the proximity of death. Two conclusions concerning the nature of this suicide are possible. First, one could surmise that the presence of these people is indicative of Dionysius's lack of desire actually to carry his intention through. Perhaps he hopes one of them will dissuade him. The second point is that this audience is admitted to provide a public affirmation of Dionysius's intended action. Dionysius wants them present to see him, to affirm and witness his decisiveness, his choice, and his plight—to commend, that is, his individuality and his selfhood. I think that the same point could be made of his calm attention to the details of his funeral. Real despair is a private matter. His actions actually affirm his sense of individuality. Dionysius's actions seem stage-managed.[21] I have made exactly the same point concerning Chaereas's jumping into the sea. By attempting suicide, Chaereas denies publicly the rights over him of the claims of Callirhoe and his parents. By attempting suicide in such an extravagant manner, he underscores what we might call his volitional independence.

Were we to check through the remainder of the suicides in Chariton's *Chaereas and Callirhoe*, we would find that in most cases (except perhaps when Callirhoe contemplates suicide at 2.11.3–4 and 3.10.4), we are dealing with occasions that match, in their self-display, these two passages.[22] The suicide is usually stopped because there are friends nearby to catch the performance. Chaereas always has such an audience handy in the person of his shadowy friend Polycharmus. (How often do we watch the patient Polycharmus rescue his friend?) Despite the exuberant theatricality of all of these suicide attempts and despite their paradoxical affirmation of the victims' selfhood, they are sorry affairs. Most readers, on first encountering Chariton, find Chaereas a mildly repellent character. This is not just because of the brutal kick that he delivers to Callirhoe. It is because of his passivity, his helplessness, and his too frequent attempts at self-destruction. He is, as David Konstan dubs him, a hapless hero. New readers to this novel usually feel the same way about Dionysius and even the cagey Mithridates. But I think that part of the usual distaste felt for these characters may relate to their enthusiasm for suicide. It seems, in their cases, to be such a phony remedy, one designed not as a desperate response to a desperate and debilitating emotion but as a means for shoring up a battered sense of self.

Before continuing with other (Roman) authors, I would like to reemphasize some of my main points. Because I have found that many people find these repugnant, they need all the more stress and clarification. My first point is that as far as Chariton is concerned, there is no such thing as suicide. Rather than providing a route to oblivion, an escape from grief through death, these apparent suicides aim paradoxically to affirm the will to life, the volitional independence of these characters. Suicide, that is, offers through its public display a means for guaranteeing psychic integrity. My second point is that the melancholia, ennui, boredom, anorexia, and lovesickness that seems to appear willy-nilly across the Mediterranean in this century does condition the circumstances in which these suicides are represented. The general emphasis on suicide in an author like Chariton reflects this tendency. At the same time, however, it offers an alternative or solution to these tendencies. Chariton's suicides aim to remedy the effects of these lugubrious conditions. My third point relates to Rome (to which I will shortly turn): Roman literary suicides, though far more theatrical, are driven by the same circumstances as are the Greek ones. A final point is that these suicide attempts, because they often resolve the public claims of an acute dilemma, are all about control. They often dramatize an actor's desire to assert control over his or her own circumstance, when faced with others' desires to do just that to him or her. Perhaps the best way to put this is to use that faddish, but useful, verb *problematized:* control, in these instances, has been problematized.

The famous black-figure depiction on the pot by the Attic potter Exekias in figure 7 captures the Homeric Ajax just as he is on the point of committing suicide (I have recounted the details of his story in chapter 1). The painting dates to ca. 530 B.C.E. It predates Sophocles' play entitled *Ajax* by approximately ninety years. Exekias's alarming portrait conjures an image of suicide that is completely at odds with that evoked within Chariton's novel. Above all, in Exekias's version the hero is alone. Ajax is drawn at a distance from his ship (just visible to the right). His only onlooker, as is pointed out by Shapiro (1994, 152), is the "ghostly" image of Ajax's helmet "propped on the big Boeotian shield" (to the right of the picture). His solitude is enhanced by his vulnerability. He crouches forward, cowed almost, completely naked and by a barren shore. This shoreline seems to reflect his inner state in much the same way as has been said of the palm tree, drooping in melancholy sympathy for the hero (Hurwit 1982). Anxiety lines are etched on Ajax's forehead. His sword—the very weapon that the hero should wield against his enemies—is set up threateningly

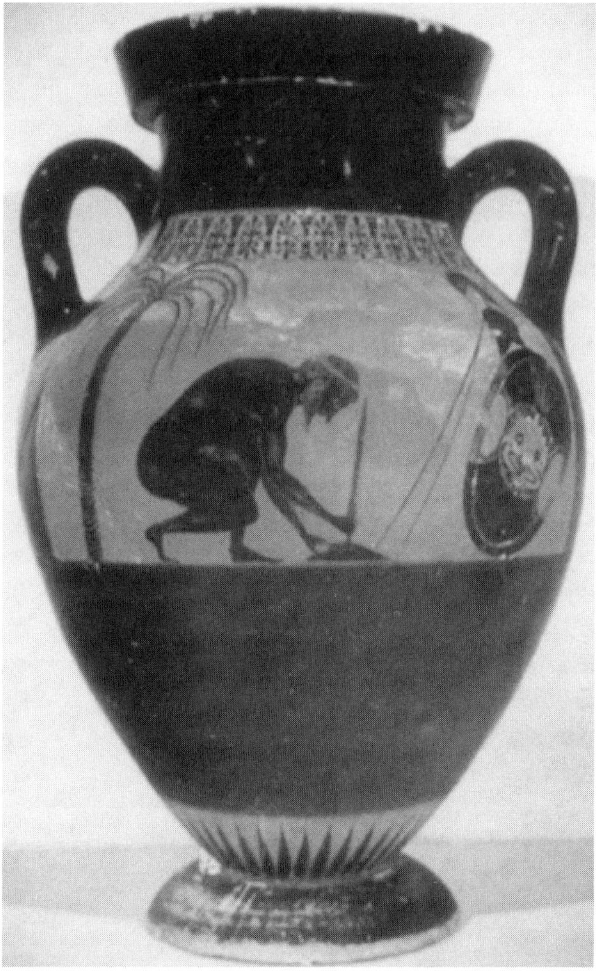

FIG. 7. Exekias, "The Suicide of Ajax" (ca. 530 B.C.E.). (Courtesy of Chateau-Musée, Boulogne-sur-Mer.)

near his head. Soon Ajax will cast himself belly-first onto this weapon.[23] The utter solitude is also emphasized by Sophocles in his version. In the *Ajax*, Sophocles has his protagonist trick his companions into allowing him to seek solitude for his suicide. There is no theatricality or self-display in this death. It is swiftly realized, completely private, and accomplished with no warning. There is in Ajax's death something that is not just pathetic but disgraceful, even demeaning. How could a great warrior sink this low, become so vulnerable, be so swayed by emotion?

Ajax was probably mentally ill. Sophocles skews the picture (see my discussion in chapter 1) by stressing the solitary heroism of the hero and his resistance to the new sophistical social values of Odysseus. So, too, does the *Problema* (see my discussion of this in chapter 1). The illness behind the play, behind the painting, behind the *Problema*—the life situation that these exploit—is likely what Collinge recognized as manic depression, or perhaps it is what now might be termed schizoaffective. This is because of Ajax's delusions. The successful rate of suicide among such sufferers is alarmingly high. Such suicides are seldom carried out in the theatrical mode of Chariton's melancholy heroes. Depressives like Chaereas seldom achieve successful self-immolation.[24]

I have dwelt on Ajax's death to reemphasize the points made at the outset of this chapter, but within a context of ancient literature. People killed themselves in ancient life, just as they do now, because they are mentally ill, not because they are depressed, lovesick, bored, or in pain. The valueless notion of suicide masks other problems. Successful suicides are not theatrical, unless they are enforced. It will not do to say, of Dionysus for example, that privacy was nearly impossible in the ancient or premodern worlds. In day-to-day life this was undoubtedly the case. (It is not easily had in the modern world either, for that matter.) But Ajax found it, despite his slaves. No doubt many others did too when the mind-forged manacles demanded it.

Encolpius is the starting point for Rome. He is a character in Petronius's *Satyricon*. Petronius's narrative, which, with a little chronological liberality, may be dated to approximately the same period as that of *Chaereas and Callirhoe*, has as one of its intentions the parody of the Greek novel, of which Chariton's novel is one of the few complete surviving examples. The *Satyricon* inverts many of the habitual circumstances of the Greek novel: for wellborn Greek heterosexual lovers, it substitutes down-at-the-heel Roman homosexuals; for faithfulness, it substitutes promiscuity; for an upper-class milieu, it substitutes a low-life one. In fact the *Satyricon* is replete with the sorts of event that the Greek novel eschews: murder, blasphemy, child sex, cannibalism, gluttony, and bad taste on an extravagant scale. One of Petronius's more trenchant parodies of the Greek novel—and it is hard not to think that this is a parody of Chariton in particular—is a very amusing failed suicide that upends all of the apparent seriousness of Chariton's many attempts. One would like to see Petronius's target here as Chariton's novel, with its noteworthy overrepresentation of suicide. What is so interesting about Petronius's parody is that it preserves the key characteristics of Chariton's suicides, their self-display and the self-affirmation of those who attempt the act. In the scene that I quote from shortly, Encolpius, the protagonist of the *Satyricon,* seems to be about to have his boy lover, Giton, abducted. Eumolpus, a seedy, out-of-work academic poet, has just declared his infatuation to Giton in front of Encolpius, whose understandable anger caused Giton discreetly to leave their doss-house bedroom on the pretext of looking for some water. Shortly afterward, Eumolpus slipped from the room to find Giton, but not without locking Encolpius inside. The prospect of losing Giton (it has happened before) causes Petronius's protagonist to attempt suicide. The prospect of losing Encolpius and having to take Eumolpus for a lover, Giton pretends (his suicide attempt is a bogus one), causes in him the same emotions. Here, at any rate, is the core of the scene in which we watch Encolpius's attempt to do away with himself (*Satyricon* 94.23) (Penguin translation).

> Shut up inside like that, I decided to finish everything by hanging myself. I had already put the bed frame against the wall tied a belt to it and was inserting my neck in the noose when the door was unlocked and Eumolpus came in with Giton and in a race against death brought me back to life. In his grief Giton, unlike Eumolpus, went mad with rage; he raised a great outcry and, pushing me with both hands precipitated me on top of the bed.
>
> "You're wrong, Encolpius," he said, "if you think by any possible chance you can die before me. I tried first: I looked for a sword in Ascyltus' rooms. If I had not found you, I was going to throw myself to my death. To make you realize death isn't far away if you look for it, see in your turn what you wanted me to see."
>
> With this he snatched a razor from Eumolpus' hired servant and slashing his throat once and then twice collapsed at our feet.
>
> Thunderstruck, I let out a cry and following his collapsing body to the floor, I looked for a way to die with the same instrument. But Giton showed not the slightest suspicion of a wound nor could I feel any pain myself. It was a practice razor and blunted for the purpose: to give apprentices courage, it had a sheath fitted round it. This was the reason why the servant had not panicked at his snatching the razor and why Eumolpus had not intervened in this fake death scene.

The bathetic inversions (they are also parodic—Encolpius's excessive second suicide attempt demonstrates this) should be apparent. The love triangle is homosexual for a start. Encolpius attempts (somehow or another) suicide from, of all places, a bed frame. Giton, the catamite, tries to upstage his lover's suicide. His attempt, however, is performed with a harmless instrument. (Did Giton realize that the razor was blunt? The scene seems to suggest that this is the case.) As if one suicide attempt were not enough, Encolpius then repeats the action. (The surfeit undermines credibility.) Encolpius's rival, Eumolpus, makes no attempt to intervene. Above all, both suicide attempts seem to have been designed for show rather than for effect.

Public show, rather than private grief, drives both death attempts. Both aim to resolve a dilemma. Both assert, in the manner of Chariton's suicides, volitional independence. Giton's is the more obvious. His attempt is a very public affair—it is performed in front of Encolpius, Eumolpus, and the hired servant. Giton's dilemma is to be caught in between the demands of the two lovers. The suicide attempt reasserts his devotion to Encolpius and independence of Eumolpus. Its phoniness, however, demonstrates his recognition of Eumolpus's claims. The suicide attempt also asserts the youth's volitional independence. Giton seems to know that it will fail (as must Chaereas's when he jumps into the sea). But the attempt aims to distance his lovers and to assert his own control.

Encolpius's despair, on seeming to lose Giton, is such that he initially tries that most despised of suicide modes, hanging. (The scene has a close parallel in *Chaereas and Callirhoe* 5.10.6 ff., where Chaereas, despairing of ever regaining Callirhoe, "was seized with an inconsolable grief" and, "left alone, . . . fastened a noose." After a lengthy soliloquy, Chaereas "kissed the noose" and began to place it around his neck. Polycharmus arrived just in time and "forcibly restrained his frantic struggles.")[25] Before his second attempt, Encolpius seems (just like Chaereas) to swoon from emotional excess (he is "thunderstruck").[26] How should we understand Encolpius's suicide? The first attempt, ostensibly driven by grief, is as self-serving as are the sad Aboriginal suicides alluded to in the second epigraph prefixing this chapter. Helpless and frustrated Encolpius may be, but his death attempt is designed in part to punish Giton and Eumolpus (as it were: "I'll neck myself, and you'll lose your job") and paradoxically to assert his volitional independence. Encolpius has no audience now, but he soon will have. The audience is implied. The second attempt—out of grief or frustration?—makes the same point again to Eumolpus.

Petronius makes mockery of the whole scene by having his attempted suicide performed with a blunt razor, then leaving the gullible Encolpius to replicate the action, no doubt much to his subsequent embarrassment. Petronius's parody is built upon faithlessness, Chariton's on faithfulness. Petronius's psychologically realistic vignette substitutes amoral bathos for romantic pathos. But note that in this instance from Petronius, suicide is flamboyant and, as in Chariton, a theatrical event. Giton, in particular, requires an audience for his charade, a charade that is designed mockingly to demonstrate his personal independence. Giton renders problematic the issue of control.

It is chilling when literary representations prefigure events within an author's life. Petronius's own suicide attempt was far more successful and far more spectacular than that of his fiction Encolpius. What makes his death so alarmingly relevant to the present discussion is that it preserves, as it is reported by Tacitus (*Annals* 17–20), the parodic element of our *Satyricon* passage while remaining the most public of performances. Petronius, formerly favorite of the emperor Nero, had aroused the enmity of the emperor's confidant, Tigellinus. He connived at Petronius's death by accusing him of being an intimate of Scaevinus, who had been implicated in plotting against Nero. Petronius, facing certain death, determined to forestall the emperor by taking his own life.[27] It was the manner of his death that was so extraordinary. Here is Tacitus's description (*Annals* 16.19).[28]

> The emperor at this time happened to be on a visit to Campania. Petronius got as far as Cumae and was prevented from going any further. He refused to prolong the suspense that hope or fear involved. Not that he was hasty in taking leave of life. On the contrary, he opened his veins and then, as the fancy took him, he bound them up or reopened them. Meanwhile he talked with his friends, but not on serious topics or anything calculated to win admiration for his Stoicism. He listened to their contributions—not discussions about the immortality of the soul or the views of the philosophers, but simply gay songs and light verse. He dealt out rewards to some of his slaves and floggings to others. He had a good dinner served and slept for a while, so that his death, though forced upon him, should appear natural. Even in the codicils to his will, he refused to put down any of the deathbed flatteries for Nero or for Tigellinus or any of the other courtiers. Instead he wrote out a full description of the emperor's vicious activities, prefaced with the names of his male and female partners and specifying what novel forms his lust had taken. This document he sent under seal to Nero. Then he broke his signet ring in case it should be used later to endanger others.

The calculated indifference to death in this suicide scene appears to have two targets. First, there is the emperor himself: Petronius's apparent fearlessness seems designed to thwart Nero's taste for cruelty and for instilling fear into his subjects. Second, Petronius's death (at least as Tacitus tells it) seems to have been stage-managed to parody the pretensions of the Stoic deaths of men like Seneca and, before him, Cato the Younger. Petronius's death, as Griffin suggests (1976, 199), is designed to exemplify a dislike for the "element of self-glorification in the long philosophical discourse and the imitation of Socrates and Cato." Griffin goes on to point out:

> There developed the anti-philosophical tradition of death with panache. Here the fearlessness and rationality were shown by attention, not merely to ordinary matters like Seneca's will, but to the positively trivial. So Tacitus shows us Claudius' victim Valerius Asiaticus checking the location of his funeral pyre before opening his veins to ensure that the flames would not damage his trees (*Ann.* 11.3). But his triumph in this style is the death of Petronius, carried out on Nero's order and clearly regarded by victim and writer as the answer to the *iactatio* [the vaunt] of people like Seneca (*Ann.* 16.19).

There is an unexpected similarity between Chaereas's leap into the sea in *Chaereas and Callirhoe* 3.5 (and indeed most of Chariton's suicides) and Petronius's leisurely death. Chaereas was caught in a dilemma, between the demands of his parents and those toward Callirhoe. By his theatrical leap he declared publicly his independence of both. He asserted, as I have been suggesting, his selfhood. Petronius's dilemma, I suppose, consisted in the conflict between demonstrating intellectual distance between himself and what he seems to have seen as the pomposity and falseness of the philosophical suicide, on the one hand, and the need to display indifference to Nero's arbitrary exercise of power, on the other. His solution (a feigned indifference to the whole process of death), which we have just witnessed, neatly solves the dilemma, as Chaereas's leap solved his. At the same time, Petronius's suicide produces, in its utter, if low-key, self-display, a profound affirmation of individuality and of what I have termed volitional control.

The comparison with Chaereas deserves emphasis. The differences between Chaereas and Petronius are marked. For Chaereas the "why" of suicide is important. For Petronius the "how" is what is important. But of equal significance is the presence and absence of helplessness and frustration. Chaereas's literary context is frequently a melancholic one. Petronius's is not. Petronius's aristocratic Roman world is habitually built upon self-display. Chaereas's bourgeois one is built on no such show. Chaereas's death may be fiction, and Petronius's may have been historical fiction,[29] yet the posture that both produce is of a kind. Both use the display involved in suicide as a means for reformulating or reaffirming the volitional power of the social self.

One final point concerning Petronius's death needs to be made. It is Tacitus who tells us the story, not a coroner. There can be no doubt that he shapes and adds nuance to this in accordance with his own particular response to suicide. This response will be as much the product of his own ear (forty years subsequent to Chariton and Petronius) as it will be of his psychology and conscious beliefs and, especially, of the generic and the discursive traditions shaping his writing. I stress this point (and will repeatedly come back to it) because it makes more clear how the description of Petronius's death provides further evidence for the trends noted in *Chaereas and Callirhoe* and in the *Satyricon*. (We are not muddling real life with fiction in this instance—or in the instances to follow.)

At any rate, the type of modish, Stoic suicide that Petronius seems to have targeted (or that Tacitus targeted) through his own death is exemplified in the famous *mors voluntaria* of Seneca.[30] Tacitus's description of this ought to make clear precisely that at which Petronius had taken aim. Following is Tacitus's description (*Annals* 15.61–64, epitomized by Griffin [1976, 65]; this description will be subject to the same constraints, discursive and other, as the last one). Seneca has just denied the charge of plotting against the emperor. (The "republican" poet had conspired against Nero with a group gathered about Calpurnius Piso. The conspirators intended to assassinate Nero and to appoint a new emperor. The plot backfired. Among others, Lucan and his uncle Gallio, were condemned to death. Lucan's father, Mela, also perished in the cross fire.) Tacitus reports that Nero subsequently questioned the praetorian officer who had delivered this edict to Seneca, asking "whether Seneca was meditating suicide." Tacitus continues:

> Upon this the tribune asserted that he saw no signs of fear and perceived no sadness in Seneca's words or looks. He was ordered to go back and announce the death sentence . . . Seneca, quite unmoved, asked for tablets on which to inscribe his will. When the centurion refused his request, he turned to his friends, protesting that, as he was forbidden to reward them, he bequeathed to them the only thing he still possessed, yet the finest of them all—the pattern of his life . . . Then he rebuked them for their tears, asking "where had their philosophy gone?"

At this point Tacitus goes on to narrate how Seneca and his wife severed their veins (and how Seneca had attempted and failed to dissuade his wife from imitating him).[31]

> Even at this last moment Seneca's eloquence did not fail him; he summoned his secretaries and dictated much to them, which, as it has been published for all readers in his own words, I forbear to paraphrase.

Griffin (1976, 65) suggests it is probable that what Seneca dictated was likely to have been philosophical, "perhaps about the immortality of the soul." She believes that this can be "inferred from the suicide of Thrasea Paetus, in the next year." This was an imitation of Seneca's "in several respects." But let us return to Tacitus.

> Seneca, meantime, as the tedious process of death lingered on, begged his doctor to produce a poison which he had previously procured for himself, the same drug taken by those condemned by public sentence of the people of Athens (i.e., hemlock). It was brought to him and he drank, but in vain, for his limbs were cold and impervious to the poison . . . At last he entered a bath of warm water, from which he sprinkled the nearest slaves, saying, "I offer this liquid as libation to Jupiter Liberator." He was then carried into a vapor-bath, where he suffocated.

The "key themes" that seem to be displayed by Seneca's suicide are easily isolated (cf. Griffin 1976). Seneca's death is above all calm, brave, and resolute. He does not waver in his intent, nor will he allow his friends to. The death is also philosophical, both in that it uses philosophical models, above all that of Socrates, and in that philosophical discussion seems to have been an important part of the proceedings. Seneca's death is a reaction to limited options. But in choosing to die according to a pattern selected by himself, Seneca, as Tacitus depicts him, has a volitional triumph of a sort—though it could hardly compare to that of Chaereas when he leaps off the trireme, for Chaereas was under no compunction to die. Tacitus's Seneca exhibits a degree of control over the manner of his fate, therefore, but his position is an utterly helpless one. Seneca's mode of death offers a solution to his dilemma—the necessity of death without pandering to the emperor's cruel willfulness. In keeping with this notion of display of will and, in the face of crushing tyranny, a display of selfhood, Seneca's death is carried out in public, in the most theatrical of manners. I suppose that Tacitus's depiction of Seneca's death is an admirable one. It has certainly been much admired.

Seneca's death, contrived philosophically according to Tacitus's romantic description, contains, in many ways, the advice on suicide and the idealized portraits of suicide that are scattered throughout his writings. Of suicide Seneca believed, as did most Stoics, that "provided the *moment* and the *reason* were right . . . [when according to nature life was no longer possible] . . . a man was justified in making a rational departure from life" (Griffin 1976, 72).[32] Diogenes Laertius (7.130) states, and Seneca does not seem greatly to disagree (Summers 1952, 253), that "the wise man will make a rational exit from life either on behalf of his country or for the sake of his friends or if he suffers intolerable pain or mutilation or incurable disease." Seneca vividly suggested that the "body is a guest house and that we must depart as soon as we find we are a burden on our host" (*Epistles* 120.14). Why prolong life unnecessarily (*Epistles* 4.4)? Intolerable hardship can render suicide a freedom (*De ira* 3.15.4). If the future looks doubtful, then the issue is not "of dying sooner or later but of dying well or ill" (*Epistles* 70.5). In Seneca's eyes one may choose an "easy, rather than a hard, death" provided, naturally, that an easy death does not compromise one's Stoic morality. This is not to say that Seneca offered a carte blanche for suicide. He disapproves of the contemporary fad for death and suicide—evident in a contemporary *libido moriendi* [lust for dying] (*Epistles* 24.5)—which seems to have been driven by a disgust or weariness or boredom with life (an *odium* or *fastidium vitae: Epistles* 3.5, 77.6; *De tranquillitate animi* 2.14–15). Seneca also disapproves of men such as the gourmand Apicius, who committed suicide rather than face a life without good cooking (*Ad Helviam* 10.8.11). Elsewhere he shows a marked disapproval of suicide when it is motivated by desperation (as was Jocasta's at *Oedipus* 1024–39 or Hercules' at *Hercules furens* 1202 ff.) or by a desire for revenge (as was Phaedra's at *Phaedra* 1159–1200).

If Seneca's death has its philosophical underpinning in such writings as *Epistles* 70 and 77 (cf. *Phoenissae* 63–215), it has its dramatic counterpart in the notable Stoic suicide of Hercules in the *Hercules Oetaeus.* In this play, Hercules, accidentally poisoned by a cloak meant by his wife, Deianira, as a love charm, chooses to immolate himself on a pyre built on Mt. Oeta. He sees this fiery suicide both as a release from the intolerable pain caused by the poison and as a fulfilment of the will of Jupiter that had foreordained this death. Philoctetes, in a description that would have made any informed Stoic envious, depicts Hercules' last moments on the pyre in this manner (*Hercules Oetaeus* 1683–90):

> What victor ever stood in his chariot so joyfully
> Triumphant? What tyrant with such a countenance ever gave laws
> To nations? How calmly he bore his fate!
> Our tears stopped; grief's shock subsided
> In us. No one grieved that he should perish.
> Now we were ashamed to weep; she whose sex
> Bids mourning, Alcmena, with dry cheeks
> Stood, a mother almost the equal of her son.

Had Seneca been able to envisage his own death, I am sure that it would have been modeled on this exemplary Stoic ending.

It was not just myth that provided for Seneca a rich store of these types of resolute, theatrical, and Stoic death. Real-life Roman aristocrats offered examples. (The depiction of their ends, however, are subject to the same discursive constraints as were those of Tacitus.) In the long discussion of suicide in *Epistle* 70, Seneca cites the famous Stoic Cato the Younger, who, having lead the resistance against Caesar in North Africa, declared after his defeat that he was unwilling to ask a pardon of Caesar. To accede to such a request would be tantamount to an admission of the legality of Caesar's position. Instead he chose to stage-manage his death: he read Plato's dialogue on the afterlife, the *Phaedo,* twice on the eve of his death, slept, then, after waking near dawn, stabbed himself (Plutarch *Cato Minor*). Tullius Marcellinus's death was less spectacular but no less resolute and theatrical. In *Epistle* 77 Seneca tells us that this man, prematurely aged and ill, determined on suicide as a means of foreclosing a joyless existence. Marcellinus, after consulting his friends, starved for three days, then lay in a warm "bath and had hot water continually poured over him." Seneca continues, "The sensation of gradually dying, he pointed out to his attendants, was not without certain pleasure."

Deaths less attractive but no less spectacular or admirable could be exemplified from the lower classes. A German gladiator, Seneca tells us in *Epistle* 70.20–21, so loathed the captive's life in the arena, that he choked himself to death with a toilet sponge normally used for anal cleaning. Of such a mode of death, Seneca notes that it was *parum munde et parum decenter* [scarcely clean and decent]; but, he queries, *quid est stultius quam fastidiose mori* [what is more stupid than to die fussily]? The suicide of disaffected gladiators must have been common. Soon after this representation, Seneca recounts how another man took his own life as he was being conveyed to a morning exhibition in a cart. Pretending he was asleep, he allowed his head to droop so far over the side of the cart that his neck caught in the spokes of a wheel and broke. Another gladiator, in a sham sea battle in the arena, thrust his sword into his own neck rather than continue with the nautical charade.

The role of self-assertion is as important in these *literary* suicides as in any of those discussed so far. The dilemma for these slaves is obvious: fight in the arena and survive, after a manner, or refuse and face immediate death. The suicides provide a dire solution to this dilemma. Suicide provides a mode for the rejection of both alternatives. In so doing, these very public, yet utterly literary, deaths act as a profound, if tragic, means for self-affirmation. Note, too, the remarkable match between the control exerted by Rome over these slaves and the reassertion of control that they represent. These deaths, just like the others we have examined, highlight the difficulties related to the issue of control.

The route from Chaereas to Seneca may seem to be a long one, and the types of death may seem quite different. As I have stated, for Chaereas it is "why" that matters, and for Seneca it is "how." Yet there is more to the Silver Latin suicide than the mere "how." There is a persistent fascination with self-killing that goes beyond Stoic posturing. The fascination seems to match that of Chariton. As I have stated at the outset of this chapter, all of this talk does not provide a link between frustration and helplessness and suicide. Rather, it offers a link between suicide and self-affirmation. For reasons too complex to canvass here, the first century of our era seems in Mediterranean culture to have brought with it a challenge to the social integrity of the personality. The best that I can do here is to suggest that this is the result of an increase in private freedom that is balanced by a curtailment of public freedom. Control thus becomes put at issue. At any rate, one of the means by which this psychological challenge was met was through the paradoxical self-affirmation involved in all of this talk about suicide.[33]

So it is that, despite the rationality of Seneca's discussion and depiction of suicide, one is justified to suspect, as does Gordon Williams (1978, 177), that Seneca is more than usually concerned with, and even interested in, suicide and death:[34] fascination, that is, displaces disinterest. Williams refers us to Seneca's view (*Epistles* 61.4) that life is but a preparation for death and observes, citing Leeman (1971), that the theme of death is present in over half of Seneca's surviving 124 long letters. It is significant that most of Seneca's suicides are carried out in the face of certain death. This is not like Chariton. There do exist, however, unexpected similarities between Seneca's representation of suicide and that of Chariton and, for that matter, of Petronius.[35] These similarities cluster beneath four lemmas. First, all of these deaths are performed in public and their details are almost stage-managed. These suicides are theatrical events. Second, these deaths and death attempts are driven not by desperation but by choice. (This is not true of the gladiators; their situation is truly desperate, and their deaths are achieved by stealth; that they are public is an avocational inevitability.) Third, the mode by which these deaths are achieved provides a resolution to a pressing dilemma. (I stress the term *mode* here, for it is not suicide or even attempted suicide per se that resolves the dilemma. It is how suicide is staged. So it is that Chaereas's dramatic leap into the sea resolves the conflicting demands created by his parents and Callirhoe's abduction and that Seneca's stagy and public mode of suicide provides a resolution for the conflicting demands of the emperor's death sentence and the need to display indifference to his arbitrary exercise of power.) The fourth point relates closely to the third. These dramatic, stage-managed suicides foreground what I have termed volitional control. I could put it in another, more familiar way. These dramatic modes of suicide involve a remarkably public and deliberate display of self. These modes of suicide thus cast into relief the problems related to control (whether it is that of the emperor, the family, or the individual) and, in so doing, present a realignment of personal values, commitments, and loyalties. The end product is the highlighting of the need for the individual to be able to exhibit personal control; power, that is, ought to be shifted from the group to the individual.

Let us spread the net more widely still. Let us test these conclusions against some of the depictions of suicide in another of the writers from this period, Seneca's nephew, Lucan, the author of an incomplete, ten-book epic, the *Civil War*.[36]

Lucan's most remarkable suicide occurs within his gory description of a sea battle. This battle occurs early in the conflict between Julius Caesar's invading forces and those Romans and allies who were loyal to the traditional Roman senatorial classes. In the sea battle to which I am referring, the Massilians (Greek inhabitants of the modern Marseilles) are resisting the attempt of Caesar's forces to dominate the littoral between Italy and Spain. This sea battle represents the culmination of the key conflict between the Gallic city and Julius Caesar's forces (*Civil War* 3.509–762). Young Argus was a Massilian and was fighting in hopeless defense of his city. He was mortally wounded by a shaft cast into his lower abdomen. At the other end of the ship stood Argus's father, watching this event with horror. The father's reaction, by twentieth-century standards, was peculiar. Disregarding Argus's silent plea for terminal comfort, the old man stabbed himself in the throat and, in case this method might fail, leaped overboard to drown. At the same time, he muttered to his son (3.742–47):

> I will not waste
> The time allowed by the cruel gods: I will pierce
> My aged throat. Grant pardon to your unhappy parent,
> Argus, for running away from your embrace, from your last kisses.
> Not yet has the hot blood left your wounds
> And only half dead do you lie: you can still outlive me.

Argus's father, to an exaggerated degree, reflects a typical ancient fear of outliving one's children. This father's suicide, carried out in such a way as to leave no room for error, was designed to avoid the situation. Although the death is bizarre, almost to the point of becoming comical, it does share important features with the other suicides we have witnessed so far. Philosophically speaking, on the face of it, this death—despairing, precipitate, overemotional—is the direct opposite of the type of death recommended by Seneca. Yet it does exhibit the traits of a Stoic, Senecan tradition: above all it recognizes that there is little value in preserving a life that has become intolerable. Seneca persistently recommends this course. It is important to recognize, however, that Lucan, himself a Stoic, clearly disapproves of this death and views it as excessive and as an unnecessary hastening of the end.

What interests most, however, is the fact that this literary suicide reflects the four qualities that I highlighted at the conclusion of the previous section of this chapter. First, the death of Argus's father is a thoroughly public event. It takes place within sight of the dying son and on a crowded ship's deck. Second, however desperate the father may feel, he has chosen this death. It is very difficult to view this bizarre death, in fact, as a reaction to grief. Were grief involved, we would expect the father to expend a little more affection on his suffering, deathbound son. It is almost as if Argus's father were driven by what he understands as the popular estimation of a father who survives his children (negative); his choice, that is, seems almost more intellectual than emotional. Third, the suicide represents a neat solution to what was an acute dilemma. This dilemma consists in the tension between his natural desire to comfort his son and his perhaps less natural desire to avoid the grief attendant on outliving one's own child. Suicide provides a useful way out and, at that, one sanctioned by Stoic philosophy. Fourth, Argus's father's suicide is as theatrical an event as we have seen so far. More than problematizing control, it aims to demonstrate the volitional power of the old man. It stands, at the expense of the poor son, as a very emblem of the triumphant assertion of self, of the shoring up of the self in the face of potentially overwhelming grief and frustration.[37]

The death of Argus's father, therefore, represents one tessellated motif within a larger affective mosaic. Other elements are provided by Seneca, by Chariton, by Petronius, and by Tacitus. We should not think of this mosaic as representing a suicide epidemic. Instead we should think of it as representing a *literary* epidemic of suicide, as a kind of unconscious textual dialogue taking place on the subject of suicide between a number of writers in this period. The parameters of this dialogue were narrow. They were set by a need to query the concept of individual volitional control, of the autonomous self. Suicide—the private, pain-driven action to which I alluded at the beginning of this chapter (exemplified by Ajax's death)—is hardly at issue here. Argus's father is making a point for all those about him. This has to do with his own independence of spirit.

This concept of an *unconscious* textual dialogue deserves emphasis and clarification. It is clear that Lucan approaches these suicides and suicide attempts in a deliberate, if ambivalent, manner. He seems attracted to the Stoic resolve it may embody, but he feels that, as often as not, it exhibits a total lack of control, an arrogant reaction to dangerous circumstances or emotional frustration.[38] For Lucan, suicide is above all a sign of weakness. It is this, I suggest, not because of the despair that drives it but because of the arrogant selfishness and self-sufficiency that it entails.

Not all suicides are so. When a suicide is faceless, the public aspect is preserved, but despair and pain can come to the fore. Take, for example, the following description of the reaction of Romans to the threat of proscription by Sulla, a Roman general who invaded and "ruled" Rome in the late seventies B.C.E. (*Civil War* 2.154–59).

> One man broke his windpipe with a noose and choked his throat,
> Another headlong hurled himself and split apart
> When he smashed on hard ground, and so they deprived the bloodstained
> Victor of their deaths; another personally piles up
> The wood of his own funeral pyre and leaps into the flames
> Before all his blood has poured away, and he takes the fires while he can.

Two of the types of death described here, hanging and jumping from heights, are among the most despised forms of suicide.[39] The third, I suppose, is a travesty of the typical dignified Roman funeral. These deaths, in Lucan's eyes, are driven by emotion, frustration, and fear (would Sulla necessarily have proscribed these individuals?). As Lucan depicts them, they are precipitate and indicate a lack of control. Worst of all, they have no philosophical substance. This attitude of Lucan is mirrored elsewhere, but perhaps even more extravagantly, by the starved and fluid-deprived troops of Afranius and Petreius, two republican commanders who were on the losing side of the Caesarean military maneuvers in Spain. After being bottled up and deprived of sustenance for some time, they eventually broke out and, in desperation, moved on Caesar's troops. They were terrifying, for they were driven by despair and a desire to perish (a *velle mori*, as Lucan puts it).[40] There is, in Lucan's eyes, something utterly unhealthy in such actions even when performed by troops on the side that he supports.

Lucan did not understand the motives of his own subjects. Compared with the deaths already surveyed, these evidence the same pattern of self-display, volitional independence, the desire for a resolution of a dilemma, and the assertion of self. Rather than exhibiting despair and solitary hopelessness, these deaths are best understood as proud assertions of individual autonomy. Whatever Lucan's intention (or that of his narratological mouthpiece) in these scenes, the dominant and lasting impression is of the problematization of control. It is as if this textual dialogue on control, carried out between Seneca, Petronius, Lucan (and, whether we like it or not, Chariton) set the parameters for Lucan's representation.

Lucan, then, almost willfully misconstrues suicide. This is exactly what we would expect when discourse rules. Lucan persistently views suicide as either a refuge for cowards or a refuge for those for whom living longer holds no attractions. The next example I would like to cite from Lucan's epic embodies this miscomprehension. Yet its depiction chimes in with this chapter's themes of volitional independence and problematized control. It comes from the central section of *Civil War* 4. The Caesarean Antonius, besieged in Illyria by the loyalist Roman forces of Pompey, tries to escape with his soldiers aboard three rafts (4.402–52). When one of these is checked, the soldiers on board, rather than surrender, kill themselves at the urging of their commander, Vulteius (4.452–581). Here is how Lucan depicts their determination (4.532–41).

> Determined to die, the soldiers stood
> With life already renounced, fierce, indifferent to the battle's outcome
> Because the end was promised them by their own hand, and no
> uproar
> Shook the warriors' resolve, prepared for the worst;
> And few in number, they resisted countless hands at once
> On land and on sea; so great is their confidence in death.
> And when they thought that blood enough had flowed in battle,
> They turned their frenzy from the enemy. The vessel's captain,
> Vulteius himself, was the first now to demand death with throat laid
> bare.

Vulteius and his followers display, it seems, a no-nonsense Stoic resolve (4.573–581). But in this instance the suicide, though admirable, is wasteful, even futile (Saylor 1990), or so it seems to Lucan. Suicide here has been enacted by forces prolonging civil war and hostile to the survival of Rome. The soldiers would have been better put to devote such resolute determination to the protection of Rome rather than to their own "freedom." Lucan makes his two-sided judgment of their spectacular suicides (something he might have said of his own death) in the following lines (4.573–79):

> Fame, running through all
> The world, spoke of no craft with a louder voice.
> Yet even after the example of these warriors, cowardly
> Races will not grasp that to escape slavery by one's own hand
> Is not an arduous act of valor; but that tyranny is feared
> Thanks to the sword and liberty is chafed by cruel weapons,
> And they do not know that swords are given to prevent slavery.

Lucan's narrator ignores the theatricality of the death of Vulteius's men. He misses its proud self-assertion of volitional control and individuality. The narrator displays little sense of the problematizing of control evident in this passage. His carping republicanism diminishes the selfish, self-assertive heroism of these Pompeian soldiers.

The *Civil War* provides us with one suicidal figure who throws into relief the distressing falseness (and subservience to discourse) of so much of what we have viewed to this point. For this figure, suicide is rejected as being unworthy, as somehow playing false to the dilemma in which she is trapped. If death must come, it can only be through grief, through wasting. We witness this in those three scenes where Pompey's unhappy wife, Cornelia, seems set to commit suicide. Pompey was the loyalist Roman general and is one of the three main characters of Lucan's epic. In some ways he is its star. At 5.774 Cornelia avers to her husband that she will commit suicide if he dies. When Pompey is eventually murdered by Achillas, in front of Cornelia's very eyes, she understandably wants to do away with herself (*Civil War* 8.652–56).

> Traitor, were you being kind? As you approached your final destiny,
> Did I deserve to die? I shall die, and not by the favor of the king.
> Allow me, sailors, to make a headlong leap, or fit
> The noose and twisted ropes around my neck, or let some comrade,
> Truly worthy of Magnus, drive the sword right through.

It appears in this scene that Lucan views Cornelia's death wish with considerable reserve. Coming so close after Pompey's speech expressing a resolute, Stoic acceptance of death, Cornelia's speech inclines one to think that she needs to imbue herself in more of her husband's spirit. This is, as we learn, precisely the spirit in which she is imbued. At 9.104–16 Cornelia rejects suicide as unworthy of the wife of Pompey and indicates that death will come to her through grief alone.

> "Great Pompey, it [my soul] could see your pyre and not take refuge
> In death. I'll crush it in my breast with the pounding strokes
> Of grief. I'll distill it in my tears. I want no sword,
> No rope, no drop headfirst through empty air: heartbreak
> Alone must kill Great Pompey's widow." Saying this,
> She veiled her head in funereal black and, sworn to shun
> The light, interred herself in cavernous depths of the hull
> To hug her bitter pain. Her very tears become sweet
> To her and, with no man to love, she loves her grief.
> The rising swell, the east wind howling in the ropes,
> The sailors' shouts as sheer disaster threatens, leave
> Her unmoved. She prays for what they dread, invokes the storm
> As friend, and lies composed for her death.

The rejection of active suicide seems based on the realization that its self-display, its volitional control, and its assertion of self would in this case tell more of the person committing the suicide and of her individuality than of her devotion to another. It is as if Lucan intuits that Cornelia rejects suicide precisely because its self-assertion would dim—even upstage—the tragedy of the death of her husband, Pompey. It would demean the *selflessness* of her love. The passivity of wasting is all that is left open to her.[41]

Lucan's take on suicide has its most startling reflection in real life. Lucan committed suicide at approximately the same time as Seneca and as a result of the same conspiracy. He was just twenty-six. The circumstances of his death, as Tacitus describes them (*Annals* 15.70), display some of the Stoic resolve of his uncle.

> Then he [Nero] ordered death for Annaeus Lucan. When, because of loss of blood, he felt his feet and hands going cold and life gradually leaving his extremities (though his heart was still warm and his brain clear), Lucan remembered the poem he had written in which a wounded soldier died a similar death. He recited the verses. That was his last utterance.

The quotation of the words of the dying soldier are a fetching touch. The nobility of this scene, however, was compromised by reality. It seems somewhat to match Lucan's own jaded interpretation of his epic suicides and suicide attempts. In Suetonius's life of Lucan and in Tacitus (*Annals* 15.56), it is said that after his arrest, Lucan denounced his mother, Acilia, in the expectation of gaining pardon (but see Getty 1940). Lucan hoped this might evoke fellow feeling in the matricide Nero. Acilia was neither pardoned nor punished. The tale does not end here. Lucan's father, Mela, in pursuit of his dead son's personal fortune, was falsely implicated in the Pisonian conspiracy by one of Lucan's friends. At the urging of Nero, Mela took his own life. Lucan's uncles, Seneca (as we have just seen) and Gallio, perished in the same circumstances. The only glimmer of light in this black landscape appears with Lucan's stage-managed death, as Tacitus reports it. Perhaps all this demonstrates that the discursive representation of suicide bears scant relationship to the actuality.

Behind all of these deaths from this period, whether they are apparently real-life or fictional, idealized Stoic or panic-driven, sentimental or parodic, there seems to exist an underlying set of rules, a syntax, as it were, that determines the modes and motives for suicide. The suicides of Chariton and Seneca, for example, do differ on several key aspects: Seneca's Stoic suicides are often compelled, whereas Chariton's are chosen; the Stoic deaths exhibit calm, resolve, and philosophic detachment, while Chariton's lovers display haste, indecision, and excessive emotion; Seneca's suicides focus on the "how," Chariton's on the "why." Yet the similarities between the various suicides and suicide attempts are both striking and compelling. The main "syntactical" similarities may be listed as follows:

1. These suicides and suicide attempts are motivated by a profound sense of constraint or frustration.
2. Suicide, in its immediate context, is usually designed to provide a solution to a dilemma presented by constraint or frustration.
3. To achieve the end of resolving this dilemma, the suicide or suicide attempt usually is carried out in such a manner as to create public display.
4. Such a display is normally designed to elicit strong emotions from its audience.
5. We find that this display, directed at some form of immediate audience, can be designed to exhibit weakness or strength, depending on which is envisaged as most useful at the time.
6. This display of strength or weakness, perhaps because it is a chosen thing, problematizes the concept of control (even if this is, as is usually the case in fact, to stress its complete lack).
7. This display of strength or weakness also aims to affirm the actor's apparent volitional control; his or her action, therefore, demonstrates will.
8. Thus, the suicide or suicide attempt is above all a demonstration of the integrity of an individual's selfhood.

The eight rules can be fleshed out in such a manner as to provide a "map" by which we may trace the etiological origins of some of the forms of suicide that have been described in this chapter.[42] The "map" runs as follows. When faced with an insoluble and enduring cause of frustration,[43] caused by shock, overwhelming emotion, unendurable social pressure, confinement, or sense deprivation, an individual, depending on their station within their society or their group and their gender, may react in a passive or self-directed manner. Typically this will produce a physical reaction.[44] There will be astonishment, blanched cheeks, glassy eyes, distorted facial expressions, voicelessness, spasms, and swooning and collapsing to the ground.[45] Either of two subsequent reactions are possible. Sickening may follow. This is accompanied by fretting, wasting, a rejection of food, and, eventually, a withdrawal from the community or group. In such cases death soon follows, as a result, it seems, of a psychic disintegration. (This type of reaction more or less resembles that of Sophocles' Ajax.) A sufferer, however, may react in such a manner that leads to psychic reformulation. Such a course, as we have seen throughout this chapter, will in some way put at issue control or power (whose exercise has caused the individual this trouble in the first place). To achieve control or power, the individual challenges his or her community by some form of a public self-display. In the examples in this chapter, such a theatrical display was achieved through a very public and stage-managed suicide or attempt at suicide.

What we are dealing with here in this "map" and in these rules is not reality but the cliché of compounded literary representation. (It is for this reason that I have entitled this chapter "The Myth of Suicide." Real suicide is not at issue here.) Another way of putting this might be to suggest that what we are viewing is a discursive construct—in the Foucaldian sense. The rules tell us a considerable amount about the literary formulation of suicide and suicide attempts, but not about real-life suicide. (The closest thing that we have here is Ajax's death, one devoid of the usual self-promotion of the deaths and would-be deaths of this chapter.) These rules do, however, tell us about the sorts of pressure that may have given rise to this discourse. Discourses do not exist in timeless intertextual voids; they reflect reality, though not in a simple, one-to-one or reflexive manner.

It would be neat to be able to provide an explanation for the remarkable prevalence of the ancient attribution of suicide to the period of the writers discussed in this chapter.[46] To try to determine whether we are dealing with a sociological reflex rather than with a contemporary literary enthusiasm, however, is unconvincing. Occasionally one sees this interest in suicide attributed to the "decadence" of the period: it was, that is to say, a sociological reflex. Such speculation is provided with its most vivid testimony from certain passages in Seneca. I will repeat some of these here, primarily to illustrate just how unhelpful such claims can be.

The Latin phrase *fastidium vitae* is used occasionally by Seneca. It represents a satiety—even a disgust with life—that is produced by the predictable and repetitive sameness of things (*quousque eadem?* [More of the same?], asks Seneca). This emotion is alluded to often in Roman literature. The restless and unsatisfied emotion to which Seneca refers here is perhaps to be linked with the bored restlessness of the wealthy to which Lucretius and Horace refer and that I have discussed in an earlier chapter. (It may also be linked with the *aegritudo animi* discussed by Cicero in the *Tusculan Disputations.*) But for imperial writers such as Seneca this emotion takes on a far more dangerous allure. The condition can engender in people a type of a "death wish," a *libido moriendi* or a *velle mori*. So Seneca tells us at *Epistles* 24.25.

> . . . and above all let that emotion be avoided that has taken hold of many, a death wish *[libido moriendi]*. For, Lucullus, just as there is an unreflecting inclination of the mind toward other things, so there is to death. This often gets hold of the most noble and most gifted men, and often the lazy and ignoble. One group despises life; the other is wearied by it.[47]

It seems that death, usually by one's own hand, offers the most potent cure for this illness (surely an extreme form of what we would call ennui). If we can believe Seneca's descriptions, then the emotion of *libido moriendi* was widespread in his era and was, in some cases, a product of *fastidium vitae*, a weariness with life.[48]

It is possible to provide a more detailed description of this illness or *morbus*. The malady is neatly characterized, as we have seen earlier, by Seneca at *De tranquillitate animi* 2.15 (Loeb translation adapted).

> And so we ought to understand that what we struggle with is the fault not of the places but of ourselves; when there is need for endurance we are weak, and we cannot bear toil or pleasure or ourselves or anything for very long. This has driven some to death, because by often altering their purpose, they were always brought back to the same things and had left themselves no room for anything new. They began to be sick of life and of the world itself, and from that self-indulgence that wasted them was bound the thought "More of the same *[quous que eadem]*?"

A supplement to this passage is provided shortly after by Seneca in *Epistles* 24.26 when he suggests:

> [T]he same satiety for doing and a disdain *[fastidium]*—not boredom *[odium]*—for life assails certain individuals. We are driven into this, philosophy itself forcing us, when we say: "How long the same things? Surely I will yawn, I will sleep, I will eat, I will be thirsty, I will be cold, I will be hot. Is there no end? But do all things go in a circle? Night overcomes day, day night, summer gives way to autumn, winter presses on autumn, which is checked by spring. All things pass that they may return. I do nothing new, I see nothing new. Sometimes this makes me seasick *[fit aliquando et huius rei nausia]*. There are many who judge living not painful but empty."

Suicide, according to Seneca, may be the result of an extremely oppressive form of boredom. It is unlikely that Seneca was correct. I know of no certain link between suicide and decadence (and anyhow, most of Chariton's romantic and suicide-prone heroes show little evidence of decadent Roman habits).[49] Suicide is the product of unendurable frustration, of extreme psychological trauma, or of psychosis. There is little evidence to suggest that it is ever the product of ennui or even of depression. Seneca's unconvincing romantic—or is it world-weary?—speculation suggests that the notion of suicide must have been a topic of considerable concern and of interest to Romans during this period. That is all.

Suicide was of such appeal because it provides a superlative demonstration of the problematization of personal control. In the case of many of our Stoics, the problem is the result of their subservience to an emperor, a slave master, even a god. In the case of Chariton's heroes, the other extreme, it is the result of subservience to an overwhelming emotional demand. The powerlessness may result in a profound sense of helplessness—we witness this frequently in the cases of Chaereas and Dionysius—and, often, in *seemingly* utter passivity. The suicides and suicide attempts so often represent means for solving dilemmas. We have seen how Chaereas's leap into the harbor in Syracuse resolved the conflicting demands of his parents and Callirhoe; we have seen how Seneca's death resolved the demands of self-pride and an arbitrary imperial cruelty. These dilemmas are normally the product of forces outside the victim (parents, Callirhoe, or Nero). It is important, therefore, that the solution to the conflicting demands involves a public display—even an eye-catching element of self-display. How else, other than through display, can our potential suicide demonstrate to those causing his or her problems that he or she can rise above them? It follows that these deaths are designed to elicit strong emotional responses from their viewers—whether these are Dionysius's retainers, Chaereas's friend Polycharmus, or the crowd of admirers who thronged Seneca's death performance. This emotive display, if one is a Stoic, exhibits strength and resolve; if one is a Roman facing Sulla's proscriptions, it highlights one's individual defiance, even within a situation of apparent powerlessness and helplessness. Circumstances dictate the sort of response required. The issue that these displays render problematic is power and control: one questions this external power (whether it is Eros's or Nero's) by pitting one's own power against it; or one highlights the arbitrariness of this external power by making publicly prominent one's helplessness. It follows, therefore, that in these suicides and attempted suicides we witness from the actor great displays of willpower, or, as I have termed it, volitional control. Naturally this display is ultimately futile, for extinction renders the suicide a gesture of powerlessness. (Thus, these suicide and suicide attempts represent above all powerful demonstrations of selfhood. The paradox in this is acute.) But perhaps even more importantly, these literary suicides and suicide attempts represent a problematization of control and of power.

The frequency of these modes by which these suicides and suicide attempts are enacted in the literature of this period therefore points not so much to an upsurge in the desire of people to do away with themselves but to some form of a crisis in the way individuals perceived authority and thus registered their own selfhood. I doubt that this crisis is the result of the periodic excesses of the principate or of anything as banal as "decadence," for this crisis seems Mediterranean-wide.[50] It is registered in regions with a more tangential relationship to the principate and in regions where decadence can hardly have been an issue. Rather, it must be the result of a number of interlinked factors, such as urbanization, the centralization of control structures, the multicultural nature of the large Mediterranean cities, the eroding of traditional class structures, and so forth.

What we may be able to say with a little more confidence still is that this apparently literary epidemic fits very well into a larger attitudinal framework, one that highlights those states of passivity and interiority that we have seen given such prominence in a number of the conditions discussed in earlier chapters.[51] With the type of suicide discussed in this chapter, we seem to be sharing in a dialogue that embraces a broad range of passive affective conditions—melancholia, lovesickness, and, as will become apparent in later chapters, a revaluation of the way that time should be employed. It is a dialogue within which suicide plays a small, though noteworthy, role. It is my suggestion that the frequency of suicides, as they are depicted in literary texts, is so pronounced in this period not just because of this problem of control but also because it so matches the formulation of the dialogue of passivity that I have attempted to register throughout this book. Had it not fitted so easily within this textual discourse, it would not have become so prominent.

It may seem to be extreme to speak of suicidal epidemics (especially those represented primarily in the minds of writers). They have existed in eras other than the classical.[52] There was a notable example in fin de siècle France. It offers neat correlation for the forces behind this classical outbreak. At the same time, it emphasizes the striking affective similarity between Greece and Rome of the first century of our era and recent history. Allow me to stress again, however, that we can hardly be dealing here with anything other than a *literary* epidemic of suicide. As I have stated earlier, we should think of this as a kind of unconscious textual dialogue taking place on the subject of suicide between a number of writers in this period and as a dialogue whose parameters were narrow and were set by a need to problematize the concept of individual volitional control, of the autonomous self. Suicide—the private, pain-driven action to which I alluded at the beginning of this chapter (exemplified by Ajax's death)—is hardly at issue here. At any rate, I base my brief epitome of French *fin de siècle* suicide on Alvarez 1971.

"I dreamed of suicide," wrote Flaubert of his youth. He goes on to describe how he and his provincial friends "swung between madness and suicide; some of them killed themselves . . . another strangled himself with his tie, several died of debauchery in order to escape boredom; it was beautiful!" (Alvarez 1971, 221). Flaubert's enthusiasm (something carried on in the literature of the nineteenth and the early twentieth centuries) provides a vivid and instructive tableau with which to finish this chapter. In this period the Romantics and the Decadents and, later, the surrealists and the dadaists lavished particular attention upon suicide. It was as if they had invented it. What is remarkable, however, is just how close these deaths are, in "syntactical" terms, to those we have already confronted in this chapter.

Suicide did not always resemble Flaubert's version. It did not necessarily require the dignification of boredom and madness. De Vigny's *Chatterton* was credited with doubling the suicide rate in France between the years 1830 and 1840 (Alvarez 1971, 210). Given the unreliability of statistical collection in this period, however, the high incidence of morbidity associated with this epidemic (not of a sort to be confused with the affective epidemics represented by acedia) can have existed only in the minds of journalists and the credulous. So we hear that in the same period a young man, accused of pushing his pregnant mistress into the Seine, defended himself in court with the statement "we live in an age of suicide; this woman gave herself to Death" (Alvarez 1971, 211). A character in a popular contemporary novel summed it up neatly: "suicide establishes a man. Alive one is nothing; dead one becomes a hero . . . all suicides are successful; the papers take them up; people feel for them. I must decidedly make my preparations" (Alvarez 1971, 212). These preparations were at least made on the page. Keats died at twenty-five. The Romantic association between youth, poetry, and death encouraged the aberration. Shelley died two years later at age twenty-nine, Byron at thirty-six with the heart and cerebellum of an old man; Coleridge solaced unexpected longevity with opium; Baudelaire finished himself off with syphilis, Rimbaud, literary career complete at twenty, as a *littératuricide* (Alvarez 1971, 203). The theatricality and self-display involved here hardly needs to be underlined. Alfred Alvarez, discussing this Romantic angst in his book *The Savage God* (whence I have taken these illustrations), acutely remarks that "suicide *à la mode* had one element in common: the belief that the suicide himself would be present to witness the drama created by his own death" (Alvarez 1971, 210). Suicide had become a thoroughly literary affair. It was a metaphor, a "supreme, dramatic gesture of contempt toward a dull, bourgeois world" (Alvarez 1971, 210).

The enthusiasm for suicide was carried on past the Romantics and past the Decadents well into the twentieth century.[53] The dadaists and the surrealists enacted their own version of the suicide cult in Paris. Suicide became a metaphor enlisted in the service of art. We read, "Sir, allow me to reply to your question by copying out the notice on my bedroom wall: enter without knocking, but you are requested to commit suicide before leaving." So ran one of the responses to a 1933 symposium on the theme "Is suicide a solution?" (Alvarez 1971, 232). It was published by the Parisian arts magazine *La révolution surréaliste.* Most contributors answered in the affirmative. Dada, on Alvarez's explanation, entailed a destructive agitation against everything: established values, the bourgeoisie, art, even life itself. It was, Alvarez believes (1971, 226), a product of the "sense of universal moral bankruptcy which followed the First World War." For the Dadaist, meaningless art reflected a meaningless world. Suicide inevitably became the most representative work of art.

A death marked the movement's beginning. For the exquisite and influential Jacques Vaché, life and death were art. He took his life with an opium overdose shared with two unwitting friends. "I object to being killed in the war," he wrote, ". . . I shall die when I want to die, and then I shall die with somebody else." Vaché's death, notes Alvarez (1971, 239), was the "supreme Dada gesture, the ultimate psychopathic joke: suicide and double murder." The demise of Jacques Rigault in 1929 is said to mark the end of the movement (Rigault observed that "suicide is a vocation"). Rigault, who consistently destroyed everything he wrote, did leave the following comment: "the only way left to us of showing our contempt for life is to accept it. Life is not worth the trouble to leave it" (Alvarez 1971, 231)

As Alvarez describes things, we can descry in these passages several characteristics that we have already isolated in ancient literary contexts. That we are witnessing an essentially literary event deserves highlighting at the outset. These suicides appear to have been more written about than acted upon. Their representation in words, however, emphasizes other aspects. These vaunted deaths are all determinedly public and, to follow Alvarez's descriptions, determinedly theatrical, even stage-managed. Above all, these deaths rely for their impact upon an audience, even if it is only a reading one. The deaths, furthermore, represent freely chosen actions. So Vaché states, "I shall die when I want to die." Another writer states of suicide, "I must decidedly make my preparations." With this assertion of volition is problematized the notion of control. Above all, these Frenchmen are insistent upon their right to control their actions and, in particular, the manner by which they will die.

Following from this self-display, the assertion of volition, and the problematization of control is, most obviously, the assertion of self, its assertion as an entity separate from the world about. How could this have been better expressed than by that Gallic aficionado who maintained: "suicide establishes a man. Alive one is nothing; dead one becomes a hero . . . all suicides are successful."

6

Time's Passing

Catastrophes, Trimalchio, and Melancholy

> There are two possible ways of viewing the passage of time: that everything is in a state of constant and unrecognizable change. And everything remains unchanged. There it is, the supreme contradiction. Linear time and circular time. Linear time is envisaged as a huge, endless knife-blade scraping its way across the universe . . . Circular time sees the world as remaining more or less the same . . . I believe that virtually all of the existing books on time, deep down, are certain that it is linear. That it passes and is then, irrevocably, gone . . . The life of every person possesses a linear trait . . . And yet, life is full of repetition . . . Read books about the history of time and you will find all of them agree that linear time triumphed along with Christianity . . . Even though linear time has triumphed, it is as though cyclic time is what counts . . . In 1865 Rudolf Clausius suggested the word "entropy" as a scientific term for the fact that time was linear, irrevocable, irreversible . . . Up to that point, even in biology, no one had really been sure of anything other than that living creatures kept on reproducing themselves; that nature was cyclic.
>
> —PETER HØEG, *Borderliners* (1994, 201–3)

I have used for the epigraph of this chapter a quotation from Peter Høeg's novel *Borderliners* (1994, 201–3) because it so neatly embodies popular perceptions of linear and circular time. The primary focus of this chapter will be on time, linear and circular; its relation to the body and to the mind; and how individuals may register their experience particularly of linear time. This will mean that we must reconsider the concepts of circular and linear time. Unfortunately I have found that, among the sorts of readers this book is liable to find, circular time is viewed as, if not an aberration, at least a fiction of overimaginative scholarly minds.[1] This should not be the case, as I hope the extract from Høeg's frightening fiction may demonstrate. There are many devotees of circular time, not the least of whom are children.

Høeg's narrative speculations are useful in another way. They provide a striking example of the localization of the apparent triumph of linear time to within the period of the rise of Christianity and then to the century following the Enlightenment. Høeg's conceptualization mirrors many others. Time, yoked with insanity (so we might consider melancholia), owes its modern formulation to the Enlightenment. (For madness see Foucault 1973. For time see Elias 1992; Borst 1993; Foucault 1977, 149 ff.) Foucault argued that madness was incompatible with the new mercantile economy. It was therefore conceptualized and then banished to the new "clinics": "in the bourgeois world . . . the cardinal sin . . . had been defined . . . [as] . . . inability to participate in the production, circulation, or accumulation of wealth (whether or not through any fault of their own [i.e., of those who are mad]). The exclusion to which they [sc., the mad] were subjected goes hand in hand with that inability to work, and it indicates the appearance in the modern world of a caesura that had not previously existed" (Foucault 1987, 68; see also Foucault 1973; cf. Porter 1987, 6–10). It is easy to see how Foucault and others imagined that time had become reconceptualized under the same forces.[2]

Time and its articulation within a key period in the ancient world will be the focus of this chapter. I will attempt to demonstrate that time's passing (as we see it in the literature of the first century of our era) can best be understood as part of a dialogue that engrosses boredom, melancholia, and lovesickness. I hope to demonstrate not just that time exhibits a periodization that runs parallel to that of madness (as I have just indicated, I am using the term *madness* as an equivalent of melancholia) but that these particularized states also manifest patterns and relations that are shared and that are applicable not only to one another but also to the worldviews that this book has considered. I will also argue that, at least in one case, the experience of time's passing could be registered in a corporealized fashion. As melancholy could be linked with conditions such as quartan fever (chapter 1), love with fevers and wasting (chapter 2), or boredom with nausea (chapter 3), so could time be linked with intestinal disquietude. Time itself is no affective state. But the way we react to it most certainly is. Its passing can provoke mood or affective responses of lesser or greater strength; this experience of time can become, that is, the equivalent of a mild affective disorder, just as can the experience of love or boredom.[3] This affective disorder, like most others, can become internalized or corporealized. The mode that this corporealization takes most commonly involves a physical ailment that mirrors the psychological affliction (depression, love, boredom). This, we will see, is markedly so in the instance of time. In Trimalchio's case, as will become evident, time's apparently uncontrolled linear thrust is ironically mimicked by his uncontrolled digestive tract. Trimalchio's remarkable attempts to control his digestion have their image in his extreme attempts to control time's passing.

So Trimalchio returns obsessively to the themes and motifs of time's passing and, as we will see, even acts it out by staging a mock version of his funeral. Through action such as this he aims to punctuate and control its course.

Trimalchio has been absent for some time from his famous banquet. He seems to feel that his guests deserve an explanation (Petronius *Satyricon* 47). Constipation was the excuse, and the cure was pomegranate, resin, and vinegar. Constipation makes Trimalchio think of dying.[4] "The doctors," he explains to his friends, "forbid you to hold back . . . Believe me if the gas goes to your head it produces feebleness throughout the whole body too. I've known many to die that way, because they were unwilling to be honest with themselves."[5]

The passing of time and death provide persistent organizational motifs within the banquet scene of the *Satyricon* (Arrowsmith 1966; Slater 1990, 54–55; the novel is usually dated to the first century C.E.). Trimalchio's anxiety over constipation exemplifies these themes.[6] I believe that how Trimalchio describes his condition echoes the language and conceptual formulation used of some forms of madness in contemporary literature. In a previously published article (Toohey 1997c), I looked at how the themes of time's passing and death are intertwined within the *Satyricon*. For the sake of clarity I will go through some of this material again. At the very beginning of Trimalchio's banquet (*Satyricon* 26), we learn that Trimalchio has a "clock *[horologium]* in his dining room and a well-dressed trumpeter to tell him how much of his life he's lost." The trumpeter lets forth timely blasts that notify the millionaire how much remains of his thirty years, two months, and two days (we learn of Trimalchio's residual life span in section 77; cf. Seneca's near contemporary Manilius and his computation of life spans at *Astronomica* 3.560–617). Trimalchio's "morbid, although whimsical, preoccupation with death," as Smith (1975, 53) puts it, is made even more plain in the closing scenes of the banquet. In section 77 he gives this remarkable command: "Stichus, bring out the material in which I want to be laid out. Bring some unguent too, and a draught from that wine jar in which I want my bones to be washed." Trimalchio experiments with the nard and urges his guests to try it too. He even opens the wine in which his bones will be washed and seems set to share it. Worse still, after showing the guests his shroud, he lies along the couch as if he had already passed away. "Imagine I'm dead," he announces, "and say something nice." He then has his cornet players blow a funeral march (section 78). Petronius therefore concludes his depiction of Trimalchio's banquet with an evocation of death, time's ultimate threat (cf. Arrowsmith 1966, 306–7).

The motifs of time's passing and death can be observed in other places within the banquet scene. Early on in the banquet (section 34), Trimalchio's slave brings in a miniature silver skeleton with flexible joints. This leads Trimalchio to muse, in poetry, on the universality of death. Later Trimalchio brags (section 48) that he has seen the Sibyl at Cumae and that she said, "I want to die." Trimalchio reads his will in section 71 and later, in section 74, quarrels with his wife, then denies her cohabitation with him in his tomb (to avoid postmortem quarreling). Trimalchio seems to surround himself with the symbols of time and mortality or with associates who like to allude to them. In the colonnade to his home (section 29) is a golden casket containing Trimalchio's first beard; in section 73 we learn that one of Trimalchio's slaves has just had his first shave. There is also the zodiac dish, a bizarre, celestial timepiece (sections 35, 39). One of Trimalchio's guests (referred to in section 38) has been an undertaker. Habinnas and Scintilla arrive late at the banquet (section 65) because they have been at a ninth-day funeral feast for a slave called Scissa. Conversation at the banquet is often about death. Seleucus (in section 42), after recounting aspects of the funeral and of the life and death of his friend Chrysanthus, concludes lugubriously on human longevity that "we're nothing more than bubbles." When Ganymedes puts in his piece (section 44), he speaks on contemporary decline, while Echion, the sadistic rag merchant (section 45), talks of the death struggles at gladiatorial shows or of killing off a young boy's pet birds.

It is through this prism of time and mortality that we ought to interpret Trimalchio's constipation. Trimalchio's intestinal regularity seems to provide a bizarre means for calibrating the proper advance of time. Just as does the regularity of the clock and the trumpet, so, too, does bowel routine provide for Trimalchio's life a series of foreseeable punctuations and predictable events. Their regularity, their predictability, and the fact that they can be controlled does in some degree mitigate the depressing, unpredictable, and uncontrollable reality of death. I doubt that Trimalchio (or Petronius) was conscious of this, at least when all was normal. But irregularity of bowel movements, which Trimalchio has been suffering, threatens his attempt at controlling death. Irregularity may even hasten one's death. It is little wonder that Trimalchio and his friend Habinnas are so conscious of what they eat. Although Petronius's discourse represents humans as time's playthings, and although they register time's passing passively (for them its climax is death), Trimalchio's comic, but understandable, attempts to manage and to master time through incessant protestations and bizarre temporal calibrations aim to master a fear of an unrelenting, linear time that climaxes only in death.

We could say that Trimalchio registers time through illness and through the body.[7] The passing of time for Trimalchio produces an actual *debilitating* and *physical* manifestation.[8] This is, as I have stressed in a number of contexts in the book (in chapter 1 with melancholia and quartan fever, in chapter 2 with love and wasting and fevers, in chapter 3 with boredom and nausea, in chapter 4 with "boning"), a common, predictable, and very modern way to mark affectivities and affective registers such as time. Trimalchio's constipation therefore forms a part of a larger textual dialogue on the experience of time's passing.[9]

Time's passing was not always expressed in this strange and maudlin fashion. Trimalchio's linear time is a long way from the conception of time broadcast by Alexandrian writers such as Virgil, Horace, and Ovid (in the *Metamorphoses*) and by earlier epic poets such as Naevius and Ennius.[10]

The sense of the immanence of the distant past is a constant theme of Roman literature. It is based on a feeling of the circularity or of the repetitious nature of past history and of time itself. We can observe this as early as the writing of Gnaeus Naevius (ca. 270–201 B.C.E.). Naevius wrote what is usually termed as the first Roman national epic. His poem concerns the First Punic War (264–241 B.C.E.). (For texts see Strzelecki 1964; Marmorale 1953; Morel 1975. For a translation see Warmington 1935. Cf. Toohey 1992, 92–95.) Beginning with the mythological origins of Rome in Troy, it produces a narrative climaxing in the victory of the Romans over the Carthaginians in the First Punic War. Sixty-odd lines of the poem are extant (see Rowell 1947). The poem, composed originally as an unbroken narrative, was apparently divided into seven books in the second century B.C.E. by C. Octavius Lampadio. Fraenkel (1935) suggested that the first book of Naevius's *Punic War* provided an account of events of the war down to the capture of Agrigentum in 262 (Rowell 1947). At Agrigentum was a temple to Jupiter on whose pediment the foundation legends of Rome were depicted. The poem may have provided a description of this pediment, beginning in book 1 and extending at least until the conclusion of book 3.[11] Book 2 seems to have concentrated on Aeneas and his arrival in Carthage—and possibly on his love affair with Dido. Book 3 has Aeneas in Italy. The book may also have contained narratives of the Roman regal period. Books 4–7 then narrate the First Punic War and may have outlined the years 260–241, with each book embracing approximately a five-year period. If Naevius really did include Aeneas and his Trojans within his narrative (cf. Waszink 1972, 906 ff.; Strzelecki 1964; Marmorale 1953), then we could speculate (1) that his *Punic War* exhibits, through its vigorous juxtaposition of past and present, a belief in the vital continuity of Roman history and (2) that

Aeneas, the early kings, and their dilemmas provide prototypes for contemporary leaders and heroes. History thus repeats itself.

Naevius's epic successor Quintus Ennius (239–169 B.C.E.) wrote his *Annals* about the Second Punic War (218–201 B.C.E.) and seems to have adopted the same strategy as Naevius. In his *Annals*, we witness this same sense of the circularity of time and history. This can best be illustrated by outlining briefly the contents of his fragmentary poem (the fragments amount to not much more than six hundred lines, less than a twentieth of the final scope of the eighteen books: for the text see Skutsch 1985; for a translation see Warmington 1935). Fifteen books spanning the thousand years from 1184/3 to 187/184 B.C.E. represented the original ambit of the poem. The fifteen books may have been grouped into triads (I am following Gratwick 1983, 60 ff.). The first triad (books 1–3) covers, in book 1, events from the sack of Troy, via Aeneas, to Romulus and Remus and the foundation of Rome. Books 2–3 seem to have narrated the events of the legendary period during which Rome was said to have been ruled by kings (the so-called regal period). The second triad (books 4–6) describes, in book 4, events from the foundation of the Republic (510 B.C.E.) to the Gallic invasions (390 or 387 B.C.E.). Book 5 narrates events down to the end of the Samnite wars (295 B.C.E.), book 6 the war against Pyrrhus (281–271 B.C.E.). The third triad (books 7–9) deals with, in book 7, events leading up to the invasion of Hannibal (218 B.C.E.). Books 8 and 9 describe the rest of the Second Punic War (218–201). The density of narrative detail increases considerably in the fourth and fifth triads (books 10–12, 13–15). Within the fourth triad, book 10 outlined the war against Philip of Macedon (201–196 B.C.E.), while books 11 and 12 carry the narrative down to the commencement of the war against Antiochus III of Syria (191/2 B.C.E.). The final triad of the original edition seems to outline events as follows: book 13, the war against Antiochus (191 B.C.E.); book 14, Scipio's victory at Magnesia and the naval war (190 B.C.E.); book 15, the actions of M. Fulvius Nobilior, Ennius's patron. The final, appended triad (books 16–18) described the events of the Istrian war and ran to 171 B.C.E.[12]

The concept for a poem that leapfrogs back from Hannibal to Numa to Troy belongs to Naevius. So, too, does its meaning. On the simplest of levels, the *Annals* represents a national encomium. Like Naevius, Ennius seems to admire the successful warrior. The position of Rome's power within history, however, is at the heart of the concerns of the *Annals*. Through the depiction of a series of Roman heroes (culminating in the present), Ennius demonstrates the immanence of the Roman past in the Roman present. Ennius's alleged Pythagoreanism may support this conclusion. Pythagoreanism, in which doctrine it is sometimes said Ennius was instructed, believes in the transmigration of souls (metempsychosis). An instance is provided by Ennius's dream at the beginning of the *Annals:* Homer has transmigrated into the soul of Ennius. The progress of Roman history is ordained, Ennius may have believed, by the metempsychosis of a heroic soul from one generation to the next. If Ennius did believe in this historical circularity, he would not be alone. Compare Ovid's Pythagoras in *Metamorphoses* 15 and Anchises' lore in Virgil's *Aeneid* 6. There are also Valerius Flaccus's Argonauts (to cite another epic example, but this time from the end of the first century C.E.). If we follow Jupiter's prediction at *Argonautica* 1.531–60, Jason and the Argonauts are the first in a chain of individuals who will climax in Domitianic Rome. The speech occurs within the divine assembly of 1.498–573: Jupiter's speech implies that the Argonauts are harbingers of the Roman Empire; their voyage, Jupiter explains, will shift the balance away from the East to Greece and from Greece eventually to the West, presumably to Hesperia; Jason becomes, therefore, a proto-Roman, proto-Aeneas, and emperor.[13]

A comparable version of time is at the base of the ideological design of Virgil's *Aeneid* and Ovid's *Metamorphoses.* In Virgil's *Aeneid* 6, Aeneas, through consultation with his father, Anchises, learns the theory of metempsychosis and of Rome's history to come (6.679–901). Anchises (6.679–702), when Aeneas meets him in Hades, reveals the future generations of Roman heroes. But before outlining these, Anchises details his famous theory of transmigration (6.713–51, 756–886). The purpose of this speech is to explain how the past lives on in the present, how a leader such as Augustus embodies Aeneas, how the progress of Roman history is made constant—or better, is made cyclical—by the metempsychosis of a heroic soul from one generation to the next. (So Anchises points out to Aeneas the souls of famous Romans [6.752–853]: the Alban kings, Romulus, Augustus, the Roman kings, and many heroes who lived during the Roman Republic. The roll of heroes concludes with a description of Marcellus, the son of Octavia, Augustus's sister.)[14] While the implication of all of this is that Augustus and Augustan Rome are but another element that reenacts the past values and triumphs of Rome, the vision is essentially cyclic, for, although faces change, the essence keeps on coming back. Anchises, in Virgil's *Aeneid,* offers a real link between Aeneas and his followers and contemporary Romans, particularly between Aeneas and Augustus. He, too, does this through a theory of metempsychosis. So the Roman Empire is achieved by a cyclical reenactment of a past established by Aeneas.

Ovid's *Metamorphoses,* using the motifs of metamorphosis and metempsychosis, creates a narrative that, commencing with creation, traces history down to contemporary times: creation (beginning book 1) leads to the apotheosis of Julius Caesar and the prediction of the apotheosis of his nephew, Augustus (15.745–870). This is buttressed by the Pythagorean speech of 15.60–478. This provides a rationale for the theme of metamorphosis: through the flux of history, the constant is the human soul changing from one form into another. Pythagoras's doctrines provide a unifying link for the *Metamorphoses* as a whole. They place the poem firmly within a tradition of time that we have just witnessed in the *Aeneid* (and will shortly see in the *Fasti*). Ovid uses metempsychosis, the doctrine of universal change (15.176–272), the section on the rise and fall of cities and the predictions of Rome's greatness (15.418–52), and the section on the transmigration of souls (15.453–78) to provide a clear link between such mythological or nearly mythological heroes as Hercules, Aeneas, Romulus, Julius Caesar, and Augustus.[15] Time therefore moves in self-fulfilling circles.

This traditional Roman attitude to time is also evident in Ovid's poem on time and the calendar, the *Fasti*.[16] The *Fasti*, perhaps the most striking Roman exemplar of the cyclicality of history, details the major events of the first six months of the Roman calendar. For the *Fasti*, time is social and cyclical.[17] (For this type of "social" time see Elias 1992; Borst 1993, 1 ff. For time as a social construct see Bettini 1991.) It is not progressive (i.e., linear, as it is for Trimalchio), nor is it degenerative (despite Janus's halfhearted reference to a decline from the Golden Age at *Fasti* 1.247 ff.). Ovid's calendar reenacts and re-creates the past through religious ritual: Roman origins and the mythological and historical or quasi-historical events of Rome's past are annually re-created in the festivals of the calendar. Such events are persistently related to contemporary events (see Beard 1987; Newlands 1995). Thus is created a cyclical link, through ritual and the calendar, between mythological time and time now. We could exemplify this with the festival of the Megalesia, where Augustus's family is linked with the mythological past (*Fasti* 4.179–372). Transplanted from Greece to Rome, this festival early on gained particular connection with the imperial family of Augustus (4.293–348). It is still practiced (4.349–72) and is still relevant now. Thus, too, for example, the "Trojan" legend concerning Dido's sister, Anna (3.523–710), leads imperceptibly to Roman foundation legends and, significantly, is juxtaposed with a brief lament on the murder of Aeneas's descendant Julius Caesar (3.697–710). Anna and Caesar, both victims, become, eventually, divine beneficiaries.

A systematic appraisal of time's passing within Ovid's calendar would be impossible within the constraints of the space I have available here (cf. Wallace-Hadrill 1987 and Zanker 1988 on the politics of the calendar). But allow me to offer, through the Carmentalia, one further example of how this circularity is operant (and thus offer a hermeneutic template that may be applied throughout much of the rest of the poem). The Carmentalia was a festival begun on January 11 for Carmentis, the mother of the first inhabitant of the site of Rome,

Evander (*Fasti* 1.461–586). It begins with a straightforward description of Evander's birth and exile (for crimes not of his own making) from Arcadia in Greece (1.469–508). Then it shows us Carmentis, after arrival at Tarentum, enthusiastically greeting the new homeland (Rome itself—Carmentis and Evander have sailed up the Tiber) and predicting its future greatness (1.509–42). What does Carmentis tell of Rome's future? After greeting Rome and exclaiming in a generalized fashion on its future (1.509–18), she prophesies the arrival of the Trojans (1.519); subsequent war (1.520); Lavinia, Aeneas's bride-to-be (1.520); the death of Pallas, Evander's son (1.521–22); the belated triumph of Troy over Greece (1.523–26), and Aeneas (1.527–28). At this point Carmentis jumps one thousand years *(in annos nostros)* and forces, arbitrarily, a comparison between the family that includes Julius Caesar, Augustus, Tiberius, and Germanicus, on the one hand, and the founders of Rome, on the other (1.529–30; note the reference to Vesta in 1.528). Augustus's clan thus comes to be seen as another instance of the sorts of thing that were manifest in Rome even from its beginnings. Ovid drives home the point. He goes on to link in Augustus, Tiberius (1.530–34), and Augustus's eventually deified wife, Livia (1.535–36).[18]

Notwithstanding such evidence, it is difficult for many modern readers to accept that different cultures, different periods, and different individuals may conceive of time in different ways. To us, especially when we think of mortality, the linearity of time seems self-evident.[19] Yet it is quite clear that for us to insist upon such a conception is to be purblind. Cyclical time, which may stress not just a recurrence of events but more particularly an immanence of the past in the present, is a common, alternative means for the registering of the movement of time.[20]

Cyclical time is associated primarily with illiterate and with agricultural societies (Lévy-Bruhl 1923)—with the illiterate because linear time requires measurement for its reckoning and because measurement of any complexity requires writing; with the agricultural because farming, particularly crop farming, relies on the repetitive nature of the seasons for its success.[21] Cyclical time, as has often been argued (Ong 1977, 1982; Goody 1987; cf. Lévy-Bruhl 1923), may be seen above all in myth (which in turn has its genesis in illiterate societies).[22] Pindar's epinicians perhaps provide the earliest and most striking example of a conception of mythology that relies on a cyclical, nonlinear concept of time. For Pindar, as has often been noted, the significance of the competitor's victory resides to a very large degree in that it is envisaged as repeating or reenacting, in the present, past mythical victories such as those of Heracles or Perseus, among many others.[23] The past in this way becomes immanent in the present, through the recursive force of the triumph of the games victor. The present thus repeats again and again seminal actions from the past (cf. Eliade 1954).

This conception of time is not just the preserve of preliterate agricultural or premodern cultures.[24] It also played a surprisingly prominent role in ancient, specifically Stoic, philosophical thought.[25] To illustrate this I will quote Long and Sedley (1987, 1:311 ff.) on what they term "circular or closed time" (as opposed to linear time), a concept that is built on an "everlasting cycle of world-order and conflagration" (on the notion of *ecpyrosis*, to which I will return).

> What presses harder for clarification and philosophical assessment is everlasting recurrence itself. The doctrine which Chrysippus canvassed as a possibility, if not a firm thesis, was "our return to the shape we are now" in a future world after our death; and in the most detailed summary this hardens into the claim that there is an everlasting sequence of worlds and conflagrations in which the individuals and actions of any one world are exactly the same as those of every other world "down to the smallest details." Such a cosmology is asserted rather than proved in our surviving evidence, but it appears to be an inevitable consequence . . .

This conception is not quite the same as the ideas of immanence that we have observed in the poets, but its popular basis may well be the same. Long and Sedley nicely sum up the philosophical ramifications of this idea as follows:

> Just as Nietzsche probably regarded everlasting recurrence as a way of saying that any other life one had would always be just the same—for how else could it be *your* life?—so in Stoicism the doctrine may have served to underline the necessity of accepting one's present situation. For that will be one's situation time and again in the everlasting nature of things.

The contrast between Petronius and the tradition represented by the writers of epic so far discussed could not be greater. In Ovid (who lived from 43 B.C.E. to 17 C.E.) we noted the refraction of a way of looking at time's passing that implies that one participates, collaborates, or plays a partner with time and its restoration of the Roman state. In Petronius (d. 65 C.E.) Trimalchio's representation of the experience of time's passing is utterly passive: time controls, it humiliates, humans attempt to escape its net, and time is named. Time, furthermore, is a linear, serial, and cumulative process (Slater 1990, 55). The contrast between a point of view that respects individual participation in a cyclical temporal movement and one that sees subjects as passive victims of an essentially disinterested (but potentially malevolent and degenerative), linear, and serial temporal movement is marked.

Melancholia—or madness, as some might term it—seems to evince a periodization resembling that of the experience of time. Consider again the pseudo-Aristotelian *Problema* 30.1. It placed melancholics into two broad groups, those in whom the black bile becomes very hot and those in whom the black bile becomes very cold. Where the black bile is hot, one would expect what we term the *manic phase* of this condition; where the black bile is cold, one would expect the *depressed phase*. Subsequent theorists, whether humoralists or not, reproduce this distinction. The literary depictions of melancholia, I have argued, indicate that these two forms predominate in two different periods. The more common literary depiction of melancholia is of the manic variety (Cicero states typically at *Tusculan Disputations* 3.5, "what we call *furor*, the Greeks call *melancholia*"). Manic melancholia, except for a brief efflorescence of the depressive form in the early Hellenistic era, dominates until the time of Seneca. The second form of melancholia, the depressive variety, does not assume any prominence in literary experience until the era when Celsus, Soranus of Ephesus, Aretaeus of Cappadocia, and Galen began their analysis. So we find Trimalchio's contemporary M. Annaeus Serenus, the addressee of Seneca's *De tranquillitate animi*, suffering from this condition. He has companions in the addressee of Persius's *Satires* 3 and in the lead characters of Chariton's novel *Chaereas and Callirhoe*.

With melancholia, we witness what seems to be the periodization of an emotional state. This periodization may be localized: to speak approximately, acute frustration tends to provoke a manic melancholic reaction throughout the literary experience of antiquity. But, beginning with the third century B.C.E. and more pronouncedly within the literary experience of Rome in the early empire, acute frustration may produce a reaction best described in terms that match those we nowadays use of melancholia. It "becomes" a passive condition, an utterly depressive and fretting condition. What is notable, however, is that this invention displays no clear stratigraphic line of demarcation. It begins to become prominent in Alexandrian literature for the first time. It disappears. Then, displaying a pendulumlike motion, it reappears in the first century of our era. Of its own, this melancholic periodization is, I believe, a rather interesting thing—if, that is, my rough and schematic diagnosis is correct. Depression, something to which nearly all of us are prone, was, as it were, "invented" in a more systematic way twice, first in Alexandria and then again sometime in the first century of our era. I use the word *invented* with all due caution. What I mean by this term is merely that depression seems suddenly and unexpectedly to have been judged a topic worthy of serious textual contemplation. Real life is another matter.

Earlier in this chapter I spoke of the need to demonstrate how a single set of rules defines the relations between madness and time. Trimalchio's temporal concerns have much in common with the depressive formulation of melancholia. Not unexpectedly it also has much in common with the literary experience of boredom. Greek literature to the Hellenistic period seems to lack reference to anything more than the simplest form of boredom. Serious or unequivocal consideration of boredom begins in the first century B.C.E. in Rome, but here it is limited by the absence of a clear-cut term or conception for the condition. A psychic or inner form of boredom is first referred to in the first and second centuries C.E. In Seneca, for example, boredom is depicted as an emotion that not only can affect a person's life sporadically but can spread to influence one's every waking action. In Seneca, Persius, and Plutarch, as I have argued in chapter 3, there is registered the "invention" of the modern concepts of the emotion. The incidence of boredom in ancient literature seems not unexpectedly to match the literary "invention" of melancholia. Do we witness the operation of a generalized affective formulation, one whose very hallmark is passivity, one that inscribes the world as something one merely registers, something that acts upon one, something over which one has no ready control? Can we link to this Trimalchio's constipation?

What intrigues in the instances of boredom and melancholia is that, like most psychological conditions in the ancient world, these emotional states could manifest themselves in somatic terms. We have seen this corporealization in, say, the instances of quartan fever or nausea, to name but two. Trimalchio's constipation represents, I have argued, a corporealization of the registering of time's passing. This is represented, remarkably, in terms that echo those used by medical writers for melancholia. Constipation, we learn from Petronius's near contemporary Celsus (*De medicina* 3.18.17), is to be associated with melancholia *(tristitia)* or an excess of black bile (*bilis atra*, the very substance that causes melancholia) (cf. Jackson 1986, 38):[26] "there is another sort of insanity . . . depression which seems caused by black bile. Bloodletting is here of service; but if anything prohibit this, then comes firstly abstinence, secondly, a clearance by a white hellebore and a vomit" (trans. Spencer [1935–38, vol. 1]). A few lines later Celsus points out that if health is to be maintained, then "the motions are to be kept very soft." Trimalchio, though alluding to constipation and to purges, does not use as an emetic hellebore *(veratrum)*, the standard treatment for insanity (Celsus 2.12; see also Spencer 1935–38, 2:lviii–lix) and melancholia (Starobinski 1962, 16–21; Toohey 1990b, 159–60). He uses pomegranate, pine resin, and vinegar. We know from Caelius Aurelianus (*On Chronic and Acute Diseases* 1.184) that pomegranates (in this case combined with vinegar- or wine-soaked Theban dates) were curatives for melancholia. We know too from the Hippocratic text *Regimen in Acute Diseases* (61) that the dissipation of black bile is assisted by vinegar. Then there is the constipation. Of itself it is no proof of melancholy (Celsus described its symptoms and cures at 1.3.23–27). But it was associated with melancholy (by such physicians as Aretaeus: see Starobinski 1962, 23), as was flatulence.[27] Aretaeus, for example, makes this clear when he states, "in certain of these cases, there is neither flatulence nor black bile, but mere anger and grief, and sad dejection of the mind; and these were called melancholics, because the term bile and anger are synonymous in import, and likewise black with much and furious" (trans. Jackson [1986, 40], following Adams [1856, 298]).[28] This link between melancholia and Trimalchio's constipation is made more clear by Trimalchio's suggestion that the stool may overheat and send up an exhalation that may damage the higher portions of the body. Although such damage is an expected concomitant of excessive constipation (according to Celsus 1.3.23–27), Trimalchio, by describing the dangerous vapor produced by the constipation as *anathymiasis*, must inevitably point to a humoral context. Galen uses that word of "an exhalation from the humors being drawn to the head" (Smith 1975, 128). (For Galen the combustion within the body of black bile and the resultant dangerous vapor cause insanity: see Starobinski 1962, 25–26.)[29] What other humor would an ancient physician associate with this condition than the black humor (melancholia) associated often with constipation?[30]

Petronius, therefore, through the descriptors used of Trimalchio's constipation, reflects the language and concepts used of melancholy. What are we to conclude? The concept of time, as it is embodied here, forms part of a larger textual dialogue engrossing boredom, melancholia, and the experience of time's passing. Trimalchio's condition does not just help us in the search for patterns. It also provides a suggestive match for the periodization I have attributed to madness as it is manifested in melancholia and boredom. Trimalchio's fears manifest themselves precisely within the period during which Seneca's Serenus and, possibly, Chariton's doleful heroes make their melancholic, depressive, and passive laments.

I would like to take this intriguing link between time, the body, and melancholia a step further—this time into the more speculative realms of contemporary psychological description. The link between time and the body is perhaps more peculiar than we might have imagined.[31] Let me explain.

Organizing time for cyclothymiacs or manic-depressives can be a fraught event. Their subjective temporal experience of time seems to involve a sense of the expansion or contraction of time, two perceptions that follow the cyclical movement of the phases of the illness. So time speeds in the hypomanic phase but slows in the corresponding, depressive phase.[32] Thus sufferers appear to be unable to adjudicate the length or shortness of the time required to navigate what for nonsufferers are only mildly complex activities. The many complaints (especially in the case of victims of cyclothymia) of the slowness of their companions or the intolerable haste that they feel their speedier companions are forcing upon them points to the affective basis for the registering of time's passing. (Time, we could speculate, may be conceptualized of as an emotion even, rather than merely representing an emotional register). The precise measurement or demarcation of time for sufferers when they are in the acute phases of the illness can bring on the most anxiety-ridden, anxious, and even aggressive of reactions. This is notably so in the case of the quarrelsome cyclothymic.[33]

As a means of controlling this anxiety brought on by the oppressive slowness or speed of time, some sufferers (again, especially cyclothymiacs) will sometimes involve themselves in the most painstaking of temporal measurements: lists, a variety of alarms, detailed calendars and almanacs, and a crazy collection of calibrations. The relevance of this for Trimalchio (and perhaps for Giorgio de Chirico, whom I discuss in the appendix) ought to be plain. Time and the body, through the dire influence of these melancholy phases, can enjoy a symbiotic relationship.

Entropy is a measure of the disorder among the atoms making up a system. We are told that any initially ordered state is certain to become more random over time. That is one formulation of the second law of thermodynamics. In everyday speech, entropy is taken to mean not the measure of the state of disorder in a system but the tendency for all things, as time progresses, to become more disordered, chaotic, and even prone to catastrophe. Peter Høeg's narrator is referring not just to atoms but to the very material of civilization and society. As he states: "In 1865 Rudolf Clausius suggested the word 'entropy' as a scientific term for the fact that time was linear, irrevocable, irreversible, and that nothing could ever be the same again. Up to that point, even in biology, no one had really been sure of anything other than that living creatures kept on reproducing themselves; that nature was cyclic" (Høeg 1994, 201). Such an entropic temporality has an alarming end point. It envisages that not just civilization and society but also the universe consume themselves through a catastrophic state of total disorder.

We are not alone in this estimation of the course of time. It held considerable appeal for the ancient world, especially for Stoic thinkers such as Trimalchio's contemporary Seneca and for the poet Lucan.[34] It represents an extreme form of the registering of time to which Trimalchio was subject. Seneca believed that the earth and the universe itself would, in time, perish in a mighty catastrophe (sometimes termed *ecpyrosis* or conflagration).[35] The theme of the universal catastrophe seems to have held more than just philosophical appeal for Seneca and his nephew, Lucan. It becomes, in a series of variations, a leitmotiv of their writings, whether they are occasional, dramatic, epistolary, epic (in Lucan's case), on science, or on philosophy. It is another variant of the time corporealized in Trimalchio's constipation, and it offers further support for the discursive typicality of Petronius's time. It is, furthermore, a version of time shared by ancients and moderns.

Let us begin with Seneca. His most vivid description of the universal catastrophe follows (it comes from the *Consolation to Marcia* [26.6–7] and is uttered by Marcia's dead father, the historian A. Cremutius Cordus) (Loeb translation).

> For, if the common fate can be a solace for your yearning, know that nothing will abide where it is now placed, that time will lay all things low and take all things with it. And not simply men will be its sport—for how small a part are they of Fortune's domain—but places, countries, and the great parts of the universe. It will level whole mountains and in another place will pile new rocks on high; it will drink up seas, turn rivers from their courses, and, sundering the communication of nations, break up the association and intercourse of the human race; in other places it will swallow up cities in yawning chasms, will shatter them with earthquakes, and from deep below send forth a pestilential vapor; it will cover with floods the face of the inhabited world, and, deluging the earth, will kill every living creature, and in huge conflagration it will scorch and burn all mortal things. And when the time shall come for the world to be blotted out in order that it may begin life anew, these things will destroy themselves by their own power, and stars will clash with stars, and all the fiery matter of the world that now shines in orderly array will blaze up in a common conflagration. Then also the souls of the blest, who have partaken of immortality, when it shall seem best to God to create the universe anew—we too, amid the falling universe, shall be added as a tiny fraction to this mighty destruction, and shall be changed again into our former elements.

The description is clear enough for it not to require significant paraphrase. Like any organism, Seneca's universe will die in time. The earth will "die" by suffering vast inundations. The firmament in turn will "die" by burning up (and with it will be destroyed creation itself). For the Stoics this was not the complete end of things. From the destroyed universe will grow eventually a new version, perhaps, in the infinity of time, repeating precisely the conditions under which Seneca's contemporaries lived. Stoic time, therefore, was both linear and cyclical. But there are local constraints. Cyclical as Seneca's adopted philosophy of time may have been, there is to his depiction of catastrophe a persistent sense that we are dealing with something that is final. Seneca speaks as if the *ecpyrosis* really were the end of all things. His stress is not so much on regeneration as it is on destruction. It follows that, throughout Seneca's prose and poetry, there is to be derived from knowledge of the final conflagration a bleak romanticism.[36]

Seneca's Stoic catastrophism strikes a curiously modern chord. For those of us, like Høeg, who came to maturity during the cold war, universal catastrophe seems the only possible way for the world and our time to end. To underline that curious congruity between this ancient formulation and modern prejudice is one goal of my brief.[37] But, for the present context, there is a more important point to be made. The vision of time that Seneca repeatedly offers matches, at root, that which we have observed in Trimalchio and will see in Lucan.

But this is to assert too much too soon. First I need to demonstrate some of the contexts in which Seneca makes appeal to this vision of the destruction of the earth and how these may relate to his view of time. Descriptions of the end of the earth (the so-called *ecpyrosis*)[38] occur in several places within Seneca's writing. We have just read one. Others occur in his plays (*Octavia* 391–96; *Hercules Oetaeus* 1100–27; *Troades* 382 ff.; *Thyestes* 830 ff.), in his occasional writing (*Consolation to Polybius* 1.2), in his philosophical writing (*De beneficiis* 6.22), and in his scientific writing (*Natural Questions* 3.13.1–2, 3.27–30). The most extensive of these is presented at *Natural Questions* 3.27–30. In this long sequence, Seneca speculates in detail on how the universal catastrophe will come about ("will it be by the force of the ocean and the rising of the outer sea against us or will heavy rains fall without ceasing and persistent winter eliminate summer and hurl the full force of water down from burst clouds?" 3.27.1), on the stages by which this will happen (3.27.4 ff.: rain, famine, floods, storms), on the true extent of the damage to be caused by the deluge (3.28.1 ff.), on the ability of astrologers to predict the length of the life of the earth and the universe (3.29.1–2), and on the cause of this *ecpyrosis*. It seems, furthermore, that Seneca believes that this universal destruction is imminent (3.30.5 ff.). There is, in one of his summaries within this long sequence, a malevolent, yet elegiac, tone that is typical of his catastrophic imagery. Seneca laments the loss of all things human, yet, strangely, he seems to exult in its passing. Here is his description of the end (3.29.8) (Loeb translation).

> As if this were not enough, winter will hold strange months, summer will be prohibited, and all the stars that dry up the earth will have their heat repressed and will cease. All these names will pass away: the Caspian and the Red Sea, the Ambracian and Cretan Gulf, the Propontis and the Pontus; all distinctions will disappear; all that nature has separated into individual parts will be jumbled together. Neither walls nor towers will protect anyone. Temples will not help worshippers, nor will the heights of cities help refugees, since the wave will anticipate the fugitives and sweep them down from the very citadels. The destructive forces will rush together, some from the west, some from the east. A single day will bury the human race; all that the long indulgence of fortune has cultivated, all that it has lifted to eminence above the rest, all that is noble and beautiful, even the kingdoms of great nations—fortune will send all down to ruin at the same time.

Tarrant (1985, 209) acutely notes the un-Stoic slant that, in passages like this, Seneca places on *ecpyrosis:* "In orthodox Stoic thought *ecpyrosis* brought about purification and renewal . . . but even in his philosophical writing Seneca can focus exclusively on the prospect of annihilation." Passages such as this one tempt us to go further: it is almost as if Seneca rejoiced in this imminent destruction.

Seneca's fascination with this theme of catastrophe spills over into other contexts. He is very fond of depicting cities in calamitous ruin. So the *Troades* begins in the very ruins of Troy (vv. 6–21; cf. vv. 739 ff., 885 ff.).

> Overthrown and fallen is the prop
> Of mighty Asia, famous work of the gods
> . . . .
> Pergamum has fallen upon herself.
> See! The towering glories of her high-piled wall lie low,
> Her dwellings consumed by fire; flames lick around her palaces
> . . . .
> The very sky is hidden
> Because of the billowing smoke; as if smothered by a thick cloud,
> The black day is foul with the ash of Ilium.

The *Oedipus,* too, commences in a gloomy, smoky, plague-ridden city. Fire, whether in the firmament or in a city, seems also to have fascinated Seneca. In *Epistle* 91 Seneca draws lessons from the disastrous conflagration that has leveled Lyons. Catastrophe can happen through other means: in *Natural Questions*

6.1.1 Seneca dwells on the ruinous effects of an earthquake at Pompeii (cf. 6.27.1). The imagery of catastrophe (if not outright references to catastrophe or to the calamities of cities) permeates Seneca's prose writing and poetry. Among those passages one could single out are Oedipus's description of the plague at Thebes (*Oedipus* 110 ff.), Hercules' references (*Hercules Oetaeus* 1150) to the *mundi ruina* (in which he will be buried), the stress of the narrator of the *Natural Questions* on the ominous nature of comets (*Natural Questions* 7.15.1, 7.13.3; they are often associated with periods of great disaster), or the focus generally in book 6 of the *Natural Questions* on the terrifying nature of earthquakes One should also link with this catastrophic imagery the peculiar Stoic notion of *sympatheia:* evil deeds will produce their echo in the very physical constitution of the universe (thus great evil deeds may produce catastrophic natural reactions). So at *Troades* 168 ff. the earth itself revolts against human wrongdoing. In the *Hercules Oetaeus* (v. 1017) poor Deianira thinks that the universe itself is reaction against her complicity in Hercules' destruction (that is precisely the wish made of Hercules at *Hercules Furens* 1054 ff. and 1202). Elsewhere in this same play, we learn that the earth now roars in reaction to Hercules' death (*mundus sonat,* v. 1595).

Seneca's fascination with catastrophe is something that seems to go beyond mere Stoicism and a literary interest in universal destruction. It is as if this reflects his own inner drives and his narcissist horror at the prospect of personal extinction (the very worst aspect of linear time). This is very close to the emotion that drove Trimalchio to insist that his friends participate in his mock funeral.[39] To substantiate this point I will cite three passages, the first spoken by Medea (*Medea* 426–28), the second spoken by Hercules (*Hercules Oetaeus* 1131–37), and the third uttered by Seneca himself (*Natural Questions* 6.2.9). The sentiments embodied in these passages, despite their various speakers and contexts, all seem ominously to match one another. Here are Medea's words.

> My one solace is this:
> To see everything destroyed and in ruins with me.
> Let everything perish with me! Destroying all is pleasure if you must perish.

Medea is referring to her plan to kill her children. This, in Seneca's play, is motivated by Jason's having abandoned her for a new marriage. Medea's startling lack of empathy with creatures other than herself, her desire for universal destruction if she must suffer, and her pessimism and narcissism match the elegiac pessimism we noted earlier. Her selfishness also has a curious analogue in Trimalchio's own bizarre funeral rehearsal and his insistence on the participation of all those around him. It also has a further parallel in the mock funeral of Sextus Turannius reported at the conclusion of the *De brevitate vitae.*

Hercules also echoes Medea's dire selfishness. So great is his own estimation of his terrestrial import that he hopes that the world will suffer destruction on his death. In a passage that reeks of images of *ecpyrosis* (Lapidge 1979), Hercules tells us:

> Turn back, gleaming Titan, the panting horses;
> Send forth night. For let the world let this day perish
> On which I die. Let the pole shudder, wreathed in black cloud.
> Foil my stepmother. Now, father, black chaos
> Should return. On all sides, its framework
> Shattered, the pole should be sundered.
> Why spare the stars? You're losing Hercules, father.

Once again we witness a total lack of empathy with fellow humans, a thoroughgoing narcissism, a remarkable selfishness and self-absorption, and a childish desire for universal destruction—if Hercules himself must suffer: "for the world let this day perish on which I die."

Here is the companion passage from Seneca's *Natural Questions* (Loeb translation).

> The earth is split and burst by the great power of I know not what calamity and carries me off into the immense depths. So what? Is death easier on a level surface? What do I have to complain about if nature does not want me to lie in an ordinary death, if she places upon me a part of herself? My friend Vagellius expresses it well in that famous poem of his:
>
> "If I must fall (*si cadendum est*),"
>
> he says,
>
> "From heaven I'd wish to fall (*e caelo cecidisse velim*)."
>
> I might say the same thing: if I must fall, let me fall with the world shattered *[si cadendum est, cadam orbe concusso]*, not because it is right to hope for a public disaster but because it is a great solace in dying to see that the earth, too, is mortal.

Seneca's adaptation of Vagellius's words (on which see Courtney 1993, 347) is bizarre to say the least. Vagellius seems to be saying that if he must fail, it is better to have failed attempting great deeds (rather like Phaethon). Seneca, ostensibly echoing the sentiments he used for Marcia (*Consolation for Marcia* 26.6), turns the wish solipsistically upon himself: "if I must fall, let me fall with the world shattered." Does he not realize that others would perish in this conflagration? Seneca exhibits the same selfishness, narcissism, and total lack of human empathy as do Medea and Hercules.[40] Seneca's disclaimer ("not because it is right to hope for public disaster") rings false. His sentiment matches utterly those of his alter egos Medea and Hercules. In its peculiar way, it also matches—on a much larger scale—the emotions of Trimalchio. This is a worldview, we should now be able to see, that is based on linear time (at *Natural Questions* 6.32.10–11 Seneca magnificently states that he "hangs on an instant of fleeing time" *[in puncto fugientis temporis pendeo]*).[41] In fact, so linear is this time that Seneca mentions that astrologers are capable of computing the time when the *ecpyrosis* will take place (*Natural Questions* 3.29; cf. *On Providence* 5.7).[42] These computations represent variants of the calculations of which Trimalchio was a devotee. Above all, however, Seneca's desire for a universal cosmic dissolution, apparently designed to assuage his own doleful recognition of personal extinction, represents a revolt, albeit a hopeless one, against the all-powerful linearity of time. This was Trimalchio's strategy in his mock funeral.

This theme of catastrophe can have peculiar referents in real life—nondiscursive referents, we might say. It is hard not to think of the woeful emperor Caligula at this point. Suetonius (*Caligula* 31) tells us:

> He used to complain[ing] how bad times were and that there had been no public. The Varus massacre under Augustus or the collapse of the amphitheatre at Fidenae under Tiberius made their reigns memorable. The prosperity of his own reign, he said, would lead to its being forgotten, and he prayed again and again for a great military catastrophe or some famine, plague, fire, or earthquake.

The same feeling, to follow Suetonius, seems to have impelled Nero to stage his own mini-*ecpyrosis* when he purportedly set fire to Rome.[43] So we read (*Nero* 38) (Penguin translation):[44]

> Once someone quoted the line
>
> When I am dead, may fire consume the earth
>
> but Nero said that the first part of the line should read "While I yet live," and soon converted fancy into fact . . . he brazenly set fire to the city . . . He also coveted the sites of several granaries, solidly built in stone, near the Golden House; having knocked down their wall, he set the interiors ablaze . . . Nero's men destroyed not only a vast number of apartment blocks but mansions which had belonged to famous generals . . . temples too, vowed and dedicated by the kings . . . Nero watched the conflagration from the Tower of Maecenas, enraptured by what he called "the beauty of the flames"; then put on his tragedian's costume and sang *The Sack of Ilium* from beginning to end.

Seen from the perspective of Seneca's writing, the line "When I am dead, may fire consume the earth" takes on an especial urgency. Read within the context of this chapter, it is as if Nero were in revolt not so much against Rome as against the very destructive linearity of time itself.

I would like to pursue the theme of temporal degeneration and of the revolt against the linearity of time one stage further. It is something that was vividly exploited by Lucan (39–65 C.E.), Seneca's contemporary and nephew. His *Civil War* (sometimes called the *Pharsalia*), a historical epic, likens the fall of the Roman Republic and the destruction of its forces under Pompey to the end of the world, to *ecpyrosis*. Do we not have in this a variant of those emotions with which we began this chapter, those to which Trimalchio gave rein in his funeral scene within the *Satyricon*?

The Albertan Michael Lapidge, in a splendid article published in 1979, takes us through the key information on the topic of Lucan and *ecpyrosis*.[45] Lapidge (1979, 359–60) explains that the key themes of the *Civil War*, fratricide and martial blood lust turned on blood relatives, are to be seen from both a human and a cosmic perspective.

> The dissolution of the universe is viewed as parallel to (and, in poetic terms, a result of) the destruction of the state. Lucan is able to keep this parallelism present in the minds of his audience through the use of a vocabulary inherited from Stoic cosmology which . . . had both political and cosmological connotations by the first century A.D.

This remarkable parallelism is best seen in *Civil War* 1.72–80.

> Thus, when, with its framework shattered,
> So many areas of the world the final hour will draw together,
> Seeking again its primeval chaos, and all
> The stars will run in upon all the others, and the sea
> Will the fiery stars seek, and earth will be unwilling to extend its
> shoreline,
> And it will shake off the strand, and contrariwise to her brother
> Phoebe
> Will go to drive the chariot across the far horizon,
> Will she demand, disdaining day, and the whole discordant
> Mechanism will disorder the laws of the disrupted world.

This passage, occurring shortly after Lucan's eulogy of Nero, aims to provide some cosmic rationale for the war. It was, it seems, designed to hasten the eventual process of cosmic dissolution. This is a description of *ecpyrosis*. Although it is not a doctrinaire description of cosmic dissolution, Lapidge (1979, 362) can argue from this passage:

> Lucan was conversant with all of the intricacies of Stoic cosmological theory . . . he was conversant with and stimulated by the vocabulary which the Stoics had employed to illustrate that theory. Lucan clearly employed the Stoic imagery of dissolution because it was germane to the central theme of his poem: that the destruction of the state through civil war is a disaster on a scale commensurable with the dissolution of the universe at *ecpyrosis*.

There are a number of passages that Lapidge highlights in order to demonstrate his case. I will select here just a few to illustrate his claims. *Civil War* 4.98–101 describes floods in Spain.

> Now hills and mountains disappear; now one mere
> Draws all rivers together and submerges them in a huge whirlpool.
> It engulfs completely mountain crags and the homes of beasts.
> It carries these away. It swallows the animals down.

As Lapidge notes, the imagery of the whirlpool, engulfing and swallowing, echoes Seneca's picture of the *ecpyrosis* in the *De beneficiis*. This is no mere flood that we witness; its cosmic overtones color the battles in the books to follow (the real beginnings of the civil war). These battles, then, are initiated by a vision of cosmic dissolution.

Later in the poem, Caesar attempts to cross the Adriatic in a skiff during a storm. The depiction here of the violence of the seas uses the same Stoic terminology of the *ecpyrosis*. It is as if Caesar's voyage presages the imminence of cosmic dissolution (5.632–36).

> Then on high the vault of the sky trembles and the steep poles
> Thunder and labor at the shaking of the framework of the celestial
> axis.
> Nature fears chaos. The elements themselves seem
> To have broken their harmonious unity. And again
> Night seems to return to mingle spirits with gods.

Later, just as the climactic battle of Pharsalia is about to begin, the images of universal dissolution again crowd in (7.134–37).

> Who, having seen the seashores
> Destroyed, who, having seen the ocean on mountaintops
> And the sky sinking onto the earth and the sun vanished,
> An end of so many things, would not fear for himself.

Again after the battle, the enormity of the conflict and its outcome is made clear in Lucan's persistent use of comparable imagery (7.812–15).

> These people, Caesar, if fire won't burn them now,
> It will with the earth and with the ocean depths.
> A shared pyre remains for the earth, one that will mix
> Stars with human bones.

Lapidge (1979, 370) sums his striking study up with the following words:

> During the first seven books . . . the imagery of dissolution occurs in an amazing variety of forms, and it is not misleading to describe it as central to the meaning of the poem. Its use in the *Pharsalia* does not demonstrate that Lucan was a doctrinaire Stoic, but it suggests at least that he was the inheritor of a rich tradition of Stoic cosmological vocabulary stretching back to Chrysippus, and that in the application of this Stoic vocabulary, he displayed striking originality.

Lucan's imagery of cosmic dissolution may seem to be a long way from Trimalchio's constipation. Yet when we view both from the perspective of time, the distance is not so great as at first sight. Trimalchio (through his funerary reenactment), Seneca (through his desire for a universal conflagration to assuage his own mortality), and Nero (through the salve of his *ecpyrosis*) all seem to wish to revolt against time and its destructive linearity. Does Lucan revolt too? For him the linearity of time is above all associated with Julius Caesar and the cataclysmic defeat of the republican forces at the battle of Pharsalia. Lucan's poem, above all else, is a perfervid protest against these events and their outcome for Rome. In this sense his poem is the very embodiment of a revolt against the constraints of a linear time that produced Julius Caesar. It is through this revolt that all these men attempt what I have termed a reformulation of the social personality.

My comparison of examples concerning the representation of time, of madness (or affective disorder at any rate), and of the end of the world is designed to illustrate what is best understood as a textual dialogue between three affective registers. The discursive link between Trimalchio's conception of time and that of Seneca and Lucan should be apparent. This link, however, does go deeper. I have suggested that the corporealization of time in Trimalchio's case provides evidence that for him the experience of time's passing could be understood as equating almost to a mood or affective disorder (a mild form of madness, we might say). I would like to suggest that Seneca's attitude toward time is so intense and so morbid that it, too, points toward affective disorder. Can Seneca's desire for a universal destruction designed to assuage his own personal death be understood in any other way? We would not doubt this of Nero. Why, then, should we doubt it of Seneca?

For the sake of clarity, it may be valuable to reprise the argument of this chapter. My initial point was that the two most generally registered forms of time, the cyclical and the linear, have their representation in ancient experience as surely as they do in modern or early modern experience. There was no need for an Enlightenment or an early capitalist form of economy for the "invention" of linear time. I ought to emphasize, in regard to these two modes of registering time, that I am not necessarily speaking of real-life conditions. Rather, I am referring to the way time could be or predominantly was registered in a number of popular or at least widely read texts. The cyclical time to which I am referring might also be termed "mythological time." Throughout antiquity, it persisted alongside the more prosaic "straight-line" forms of time (which are discussed by philosophers). It was significantly displaced (and this is what I am really arguing) as part of a larger and changed affective and somatic discourse in the first century of our era.

Trimalchio, in Petronius's *Satyricon,* provides one striking embodiment of this concept of linear time, both in his obsession with the measurement of time and, in a somatic fashion, in his attempt to remedy his disordered digestive process. Trimalchio's concern with the linear, serial nature of time also entails a view of temporality as a degenerative agent. Put simply, this means that time leads to personal extinction. Trimalchio's revolt against this (his attempted reformulation of the self) consists in his obsessive measurement of time and in the staging of his own funeral. A parallel to Trimalchio's degenerative time seems to exist in the works of Petronius's contemporaries Seneca and Lucan. Their reactions to the concept of a universe that ends in cosmic catastrophe, or, as the Stoics termed it, *ecpyrosis,* may be contrasted. In Seneca's case there is a willful desire to see his personal extinction accompanied by a universal conflagration. Rather than revolting and pursuing a reformulation of the personality thence, Seneca and his mouthpieces acquiesce and despair. In Lucan's case degeneration is rejected. His poem itself represents the protest and the reformulation. Its passionate preference for republican values represents a rejection of the cosmic dissolution unleashed by Julius Caesar. This protest, then, which is evident in Petronius, Seneca, and Lucan, represents one means by which the boundaries of the self are established firm and upright.[46]

It is striking that this theme of the destructive linearity of time becomes so evident in three authors and in this very period. This, as we have seen in earlier chapters, is the period in which melancholia, lovesickness, boredom, and a theatrical form of suicide became prominent. I have suggested that the somatization of time, in Trimalchio's case, offers a set of symptoms, some of which may be applied as readily to melancholia as to constipation and to time. We witness, therefore, a large affective "domain" (to use rather shopworn jargon) taking in time, passive affectivities such as melancholia and boredom, and, curiously, the body itself. This textual dialogue, as may now be clear, engrosses a number of characterizing polarities, such as the contrast between activity and passivity, between assertion and yielding, between participation and withdrawal, between complicity and estrangement, between the cyclical and the linear, between the mark (the visible) and the sign (the hidden), between body and mind. The list could be continued. We will encounter this again.

7

Passing Time
Hunting, Poetry, and Leisure

> *Vladimir:* That passed the time.
> *Estragon:* It would have passed in any case.
> *Vladimir:* Yes, but not so rapidly.
>
> —SAMUEL BECKETT, *Waiting for Godot*

Preserved for us on an amphora in the Vatican Museum under the name of the black-figure painter Exekias (fig. 8) is a remarkable evocation of ancient leisure.[1] Two men, the greatest of the Greek warriors at Troy, sit opposite one another playing at a game on a board. These warriors are Achilles and Ajax. The scene in Exekias's painting takes place during the Trojan War. It is situated in what must be a brief interlude during or immediately before the fighting around the walls of the citadel.[2] Exekias (who flourished in third quarter of the sixth century B.C.E.) makes unequivocal this temporal location. Achilles is fully armed. His helmet is on, as if he were ready at any moment to go to battle. His two javelins rest instantly available on his left shoulder, and his hand grasps them. His shield, propped just behind him, is within easy reach. The lesser figure of Ajax mirrors that of Achilles in all respects except one: his helmet rests on his nearby shield.[3] Despite the absence of a helmet, Ajax, too, is ready for battle: the pair of javelins resting on his left shoulder makes this quite apparent.[4]

The focus of the picture, however, is not on the two warriors. It is on the box where their game is being conducted. We can barely make out the game. But it is quite clear what they are doing. The warriors' concentration on that box is total. The viewer is drawn toward it with them. Our eyes are led to the game by the way that their figures (their very backs and even their musculature) curve inward toward it, by the way that their arms reach toward it, by the way that their eyes, noses, foreheads (and Achilles' helmet plume), thighs, lower legs, and feet point toward it. The bases of the two pairs of javelins are

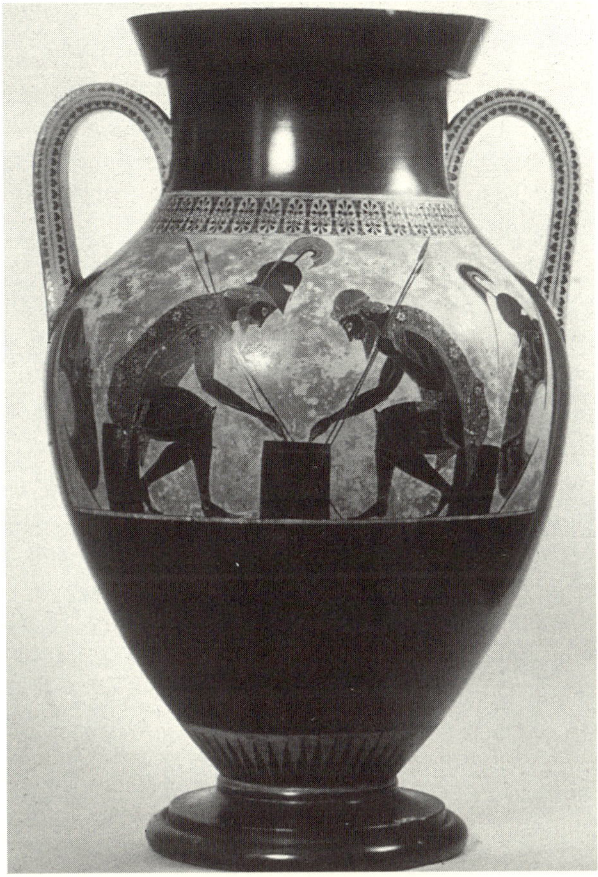

FIG. 8. Exekias, "Achilles and Ajax" (ca. 530 B.C.E.). (Photography courtesy of Vatican Museums.)

fixed on either side of the game box, as if more firmly to anchor the viewer's concentration on the game.[5]

The hands of Achilles and Ajax are poised over the board with striking deliberation. We sense that this very deliberation will shortly be produced for their many victims on the battlefield. The contrast that this brings out, between the pacific and trivial nature of the game and the terrible and bloody events in which Achilles and Ajax are about to participate, is breathtaking.[6] These two heroes will shortly abandon this most convivial of pastimes and participate in the most protracted, bloody, and famous of all ancient conflicts. This war will eventually claim both Achilles' and Ajax's lives.[7] It will cause untold sufferings for the Trojans, as well as the destruction of their city. But not for the present.

At this moment, the two heroes, distracted and content, seem to have no consciousness of the terrible events in which they are key players. The enormity of this realization is to be contrasted with the calm and apparent unimportance of their current activity, the game.

Exekias's vision of how free time may be occupied is constructed around a series of polarities or juxtapositions. This is evident in, for example, the simple contrast between the threatening and purposeful martial habiliment of Achilles and Ajax, between the striking physiques of Achilles and Ajax and the triviality of the game, between the ornate beauty of their dress and its martial purpose. There are also polarities evident between the calm of the warriors and the disordered world of war that they will soon enter, between the board game itself and the serious business of war that is soon to come, between the weapons and the game board, between the way the fighters' hands are outstretched in this picture and how we know they will soon be outstretched on the battlefield. These juxtapositions emphasize the deliberate purposelessness of their play.

It would be easy, when viewing Exekias's remarkable evocation of leisure, to interpret it in some way as expressing a tragic vision of human life. Such an interpretation would go something as follows: War rages around the doomed pair, Achilles and Ajax. The contrast between the insignificance of their game and the momentous nature of events that enfold them highlights their impending deaths. It is as if Achilles and Ajax were the game pieces on the board and the Trojan War was the board itself.

That is far too sentimental an interpretation. Exekias, rather, seems to me to be commenting on the power of play and of games. Despite the chaos around them, Achilles and Ajax are totally absorbed by their game and, presumably, become oblivious to their surrounds. Such leisure activities therefore exist in spite of the surrounds. So leisure in this portrait is something slotted in between other momentous events. Part of its allure, for us viewers at any rate, resides in its acting as an alternative to (not an escape from) war. But that is our reaction. For the two players, the attraction of the game must consist not in such metaphysical implications or in its capacity to provide for them an escape from the savage reality of the war and the proximity of their own deaths but in the simple fact that the game in itself is pleasurable.[8]

There are other aspects of this vase painting that must be highlighted. Exekias's evocation of leisure marks it as no *passive* affair. Leisure requires activity, however slight, as the outstretched arms and the visible musculature beneath the cloaks indicate. The body itself is engaged in this game. Even more important than the complicity of the body itself in Achilles' and Ajax's leisure activity is mental concentration. The very focus of the bodies and of their gestures implies this. It is their concentration that renders irrelevant, for a time, both the war and time itself. Exekias's game requires, furthermore, a form of complicity, of community, and of association: the game requires more than one person to play it. It is notable that this game, furthermore, is a public affair. The dress of the warriors indicates that their game is no secluded pastime but is probably carried out in the open air very near to or even at the marshaling place for the massed fighters; their game, that is, takes place within the melee of public activity, almost within the midst of the war itself. The game asserts vigorously a type of "exteriority." So it is, too, that this form of leisure is both competitive and assertive. Achilles asserts his dominance, not just physically, but, as the painter tells us, by defeating Ajax in this round of the game.

What do Exekias, Achilles, and Ajax have to do with this portion of my study and with this book as a whole? This evocation of leisure and, through this, of how free time may be employed acts as a benchmark against which subsequent formulations or manifestations of the use of free time may be gauged. This chapter will focus on some of the registers of free time and leisure in antiquity. Their changing temporal conception, I will argue, closely mirrors that of those other affectivities and registers that have already been discussed, especially that highlighted in the previous chapter. Their various reflections change markedly within ancient culture. The most notable experiential shift occurs, we will see, approximately at the same time as another major fissure begins to emerge, that between the active and the passive registering of melancholia or lovesickness (see chapters 1–2). This occurs sometime toward the middle of the first century of our era. I will argue, as is in keeping with the three chapters in this part of my book, that leisure is construed in accordance with a desire to protect—even reformulate—a self that is seen as under stress from a variety of societal pressures. It will follow from this that I am asserting a periodization for the construction of leisure. This assertion of a periodization for the utilization of free time (and, perhaps, leisure itself) should come as no surprise, for its perception and use are intertwined intimately with, for example, how it is that the body, the mind (see chapters 1, 2, or 6), and, crucially, time itself (see chapter 6) are felt.

The entirety of the perceptual register of free time and leisure cannot possibly be surveyed within the short space available here (see Balsdon 1969; Veyne 1987; Toner 1995). It is possible only to point to trends and to tendencies. These are best illustrated by tracing the historical development of one mode through which time, in a leisurely manner, may be filled. Such an approach may offer clues to the changes evident in the larger affective field. Elsewhere, in my discussion of the history of didactic epic poetry (Toohey 1996), I have offered some tentative conclusions on this matter. Here, it is my intention to repace some of that material and to reformulate it in accordance with the conclusions this book is attempting to press. By charting the association that a number of didactic authors display toward the use of time in leisure and play, we may come better to understand how one of leisure's ancient forms may have changed and, further, how this may demonstrate the various societal cultures within which it was nurtured.

First let us try to pin down, using Exekias's painting as a model, a more systematic description of leisure and thus the use of free time. The definition offered here is not intended to be timeless but, rather, applies essentially to Exekias. As I trace later historical representations of how free time may be used, we will find that the vision changes markedly.[9]

The preconditions for leisure are free time and the freedom to choose to utilize this. Leisure must also entail pleasure, constitute an end in itself, and involve the application, if not necessarily of some degree of intelligence, at least of a marked degree of mental concentration.[10] I doubt that we need to expand on the need for pleasure in a satisfactory leisure activity (although Aristotle, in his *Politics,* felt obliged to assert the link). If it does not please, would Achilles and Ajax be devoting such considerable attention to it? But what type of activity constitutes an end in itself? Many believe, and it is hard to reject their conclusion, that activities pursued with an end in mind are best thought of as utilitarian, ultimately as little more than work (Aristotle *Politics* 1337b; de Grazia [1962] 1994, 15). They are the sorts of things we do (or hope we do) to keep alive. It is probably true that any activity that functions as an end in itself cannot be thought of as work. Leisure has nothing to do with work or with survival. It is done for its own sake: the board game of Achilles and Ajax could not be further from the utilitarian backdrop of war. That a satisfactory leisure activity should engage the mind was Aristotle's position (in the *Politics;* cf. Pieper 1952). He believed successful leisure *(scholê)* and the exercise of the mind were closely related (*Ethics* 1177b). Although Aristotle probably exaggerates the importance of this element, we ought to note that the intellectual component, while not needing to be profound, must be such as to generate in an individual a marked level of mental concentration. This element of concentration is vital, for without it there cannot be achieved that sense of otherworldliness, that sense of distraction or escape from the quotidian, that is such a notable feature of satisfying and therapeutic leisure.[11] The concentration that Achilles and Ajax display toward their game is made quite apparent in Exekias's rendering of leisure and of the use of free time. Two other qualities, neither of which are stressed in the Aristotelian scheme of things but which are prominent in Exekias's vase, are constants in leisure: first, leisure is most often pursued in a bodily position that is the opposite to that of work (hence one that is nonquotidian, often sedentary);[12] second, leisure is frequently, though not exclusively, pursued in company with others.[13]

Leisure, as Achilles and Ajax show, is closely related to play. I have suggested (Toohey 1996) that they are siblings (cf. Huizinga [1949] 1971; O'Loughlin 1978). Because the concept of play will prove important to my discussion, I offer here a few summarizing comments (see too Bruner 1975). These are, again, based on Exekias. I suppose that the simplest distinction between leisure and play is that leisure owes its existence to work, while play does not. Leisure is conceived as an alternative to work. It is probably fair to say that a child can have no leisure. Not being subject to work, a child cannot have leisure from something. The same could be said of the unemployed. Play, however, does not exist in contradistinction to work. A child's life or that of any unemployed person may be full of play. Play seems dependent on the pleasure inherent in leisure (cf. Aristotle *Politics* 1337b). In play "the player leaves his everyday world and enters one in which for the moment he is free of necessity, namely in his free time, his time of recreation" (de Grazia [1962] 1994, 375). Play is inherently "otherworldly." It usually has rules, against which one often can pit oneself. It usually involves interaction with others (in person or through instructional material). Because play is not concerned with the here and now, it also seems to exploit the gulf between signifier and signified, between subject and object. Play can be a game, though this is not necessarily so. Games, often mere contests, are so frequently and so vigorously predicated on winning and losing that they may forfeit their autonomy.[14] Loss and victory easily undermine the self-referentiality and come to function as economic or social "ends."[15]

Leisure, in the model I have suggested, is built upon purposelessness, upon a disjunction between action and realization—perhaps more properly, upon a disjunction between the subject and the world (the object). Leisure here derives its resonance from the chosen inability of the individual to influence the world by practicing its particular modality. In the most peculiar of manners, it is as if leisure recapitulates the infantile rupture that took place between the individual and the world. It is at this point that play becomes important. For the child, it helps overcome the trauma of that rupture by teaching a limited mastery of the physical worlds and thus a pleasurable tolerance of the disjunction between self and other. Leisure, because it is so often and so easily perceived as frivolous (as purposeless, as forging no link between subject and object), is frequently disapproved of or rejected out of hand. Play provides its rationale, its excuse, and even its justification. Play restores the balance potentially offset by leisure's purposelessness. This is inherent in the model based on Exekias that I have sketched.

To chart the changes in such a slippery experience as the use of free time or such an intangible concept as leisure itself, we need to focus on some discrete mode of its construction (e.g., a toy, a game, a spectacle)[16] and to allow this specific instance to speak for the general. It has often been argued that ancient didactic poetry, in many, if not all, of its incarnations, functions as an adjunct to the leisurely use of free time (Effe 1977; Toohey 1996). On the simplest level, it may provide instruction on such essentially leisure activities as hunting with dogs, fishing, the theater, love, and gardening (Dalzell 1996).[17] On a more complex level, didactic poetry may function, in itself, as a form of intellectual play—displaying those characteristics adumbrated in the previous paragraphs (Toohey 1996). Were we, therefore, to chart the interaction between examples of didactic poetry that focus explicitly on leisure activities and the use of free time, it might be possible to descry the lineaments of a reasoned sequence, or periodization, for the manner by which the leisurely use of time, in this arena at any rate, may be registered:[18] the concrete instance of didactic epic, that is, may provide clues for the general.

Hunting may provide the most comprehensible example.[19] It is in many, if not all, eras a leisure activity, while being one of the more popular topics within the extant ancient didactic corpus. For what it is worth, opinions on the status of hunting as a leisure activity differ in prose. Xenophon (*Cynegeticus* 7), describing hunting with hounds on foot, sees the activity not as leisurely but as utilitarian, as good preparation for war (see Hull 1964). Arrian, describing a hunt that uses horses with the dogs, sees no particular morality in hunting (Anderson 1985, 119). Pleasure drives its practice. The Celts, who provide much of Arrian's focus, are said to hunt "for the sheer pleasure of it" (Hull 1964, 164). At any rate, to follow is a very simple evaluation of the worth of hunting. It comes from Rutilius Namatianus's poem *De reditu suo* (vv. 615–30).[20]

And now, returning to Triturrita from the city of Pisa
  I was setting the hanging sails to a gleaming South wind,
When, shrouded by sudden clouds, the sky turned foul.
  The broken clouds scattered their wandering lightning.
We stopped. For who, in such a terrible storm,
  For who would dare to travel on seas soon to be raging.
We pass our leisure from the sea in the neighbouring woods,
  And it pleases us to exercise in the pursuit of game.
Our hospitable bailiff prepares the hunting instruments
  And the dogs who know how to recognize the strong scented
    furrow.

By ambush and by the snare of wide-meshed nets
  The boar, with his terrifying flash of tusk, is overthrown and falls.
A boar that Meleager's might would have feared to approach,
  That would have weakened the joints of Hercules.
The hunting bugle rings back from the echoing hills
  And song makes the booty light for carrying.

We have met Rutilius before and examined his comments on the problems suffered by anchoritic monks and on Bellerophon. In this phase of his poem, he is no longer at sea and reflecting on melancholy. He has broken his sea voyage to Gaul to stay in a country house, probably that of a friend. Hunting has been undertaken here as a means, we would say, for relaxation, as a means for leisure. The passage, I think, speaks for itself. Note especially verse 621, "We pass our leisure from the sea in the neighbouring woods." Neither the replenishment of food supplies nor the acting out of ideological posture seems to be at issue here. It is just a matter of passing time pleasurably, of play, of purposelessness.

There survive didactic poems on this topic of hunting, written by Ovid, Grattius, Oppian, and Nemesianus, that reflect, in very different ways, the leisurely tradition encapsulated in these lines by Rutilius.[21] The didactic poetry written on hunting (and, to a lesser extent, on fishing)[22] is obviously dictated by the exigencies of leisure. While these texts do aim to impart some information on technical topics,[23] they have as their target more the amusement of those people who would wish to enjoy very popular leisure pursuits.[24] What I propose to do in this section is to look at the attitudes displayed by these hunting (and fishing) poems and then to attempt to demonstrate how these may relate to one another and in turn to the idealized template for leisure within Exekias's painting. Thence may emerge the periodization to which I have referred, one that will allow us to compare the modes by which leisure is experienced and the modes by which we may relate to leisure the other affective registers surveyed up to this point in my book.

Before we begin with the didactic poems, there remain a few general comments that ought to be made concerning hunting. Its practice in antiquity was not always based upon the exigencies of leisure.[25] If we survey, briefly, the prose and pictorial depictions of hunting, a trajectory becomes apparent: hunting shifts from a subsistence activity, to one providing education, to one pursued particularly as a means of affirming power, to, finally though not exclusively, one that simply fills in time in a pleasurable manner. Several of these elements may be present at one time, but the pattern I have indicated here is operant, in the most general of senses.

Let me explain this trajectory in a little more detail. In its earliest practice—as we see it in Homer, for example—hunting seems to have been firmly utilitarian, an activity unrelated to leisure. The Homeric hero, according to Anderson (1985, 15), hunted to provide himself with a meal. The skills required—cunning, patience, physical endurance, and, in the case of the hunting of larger animals, courage—not unexpectedly came to be associated with the battlefield. While we may wonder at the worth of hunting as preparation for taking part in war as a hoplite in a phalanx or an oarsman in a trireme, such a writer as Xenophon (*Cynegeticus* 7) asserts the educational value of hunting and claims that "hunting brings bodily health, improves sight and hearing, is an antidote to senility, and excellent training in the art of war."[26] Plato, in the *Laws*, provides an echo of Xenophon's utilitarian explanation when he praises hunting "of four-footed beasts" with horses and with hounds and with "men's own bodies." Plato admires the chase and the shooting and believes that "those who hunt in this way have their thoughts fixed on god-like manhood" (Anderson [1985, 22]). Whether representative of manhood or war, the vision is utterly utilitarian.

It is telling that Plato despises the banausic forms of hunting, such as fishing and fowling (see Longo 1989). These vigorously utilitarian activities make no claim on the time of a person who had the leisure to frequent the Academy or Socrates' company. Hunting with dogs or on horseback was no pursuit for the poor. Indeed it could not be practiced by the poor. Breeding and maintaining dogs was a full-time job. It is not surprising, therefore, that hunting became associated in Greece not just with wealth but with the sort of display associated with the aristocracy.[27] This association is well illustrated in Xenophon's *Cyropaedeia* where the hunting abilities of the Persian noble Cyrus—above all, his abilities on horseback—are extolled. Xenophon no doubt wishes the same abilities for his own Greek class. Two aspects of Persian hunting are worth noting, in passing, in this context. First is the imperial habit of establishing, within the palatial precinct, large walled enclosures in which emperors and nobles could hunt undisturbed on horseback. That practice illustrates the link between class and hunting as a leisure-time activity. Second, there was the strange link made by the Persians between hunting and empire (Anderson 1985, 67). The emperor, depicted on stone relief and in prose, is cast as the mighty hunter, the "protector of the people." The class-based ideology underlying Persian hunting is inevitably present, in spirit at any rate, in classical Greece. The various Greek pots, made to be buried in graves, that associate life (especially those of the young) with hunting make apparent this link between social power and hunting (Anderson 1985).

During the Hellenistic period, a specific type of hunting, termed by Anderson (1985) as the "royal hunt," became very popular among Greeks of the ruling classes. Hunting, particularly on horseback and often within game-stocked regal parks, was practiced constantly and enthusiastically by monarchs. It could often be accompanied by considerable and expensive trappings. A variety of animals might be shipped in especially for the hunt, and these might be paraded publicly before the event. Anderson (1985, 81) details one such parade.

> A procession [was] organized by Ptolemy Philadelphus of Egypt (283–247 B.C.) . . . and included hunters with gilded spears, 2,400 hounds of the Indian, Hyrcanian, and Molossian breeds, trees with beasts and birds dangling from them, and caged parrots, peacocks, guinea fowl, pheasants and "Ethiopian birds" . . . sheep of exotic breeds, white Indian and Ethiopian oxen, a large white bear . . . leopards, panthers, and lynxes . . . and this section of the procession was closed by a giraffe and a rhinoceros [Athenaeus 5.201b–c].

These were creatures all destined eventually for the royal hunt. Such a remarkable display cannot be motivated simply by an overenthusiasm for leisure-time activities. Its motivation is in the display itself. That, at root, is designed to exhibit power. Such displays, one must conclude, were another means used by the Hellenistic monarchs to shore up their novel and insecure regal positions. Hunting, while apparently a leisure-time activity for the very rich, is in fact as practical an activity for them, but in a different way, as it was for Homer, or Plato, or Xenophon.

In Rome, I suspect, this link with class became less pressing. Hunting became part of the normal aristocratic lifestyle and, unquestioningly, became associated with passing time pleasurably, with leisure. This pastime of hunting, imitated on the grand scale from Greece, seems to have taken root in the 170s and 160s B.C.E.[28] The ethos that seems to have become associated with hunting in Rome may be viewed, as neatly as anywhere else, in the description given to us of hunting by Rutilius Namatianus, cited in the last section of this chapter. I will have more to say on this in the next section of this chapter.

Things are seldom as simple as they ought to be. This is as true of the poetical descriptions of hunting as of any other activity.[29] The sorts of ideological or discursive underpinnings that may influence the depiction of hunting and of leisure in Rome may well be illustrated by a poem of Martial. The poem that I have in mind is 1.49. It was published in 80 C.E.

Martial's poem acts as an invitation to a Licinianus to come for a summer visit to the poet, his fellow countryman, on his regional estate in Spain. The visit is more than just that. Martial is urging Licinianus to abandon Rome and to take up residence in his native Spain. A crucial part of the attraction of Spain, according to Martial, is the hunting. The poem is a long one but deserves quoting in full.

Worthy to be acclaimed by the Celtiberians,
    Glory of our Spain,
Licinianus! You will see lofty Bilbilis,
    Famed for horses and weapons;
And old Caius with its snows; and sacred Vadevero
    Set in rugged hills;
And the pleasant wood of pretty Boterdus,
    Beloved of generous Pomona.
You'll swim in the gentle shoals of warm Congedus
    And the smooth lake of the nymphs,
And, relaxed, you'll brace yourself in shallow
    Salo, which freezes steel.
There Vorberca will provide you freely with animals
    To shoot at close range while you lunch.
You will break the cloudless heat in golden Tagus,
    Hidden in the forest's shades.
Chill Derceita will slake your raging thirst,
    And Nutha, which is colder than snow.
And when frosty December and wild winter
    Howl with the hoarse north wind,
You'll go back to the sunny shore of Tarraco
    And your own Laletania.
There you will slaughter deer snared
    In soft-meshed nets, and native boars,
And run the cunning hare to death with your stout horse.
    Stags you'll leave to your bailiff.
The neighboring forest will come right down to your hearth,
    And its crowd of grimy children.
The hunter will be invited, and he'll come
    As a dinner guest called from nearby.
Nowhere will you see a crescent shoe buckle or a toga
    Or clothes smelling of purple dye.

There will be no litter bearer or grumbling client
 Or imperious widow.
No pale defendant will interrupt your deep slumber.
 Instead you'll sleep the whole morning.
Let someone else win the big, mad "Bravo":
 You should pardon the successful *[felices]*.
What you must do is to enjoy real pleasure *[gaudium]*.
 Let your lawyer friend Sura get the public praise.
It's only right that life seeks what else is in store,
 When fame has been sated.

Martial goes to great lengths to induce Licinianus to visit his estate. He stresses (vv. 1–18) the various summer attractions of his region. In doing so he heaps up, almost sensuously, local nomenclature and characterization (of towns such as Bilbilis, Vadevero, Boterdus, and Pomona and of rivers such as the Congedus, Salo, Vorberca, Tagus, Derceita, and Nutha—these are all vividly invoked). Part of this appeal resides in stressing the ease of hunting in the region (vv. 13–14): so plentiful is game that it might be had even while lunching—in a state, that is, of remarkable passivity. In Licinianus's region of Tarraco, the hunting (vv. 23–26) is more vigorous than on Martial's estate. In Laletania there are deer and boars and hares for hunting on horseback (cf. also vv. 23–25). Hunting here, however, is not as active an affair as it was for Homer, or Xenophon, or Plato. This is not hunting for subsistence, or education, or display. It is a game. Stags are left to the bailiff (v. 26), and Licinianus is to concentrate on hares or deer caught in "effete" *(mollia)* nets (v. 24).[30]

The appeal of Martial's and Licinianus's Spanish countryside is in its nonquotidian nature. It is as far from the life of the city as could be imagined. This is a point made forcibly again in the final four lines of the poem. Licinianus is clearly still resident in Rome, where he practices, actively and vigorously, as an advocate (vv. 31–34). The attraction of a life in Spain, argues Martial, is that it will provide a release from such a grueling regime (v. 37: "let someone else win the big, mad 'Bravo'"). The key to Martial's argument is provided in verses 38–42. Licinianus has fame (v. 42), thus success enough (v. 38). He should devote himself to real pleasure *(verum gaudium)*. That is Spain, the rural life, and, especially, hunting. As we can see, hunting becomes the very embodiment of the leisured life. Martial would have Licinianus practice a form of life that embodies a complete disjunction between action (the Roman life of the advocate) and realization (the easy hunting on Martial's or Licinianus's estates).

To what extent does Martial's vision match that of the Exekian template? Many of the elements are there. Licinianus is urged to devote himself to the pursuit of not only free time but a free time that is chosen and pleasurable. His hunting, furthermore, is purposeless, playful, and companionable. There is here no place for subsistence, for education, or for the display of power. Yet there is a key difference, and in this regard we may contrast Martial with Rutilius Namatianus as well. There is, in Martial's advocacy of verses 31–36, a recommendation for hunting that is based on an escapist appeal. Hunting and the Spanish way of life are valuable precisely in their contrast with Rome. There is in this contrast an implicit regret that Rome could not be better—more like Spain. Public life in Rome, Martial implies, is in some way or another a threatening process. It is something inimical to human happiness. Martial argues to Licinianus that if he is to achieve true happiness, then Rome and his legal life must be abandoned. Hunting comes to symbolize the happiness that an alternative mode of life in Spain could offer. Martial's leisure activity therefore has an implicit end, despite its apparent purposelessness. Thus there is the idea of escape, of the alternative offered by leisure through hunting.

It is too soon to be positing links and changes. But, for the sake of clarity, I would like to anticipate my contentions and conclusions concerning this theme of filling in time. The contrast between Exekias and Martial represents more than a mere difference in outlook toward the use of free time. It represents, in my opinion, a fundamental shift, above all, from the active to the passive. This is precisely the shift we have witnessed in other affective registers: melancholy, love, suicide, and time itself. The focus of this and the last two chapters has been on the notion of "reformulating the personality." Licinianus's social self may be under no imminent threat from his Roman legal practice. Martial seems to believe his happiness is. Hunting, in Martial's eyes, offers a means for recalibrating and reformulating Licinianus's hold on happiness. That conceptualization has no parallel in Exekias's vision.

To take the preceding simple conclusions further, I would like now to turn to didactic epic proper and to Ovid's poem on fishing. In Ovid's poem, the Exekian vision of things is operant. At any rate, the 134 lines of Ovid's *Halieutica* represent but a portion of the original poem. There is no proper introduction and conclusion, nor are there, as part of the body of the poem, the sorts of didactic elements that we might expect: descriptions of dangerous fish, their and other fishes' social habits, the tools that fishermen use to catch them, and so forth.[31] Yet there is enough of the *Halieutica* to enable us to gain an idea of how it went about things.[32] It is as if Ovid had asked himself the question, how do you turn a practical manual into something impractical—something purposeless; or, to put it another way, how does instruction become play?[33] Part of the answer is to put the instruction in verse. Another part of the answer is to write about something that may involve play. The other part of the answer lies in irony and in the mock serious. Both signal apparent purposelessness.

How fish protect themselves is the subject of verses 10–48 of the *Halieutica.* Unlike land animals, who exercise self-protection through instinct (vv. 49–81), these fish exhibit a remarkable level of self-knowledge, of, we might say, *notitia sui.* This self-knowledge is exhibited—or better, gained—through adversity. This is a simple notion, one that has a direct parallel to that for which I have argued, in more complex circumstances, in relation to the self.[34] Ovid provides us with a number of examples of piscine self-knowledge. The lamprey *(muraena),* for example, is cited twice in this regard. Here is what Ovid says first (vv. 27–30).

> The fierce lamprey, conscious of[35] his smooth back,
> Struggles more against the loosened apertures of the net,
> And, finally, by means of his many twists, slips out to escape,
> And does harm by his example: he offers an escape for all.

The lamprey's self-knowledge is of a very limited sort—a consciousness of his physical advantages. Yet, as Ovid has it, the lamprey *understands* this advantage and acts upon it quite deliberately. He knows how to get out of trouble by using his key physical attribute.[36] Using his knowledge of his slippery back, he wriggles through fishing nets. The lamprey's exemplary self-knowledge is stressed again later (vv. 43–45).

> Nor is the lamprey unknowing of his own strength at harming,
> Nor in self-assistance and in fierce biting at close quarters
> Is he found wanting, nor when captured does he lose his threatening
> spirit.

Notice how, in this second passage, Ovid places stress on knowledge and understanding (v. 43: *nec nescit* [nor is he unknowing of . . .]). The strength of the lamprey again resides in self-consciousness and in deliberate exploitation of its own best features.

Contrast land animals (vv. 49–81). They are driven by instinct to self-preservation, unlike the thoughtful fish. Forest dwellers are worst, states Ovid (vv. 49–52).

> Other creatures that live in thick forests
> Are frenzied and terrified constantly by baseless fears
> Or are drawn headlong by crazed daring.
> Then nature urges them to hunt or to fight at close quarters.

So it is that creatures such as the lion, the bear, the boar, the hare, the hind, and the stag fight or flee, frenzied or terrified, instinctually and uncontrollably. There is no self-knowledge here. Look at what the boar does (vv. 60–62).

> The hunted boar displays his anger with his hairy bristles.
> He rushes vigorously onto fixed, wounding steel.
> Checked by a spear thrust through his guts, he dies.

Even horses and hounds, both of whom Ovid admires, are driven by a comparable thoughtlessness.

But can we take this partisan moralizing seriously? The tone of these lines can allow us only to answer this query in the negative. In the broadest of senses, a passage that attributes such self-conscious and humanlike intelligence to such unlikely recipients as fish is pulling our leg. This suspicion is reaffirmed by some of the descriptions of the fish. Some are too bizarre to take seriously (e.g., at vv. 16–18, one scarfish rescues another by grabbing its tail and dragging it from the trap) or too histrionic (e.g., at v. 20, the squid's very gizzards, *hilla*, fear "snatching hands" *[manus rapaces]*). Ovid mocks more than he instructs. The mockery is no doubt directed toward poems such as that of Grattius to be discussed shortly. Ovid has no pretension to practicality. He is more interested in writing an amusing poem than in providing instruction. His focus, thus, is on his own poem. Ovid conveys this nicely when he states, "our task is dependent on *ars*, all our hope is in this" *[noster in arte labor positus, spes omnis in illa]* (v. 82). *Ars* here implies not just the skill required of a successful fisherman but also that required of a poet (a practitioner of *ars poetica*). Such self-referentiality deliberately exploits the gap between the means (Ovid's verse texture) and the advice (instruction to fishermen). It highlights the medium (the poem itself) and so stresses the importance of play and purposelessness in Ovid's overall design.

It is in this spirit of play that we come to read the remaining sections of the poem (vv. 82–93, on where to hunt for fish, and vv. 94–113, a list of fish to be hunted). The extensive, learned catalog has its force not in instruction but in its playful display of erudition. How else than as playful should passages such as the following (vv. 107–10) be taken?

> And the ruddy Pager, and the tawny Snoods, and
> The self-conceiving Channe, playing both parents to itself,
> Then the green-scaled, small-mouthed, rock-dwelling,
> Seldom seen Dory, and the painted Morays . . .

It must be very difficult to set such extravagant lists to verse.

The spirit of parody that so permeates Ovid's poem highlights other aspects of its "leisurely" nature—a nature that has its analogue in the vision of Exekias. These relate to the pleasure side of leisure. The strain of parody enforces a marked gap between the signifier and the signified. It is difficult, if not downright impossible, to believe that Ovid intended the instruction of the *Halieutica* to be read and used by the sorts of men and women for whom he wrote. They would have had their own authorities. While I have no doubt that his information was reliable, I doubt that we should read them in anything other than the playful and ironic spirit in which they were conceived. The poem also offers rules against which to pit oneself, and it implies the eventual interaction with other people.

We can go further. Leisure as it is *embodied* in the *Halieutica* is the most purposeless of things. We could also say that a leisure that is devoted to reading about fishing is frivolous. The accusation that could be leveled against the poem, of purposeless frivolity, is mitigated by play, however, in two ways: first because it insists upon the pleasurable (nonharmful) nature of the experience; second because it focuses attention at the same time onto the poem itself. As I have just noted, the *Halieutica* parodies instructional literature. In so doing, it forces attention, at least for a time, away from its advice (the activity of fishing) and onto its means (the poem as a generic parody). Thus parody forces a gap between the subject (the poem) and its object (fishing). But this is done in such a pleasurable manner that it produces enjoyment. The *Halieutica* therefore plays upon purposelessness. Play restores the balance potentially offset by the purposelessness of leisure and at the same time answers definitively any accusation made against the *Halieutica* of utter frivolity. In this way Ovid's poem provides a striking, albeit much lighter, analogue to Exekias's painting. The purpose of the poem is thus pleasure, not sensual, but intellectual and mental, very much of the same order as that attributed to Exekias's game players, Achilles and Ajax.[37]

The focus of this chapter is not just leisure but, specifically, the modes by which leisure can be conceptualized in didactic poetry and how leisure occurs in didactic poetry that has hunting as its theme. One of the least expected places within the corpus of poetry that has instruction in hunting as its aim is again provided by Ovid. The concern of this poetry is not fish but sexual relations.[38] Ovid, in his didactic poetry on love, pursues the metaphor of hunting into amatory contexts (see *Ars amatoria* 1.43–50, 277–82). What may surprise (initially at least) is that in these poems the real focus is on the act of creating poetry on "amatory hunting," rather than on the amatory process itself. These "hunting" poems are in no way utilitarian (aiming to assist in seduction). Mirroring Exekias's vision of leisure and that which we have encountered in the *Halieutica*, this poetry is resolute in its salutary uselessness.

Ovid's *Ars amatoria* embodies this Exekian tradition. The merest summary of its contents will illustrate its comic and leisure-related nature. Book 1 (telling how to catch a woman) divides, after its introduction (1.1–40, which asserts this poem's status as a legitimate didactic product), into two parts. The first (1.41–262) outlines the best places in Rome, primarily, to pick up a lover: colonnades, foreign temples, the theaters and the Circus, processions, dinner parties, coastal resorts, and Diana's forested shrine near Aricia. The second part (following a bridge at 1.263–68 and a postscript at 1.755–72) offers various means for gaining the favor of the woman met in the places listed in verses 41–262: insinuating oneself with her maids, love letters, personal presentation, behavior at dinner parties, promises, tears, violence, and looking lovelorn (1.269–754). Success in seduction is assumed for the predominantly male audience of the second book of the *Ars amatoria*. It aims to impart the self-knowledge (the *notitia sui* of the lamprey), the self-control, and the humility necessary to retain one's lover. Ovid teaches us how to sustain and cultivate a relationship. Thus, after the introduction of 2.1–98, we are instructed in the avoidance of aphrodisiacs (2.99–106), then on the need for persuasiveness (2.107–44), tolerance (2.145–76), and an accommodating nature (2.177–232). Shower the woman with gifts (2.255–86), flattery (2.247–314), and attention when sick (2.315–36), and, if necessary, fuel her enthusiasms with discreet absences (2.357–408), Ovid advises his seducers. Encouraging jealousy can be useful (2.435–60), as can settling quarrels with lovemaking (2.461–92). Ovid offers advice on coping with infidelity (2.535–640) and encourages his pupils not to criticize a lover's shortcomings (2.641–702). The book finishes with advice on lovemaking (2.703–32) and a brief conclusion (2.733–46). As should be evident, the conceit generating all of this is hunting. The opposite sex becomes the quarry.

Books 1 and 2 of the *Ars* were composed as a pair. Perhaps their popularity caused Ovid to rethink his design and to add a third book of advice, this time for the quarry, women. The material within this book (surely written for male readers) combines advice on hunting and on *cultus*. There are two halves reflecting approximately these two concerns. The first (3.101–524) outlines a variety of necessary personal accomplishments: dressing up (3.101–32), hair (3.133–68), clothing (3.169–92), personal hygiene (3.193–208), cosmetics (3.209–50), poetry (3.311–48), dancing and games (3.349–80), where to appear in public (3.381–432), and the sort of man to avoid (dandies: 3.433–66). The second half of the book (3.553–808) dwells on how women ought to deal with their lovers—whether inexperienced, experienced (3.553–76), or suspicious husbands (3.611–58)—then how to fan jealousy (3.577–610), how to eat (3.747–68), and how to make love (3.769–808).[39]

I have written in more detail about this aspect of Ovid's depiction of leisure elsewhere (Toohey 1996). It would be too repetitive to reproduce the material here. Play, leisure, and the use of free time are at the very heart of the *Ars amatoria* (Myerowitz 1985; Citroni 1989; cf. Hollis 1973, 93). In his comedy on love, Ovid has made leisure prominent and has ironically enshrined its pursuit through the metaphors of love and hunting. The *Ars amatoria* could be read as a specialist leisure guide: not only does it envision the life of the lover as sensually gratifying and as an ideal means for passing time, but Ovid believes that *writing* and *reading* about love represent an ideal pastime.[40]

The sorts of conclusions that I have suggested for the *Halieutica* therefore apply with the same force and vigor to the *Ars*. The latter's direct focus on amatory dalliance makes it even more palpably a leisure manual. It is, however, an utterly frivolous poem. Its subject matter is completely purposeless (especially when viewed from the perspective of an emperor such as Augustus), and its treatment is completely frivolous. As with the *Halieutica*, the notion of play in the *Ars* interposes itself between us and the acceptance by the reader of the poem's advice as seriously meant. Perhaps even more than in the *Halieutica*, Ovid has, both through the parodic nature of his poem and through his emphasis on its persuasory attraction, highlighted its existence as a subjective entity. In many a passage, Ovid makes plain the gap between subject (the poem) and object (its instruction).[41] He thus highlights the purposelessness of his poem, but he excuses this through the pleasure inherent in the playful texture of the poem. (Once again play comes to the rescue of purposelessness.) The purpose of the poem is thus pleasure—again, not sensual, but intellectual or even psychological and very much of the same order as that of Exekias's Achilles and Ajax. Play is therapeutic. Ovid's seemingly frivolous poems are profoundly so.

The *Remedia amoris* continues the comic tradition of the *Ars amatoria* (cf. Conte 1994b). Its primary reason for composition was parodic (I would place this above any didactic pretense). Not content with the joke of the *Ars Amatoria*, Ovid attempted to cap it with a repeat performance—one that parodies Ovid's own poetry as much as the subgenre within which it is composed. In the *Ars* he had taught how to hunt out a partner and how to fall in love, while in the *Remedia* he teaches how to remove the snares put in place by the hunter. This poem stands as a fourth book to the *Ars amatoria*. A brief summary of the contents of the poem will once again illustrate its instructive nature and how this links with our theme of leisure and the use of free time. After a preface (to Cupid) and a statement of aim (to help those who are crossed in love) (vv. 1–40) and following a type of invocation (vv. 41–98, directed to the audience and to Apollo), Ovid outlines a variety of means for countering infatuation: initial caution (vv. 79–134), avoiding idleness (vv. 135–50), business (vv. 151–248), avoidance of magical assistance (vv. 249–90), and just about anything that will cast one's lover in an unattractive light (vv. 291–340). A defense of the *Ars amatoria* bisects the poem (vv. 356–98: Ovid has been accused of being insufficiently "epic"). The second half of this very funny poem continues with advice on tactical ploys: how to cast one's lover in the worst of lights (vv. 399–544), means for distracting oneself (vv. 545–602), how to avoid one's lover (vv. 603–64), how to behave in front of her (vv. 665–90), places to avoid (vv. 699–784), and advice on diet (vv. 785–800). The poem finishes with a brief epilogue (vv. 801–4).

The utilization of free time dictates the choice of subject matter for Ovid's erotodidactic poems. But this choice of subject matter is also reflected in the very texture of this poem—something quite obvious from my summary. Instruction, to restate the point, has always been the sine qua non of didactic poetry, and Ovid attempted instruction in his long poems on eros. Yet instruction seems primarily to provide the excuse for the poetry. Its raison d'être exists above all within the poetic texture itself.[42] The pleasure that these poems offer resides not so much in their ends as in their process. The elements of play within the *Remedia* (the process) seem not so much to undercut as to complement the purveyance of information (the ends). Play and pleasure are key constitutive elements of leisure. Like proper artifacts of leisure activity, these poems also exhibit self-containedness and intellectual complexity. Let me also reemphasize that Ovid's poetry is totally purposeless. The activity on which it instructs is purposeless (it does not aim for any utilitarian end), and the medium through which this message is delivered is also purposeless (it aims to produce a pleasure that is specifically text-orientated).

We should now return to the central theme of this chapter, hunting, and see how, in didactic poetry, it fares after Ovid. But before doing this, I would like to put one more query: what does this discussion of Ovid have to do with my theme of the reformulation of the personality? Exekias and Ovid provide a remarkably compelling model for the means for such a reformulation. The personality is most threatened by the widening of the fissure between subject and object and, with this, the replication of the childhood rupture between the self and the world. Exekias's and Ovid's strategy is first to highlight the fissure (in Exekias's case, in the contrast between the war and the game; in Ovid's, by highlighting the existence of his poem less as an instructional manual than as a poetic artifact), then to demonstrate how the fissure is bridged, through play and through purposeless pleasure.[43] The reformulation offered by later writers on hunting is of a completely different order. It echoes the end-orientated Martial 1.49.

Ovid's contemporary Grattius (cf. *Epistulae ex Ponto* 4.16.34, dated to 8 C.E.) has left us 541 lines of an incomplete poem on hunting with dogs, the *Cynegetica*.[44] Instruction, rather than play, conditions Grattius's text.[45] The utilitarian dominates poetic textures. Whimsy and wordplay are excluded (there is none of that Ovidian humor or misdirection that calls into doubt the applicability of the material being broadcast). Grattius exhibits a number of interesting ideological tics that betray what might be termed subjective camouflage or even a censoring of the ego.

To illustrate this, the best method is to begin with Grattius's striking approach to the Hellenistic equation between empire and hunting. At verses 307–25 Grattius complains of the effects of excessive luxury and greed (v. 308). He illustrates this, as we might expect, first with dogs: luxury and greed should be avoided when raising pups ("such pandering comes at great cost," v. 309). Grattius attempts to back this up by highlighting the vices of luxury-loving Egyptian monarchs, Lydians, and Greeks generally. The Romans of the early Republic are offered as exemplars of the advantages of a life without the trappings of luxury (vv. 321–25). It was these early Romans who made Rome a world power *(imposuere orbi Romam caput)*. Grattius's rearing methods for animals match, microscopically, the triumphant methods used by Rome to dominate the world (at v. 328 the hunter's rule over pups is termed an *imperium*). The lines in question run as follows:

> You must sustain the young brood with a mild and simple pap:
> And do not let them know the other luxuries and the outlays of
> The gluttonous life: such indulgence comes home at a mighty cost.
> This is not surprising: no other life eats more into the senses of
>   mankind,
> Unless reason *[ratio]* banishes it and bars the way against the
>   approach of vices *[vitiis]*.
> Such was the fault that ruined Egyptian kings,
> As they drank old Mareotic wines in goblets of precious stone,
> Reaping the perfumes of nard-bearing Ganges and ministering to
>   vices *[vitiis]*.
> By this sin you fell too, Lydia, to Persian Cyrus—
> And you were rich and golden in the veins of your river.
> In fact, so that you might have nothing left to possess,
> While you were gathering together the arts that luxury fashioned,
> And while you were madly following the faults of other nations,
>   Greece,
> How much and how often did you fall short of ancestral honor?
> But of what sort, and how simple, was the table of our Camilli?

What was your dress, Serranus, after so many triumphs?
These were the men who, in accord with the bearing and endowment of ancient virtue,
Set over the world Rome as its head; and by them
Was virtue *[virtus]* exalted to heaven; thus did she reached the highest honors.

This unexpected ideological underpinning of Grattius's *Cynegetica* is far more extensive than it may appear at first sight. It is crystallized in an opposition between *ratio* (reason) or *ars* and *violentia,* an opposition made plain from the proem (vv. 6–9). Thanks to *ratio,* we learn in verse 9, *demens cecidit violentia retro* [mad violence falls to the rear]. *Ratio* and Rome receive their implicit link in verses 24–60. Lavishness in the making of nets is rejected (with another shot at the Egyptians, at vv. 42–45) in favor of the sorts of products constructed by poor, hardworking Italian farmers (vv. 45–48). Roman *paupertas* (frugality) makes a stronger net. Hunting, Rome, world domination, and frugality are set against *violentia,* a taste for luxury, being foreign, and ultimate powerlessness (manifested in a different way in vv. 344–98, where wounds and disease are described: *ratio* is the only answer for these; note, too, that the training of the essentially unruly spirits of dogs is tantamount to the action of hunting itself—extirpation of the wild).[46]

Hunting, *ars* and *ratio,* furthermore, may be associated with civilization (at v. 284 *natura,* that which hunting confronts, is *impatiens* and given to *furor*). That great civilizer and mythic hero Hercules was a hunter. He took his most famous adornment, the lion skin, from the hunt (vv. 69–74). Hunting, civilization, *ars* and *ratio,* Rome, world domination, frugality—we are forming a heady brew. It does not surprise that Grattius continues to cast his net wider still. Dercylus, the ingenious first hunter, learned his art from a god—as did another primeval hunter, Hagnon (vv. 249–50). The god was Diana, who is also at the fore at verses 480–96. We could add, therefore, respect for the gods (v. 105) and *industria* (v. 95) to qualities clustering beneath *ratio* (vv. 95–110). To these divine references one ought also add the digression-like description of the curative powers of Vulcan's grotto in Sicily (vv. 430–66). Here beast and human alike, provided they are pure of heart, can count on the assistance of the god (vv. 446–49).

His priest, with pallid hand waving the olive branch
Proclaims: "In the presence of the altars and in the presence of god,
I ordain that all go out of the land, and go far from here,
Those who have put their hands to crime or contemplated it in their heart."

It is as if *ratio* (here manifest as devotion to the gods) can master the universe. Grattius sums this up very nicely at verses 326–29: "Experience, careful in action, how great the benefit you have lavished on humans, if only they see to their laziness and, by action, stick to their ideals."

What is it that so drives Grattius to stress this almost puritanical (as it is formulated) link between hunting and empire? Why does he instrumentalize free time and, by implication, see it as a threat to the boundaries of the self?[47] The answer, I believe, lies one step back from the analogy between hunting and empire. It resides in his concern with the deleterious effects of *indulgentia* and *luxuria*. Grattius regularly sees these two modes as capable of undermining the training of animals (dogs or horses), their behavior, and also human behavior and institutions. What Grattius seems to fear is lack of control. Again and again he chides indulgence, luxuriance, overenthusiasm—in plants even, as well as dogs, horses, and humans. It is almost as if he felt ill at ease with the societal purposelessness of hunting. As a free-time activity it could become particularly driven by *indulgentia* and *luxuria*. To play this down he attempted to analogize it with the maintenance and acquisition for Rome of empire. Thus is removed any possibility of an accusation of frivolity. At the same time are removed the pleasure element and play, as they apply to the activity of hunting (and as they apply to the poem itself). This produces a curious flattening of the texture within the *Cynegetica*. Grattius's poem, therefore, steps back from Exekias's and Ovid's model for leisure and seeks to impose the societal sanction of purpose on free time. That purpose manifests itself through exercise of power is all the more depressing.

Grattius seems driven by a fear of a lack of control. This lack of control (or powerlessness) becomes acute in the area of free time and leisure—and, one might guess, in the realm of pleasure. A lack of control threatens his capacity for self-definition. To reassert control, he insists on a pragmatic approach to leisure. This pragmatism is made concrete by anchoring it in imperial ideology.

It is much easier to see what Oppian was afraid of and how he used leisure to combat it. For the poet of the *Cynegetica*, leisure is, as it was for Grattius, a very purposeful thing, if we may judge from the underlying ideas that seem to bind together the various elements of his poem.[48] (I have already discussed some of these in my chapter on lovesickness. My remarks here should be taken as a supplement to that discussion.) Oppian, as I showed in chapter 2, is obsessed with sexual relations. Why, when he might have provided his ancient readers with useful technical information on hunting, does he focus so relentlessly, and with such patient disdain, on the mating habits of his quarries? Why has he felt so driven to ignore the claims of leisure and the enjoyment of free time and to focus so relentlessly on what is best understood as a warped concern with sexuality? There is, if we look closely, a logic behind Oppian's interest in hunting, fishing, and uncontrolled eros. This provides a part of the answer. We can detect this best in the tale of Heracles and the Orontes (2.109–58; cf. Hollis 1994). The river Orontes, obsessed with a young woman, Meliboea, lingered to find her in the high country and, blocked in by mountains, flooded the plain there and even Oppian's hometown (*Cynegetica* 2.115–22).

> For once upon a time, by the foot of Emblonus,
> All the plain was flooded; since always massive Orontes was,
> In his eagerness, forgetting the gleaming sea
> And burning for the dark-eyed nymph, the daughter of Ocean.
> He lingered amid the heights and he covered the fertile earth,
> Unwilling to abandon his ill-desired love of Meliboea.
> With mountains on either side was he encircled round;
> Mountains on either side leaned their heads together.

Heracles' labor (done as a favor for Archippus) was to cut through the mountain barrier and provide egress to the sea for the Orontes. This made the plain of Heracles fertile for the region of Chersonese (2.150–53).

> And everywhere to this day the fields flourish with corn
> And everywhere the works of oxen are heavy on the prosperous
> threshing floors
> Around the Memnonian shrine, where the Assyrian dwellers
> Mourn for Memnon.

It also provided some sort of a conclusion for Orontes' frustrated eros. So we read of the river's egress (2.145–49):

> So the mighty river Orontes bellowed about the shores,
> A dread noise, and mightily roared the headlands
> When they received within their bosom the swell of the newly come
> sea;
> And the black and fertile earth took heart again,
> Arisen from the waves, a new plain of Heracles.

The message in this vignette is that unbridled eros, such as that of Orontes, is utterly destructive. Heracles, the prototypical hunter, turns this eros to something profoundly profitable (the subsequent plain). Thus are linked fertility, the control of lust, and the activities of a hunter: these links underpin Oppian's thinking, thus his endorsement of hunting and his loathing of animal sexuality. Hunting is an exercise in the eradication of profligate, uncontrolled animal eros. Hunting is also for god. In a prayer to Zeus at 1.409–20 we hear (cf. 2.1–42): "O Zeus, in you and by you are all things rooted . . . with what loving kindness *[philotês]* you have marked out and divided the bright sky and the air, the fluid water . . . and established them apart from one another, yet you have bound them all, one to another, in a bond of amity."

The clash between reasoned, learned behavior (*technê* or, in Latin, *ars*) and passionate, uncontrolled emotional drive (*lyssa* [*Halieutica* 3.622] or, in Latin, *impetus* or *furor*) is at the heart of Oppian's poem. I have said enough already (both here and in chapter 2) of Oppian's attitude toward uncontrolled emotional drives. What can we determine of his attitude toward reasoned and learned behavior? Oppian's take on *technê* may best be understood by considering the *Cynegetica* as a whole. It aims, through its didactic instruction, to provide individuals with the *technê* sufficient to master the *lyssa* of the animals to be hunted. Thus it is clear that humans conquer by an intelligence and cunning that are not possessed by the members of the animal kingdom. Conversely, animals are conquered precisely because of their enslavement to emotion (exactly the point Ovid makes of women at *Ars amatoria* 1.372 and of land animals in the *Halieutica*). Human cunning and intelligence, Oppian claims, places humans next to the gods in power. Hunting therefore exhibits not just the superior intellectual and moral strength of *technê* but also the divine order of things within the universe. Animals are divorced from the divine precisely through their enslavement to passion or *lyssa*.

Hunting above all entails the application and display of *technê*. For Oppian *technê* is most usefully applied in the extirpation of animal *lyssa*. Hunting is, even for Oppian, pre-eminently a leisure activity—one assumes, given his choice of subject matter, *the* pre-eminent leisure activity. We may assume, therefore, that the value of leisure for him resides in its practical worth, its ability to combat animal lust.

For Oppian the occupation of free time becomes a very practical and purposeful affair. I am not for a moment claiming that he saw hunting as anything other than a leisure activity. Rather, like many other individuals, he saw in his preferred form of free-time activity a higher, moral (or moralistic) text. For Oppian hunting affirms a divine order that appears to excoriate wanton and lustful behavior. The hunter, by dominating the animal world, insists on a very moral order.[49]

The Oppian of the *Cynegetica* comes close to psychological instability. He is clearly projecting his own human anxieties onto animals. His obsessive desire to expunge all traces of unbridled eros speaks to unstable drives within his own psychology. Leisure and hunting serve the purpose for him, therefore, of controlling his own unstable inner drives (to state it again, his reading of the animal world must parallel an unstated one of the human). But Oppian cloaks the personal instability under the mantle of religion. Leisure and hunting, by combating license, affirm the will of god. We should also note that for Oppian, leisure affirms the integrity of the personality.

Ovid's erotic poems offer a version of leisure that implies participation. One is intended to learn the techniques purveyed in these poems and to participate in their arts. But, more importantly, one also participates in the game embodied by the *artes* of these poems—their poetic texture. One is intended to enjoy the poems for themselves, just as one is intended to enjoy the end to which they instruct. The gap between message and medium is highlighted but is bridged by play and by pleasure. Grattius and Oppian use didactic literature and its related pursuits to instruct us in the use of leisure. How these poets differ from Ovid is that leisure and play are qualities that exist *outside* their poems. They reside out there in the real world of hunting or fishing or gardening. These poems are translucent. They mean what they say. They are handbooks (Hopkinson 1994, 205). However, Oppian, though a far more exuberant poet than Grattius, shares with him a pragmatic attitude toward leisure. Oppian renders hunting purposeful by viewing it as the reflection of the will of a higher order. But he does so to expunge a fear of uncontrolled eros, something as dangerous in himself as in animals. So, too, did Grattius attempt to distance himself from the lack of personal control that was latent in free-time activities. He did this by pressing the unconvincing analogy between hunting and empire. So it is that the effect for the *Cynegetica* is none too different from that for Grattius's poem. Oppian, like Grattius, steps back from the model for leisure offered by Exekias and Ovid and imposes on leisure the moral sanction of purpose.

Marcus Aurelius Olympius Nemesianus, a Carthaginian who wrote during the third century of our era, has left us a *Cynegetica* that was composed possibly in 283/4 C.E. and at any rate in the period between the death of Carus in 238 C.E. and that of Numerianus in 284 (for text and translation see Duff and Duff [1935] 1982; cf. Volpilhac 1975 and Williams 1986). (Nemesianus was writing between thirty and eighty years after Oppian.)[50] Nemesianus's hunting poem survives in 325 hexametric lines and breaks off, unfortunately, just as the hunt is about to begin. What survives of his *Cynegetica* treats preparations: dogs, how to train and rear them, their breeds; then horses, their breeds, and their handling; and finally the implements of the hunt.

Nemesianus exhibits none of Oppian's strange psychological mannerisms or Grattius's taxing concern for *ratio.* His fragment, however, could not be called a practical manual on hunting. Nor is it one that embodies a spirit of recreational leisure. The ideas of the poem run too close to its surface and present too pragmatic an approach to leisure. At any rate, the following lines (*Cynegetica* 99–102) may give some indication of the importance of leisure for Nemesianus's work.

> So, come with me, whoever is love-struck
> With hunting and abhors lawsuits and terrible chaos
> And shuns civil war and the crash of battle,
> Nor pursues prey in the depths of the greedy sea.

Nemesianus envisages his preferred leisure hobby, hunting, as an alternative to the woe brought on by city life (above all litigation and civil discord) and, curiously, as an alternative to halieutic activities. As is the case with Martial 1.49, it is this pervasive sense of withdrawal and psychic sequestration that makes Nemesianus's conception of leisure and of the use of free time (based upon a desire for escape) so thoroughly different from that of Exekias and Ovid. Nemesianus rejects the pressure of the city and of engagement with the world. He recommends sequestration within an escapist world of the hunt. Nemesianus's escapism is driven by an anxious desire for solace (and even order) in a seemingly hostile universe.[51] In that sense he is very close to Martial, but without the buoyancy.

The idea of escape is woven into the texture of the poem. The proem begins conventionally with a claim to poetic novelty (vv. 1–14), albeit utilizing an imagery redolent of the hunt. Then follows a long rejection of mythological themes (vv. 15–47): Nemesianus will not sing of Niobe, Semele, Bacchus in Jupiter's thigh, Pentheus, Dirce, Hippodamia, Danaus and his daughters, Biblis, Myrrha, Cadmus, Io, Hercules' labors, Tereus and Philomela, Phaethon, Cycnus, Tantalus, Medea, Scylla, Circe, or Antigone. Nemesianus's examples are all of harsh treatment by the gods, sudden death, sexual intrigue, or bizarre transformation. The rejection of myth in poetry is conventional. But Nemesianus seems to be indicating that his poetic fare requires the removal not just of myth but also of unsavory and unsettling tales. This is important, for a literature of leisure and of escape might well be judged as the improper medium for such unsettling and salacious material. It follows that his evocation of hunting borders on the idyllic and stresses, in part, the peaceful nature of hunting (hunting is carried out over green fields [v. 48] and riverbanks [vv. 54–55], in pursuit, as often as not, of less-than-dangerous creatures such as hares, does, ichneumons, and hedgehogs). The context is worth quoting in full (vv. 48–62).

> The glades, the green tracts, the open plains,
> We search; swiftly we course all over the fields,
> And eager are we to catch varied quarries with docile hound.
> Shafting nervous hares, passive does,
> Daring wolves, or capturing the crafty fox
> Do we enjoy. To wander along the river-side shades
> We enjoy and hunting the ichneumon on the quiet banks
> Among the crops of bulrushes, piercing with the long weapon
> The threatening pole-cat on a tree-trunk
> And bringing home the hedge-hog entwined in the coil of
> Its prickly body: for such a task it is our resolve to set sail,
> While our small vessel, accustomed to be moved along neighboring
> Shores and run across safe bays with the oar,
> Now first spreads its canvas to southern winds. Trusty havens does
> It leave and dares to try the Adriatic storms.

It is no surprise that, for the time being, Nemesianus rejects imperial eulogy (of the emperor Carus and his sons Carinus and Numerianus) and its connotations of commitment to the "real world" of which his sequestered vision of hunting does not form a part (vv. 63–85). Here are some of the lines in which he does this (vv. 63–78).

> Presently the preservation on the lyre of your triumphs,
> I'll attempt, you gallant sons of deified Carus,
> And of our sea shore beneath the twin boundaries of the world,
> I'll sing, and of races subjected to the brothers' divine power,
> Which drink from the Rhine or the Tigris or the Arar's
> Source or view the very origins of the Nile;
> Nor let me be silent concerning the recent northern wars
> Which for the first time you victoriously concluded, Carinus,
> Almost outstripping even your divine father, and concerning how
>   your brother seized
> Persia's very heart and the citadels of Babylon,
> In vengeance for the outrages done to the dignity of Romulus' race.
> I shall also tell of the feeble flight and the unopened quivers,
> Of the Parthians and the unbent bows and absent arrows.
> These shall my Muses consecrate to you both,
> As soon as it is my fortune to see your holy faces,
> Kindly divinities of the earth.

The conclusion to this proem consists of a prayer to Diana (quoted in full later in this discussion). The prayer to the goddess breathes a kind of relief, as if

Nemesianus were anxiously grateful to be done with such imperial matters—and, I suspect, to be done with the possibility of having to treat unsettling and lascivious tales from mythology. It is here that we find hunting described as an escapist pursuit (vv. 99–101, quoted earlier).

There is a pattern to Nemesianus's logic of escape. We could explain this most simply by categorizing Nemesianus's likes and dislikes. The resulting picture ought to provide a map for his overall thought habits. As is indicated in verses 1–3, hunting is a type of recreational labor (*hilaris labor,* v. 1) carried out in a safe, rural landscape (*securum rus,* v. 2).

> The thousand modes of hunting I sing; the happy labours,
> The swift chases, the battles in the safe countryside
> Do we reveal.

It is associated, furthermore, with acquiescence in the will of god (vv. 10, 86–102—the latter quoted elsewhere in this section) and (not surprisingly, given its context) with poetry, another leisure activity. For Nemesianus, furthermore, hunting is an innocent type of *amor* (v. 99). Its practice involves no anger, passion, or violence (see the many myths alluded to in vv. 15–47), no war, imperial conquest, or real danger (cf. the *recusatio* of vv. 63–85—partially quoted earlier). Hunting is also the antipodes of the disorderly and litigious life of the city (vv. 99–102; cf. Martial again). Above all, hunting embodies the private; its antinomies are all public. This contrast is captured in the opposition between the type of poetry Nemesianus creates (his didactic mode) and that which he has rejected (encomiastic epic and a poetry based upon epic).

This much we can extract from the proem itself. The remainder of the poem confirms and expands this ideational grid. Elsewhere hunting is associated with youth (*vigor iuvenalis,* v. 280), morning, health and strength (v. 253), obedience (*obsequium,* vv. 188, 267), freedom (v. 264) and, perhaps not surprisingly in this context, love of right behavior (*amor virtutis,* v. 188). All of these qualities are to be contrasted with those associated with city life: age (*senectus,* v. 117), illness (the canine rabies and mange of vv. 117 and 196 ff.), restraint (as opposed to the obedience learned through training [v. 179]; see the description of the puppies at v. 166), and a general lack of civilization (exhibited above all by beasts of prey). This predictable register could be continued, but I doubt that would change what I have suggested. The pursuit of hunting and the training of animals for hunting aims to inculcate the virtues associated with this world of escape and sequestration. There is an ideational grid, a system of thought behind Nemesianus's poem. This enables us to predict its thematic choices.

One last point concerning Nemesianus's *Cynegetica* deserves to be made. Hunting and the life of sequestration give evidence to an *amor virtutis,* a love of right behavior. The *virtus* to be associated with this mode of life is also, remarkably, to be associated with an acquiescence with the will of god (vv. 10, 86–102), as is evidenced in Nemesianus's prayer to Diana (vv. 86–98).

> You only, who roam the peaceful glades and woodland,
> Diana, great glory of Latona, ah, come quickly,
> Assume your ancestral garb, bow in hand, and hang
> The coloured quiver from your shoulder; let your weapons be golden,
>   your arrows;
> Let your gleaming feet be fitted with purple buskins;
> Let your cloak be richly decorated with gold thread,
> And let a belt tighten the wrinkled tunic-folds with jewelled
> Fastenings: restrain your entwined tresses with a band.
> In your train let docile Naiads come and, ripening in fresh youth,
> Dryads and Nymphs who give the streams their water,
> And let the apt pupil echo the Oreads.
> Goddess, arise, lead your poet through the pathless wilds:
> We follow; you show us the wild beasts' homes and lairs.

Nemesianus does not bring this aspect of his belief system to the fore. Yet its logic is apparent from the template I suggested earlier. The *virtus* that accrues to the dogs and to the hunters sets their action in line with god. The invocation to Diana, though typical enough of its type, breathes a sincerity. Diana, huntress goddess and emblem of the divine, is invoked as protectress and patron of Nemesianus's escapism. The gods, it appears, admire his sequestration and, in his eyes at least, associate it with right behavior.

Leisure, for the Aristotelian, challenges. This is the intellectual component. But leisure, for most of us, is more normally a type of escape (Rybczynski 1991). The concept of leisure implicit in Nemesianus's formulation more closely resembles the modern one. Escape is all-important. For Nemesianus, the hunt represents an antidote for the insecurities of everyday life (vv. 99–102). Thus Nemesianus's play, though a source of profound pleasure to him, is no end in itself. Hunting serves as a means for distracting one, as a means for rescuing one from the distressing hurly-burly of public life. One may make one other observation of this stance taken by Nemesianus. For Nemesianus the use of free time and leisure involves the problematization of the place of power in human life (on the historicity of leisure see Burke 1995). As is evident from the preceding quotation, it is the intrusive exercise of power that he finds so difficult to cope with in his normal public life. His alternative (exercising power over the nonhuman world) highlights the difficulties related to, rather than challenges, the role of power in society (with Nemesianus cf.

Grilli 1953; André 1966). Nemesianus, just like Grattius and Oppian, saw his pragmatic and moralistic form of leisure as another means for shoring up a very fragile social personality.

Nemesianus's formulation of free time and of leisure stands at the opposite end of the spectrum to that of Exekias and Ovid. If the link between subject and object was fractured in the hunting poetry of Grattius and Oppian, it has been irrevocably set apart within the poetry of Nemesianus. The leisure act (the object, as it were) has no existence in itself. It is registered only insofar as it affects the person experiencing it (the subject). It is absorbed into the needs and demands of the subject. It is reformulated as part of the psychological requirements of the subject. Play and leisure have no role here. Leisure and free time are to assuage the asperities of felt experience. They have, for the subject's inner stability, an important and purposeful role to play.

Consult the leisure pages of your local newspapers. Leisure is inevitably confused with escape. The provincial capital Noumea, say, exists not in its own right (as an object) but only as a tool for "recharging" the run down "batteries" of the Sydney worker (the subject). The object is, with us as with Nemesianus, absorbed within the psychic requirements of the subject. The chasm, thus, between the reality of the object and the needs of the subject is set firm.

I will now recapitulate the main details of the trajectory, as I have seen it, of the development of the concept of leisure (of filling in time) as it has been evident in Exekias, then in Ovid, Martial, Grattius, Oppian, and Nemesianus.

Exekias's vase painting has been singled out because it provides such a striking template against which later versions of leisure may be understood. Exekias's version represents a type of leisure that entailed, as preconditions, free time and the freedom to utilize this. Leisure for Exekias also includes pleasure, constitutes an end in itself, and involves the application of some degree of mental concentration. I have also stressed the importance of play in Exekias's case. Play, I suggested, was "otherworldly," had rules against which a participant could commit themselves, and entailed interaction with others.

Ovid's didactic poetry on love, remarkably, captures the conceptual underpinning of the vision of leisure apparent in Exekias's painting. It is based on the vigorous utilization of free time and is devoted wholly to pleasure. Love, of its nature (unless it is purely procreational), constitutes an end in itself. It certainly does for Ovid, and it may even have hastened his banishment to Tomis. Love, furthermore, requires considerable intelligence—if not, why should these instructional manuals exist?

Consideration of the importance of play for these poems leads us away from the purely instructional. Ovid's erotodidactic poetry is otherworldly insofar as it seems to function at more than one level. Just as important as instruction is the aesthetic life of the poems qua poems. (We are to enjoy the experience of reading Ovid's poetry as much as—perhaps even more than—learning from it.) Our interest in the poems themselves undercuts an interest in their referent, love. Are there rules describing this? There are those of love itself, but there are also the various levels at which persuasion functions within these poems (that of the lover, the poet, and the poem). These poems, furthermore, imply interaction with others on two levels: between the lover and the beloved and between the addressee of the poem and its speaker. The gap between subject and object is narrowed, however, by play and pleasure. These qualities, evoked by the poem's self-referentiality, counter the accusations that might be made against the poems for purposeless frivolity.

Ovid's remarkable vision seems quickly to fade. His contemporary Grattius has different ideas. In his conception of leisure as it is embodied in hunting (for him no subsistence activity), it is pursued for pleasure and during free time. As Grattius exemplifies hunting, however, it functions as no mere end in itself. Grattius's hunting seems to have an intensely practical end residing outside or beyond itself, that of the affirmation of the values to be associated with empire and, with this, Roman civilization and societal order. As we can see, his mode of hunting has little of the spirit of play so evident in Ovid. It is hardly otherworldly, and, in its imperial aims, it plays little on the gulf between subject and object. Leisure thus becomes purposeful. The play element, both in hunting and in Grattius's poem itself, begins to vanish. As this happens, a gap between the subjective, purposeful experience of hunting and the leisurely act of hunting itself begins to widen.

Grattius's leisure, just as was the case in Martial 1.49, is pursued not just for practical reasons. The self, threatened alternatively by the pressures of uncontrol or by the city (Martial), is recalibrated by an almost irrational means: control through empire (in Grattius's case) or escape (in Martial's case).

Oppian reflects the practical and restorative concerns of Grattius and Martial, though his efforts are directed not toward an affirmation of imperial destiny or of a self-protective personal morality but toward the extirpation of personally dangerous internal drives. Oppian's poem, ostensibly, aims to provide us with instruction on a pursuit that occupies free time and provides considerable pleasure. The persistent focus on animal behavior (rather than on that of the hunter) and, at that, on the sexual behavior of animals (their *philotesia erga*) does not allow us to state that the leisure activity of the *Cynegetica*, or indeed its poetic depiction, has an end in itself. Hunting and the hunter master animal sexuality and, as I have said, bolster the immanence of the divine order in the universe. For Oppian, as I have stated earlier, hunting affirms the divine order that appears to excoriate wanton and lustful behavior. The hunter, by dominating the animal world, insists on a moral order. But he also keeps at arm's length the dangerous forces of eros. Hunting thus, as a purposeful activity with no end in itself, has very little to do with play. Hunting seems designed to keep this deranged didactic poet sane.

Nemesianus, the last of the didactic poets considered in this chapter, presents the same concerns with free time and with leisure. Hunting, however, is for him a purposeful activity possessing an end in itself. It offers an escapist alternative to the real or public life that Nemesianus apparently finds so difficult to tolerate (Nemesianus is close to Ovid). For Nemesianus, I have suggested, hunting provides an alternative to the stresses of public life and its concomitant exercise of power. In so doing, it problematizes the very notion of power itself. His version of leisured hunting shows much in common with the versions of Grattius and Oppian. The gap between subject and object, the alienation of the hunter from hunting, we might say, is complete in Nemesianus. Hunting is not pursued for its own ends or even for play and pleasure. It is pursued to restore the troubled inner state of the alienated subject.

These didactic poems, from Ovid through Nemesianus, seem to present a version of leisure that, though directed toward the use of free time and pleasure, increasingly implies that the filling of free time is something that should be of a purposeful nature. Oppian and Nemesianus particularly register this purpose as something interior to a creature, as something almost private (the establishment of moral purity or corporeal escape). Nemesianus represents something of a final point in this evolutive process, with his stress on passivity, yielding, withdrawal, isolation, privacy, interiority, and the problematization of control. His absolute antipodes is perhaps to be found in Exekias, with his version of unpurposeful leisure and its stress on activity, assertion, participation, complicity, the public, exteriority, and the surface of things. For Nemesianus, leisure, embodied in hunting, exists to keep him sane.

Is there any link between the conception of time argued for in chapter 6 and that exhibited by the preceding didactic approaches to leisure and the use of free time? To attempt to answer this question, I would like to look at a passage describing Seneca at the games, watching others watch the combatants. It provides us with a very graphic picture of the Roman utilization of free time. Here is Seneca's description of events in the arena, of the "hunting," in a public space, of criminals (*Epistles* 7.2–6) (Loeb translation).

> But nothing is more damaging to good character as the habit of lounging at the games; for then it is that vice (*vitia*) steals subtly upon one through the avenue of pleasure (*per voluptatem*). What do you think I mean? I mean that I come home more greedy, more ambitious, more voluptuous, and even more cruel and inhuman—because I have been among human beings. By chance I attended the mid-day exhibition, expecting some fun, wit, and relaxation,—an exhibition at which men's eyes have respite from the slaughter of their fellow-men. But it was quite the reverse. The previous combats were the essence of compassion; but now all the trifling is put aside and it is pure murder. The men have no defensive armor. They are exposed to blows at all points, and no one ever strikes in vain. Many persons prefer this programme to the usual pairs and to the bouts "by request." Of course they do; there is no helmet or shield to deflect the weapon. What is the need of defensive armour or of skill? All these mean delaying death. In the morning they throw men to the lions and the bears; at noon, they throw them to the spectators. The spectators demand that the slayer shall face the man who is to slay him in his turn; and they always reserve the latest conqueror for another butchering. The outcome of every fight is death, and the means are fire and sword. This sort of thing goes on while the arena is empty. You may retort: "But he was a highway robber; he killed a man!" And what of it? Granted that, as a murderer, he deserved this punishment, what crime have you committed, poor fellow, that you should deserve to sit and see this show? In the morning they cried: "Kill him! Lash him! Burn him! Why does he meet the sword in so cowardly a way? Why does he strike so feebly? Why doesn't he die game? Whip him to meet his wounds! Let them receive blow for blow, with chests bare and exposed to the stroke!" And when the games stop for intermission, they announce, "A little throat-cutting in the meantime, so that there may still be something going on!"

Seneca's vision of free time is conditioned by an abhorrence of gladiatorial combat, and this passage, to be sure, is as much a confirmation of that as it is of anything else. Yet the focus is preeminently on the spectator and, at that, on the deleterious way that these spectators have chosen to occupy their free time (and thus on how they have forced Seneca to ruin his). Seneca's characterization of the way these individuals at the games occupy their free time stands at the very opposite end of the continuum to that of Exekias. For example, what Seneca seeks at the games is "fun, wit, and relaxation," pleasure, in other words, of a form that we could readily identify with the pursuits of Achilles and Ajax in Exekias's representation (or with those described by Ovid, for that matter). Seneca's spectators, by contrast, are driven by a corrupt pleasure *(voluptas)*, which he judges as little more than a perversion. Along with this lack of pleasure goes an absence of play: the closest thing to play in this vignette is the contest between the combatants. But, as it is to the death, it can hardly be termed play. Most alarmingly, the "games" viewed here are not self-sufficient—they do have a purposeful end. That is death, which is desired by the spectator and suffered, invariably it seems, by the combatants. The spectators, as I say, become awful and passive hunters.

The free-time experience of these spectators is markedly different to that of Achilles and Ajax in other ways. The intense concentration that Achilles and Ajax exhibit as they play their game is not apparent in the game's spectators. The Romans, so Seneca accuses, lounge about as they watch others perform. This occupation of free time also does not entail the mild social interaction afforded by the board game. The focus of the spectator is above all on the combatants, as Seneca describes it. Other spectators are irrelevant to the game. The complicity of Exekias's contestants, which brings with it a personal involvement in the game (through competition with the other contestant) and even a mild physical involvement with the game, is absent from the experience of the leisure seekers in Seneca's evocation. Seneca's Romans watch; Exekias's Greeks participate. Furthermore, the Roman spectators are denied, as Seneca states, even relaxation of the form that could flow from their game. The best that one could say of the Roman spectacles, as Seneca depicts them, is that they provide a form of escape through their being utterly different to the forms of quotidian experience that constitute the basis of the spectators' lives.

The stress on eyes and on watching in Seneca's passage is striking. It demonstrates, on the part of the spectators, a remarkable estrangement or alienation from their chosen form of leisure.[52] The occupation of free time for these spectators, because it ceases to be participatory, because it is characterized by the eyes, becomes a passive experience, one of watching and of mere entertainment. At the Roman games the emphasis shifts from spectacle to spectator. Rather than providing an alternative to the stresses of daily life, this, we assume, becomes a real escape. Seneca's vignette, therefore, offers us an evocation of free time that, were we to look back to the various forms of didactic leisure, seems most closely to resemble that of Nemesianus. There poetry ceases to become a participatory form of leisure activity and recommends a form of estranged leisure that is external to itself and that offers an alternative to mundane life.

One other important link between Seneca's passage and the works of Grattius, Martial, Oppian, and Nemesianus exists in the problematization of power. What do I mean by this? Consider Seneca first. His leisure seekers attempt to exercise considerable power. The combatants are "thrown" to the spectators, who "demand" the mode that the fight is to follow. They insist, in the morning sessions at least, on high and murderous standards from their combatants ("Kill him! Lash him! Burn him! Why does he meet the sword in so cowardly a way? . . . Whip him to meet his wounds!"). In the lunchtime sessions, they demand "a little throat cutting." Thus their power is, even if vicariously, of the highest order, for they control life and death. No doubt their lives outside the game place had no such privilege. This desire to exercise power and control within their free-time activity places a remarkable slant on leisure, for, despite the violence in the arena, the experience of the spectators is utterly passive. Our spectators seek passively in the arena that which they are denied in daily life. Grattius, Martial, Oppian, and Nemesianus exhibit this absence of control as well. The stark contrast, then, between the passivity of these powerful, hunting spectators and the terrible activity of the powerless, hunted contestants highlights the twin notions of power and control. In life outside the arena the majority of these spectators exercise no such prerogatives. The arena, it seems, offers an alternative, an escape from the arbitrary powerlessness of their own lives. (The arena, we could guess, provides an affirmation for fragile senses of the self.) In this they can, vicariously, play out the puzzles and inequities forced on them by real life (cf. Barton 1993; Toner 1995). It is hard, once again, not to compare the didactic poet Nemesianus (or even Martial in 1.49). The chaos and violence of an everyday life to which he felt victim drove him to a surrogate form of leisure violence, hunting. Can it have been so different for these spectators?

It is possible to tie the conclusions reached in this chapter with those of the preceding chapters. The implied concomitants of the form of free time described by Seneca—and by Grattius, Martial, Oppian, and Nemesianus—are of a type with those that we have observed repeatedly when surveying such conditions as melancholia, boredom, eros, suicide, and the experience of time's passing. The qualities of which I am thinking are passivity, yielding, withdrawal, isolation, and estrangement. These qualities could be said to characterize the relationship of Seneca's spectators to the contestants, just as well as they could be said to characterize Nemesianus's conception of didactic leisure or the psychology of one of Chariton's lovers or even of one of St. John Chrysostomos's enervated monks. But there are other qualities worth mention as well. The experience at the Roman games is urban, quintessentially so, and time-bound, and it is for the contestants an individualist experience. It is also one marked by signs—the presence or absence of armor displays the legal standing of a fighter and whether or not he may be allowed to fight in the morning or at lunchtime. Above all, however, the experience that we witness with these spectators and contestants is the problematization of control. Nemesianus's leisure, therefore, reflects the discursive continuum that we have witnessed progressively in each of the chapters so far.

What does this have to do with the affirmation of the self and with the reformulation of the social personality, the themes of the second part of this book? The answer, not unexpectedly, lies in these escapist formulations of leisure activity (something conceptually to be related to Seneca's game spectators). Each of these authors, with the exception of Ovid, finds himself under threat from a hostile world. The means of shoring up his self-esteem and self-identity, of protecting what is an utterly fragile self, of affirming the boundaries of self, is withdrawal, personal sequestration, or the extirpation of forces entailing a lack of control. This may also have been the strategy of Seneca's spectators. It represents a completely subjective experience, one whose success is built upon the estrangement from the objective. The reformulation of the self is achieved through alienation. Indeed, the self itself is built and fed upon such a sense of alienation. In the next chapter I will focus on one of the greatest Roman exemplars of this form of alienation, Hostius Quadra.

PART III

The Alienated Personality

8

The Mirror Stage
Hostius Quadra and the Alienated Self

> Brutes cannot reflect upon themselves. Bees indeed make neat and curious workes, and many other creatures besides, but when they have done, they cannot judge on them.
>
> —ROBERT BURTON, *The Anatomy of Melancholy*

In the last portion of the first book of his tract on natural history, the *Natural Questions*, Seneca examines the physical properties of mirrors. The discussion climaxes unexpectedly with a *fabella* describing how mirrors can be put to evil use. Seneca's moralizing tale concerns the bad habits of one Hostius Quadra, a wealthy Roman aristocrat who lived at the time of the emperor Augustus.[1] The profligate nature of Hostius Quadra's sexual enthusiasm was such that it led to his murder at the hands of his disgusted slaves. The emperor's response to the murder was unexpected. The normal punishment meted out to slaves who performed such a deed was swift and exceptionally brutal. The murdered master's slave estate, whether involved in his murder or not, could expect to be executed. In the instance of Hostius Quadra, however, so great was Augustus's distaste for the man that he refused to sanction legal retribution against the guilty slaves.[2] Here is the beginning of the *fabella* (*Natural Questions* 1.16) (Loeb translation, and following passages).

> At this point I want to tell you a little story so that you may understand how lust scorns no instrument for rousing passion and how ingenious it is for inciting its own aberration. There was a man named Hostius Quadra, whose obscene acts even became the subject of theatrical performance. He was rich, greedy, a slave to his millions. The deified Augustus did not consider him worth being avenged when he was murdered by his slaves, and [Augustus] almost proclaimed that he seemed to have been murdered justly. He was vile not only in relation to one sex alone but lusted after men as well as women. He had mirrors made of the type I described (the ones that reflect images far

> larger) in which a finger exceeded the size and thickness of an arm. These, moreover, he so arranged that when he was offering himself to a man he might see in a mirror all the movements of the stallion behind him and then take delight in the false size of his partner's very member just as though it were really so big.

Several themes stand out in this first section of Seneca's diatribe. Each of these relates to the central strand of this book, the emergence of self-consciousness and a perception of self through a process of psychic isolation and "alienation from the self." Melancholia, love, boredom, and acedia were all built on, or at least were companions of, a heightened, though ill-adapted, sense of self. Suicide, time, and leisure were registered in a comparable manner, though in their cases the adaptation to the sense of self was more fruitful. In both groups this sense of alienation went hand in hand with a stronger sense of self, of, as Seneca termed it, *notitia sui*. A delicate balance was involved. Too great a sense of self could lead to a dangerous level of depression; with too little, an individual ran the attendant risks of mania. Hostius Quadra and his life of metaphor, as it were, seem to embody these dangers.

There are a number of themes that we may coax from this remarkable sequence. (These, as I hope will become apparent, encapsulate the concerns of my book as a whole.) There is a contrast between doing and watching, between activity and passivity. Hostius Quadra builds his mirrors so that he may watch himself as he has sex performed upon him. Not only is he passive in the sexual sense, but he also passively gazes upon himself as he is being entered and copulated upon. What else does Hostius Quadra attain by his lustful gaze than an acute (even exquisite) sense of himself (a *notitia sui*, as Seneca later puts it), his physical independence, and his separate but linked relation with others.[3] Does he not, with his mirrors, display a remarkable level of self-awareness and, through this, a heightened sense of selfhood? This is made especially clear through the act of gazing upon oneself. It is as if a sense of self is gained only by standing outside oneself, by watching oneself whole. But there is, it seems, an inevitable alienation to be linked with Hostius's bizarre perception of himself. The being on which Hostius gazes is, after all, an illusion.

A few other observations concerning this passage need to be made. A simple contrast exists between purity and desire and between poverty and wealth. It is exactly as I have noted throughout this book: wealth and desire lead to a dangerous and overly strong consciousness of self. Finally, there is the fact that Hostius Quadra was murdered. To be sure, his sexual antics may have caused this. They may also have caused the emperor Augustus to overlook his death and to relinquish punishing his slaves. From the vantage point that I have established at this point in my book, however, it is difficult to see how Hostius Quadra, with his mirror-clear *notitia sui,* could have ended up any other way than dead. Such a flaunting of the self, of its independence, and such a basking in psychic isolation can only enrage others. They in turn will demand retribution. In the mental sense, taken metaphorically, it bespeaks a sense of self that is so heightened as almost to resemble autism.

This "autism" is emphasized by another of the motifs in this passage, that of illusion. Hostius Quadra has developed an advanced and remarkable sense of his own person. He exhibits this for us through, above all, his manipulation of the medium of lust. When it comes to sex, Hostius Quadra is a champion of illusion—so much so that he became, following his death, a subject for the theater, the most extreme locus for illusion. Hence emerges the first of the themes, the contrast between reality and illusion. Illusion is not limited to the theater. Hostius's devotion to illusion also manifests itself in his eschewing of gender boundaries: he was enthusiastic for sexual relations with both men and women; with other men, he offered himself passively, like a woman. With women, presumably, he played the man. Seneca even compares him to a mare, thus confusing not only Hostius's gender claims but also his claim to human status. Illusion is evident above all in the trick mirrors. These render the genitals of Hostius's partner much larger than they really are. It is as if, in constructing a self that is all facade or illusion, Hostius Quadra has risked the extinction of the personality. He did, in fact, as his murder demonstrates.

But let us return to Seneca's narrative.

> In all the public baths he would recruit favorites choose men by their obvious size, but none the less his insatiable evil took delight in misrepresentations. Go on now and say that the mirror was invented for the sake of touching up one's looks! The things that monster said and did (he ought to be torn apart by his own mouth) are detestable to talk about. Mirrors faced him on all sides in order that he might be a spectator to his own shame. Also, secret acts which press upon the conscience and which every man denies he has done, he not only presented to his mouth but to his eyes as well.

What is so utterly shameless about Hostius Quadra is his total inversion of the norm. He brazenly displayed not just his sexual preferences but his strange concept of self. So at the baths Hostius openly chose his partners (large-penised men), and at home he again made the invisible visible (acts of coition that were normally invisible were made visible through and magnified in his concave mirrors). Hostius Quadra makes the unsaid said: he vaunted about his sexual acts ("the things that monster said"). Seneca makes much of the image of the mouth. It is the means by which Hostius Quadra did his bragging. But he was also inordinately fond of fellatio. (His preference for this passive act unmans him, in Seneca's eyes. It makes his gender unspecific. It ought to render Hostius Quadra's selfhood in doubt. Yet Seneca knows that it does not, thanks to those mirrors.) Seneca reserves particular vitriol for Hostius Quadra's mouth: "he ought to be torn apart by his own mouth." Not only does it render the invisible visible, but it also challenges contemporary norms of self.

What strikes the reader most forcefully about this passage is that Hostius Quadra's identity, his brazen sense of self, is built upon a shameless passivity. That, we have seen, is the hallmark of the "new" way of registering the world that I have attempted to illustrate in each of the preceding chapters. This passivity is given emphasis in other ways within this snippet. Making the invisible visible is a process that, again, we have witnessed repeatedly in the chapters of this book: the medical interpretation of passive conditions such as lovesickness does just this; the corporealization of melancholia or the registering of time provide other powerful instances. Linked to this is the making of the unsaid said.

The establishment of selfhood paradoxically through the "alienation from self" is as apparent in this passage, therefore, as in those before. Hostius watches himself in his mirrors. His mouth, too, becomes "alienated." Rather than serving its proper purpose as communicator, it is devoted to sexual acts. So, too, are his eyes.

> But, by Hercules, crimes avoid the sight of themselves! Even among those who are degenerate and inured to every disgrace there is still some modesty, very tenuous, at what the eyes see. As though it were not enough to submit himself to unheard of—even unknown—acts he summoned his eyes to witness them. Not content to see how greatly he sinned he surrounded himself with mirrors by which he separated one by one and assembled his vices. And, because he could not watch so attentively when his head dipped in and clung to his partner's private parts, he displayed his own doings to himself through reflections. He used to look at that obscene lusting of his own mouth. He used to watch men admitted all alike to his person for all the doings. Sometimes shared between a man and a woman, and with his whole body spread in a position for submitting to them, he used to watch the unspeakable acts.

Hostius Quadra's selfhood is produced through alienation and also through an inversion of the norm. So it is that his sexual preferences defy gender classification both through their completely passive nature and through their simultaneous turning to both males and females (so we hear that he was "sometimes shared between a man and a woman"). Hostius forces his very eyes to participate in this sexual alienation. Eyes cannot normally view the acts to which he was devoted ("because he could not watch so attentively when his head dipped in and clung to his partner's private parts, he displayed his own doings to himself through reflections"). Thanks to the angles at which his magnifying mirrors are placed, this becomes possible.[4] Hostius watches himself, magnified and from all imaginable angles. His ability to see all of his actions and all of his body produces a bizarre form of self-mastery and, with this, a strange form of self-knowledge *(notitia sui)* that is gained (even asserted) through his ability to see himself whole, something denied to most people. But observe again the process of alienation that this entails. Hostius's "self" is registered through the mirror. It resides in the mirror. His self, we must say, is other than his body. As we have seen repeatedly within the chapters of this book, the self is established through a process of stepping back and viewing, of alienation. The danger resides in stepping too far back. The self then can become completely other, a mere illusion. That is what Hostius Quadra risks here—and no doubt falls victim to: his "self," that is, may become an illusion.[5]

> What did the foul creature leave for performance in darkness? He did not shrink from daylight but even showed himself monstrous coitions, and gave approval of them to himself. You would not suppose that he would not have been willing to have his portrait painted in such a position! Even among prostitutes there exists some sort of modesty, and those bodies offered for public pleasure draw over some curtain by which their unhappy submission may be hidden. Thus, toward certain things even a brothel shows a sense of shame. But that monster had made a spectacle of his own obscenity and deliberately showed himself acts which no night is deep enough to conceal.

Once again there is the theme of the "invisible made visible": Hostius performs in the daylight what is normally left unseen and for the night. Not for him is even the veiled modesty of a brothel. Hostius made manifest acts "that no night is deep enough to conceal." Notice, too, his strange self-assertion that is gained through a type of alienation. Hostius, for example, "gives permission to himself" (as if the self were other) and would have himself, Seneca opines, captured in portrait in these odd postures (again the self becomes other).

It is a wonderful touch for Seneca, in the next section of his narrative, to have this villain speak directly to us.

> "At the same time," he said, "I submit to both a man and a woman. Nevertheless, also with that part of my body not occupied I perform the role of a male in the violation of another person. All my organs are occupied in the lechery. Let my eyes too come into their share of debauchery and be witnesses and supervisors of it. By means of a device let even those acts be seen which the position of our bodies removes from sight, so that no one may

think I do not know what I do. Nature did poorly in providing scanty accessories to human lust. She better arranged the coition of other animals. I will discover a way to deceive my sick wants and satisfy them. To what purpose my depravity if I sin only to the limit of nature? I will surround myself with mirrors, the type which renders the size of objects incredible. If it were possible, I would make those sizes real; because it is not possible, I will feast myself on the illusion. Let my lust see more than it consumes and marvel at what it undergoes."

It is very difficult not to think that Seneca is speaking of himself, so vivid and so suggestive is his characterization of Hostius Quadra. But that is a claim for another occasion. In this passage Hostius does not deepen our conceptual understanding of his assertion of self. He does make it more plain. His inversion of the norm is again prominent: his defiance of gender, his "misuse" of his organs (all "occupied in the lechery"), his allowing his gaze to take charge over his conduct ("Let my eyes . . . be . . . supervisors of it"), his making the invisible visible, his paradoxical assertion of control ("that no one may think I do not know what I do"), and his utter fascination with his mirrors and images ("Let my lust see more than it consumes and marvel at what it undergoes"). Another aspect of this passage that may not be immediately apparent is Hostius Quadra's alarming concern for his inner, rather than his outer, life (for interiority, as I have termed it, rather than exteriority). This may seem paradoxical. Are not all of Hostius's actions designed to heighten his corporeal gratification? Reconsider, then, his speech as Seneca conceives it. Hostius's assertion of self through his control over his body ("I submit," "I perform," "my organs," "let my eyes," etc.) seems more important than any physical gratification gained through this: Hostius is determined to *invent* a means for increasing his sexual pleasure. The pleasure, however, is all in his head. Sex becomes the life of the mind. As Hostius tells us: "I will feast myself on the illusion."

Seneca concludes his sequence on Hostius with the following expostulation.

Shameful behaviour! Perhaps he was murdered quickly, even before he saw it; he ought to have been immolated in front of a mirror of his own.

This is a nice touch—to imagine Hostius murdered in front of a mirror. How else could he perish? His identity, after all, was a thoroughly alienated thing, an other; it was something formed in illusory fashion in front of his eyes. Hostius's self was registered and given meaning only though the mirror. Could his self be finally mastered in any way other than by being extinguished within a mirror?

Were we to follow Seneca into the final sections of this first book of the *Nat-*

ural Questions, those following the end of Hostius Quadra, we would find less startling material. It is, for all that, no less instructive. In this section of the *Natural Questions,* Seneca complains that mirrors, the product of hard labor, have been devoted to luxury (1.17). Seneca lists some of the benefits of our possession of mirrors: they enable us to watch the rising and setting of the sun; they enable us to view the conjunction of the sun and the moon. Above all, he maintains, mirrors exist so that we may know ourselves (*inventa sunt specula ut homo ipse se nosset,* 1.17.4). Knowledge of self—or, as we might generously translate it, self-consciousness (*notitia sui,* 1.17.4)—is conjoined, continues Seneca, with the advantage of "good sense" (*consilium,* 1.17.4). This second quality, he explains, encourages self-consciousness *(notitia sui):* so it may cause "the handsome man to avoid infamy, the homely man to understand that what he lacks in physical appearance must be compensated for by virtue," and so on. But Seneca argues that these advantages brought to us by mirrors come at too great a cost. In the ancient times, before mirrors had been invented, humans were better behaved (1.17.5): "that was a simpler age, content with what chance offered, and it had not yet twisted benefits into vice nor seized upon the inventions of nature for the purpose of lust and extravagance."

Why are mirrors so dangerous? With their use, *notitia sui,* self-knowledge, is displaced by an almost erotic infatuation with self *(amor sui).* Mirrors and their discovery are to be linked with the increased prevalence of vices associated with *amor sui,* luxury and vanity. Men of old washed in streams, brushed their hair and beards themselves, then let them stream loose. This simplicity was displaced by mirrors. At first simple implements, they soon evolved to become full-length creations "carved of gold and silver, then adorned with jewels" (1.17.8). Such is contemporary extravagance, argues Seneca, that the cost of a single mirror is greater than the whole dowry of a woman who lived during the early days of the Republic. Seneca sums up his qualms as follows (1.17.10):

> Luxury, encouraged by sheer opulence, has gradually developed for the worst, and vices have taken on enormous growth. All things are so mixed up by the most various refinements that what used to be called the ornament of a woman is now a man's accoutrement; I mean all men, even soldiers. Is a mirror now used only for the sake of good grooming? There is no vice for which it has not become indispensable.

Self-consciousness (as I have paraphrased the Latin *notitia sui*) is provided with a remarkable malevolent context. While mirrors may confer on us *notitia sui,* they bring in their train such dangers that it seems that the only outcome can be to create characters like Hostius Quadra. But rather than focusing just on mirrors and *luxuria,* I would like to look at the contexts with which *notitia sui* is associated. This will allow us to link Hostius Quadra more clearly back into the concerns of this book.

Notitia sui is above all associated with time. The passing of time allows the unearthing of mirrors, and with these emerges self-knowledge. But, alas, time's passing, thanks to *luxuria* and attendant extravagance, leads to degeneration and moral bankruptcy. Self-consciousness is also associated with desire. While mirrors may confer some psychological advantages, they breed in their owners an infatuation with self *(amor sui)*. One further point, to be linked with time, deserves mention. Mirrors are associated with "adulthood." Men of old, those who washed their hair in rivers and then let it stream loose, are associated with the earth's juvenescence, when our race was new, even infant. Mirrors, the sign of our corruption, are associated with the present. We are grown-ups, and through our self-awareness, we have become self-infatuated.

Hostius Quadra is a remarkable character. He pushes things to extremes and, in so doing, rejects and resists the disintegration of his sense of self. Hostius Quadra's characterization picks up some of the key motifs of this book as a whole. The simplest of these motifs is the contrast between activity and passivity. Its relevance for the sexually passive Hostius is quite obvious. So, too, is the contrast between assertion and yielding. Hostius's corporeal antics are by and large built upon his taste for yielding. It is a taste, too, that, despite its penchant for bathhouse pickups and daylight sex, is gratified in private in a room full of mirrors. This gratification, furthermore, is based on estrangement rather than on complicity and on being hidden rather than on being visible. It is a world based more upon the mind than upon the body. Paradoxically, this world of the body is built upon signs (the mirror and sexual gratification as symbols of the assertion of self). All of these features have figured in previous discussions within this book. They find a remarkable focus within the figure of Hostius Quadra. All of the features, furthermore, are to be associated with the various passive conditions that, I have argued, became pronounced in this period.

I would like to make one further point concerning these motifs. They highlight a curious contradiction. Hostius Quadra's sexual passivity is paradoxically offset by his hilarious choice to display it. Trapped, we could say, by an ideology that judged his sexuality deviant (on sexual passivity see Richlin 1997; Halperin 1990; Foucault 1986), he pitted himself against the arbitrariness of this ideology by flaunting his passivity. His display, as Seneca's dramatic speech demonstrates, indicates considerable desire not just to revolt against societal constraint but to exhibit volitional control. This desire for control is designed to counter those who would judge the passive as lacking in control. Naturally this display is ultimately futile (not unlike the suicides and suicide attempts of chapter 5). Illusions satisfy no one. It is undeniable, however, that by flaunting his passivity, Hostius Quadra asserts and achieves his reformulated self. Further, his conduct renders problematic the twin notions of power and control. The mirrors, therefore, provided Hostius with a means for responding to the ideological impasse into which he had been thrust. The solution to his dilemma, rather like that adopted by the suicides of chapter 5, was designed to create an aggressive personal display in front of a hostile audience.

Not just the key motifs of this book but also its key themes are captured by Hostius Quadra and his mirrors. These warrant the inclusion of his story within this final chapter. Let us, therefore, briefly recapitulate them. In part 1 of this study, I examined psychological estrangement. This meant, specifically, how it is that an individual's sense of self can disintegrate and, with this, lose its physiological integrity. I suggested that such a disintegration of personality entails the loss of the multiple reference systems produced by family and by community. Such dangerous affective (and conceptual) estrangement was the product of psychic trauma that could manifest itself in a variety of dangerous psychopathological conditions (discussed earlier in this book): melancholia or depression (chapter 1), boredom (chapter 3), lovesickness (chapter 2), and acedia (chapter 4) were typical. The nature of the emotional traumas could vary. Typical of those that we have observed are grief, isolation (physical and psychic), loss of family and community, thwarted desire, and the varying constraints of age, sex, or community standing.

In part 2 I examined some of the means by which individuals countered this disintegration of personality. This "reformulation of the self" is based upon an emotional and intellectual acceptance of personality disintegration. In such cases the grammar and language habitually associated with psychic disintegration is subject to an inversion. So it is that, on the matter of leisure, it can as readily lead to the valuation of a form of leisure based upon the admittedly pessimistic estimation of free time as a medium for escape (the conclusions of chapter 7). Even such a doleful matter as suicide can be viewed in this manner (as in chapter 5). Suicide can be utilized as readily as a means for the assertion of the independence of the personality as it can as a means for extinguishing this. (Chariton's suicides are not only most public affairs but are also designedly unsuccessful.) Time, in similar manner, can be seen (as in chapter 6) as a degenerative or restorative agent: it may restore Rome to its pristine glories, for example, or it may lead to personal extinction. As we have noticed in the instance of Trimalchio, overstressing or ironizing the destructive elements of time can be used, paradoxically, as a means for reinforcing personal immunity to its dangers.

How are these themes reflected in the conduct of Hostius Quadra? We might have expected Hostius to have suffered such psychopathological conditions as melancholia or depression, acute boredom, lovesickness, or even a proleptic attack of acedia; so thoroughly does he seem to have been deprived of the multiple referents and supports offered by community. On the face of things, this sexual renegade may have undergone some of the conditions inflicted on that group of pariahs whom we have seen become subject to curses or hexing or boning. So it is that Hostius experienced the withdrawal of community concern and interest (which he has forfeited because of his sexual passivity), and he was viewed and perhaps treated as a source of danger to this community (his passivity and his flagrant disregard for current sexual values were perceived as a danger; Seneca's testimony gives witness to this). Hostius may not have lost his legal rights while alive, but after his death he seems to have been treated by Augustus as a nonperson (there was no official punishment for his killers). I wonder if, while he was still alive, he experienced this state of being "dead in life"?

Yet Hostius flourished and, as far as we can tell, avoided the depredation of melancholia and related conditions. Hostius Quadra, to use the terms emphasized in this book, reformulated his sense of self. He did this above all by a parodic inversion and exaggeration of the values of which his society seems so to have disapproved. The simplest means by which he accomplished this was in his extravagant sexual posing (bathhouse pickups and daylight sex) and through his assertion of personal independence. We can also see this parody and exaggeration through the traces of the imagery associated with those themes of reformulation that were examined in the second part of this book. So it is that Hostius Quadra makes a remarkable use of reading.[6] How else does he use his mirrors but as a means of "reading" (interpreting the signs of) his sexual activity, his sexual prowess, and, ultimately, his means of social transgression? Hostius, after his death, was "read" by others for the purpose of stage plays, both as an object of negative moral exemplification and as an object of ridicule. Leisure, too, enters into the picture. Sex (as it was for Ovid in his *Ars amatoria*) was for Hostius, above everything else, a leisure pursuit. It was something utterly useless that provided an end in itself, offered play and pleasure, and required a high, if bizarre, level of intellectual input. His conduct, as it was portrayed on stage, provided leisure for the Roman community—how else should we understand the function of the theater? Hostius may not have been tempted by suicide, but his profoundly antisocial conduct was something that, we cannot but suspect, courted death. Augustus was so little shocked by Hostius's death that he invited no retaliation against the murderers. Does time and its relationship to the body enter into this metaphorical matrix of the reformulation of self? Hostius, in his desire to transcend the sensual limitations of his body (to turn each of his faculties into a sensual organ), seems to have wished almost to transcend the limitations of the body and, through his superhuman sexual feats, to transcend that final limitation of the body, time itself.

Jacques Lacan is (or was) a very fashionable figure—perhaps too much so to cite in this context. But a comparison of Hostius's mirror techniques and Lacan's famous "mirror stage" is as inevitable as it is instructive. To those who are understandably jaded with the Parisian speculation of the sixties, all I can say is, be patient. Here is a straightforward description of Lacan's formulation of the mirror stage. Its relevance will be immediately apparent.[7]

> At a certain point, around six months, and presumably when the perceptual apparatus has reached a certain stage of development, the infant becomes aware, through seeing his image in the mirror, of his own body as a totality, a total form or *Gestalt*. The mirror image is held together, it can come and go with a slight change of the infant's position, and his mastery of the image fills him with triumph and joy. The mirror image anticipates the mastery of his body that the infant has not yet objectively achieved. He falls in love with his image and, in contrast to the auto-erotic stage, in which he has an erotic relationship with his fragmented body, he now takes the image of his whole body as his love-object . . . Thus the infant's *imaginary* mastery of his body anticipates his biological mastery. In Lacan's view, any future relation with reality will be marked by this imaginary anticipation. "The mirror stage is a drama whose internal thrust is precipitated from insufficiency to anticipation" . . . There is then a fundamental "alienation" in this action. The infant's mastery is in the mirror image, outside himself, while he is not really master of his movements. He sees only his form as more or less total and unified in an external image, in a virtual, alienated, ideal unity which cannot be touched. Alienation is this lack of being by which his realization lies in another actual or imaginary space.
>
> This image of unity is not disturbed by the turbulent movements of the infant's uncoordinated body. It is a mirage in a *Gestalt,* that is, an external form, which the mirror reflects back in reversed symmetry and perspective. The infant's movements and bodily prematurity are reversed in the fixity of a big "statue" of himself. "This *Gestalt* . . . in these two aspects of its appearing [of fixity and stature] symbolizes the ego's mental permanence and at the same time prefigures its alienating fate, the statue into which man

> projects himself" . . . In Lacan's view the formation of the ego commences at the point of alienation and fascination with one's own image. This image is the first organized form in which the individual identifies himself, so that the ego takes its form from, and is formed by, the organizing and constitutive qualities of this image . . . The ego for Lacan is thus formed on the basis of an *imaginary* relationship of the subject with his own body. The ego has an illusion of autonomy, but it is only an illusion, and the subject moves from fragmentation and insufficiency to illusory unity.

Hostius Quadra is no infant, and his "mirror stage" is hardly the accidental and metaphorical process of self-discovery undergone by Lacan's putative six-month-old.[8] Yet the experiences of Hostius, as Seneca paints them and as I have just now paraphrased them, catch, in a most alarming manner, the imagery of, and even aspects of the significance of, what we have seen designated as the mirror stage.[9]

So, when it is suggested by Lacan that the infant derives his or her first knowledge of the body as a whole from the mirror, it is difficult not to think of Hostius's antics. Through the use of mirrors, he is able to devote all of the organs of his body to a single purpose. (Thus even sight plays a role in his lubricious conduct.) The body becomes, as it were, a perceptible unified register devoted to a single, unified purpose. The knowledge that Hostius gains through his concave mirrors is not as sensually specialized as might seem at first sight, for it is his body as a whole, as a unified, single-purposed organism, that he comes to know. What's more, the image of himself fills Hostius, just like the infant, with an enormous sense of pleasure and joy. Perceiving himself whole, Hostius, just like Lacan's metaphorical six-month-old, falls in love with his image (his own body becomes the real love object).[10] Desire, therefore, is directed inward toward himself as *amor sui*.

The extent to which ego—or, as we might say, self—is perceived and demarcated by Hostius through these mirrors is more easily determined. We have the term *notitia sui*. Hostius derives this from the mirrors.[11] His knowledge of the body may match that which is vouchsafed the infant and which, according to Lacan, comes through the mirror to lead, in turn, to the development of, or at least the assertion of, the ego. It may not be stretching probability to take this one step further and to claim for Hostius Quadra, as does Lacan for the infant, that the "formation of the ego commences at this point [i.e., the mirror stage] of alienation and fascination with one's own image."

We may, with even more confidence, claim that Hostius, like Lacan's imagined infant, does seem to develop, through his concave mirrors, an illusion of autonomy, or, as we might put it, of control. The mirrors enable him to control and to augment his desire, to view his body whole and to manipulate sensation. (Could we state also that he moves from a sense of corporeal fragmentation to one of unity?[12] The mirrors, after all, enable him to bring all of his senses into erotic play and to see them acting through one organism.) But Hostius, like Lacan's infant, develops an *illusion* of corporeal autonomy and of self-control. I stress the term *illusion* because the control and autonomy provided for him by the mirrors is but an image. It was one, furthermore, that was no proof against his murderous slaves. So it is that we could say of Hostius, echoing Lacan, that his realization and perception of self is achieved through an illusion and that his very ego may thus be formed on the basis of an imaginary relationship between the subject and his own image. That this sense of a mastery of self ultimately leads to death is also significant.

The final point to be made is that this imaginary mastery of self and the body, procured for the infant and for Hostius through this mirror stage, is based on "alienation." How does alienation enter the picture? The perception of self, according to Lacan's model, is based upon the recognition not just of an illusion but of the self as another, as "out there." In Lacan's estimation of things, the development of a sense of self is based upon one's identification with "another" (the mirror image). I am in no position to adjudicate on the validity of this speculation. But the match between the type of self-perception I have been highlighting in this book—the notion, that is, of "alienation from self"—bears a striking relationship to Lacan's conceptual postulate. This form of self-perception, I have argued, becomes a discursive reality in the very period during which Seneca wrote. It is as if, during this very period, the psyche of the Romans and the Greeks underwent its "mirror stage." Hostius Quadra's bizarre and fruitful actions become emblematic of this change. I would like to add one final observation to this line of speculation. Lacan's understanding of self-knowledge through this process of alienation has been put to a use completely different from that which I intend here. Teamed up with Foucauldian discourse and Kristevan intertextuality, it produces the idea—argued for by Wiles (1997, 14) or illuminated by Klossowski (1947), among many others—that the notion of the stable self is illusory. Alford (1991, 4) notes that Lacan "transforms the unconscious into a type of text, arguing that it is not the case that the self uses language; rather, language uses the self." That is not my argument at all, nor is it the use to which I would wish to put Lacan's mirror metaphor. My point is far more pedestrian: self-awareness is built on distance, on a capacity to observe oneself. This is a type of alienation. I have also suggested that should the distance become too great, the risk run represents a type of psychological disintegration to be associated with depression; should the gulf become too narrow, even negligible, the risk run is that of mania and autism.

I would like to present one more piece of evidence for the type of affective experience that I have attributed to Hostius Quadra. Basing my comments on the fertile hint offered by Sandra Citroni Marchetti (1991) linking Hostius Quadra and Narcissus, I would like to compare with Hostius a well-known image of Narcissus staring fixedly at his own reflection in a destructive spring. The version of Narcissus to be examined is not that of Ovid (*Metamorphoses* 3.339–510, discussed in chapter 2). It is that provided by a well-known Pompeian wall painting (fig. 9),[13] dating approximately to the period in which Seneca was writing about Hostius Quadra.

In this picture, Narcissus, with his clothing draped across his thighs but naked above, is seated on a large flat rock. Leaning left, he takes his weight on a straightened, vertical left arm. Resting along his right arm is what seems to be a very long javelin (as if he has just come from hunting). His head is garlanded with a wreath. The hair beneath displays ringlets, as if they were ribbons, which hang over his slight shoulders (as if he has just returned from a party). Narcissus peers, calm but rapt, down into the water of a spring, at the reflection of his neck and head.[14]

Narcissus is pretty in a feminine way and is perhaps twelve or thirteen years of age. He appears to be just on the verge of puberty. His groin exhibits, inconclusively, very small genitals. (The javelin in his right hand, however, is determinedly phallic.) There is a single fold of flesh on his soft stomach, just above his navel. This is, according to the conventions of this type of painting, vagina-like.[15] His portrait exhibits a confusing mixture of innocence and erotic charm. A few years ago we might have said that Narcissus's status was "liminal." Certainly that adjective nicely fits his depiction in this picture. He is neither quite male nor quite female, child nor adolescent, innocent nor erotic.[16] The groin, overmature for one so young, captures this ambivalence well.[17] Narcissus, furthermore, is mesmerized by his own reflection. That he is in love with this is indicated in part by his intent and charmed contemplation of his own image and in part by his suggestive, charming nakedness.

What help does the idea of the mirror stage provide for a "reading" of the painting of Narcissus?[18] I appeal here to the two notions of liminality and the erotic—liminality first. The Narcissus that we have observed is not a fully formulated creature: prepubescent, of almost androgynous status, but yet a man, he is now on the point of shedding these ambivalent characteristics. His mirror, the spring, may well provide him with a sense of autonomy, of a selfhood that will enable him to leave behind his liminal status. Through his reflection in the water, Narcissus for the first time gains a sense of his body as a unified, single-purpose organism. The image in the spring enables Narcissus to move from a sense of physical and psychic fragmentation—liminality—to one of

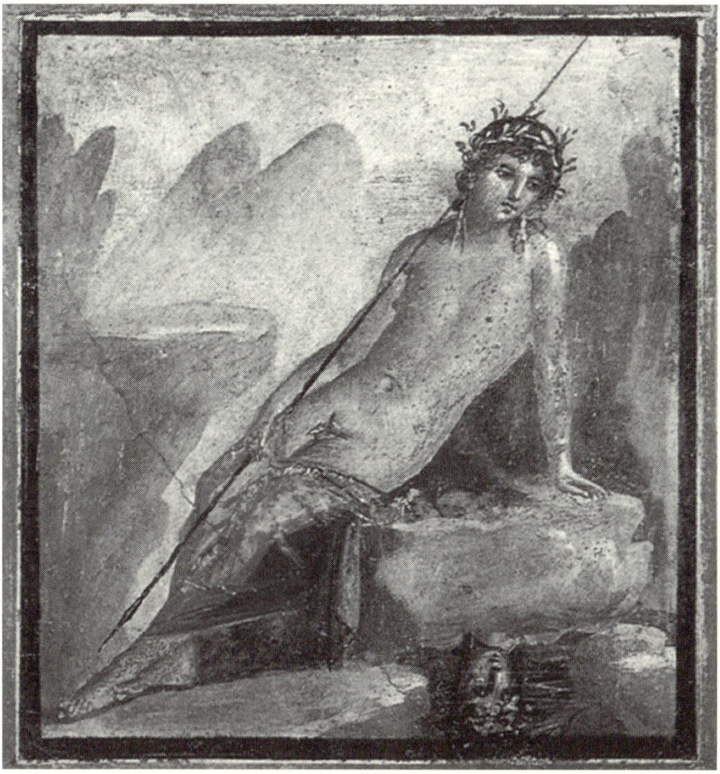

FIG. 9. Pompeian wall painting of Narcissus (ca. 69–79 C.E.). (Courtesy of Museo Nazionale di Napoli.)

unity. Narcissus develops his sense of self *(notitia sui)* and self-unity through his mirror image.[19] From this, we might speculate, develops his sense of ego.[20] The image in the spring enables Narcissus to bring all of his senses into erotic play and to see them acting through one organism.

Narcissus, in the myth and in its pictorial representation, falls in love with his own body. Why would he not, after all, if this is his first encounter with it whole? This *amor sui* becomes part and parcel of the understanding of his own autonomy. (There can be little wonder that poor Echo is left to her own devices, in myth and in lived experience.)

The myth of Narcissus, especially as it is given form in this fascinating painting, seems to act as a metaphor for the establishment of the personality, through alienation and otherness—the type of personality, strong but hard to sustain, that I have emphasized again and again throughout this book.[21] Sexual attraction countered by a sense of personal incompleteness seems to be the basis on which this change, this alienation, takes place. It is tragic, but metaphorically accurate, that this change so often results in death.[22]

Let us leave Hostius, Narcissus, and their and the Roman "mirror stage" for the moment. We will return to them soon. I would like in the meantime to provide an affective map, as it were, that attempts to illustrate the relationships between the symptoms of the various mental states and conditions I have surveyed in this book. Subsequently Hostius Quadra and Narcissus can be positioned within this affective matrix.

The symptomatology begins in one of two ways. Either it begins with the sudden and usually unexpected appearance of strong or overwhelming emotion requiring resolution (e.g., love, fear, jealousy, hate, bereavement, or even the pressing need to make a very difficult decision), or it begins with the persistent bafflement caused by prolonged confinement or sense deprivation (conditions in ample supply in monastic communities subject to the depredation of acedia or in less-than-salubrious Australian lockups). The various affective problems examined in this book take root when an individual who is subject to either of these two states is faced with their persisting irresolution: so the lover finds no union, the hater no revenge, or the overheated and constrained monk no release from his cell.[23]

Reaction to this frustration can be either active or passive. Let us consider the active reaction first. Its most common form is a combination of anger and violence.[24] So it is with Medea or Dido when their love for Jason or Aeneas is threatened. They become enraged bacchantes and storm through their hometowns.[25] The pseudo-Aristotelian *Problema* 30.1 understood such a reaction as the product of overheating of the black bile and its exhalations to the brain. It noted a number of examples of this type of reaction, from Heracles, Ajax, and Lysander. In such cases, if anger and violence produce the desired result (e.g., union with the beloved), then the frustration is resolved, psychic stability is returned, and the individual attains a unity with his or her community. But if frustration endures (as it does, say, for Sophocles' Ajax, whose resolution was thwarted by his comrades) and if it allows no apparent resolution, then the anger and violence is turned dangerously inward. Wemelsfelder (1989) has pointed out that animals who have been caged too long indulge in monotonously repetitive acts liable to cause self-harm.[26] In humans comparably self-directed violence may manifest itself as suicide (so it is with Virgil's Dido or Sophocles' Ajax). For humans the problem becomes particularly acute when this frustration is allied with community disapproval. For better or worse we tend to associate such reactions with earlier historical periods, with nonurban communities, with the nonliterate, with indigenous and with premodern communities. We associate, no doubt judgmentally, such reactions with animals.[27] This association is only approximate. The Australian Aboriginals are both "earlier" and nonurban, but their reaction to boning is utterly passive. We tend—at least I have tended in this book—to associate certain broad qualities with this response to stimuli. So we may expect to characterize this with descriptive attributes such as activity, assertion, participation, complicity, cyclicality, the mark, the public, exteriority, lack of control, and the body.[28]

The other reaction to insoluble and enduring frustration is passive. Its clinical manifestations are more vivid and more interesting. Basedow's description of the symptoms resulting from the Australian Aboriginal practice of boning is very instructive. It produces a graphic register of how insoluble and enduring frustration exhibits itself in such cases[29] (and its registers are repeated again and again in classical literature in contexts as various as melancholia, love, madness, or even being subject to the evil eye).[30] The initial symptom is astonishment. Then follow blanched cheeks, glassy eyes, distorted facial expressions, voicelessness, spasms, and swooning and collapsing to the ground. The suffering individual may subsequently react in one of two ways. Psychic disintegration may follow—this is especially the case when the person seems to have transgressed (or to have wished to transgress) acceptable societal mores. Or psychic reformulation may follow. In some cases of disintegration (most typically the Aboriginal victim of boning or the lover irremediably in thrall to lovesickness) the subsequent symptoms may be outlined succinctly: there will follow sickening, fretting, abstention from food, withdrawal from the community, and finally death.[31] Death may result from starvation or suicide.

Psychic disintegration is not the invariable result of this passive response to frustration. That is why Hostius Quadra is such an important individual. He exemplifies how it is that the personality may survive (at least for a time) and undergo a process of reformulation. The process of the reformulation of the personality (I have devoted three chapters to various aspects of this topic) seems to run through the following stages. Initially the sufferer seems to sense a need to problematize the issue of control. This is to display volitional strength and weakness. This display may involve challenging community expectations. Thus it is with Hostius's passive sexual posturing: not only does it problematize the notion of control, but it also vigorously challenges community expectations. The simplest examples of this process are to found in the staged suicide attempts (whether in Petronius or in Chariton) that we observed in the chapter on suicide. Problematizing is achieved there through grandiose public display—Chaereas, grief-stricken and attempting to throw himself overboard in front of the massed Syracusan citizenry (*Chaereas and Callirhoe* 3.5), offers a fine example. It needs stressing that such suicide attempts were normally performed in front of others and that they were rarely successful. In those cases the public display was what really mattered. It is as if the sufferer, through this exhibition, aimed above all to elicit from his or her audience a strong response. Why should this response matter so? It was against this audience that the individual was to differentiate his or her values from the rest of the community and, more importantly, his or her sense of self or personal identity (Baumeister 1986 is useful on this matter). To achieve this differentiation, Hostius Quadra used passive sex and mirrors and, presumably, a total indifference to the negative public valuation of his activities. As I say, what was crucial in these cases was the eliciting from the audience of a strong response. Justification of the sufferer's predicament or personal choices was not at issue. Agreement, after all, undermines differentiation.

Following the differentiation from the community is a realignment of the individual's values and, from this, the individual's sense of personality. This is particularly marked in the case of Hostius Quadra. Such an individual perceives that there is no cohesive relationship between the aims of the community and those of the individual. Thus he or she may come to realize at this point that there is little coherent relationship between aims and outcomes, between planning and actualization, between words and things. The sense of self displayed by a man like Hostius Quadra or by a man such as Seneca's Lucius Annaeus Serenus is, I have argued, based upon such alienation, not just from the community, but also from themselves. This melancholy form of differentiation provides them with their remarkable sense of self and, paradoxically, with their strongest tool for survival. From this sense of alienation emerges the psychic stability needed to counter the dangers of the socially sanctioned disintegration of the personality. It appears, however, that though Hostius Quadra's attempts were successful on the metaphorical level, real life was another matter.

Hostius Quadra may seem like a bizarre end point for the theme of this section of this study and, indeed, for the conclusion of this book. How can such an asocial debauchee become a model for the emergence of a type of self-consciousness? If I were to attempt to sum this up in just a few words, my explanation would run something like this: Hostius Quadra is one of the few characters—if not the only one—who has been able, partially at least, to negotiate an acceptance of the arbitrariness of the relationship between himself and the world about.[32] It is this negotiation, I believe, that enables his bizarre, but effective, reformulation of the self and, as a consequence, the emergence of a saving self-consciousness.

This reformulation may be spelled out in a little more detail. Its crucial stages run, to detail them abstractly, as follows: there is, first, a problematization of control, followed by a public display of self and, as a consequence, a differentiation from the community. This leads to a realignment of values. The conception of self that results from this is built, therefore, upon an alienation from the community and from the self and upon a psychic reintegration or reformulation that is in turn built upon an acceptance of the arbitrariness, as we interpret it, of the relationship between the subject and object.

Let me reemphasize how it is that these qualities are specifically to be found in Hostius Quadra's story as Seneca recounts it. It is true that it can never be known whether or not Hostius suffered the form of crisis reaction to frustration that is typical of the unfortunate characters within the Greek novel. But it is quite apparent that he suffered a form of social pressure that was every bit as extreme. The mode of sexual behavior that Hostius practiced was not something that was acceptable at Rome.[33] The pressure on him to modify was considerable: why else would he have been so parodied on stage, so much the recipient of the enmity of his slaves, so publicly the object of the hostility of the emperor Augustus, and, many years later, so greatly the butt of Seneca's fascinated, prurient scorn? It is remarkable that Hostius Quadra's reaction to this (no doubt extreme) pressure was not psychic withdrawal. It is remarkable that Hostius did not undergo some form of psychic disintegration. It appears that Hostius inoculated himself against the destruction of personality by continuing defiantly to do what he liked best. In acting thus, at least as Seneca tells the tale, Hostius was forced to undergo his process of psychic reformulation—what I have termed his "mirror stage."

What did this entail? The problematization of control is at the very heart of Hostius's sexual behavior. His desire was to make as many of his senses as possible capable of sexual behavior. Yet to gain this corporeal and sensual control, it was necessary for Hostius to render himself the passive and dominated subject of others' sexual advances (those of males and females). The paradox in this is apparent. Through this passivity and this relinquishing of control, Hostius established a form of control of his own. In embarking on such a seemingly self-contradictory form of behavior, does he not throw the whole notion of control into the ring? Who is it that really has the control, his behavior seems to ask? Is it the active partner? Or is it the passive partner, who owns the mirrors and controls the performance and the performers, who wills himself to sexual excess, and who blatantly flaunts the sexual ideology of his society?

We can guess at the extent to which Hostius made his behavior a public display. The virulence of contemporary and historical reaction directed against him underscores the fact that he flaunted his habits. So extravagant was his display of himself that he even became the subject of theatrical representations. Could his behavior have assumed a more public role? We might also stress that this public display was built by him upon a willful differentiation of his chosen mode of behavior (and self-estimation) from that of the community: so he exhibits an asocial sexual passivity, an asocial desire to view (and to vindicate) this in front of mirrors observable not just to himself but also to his partners, and a willingness to flaunt his difference before an uncomprehending and hostile community. The resulting community hostility is most obviously to be seen in the vigor of the reaction directed toward him at the end of his life. While alive, however, Hostius saw himself as a man apart, as one who redefined the parameters of what constitutes the body and the self and even what it involves to be human. It follows from this that he underwent personally a realignment of values. We need not linger over this, for his pursuit of sense gratification at the expense of his social standing and reputation is evidence enough. The result of all of this is a remarkable alienation from the community and, paradoxically, an alienation from the self, which is symbolized through Hostius's re-creation of self within his mirrors. That Hostius's psychic reintegration emerges from this acceptance of the otherness or alienation of self is both remarkable and the point of this chapter and this book as a whole.

There are also to be noted in this context of self-actualization a remarkably consistent, if not wholly unexpected, series of qualifying descriptors. We associate Hostius's condition (and all others subject to a passive reaction toward frustration) with specific qualities. It is inexorably to be associated with a *human,* not an animal, sphere and often with those preeminently human activities of *reading* and *interpreting.* Thus it is, too, that the *sign,* rather than the mark, becomes important in this condition. A doctor must learn to read the signs of melancholy or lovesickness; he cannot diagnose the condition, as if it were a broken leg, from the mere outward manifestation of things. This condition is to be linked, furthermore, with an *urban lifestyle,* one often associated with *recent history* and with a more *civilized way of life.* It follows, then, that such a condition concerns itself more with *linearity* through time (that which makes present history an evolutionary telos), rather than *cyclicality.* It comes as little surprise that such other features as *passivity* and *yielding* (in the existential, emotional, psychic, and sexual sense) and *withdrawal* and *estrangement* (with the same range) are normally allied with these. Those liable to fall victim to a condition such as this are more often than not societies or groups or individuals whose mode of living tends to display a greater than normal degree of *interiority* (inward-lookingness), of fondness for *privacy* and for activities associated with the *mind.* The most paradoxical of all of these qualities is that of *control.* The end product of the passive reaction to excessive frustration is either to gain or to problematize control.

The self-awareness that I have attributed to Hostius Quadra and his startling reformulation of the self is, to our modern eyes, no remarkable thing. It is merely the realization of an awareness of what these days nearly all of us possess. Yet a number of features of his affirmation deserve stressing. They are aspects of selfhood that are easily ignored and easily forgotten. The process of achieving selfhood, based so firmly on the acceptance of the arbitrary relationship between the self and the world, can be a fraught process. The inevitable frustrations involved run the risks of virulent forms of boredom and, if it is prolonged, of melancholia. They are well illustrated by reconsidering Hostius Quadra. There is always the danger of a slip into psychic disintegration—we see this most graphically in the instances of those who, unexpectedly and unaccountably, fall ill with lovesickness. This can also involve an acute psychic withdrawal, even, in some cases, a withdrawal that is comparable almost to a form of autism. Less acute forms of this process can be seen in the instances of those suffering from acedia.[34] There are also many examples of this problem in the instances of those who are subject to lovesickness. As we note in the case of Hostius Quadra, there is a risk of total community hostility formed by the utter distance from community standards that is involved in the process of frustration and alienation attendant upon this process of defining and differentiating the self.

Things do not end here. As well as the dangers, there are what we might call the costs of self-awareness. These can be cataloged easily. Self-awareness brings with it a propensity, in the person undergoing it, for boredom and melancholy. This may induce him or her even to contemplate suicide. Leisure becomes a problem for such an individual. The nagging certainty and burden of self distracts one from alterity. Alcohol (or any dopamine-inducing substance) offers relief, but, as a leisure pastime, it has its dangers. Love, too, may become impossible: self-awareness may render love an anodyne, a form of public protest, or, worst of all, a locus for extreme emotional danger because of the ever present danger of becoming subject to lovesickness. All of these experiences take place within a community from whom the subject is liable to experience immense disapproval and from whom the subject is bound to encounter enormous hostility.

The advantages flowing from such self-awareness seem petty. Self-awareness is a kind of truth, if there is ever comfort in truth.[35] Such a conception of self may offer proof, however temporary, against psychic disintegration, as it may also offer proof against self-directed violence and possession.[36] Self-awareness, the self itself, comes therefore at a considerable cost—boredom, melancholy, intimations of suicide,[37] a dangerous passivity, unsatisfactory leisure, and a sad inability to love except through the lens of one's own needs.[38] But can there be any other way?[39]

APPENDIX

Giorgio de Chirico, Time, Odysseus, Melancholy, and Intestinal Disorder

with Kathleen Toohey

Giorgio de Chirico (1888–1978), the Italian surrealist painter, is known well for his studies of melancholy and to a lesser extent for his interest in time. He is even less well known for his abominable digestion. In the phase of his career immediately before World War I, de Chirico painted a number of very powerful and often beautiful canvases focusing on the theme of melancholia (a few are reproduced in this appendix). Some of these make the link of melancholia to time apparent—above all by the inclusion of clocks. De Chirico does not necessarily link these with digestion, but he does seem elsewhere rather more concerned with food than might have been expected. We note the regular presence in his prewar painting of bananas (notably in *The Uncertainty of the Poet* [1913]), artichokes, pineapples, pomegranates, and eggs, then later of fish, biscuits, bread, and wine.[1] Occasionally one reads that his continuing fascination with the theme of melancholy may have been the result of the "intestinal disorders which plagued him from his youth" (Soby 1955, 31). We will return to de Chirico's Petronian—or, more correctly, Trimalchionic—gizzards. To start we would like to demonstrate how some of the key themes of chapter 6 (death and the destructive linearity of time) are to be seen in his *The Delights of the Poet* (1912) and how these, through Greek and Roman precedent, have classical origins and a remarkable link with melancholia, both classical and modern. De Chirico, we will therefore suggest, offers a very striking instance for the continuity of the ancient themes that have been discussed within chapter 6 and throughout this book. He also provides a remarkable example for what has been termed the corporealization of affective registers. In de Chirico's case, time and melancholia blend viscerally, on his own say-so, with a purportedly dire indigestion (see Soby 1955, 34, 36). A number of the motifs that we have seen in chapter 6 are apparent in his painting. It provides, as it were, an expressive and affective mirror reflecting back, though no doubt unintentionally, to the Trimalchionic and the Senecan vision of time and its passing and to one of their chief means for affirming the integrity of the self.

The place to begin to illustrate this is with *The Delights of the Poet* (fig. 10) and, within this painting, with de Chirico's clock. Time, through this piece, stands at the near center of the picture. The clock looks down from the railway-station building in *The Delights of the Poet* and across the empty piazza toward its viewer. The picture demands that we interpret time's significance. That the hour is 2:00 in the afternoon is telling. The direction of the shadows indicates that the sun is now off its zenith and that, therefore, we are looking, past the clock, toward the south or southwest. The sun streams in from the southwest. That, too, is important. The ghostly wraith in the mid-background, gaze fixed on the ground, is turned toward the place where the sun will set. The wraith is turned to the directive distance traditionally associated with death.[2] Time, therefore, both through the angle of the sunlight and through the gaze of the wraith, is firmly, if not unexpectedly, linked with death. Time in this picture, on such a reading, is an absolutely linear affair. It has as its end point human death.

That knowledge makes the train more comprehensible. The train is a familiar motif in de Chirico's painting.[3] Soby links it with a favorite childhood train set of de Chirico's. It is also true that from his childhood garden in Volos, Greece, de Chirico could see trains passing by. His father, moreover, was an engineer who worked on the railways in Thessaly. The train was also de Chirico's means of escape to Paris from the Italian military in Turin, whither he had been summoned and charged with desertion in 1913, the very period in which *The Delights of the Poet* was composed.[4] Whatever the case, the train functions as a symbol for youth, life, expectation, and fulfilment. It is not a symbol, however, that is always unambiguous.[5] In this picture the train, moving away from the west and death, draws into the railway station (as is indicated by the vertical direction of the ghostly clouds of steam that it produces). Is it fleeing the death that we can speculate is embodied in the wraith and implied by the distant vista taken in by the wraith's gaze? Is the train about to take on the wraith as a passenger and so vitiate its escape?

Consider once again the linearity of time as we have described it in the penultimate paragraph. The train moves on a fixed line in one direction. Its motion is mirrored again in the sharp lines created by the interplay of light and shade. These serve to illustrate this linearity of time. They may be contrasted with the fountain in the middle of the painting, directly beneath the clock. The

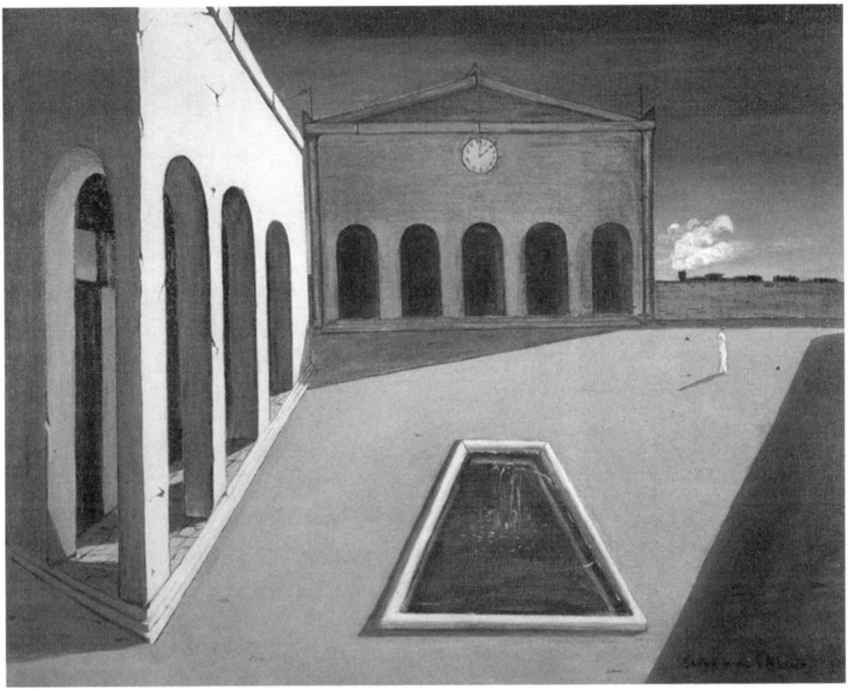

FIG. 10. Giorgio de Chirico, *The Delights of the Poet* (1912). (© Estate of Giorgio de Chirico / SIAE [Rome] / SODRAC [Montreal] 2002.)

fountain is also to be associated with time and death, although in the most ironic of manners. This fountain, set in the near foreground and—along with the train, the clouds of smoke, and the flags—one of the dynamic images in the composition, represents a metaphysical theme that de Chirico reworked a number of times. According to Baldacci (1997, 57) it is linked by de Chirico with Nietzsche's concept of the "eternal return" (alluded to in the quote in chapter 6 from Long and Sedley 1987, I:311 ff.), or, as chapter 6 has it, of circular time. The fountain presents, therefore, an unresolved temporal alternative—what might have been, we could say—to the linear thrust of the painting as a whole. The fountain reemphasizes the theme of linear time, by obverse. Its unexpected significance can be seen clearly again in *The Enigma of the Hour* (1911), which painting we will briefly discuss later in this appendix.

Time and death are linked with melancholy, with a profound boredom, and with loneliness. This is the sense projected by the empty and eerie piazza and its shaded colonnades. Any doubts that might be had on this matter are allayed by those telling colonnades in *The Melancholy of a Beautiful Day* (1913) and *The Lassitude of the Infinite* (1912) (both reproduced later in this appendix). In these two pictures, both painted very close in time to *The Delights of the Poet*, the colonnades and their shade are irrevocably associated with such an emotion. The architecture of the piazza reinforces our sense of the immanence of these emotions. "The nostalgia of the infinite is revealed beneath the geometric precision of the piazzas," wrote de Chirico when describing Turin (quoted by Baldacci 1997, 128). We take it that Baldacci is referring here to a longing for the infinite—for the timeless, that is. The monumental and motionless piazza suggests a world without time. The timelessness of the piazza is, however, one that is doomed to failure, insofar as the buildings are human creations. Do the long and starkly imposing shadows indicate that the life of the buildings we create is as finite as our own lives? Do their cracks and crumbling stone further suggest their finite nature?

Unlike later works by de Chirico, *The Delights of the Poet* does not have an extremely anxious or dramatic tone. What is apparent, however, is its overwhelming sense of loss. This is emphasized by a number of features. The lack of horizon and the conflicting scale create a sense of emptiness. The oversized colonnade stresses the fragility of the wraith and again creates an overwhelming sense of emptiness. This impression is underscored, furthermore, by what is not to be seen: there is a dramatic lack of people in the piazza; the shadow spanning the right vertical is cast from an *unseen* building; note, too, that the buildings themselves are as empty as the shadows they cast. An interesting feature that adds to this impression is the shaft of sky that is visible through the first colonnade on the right. The space of surreal green sky is the only glimpse that de Chirico gives us into the buildings' interiors. These interiors reveal nothing. They are as empty as the square. The green space balances the painting and emphasizes the movement of the train from right to left. This movement is reinforced by the flags. They indicate that the wind also moves in the direction of the train, from right to left. It also invokes the emptiness of the piazza and enforces our comprehension of the fragility and finite nature of the buildings. This sense of loss and emptiness complements the vision of linear time embodied in this painting.

The Delights of the Poet is a simple, albeit powerful, picture that collects and represents a series of favorite motifs. There is no necessarily unifying theme to the picture. Rather, the polyphonic motifs cluster about a series of ideas: the linearity of a time that leads irrevocably to death and that is associated in some manner or another, we sense, with a profound feeling of melancholy and, probably, alienation. All that is (apparently) missing from these paintings, from the point of view of chapter 6, is the Senecan sense of catastrophe.[6] Yet some views of *The Delights of the Poet*, perhaps unfairly and with too much foreknowledge, sense catastrophe in the dark shadows of the colonnades. A sense that catastrophe is about to happen is certainly projected by the famous shadows of the well-known painting *The Mystery and Melancholy of a Street* (1914). This canvas depicts the shadow of a young girl driving a hoop from the shadows of a street toward an open and bare piazza, while another shadow stalks her and forebodes who knows what.

The classical origins for much of de Chirico's iconography are as striking as they are unexpected. To illustrate these we need to turn back to the Swiss painter and mythological enthusiast Arnold Böcklin (1827–1901), a resident of Tuscany and a profound influence on the young de Chirico. In an attempt to illustrate this point, we have reproduced in this appendix Böcklin's *Odysseus and Calypso* (1882) and de Chirico's *The Enigma of the Oracle* (1910). A juxtaposition of these two not only makes clear the Greco-Roman origins for much of the conceptual imagery in de Chirico's metaphysical phase but also makes more clear how melancholia assumes a part within this imagistic web.[7]

Odysseus, in classical mythology, is a victim of nostalgia.[8] In fact, he may be the first person in Western literature to suffer from the condition. His nostalgia was not, however, the flaccid and passive longing implied by the modern word.[9] His is a strong and debilitating and grieflike emotion. Toward the beginning of the second tetrad of Homer's *Odyssey*, the depth of Odysseus's emotion, driven by his longing to return to Ithaca and to his wife, becomes clear (*Odyssey* 5.82–84).

> But he sat weeping by the seashore, as he had before,
> Breaking his heart *[thymos]* in tears, groaning, and grief.
> He looked out across the barren sea and wept.

This description is sufficiently vivid for it to require little paraphrase. Note the apparent passivity and lonesomeness of the hero. He sits, rather than stands, and does so on the seashore, the most deserted of places in antiquity. His emotions are made evident in the reference to the broken heart, the groaning, and the grief. Their sterility has its parallel in the barrenness of the sea itself. Odysseus's emotion could easily be associated with depression. Böcklin's *Odysseus and Calypso* (fig. 11) has seized upon this insight and dramatized it in the remarkable portrait of a shrouded, seemingly grief-stricken Odysseus staring out across the barren and faraway distances of the ocean. (The sea seems to act as an objective correlative for Odysseus's state of mind.) Seated outside a sea cave, Calypso, possessing the face of a hausfrau on the body of a teenager, looks sympathetically, if disconsolately, at her distant lover. She is naked and, according to the myth, available. Odysseus is clothed and closed off to her.

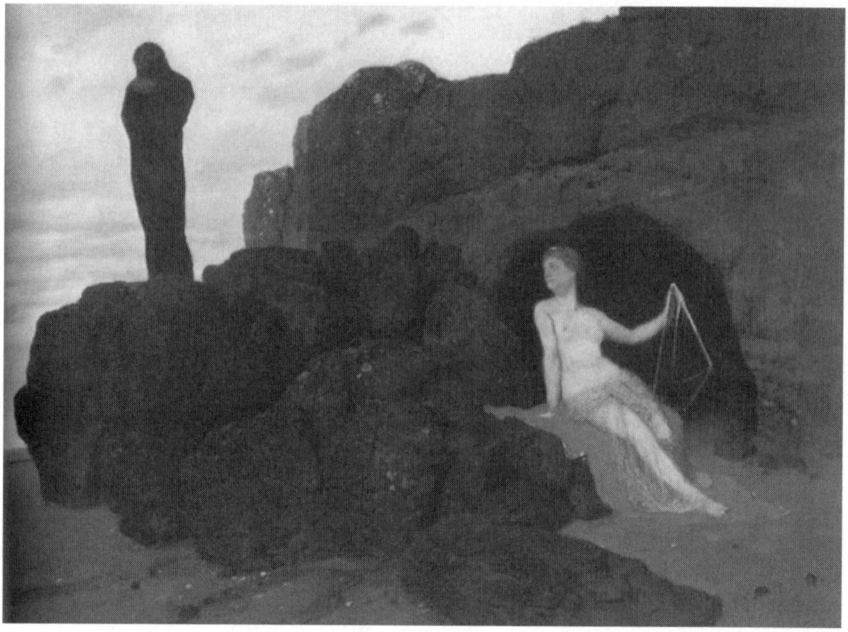

FIG. 11. Arnold Böcklin, *Odysseus and Calypso* (1882). (Photo: Öffentliche Kunstsammlung Basel, Martin Bühler. Courtesy of Öffentliche Kunstsammiung Basel, Kunstmuseum.)

Unlike Homer's hero, Böcklin's stands upright, as if to assert his grief. His despairing head droops, and his shoulders are hunched in sorrow.

If you compare de Chirico's *The Enigma of the Oracle* (fig. 12) with *Odysseus and Calypso,* you can see how much de Chirico has relied on, though adapted, Böcklin to place a melancholy, grieving Odysseus within a new context. Böcklin's Odysseus has become an unnamed, melancholy, and grieving everyman. He stares out across a lowland from which he is cut off and across the ocean. The city and the lowland are new. The ocean is Homer's and Böcklin's. The rock outcrop separating Odysseus and Calypso has become a wall in *The Enigma of the Oracle.* "Calypso," veiled off, has become an oracle—the male god Apollo, presumably. Unlike Calypso, he stares away from the Odysseus figure. The grief and nostalgia of "Odysseus," therefore, may be the result of being cut off from human concourse (in the city below) and from the enigmatic god veiled off and turning away in the right of the picture. It is as if Calypso becomes an Apollo figure, but one standing, presumably, for the gods in general. The gods know (or God knows) how to cure our nostalgia and melancholy and how to "get us home." But they will not provide us with the

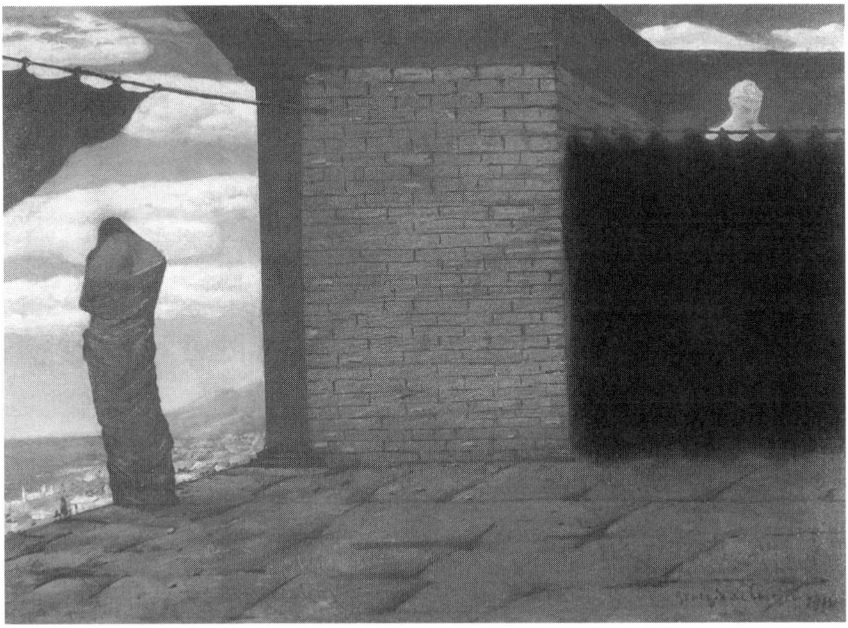

FIG. 12. Giorgio de Chirico, *The Enigma of the Oracle* (1910). (© Estate of Giorgio de Chirico / SIAE [Rome] / SODRAC [Montreal] 2002.)

answer. Thus Apollo looks away and is veiled off from the grieving everyman (who stares brooding from a Mediterranean Delphi—note how the sea is present in the distance). De Chirico thus has made a general statement about human alienation from the transcendent (and its immanence) and from human society, basing his vision on the saccharine and romantic specificity of Böcklin's picture.

At any rate, this Odysseus figure appears elsewhere in de Chirico's pictures from this period. So we see him depicted shrouded in *The Melancholy of a Beautiful Day* (1913), duplicated as tiny figures in *The Lassitude of the Infinite* (1912), and, quite alarmingly, rendered white in *The Enigma of the Hour* (1911). (All these paintings are reproduced later in this appendix.) We suspect that the wraith of *The Delights of the Poet* (1912) is none other than this grieving, melancholic Odysseus, rendered white.

Böcklin's picture helps in other ways. The ocean, the object of Odysseus's gaze, is the proximate cause of his nostalgia. The water of the sea is perhaps what is behind the presence of the fountain in de Chirico's melancholy prewar paintings. The sea is infinite, like linear time. Water becomes associated with

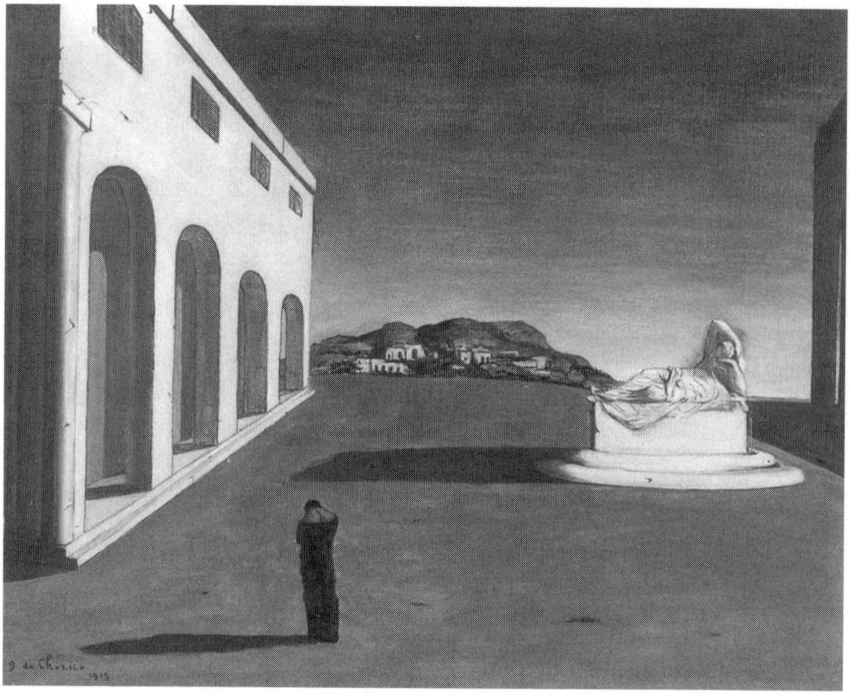

FIG. 13. Giorgio de Chirico, *The Melancholy of a Beautiful Day* (1913). (© Estate of Georgio de Chirico / SIAE [Rome] / SODRAC [Montreal] 2002; the Royal Museum of Fine Arts, Brussels, Belgium.)

the etiology of melancholy and alienation, despite its link, through Nietzsche, to circular time. In *The Enigma of the Oracle*, this proximate cause of melancholy is transformed into a seemingly infinite land and sea vista.[10] This motif occurs again in the other pictures that we have reproduced in this appendix.

Calypso is the ultimate cause of Odysseus's melancholy. She keeps Odysseus away from Ithaca and Penelope. As we have just stated, she "becomes" Apollo in de Chirico's *The Enigma of the Oracle*. There is a stark contrast, in both Böcklin's painting and de Chirico's, between the dark, shrouded, alienated, and melancholic figure and the white figure, the agent of alienation, nostalgia, and melancholy. The polarity is maintained in *The Melancholy of a Beautiful Day* (fig. 13). The powerful white female figure here, again agent of alienation, is, in origin, none other than Böcklin's Calypso. Elsewhere in de Chirico's paintings, she transforms into a figure known as MELANCONIA, melancholia itself, or, not infrequently, Ariadne (see figs. 14–15).[11] It is not hard to imagine why Ariadne should become MELANCONIA. How else can she

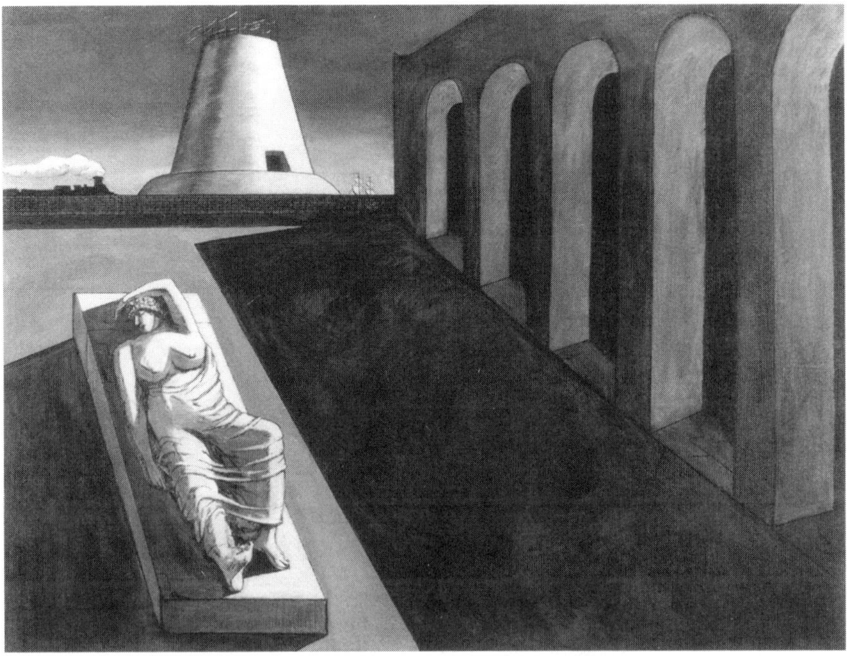

FIG. 14. Giorgio de Chirico, *Ariadne* (1913). (© Estate of Giorgio de Chirico / SIAE [Rome] / SODRAC [Montreal] 2002.)

have felt, abandoned by Theseus and left to stare out grieving and melancholy, Odysseus-like, across the sea? In *The Melancholy of a Beautiful Day*, however, the Ariadne figure stands in for Böcklin's Calypso and for the Apollo figure of *The Enigma of the Oracle*. Perhaps the Calypso-Ariadne-MELANCONIA figure is not so much the embodiment of the emotion as the cause and progenitor for melancholy and grief. (In figures 14–15, the Ariadne figure is unaware of her abandonment.)[12] These melancholy gods inflict melancholia on humans by refusing to communicate their knowledge (oracles) and by keeping them away from home. (The Ariadne figure of *The Melancholy of a Beautiful Day* seems to block off the Odysseus figure from the human settlement in the distance, thus enforcing his melancholia and nostalgia.)

At any rate, these figures seem, as we suggest, to stand for the silence of the gods and for the alienation and melancholy that their lassid indifference forces upon us. This indifference is embodied in death itself. The language of *The Lassitude of the Infinite* (fig. 16) should by now be plain—the melancholy, the threatening shadowed colonnades matching Böcklin's rocks and the wall of *The Enigma of the Oracle*, the two mourning Odysseus figures, the massive

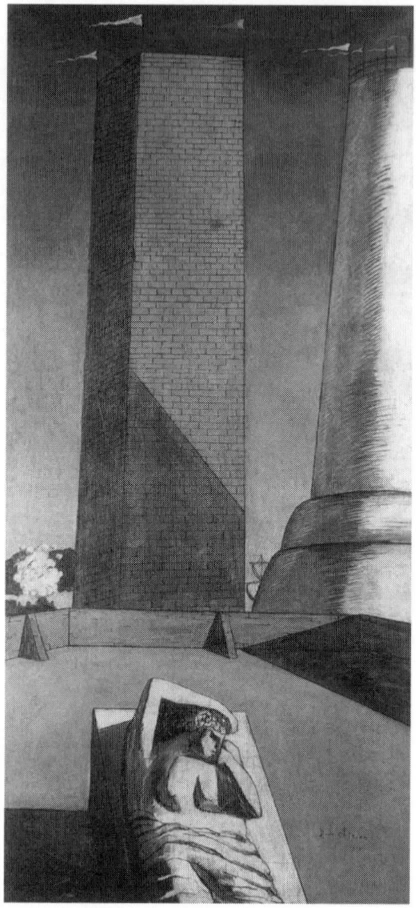

FIG. 15. Giorgio de Chirico, *Ariadne's Afternoon* (1913). (© Estate of Giorgio de Chirico / SIAE [Rome] / SODRAC [Montreal] 2002.)

Calypso-Ariadne figure (the apparent agent of alienation, death, and divine indifference), the train of youth and freshness hurtling toward the tower of death and time, and the infinitude of the endless regressive vista of the painting. The two pictures are powerful variants on the same theme.

The last of the paintings that we would like to address here is *The Enigma of the Hour* (fig. 17). The imagery should be becoming clear. The colonnade, a wall, stands in for Böcklin's rocky outcrop or for the brick wall of *The Enigma of the Oracle* and symbolizes human alienation from the divine. The clock within the structure of the colonnade stands for death, the final alienator. On the piazza, below the clock, is the spring, the symbol for circular time. It stands at counterpoint to the rest of the picture and points to what humans have

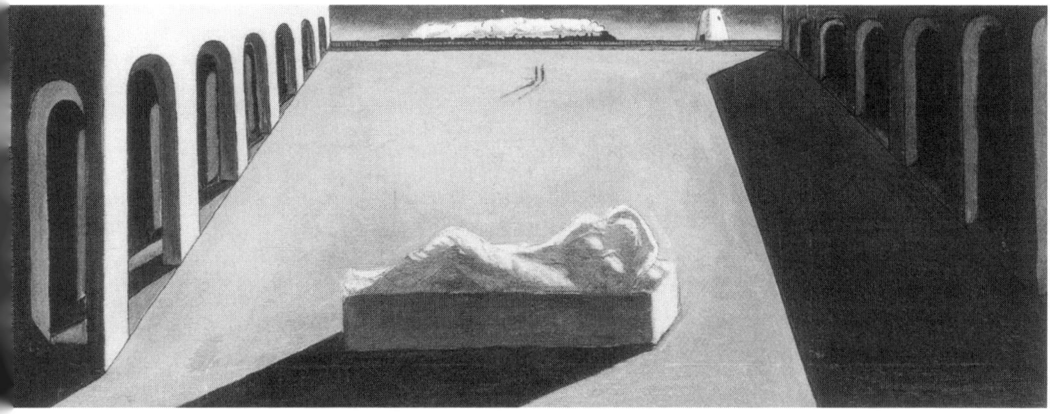

FIG. 16. Giorgio de Chirico, *The Lassitude of the Infinite* (1912). (© Estate of Giorgio de Chirico / SIAE [Rome] / SODRAC [Montreal] 2002.)

lost. The two figures (one white, one dark) in the bottom of the picture, both apparently staring with sorrow at the spring, are Odysseus figures, representing the melancholy, grief, and nostalgia of humans alienated by time, death, and the indifference of the gods. Is the small figure upstairs in the colonnade, to the left of the clock, an obscure version of Apollo-Calypso? *The Enigma of the Hour* joins with de Chirico's *The Enigma of the Oracle*, *The Melancholy of a Beautiful Day*, and *The Lassitude of the Infinite* to establish a remarkable imagistic, thematic, and ideational chain, via Böcklin, right back into classical antiquity.

It would be dreadfully reductive to attribute to intestinal disorder de Chirico's remarkably clear vision of melancholy, alienation, nostalgia, time, death, and the silence of the gods. De Chirico's ideas have ample parallels in other paintings and writings of this period, and for this reason alone they require serious treatment.[13] Yet the parallel between de Chirico's and Trimalchio's intestinal disorders and the likely links between de Chirico's disorder, his take on time, and melancholia is striking. Intestinal disorder played a very great part in the life of de Chirico in the prewar years. He linked it with melancholy and, it seems, with linear time. This is something that Trimalchio did as well. It suggests, in my opinion, a very strange continuity in the understanding of the link between the body, time (of a linear sort), and melancholy. The continuity has no basis in reality. De Chirico's ideas are too powerful for them to be subject to removal by a digestive aid. Rather, we suggest that there is a popular conceptual continuity between Trimalchio's complaint and that of de Chirico. The

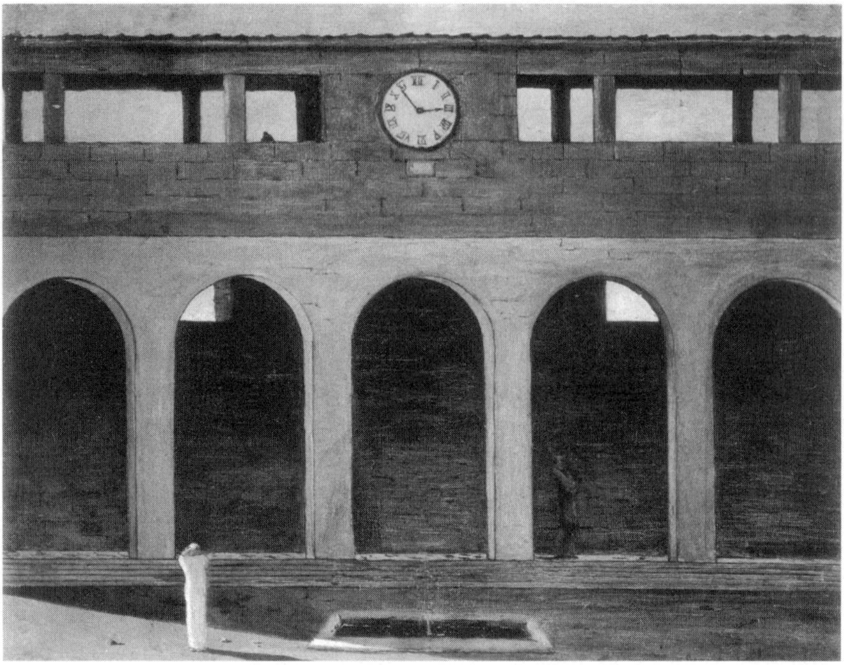

FIG. 17. Giorgio de Chirico, *The Enigma of the Hour* (1912). (© Estate of Giorgio de Chirico / SIAE [Rome] / SODRAC [Montreal] 2002.)

continuity is *discursive* and begins in the first century of our era. Trimalchio acted out time and death as a means to neutralize the fear and affective disorder with which they seemed to threaten him. De Chirico's paintings of 1911–12 and especially 1913 cannot be written down in such a reductive manner. Nonetheless, we have no doubt that they did provide for him a means by which he held together a delicately balanced sanity.

In conclusion, de Chirico's painting demonstrates the strange symbiosis of many of the affective conditions and responses examined so far in this book. It also demonstrates their continuity and, indirectly, the inadequacies of the periodizations favored in popular literature by the likes of Høeg or, in philosophy and cultural studies, by such scholars as Michel Foucault. Further, the paintings, by their articulation of de Chirico's visceral fears, provide a means for countering this and for affirming the boundaries of the self.

Notes

The epigraph is taken from Burton 1931, 65.

1. To some degree this change was, to use a very handy piece of jargon, a *discursive* shift, one to be observed in written texts. I will, however, modify this claim later in this introduction.

2. The discovery of the "inner self" has been claimed for a variety of eras. Compare, for example, Phillip Cary's evocatively titled *Augustine's Invention of the Inner Self* (2000). Foucault, as is well known, terms the inner self "man" in the final section of *The Order of Things* and, positing its invention in the Enlightenment, looks to its imminent demise.

3. The model for societal change that I am using is drawn, to some extent, from childhood developmental psychology. It would not be wide of the mark to state that I analogize the manic reaction to psychological trauma (the dominant mode, I suggest, in nonmedical literature before the Senecan era) with childhood (driven, I suggest, by the "centered," "egocentric illusion"). Nor would it be wide of the mark to state that I analogize the depressive reaction to psychological trauma (the dominant mode, I suggest, in the nonmedical literature of the post-Senecan era) with adulthood. But that is as far as things should go. The movement from a manic to a depressive mode of consciousness could hardly be said to represent development or progress. It represents, merely, change. Proponents (in varying ways) of the childhood analogy (Lévy-Bruhl [1923], Piaget [1929, 1954], Dodds [1968], Snell [1953], or even Heidegger) usually highlight progress or decline. As should be apparent, I can see no progress or decline here, only change. Either mentality can easily court madness. I will have further explanatory and justificatory comments to make on this matter.

4. Kennell (1997) objects that he finds exceptions to my claims that vitiate their validity. Swain (1996) suggests that I have not surveyed all of the evidence (as if this were humanly possible). Both imply that I have not established historical truths or laws. This is not my intention. My aim is to establish discursive and heuristic patterns and tendencies. I must insist upon this: if several texts in discrete intellectual domains are using the same analytic method, then we have a discursive "truth" or, if one prefers, at least a heuristic tool.

5. Furthermore, the exceptions to my model of discursive change are evidence for the failure of any new paradigm to wholly erase its competitors by the achievement of discursive hegemony.

6. Compare Oehler's *Subjektivität und Selbstbewustsein in der Antike* (1997).

7. The social self can even be a "national" self; see Syed 1997 on the Roman self.

8. See Hollan 1992 on the "cross-cultural" self.

9. We moderns tend to correlate the thickening of the sense of self with the generic

dissolution of bonds entangling the individual within a wider network of social relations and duties.

10. We might conclude that various illnesses and physical interferences can erase the self. Other conditions (e.g., alcoholism) reduce the complexity and range of our identity to a slimmer, less flexible entity.

11. The Australian prime minister (1969–71) John Grey Gorton was once asked by an interviewer what sort of man he considered himself to be. In response to that query concerning his self, Gorton replied, "I am six feet high and weigh about 12 stone" (Mungo MacCallum, *The Age,* March 19, 2002). That response, I think, provides a useful commentary on some of the confusion and, dare I say it, the humbug associated with definitions of the self.

12. Donaldson (1978, 27) uses the terms *self* and *self-awareness* in much the same manner as I do here. Of the self of the child, she observes, "You cannot think of a universe of stable enduring things, moving around in space and time, unless you have made the crucial distinction between self and not-self by which you award things their independence—and at the same time achieve your own."

13. The most powerful revision (with which I am familiar) of Piaget's idea is Donaldson 1978. That I believe Donaldson's admirable common sense is exaggerated should be apparent. I should detail here my objections to her formulation, if only because the societal model that I have adopted in this book owes some of its lineament to the Piagetian formulation. It appears to me that Donaldson creates a psychological model for the child that comes very close to representing it as a "little adult," one who seems to be possessed of a conceptual and moral ability that is in many ways comparable to that of an adult. Donaldson seems to believe that if a conceptual or moral conundrum is put to a child in the right language (it must be "decentered," or couched in a language that is not adult-centered), the child is capable of formulating a proper response. This argument seems to me to be somewhat strange. If a child's command of language is so primitive that he or she cannot understand an adult's formulation, must not the child's conceptual and moral sense be comparably inchoate? (The development of a self-awareness that includes, nonegotistically, other individuals is surely to be linked with one's increased linguistic ability and to the abilities of one's linguistic system—not all languages were born equal; early Greek, e.g., is abstract poor.) Donaldson seems to me almost to make a straw man of Piaget. The belief that the "egocentric illusion" (as Piaget terms the child's apparent inability of "making any distinction between himself and what is not himself") consistently dominates a child's psychology up until the age of approximately seven, then vanishes (which view is imputed to Piaget) seems to me to be odd. The movement away from any "egocentric illusion" ought to be gradual: such an illusion, thus, would be very powerful in the neonate but nearly or completely nonexistent in the seven-year-old. I have a little more to say on the development of the child's psychology in the next note.

14. An interesting report in Toronto's *Globe and Mail* (Abraham 2001) suggested that very young children more frequently use the deep, older structures of the brain, those associated with instinct. Older children appear to display more activity in the prefrontal cortex, the brain's "chair for controlling impulses." The child's immediate sense of identification with the world, we could paraphrase, is disrupted, or becomes subject to an alienation, through this prefrontal cortex.

15. Sanity and madness can be readily understood by contemplating these boundaries of the self. If the boundaries between an individual and the world about are insufficiently firm, the response can resemble something close to a manic exaltation or a mystic afflatus. If the boundaries are too watertight, then an individual runs the risk of an internal dialogue that in its solipsism resembles autism. Madness exists at either extreme. Sanity—Horace's *aurea mediocritas*—sits somewhere in the middle.

16. Foucault, at least in *The Archaeology of Knowledge* (1972), uses the term *discursive* of essentially written networks. Wiles (1997), like many others, apparently has broadened the notion to include speech as it is practiced in a particular culture. James Davidson, in the introduction to his *Courtesans and Fishcakes* (1997), provides a very readable and sensible explanation of the term *discourse.*

17. My colleague Dr. Hanne Sigismund Nielsen has described depression to me as a "drive" (rather like lust or gluttony, I suppose). This seems to me to be a very helpful way of conceptualizing melancholia. The "drive" represented by melancholia directs itself toward the striking of an equilibrium between the two poles of the autistic self-absorption represented by mania and its melancholic opposite. Depression, at least in its milder form, aims to assert the autonomy of the self against these polar dangers. In this controversial mode of understanding, I take heart from a curious report in *Calgary Herald* (Trueman 2002) of a study from a "current" issue of the *American Journal of Geriatric Psychology* by a researcher from Duke University, Dan Blazer. Older women with mild depression "are likely to live longer than their non-depressed neighbours," the research report argues. Trueman explains: "[Blazer's] research followed a group of 2,401 women and 1,269 men, all over the age of 65. The group was ranked on a scale from 'depressed,' 'mildly depressed,' to 'not depressed' . . . Over an 11-year period, from 1986 to 1997, the women who were 'mildly depressed' were 60 per cent less likely to die during any three year interval."

CHAPTER 1

1. For a recent discussion of this pot and a related series of pottery representations (with bibliography) see Shapiro 1994, 142–48.

2. Shapiro (1994, 146) describes Orestes' expression as one of "quiet reverie."

3. Compare the face of this Fury with that of the mourning woman produced as figure 3 in chapter 3. The mouth, the eyes, and the tilt of the head all seem to match. This, I think, helps us in turn to interpret the mood projected by Orestes.

4. Two of the Furies are awake because Clytemnestra (whose form is partly visible at the top left) is rousing them.

5. Shapiro (1994, 147) states, "the third Fury emerging out of the earth can be read as a learned allusion to their chthonic nature."

6. The frontal depiction of the Fury in the bottom corner of the picture does not allow the representation of emotions. But note the slight downturn of the mouth and the position of the left arm, which, minus the sword, matches that of Orestes.

7. See *LIMC* s.v. "Orestes" for a discussion of this pot and some of the matters I am raising here.

8. Psychiatric literature describes this form of melancholy as a "mixed state." See the

now classic discussions of Kraepelin 1921, chapter 6 and pp. 106 (on "manic stupor") and 107 (on depression with "flight of ideas"). On this aspect of the illness see also Koukopoulos and Koukopoulos 1999; Goodwin and Jamison 1990.

9. Kraepelin (1921, 107) describes the woman as follows: "In the rigid expression of countenance of the patient who always remains standing on the same spot, the constraint can be distinctly recognized, which for many months has dominated her and made her dumb. But at the same time, there appeared in the almost invincible tendency to destructiveness and filthy habits, the fundamental feature of the disorder, which in the adornment of torn-off leaves and twigs is recognized also in the picture."

10. The painting of Orestes exhibits, however, none of the same hostility. We must make allowances for the fact that in the case of Kraepelin's patient, one is dealing with clinical insanity, rather than with an artist's conceptualization of the illness.

11. I can see no indication of a comparable depiction of illness in Aeschylus's version, to which our poet is most indebted. Aeschylus seems to take Orestes' madness for granted and allows the Furies to corporealize it without an indication of comparable symptoms in Orestes.

12. Translations are normally my own. Where they are not, they are taken from the relevant (if reliable) Loeb editions.

13. For a description of this type of manic behavior in a context of the manic-depressive illness see Kraepelin 1921, 28–31.

14. The distinction is made very clearly by Kraepelin (1921, 36), who describes the exhaustion that necessarily follows a manic episode. See also Kraepelin 1921, 73: "very often after the disappearance of manic excitement a more or less marked condition of weakness appears, which is generally regarded as exhaustion after the severe illness."

15. Epilepsy and melancholia can be linked. The connection between the two was "an idea which appears in the *Epidemics* of Hippocrates (6.8.31) and which was accepted by all ancient doctors" (Ullmann 1978, 75). Ullmann cites in support Temkin 1971, index s.v. "melancholy." Add Goodwin and Jamison 1990, 116–17. See too the discussion of Cydippe's symptoms in chapter 2 and the linking of Heracles' melancholia to this in *Problema* 30.1. See also Jacques 1998, 224.

16. For a brief discussion of mania and delusion see Kraepelin 1921, 65.

17. I suppose that genre plays its part: tragedy, that is, focuses on the "political." This is, however, only true in part, for the very existence of Euripidean characters such as Orestes points to a tradition straining against the bounds of the apparently "political" basis of the genre.

18. Perhaps the emotions expressed by the Eumenides Painter's pot would be best rendered in personal poetry (they eventually are rendered, to some extent, in Catullus's poem 76 in the sixties B.C.E.).

19. Compare Flashar 1966, 47 for this definition; Flashar cites the Hippocratic treatise *Epidemics* 6.23 [4.568.11.f.L].

20. This position is improbably maintained in Deleuze and Guattari's *Anti-Oedipus* (1977), where it is suggested that "depression and Oedipus are agencies of the state" (xx). The representation of melancholia receives a comparable straitjacket from Schiesari (1992), who attempts to make the term gender-defined. Melancholia (which is far more than an appropriated male version of depression) knows no gender boundaries in antiquity, in experi-

ence or literature. The desire to associate melancholia or depression with capitalism or phallocentrism is both mendacious and ahistorical.

21. For a survey of the shifting perceptions of madness through history, looking at literary texts and the history of medicine, see Thiher 1999.

22. Depression can be bipolar, exhibiting at different times active hilarity (or violent aggressive behavior) or passive (regressive) "depression." On the Democritean tradition of the laughing melancholic see Rütten 1992.

23. The basis of this physiology seems to represent an earlier version of the Galenic humoral theory (Jackson 1986, 30).

24. Solomon (2001, 196) notes that PET (positron emission tomography) scans produce an image of the depressed and manic brain that curiously echoes this Hippocratic speculation. The depressed brain shows up as literally blue, the manic as yellow and orange and red.

25. Griesinger (1845; note also Marneros and Angst 2000 passim) described "seasonally affective disorders" and, like the Hippocratics, noted that melancholia may begin in autumn and winter, mania in spring.

26. For the following survey, I have relied upon Jackson 1986 and Klibansky, Panofsky, and Saxl 1964. Starobinski 1962 was also helpful. More generally I have found useful Milns 1986; Simon 1978, especially 228–37; and Rosen 1968, 71–136, especially 92 ff. and 98. Simon (1978, 317) cites Kudlien 1967 and 1975; Lewis 1967; and Leibbrand and Wettley 1961, 43–89.

27. On melancholy and the Hippocratic writers see Müri 1953 and, more generally, Smith 1979; compare Neuburger 1909.

28. See Jackson 1986, 30–31, quoting from Jones and Withington 1923–31, 1:236, 4:185.

29. There is something to be said for the view of Lewis (1971, 73) on writers such as Aristotle/Theophrastus: "it is proposed to abstain here from those citations out of non-medical writers and discussions about the madness of famous personages, from Hercules onwards, which are common in articles of this kind, but belong less to the history of psychiatry than to its *belles-lettre*."

30. A recent discussion of this passage is contained in Rütten 1992. See also Roussel 1988; Van der Eijk 1990.

31. There was a tradition linking melancholia with inspiration. It is associated with Democritus of Abdera (see Rütten 1992; Padel 1995) but relies on the link between mania and melancholy. Plato, in the *Phaedrus*, had spoken of the prophetic capacities of mania. These, it appears, were transferred to melancholia, insofar as this is identified with mania. The confusion may have been accidentally strengthened by *Problema* 30.1, which stresses the link between intellectual acumen and melancholia.

32. This bipolarity is acknowledged elsewhere in ancient thought. The following passage on the bipolarity of emotion comes from Seneca *Epistles* 92.8.

> inrationalis pars animi duas habet partes, alteram animosam, ambitiosam, inpotentem, positam in adfectionibus, alteram humilem, languidam, voluptatibus deditam; illam effrenatam, meliorem tamen, certe fortiorem ac digniorem viro reliquerunt, hanc necessariam beatae vitae putaverunt, et enervem et abiectam. Huic rationem servire iusserunt . . .

[the irrational portion of the soul has two parts, one animated, ambitious, violent, and seated in the emotions, the other lowly, languid, and given to pleasure; the former, though uncontrolled, provides a man with a better, bolder, and more worthy nature; the latter, necessary for the good life, [philosophers] consider to be weak and lowly. They have ordered reason to serve the latter . . .]

33. Jamison (1999, 200) notes that "most people who suffer from depression . . . do not kill themselves." Kraepelin (1921, 78) is as illuminating as ever. He divides depressives into a number of categories (*melancholia simplex,* stupor, *melancholia gravis,* paranoid melancholia, etc.). Only *melancholia simplex,* if I understand things correctly, exists in a unipolar state. It is what we term, popularly, as depression. Of this condition, Kraepelin writes: "just because of this severe volitional disorder [sc., *melancholia simplex*] it relatively seldom comes to more serious attempts at suicide, although the wish to die very frequently occurs. It is only when with the disappearance of inhibition energy returns while the depression still continues, that the attempts at suicide become more frequent and dangerous."

34. Sophocles' character Philoctetes, in the play of the same name, is sometimes accused of suffering depression or at least a severe form of boredom. He deserves comparison. See Kuhn 1976; compare Worman 2000.

35. Books such as Jamison's *Touched with Fire* (1993) tread a thin line between the sensational and the scientific.

36. Klibansky, Panofsky, and Saxl (1964, 49) makes this statement as part of a general discussion (48–55) of Rufus of Ephesus. Rufus's work on melancholy is reconstructed from (Arabic) fragments and citations: see Klibansky, Panofsky, and Saxl 1964, 49; Ullmann 1978, 36–38. The Greek text for Rufus is Gärtner 1970. The most accessible translation is by Daremberg and Ruelle (1879). For a discussion of the Arabic material see Ullmann 1978, 36–38, 72–78.

37. Rufus's influence on Arabic medicine, especially as this relates to melancholy, appears to have been considerable (Ullmann 1978, 72–78).

38. Klibansky, Panofsky, and Saxl (1964, 49) quotes a fragment of Rufus in Latin to support this: *illi sunt qui subtilis ingenii et multae perspicationis, de facili incidunt in melancholicas, eo quod sunt velocis motus et multae praemeditationis et imaginationis* [those who are of subtle ability and of great insight, easily become melancholy, in that [their characters] are swift, full of foresight and imagination].

39. For a discussion of Celsus and a bibliography see Klibansky, Panofsky, and Saxl 1964, 45 f. The authors point out that Celsus bases his work on that of Asclepiades of Bithynia, who came to Rome in 91 B.C.E. and went on to become a friend of Cicero (cf. Vallance 1990). Jackson (1986, 33) believes that Celsus may have been influenced by humoral theory.

40. Soranus survives in a Latin translation made at the end of the fourth century by Caelius Aurelianus *(De morbis acutis et chronicis)*. For a text see Drabkin 1950.

41. Drabkin (1950, 561) quotes the text: *melancholia dicta, quod nigra fella aegrotantibus saepe per vomitum veniant . . . et non, ut plerique existimant, quod passionis causa vel generatio nigra sit [sint] fella; hoc enim est aestimantium magis quam videntium veritatem, vel potius falsum, sicut in aliis ostendimus.*

42. There is a useful, though aged, text and translation of Aretaeus by Adams (1856).

43. Siegel (1973, 273) asserts that it is mistaken to see bipolarity in Aretaeus's descriptions. Such a claim seems to fly in the face of Aretaeus's own words.

44. Marneros and Angst (2000) provide a most illuminating historical overview of interpretations of bipolar illness and, in so doing, demonstrate Aretaeus's honorable place within this history.

45. For literature on Galen see the next note, plus Siegel 1968 and Temkin 1973. Smith (1979, 66 ff.) discusses the relation of Galen to the Hippocratic writings.

46. Galen's comments on melancholy may be found in book 3 of *On the Affected Parts.* For a translation see Siegel 1976. On Galen and melancholy see Jackson 1986, 41–45; Jackson 1969; Siegel 1968, 300–304; Klibansky, Panofsky, and Saxl 1964, 57 ff.

47. Rosen (1968, 92–94) offers useful comments on the colloquial use of the term *mania* in Greece and Rome. See too Müri 1953, 38.

48. Jacques (1998) makes the fascinating deduction that the verb *melancholan* is older in usage than the noun *melancholia.* The former, then, suggests anger and mania (being "mad at someone," in our sense); the latter—developing under the pressure of medical speculation, perhaps—suggests depression.

49. Padel (1995, 48 n. 3) offers parallels from Aristophanes (*Birds* 14; *Wealth* 12, 364–66, 903).

50. Padel (1995, 48 n. 5) offers other parallels from Menander (*Samia* 218; *Epitrepontes* 217, 560–61) and from Plautus (*Amphitryo* 727; *Captivi* 596).

51. Athamas is characterized as violent at Ovid *Metamorphoses* 4.416 ff., as is Ajax at *Metamorphoses* 13.1 ff. Orestes appears in this manner in Horace *Satires* 2.3.137 ff. (Varro wrote a *logistoricus* entitled *Orestes de insania* [Rawson 1985, 287]. The ancient source is Aulus Gellius 13.4.1.) Alcmaeon, like Ajax, murdered his mother and suffered in much the same fashion (Euripides wrote an *Alcmaeon*). On Ajax, see the discussion later in this chapter.

52. Goodwin and Jamison (1990) add Herod the Great to the list.

53. Useful for this play and for the Heracles tradition generally is Galinsky 1972. More precisely on Heracles *melancholicus* is Wilamowitz-Moellendorff 1959, 92–95. For an interrelation of Hippocratic theories of black bile and of tragedy (and of Aristotle) see Tate 1937. See also Yoshitake 1994.

54. The quote is from Collinge 1962, 48. Bond (1981, 309) seems to share this verdict. Wilamowitz-Moellendorff's theories of "megalomania" may be equally wide of the mark; see Bond 1981, xix and n. 9. Comparable language is used, for example, of Creon's daughter—no melancholic—after the application of Medea's poison (*Medea* 1173 ff.).

55. Depiction of this manic melancholia is furthermore constrained by the conceptual force of Heracles and his madness within the drama. One plausible type of interpretation for the play is to maintain that its logic is to exhibit the moral change that takes place within its hero. (Typical exemplars of this "humanistic" interpretation of the play are Chalk 1962; Conacher 1967, 78–90; and Simon 1978, 130–39. Conacher includes within this critical tendency the remarks on the play by Kitto in his *Greek Tragedy.* This position is criticized by Adkins [1966, 193 ff.] and implicitly by Bond [1981, xxiiiff.].) Previously valuing an *aretê* based upon lineage and simple physical ability, Heracles learns, through the madness visited upon him by Juno, an *aretê* of the spirit. Heracles assimilates a spirit of perseverance and, with this, a type of internal heroism and fortitude.

56. Seneca's version of the legend is also delimited by the same constraints. Hercules' condition, if melancholic, is to be interpreted as manic. (Seneca's Hercules is related to that of Virgil.) The *atrum fel* of this passage is usually taken to mean melancholia. It is firmly within the pseudo-Aristotelian tradition of melancholia as mania. Seneca does not name Hercules' condition, but when, at *Hercules Furens* 939 ff., madness comes upon the hero, it is described in atrabilious terms (analogized with darkness, confusion, etc.: so we read the words *tenebrae, obscuro nube, diem fugat, nox atrum caput,* etc.). Compare Heracles' similar comments (vv. 867 ff.) in Euripides' play. The function of the madness in the play is primarily of a symbolic nature. (Heracles' madness in Seneca's play is thus provided with a clear etiology. This is not the case for Euripides' hero.) In Seneca's *Hercules furens* Juno blights a hero driven not by divine caprice but by a resentment of the violence with which he pursues his claims (vv. 1–124)—especially that of reaching heaven (vv. 89–91). In one sense Hercules represents the life of overweening ambition—to be contrasted with the life of tranquillity urged by the play's first choral ode (cf. vv. 192–201; contrast the light imagery of this ode with the darkness associated with his madness). His madness, because of his violence and lack of Stoic calm, is in a sense another example of his moral failing. It is, as Galinsky suggests (1972, 170; cf. Pratt 1983, 24 f.), "the logical consequence of his will." The Hercules in this play contrasts dramatically with the eponymous hero of *Hercules Oetaeus.* The latter is a powerful portrait of the idealized Stoic hero who, like Seneca in Tacitus's description of his death, understands *bene mori.* The theme of madness is not, however, apparent in this play. Nor is there any reference to the sores mentioned in the *Problema.* The madness of Heracles is as symbolic in Seneca as it is in Euripides. Melancholy is of the manic variety described in the *Problema,* in spite of the fact that current medical opinion—Celsus, for example—interpreted the condition as essentially depressive. Can it be assumed, then, that the determinants for Seneca's conception of Hercules are those of Euripides and, above all, the *Problema?*

57. Plutarch's interest in humoral theory can be observed elsewhere. In *Alexander* 4 Plutarch ascribes the pleasant odor of Alexander's body to the heat of his blood. This would also imply, under the humoral scheme of things, that Alexander was choleric. Plutarch does point this out. Ian Worthington points out to me that elsewhere Alexander was accused of being subject to melancholia. So Ephippus (*FGrH* 126 F 5 = Athenaeus 12.537e–538b) notes: "And Alexander used to have the floor sprinkled with exquisite perfumes and with fragrant wine; and myrrh was burnt before him, and other kinds of incense; and all the bystanders kept silence, or spoke only words of good omen, out of fear. For he was a very violent man, with no regard for human life; for he appeared to be a man of a melancholic constitution." (Ephippus, something of a scandalmonger with a great interest in Alexander's drinking habits and divine pretensions, was a contemporary of Alexander's.) Ephippus's understanding of melancholia is clearly of the traditional, popular, mania-based sort.

58. References from Plutarch to Lysander's anger and violence occur at *Lysander* 19 (to his cruelty *[chalepotês]*), 22, and 27 (to his anger). An interesting parallel for Lysander is provided by Diodorus Siculus's depiction of Dionysius of Syracuse (15.7.2–3). Dionysius, an enthusiast for poetry, had his own work performed at Olympia. This was received with derision. The experience seems to have unhinged him. Diodorus says that in his madness he came to suspect his friends of plotting against him. He slew many of them. (Diodorus describes him as *maniôdês* and as suffering from a *hyperbolê lupês.* The term *melancholê* is not used however.) Madness, therefore, is associated with extreme violence.

59. On Bellerophon see Strömberg 1961 and Rütten 1992, 56–61.

60. If Bellerophon had lived in the late nineteenth century, his condition would have been diagnosed as fugue (Hacking 1998). Fugue was an apparently faddish hysterical (or melancholic) condition that caused its victims to wander excessively, without resource, over much of Europe or even further. The psychological malaise appeared suddenly and, according to Hacking, disappeared as suddenly. We are not dealing here with an invented or culturally constructed psychological condition (in much the same way as depression has occasionally been argued to have been invented or culturally constructed). That Bellerophon may well have been a victim of fugue points to the longevity and persistence of the illness. What changes is not so much the existence of the illness as the willingness of the contemporary literary and discursive climate to accommodate it and, most importantly, to encourage its communicability by publicizing it. We will encounter such matters again in my later chapters on acedia and on suicide.

61. Naturally there is more to this madness than a mere clinical portrait. It does have a symbolic import. Winnington-Ingram (1980, 11–56), for example, convincingly links Ajax's madness with a lack of mental balance, self-knowledge, and *sophrosynê*. It was the lack of these qualities, he argues, that nullified his preeminent *aretê*. In the imbalance between *aretê* and *sophrosynê*, highlighted by the madness brought on by Athena, consists Ajax's tragedy. Such symbolic understandings of the madness do nothing, however, to diminish the purpose and force of what may have been to contemporary eyes an accurate clinical portrait.

62. Collinge 1962, 47; see too Simon 1978, 124–30. Simon (303) cites Starobinski 1974; Faber 1967; Seidenberg and Papathomopoulos 1961.

63. Some other discussions of Ajax's madness and its contemporary medical basis are Harries 1891; Miller 1944; Mattes 1970; Ferrini 1978; Hartigan 1987. (I owe this reference to Cerri 2000, 251 n. 37.)

64. Let us leave Ajax and return to the *Problema* and to its anger and melancholy. There is a final trio of characters mentioned in the *Problema:* Empedocles, Plato, and Socrates. Here is what the text says (trans. Klibansky, Panofsky, and Saxl [1964, 19]):

> Among the heroes many others evidently suffered in the same way, and among men of recent times Empedocles, Plato, and Socrates, and numerous other well known men, and also most of the poets. For many such people have bodily diseases as the result of this kind of temperament; some of them only a clear constitutional tendency towards such afflictions, but to put it briefly, all of them are, as has been said before, melancholics by constitution.

There is little that can be profitably made of these assertions. The biographical tradition of these philosophers is too unreliable. It might be worth observing, however, that if Aristoxenus were correct in saying that Socrates, if contradicted, could fly into anger and violent language (alluded to by Guthrie [1969, 70]. The ancient source is Wehrli 1945, fr. 54), and if Diogenes Laertius were correct in stating that Empedocles perished by leaping into Mt. Aetna (*Vita Empedoclis* 8.2.69), there might be some grounds for the speculation of pseudo-Aristotle (another more scientific link is offered by Flashar [1966, 57 n. 14]). But, in a sense, all that is beside the point, for it is quite clear that the common denominator between these characters and those that we have already examined is mania. Depression plays an unimportant role in their conditions. Their illnesses were characterized above all by anger and violence. Despite the understanding of the bipolarity of melancholia that the *Problema* displays, its preferred illustrations reflect the popular understanding of *melaina cholê* as a violent, angry, and mania-driven sickness (for a discussion of the origins of the equation of *melancholê* with *mania* see Müri 1953, 34–38).

65. There may be more to this than mere discursive privilege. Kraepelin (1921, 171) voices something most of us suspect, that premodern societies experience more mania than depression. Kraepelin asserts that this was the case among nineteenth-century Javanese. This claim is treated with caution, however, by Goodwin and Jamison (1990, 179, 181). They note that Tan 1977 supports Kraepelin's conjecture.

66. I take this idea of the "epiphenomenon" from Hacking 1998 (see also Toohey 1999b). It means that in the case of an illness such as manic depression, some societies or groups will privilege one or another manifestation and, in their speech, diagnosis, or description, declare the other a mere epiphenomenon. This downgrades and skews the mode by which we understand, socially, the true state of the illness.

67. For a discussion of self-consciousness focusing primarily on Greek literature, philosophy in particular, see Oehler 1997.

68. Beye (1982, 81) says of Jason that "his leave-taking is marked by a melancholia which distinguishes him from his exuberant fellow crewmen." Beye (183 n. 8) cites the support of Couat 1931, claiming that melancholia is an "emotional attitude common to the poem." Couat (1931, 337 n. 2) cites the following passages as indicative of the emotional attitude: 1.1172 ff.; 2.541 ff., 1001 ff.; 3.291 ff., 744 ff.; 4.1062 ff.

69. The deposition of Jason's lugubrious disposition finds parallels in the marked tendency of Theocritean lovers, especially the male ones, for pining and wasting and suicide under pressure. More discussion on this topic will be provided in the next chapter.

70. Heracles' anger at the loss of Hylas is expressed by Apollonius in language redolent of the manic phase of melancholia. At 1.1262 Heracles' *kelainon haima* is said to have boiled *hypo splangchnois*. Hercules is the old type of hero. It is fitting that he should suffer an "old" illness.

71. The term *katêphioôn* is often used in contexts relating to a very "depressed" state of mind. On *amêchaniê* see Green 1997, 39.

72. At 4.1279 all of the Argonauts (Jason included) are said again to be in a similar state.

73. This translation and those that immediately follow are adapted from Green 1997.

74. For the mournful reaction of Achilles to Patroclus's death, see, for example, *Iliad* 18.22 ff.

75. Indecision and depressive behavior on Jason's part are more pronounced in books 1 and 2. In book 3 and to a lesser extent in book 4, the focus is on Medea. This may have blurred the presentation of Jason's personality. Anyhow, he now has Medea's help, especially in the scene of the contests at the end of book 3.

76. Compare Odysseus's far more positive reaction to disaster in the Aeolus episode of *Odyssey* 11. For a different evaluation of Jason's character see Hunter 1993.

77. Not all of Soranus's qualities of a melancholic are present. There is no animosity toward members of the household. (Notice, however, the peculiar simile used of Jason's mother at 1.268 ff.) Nor are there conflicting desires to live and to die. Idmon, who often acts as a doublet for Jason, perhaps avers to the latter theme at 1.440–44. He is referring mournfully to the danger of death far away from home, in a strange land.

78. Green (1997, 39) makes some suggestive remarks concerning the melancholic tone of the *Argonautica* as a whole: "judged by these criteria, Jason's much debated 'inadequacy' or 'resourcelessness' *(amêchaniê)*, far from being a flaw (tragic or not) could be interpreted as a realistic acceptance of man's limitations—a view supported by the constant subversion of the poem's initial heroic optimism." Green goes on to cite Pike (1993, 29) with approval: "heroic promise is constantly cast into shadow by what can only be called a negative, melancholy, almost 'autumnal' tone."

79. The relationship between *aegritudo animi* and depression is examined by Michel (1993).

80. The Stoics had much to say of considerable interest on emotions *(de affectibus)*. Cicero reflects this tradition. The material relating to this fascinating tradition can be found in *SVF* 3.92 ff. The term to look for above all is *lypê*, the equivalent of Cicero's *aegritudo* (for a useful list of the types of *lypê* see *SVF* 3.151, 12). What disappoints in these Stoic discussions, as it does in Cicero, is the equation of mental illness with moral infirmity. Cicero and Horace and Seneca regularly preach this line (see *SVF* 3.167 ff.). It is related to what Mayer (1994, 93–94) terms the Stoic analogy between physical and moral health. Mayer (94) cites as exemplifying this analogy Horace *Epistles* 1.28–32, 33, 36, 37, 101, 108; 2.33–37; 6.28–29; 16.21, 40, 101. I notice a vigorous criticism of this kind of pernicious moralism (which dogged ancient thought) in Caelius Aurelianus's discussion of mania (trans. Drabkin [1950, 541]): "Those who imagine that the disease *[mania]* is chiefly an affection of the soul and only secondarily of the body are mistaken. For no philosopher has ever ever set forth a successful treatment for this disease; moreover, before the mind is affected, the body itself shows visible symptoms."

81. Comparable definitions are provided at *Tusculan Disputations* 3.16–19, 22–23.

82. The link between somatic and psychological conditions fascinates. Grief could be expressed as a physiological illness: so in the Hippocratic *Epidemics* (3.15) there is a woman from Thasos, the wife of Delearces, who develops a high fever from grief.

83. This occurs in Freud's *Mourning and Melancholy*. Julia Kristeva (1987) and Melanie Klein continue the tradition.

84. In 58, Cicero's year of exile, he describes his condition in terms of mourning (*dies non modo non levat luctum, hunc sed etiam auget* [the passing of time does not alleviate grief but makes it worse]. His mourning of his daughter Tullia is expressed in comparable manner (*itaque solitudinem sequor*—precisely the course of action followed by the melancholy Bellerophon at *Tusculans* 3.63.)

85. In chapter 3 we will look at Lucretius *On the Universe* 3.1060–67, a passage that contemplates the ennui-ridden life of the Roman aristocrat who tires of being at home, goes out, then returns again dissatisfied. Lucretius does not attribute this restlessness to anything as trivial as ennui. He believes that the aristocrat is attempting to escape his fear of death. Does Lucretius therefore provide evidence of how trivial such actions may have seemed. Is this why Cicero may have ignored them?

86. See Pigeuad 1981 on the opinions of the other Stoics on madness—they, too, favor a simple causation for this illness. See *SVF* 3.92 ff.

87. The manic form of melancholia can appear in Horace. Is the mad poet at the end of the *Ars poetica* a melancholic?

88. Porphyrio, glossing Horace's use of the term, suggests a Greek parallel in *lethargia*.

Lethargy and sluggishness seem to be the usual implications of the term (Seneca *Epistles* 82.19.7, 88.19.3, 115.7.2). Catullus uses it at 17.24 of an old man (*nunc eum volo de tuo / ponte mittere pronum, si pote stolidum repente excitare veternum . . .* [now I'd like to throw you headfirst from your bridge, if it were possible to wake up suddenly a leaden, *veternus* victim . . .].

89. The *Oxford Latin Dictionary* glosses *Veternus* it as a "morbid state of torpor or lassitude."

90. Seneca's *De tranquillitate animi* and its addressee, Marcus Annaeus Serenus, victim of *fluctuatio animi,* falls within this Horatian tradition. I will defer discussion of this key text until chapter 3 and its survey of boredom. There is no "sorrow without cause" in Serenus's instance.

91. I use the name *Persius* with full knowledge of the various offenses I have committed, biographical, historical, deconstructive, intertextual, and otherwise. The literature on the use of the persona in Roman satire is large and often dispiriting. It is simplest to call the authorial voice Persius, and for all we know, it might be. We are listening, at any rate, to a poet with an interest in philosophy (cf. Hooley's intertextual "authorless" reading [1997]). The Persius that I find most stimulating is the old-fashioned one of Antonio La Penna (1995; see also Toohey 1997b).

The best commentary on this poem is still that of Conington (1893). Jenkinson's translation (1980) is extremely helpful. Harvey's commentary is useful but is rather on the Olympian side for my tastes: *Satires* 3 is a very hard poem to translate and to construe and requires a more pedestrian explication.

The allocation of lines to speakers, I take it, is as follows (following Jenkinson 1980): Persius, 1–4; Friend, 5–6; Persius, 6–7; Friend, 7–8; Persius, 8–14; Friend, 15–43; Persius, 44–47; Friend, 48–51; Persius, 52–55; Friend, 56–106; Persius, 107–9; Friend, 109–18. For a different set of allocations see, e.g., Reckford 1998. Morford's no-frills paraphrase (1984) is also very instructive.

92. If we must have intertexts for this poem, then, pace Hooley (1997), perhaps they lie in the remarkable manipulation of authorial persona as it is achieved by Horace in *Epistles* 1 or, particularly, in the characterization of Serenus by Seneca in *De tranquillitate animae* 2.6–15. Horace and Seneca are discussed in chapter 2.

93. On Persius's apparent penchant for the melancholic see Squillante 1995.

94. That the illness is of a psychological variety is stressed by periodical references to inwardness. See v. 30: "I know you inside and out" *[ego te intus et in cute novi].*

95. Compare the term *effluis* in v. 20. Harvey (1981) compares Silius Italicus 6.245.

96. Persius is again relying on Horace *Satires* 2.3.137 ff. On medical references in Persius see Lachenbacher 1937.

97. Jenkinson (1980) understands this as referring to some form of blistering in the skin. The text seems to me to be inconclusive on this matter and to aim to link more with the imagery of swelling. Were blisters involved, however, the condition might have a melancholic parallel in the sores attributed to those other two melancholics, Heracles and Lysander, at least as they are depicted in the *Problema*.

98. For a brief and recent discussion of hellebore and an attempt to provide a botanical distinction for white hellebore see Amigues 1999. Amigues also has a useful bibliography on the plant (8 n. 6) and cites the discussion of Pliny 25.47.61 on the plant.

99. The effects of hellebore could be gruesome. Aretaeus speaks of the need to accustom a patient to the drug because of the paroxysms it induces. Here is Aretaeus's description of these effects (Adams 1856, 465):

> In the interval between each remedy, the patient is to be supported, in order that he may be able to endure what is to be given in the intermediate periods. The patient is to be assisted during the paroxysms thus: the legs are to be bound above the ankles and knees; and the wrists, and the arms below the shoulders at the elbows. The head is to be bathed with rose-oil and vinegar; but in the oil we must boil wild-thyme, cow-parsnip, ivy, or something such. Friction of the extremities and face. Smelling to vinegar, penny-royal, and mint, and these things with vinegar. Separation of the jaws, for sometimes the jaws are locked together; and tonsils to be tickled to provoke vomiting; for by the discharge of phlegm they are sometimes roused from their gloom. These things, then, are to be done, in order to alleviate the paroxysms and dispel the gloomy condition.

100. On the medical imagery of the poem see Reckford 1998.

101. Celsus states: "now quartan fevers have simpler characteristics. Nearly always they begin with shivering, then heat breaks out, and the fever having endured, there are two free days; thus on the fourth it recurs."

102. "Quartan fever has its highest incidence in the autumn and in those between the ages of twenty-five and forty-five. This is the time of life when the body is most subject to black bile, and the autumn is the corresponding time of year. If quartan fever occurs at any other time of the year, or at any other age, you may be sure that it will not be chronic unless some other malady be present" (Lloyd 1978, 271).

103. Depression in real life, as we have seen, no doubt was common. Within different literary traditions the condition may appear at different times. In the Hebrew tradition, for example, Antiochus IV is pictured in 164 B.C.E. (at I Maccabees 5.68.8) suffering from what is clearly something like depression (the Greek term is *arrôstia*). The passage runs as follows: "and it happened that when the king heard these words, he was astounded and distressed and fell on his bed, and fell into despondency [*arrôstia*] because of his grief [*lupê;* Goldstein [1976] translates this anachronistically as "melancholy"], because it did not come about for him as he had intended. And he was there for many days, because the great grief kept on at him, and he thought that he was dying." As we will see in later chapters, his symptoms are reproduced in later Greek contexts. One might also wish, in this context, to compare Ecclesiastes.

104. If there is a reason for the appearance and disappearance of these conditions, it may well be what is suggested by David Konstan (1997) in his piece on public versus private in monarchical states. The necessity of public toadying (think of Callimachus's verse on Berenice or Theocritus's praise poems for Ptolemy) can cause individuals to privilege the private and all that it stands for. This may in turn register itself, in the literary sphere at any rate, as the preference for the depiction of a variety of passive, affective conditions, among which melancholy could be placed.

105. See Kraepelin 1921, 171; note also Tan 1977. Compare, however, Goodwin and Jamison 1990, 179, 181.

106. Jamison (1993, 46) provides the following quote from Shelley that well illustrates mixed-state melancholia—its outward calm and inner turmoil:

There would I stretch my languid frame
Beneath the wild wood's gloomiest shade,
And try to quench the ceaseless flame
That on my withered vitals preyed;
Would close mine eyes and dream I were
On some remote and friendless plain,
And long to leave existence there,
If with it I might leave the pain
That with a finger cold and lean
Wrote madness on my withering mein.

107. I am not speaking here of the moralistic, Socratic, "Know thyself" type of "self-awareness." I am speaking of the sort of self-awareness a child feels when he or she notes the chasm between himself or herself and the world about. This is a sense of interiority that, at its crudest level, distinguishes most humans from animals.

CHAPTER 2

1. Erwin Rohde (1914, 157 n. 2) lists the symptoms of lovesickness. Nussbaum (1994, 143–44) flattens the historical experience of love, but, as always, in a fresh and provocative manner: "obsession, madness, attempted escape, suicide—all the ingredients of romantic/erotic love are there, ingredients that have provided the plot of love stories from *Aeneid* Book 4 to the *Sorrows of Young Werther*—and of countless stories both before and after these."

2. Persuasion is the first route to follow according to *Amores* 2.3.17: *aptius at fuerit precibus temptasse* [it would be better to try with pleading]. See too Amores 2.1.22 and 23–28, 2.17, and, perhaps, Anio's pleas at 3.6.53 ff. Compare also *Amores* 1.3. In general see Gross 1985; Toohey 1997a.

3. This pattern is seen most neatly when divine amours are the subject of poetic attention. The god usually indulges in a small amount of persuasion, then, at the least signs of resistance, rapes the object of his desire. See *Amores* 3.6 (Anio and Ilia [e.g., vv. 81–82]; compare *Metamorphoses* 1.490 ff. [Apollo and Daphne] and *Ars Amatoria* 1.703–4); compare Pindar *Olympian* 1 and the story of Pelops and Poseidon. The tale of Romulus and the Sabine women at *Ars amatoria* 1.101–34 offers a human version. (Cf. Fantham 1975.) I presume the violence of *Amores* 1.7 is to be seen in this light, as may well that of 2.5.45–46. Perhaps the best, albeit most cynical, example is the advocating of the use of force at *Ars amatoria* 1.673–722. Compare also Plutarch *Eroticus* 751D, 768B.

4. On age see Ibycus 287; Anacreon 358 Campbell. On death compare Aegialeus, the old fisherman of Xenophon of Ephesus's *Ephesian Tale* 5.1, who keeps his dead wife, Thelxinoe, embalmed in his house (note Propertius 4.7; Ovid *Amores* 3.9.15–16). On distance see Horace *Odes* 3.7; Propertius 4.3; Ovid *Amores* 2.16 (cf. 2.11). On conclusive rejection see Ovid *Amores* 3.11A, 11B, 12, 14; seemingly 1.12. On physical infirmity see Ovid *Amores* 3.7.

5. See Ovid *Ars amatoria* 1.283 ff., 2.373 ff. Virgil's Dido and Apollonius's Medea,

when rejected, present other instances, as do the persuasive exempla with which Gyges is plied in Horace *Odes* 3.7.

6. See Toohey 1992b; Wack 1990.

7. The overwhelming impression created by Cyrino (1995) in her survey of lovesickness in early Greek poetry is of the violence associated with the onset and effects of eros. Eros is violent and makes its victims violent. The only exceptions seem to be Anticleia, who is not suffering from lovesickness but is pining for her son, Odysseus (*Odyssey* 9.200–203; see Cyrino 1995, 27), and Penelope (*Odyssey* 1.340–44; see Cyrino 1995, 23), who may be pining for the protection and social position afforded by a husband and companion, rather than for an erotic partner. Anticleia's and Penelope's conditions are probably better associated with mourning. We could also compare Odysseus's grieflike nostalgia at *Odyssey* 5.82–84.

8. Compare also Virgil *Aeneid* 1.712, where Dido is apostrophized as *praecipue infelix, pesti devota futurae* [especially wretched and doomed to a plague to come]. Compare Valerius Flaccus *Argonautica* 7.125. Here lovesick Medea is being compared to a feverish lapdog—*aegra nova iam peste canis rabieque futura* [a dog sick with a recent illness and with a madness to come].

9. On lovesickness generally, Wack (1990) cites Biersterfeldt and Gutas 1984; Chrohns 1905; Ciavolella 1970, 1976; Giedke 1983; Rohde 1914; Schadewaldt 1985; Winkler 1990. For a more tendentious view of lovesickness and the role of therapeutic intercourse see Allen 2000.

10. There have been a number of terms used for this condition. Jackson (1986, 352) lists the following: "love-melancholy" (Robert Burton's term), lovesickness, "love-madness," *amor hereos, amor heroicus,* heroical love (*heroes, heroicus,* and *heroical* are corruptions of the Greek word for love, *erôs*), the malady of hereos, the lover's malady, erotomania. The condition of erotomania is still with us. In Sydney's *Sunday Telegraph,* the case of an English stalker was reported ("A Bad Case of Lovin' You" 1997). The medical team who cared for the man (led by Dr. Frank Farnham of London's Royal Free Hospital Medical School)—and who subsequently published a report of the stalker in *The Lancet*—diagnosed the man as suffering from erotomania.

11. I take lovesickness (or love melancholy, as it came to be known) as the product of unconsummated or abnormally frustrated love. Thus jealousy is not here at issue. Bitinna in Herondas 5, for example, exhibits neither an unconsummated nor an unseasonably frustrated love relationship. The same point could be made of the soulful and short-lived amatory frustrations of Roman elegiac poetry (Propertius 1.5, 1.9, 1.19; Tibullus 2.4, 2.6). For more on elegy see n. 60 in the present chapter.

12. On love in Apollonius see Zanker 1979.

13. This latter description of Medea's condition may be compared to the descriptions of the condition of Antiochus discussed later in this chapter.

14. She dreamed that Jason had taken on the contest not to gain the fleece but to win her. Medea even dreamed that she fought Aeetes' bulls in Jason's stead (Hunter [1989, 164] notes the sexual symbolism of fighting the bulls). In the dream, Medea must decide, her father dictates, whether to award the stranger the fleece. Aeetes would not, for Jason had not fought. Against Aeetes' wishes, Medea awards Jason the fleece.

15. I am following the order of lines as given by Hunter (1989), not that of Fränkel's Oxford edition.

16. At the beginning of the book (4.4–5) Medea flees from the palace to join Jason: the poet asks whether her action is the result of *atês pêma dysimeron* [ill-desired woe resulting from *atê*] or a *phyzan aeikeliên* [unseemly panic].

17. Fear is her motive according to Dyck (1989) and Zanker (1979).

18. Later, at *Argonautica* 6.469 ff. (not quite the same point in the narrative), Valerius Flaccus again moralizes on the destructiveness of love. Here Valerius is describing the girdle Venus lends to Juno. With this she causes Medea to fall in love with Jason.

19. Venus's intention is powerfully described with the imagery of fire: *donis furentem / incendat reginam atque ossibus implicet ignem* [she sets the queen afire, raging because of the gifts, and insinuates fire into her bones] (1.659–60). Note also 1.712–22.

20. The comparison is important. Orestes is singled out in the canonical discussion of manic melancholia, the pseudo-Aristotelian *Problema* 30.1. See Toohey 1990b. In Valerius Flaccus *Argonautica* 7.144–52, Medea, initially inflamed by the love of Jason, is compared to Orestes *furens.*

21. *Argonautica* 4.531–32: *rursusque resurgens / saevit amor magnoque irarum fluctuat aestu* [renascent love rages again and surges with a huge, boiling anger]; note that her anger is linked with love *(resurgens / saevit amor);* this is not just a matter of insulted pride or broken covenants.

22. The characters of *Eclogues* 8, too, are not passive, depressive figures.

23. Scylla, in the *Ciris,* is not Virgilian (see Lyne 1978). But she is very like Apollonius's Medea in her total surrender to love *(himeros)* and her swift betrayal of her father, Nisus, to her beloved, King Minos.

24. The lineaments of the pattern may be found in Virgil's allusion to depressive, metamorphic love at *Aeneid* 10.189–93 (the transformation of Cycnus). The allusion is perhaps too brief for proper discussion.

25. Compare the long and powerful analysis of Lucretius's diatribe against love by Nussbaum (1994, 140–91).

26. In a few random examples, we read that *Sallustius insanit* [Sallustius is mad] over freedwomen at 1.2.48–49, and amatory frustration is alluded to in a colorful manner at 1.2.71 (*mea cum conferbuit ira* [when my rage is at a fever pitch]) and at 1.2.118 (*malis tentigine rumpi* [do you prefer that I'd be ruptured by sexual tension?]).

27. These include, among others, 4, 9, 10, 11, 13, 14, 17, 20, 25, 26, 28, and 29.

28. Structurally the story resembles that of Zeus and poor Semele. Elements have been inverted: dependent male for female, a Hera-like mother for the king of the gods, the destructions of others for the destruction of self. The most obvious parallel, however, is Oedipus. For a discussion see Lightfoot 1999.

29. Periander's mother feigned fear of wasting away from unrequited love, were she not to gain the object of her desire. After being unmasked by her son and after his subsequent madness, she committed suicide.

30. Parthenius adds a variant: "the story has, however, been related by others that she threw herself in while fleeing from his pursuit."

31. Ovid's *Heroides* 4 provides us with an ironic letter from Phaedra to Hippolytus. But

here we have a portrait of a loose-living Roman matrona whose love or lust, though apparent, hardly exhibits the symptoms of real lovesickness. Jacobson 1974 (142–58) is helpful.

32. Her condition is sometimes linked with hysteria (Lefkowitz 1981, 19 ff.). But whether ancient hysteria ought be considered a manic or depressive disease (in the same way as lovesickness or melancholy) I am not sure. By the time of Galen, at any rate, some descriptions are of the depressive order (Veith 1965, 31 ff.).

33. van Hoof (1990, 45–46) argues: "inedia is the ancient method for attracting attention for grief, open or hidden. Phaedra could not reveal her unbecoming love for her stepson Hippolytus. 'I abstain from food' *(asiteô);* such will be 'the renouncing of life' *(apostasis tou biou)* . . . Frustration in love leading up to voluntary starvation is a theme in the ancient novel: on one occasion Chaereas is convinced that Kallirhoe is in love with Dionysios. He decides to abstain from food."

34. A good survey of the literature related to the identity of "Oppian" and of the background to many of these stories is provided by Bartley (2000). It is usual to link Oppian with the *Halieutica* and to attribute the *Cynegetica* to a later writer. For simplicity I refer to both authors as Oppian.

35. The compositional date for this is set somewhere between the second and fourth centuries C.E. Morgan (in Reardon 1989, 352) favors the fourth century. The conflation of the medical and the popular traditions owes its novelty in my opinion to a much earlier era, that of Aretaeus and Galen. Perhaps Charicleia's illness is evidence for a compositional date for the *Aethiopica* of the early third century or even the late second century.

36. Quoted in Jackson 1986, 353, citing Kühn 1821–33, 18B:18. Wack (1990, 7–9) provides an excellent discussion.

37. It is also worth pointing out that Galen seems to have felt that "excessive vehemence in loving" was a condition related to lovesickness (Jackson 1986, 353, citing Harkins 1963, 48). The significance of this suggestion is something to which I will return.

38. Quoted in Jackson 1986, 354, citing Bussemaker and Daremberg 1851–76, 5:413–14. See too Wack 1990, 10.

39. See Jackson 1986, 354, citing Adams 1844–47, 1:390–91.

40. Caelius made a Latin translation *(De morbis acutis et chronicis)* of a lost text by Soranus of Ephesus, who worked in Alexandria during the Trajanic and Hadrianic periods. For a text see Drabkin 1950. Pigeaud 1987 has an extensive discussion of this author. See too Wack 1990, 11.

41. See Drabkin 1950, 561. Klibansky, Panofsky, and Saxl (1964, 48) quotes the text: *melancholica dicta, quod nigra fella aegrotantibus saepe per vomitum veniant . . . et non, ut plerique existimant, quod passionis causa vel generatio nigra sint fella; hoc enim est aestimantium magis quam videntium veritatem, vel potius falsum, sicut in aliis ostendimus.*

42. Marcovich 1991 is very useful for isolating the difficulties involved in interpreting this poem and for demonstrating that the symptoms made evident by the speaker of this poem are as likely to be the product of lovesickness as jealousy. The evidence in the present book supports Marcovich's contention. Marcovich (46) provides a reasonably up-to-date bibliography. Devereux (1970), I should add, is surely right to diagnose Sappho's speaker as suffering from an "anxiety attack." What is incorrect is Devereux's etiology.

43. They closely resemble the symptoms attributed to the common real-life condition

of "panic disorder," listed by Hawley (1997) as "dizziness, light-headedness, confusion, blurred vision, feelings of unreality, breathlessness, increased heart rate, numbness and tingling in feet and hands, clammy hands, stiffness and shakiness in muscles, jelly-legs." Hawley continues, "If over-breathing persists, the next stage is severe vertigo, nausea, choking, sharp chest pains, temporary paralysis of some muscles, momentary blackouts and rising terror." See too Devereux 1970; Marcovich 1991, 40 ff.; Lucretius 3.154–57.

44. See, for example, Theocritus 2.106 ff. But this could also point to the "boning" discussed in chapter 4.

45. On envy and jealousy see Schoeck 1969.

46. We might, in this case, want to distinguish between proximate and ultimate etiologies, between, that is, the how and the why of things. The how is certainly lovesickness. The why, however, is not at all clear.

47. The final stanza of Catullus 51 is of little help, for it may be a very free adaptation. At least Catullus does not speak of mania or depression. Compare Wills 1967.

48. Compare Archilochus 112, 118 Campbell.

49. Professor Vivienne Gray of Auckland, for example, once pointed out to me that Sappho depicts lovesickness in the depressive sense.

50. Neither depression nor violence, it is noteworthy, are gendered. Ovid *Amores* 1.7 has a male dole violence out, while Propertius 3.8 and 4.8 has a male on the receiving end (for some very violent heroines see Sinonis and Calligone in Stephens and Winkler 1995, 197 and 267, respectively). As I will point out later, for every love-depressive female in the novel, there is a depressive male.

51. The point needs to be stressed that the concern here is with lovesickness, not with love in general. This is true of such discussions or expostulations as those of Plato in the *Symposium* or *Phaedrus*, of Sophocles at *Antigone* 781 ff., and of Plautus at *Trinummus* 223–75 and 668 ff. (where the stress is less on the subjective experience than it is on the deleterious effects of love on aristocratic young men and their families—though at v. 669 love is said to make men downcast *[morosi]*). The same point may be made concerning Garrison's useful discussion of love in the Hellenistic epigram (1978). Other passages, while offering witness to lovesickness, lack detail. Such a one is Horace *Odes* 3.12, a description, according to Quinn (1980), of a lovesick Neobule. Quinn terms this a "cliché" and compares Sappho 102 LP. Into this category should be placed such productions as Propertius 1.5 and Ovid *Amores* 1.6 (note also Barsby's comments ad loc.).

52. Clausen (1987) points out that the baldness is a symptom of a "morbidly excited condition" and compares Hesiod *Catalogue* fr. 133.4–5 M.-W. and Virgil *Eclogues* 6.51.

53. When Simaetha sees Delphis, her swoonlike symptoms seem to match those of Sappho's speaker in poem 31: see Theocritus 2.106 ff.

54. Another comparable example may be found in Herondas 1.49–60, where Gryllus unrequitedly loves Threissa. Unfortunately the symptomatology is too sketchy to be of assistance.

55. On the evil eye see the discussion of Heliodorus later in this chapter. See also Thomsen 1992; Dickie 1991; Yatromanalakis 1988; Rohde 1914, 486 n. 2; Faraone 1998. Parallels from anthropological literature are provided by Reid (1983, 36 ff.).

56. The numeration is that of Trypanis 1989.

57. The disease is epilepsy. Its being linked here with lovesickness is intriguing. It is as-

sociated in Hippocratic medicine with a superfluity of the phlegmatic humor (Flashar 1966, 28 ff.) and with melancholy (see Goodwin and Jamison 1990, 116–17). In the discussion of Heracles' madness in the *Problema* 30.1 (cited in the previous chapter), epilepsy seems to be linked with his manic melancholia (see also the *Epidemics* and Ullmann 1978, 75). This may provide further grounds for the association of Cydippe's lovesickness with black bile and melancholia.

58. His poem is conveniently reproduced in Quinn 1969, 13 (I have reproduced Quinn's translation).

59. Gallus's situation is an ironic reversal of Phaedria's at Terence *Eunuch* 46–49.

60. There is in poems like this the problem of "sincerity." The genre of elegy is so deliberately unrealistic, literary, and, hence, ironic that it is very difficult to take Gallus seriously (thus I follow Veyne 1988, e.g., 31 ff., 132 ff.). Compare Propertius 1.1.21 (*en agedum dominae mentem convertite nostrae, / at facite illa meo palleat ore magis* [come then, change my mistress's mind, and make her more pallid than me]). Baker (1990), for example, seems to take this as an example of the pallor brought on by wasting and lovesickness (thus another instance of Knox's topos) and cites Plautus and Aretaeus in support. But verses 33–34 of the same poem seem to identify such pallor as the result of too much lovemaking. It is that very sort of complication that makes elegy such an unreliable and ironic witness.

61. Compare Propertius 1.1.23, 1.5.12 ff., 1.6.27, 1.9.17, 1.13, 1.18.21, 2.4, 2.25.25, 2.34b.1, 3.6.4, 3.12.9, 3.19, 3.21.33–34 (where unrequited love leads to death), 4.3.28; Tibullus 1.8.53–54, 1.9.29, 1.9.79, 2.6.17–20, 3.2.27–30 (where lovesickness leads to death), 3.5, 3.10. Compare too Toohey 1999a and, on Catullus, the instructive piece by Joan Booth (1997).

62. On this theme of lovesickness see La Penna 1957.

63. Ovid, in his love poetry, offers many references to what seems almost to be lovesickness: see *Amores* 1.6, 2.5.2, 2.7.10, 2.9.14, 3.14.37; *Ars amatoria* 1.729–836.

64. Ovid does not quite depict lovesickness in his elegiac poetry, though he comes close: note *Amores* 1.6, 2.7.10, 2.9.13; *Amores* 3.14.37. In these cases lifestyle rather than affective debility seems to be the cause of the weak condition of the male lover. Compare also *Ars amatoria* 1.723–39.

65. For discussion see Beecher and Ciavolella 1990, 53–54. It is sometimes suggested of Narcissus's pining away that "the topos is the familiar one of the lover who wastes away with passion." Knox (1986, 22), who makes this claim, cites in support Ovid *Ars amatoria* 1.735; compare *Amores* 1.6.5, 2.9.14; Propertius 1.5.21–22; Theocritus 2.88 ff.

66. A Roman painting of Narcissus is represented in figure 9 in chapter 8.

67. The novelty of this description may be underscored by comparing it with another case of frustrated love in the *Metamorphoses.* Byblis fell in love with her brother (9.454–665). Declaration of love to him was followed by rejection. Her reaction was not Antiochean pining but violent and unrestrained madness—she became a bacchante (9.635 ff.). The exertion of her Bacchic travels eventually caused her to die. She metamorphized into a fountain.

68. In Longus's *Daphnis and Chloe* (3.23), Daphnis tells Chloe a variant version of the legend. Here Echo repulsed Pan's advances. In an excess of frustrated love, he caused the local shepherd and goatherds to go into a frenzy *(mania)* and rip her limb from limb. Earth buried these limbs in a variety of places, where, henceforth, echoes became possible. Pan's reaction is one of manic lovesickness, which variety I will discuss in the next section. On the history of the Narcissus legend see Vinge 1967.

69. On the historicity of some of these events see Fisher 1993.

70. Plutarch, in his version, attributes the story to a Greek physician, Erasistratus, who lived in the first half of the first century B.C.E. I see no reason why we ought to believe Plutarch's attribution. The story has the ring of the literature of the Roman Empire.

71. Beecher and Ciavolella (1990, 48–51) provide a number of these and references. See also Wack 1990, 17 ff.

72. For the text see Baehrens 1914, 112–25. For discussion see Bright 1987, 222–44; Wack 1990, 4–5.

73. A possible contemporary parallel comes from the Vandal poet Reposianus, whose miniature epic "The Intrigue of Mars with Venus" (for text and translation see Duff and Duff [1935] 1982) depicts a lovesickness (here effected by jealousy) that is both depressive and manic. The poem describes the famous affair of Venus with Mars and their punishment by Hephaestus. It is the love of Vulcan for Venus that is frustrated. When he discovers his wife's infidelity, his reaction is a bizarre mixture of depression (v. 160: "and now half benumbed" [*iam quasi torpescens*]) and mania (vv. 161–62: "he growls aloud, and groaning mournfully strikes his sides to their very depth and wrathfully heaves sigh on sigh unceasing" [trans. Duff and Duff, adapted; the Latin is: *ore fremit maestoque modo gemit ultima pulsans / ilia et indignans suspira pressa fatigat*]). But anger quickly wins the day (v. 160: *vix sufficit ira dolori* [the anger scarcely matched the grief]).

74. The tale is repeated by Aurelius Victor (*De Caesaribus* 16.2).

75. For the translation (here slightly adapted) and Latin text see Magie 1953.

76. A comparably macabre example may be found in Quintus Smyrnaeus's *Posthomerica* when Achilles develops a necrophiliac lovesickness for Penthesileia. After he has killed the Amazon warrior (1.654 ff.), he gazes on her corpse and is smitten (1.716–21; cf. 1.666–68) by love (1.719; cf. 1.671–74) and by grief (1.720: "deadly grief [*aniai*] devoured his heart"). His reaction was not violent but passive, at least until provoked by Thersites (1.722 ff.).

77. Dolphins have the strangest of reputations. Louis de Bernières, in *Señor Vivo and the Coca Lord* (1991, 148–49), states: "Quite often the dolphins save the lives of those who are drowning, and sometimes the dolphins make a mistake and try to save the lives of those who are not drowning at all, but are really diving for turtles. That is just something that one has to put up with from time to time, and it serves to prove how simpatico the animals are. The cabolcos allow the dolphins to take fish from their nets, and when the dolphins become human and emerge from the river with their different-coloured eyes and their beautiful muscles, they make love with whomever they choose, because it is bad to refuse a lover who loves so tenderly. Dolphins' children always eventually return to the water, and so there are perhaps entire districts where the dolphins are half human, which makes it doubly a crime to kill them. Another reason is that dolphins love each other so romantically, so playfully, so completely, that it is obvious that they are sent by God to teach us by their example to do the same."

78. There is an astonishing statue in the Museo Nazionale di Napoli of Cupid entwined, in the most provocative of manners, with a dolphin. A reproduction can be found in Maiuri 1957, 37.

79. Pliny (*Letters* 9.33) presents a nonerotic version of this tale. Sherwin-White (1985,

514) parallels Pliny the Elder *Natural History* 9.26 and cites a real-life parallel for Pliny's story.

80. Less striking instances may be found in Longus's *Daphnis and Chloe* after Chloe has been abducted by the Methymnaeans (2.20), when Daphnis, in the despair of frustrated love, casts himself onto the ground, languishing and waiting for death (*entautha perimenô keimenos . . . thanaton*, 2.22). This is not quite melancholy, yet the passive desire for death resembles the despair of Antiochus or Perdica. Melancholy is more evident in book 3. Here Daphnis and Chloe are kept from the pastures and their meetings by the harsh weather of winter. Longus describes how they were sleepless, sad, pensive, and longed for the return of spring (3.4). Similar reactions take place in book 4: Chloe, thinking Daphnis has forgotten her, weeps, complains, and thinks only of death (4.27); Daphnis, after Chloe has subsequently been spirited away by Lampis, sinks into a similar state of despair (4.28).

81. For more of the symptomatology see Toohey 1999a.

82. One might have hoped that this was quartan fever. On this fever see my index s.v.

83. Theagenes suffers too, though not so badly. At the banquet for Neoptolemus (3.10) he is distracted and gloomy, and later he confesses to Calasiris that he is near to death. Calasiris describes his condition at the beginning of 3.11 in terms redolent of medical depression—he is full of *chasmê adêmonousê* (presumably "troubled depression" or perhaps "troubled ennui"), and he is also suffering from a humoral imbalance (he is *anômalos*).

84. On the evil eye in Heliodorus see Yatromanalakis 1988; Dickie 1991.

85. Kraepelin (1921, 37) speaks of one variety of melancholy that he treated as stuporous (see fig. 2 in chapter 2). The notion of stuporous mania might well be applied to Charicleia, as I will suggest later in this chapter.

86. Another example of this type of lovesickness is alluded to by Hägg (1983). It is the story of Paul and Thecla in the apocryphal Acts. Hägg points out (160) that "Thecla's first reaction when she hears Paul preaching in the neighboring house—she does not touch her food or drink, she worries her family by her distracted behaviour—is reminiscent of the purely physical manifestations of awakening love in, for instance, the *Ephesiaca*."

87. It is precisely such jealousy that causes Chaereas to kick pregnant Callirhoe in the belly in Chariton's novel *Chaereas and Callirhoe* (1.4.10). This example is discussed at the beginning of chapter 5.

88. A reproduction of the Greek text with translation and comments may be found in Klibansky, Panofsky, and Saxl 1964, 18–29.

89. Gabriel García Márquez 1988, 61–62.

90. The fever was a mirage. But it recalls the quartan fevers alluded to earlier in this chapter. It also picks up the motif of the love fever described by Srì Harsa-Deva in the second of the quotations beginning this chapter.

91. Compare DiBattista 1991.

92. Marneros and Angst (2000) describe this condition as "reactive" depression.

93. A very striking example of passive lovesickness as it is described by the great poet of the Roman dialect Gioacchino Belli (1791–1863) follows. It points to the continuity of this tradition. The translation is by Peter Dale and is reprinted with his permission. (Dale uses the slang and speech idiom of Melbourne, Australia, in the 1950s to approximate that of Belli.)

2228 *Un fischio d'aria*
        È ubbidiente, è aggrazziata, è de bbon core,
Je piasce er lavorà, ppovera fijja,
Ché ttutto er po' de svario che sse pijja
È de ssceggne la sera in coritore:

        Diggiuna a ppan'e acqua oggni viggijja,
Abbada sempr'a ssé, nun fa l'amore . . .
Ché in quant'a cquesto poi, sur punto onore,
Ve la do pe l'Ottavia maravijja.

        L'unica cosa che mme tiè sturbata
È cche da un mese e mezzo, poverella,
Me la trovo un tantino sscinicata.

        Da quela santa notte, sora Stella,
C'annò ggiù pe ssentì una serenata,
Fussi l'aria o cche sso, nnun è ppiù cquella.

[2228 A draft uv air
        She's abedient, graceful, goodharted, alrite,
The poor girl likes wirk, she's always on call,
Cos the only relaxation she allows'aself ad all
Is goen down the stairs f'ra chat ev'ry nite:

        She fasts on bred'n water ev'ry vigil eve,
Looks after'aself, n' never makes luv, poor girl . . .
Cos in this regard, my wird've honour, b'lieve
Me, I'd pass'a'r off as the Eighth wunder a the wirld.

        The only thing ut tends ta wurry me sick
Is that f'ra munth'n a harf or so, Heather,
I find she's getten thin, as thin as a wick.

        Frum that blessèd nite, the wun that the poor
Girl wen' down'a lissen tw'a serenade; an whether
It was a draft or not, she ain' the girl she was before.]

94. Veyne 1978.

95. Compare Elizabeth Marshall Thomas (1993, 58) on romantic love in dogs, which she believes exists and has its biological uses, in dogs as in humans. This might be contrasted to Veyne's notion of the discovery of this emotion. There is no reason why a universalist approach cannot coexist with an opportunist/historicist one such as that of Veyne. The universalizing of Thomas might be compared to the anthropologizing of Jared Diamond in his *Why Is Sex Fun? The Evolution of Human Sexuality* (1997) or the comparable biologism of Matt Ridley in his *The Red Queen* (1993).

96. The remarkable condition of acedia, at least in its fourth-, fifth-, and sixth-century manifestations, bears a very close resemblance to depression and lovesickness. It is curious that lovesickness receives one of its best descriptions in the *Aegritudo Perdicae* in Vandal

North Africa at approximately the same time monks and lay folk were being ravaged by the *morbus* of acedia. There can be no easy explanation for this coincidence except perhaps to remark that the first and fifth centuries of our era were most dangerous and demoralized periods. In such periods, perhaps that sense of passivity that seems a congener of these conditions is especially prevalent and encourages these *pestes*.

97. Veyne has been corrected, notably, by Saller and Shaw (1984, 134–35). See also Dixon in Rawson 1991, 102 ff.; Treggiari 1991.

98. Brown (1988, 16 n. 51) states that although Saller and Shaw correct Veyne "on important points," Veyne's is "an exceptionally thought-provoking study."

99. It may be that the formulations of Jack Goody (1998) have more to offer. He maintains that romantic love is the product of literate societies (writing is needed to celebrate the beloved). Depressive love melancholy's genesis may well be connected.

100. Descola (1996, 195) briefly discusses lovesickness among the Amazonian Jivaro. The condition thus has a very wide sociological appearance. I believe that the emotion, in the literary sphere, became more prominent in the periods I have designated. It was probably always present but often not taken as seriously as we sometimes do.

101. Love melancholy, if we were to follow Melanie Klein (or Julia Kristeva, for that matter) results from the withdrawal, at a crucial stage of early childhood, of maternal affection. People who are prone to this condition are also, on their understanding, afraid of consummation—this would be to defy maternal affection and to court its loss.

102. I make no claim to be anything other than superficial in the analysis of these poems. I have no competence in (or only minimal competence in one of) the languages and literatures being discussed here.

103. Biersterfeldt and Gutas (1984) examine this phenomenon in Islamic society.

104. According to Lichtheim (1976, 7), "in the New Kingdom the education and training of scribes was expanded, and the genre known as School Texts has no counterpart in earlier periods."

105. Lichtheim (1976, 7–8) states: "lyric poetry was developed in the Middle Kingdom; but Love Lyrics seem to have been a creation of the New Kingdom. At least, no love poems older than the New Kingdom have come to light. The love poems are misunderstood if they are thought to be naïve and artless. For they are rich in elaborate wordplays, metaphors, and rare words and thereby indicate that they are crafted with deliberation and literate skill. The actual situations of life from which the poems may have arisen are concealed from our view. We do not know enough about the position of women, especially of young unmarried girls, to know how to interpret the free relations of the lovers that are depicted in so many of these poems."

106. The following translations of the Egyptian poems are those of Lichtheim (1976). There is also an attractive version by Fowler (1994).

107. Another symptom is aging (cf. "my body is young"). This depressed form of wasting that is linked with aging recalls Horace's melancholy-like condition of *veternus* (the word is linked with the adjective *vetus*, meaning "old").

108. Compare Basedow 1929, 175–79.

109. Wiles (1997, 14), as I have indicated in the introduction to this book, believes that the self is fragmentary and unstable and, most importantly, that "the self seems to be compounded of a series of discursive networks." His Lacanian view represents postmodern

orthodoxy. The self, I am suggesting, seems to react and to become prominent in a pretty predictable manner. It is, as I have suggested, the product of pain and alienation and a product of total otherness from family, community, and even the self itself. It is defined by the chasm between subject and object enforced on a child at a very young age. The sense is formulated from a basic set of constraints and manifests itself in a standard set of modalities.

110. It is worth noting that these victims of love are young people, a self-perceived marginal group. See too Goody 1998.

111. See n. 6 in chapter 8. See too Goody 1998.

112. Ingalls 1965.

113. Separation is the more probable cause. This is the theme of the following poem taken from Brough's collection (1968, poem 10):

Although my mind
Is sick with love, I find
I have acquired the gift of magic sight.
Though she is far away, and it is night,
I see her in a foreign land
From where I stand.

(Bhartrhari)

The affective state that is highlighted in this poem is designated. The speaker claims that he is "sick with love." The condition, he tells us, has been brought on by the absence of his beloved (she is "in a foreign land"). No symptoms for the sickness are provided, but we can guess readily at those that would present themselves.

114. Dropsy was a condition that some have argued was suffered by the addressee of Persius's *Satires* 3. I am unaware of a tradition linking it with either melancholia or lovesickness.

115. This is a sickness that may require medical attention, according to the following poem from Brough's collection (1968, poem 157):

When the fever is caused by her looks and her voice,
The treatment of choice
Is thrice-daily sip
Of her honey-sweet lip.
To avoid further harm,
And to keep the heart warm,
The follow-up treatment is known to be best:
The soothing and gentle warm touch of her breast.
(Professional secret, though—
Careful to keep it so!)

(Jayadeva)

There is lovesickness here, but it is designated only as a fever. There are no other symptoms. Cure, typically, is congress with the beloved.

116. Here is another very pretty example of this theme of wasting (reproduced in Ingalls 1965 as poem 719):

> Upon her body
> golden as the opening tuber of turmeric,
> appears a paleness
> born of the separation from her lover.
> As this increases
> it is as though the fawn-eyed maiden's limbs
> were made of silver
> melted down with gold.
>
> (Rajasekhara)

117. Ingalls (1965, 242) points out: "The effects of separation on the man are not very different from its effects on the woman: the same sighs (752, 804), tears (753, 792), and fevers (755, 771, 784). Indeed, he too occasionally takes to the lotus couch and is fanned, all to no avail (801–803). He may even die of love (760)."

118. A couple of other Indian examples of this theme follow. The poems are taken from Brough's 1968 collection (poems 24 and 135, respectively).

> You are pale, friend moon, and do not sleep at night,
> And by day you waste away.
> Can it be that you also
> Think only of her, as I do?
>
> (Bhartrhari)

The references here to lovesickness (a condition that is based upon absence and upon frustration) are succinct, unmistakable, and delivered with such a knowingness as to indicate a strong tradition behind their utterance. The moon (and the speaker of the poem, it is implied) is pale and wasting away. It is obsessively fixated on its beloved.

> "Well but you surely do not mean to spend
> Your whole life pining? Show some proper spirit.
> Are there no other men? What is the merit
> Of faithfulness to one? But when her friend
> Gave this advice, she answered, pale with fear,
> Speak soft. My love lives in my heart, and he will hear."
>
> (Amaru)

This poem puts a spin on the notion of a cure through sexual congress with the beloved. The speaker of the poem is "pining"—wasting away, that is—from a lovesickness brought on by separation from the beloved. This speaker may also exhibit the paleness of love (part of the force of "pale with fear"). The unexpected solution for the suffering lover (for whom union with the beloved seems to be impossible) is to find another partner.

119. Two other representative poems follow. They are poems 92 and 25, respectively, in Brough's 1968 collection. While they are imprecise on the matter of sickness and on its

treatment, the overall picture is one of a lovesickness fueled and generated by absence. The wracked lovers exhibit tears, sighing, insomnia, an obsessive fixation on the longed-for individual, and a generalized sorrow.

At night the rain came, and thunder deep
Rolled in the distance; and he could not sleep,
But tossed and turned, with long and frequent sighs,
And as he listened, tears came to his eyes;
And thinking of his young wife left alone,
He sobbed and wept aloud until the dawn.
And from that time on
The villagers made it a strict rule that no traveler
should be allowed to take a room for the night
in the village.

(Amaru)

Has God no pity, while he counts away
The endless hours of every weary day,
The endless nights, when still my sad head lies
Unpillowed by the breast of Lotus-eyes?

(Bhartrhari)

120. On looking, seeing, and watching see my final chapter in this book and also Frontisi-Ducroux 1998.

121. There are several current definitions of the self—and these are usually not made as clear as they might be. For example, the "self," in the anthropological sense, seems in practice to refer to the sets of shared psychological traits that define how individual psychologies exhibit traits of a larger social or historical psychology. So one may speak of Western or Australian or Aboriginal or even Homeric self. But sometimes the "self" is used in a complimentary way to designate a human who is capable of reasoned moral behavior. There is a "self" involved, to follow this definition, whenever we question and weigh up the ethical validity of impulse. Implicit in such an argument is the idea that some individuals (children, the mentally ill, the very old, the primitive, the illiterate, animals) must have a less developed sense of self. Paradoxically those with an interest in this type of self are usually keen to flatten difference. The selves of the primitive, the illiterate, the aged, or the Homeric hero (or even the Australian male) differ only in superficial ways. See also Westra 2001; Stock 1994. For some psychoanalytic discussions and conceptualizations of the self see Alford 1991; Kohut 1971, 1977, 1985. See too Baumeister 1986.

122. For a survey of how, apparently, the definition of self can vary between cultures see Hollan 1992.

123. Goody (1998) believes that this type of love relationship is only possible in urbanized societies with high literacy levels.

124. I offer one last observation: the periodical privileging of romantic love seems closely related to, even dependent on, the privileging of love melancholy. Romantic love's appearance is dependent, therefore, on the social pressures that I have highlighted in the previous paragraphs in text.

CHAPTER 3

1. The pot can be described as follows: white-ground lekythos, assigned or attributed by Beazley (1963) to "Group R" (*ARV* 1384, no. 15), under the heading of "Late-Fifth Century Painters of White Lekythoi." The vessel (height: 50.8 cm; shoulder diameter: 13 cm) is dated to the last quarter of the fifth century B.C.E. and is in the British Museum in London. The iconography shows a fairly standard funerary scene of a woman seated at tomb, with a man and a woman seated on either side. A black-and-white image can be found in Kurtz 1975, 222, no. 49.4.

2. For other examples of this remarkable genre of painting see Robertson 1992, 252 ff.; Arias 1962, plates 200–201.

3. Beazley 1963; Kurtz 1975. John Papadopoulos and Carrie Tove suggest to me that the clothing is that of a female. I could point out, however, that the bulk of the shoulders and the apparent youth of the face present us, as far as gender is concerned, with a profoundly ambiguous picture.

4. The link is apparent visually as well. A more sanguine examination of the Eumenides Painter's Orestes, with which chapter 1 began, could diagnose severe boredom as Orestes' problem. The pictorial representation of these emotions once again points to the curious phenomenon that the representation of emotional states in the pictorial tradition seems to antedate that of the literary (discursive) tradition by some centuries.

5. The confusion between the two is nicely captured by the related titles of two books: Kuhn (1976) wrote his classic on boredom and called it *The Demon of Noontide;* Andrew Solomon (2001) wrote his more sensational, but nonetheless moving, book on a personal account of depression and called it *The Noonday Demon*. Judd's novel *The Noonday Devil* (1986) makes the affective confusion, not to say the repetition of the title, all the more perplexing.

6. What is it exactly that is meant by boredom? The word *boredom* is used of so many disparate affective states that one is tempted to include it with such outmoded medical terms as "consumption" or "the gripe." Terms such as these engross such a constellation of disorders (John Dearin's description) that they become almost too general to be useful and, according to some skeptics, are often best passed over in silence. My former colleague Australian logician Dr. David Londey suggested to me once that there might in fact be no such thing as boredom at all.

7. Liddell, Scott, and Jones's Greek lexicon offers two early uses of the word where the meaning seems to be "boredom" or "ennui." The first comes from the Epicurean philosopher Metrodorus. Metrodorus links the verb *aluô* with the words *epi tôn symposiôn* (*Papyrus Herculanensis* 831.13 A. Körte). The context is fragmentary, but Metrodorus seems to be referring to the tedium that can be induced by a bad drinking party. Lacking a context, it is difficult to state anything with confidence. Yet here it seems not unreasonable to interpret the reference to boredom as being of the simple type. Zeno, as reported by Clement of Alexandria (*SVF* 1.58), uses the word in a manner that may be appropriate to simple boredom, or so suggests Liddell, Scott, and Jones's Greek lexicon. To judge from the following lines, it may be easier to gloss the word *alus* as "satiety": "but let there be no satiety *(alus)* of perfume, gold, or wool sellers, [for] here the women, decked out like prostitutes in a brothel, pass the day."

8. Following are some terms for boredom. In Greek there is *alus* and its verbal forms *aluo, alusthaino, alusso, alustazo,* and so on; nouns such as *apatheia, akêdia* (cf. Cicero *Ad Atticum* 12.45 and the comment of Shackleton-Bailey [1966, 337–38]), *aplêstia, asê, koros, plesmonê* (and their verbal forms); and, in some contexts, verbal forms such as *aniao, enochleo,* or *truphao.* In Latin there are words such as *taedium* and related forms, *fastidium* and related terms, *otium, satietas* and related forms, *vacare, fatigo, defatigo, defetiscor* and so on, *torpor* and related forms, *languidus* and related terms, *desidia, inertia, ineptia, piget* and related forms, *hebes* and related forms, *obtundo, molestus, odiosus, odium, vexo,* and so on. The list could be extended, had we the time, into suggestive physiological terms that can be associated with boredom: so in various contexts yawning might denote boredom. One could add to the list the various terms for "yawning": in Greek *chasko* and in Latin *oscito, oscitatio,* and *hio.* Boredom is not depression, but it does use some of the same terminology. For a list of terms applicable to mental distress see *SVF* 3.100.15 ff.

9. It would be very tempting to invoke Heidegger here and to suggest that boredom is the product of alienation from *Dasein.* The early Greeks, according to Heidegger, had not experienced this alienation. See Steiner 1989. (Such an understanding seems to inspire as various works as the Snell's Heideggerian *Discovery of the Mind* [1953] and Dupont's *The Invention of Literature: From Greek Intoxication to the Latin Book* [1999]). This sort of alienation is the sort of thing that animals cannot therefore suffer. I doubt that such an earthly paradise as one free of boredom ever existed. Twentieth-century Romantics may be right, however, to consider that the Enlightenment and the Industrial Revolution have made widespread boredom more prevalent, at least on paper.

10. The topos has a long history. Compare, from among the many possible examples, Isocrates *Panegyricus* 7; Ovid *Epistulae ex Ponto* 3.7.3; Seneca *Epistulae morales* 100.11; Quintilian *Institutio oratoria* 8.6.14, 10.1.31; Rutilius Namatianus *De reditu suo* 2.3. This rhetorical topos never clearly distinguishes between boredom, weariness, and offense.

11. The application of "being burdened" to mental conditions comes early, however. Homer (*Iliad* 11.274) speaks of "being burdened in regard of the heart." That, as Liddell, Scott, and Jones's Greek lexicon suggests, means "grieved."

12. It needs to be observed, however, that the manuscript readings are crucial. Jocelyn's text reproducing the codices (1967, 112, 333 f.) tends to remove the sense of "boredom" by reproducing the less comprehensible reading *otioso initio* rather than Lipsius's widely accepted *otioso in otio.* On this fragment and *otium* see André 1962 and, more generally, 1966. See too Jocelyn 1967; Skutsch 1968, 1157–65 (a reprint of his article in *Rheinisches Museum* 96 [1953]: 193 ff.)

13. The reading *otioso initio* is defended by Baker (1989). Baker interprets the phrase as an ablative of attendant circumstances and cites Cicero *De legibus* 3.37 (*hoc populo* etc.) as a comparable construction. The reading does produce a scannable half line (the first two metra of this trochaic septenarius are comprised of two trochees followed by two anapests), provided one allows hiatus between *initio* and *animus.*

14. It follows from this that the ancients, at least during the periods to which I have been referring, had no clearly conceptualized notion of the emotion (note that the matter of conceptualization differs from that of experience). Why this may have been the case is part of the task of this book to answer. It is my contention that they were in the process of discovering this emotion.

15. For other attempts at definitions see the surveys of Kuhn 1976, 3–13; Healy 1984; Bernstein 1975; Spacks 1995; Jonard 1998.

16. A very nice illustration of this form of situational boredom as it is described by the great Gioacchino Belli (1791–1863) follows. The translation is by Peter Dale.

1482 LA MOJJE MARCONTENTA
Nun me la sento, nò, nnun me la sento:
Queste cqui nun zò llègge da cristiani,
D'avé da stà li mesi e ll'anni sani
A mmorisse de pizzichi cqua ddrento.

Mai un po' d'aria! Ma' un divertimento!
Sempre ammuffita cqui ccome li cani!
Che mmariti! Che ccori indisumani!
E sse laggneno poi si mmuta vento.

Co cquella sscimmia tua de Lusciola
Er tempo d'annà in zònzola sce ll'hai:
Tutti li gran da-fâ ssò ppe mmé ssola.

Oh, inzomma, io drento casa incaroggnita
Nun ce vojjo stà ppiù. Ssi ccaso-mai,
Nun ho ggruggno né età de fâ sta vita.
12/2/1835

[1482 THE DISCONTENTED WIFE
I jus don' see the point, nah, I don' see the point:
The rules round here ain' a witeman's laws,
Haven ta stay here fa munths n' hole years, forced
Ta die a boredom bit by bit in this dump uva joint.

Never a breth a fresh air! Never an ounce a fun, an I'm
Stuck here moulden away like a mungrel in its hutch!
Sum ruddy husben's! Their harts lack the human touch!
An a slite wind change's anuf ta make'em all whine.

There's always spare time ta go out f'ra bidda fun
An do the Block with that munkey-faced Lucy a yors
While I'm singled out when there's hard yakka ta be dun.

Ah, now look here, this place's depressen f'ra wife
An I'm fed up be'en kept inside. If ya wanna know the corze,
It's cos neither me mug or age's cud out fa this sorda life.]

17. Elizabeth Marshall Thomas (1993, 121), commended by Spacks (1995), implies that dogs do not feel boredom (she is thinking of these animals in a natural, nonhuman environment). This claim should be juxtaposed with those made by Françoise Wemelsfelder

(1985) and with that later implied by Thomas (1993, 143). Repeated personal observation suggests that dogs, at any rate, can become profoundly bored.

18. According to Klibansky, Panofsky, and Saxl (1964, 356), Lucretius is said, in a tract on melancholy by Agrippa of Nettesheim, to be a melancholic (as are Hesiod, Ion, Tynnichus of Chalcis, and Homer). The assertion is not demonstrable. However, it makes more sense than the assertion of Kuhn (1976, 25 ff.) that Lucretius was subject to ennui.

19. Their probable wealth is stressed by Kenney (1971, 239).

20. So argue Bailey (1947, 2:1171) and Kenney (1971, 239).

21. Bailey 1947, 2:1171.

22. As a rhetorical demonstration of this fact, we could point, for example, to Cicero's letters of 59—for example, *Ad Atticum* 6.9 and 11—that do not mention or describe boredom. One might have expected them to. Similarly one might have expected Ovid in Tomis to be consumed by the emotion. Yet his *Epistulae ex Ponto* contains no such references (cf. *Epistulae ex Ponto* 1.5.8, 43–44; 3.4.57).

23. On *horror loci* in Lucretius see also Nussbaum 1994, 198.

24. The notion is also picked up in *Odes* 2.16.18–20: *quid terras alio calentis / sole mutamus? patriae quis exsul / se quoque fugit* [Why do we leave for lands that are being burned by another sun? What exile doesn't also flee himself?].

25. This is contra Kilpatrick (1986, 38–39), but compare my discussion in chapter 1.

26. This metaphorical use of *veternus* might be compared to those of quartan fever—see my index for references.

27. Recall the yawning of Dicaeopolis or of Persius's addressee in *Satires* 3.

28. Barton (1993, 51 ff.) also notes the importance of boredom for Roman experience in this period. She seems to think that boredom drove Romans to the gladiatorial games.

29. If we are to understand it satisfactorily, we must engage with it under three headings. First is the physiological: it can literally induce nausea and, moreover, can be life-threatening. Second is the psychological: it is characterized by an acute disjunction between volition and perception. Third is the philosophical: to characterize one's response to life as a kind of nausea is to make a judgment on the value of life itself. "Biliousness" can be associated with manic depression, however. See Jamison 1993, 181, on Byron, who states "I am so bilious—that I nearly lose my head—and so nervous that I cry for nothing—at least today I burst into tears all alone by myself . . . I have been excited—and agitated and exhausted mentally and bodily all this summer . . ."

30. The *Oxford Latin Dictionary* (s.v. *taedium*) allows the meaning "ennui" for *taedium* only when it stands without the genitive. This seems to me to be unnecessarily prescriptive. For *taedium* meaning "disgust" or "boredom" see, for example, *Epistulae morales* 56.9.5, 59.15.8, 100.11.5; *De ira* 3.1.5.6; *De beneficiis* 2.5.2.7, 2.11.6.2, 6.16.6.2, 7.2.4.2.

31. See *Naturales quaestiones* 4A, *praefatio* 2; *Epistulae morales* 40.3.6, 70.3.7.

32. Compare *Epistulae morales* 100.6; Martial 3.48.

33. This is not quite the same idea as is contained in Lucretius 3.79–82:

> And often so deeply because of fear of death
> Does a hatred of life and of seeing the light seize humans
> That with sorrowing heart they commit suicide
> Forgetting that this fear of death is the origin of their woes.

(Cf. Nussbaum 1994, 197 ff. See also Bailey 1947, 2:1002.) Suicide here is caused by fear of death, not by satiety *(satietas)*. Bailey compares Democritus B.203 Diels and Cicero *De finibus* 1.15.49.

34. The term *taedium* is used earlier in the letter (24.22): *Obiurgat Epicurus non minus eos, qui mortem concupiscunt, quam eos, qui timent, et ait: "Ridiculum est currere ad mortem taedio vitae, cum genere vitae, ut currendum ad mortem esset, effeceris"* [Epicurus also upbraids those who long for death as much as those who fear it and says "it is ridiculous to hasten your own death because you're bored with life, when you're doing the same thing by the way you live"]. The sense is the same. The quotation is reproduced by Usener (1966) as fragment 496 of Epicurus's remains. It would be useful to know what Epicurus said and to have a context. This might alter the conclusions concerning the earlier Greek conceptions of the emotion. As it stands, Seneca may be guilty of distortion.

35. *Epistulae morales* 16.2 has the remarkable phrase *ut dematur otio nausia* [that *nausia* may be taken away from our leisure]. The context in which this clause occurs runs as follows: "Philosophy is no trick to catch the public; it is not devised for show. It is a matter not of words but of facts. It is not pursued in order that the day may yield some amusement before it is spent or that *nausia* may be taken away from our leisure."

36. Kuhn (1976, 31) insists incorrectly that the concern of this dialogue is ennui. See too Griffin 1976, 322; Jonard 1998.

37. The following deceptively simple poem is by Gioacchino Belli and is translated by Peter Dale. The speaker of this poem chooses, ironically, a life of boredom to replace the boredom of life. The irony cannot have been lost on Belli. The very neurotic loafer of this poem, I suggest, is more like Seneca's Serenus than any other figures I have noted so far.

1357 LO STUFARELLO

Sto a spasso, grazziaddio, sto a spasso, Checco.
E inzin'a ttanto c'averò er tigame
De bbobba dar convento de le Dame
De Tor-de-Specchi, ho vvinto un terno a ssecco.

Che sserve? A la fatica io nun ciazzecco:
Quasi è ppiù mmejjo de morì de fame.
E cquer fà ttutto l'anno er faleggname
Nun è vvita pe mmé: ppropio me secco.

Sò stato mozzo, sempriscista, coco . . .
Ar fin de conti { } me sò ddisciso
De capì cche un ber gioco dura poco.

Uhm, quer zempre reggina è un brutto ingergo:
E nnemmanco annerebbe in paradiso
Pe nnun cantà in eterno er Tantummergo
29/11/1834

1357 EASILY BORED

I'm loafen, thank God, I'm twiddlen me thums, yeah Frank.
N' as long as them Ladies a the Convent a Mirror Towers

Serve me up a plate a their mush, I'll lounge away me hours.
It's like winnen a triple at the lott'ry, mate: money in the bank.

Wot's the point a wirk. I ain' cud out fa sweten on a job.
Id'ud almost be better starven ta deth fa lack uva feed.
An wod a carpenter duz all year round's garanteed
Ta bore me shitless. That ain' the life fa me, nah, cob.

I've wirked as a stable boy, a herbalist, a cook, . . .
Then, after all, I finally began ta realise
All good lurks start ta bore ya if ya wirk by the book.

Uh, it's ugly that frase ut good tail never stales, an I'll never,
If it's the last thing I do, go off ta paradise,
Anythen tw'avoid singen 'Tandem yergo' f'r ever an ever.

38. For discussions of this dialogue see Griffin 1976, 321–27; Walz 1950, 63–66.

39. On *euthymia* see McGann 1969.

40. Serenus was no melancholic in the medical or any other sense. Seneca's generalized symptomatology, while at no point presenting a condition that matches, for example, Soranus's precisely detailed *morbus,* does exhibit elements in common with the more generally described conditions of Celsus (who links melancholia with prolonged despondency) or Rufus of Ephesus (whose melancholics were gloomy, sad, fearful, and doubting). But this is beside the point, for Serenus's condition in the *De tranquillitate animi* is best characterized as a secularized form of the illness. Serenus was indeed a depressive, but in the circumscribed world of literature. His melancholy, we might adjudicate, was existential.

41. Other instances, but scattered ones, exist. See, for example, Martial 12.82.14, which refers to the boring importunities of a man seeking a dinner invitation.

42. Among others, one could cite *Eumenes* 11; *Antonius* 51; *Pyrrhus* 16; *Timoleon* 14; *Romulus* 5.

43. Descola (1996, 202) notes that the Jivaro seem to use vendettas in much the same way, as a means of alleviating the tedium of their lives. The Jivaro sound rather like academics.

44. Farquharson 1944, 46–77.

45. The hypochondria, in the modern sense, of Marcus Aurelius and his correspondent here, Fronto, could be linked with this expression of "sick in life." On their hypochondria as something symptomatic of their era, see Bowersock 1995; on hypochondria more generally as a cultural phenomenon see Baur 1988.

46. Barry Jones, a prominent Australian Labour politician until recently, claimed, in a report to the Australian Parliament entitled *Expectations of Life: Increasing the Options for the Twenty-First Century,* that for Australian workers, "boredom was one of the country's 'greatest economic problems.'" He apparently believes it has "created a 'perverse attraction' to drive long distances from home to work" (Stanaway 1992, 3). Such boredom would be described by Lepenies (1992) or by Deleuze and Guattari (1977) as depression. Perhaps it does not deserve description at all.

47. Lucan has an equally vivid term, *mens conscia* (7.784: *et quantum poenae misero mens*

conscia donat [what portion of punishment did self-awareness provide for the wretch]). (*Mens conscia* = guilt; cf. Euripides' *sunesis* in *Orestes* 396. *Donat* is usually understood as "makes a present of," "remits," or "excuses.")

48. The depressive melancholia of chapter 1 and the depressive lovesickness of chapter 2, it hardly needs to be pointed out, are built upon a similar divide.

49. See Benvenuto and Kennedy 1986, 118.

50. Various cultures may make the experience harder to cope with than do others. Agrarian societies, where there is a greater correlation between aims and outcomes, and, to an even greater extent, premodern societies, where little industrial estrangement is possible, may suffer this to a lesser degree. It has often been suggested that the difficulties experienced by premodern societies in adapting to the expectations of modern, industrialized societies result in part from their inability to cope with the privileged nature of the subject-object rupture in Western society.

51. The topic of leisure and play is recapitulated in chapter 7.

52. *Alice in Wonderland* (what can I say but that it is handily translated as *Alicia in Terra Mirabili* by Clive Harcourt Carruthers) is perhaps one of the few examples of an evocation of the state of mind engendered by the childhood rupture between subject and object. Alice is clearly caught between identity and discriminate consciousness at the outset (note that she dislikes books without pictures, preferring the visual to the discursive, and that, not surprised to hear the White Rabbit talking to himself, she only reflects on the oddness of his taking a timepiece out of his waistcoat). Falling down the rabbit hole or well takes her into the topsy-turvydom of adult logic as it is experienced by a child. La Barre 1972, 92–120, is interesting on this matter. La Barre notes (118 n. 13): "The 'fuzziness' between the self and object can best be described in terms of the voluminous empirical researches of Jean Piaget"—see Piaget 1929, 1954. See also Douglas 1966, 108: on ". . . the fumbling efforts of children to master their environment." She goes on to say: "Whether we follow Klein or Piaget, the theme is the same; confusion of internal and external, of thing and person, self and environment, sign and instrument, speech and action. Such confusions may be necessary and universal stages in the passage of the individual from the chaotic, undifferentiated experience of infancy to intellectual and moral maturity." This position is attacked by Donaldson (1978). My only comment here is this: the change that we witness in the various emotional registers surveyed in this book, whether it is real-life or discursive, is a genuine one that is more or less quantifiable. The change involves a movement away from a type of a Piagetian "egocentric illusion" to something that, while hardly "decentered" (to use the term of Donaldson 1978), at least acknowledges the separateness of the self from the world about. Societal change as I have described it thus mirrors the change posited for the movement away from or out of childhood argued for by Piaget and others. To my mind this suggests that Piaget's arguments, though perhaps extreme (like those of Lévy-Bruhl [1923] or Bruno Snell [1953]), nonetheless have a basis in real experience. In my opinion the "egocentric illusion" is real, but not as extreme as Piaget and his followers suggest. In the introduction to the present book, I have stated my views on what I see as the weakness of Donaldson's argument.

53. See La Barre 1972, 95. The themes of nostalgia and homesickness relate to this complex of ideas. See Virgil *Eclogues* 1, 3. On nostalgia see Davis 1979; Brunnert 1984; Heuser 1994 (I have not seen the last two). Boym (2001) links the "invention" of nostalgia with the

Enlightenment. On the theme of homesickness there is the Australian novel *Homesickness* by Murray Bail (1980). Sultan 1999 deserves comparison.

54. I thank Peter Dale for assistance in formulating these paragraphs.

55. On the notion of trauma, though not necessarily of the type to which I am referring here, see Leys 2000.

CHAPTER 4

1. Basedow 1929, 176.

2. The phrase comes from Reid 1983, 100.

3. See also Reid 1983, 36 (on Aboriginal sorcerers and their killing), 37 f. (on their modes of killing), 42 (on boning specifically).

4. On the practice of Australian Aboriginal magic and medicine see also Elkin 1944. Reid (1983, xiv) provides a useful bibliography on magic and Aboriginal healing. (I have not yet seen Kozak and Lopez 2000.) Reid (1983, 126 f.) quotes a very useful firsthand description of the effects of boning:

> Someone pointed the bone at me last year and I nearly died. I was very sick. I was febrile and could see mokuy and people in front of my eyes. They took me to hospital and operated and found I had appendicitis. It was due to *manggimanggi*. I wasn't afraid, though, because I was praying. The next day [the adult male *marnggitj*] came to the hospital, found the *manggimanggi* and took it out. The operation was very successful. They told me I was swearing at the nurses when I woke up! Dad knows who did it. The man lives at Yirrkala. But dad won't do anything in the legal way [implication: he will arrange punishment by sorcery].

5. See also Maddock 1974, 166.

6. For an ethnographic parallel see Reid 1983, 46.

7. Devereux (1970) would also link these with an "anxiety attack." Lucretius (3.152–58) lists these symptoms as the product of fear (was he imitating Sappho?):

> Nevertheless, when mind is stirred by a greater fear,
> We observe the whole body feel it throughout its members,
> So there are sweats and pallor over the whole
> Body, and the tongue is crippled and the voice is broken,
> The eyes cloud, the ears ring, the limbs give way.
> Then we observe, from mental terror, men often
> Falling down.

There are parallels to be found in Homer—see Marcovich 1991, 38; Page 1955, 29 n. 1. That comes as no surprise, for fear is no culturally specific phenomenon.

8. A remarkable instance of this is to be found in Aurelius Victor's *De Caesaribus* (33.5). During the era of the Roman emperor Gallienus (253–68 C.E.), such was the psychic despair *(desperatio animi)* of the Roman people, according to Aurelius Victor, that it made them prone to war and pestilence. States Aurelius Victor: "such things usually happen when one

has become bowed under great concerns, and when despair reigns in people's spirits." I draw this reference from den Boer 1968 (266) and Bickerman 1972 (24).

9. Compare Reid 1983, 54 (cf. 69 ff.: to combat sorcery there is a class of healers called *marnggitj*) and my chapter 2 generally (and the references there to the evil eye).

10. The most useful study (with which I am familiar) on long-distance sorcery is Reid 1983.

11. Peter Dale suggests to me an intriguing link between boredom and exalted religious states. He speculates that boredom, at least in Western usage, frequently refers to the tedium of talk and of language bereft of evocative power. Because object deprivation and the loss of joy in the attachment to ourselves and the world around us leads to melancholy (a passive state in which the state relates to an internalized, mourned object that cannot be located) or annoyance (active boredom that has found an external cause to blame for its sense of the void), boredom, in one sense, acts as a prelude to mystical afflatus, insofar as it points to the void that a disenchanted world appears to be in certain states of mind. Many are bored and alleviate the feeling by distraction in ephemera. The mystic insists on cultivating and staring in the face of aggravations, of sensory deprivation in order to elicit its opposite, the blinding yet ineffable experience that suddenly makes existence, even at its most banal, infused with a glow of transcendental meaning.

12. This is true in the most unexpected of places. See, for example, Aldous Huxley 1923, 18–25; Waugh 1983; Judd 1986 (reviewed in the *Times Literary Supplement*, June 26, 1987, 697).

13. The issue, for better or worse, has narrowed in on definitions: does the condition represent a form of depression, or (without canvassing the grades in between) does it represent, simply, a type of boredom? Starobinski (1962, 31–44) and Kristeva (1987, 17) see it as a type of depression. For Kuhn (1976, 39–64) and Bouchez (1973, 31–34) acedia is an enervating form of boredom, albeit one with psychological ramifications. Klibansky, Panofsky, and Saxl (1964, 75–78), after seeming to describe acedia as a severe form of depression, refuse to name the state. Following their lead, Jackson (1986, 67), who delivers one recent treatment of the problem, steers the middle course. Siegfried Wenzel (1967), concentrating on the word *acedia* itself, maintains that there is no single definition. (See also Jonard 1998, 23 ff.)

14. The business of affective somatization will reappear in chapter 6, in particular with Trimalchio. It is of considerable importance and deserves some stress here. We have, in the previous three chapters, noticed how emotions such as melancholia, lovesickness, and boredom move in time from an acted-out or externalized mode (manic almost) to, eventually, an internalized or corporealized mode (near depressive). This corporealization seems to gain prevalence in the first century of our era. So, for example, melancholy becomes associated popularly with the quartan fever, lovesickness with wasting, and boredom with nausea. In chapter 6 we will observe that Trimalchio corporealizes time itself (not an emotion, but an emotional register) as indigestion and constipation. This type of corporealization soon leads to a medicalization of these emotions and affective registers. (This notion of affective corporealization gained some popularity in the 1980s—see Joshel 1992.)

15. Showalter (1997, 17) is very helpful on this matter. She suggests that the preconditions for "hysterical epidemics [are] . . . physician-enthusiasts; unhappy, vulnerable patients; and supportive cultural environments." She characterizes hysteria as an affective condition

"that produces the appearance of disease although the patient is unconscious of the motives for feeling sick" (14).

16. By analogy, these are the conditions under which many other such psychic illnesses transmit. These are surveyed trenchantly in Showalter 1997; Hacking 1995, 1998 (cf. Toohey 1999b).

17. The use of the term *infection* may seem unnecessarily anachronistic. It is sometimes claimed that ancient medicine had no understanding of infection in the modern sense. This seems to me to be less than certain. I offer here one instance of a recognition of the communicability of illness. This is taken from Aretaeus's discussion of *elephas* (8.13.1; trans. Adams [1856, 494]): "and, moreover, there is danger in living or associating with it no less than with the plague, for the infection *[baphê]* is thereby communicated by the respiration *[anapnoês gar es metadosin rêidiê baphê]*."

18. Elizabeth Marshall Thomas (1993) speaks interestingly of the pining and sorrow that can be observed in animals, especially dogs.

19. Nietzsche's *On the Genealogy of Morals* is helpful on ascetics' will to power. The will to power is best seen as an assertion of self—perhaps if it is pushed too far we end up with the situation of acedia. Compare France 1995.

20. It cannot be stressed enough how often this emotion is "colonized" by those without a historical sense. For example, Deleuze and Guattari (1977, xx and passim), linking the state and depression, imagine that a removal of Oedipal, colonial, capitalistic, patriarchal values will free us all from this condition.

21. I have heard Australian Aboriginal leaders from the outback argue that young Aboriginal men's suicide rates increase dramatically when their football team is not operating. I have read in Canada's national newspaper *Globe and Mail*—the report was hearsay—that petrol sniffing among the Inuit young declined when as simple a thing as a ice-hockey rink was present in the community. A comparable report appeared in the *Sydney Morning Herald* (Bradley 2001).

22. *Peri tôn oktô logismôn pros Anatolion* (*Patrologia Graeca* 40.1271 ff.). The best discussion is by Wenzel (1967). (See also Arbesmann 1958.)

23. *Patrologia Graeca* 40.1273.

24. *Logos parainetikos pros Stageirion askêtên daimonônta* (*Patrologia Graeca* 47.423 ff.), written in 380 or 381 C.E.

25. Compare Reid 1983, 52. Perhaps Stagirius was a schizophrenic.

26. Cassian wrote *De institutis cenobiorum* (*Patrologia Latina* 49.53 ff.)—published 425—a description of monastic life as he knew it from Palestine and Egypt; books 5–12 treat the eight vices; book 10 (*Patrologia Latina* 49.359 ff.) is written *de spiritu acediae*. (Translations are Ramsey 2000 and Jean-Claude Guy 2001.) Cassian also wrote the *Collationes patrum* (*Corpus Scriptorum Ecclesiasticorum Latinorum* 13), pretended reports of "conferences" with the most famous desert fathers. This was published about 426–28. Generally on Cassian see Chadwick 1968.

27. *Patrologia Latina* 49.366–67.

28. Cassian seems to have adapted Chrysostomos (*Patrologia Graeca* 47.489). On the relation of Chrysostomos and Cassian see Chadwick 1968, 9.

29. I have discussed this matter at more length in chapter 1. The crucial reference is

Galen *Introductio seu medicus* 14.740.16, in which passage Bellerophon's status as a melancholic is affirmed.

30. Elsewhere (*Epistles* 130.17, *ad Demetriadem*) St. Jerome discusses the mental derangement that arises from poor surroundings: "I know that sanity can be damaged in both sexes through excessive abstinence . . . with a result that they don't know what to do, where to turn, what to say, or when to be quiet."

31. Klibansky, Panofsky, and Saxl 1964, 75 f. For discussion of medical knowledge in the early church see D'Irsay 1927. Wenzel (1967, 191–94) provides a useful compilation of links between acedia and the Galenic humoral theories of the origin of illness; he writes (193), "That acedia is sometimes related to melancholy (1), sometimes to a phlegmatic disposition (2), illustrates the fact brought out repeatedly in our survey of its history: that by 1200 acedia comprised two essentially different vices, grief and indolence."

32. The solution, as we have seen, is that advocated by Cicero and Seneca as a solution for melancholia—the exercise of the will. Such over-easy and dreary conclusions have bedeviled the diagnosis and treatment of this illness.

33. Bloomfield 1952, 73. The text is *Patrologia Latina* 80.10 ff. See also Bloomfield 1952, 358 n. 50, where, quoting Chadwick on Cassian, Bloomfield notes that Eutropius may depend for his listing on Cassian *Collationes* 5.2.10–16.

34. According to Klibansky, Panofsky, and Saxl (1964, 76 n. 23), a discussion of his views on acedia may be found in Paget 1903, 8 ff.

35. Bloomfield 1952, 77. The text is *Patrologia Latina* 83.95–98.

36. *Scala Paradisi*, *Patrologia Graeca* 88.631 ff. (for a translation see Luibheid and Russell 1982). Step 13 (*Patrologia Graeca* 88.857–61) provides an extended treatment of "despondency." Wenzel (1967, 18) maintains that although Climacus gives long descriptions of the vice, they are "mostly borrowed from earlier desert fathers."

37. See Müri 1953 on Hippocratic notions of melancholy and black bile; on the Hippocratics generally see Smith 1979. For the larger view see Neuburger 1909.

38. See Jackson 1986, 30–31, quoting from Jones and Withington 1923–31, 1:236, 4:185.

39. See Klibansky, Panofsky, and Saxl 1964, 45 f., for a discussion of Celsus and a bibliography. The authors point out that Celsus bases his work on that of Asclepiades of Bithynia, who came to Rome in 91 B.C.E. and went on to become a friend of Cicero (see Vallance 1990). Jackson (1986, 33) believes that Celsus may have been influenced by humoral theory.

40. Klibansky, Panofsky, and Saxl (1964, 49) make this statement as part of their general discussion (48–55) of Rufus of Ephesus. Rufus's work on melancholy is reconstructed from fragments and citations: see Klibansky, Panofsky, and Saxl 1964, 49. The text for the remains of Rufus of Ephesus is now Gärtner 1970. Jackson (1986, 407) refers to the translation of Daremberg and Ruelle (1879).

41. Jackson (1986, 39—41, 407) discusses Aretaeus and mentions a translation by Adams (1856). The Greek text is Hude 1958.

42. Galen's comments on melancholy may be found in book 3 of *On the Affected Parts*. The Greek text is contained in Kühn 1821–33, vol. 8. For a translation see Siegel 1976. On Galen and melancholy see Jackson 1986, 41–45; Jackson 1969; Siegel 1968; Klibansky, Panofsky, and Saxl 1964, 57 ff.

43. Soranus survives in a Latin translation made at the end of the fourth century by Caelius Aurelianus (*De morbis acutis et chronicis*). For a text see Drabkin 1950.

44. The translation is drawn from Jackson 1986, 40 citing Adams 1856, 298.

45. This parallel is pointed out by Rosen (1968, 98). The New Testament references are Luke 8:26, 29; Mark 5:3; Matthew 8:28. Demonic possession, in some of its aspects, may be compared generally—see Lewis 1971; La Barre 1972; Cohn 1957.

46. For discussion of medical knowledge in the early church see D'Irsay 1927.

47. John Chrysostomos's alarming linking of the condition with the loose—perhaps homosexual—lifestyle is such a one.

48. I would include even the mode by which we react to our capacity to read. I have a few remarks (and references) on this matter in Toohey 1996.

49. The earliest uses of the word to mean "boredom" may be Hellenistic. But these could just as easily be taken to mean "annoyance." See the previous chapter.

50. There remains a third aspect of acedia for which I have not offered parallels. This is frustration. It has been argued by Wemelsfelder (1989) that frustration precedes boredom. As far as the literary condition is concerned, this is a less easy concept to pin down. To avoid the attendant imprecision, I have omitted its consideration. It could be observed that *horror loci* may be as good an example of frustration as one is liable to find.

51. Chrysostomos, however, did not see it this way. He lists *melancholici* along with a variety of other sinners (*Patrologia Graeca* 47.451).

52. So, too, suggests St. Jerome (*Letters* 95, 97), who alludes to the melancholy that arises from poor surroundings.

53. *Patrologia Graeca* 47.426.

54. The notion of contagion has become a very popular one in cultural studies. Dan Sperber uses it of what he calls "mental representations"—beliefs and so on. (I am using it of psychosis.) Sperber's book has been published in English as *Explaining Culture* (1996; reviewed in the *Times Literary Supplement*, June 20, 1997). Sperber's approach was attacked in the *Times Literary Supplement* (July 4, 1997, 14–15) by Regis Debray, who mentions a number of other books concerned with "contagion" in the cultural sphere (e.g., Siegfried 1960). See also Cullen 1993. The popularity has spread to the natural sciences. I presume that this is the result of the relatively recent appearance of AIDS, the Ebola virus, and so forth. Paul W. Ewald (2000), rejecting both environment and genes, apparently wants to link mental illness, such as schizophrenia or manic depression, to viral infection. He links schizophrenia, for example, to the protozoan *Toxoplasma gondii*, which is, again apparently, carried by domestic cats. Ewald speculates that cats may pass it on to humans when they live in close proximity to us. Regions and periods where cats live in close proximity to humans, such as in the northern-hemisphere winter, should register higher rates of schizophrenia. I have not been able to ascertain whether Ewald has noted a very high incidence of schizophrenia among Canadians, many of whom keep their cats indoors all year round because of the severity of the climate. Nor have I been able to ascertain whether Australian schizophrenia rates are correspondingly lower. In Australia, cats are habitually kept outdoors. (Cf. the review of Ewald's book by Julius Schachter in the *New England Journal of Medicine* 344, no. 15 [April 12, 2001].)

55. The best discussion of the viral analogy and the transmission of hysterical conditions such as acedia is to be found in Showalter 1997, 60

56. Viral attacks have become rather popular in current literature: see, for example, Preston 1994; Garrett 1994.

57. McNeill 1976 is very helpful on the notions of pestilential infection and spread. For the viral analogy applied to psychological conditions see Showalter 1985, 1997.

58. For modern parallels see Showalter 1997. With less sweep, Tom Lutz's *American Nervousness* (1991) examines the "outbreak" of neurasthenia among American artists, writers, and intellectuals at the turn of the twentieth century.

59. Golden (1977) reports of a case in Littlerock, Arkansas, of an Afro-American man who had been having seizures and hallucinations and was becoming increasingly irritable and withdrawn from his family when he was admitted to a medical center for psychiatric treatment. All medical examinations, including a brain scan, found absolutely nothing wrong with him. But his condition continued to deteriorate, and within two weeks he had a massive heart attack and died. The autopsy found no cause for his death at only thirty-three. Golden believes that the man was killed by voodoo. After the man died, his wife revealed he had been seeing a witch doctor. The widow said she believed her husband had angered the "two headed," as the female witch doctor was known, and that as a result the witch doctor had caused his death. See also Cannon 1957; Mathis 1964; Milton 1973.

60. An Australian Aboriginal was brought to the Darwin hospital in April 1956, apparently dying of this type of sorcery. He was placed in an oxygen tank and fed intravenously. He gradually recovered, convinced that the white man's magic was stronger. See Arthur Morley's article in the London *Sunday Times*, April 22, 1956, 11.

61. Fugue does have implications for contemporary mental health. The big question posed by Hacking in *Mad Travellers* (1998) is this: are fugue and comparable disorders the products of our own societies and whims, or are they universals, true through time? Have people always had ME, RSI, bulimia; or are these syndromes products of the neurotic end of the twentieth century? Hacking, despite his agnosticism, leans toward social construction. (Your ME, RSI, post-traumatic stress disorder, MPD, or DID may hurt, but it is not quite real. It has been invented by your society.)

62. The "Paraquat suicides" in contemporary Western Samoa offer another disheartening parallel: "Families throughout Western Samoa are struggling to come to terms with a tragic epidemic of youth suicide . . . Demographers say the official rate of 40 deaths per 100,000, out of a total Samoan population of 160,000, is probably underestimated. The isolation of the island of Savaii and the stigma of suicide among its many Christians are reasons why some suicides are not recorded. About four-fifths of the young men who kill themselves drink the toxic weed-killer Paraquat, which means a high proportion of suicide attempts succeed. A United Nations Children's Fund report warned South Pacific countries about their suicide rates, some of which are 20 times higher than comparable figures in the United States or Australia . . . The young men sometimes commit suicide in public—drinking Paraquat as a kind of display . . . Earlier this month, Laufau, a mother with a one-year-old son, threatened to leave her husband if he did not give up alcohol. He reacted by drinking a bottle of Paraquat and died in hospital in Apia two weeks later. Her brother committed suicide in a similar fashion last year . . . Ms Moelagi Jackson, a village chief or Matai, runs the Safua hotel and saw her cousin commit suicide after he joined a religious cult and quarrelled with his family. She believes most suicides are due to the clash between the old and the new ways . . . The Reverend Nuu'Osamea, a leading Protestant churchman

in Apia, despairs of the death toll. 'At times we feel things are getting out of hand,' he said. 'We really don't know how to deal with the situation because we only hear when someone has done a successful job. You're left with a feeling of helplessness.' He believes the main cause of youth suicide is the scolding of youngsters by authoritarian parents. "The young people go through a lot of stress, and the most available option for them is to be finished off from this life" (Zinn 1995).

CHAPTER 5

The quote from Tatz is drawn from a report on indigenous youth suicide (an apparent epidemic) in New South Wales, the Australian Capital Territory, and New Zealand. The context of this quotation is as follows: "On being taken into cells the youth invariably says, 'I'll neck myself, and you'll lose your job.' My life he proposes, for your discomfort. Is he drunk? Does he mean it? . . . He says it, and in so doing, he infers that he'll be around to witness his fleeting moment of sovereignty."

1. The greatest success rate is in fiction. Nice representatives are Cleite in Apollonius' *Argonautica* 2 or Ovid's Byblis (*Metamorphoses* 9.457 ff.). On both I note (but have not yet seen) Jackson 1997.

2. I suspect that many alcohol related suicides fit this category. The life affirmation involved in the assertion of the young Aboriginal man (under the influence of alcohol) that is quoted by Colin Tatz is typical.

3. Chaereas's departure reflects a topos to be seen in Apollonius of Rhodes *Argonautica* 1.250–59 and Valerius Flaccus *Argonautica* 1.693–852. In Valerius's version the parents actually commit suicide.

4. For a different reading of this scene see MacAlister 1996, 28; Konstan 1994, 17. Perkins (1995, 96–103) links the underlying ideas behind Chaereas's leap to Epictetus's brand of Stoicism.

5. Some discussions of suicide in the ancient world are Van Hoof 1990; Plass 1995; MacAlister 1996; Hirzel 1908; Grisé 1983; Griffin 1976, 367–88; Garrison 1991, 1995; Bowersock 1995, 59–74. Compare Dillon 1994. Van Hooff (1990, 6—following Durkheim 1952; cf. Taylor 1982) defines suicide as "any case of death which results, directly or indirectly, from an act, positive or negative, accomplished by the victim himself and in the knowledge that it would necessarily produce this result." See also MacAlister 1996, 14–15.

6. Brown (1988) asserts the public importance of suicide in his discussion of the Aguaruna. Among women and the young, it can become a means of punishing antagonists.

7. This is the direct opposite of what, for example, MacAlister (1996, 56 ff.) argues in her fascinating and helpful book. She sees despair in these suicides. I see self-advertisement. See also Perkins 1995, 96–103.

8. Suicide attempts may be found in the following places within Chariton's novel: 1.5.2, 1.6.1, 2.11.3–4, 3.3.1, 3.3.6, 3.5.6, 3.7.6, 4.2.1, 4.3.6, 4.3.9, 5.10.6, 6.3.8, 6.6.2, 7.1.6, 7.5.14.

9. The only person not to suffer repeatedly from lovesickness is Callirhoe. It is notable that the more robust Callirhoe, in love but seldom lovesick, is rarely tempted by suicide. I wonder if this is evidence that Chariton may have been a woman (cf. 2.11.3–4, 6.6.2, 7.6.8)?

10. For falling see 1.1.6, 1.1.14, 2.7.14, 4.1.9; for the black swoon (designated as *achlus, nux, nephelê,* or *skotos*), 1.1.14, 2.7.4, 2.8.1.

11. See 1.1.8, 2.4.1, 4.2.4, 6.3.2–3.

12. For depression see 2.6.1, 4.2.8; for a deathlike trance, 6.1.6–12; for blushing, 4.2.13, 6.3.1; for silence, 2.4.2, 4.2.13, 6.3.2–3; for insomnia, 2.4.2, 6.7.2; for weeping, 1.1.14, 4.2.13, 6.3.2–3; for the sweats, 4.2.13. We are close to the "anxiety attacks" discussed in chapter 2.

13. For wasting see 1.1.8–9, 2.7.4, 4.2.4; for suicide by starvation, 3.1.1, 6.3.8; for hanging, 5.10.6; for cutting the throat, 7.1.6. It is worth noting at this point that this symptomatology bears a fairly close resemblance to that attributed to boning by Basedow in his description cited at the beginning of the previous chapter.

14. Jealousy may cause speechlessness (1.4.7, 1.4.10), depression (1.3.4), the swoons (1.4.6), a state resembling mourning (1.4.6), weeping (1.4.7), suicidal urges (1.4.7), and anger (cited shortly).

15. Compare Dionysius at 3.1.3, 3.7.4, 3.9.10, 4.5.9–10; Chaereas at 3.6.3–4.

16. A challenging parallel for Artaxerxes' state of mind is to be found in a remarkable painting (fig. 6) in the Museo Nazionale di Napoli, reproduced in Maiuri 1957 (84) as "Zeus malinconico" (I thank Dr. Sonia Hewitt for providing me with access to this painting). In this wall painting (which no doubt stems from the era of Chariton—I am assuming a Neronian date) is pictured a bored, even melancholic Jupiter. Why is he bored? Idleness is no doubt the cause, though this is not hinted at in the painting (Jupiter might have remarked, along with Seneca, *fit aliquando huius rei nausia*). The clue to the melancholy is probably provided by the representation of Cupid leaning over his right shoulder. Is that god present to encourage Jupiter toward further diverting love exploits among the humans who inhabit the worldly vistas to his rear? Jupiter will have none of it, the painting seems to be saying. Satiety (and idleness?) has bred a melancholy that further affairs can only prolong. If we could draw a parallel between Jupiter and Artaxerxes, then we might want to compare their mental states and even suggest that Zeus is ripe for a Callirhoe.

17. See chapter 2 for a discussion of this word.

18. Compare Homer *Iliad* 20.321, 421 (of Hector's anguish).

19. See, for example, Theocritus 2.106 ff. But we could also point to Basedow's boning.

20. See Cannon's (1957) description of the physiology of such a breakdown, reproduced in chapter 4. See too Milton 1973; Golden 1977.

21. Once again, MacAlister (1996, 57) sees despair where I see self-advertisement.

22. For this concept of theatricality see Leigh 1997.

23. What the sword will actually do to Ajax is illustrated on a black-figure vase, dated to ca. 580 B.C.E., that is reproduced as an illustration in Shapiro 1994, 151 (cf. 1153).

24. See Jamison 1999, 200; Kraepelin 1921, 78.

25. Suicide, it is worth noting, was condemned by Plato (*Laws* 871a–3d) and Aristotle (*Nicomachean Ethics* 1138a5 ff.) particularly when it involved cowardice. A despairing reaction may have come under the same rubric. On Plato and Aristotle see MacAlister 1996, 6, citing Garrison 1991, 18–19. (There is an interesting discussion of suicide in Plotinus by Dillon [1994].)

26. Giton's words to Encolpius "You're wrong . . . if you think by any possible chance you can die before me" match the sentiment, if not the actual words, that we will see

expressed to Argus by his father (who intends to kill himself before his son dies): "you can still outlive me."

27. On Petronius's death see Plass 1995, 111. See also Plass 1995, 90, on Tiberius's chagrin when someone kills himself before Tiberius can strike him ("Why, he escaped me!" Suetonius *Tiberius* 61.5). Plass (123) also provides an interesting schematic analysis of the place of suicide within the mechanics, as he sees them, of the imperial Roman power game.

28. Translation adapted from William 1986.

29. We must be honest at this point. Petronius may have been a real-life person, but as described by Tacitus he is as subject to Tacitus's historiographical bias as any characters in fiction.

30. On political suicide at Rome see Plass 1995. My discussion by and large avoids political suicide and its implications (except in the cases of Lucan and Seneca, whose death's seem to echo their prose works). I have avoided political suicide because it is forced from without. My interest has been in the suicide driven from within, such as those passive and apparently private suicides of Chariton and others. Plass (95) suggests that political suicide may be little more than imperial execution.

31. It is very hard not to think at this point of Arthur Koestler's act of personal euthanasia, accompanied also by his apparently guileless wife, Cynthia.

32. Bowersock (1995, 59–74) discusses the modes by which the early Christian enthusiasm for martyrdom, another form of suicide, matches and indeed is dependent on the Stoic ideal of the *mors voluntaria*. (Lucretius 3.72 ff. might profitably, if cynically, be compared: Lucretius believes that suicide happens because people fear death.) See also the panoptic study of MacAlister (1996, especially 84–114) for a discussion of Christian martyrdom and suicide.

33. I apologize for the brevity of these comments. I have repeated them elsewhere in this book. My apology should be applied there too. The topic is too vast—too slippery as well—for proper treatment here. I would like to be able to say that I will leave it to others for demonstration.

34. I have a discussion of other aspects of this matter in the next chapter (concerning time). Seneca's fascination with the course of time, with *ecpyrosis*, and with mass annihilation generally seems to reflect a troubled infatuation with death.

35. It is almost as if we witness here a suicidal epidemic (there was an "epidemic" of political suicide in this period). This should be compared to the epidemic of acedia discussed in the previous chapter and to the implications of the practice of boning.

36. I have found Leigh 1997 very helpful on Lucan. Plass (1995, 107) links Lucan's suicides to gladiatorial combat and the cult of the unflinching death. Compare Barton 1993.

37. The psychic danger faced by Argus's father perhaps may be associated with psychological disintegration. When Argus's father spotted his son dying, "night came over him and huge shadows covered his eyes" (3.735). This type of swoon was a typical precursor of a suicide attempt. A comparable line in Homer (*Iliad* 5.659) is used to characterize the affect of death on a Trojan warrior.

38. On the futility of suicidal resistance see Plass 1995, 83; Tacitus *Agricola* 42.3.

39. So we can see from Cornelia's utterances at 8.654–55. Hanging is associated sometimes with women—see Loraux 1987.

40. The phrase is like the *libido moriendi* used by Seneca at *Epistles* 24.25.

41. Plass (1995, 109) mentions several other instances of women who do suicide.

42. Once again, it is worth noting that we seem to witness an epidemic of suicides in this period that, as Chariton shows, owed its origin to more than just current conditions at Rome. (Showalter [1997] would term this a hysterical epidemic.)

43. I am not speaking here at all of trauma, such as sexual abuse when young. This can present a comparable set of reactions.

44. The reaction can be psychic. A psychic reaction may be, in general, more typical of premodern societies and of children.

45. They are the symptoms of the victim of boning, as Basedow describes him (cited at the beginning of chapter 4).

46. MacAlister (1996, 16), for example, links a rise in suicide to the uncertainties of the late Hellenistic age (and links this with Durkheim's notion of the "egotistic" suicide). This is, approximately, also the position of Konstan (1994). Swain (1996) sees no such uncertainties in the urban life of, at any rate, the Greeks of this period. I believe that any convincing explanation (indeed any convincing description) must include Greek and Roman evidence side by side.

47. Seneca, at *Epistles* 77.6, makes even more plain the link between suicide and *fastidium vitae* when he states that *mori velle etiam fastidiosus potest*. The term *velle mori* is also used by Lucan at *Civil War* 4.280.

48. A curious variant on this emotion is provided at Epictetus 1.9.12: Epictetus warns against the enthusiasm of young men for doing away with themselves after learning of the advantages of the Stoic afterlife. This type of an *erôs thanatou*, it seems to me, is parasitic on a widespread acceptance of self-killing as an alternative to a less than salubrious present life (cf. Griffin 1976, 387).

49. An exception is the Persian king Artaxerxes.

50. The argument goes like this: Roman emperors such as Nero were generating suicides among the elite at a distressing rate. The actions of the principate, therefore, will go some distance to explain the heightened interest in the matter (not to say its practice) by authors such as Seneca, Petronius, and Lucan. (But this will not explain Chariton's striking fascination for the matter: he wrote in Greek and did not live in Rome.) I doubt that this is a matter of cause and effect, however. We should think of it this way: the power exercised by the principate, for better or worse, highlights or, to use the expression I have favored, problematizes the issue of control. (I doubt that it matters whether you live in Rome or in Asia Minor, if power is at issue.) Most of the acts of suicide described in this chapter respond precisely to this problematization. They cannot be seen as acts of existential despair. Rather, they represent very public acts of self-assertion in contexts where personal control has been severely challenged or, worse, curtailed. That such a representation of suicide coincides with a historical period in which the principate used enforced suicide as a means of punishment and control makes the frequency of suicide and suicide attempts in literature all the more predictable. (Plass [1995, 90] looks at suicide and Roman social etiquette. Something larger still than Roman mores is operating here, as the instance of Chariton demonstrates.)

51. Epidemics of suicide did occur in antiquity, at least according to the literary sources. Plutarch (*De muliebris virtutibus* 11) speaks of a mysterious epidemic afflicting the women of Miletus. They were inexplicably hanging themselves. (Speculation had it that poisoned air deranged their minds.) The epidemic, according to Plutarch, was stopped by a law insisting

that women who had perished thus should have their bodies carried naked through the agora on the way to their funerals. See also Stadter 1965, 76–77; Bowersock 1995, 65.

52. The epidemic of acedia, surveyed in the last chapter, offers a neat parallel for the modes by which affective contagion may take place.

53. Why did this literary epidemic break out in the nineteenth century? I suspect that the answer may be found in part in the social forces identified of fugue by Hacking (1998) and Showalter (1997) and in part in the sociological changes, underscored by Bourdieu (1996), that took place in this period in the marketplace of art and artistic self-representation.

CHAPTER 6

1. Modern scientific notions of time are relevant, insofar as they point to the relativity of the concept of time. Paul Davies's popular book *About Time* (1995) is helpful here. Davies, however, has been chastised for not attempting to analyze (1) the conflict between "philosophical" time (thus the theorizing of Husserl, Heidegger, or Bergson) and scientific time and (2) the conflict between human concepts of time and scientific ones (exemplified in the "celebrated confrontation between Bergson and Einstein on this very point": see Brian Rotman's review [1996, 29] of Davies's book). More generally on time see Macey 1989; Aveni 1989; Borst 1993; Davison 1993.

2. This paragraph restates Toohey 1997c, 50.

3. This cannot be the case for animals and small children, who live in a relatively timeless zone. Randall Jarrell's poem "The Woman at the Washington Zoo" (1959) makes this point of animals and time. The relevant lines of his moving poem run as follows (the narrator is speaking of himself):

> this serviceable
> Body that no sunlight dyes, no hand suffuses
> But, dome-shadowed, withering among the columns,
> Wavy beneath fountains—small, far-off, shining
> In the eyes of animals, these being trapped
> As I am trapped but not, themselves, the trap,
> Ageing, but without knowledge of their age,
> Kept safe here [the zoo], knowing not of death, for death
> —Oh, bars of my own body, open, open!

4. Arrowsmith (1966, 307) notes of Trimalchio's circumstances, "wealth brings thoughts of defecation (for wealth is symbolically a satiety that cannot evacuate itself)."

5. Compare Suetonius *Claudius* 32. Burton *The Anatomy of Melancholy* (2.27) and Bright (1970, 11) link bad digestion to melancholy (just like Trimalchio).

6. Compare Arrowsmith 1966, 309: "food consumed to the point of satiety is an instance, a symbol, of luxuria; the end of satiety is constipation; and flatulent vapours 'go straight to your brain and derange your whole system,' and especially the reason which should, at least in the Epicurean ethics, control the appetites. 'I know someone who died . . . from holding it in.' That is, luxuria is death, extinction of the rational will."

7. Elizabeth Marshall Thomas (1993, 137) describes how knowledge through the body

is natural to dogs but not to us primates. She is speaking in this instance of death. I am suggesting in this chapter, however, that Trimalchio corporealizes time (within the body) as an illness. Understanding through the body is not quite the same thing as this process of visceral internalization that I have been discussing (following many others).

8. It is, that is to say, akin to the hysterical illnesses that I focused on particularly in chapter 4 (on acedia). There, following Showalter (1997, 14), it was suggested that hysteria implies "behaviour that produces the appearance of disease although the patient is unconscious of the motives of feeling sick." The parallels with lovesickness (discussed in chapter 2) should also be apparent.

9. Petronius's novel may be sui generis, but his concept of time is not. Seneca periodically alludes to the serial nature of time's movement. The best place to see this is in his essay *De brevitate vitae*. It may be worth noting that the essay finishes with a mock funeral, that of Sextus Turannius. Bettini 1991 has some interesting observations on Seneca and time. For Stoic time see Goldschmidt 1979.

10. Perhaps Livy should also be included here. For a discussion of cyclical time in Livy see Beard 1987. Polybius (6.5 ff.) has some very interesting observations about the cyclical nature (the *anacyclosis*) of the appearance of constitutions in human society—see Walbank 1957, 643 ff.

11. It has been suggested, however, that the Trojan material of these first three books was not an insert but, rather, was freestanding (Büchner 1967, 9–25).

12. This summary is drawn from Toohey 1992c, 96.

13. In Silius Italicus's epic poem *Punica*, Scipio is likened to Aeneas (and ecomiastically to the emperor Domitian, under whom this poem was written). History thus repeats itself when we liken Scipio's pilgrimage to Hades (13.400–895; here he learns of Rome's future and the fate of Hannibal) to that of Aeneas; compare also Scipio's celebration of funeral games in honor of his father (16.275–591; cf. *Aeneid* 5).

14. Marcellus had married Augustus's daughter Julia and was earmarked as Augustus's successor. He died at age nineteen in 23 B.C.E.

15. The same notion approximately animates Horace's *Carmen saeculare* (alluded to earlier), which was written for Augustus's centennial games of 17 B.C.E. The games were a festival to be held every eleventh decade and were designed to celebrate the preservation of the state. In this poem, at v. 49 ff., Augustus is addressed in precisely the same manner by which one would address Aeneas: "he of Anchises' and Venus' pure blood." This principle of historical recurrence is also behind Virgil's *Eclogues* 4.

16. Although temporal decline is a persistent topos (see, e.g., Virgil *Georgics* 1.463 ff., 1.121 ff.; Horace *Epodes* 7, 16 [cf. Lovejoy 1965; Dodds 1985]), much public literature affirmed a cyclical (or agrarian) concept of time. In the *Aeneid* Augustus completes a cycle in that he embodies the mythical Roman founder, Aeneas (6.752–853, 8.608–731). So he does in Ovid's *Metamorphoses*, as we learn through Pythagoras's teachings on metempsychosis (15.418–52). In Horace's *Carmen saeculare* Augustan Rome renovates time, as it were, by its continuation of ancient festival. For this theme in architecture see Zanker 1988. Is the same pattern to be found in Livy? Walsh (1961, 16 ff.) has some helpful comments on this matter.

17. A recent discussion of modern concepts of time is Davies 1996.

18. This template is drawn explicitly from Toohey 1996.

19. Young children, however, are devoid of a clear sense of mortality. Where does that leave their sense of time? I suspect (or should I say that I recall) that their time is "longer" and inevitably repetitive, not unlike that of a dog or a cat. Time has no affective dimension for children.

20. The following is quoted from Rycroft 1997, 37:

> To the primordial intelligence humanity held a central position in the cosmic order, lived in a state of intimate participation with nature (what Lévy-Bruhl called participation mystique), held a rhythmic, circular conception of time, inhabited a reality located in the world of the spirit, accepted moral values as absolute, regarded life as eternal, and believed myth and ritual to be indispensable to the health and vitality of the spirit. By contrast, to the modern intellect, humanity holds a peripheral position in the cosmic order, lives in a state of objective separation from nature, holds a progressive linear conception of time, inhabits a reality primarily located in the world of matter, accepts moral values as relative, regards life as strictly finite, and believes myth and ritual to be irrelevant to the requirements of modern life.

If this idea seems very old-fashioned now, I would remind the skeptical of the centrality of ritual in the premodern life and of the fact that it suffused most aspects and actions of an adult's life. Every deed in a ritualized world recapitulates key primal events. What is this but circularity?

21. Premodern societies that are not agriculturally based (and hence lack a strong sense of seasonal circularity) may see time differently again. Descola (1996) believes that the Achuar exist in a kind of a temporal amnesia.

22. The chapter "Primitive Worlds" in Douglas 1966 is helpful in locating, if not time specifically, at least the types of society in which such a view of time may flourish. I notice a useful contrast between time in illiterate and literate societies in Ignazio Silone's *Fontamara* (1948, 10). Of the peasant village we read: "It was always the same. There was never any change. Years passed, years piled up, the young grew old, the old died. Sowing, weeding, pruning, spraying, mowing, and harvesting went on. What followed? No change of any kind. Every year was like the last year, every season like the last season, every generation like the one before." The comparison with the literate town in the plain below the village reads: "Many things changed meanwhile down below in the plain, but at Fontamara nothing changed. The soil was meagre, dry and rocky. The meagre soil was divided and subdivided, racked with mortgages."

23. See Pindar *Olympian* 2; *Pythian* 10.

24. On the circularity of the appearance of constitutions see Polybius 6.5 ff.; Walbank 1957, 643 ff.

25. On time see Sandbach 1975, 92; Rist 1969, 273–88; Long and Sedley 1987, 304–13 and s.v. "time."

26. Compare the following quote from Margo 1996, 9: "Professor John Kellow, a gastroenterologist at Sydney's Royal North Shore Hospital, says constipation is known to be associated with depression. With depression the metabolic rate can become sluggish and the bowels can too."

27. Flatulence was linked with melancholia by Diocles of Carystus—see Flashar 1966,

50. On flatulence generally see also Seneca *Natural Questions* 5.4.2. Aristotle (2.8.366b15–20) likens flatulence to earthquakes, a very telling comparison.

28. For the Greek text see Hude 1958.

29. Compare also Siegel 1973, 192.

30. For a link between diet and melancholia see Flashar 1966, 54.

31. Solomon 2001 is helpful on how time is registered as slowing down for the victim of affective disorder.

32. Kraepelin (1921, 55) stresses as characteristic of hypomania "the lack of inner unity of the course of ideas, the incapacity to carry out consistently a definite series of thoughts, to work out steadily and logically and to set in order given ideas"—all characteristics of a haste-driven temperament. Jamison (1993, 130) alludes to the sense of timelessness (or at least the circularity or repetitiveness of time) that can accompany depression. Time for the depressive is sometimes said to slow down. See Borgna 1991.

33. For a definition of cyclothymia see Goodwin and Jamison 1990, 49–54.

34. The following discussion is based on a paper entitled "The Course of Time in the Writings of Lucan and Some of His Contemporaries" delivered in Italian as "Il corso del tempo in Lucan" at a conference entitled "Il *Bellum Civile* di Lucan, Convegno Internazionale di Studi" and organized by Emanuele Narducci at the Università di Firenze in Florence in March 1999. It was also delivered in English a week earlier at the Department of Greek, Latin, and Ancient History, University of Calgary. Emanuele Narducci (2002, 42 ff.) touches on this same subject usefully in his recent book on Lucan, in a chapter entitled "Lo sfondo cosmico." In this chapter he has two sections, "La fine di Roma e la dissoluzione dell'universo" and "Una catastrophe senza rinascita." Narducci covers some of the same passages as I do, but of course from a different perspective.

35. On the Stoic apparatus of cataclysm, *ecpyrosis*, and *sympatheia* see Lapidge 1979; Schotes 1969 (cf. Goldschmidt 1979). See also Long and Sedley 1987, s.v.; Rist 1969, s.v.

36. See Barton 1993, 55.

37. This prejudice is not just a feature of the popular imagination. It can be seen in contemporary scientific circles: see, for example, Bull's vividly titled 1995 book (*Apocalypse Theory and the Ends of the World*). In respectable popular literature there are works such as Robert Kaplan's bleak *The Ends of the Earth: A Journey at the Dawn of the Twenty-First Century* (1996) (reviewed by Kennedy [1996] as "doomsterism"). A less pertinent, but discursively typical, example (which, while pandering to the mood of catastrophism that became so prominent as we approached the end of the last millennium, offers a hostile perspective) is Arthur Herman's *The Idea of Decline in Western Literature* (1997).

38. On *ecpyrosis* see Fantham 1982 (on Troades, 386–92); Tarrant 1985, 209–10; Rist 1969, 93, 175–76; Sandbach 1975, 78–79.

39. Seneca also refers to a mock funeral, that of Sextus Turannius, at the conclusion of the *De brevitate vitae.*

40. Not everyone was this selfish. Lucan tells us that Pompey, after the battle of Pharsalia, felt no such emotions. Of Pompey Lucan says (7.654–55): "nor, as is the habit of the wretched, did he wish to pull down everything / with him and to mingle the human race with his downfall . . ." Sometimes Claudian *In Rufinum* 2.17 ff. is compared: "what remains unless to confound all things in fresh grief / and to mix the innocent with

my destruction? / I'd like to perish in a destroyed world; universal destruction will provide me with solace for my death." So, too, is Silius Italicus 8.335–37: "he drags everything down with him and fears, fool, that Rome may fall under some other consul."

41. Compare Seneca *Hercules Furens* 178–80: *properat cursu / vita citato volucrique die rota praecipitis vertitur anni* [life hastens on its swift course and the wheel of the racing seasons spins with the swift day].

42. Seneca, in a small poem represented in the *Latin Anthology* (232; a handy translation by Marcus Wilson may be found in Boyle and Sullivan 1991, 391–92), neatly links the one-way course of time ("voracious time consumes it") with "ecpyrotic," catastrophe imagery ("the sky's fair dome will blaze, the flames bursting in a flash") (cf. *Dialogues* 10.10.6.2). I am not attempting to claim, however, that Seneca's era invented this concept of time. What I am saying is that such a view of time became much more common in this period and that its representation seems to be bound discursively with a number of other related emotions (those surveyed in this book). Can we only speak usefully of "tendencies" and "discourse," or, following the lead give us by the evidence of my chapter on acedia, should we speak of real-life attitudes? I favor the latter.

43. The pseudo-Senecan *Octavia* (831 ff.) may be relevant here. It depicts Nero as responsible for this Roman *conflagratio*.

44. See Barton 1993, 55, on this passage. Barton usefully links *Natural Questions* 6.2.9 (*si cadendum est, cadam orbe concusso* [if perish I must, let the whole world perish with me]). See, too, Leeman 1971 (*Toderlebnis* in Seneca).

45. Hardie (1986, 381; cf. Feeney 1991, 276) notes, "whereas the *Aeneid* is a poem about the creation of a universe, the *Bellum Civile* is about the destruction of a universe"; Feeney (1991, 278) suggests that the destruction of the Republic is a catastrophe of cosmic proportions.

46. In a much earlier version of portions of this chapter, I finished things with the following curious piece of evidence for this periodical continuity. Think back to Trimalchio's trumpeting timepiece and the life span allotted to him by an astrologer, which the trumpet and the doomsday clock announced. Some years ago, in the *Sydney Morning Herald* (September 1, 1994, 21), I found the following report (I will let it speak for itself):

> A clock which forecasts how long someone has to live is being sold in the United States. Based on the average life span—74 years for men and 79 for women—it is programmed with the owner's age and gender and calculates his or her remaining hours and minutes.

CHAPTER 7

1. For discussions and analyses of this pot see, among others, Hurwitt 1985, 260–61; Kurke 1999, 261 ff. (with bibliography).

2. Kurke (1999, 261) notes: "most archaeologists have speculated that the image may have a literary source in an episode from one of the cyclic epics . . . Instead, I would suggest that the scene is invented in the sixth century as part of the civic appropriation of the

Trojan War story—an attempt to translate the heroes of epic into the context of the polis." That would go some distance toward explaining the fact that Achilles and Ajax wear hoplite armor. Kurke goes on to observe (263), "In content and in style, the image affirms that the heroes are played in the game of civic warfare, even as they play on the board between them."

3. Achilles dominates Ajax in height (the helmet places him above Ajax) and in the game itself. Inscribed on the pot are the current scores—four to Achilles and three to Ajax.

4. Mingazzini (1966) suggests that the heroes are so absorbed in their game that they have forgotten to return to battle.

5. The description by Hurwitt (1985, 260–61) is enormously helpful and should be used to supplement what I have to say.

6. Whether or not the same theme is preserved on the reverse side of the amphora deserves consideration. This preserves for us a family scene of the Dioscuroi—Pollux patting a horse, Castor patting a dog—in company with their parents, Tyndareus and Leda. A slave boy is present between Pollux and Tyndareus. Does the pacific nature of this family scene contrast (as does Achilles' and Ajax's game with the Trojan War) with the more normally violent and martial activities in which the Tyndaridae were usually involved?

7. The poignancy of the juxtaposition of Achilles and Ajax is achieved in yet another way. Ajax's death results from that of Achilles. When he was, soon after Achilles' death, denied the arms of Achilles in favor of Odysseus, the disappointment and shame of that decision led him to suicide. Hurwitt (1985, 260–61) also stresses the element of fate played out in this picture.

8. Part of the pleasure of this game results, initially, from its purposelessness but also because, requiring considerable concentration, it distracts and because it requires social interaction with another individual.

9. Compare the definitions offered by Toner (1995, 17–21) and Argyle (1996, 3–4). Exekias's formulation of leisure is probably as close as we can come to a beneficial and therapeutic ideal—see Argyle 1996, 79–106.

10. Argyle (1996), like many psychologists and sociologists, allows leisure to be what people want it to be—or, at any rate, what they say it is. Such catholicity opens a Pandora's box of definitional woes. Hence, for example, religion is assessed as a very significant leisure activity. While religious observance may be therapeutic for some, it is normally performed with an end in mind, that of personal salvation. On such grounds we might as well consider bricklaying as a leisure activity because Winston Churchill found it such a restorative weekend activity. For weekday laborers it certainly represents personal salvation.

11. I admit, in this instance, to be attempting to be prescriptive, rather than descriptive, of leisure. Argyle (1996, 159) attempts to describe what is satisfying in leisure as follows: "The most satisfying forms of leisure have some of the features of work: they involve varied and meaningful activities, use of skills, serious commitment to goals, and membership of cohesive working groups." Argyle's results, by and large, are based on questionnaires that ask subjects to rate the degree of pleasure they obtained from various leisure activities.

12. There are sociological determinants for a person's choice. A sedentary form of leisure is more appealing, no doubt, to a person whose work is more physically demanding. The converse may be true for sedentary academics.

13. Argyle (1996) stresses the therapeutic benefits associated with interactive or community leisure activities.

14. Mark Golden suggests here a comparison with A. Guttman's suggestively titled *A Whole New Ball Game.*

15. My intention is not to adjudicate upon the universal validity of such a definition of leisure as I have just outlined but, rather, to suggest that it is helpful for looking at the various representatives of didactic epic. The concept I have suggested is, admittedly, elitist and is ultimately founded upon a culture where the division between work and leisure is pronounced, where work is something done for you, usually by a servant or, worse, by a slave, and where a tolerably high level of intellectual attainment is the norm.

16. Gardening is a particular example. I have some very brief comments on this matter in Toohey 1996.

17. Ovid, in *Tristia* 2, refers to considerable amounts of ancient literature devoted to other subjects related to this topic. He refers, at *Tristia* 2.471 ff., to the work of other poets in this genre—in didactic poems on dice games, ball games, swimming, playing with the hoop, cosmetics, feasting, and potting.

18. In my *Epic Lessons* (Toohey 1996) I argued that didactic epic underwent six phases of development. Each of these display a notable "attitude" toward how time ought to be occupied. They may provide, therefore, a schematic basis for an understanding of its change.

1. The oral phase was associated with Hesiod (his *Works and Days,* an instructional poem written some time in the eighth century B.C.E.) and with the pre-Socratic philosophers Xenophanes (active probably toward the middle of the sixth century B.C.E.), Parmenides (ca. 515–?450 B.C.E.), and Empedocles (a Sicilian who lived in the first half of the fifth century B.C.E., ca. 495–35). This didactic poetry is rigorously instructional.
2. The Hellenistic phase is exemplified by the writing on astronomy of Aratus (active in the first half of the third century B.C.E.; his verse *Phaenomena* tells us about the significance of star signs and weather signs and survives in 1,154 lines) and by the writing of Nicander (born in Colophon, perhaps a century after Aratus) on poisons and poisonous creatures.
3. The third phase of the extant literature is represented by an early Roman "reinvention" of the genre. So Cicero (107/6–43 B.C.E.) produced a verse translation of Aratus and Lucretius composed his monolithic poem *On the Universe* (Lucretius lived ca. 98–55 B.C.E.).
4. The fourth phase is typified by Virgil's *Georgics* (composed between 36 and 29 B.C.E.) and by Ovid's *Fasti* (composed, probably, between 2 B.C.E. and 14 C.E.; this six-book poem looks at the Roman calendar). This phase is the most complex. The representative poets produce "polyphonic" texts of marked density (playing private, public, and "ludic" voices against one another).
5. In the fifth phase the texture of didactic epic seems to thin. The instructional medium is both a leisure pursuit in itself and instructs on matters associated with leisure time. Representative poets are Horace in his *Ars poetica* and Ovid in his various instructive poems on love. We read this poetry not as mere instructional text but also as a clever, playful, and entertaining artifact in its own right.

6. Most of the literature of the sixth phase aims at a reconciliation with a supreme being. (There are many representatives of the poetry of this phase: for example, Germanicus's version of Aratus; Manilius's poem on astrology; Columella on farming; the *Aetna* and its volcanic lore; and, on hunting, Grattius, Oppian, and Nemesianus). In this phase didactic poetry aims to curb instinct and to provide privilege for a learned behavior or reason *(ratio)* in which may be detected the manifestation of divine will.

19. There were prose tracts on hunting, such as Xenophon's and Arrian's *Cynegetica* or passages within Pollux's *Onomasticon.* (These, along with a very engaging and practical evaluation of their advice on technique, are provided in Hull 1964.) Instructional prose tracts have their own agendas and generic laws. Didactic poetry, something with which I am familiar, has a more discrete and graspable agenda.

20. The translation is taken from Anderson 1985, 150.

21. The interest spills over into other areas. Ovid's didactic poems on love not unexpectedly analogize the pursuit of the opposite sex with hunting. Nicander's strange pharmacological poems on dangerous creatures also touch on this theme. See also Schnapp 1997.

22. Fishing is as much hunting as was hunting with dogs (see Longo 1989, 12), though Plato did view it as banausic, and (as Longo shows) it had none of the prestige of hunting with dogs. Fowling may be compared with fishing.

23. Animal lore was popular in this era: see Beagon 1992, 124 ff.

24. Oppian (*Cynegetica* 2.7, 2.31 ff.) describes them thus; compare Athenaeus *Deipnosophists* 1.13.

25. Barringer's *The Hunt in Ancient Greece* (2001) appeared too late for me to be able to use it within the formulation of this chapter.

26. Quoted by Anderson (1985, 17).

27. This was the case in Rome (Anderson 1985, 88) despite Augustus's predilection for angling (Anderson 1985, 85).

28. So popular did this become, in fact, that it developed into a spectator sport. At Caesar's triumph of 46 B.C.E., for example, four hundred lions, Thessalian bulls, and a giraffe were hunted publicly in the arena.

29. The ideology of hunting can be turned on its head—in, for example, the famous Nile scenes of pygmies hunting. Their study in this context and in the context of Roman conceptions of leisure would be extremely fruitful.

30. Anderson (1985) is right on this point, pace Shackleton-Bailey (1993, 1: 77 n.b.)

31. That Ovid wrote this poem is denied by Wilkinson (1955, 363), for example.

32. Some of this can be deduced from examining the topical structure of the poem (following de Saint-Denis 1975; cf. Richmond 1962): (I) every animal has its means of self-protection (vv. 1–9); (II) fish protect themselves by *ars* (vv. 10–48); (III) land animals protect themselves through *timor* or *non sana ferocia;* racing horses may be compared, but dogs seem to exhibit a measure of *sagax virtus* (vv. 49–81); (IV) where to hunt for fish (vv. 82–93); (V) a list of fish that may be hunted (vv. 94–134: deep-sea fish, vv. 94–117; coastal fish, vv. 118–34). To judge from this summary, Ovid is less interested in instruction (of which the poem possesses little) than in play and in dramatizing a contrast between learned and instinctual behavior.

33. I should stress again here the usefulness of the monograph by Longo (1989).

34. The principle of self-understanding (albeit of a limited form) is stated at vv. 8–9: "assistance is given to understand the force and limit of their own weapon." This knowledge is vouchsafed by adversity: "all gain assistance in understanding their enemy."

35. The wording for "conscious of" is *conscius . . . sibi,* which is very close to *conscius sui,* a synonym for *notitia sui,* our tag for "self-consciousness" or "self."

36. Ovid's Narcissus might be both compared and contrasted.

37. I am not suggesting for a moment that Ovid took his cue concerning leisure from Exekias. There are a limited number of manners by which leisure is conceptualized and practiced. I am suggesting merely that Ovid's concept matches that of Exekias.

38. Ovid produced three poems of this sort: first the handbook on makeup for women (the incomplete *Medicamina faciei femineae* [Cosmetics for the female complexion], 2–1 B.C.E.), then three books of versified instruction on methods of seduction (the *Ars amatoria* [The art of loving], 2 B.C.E.–1 C.E.—on the dating see Murgia 1986; Sharrock 1994, 18), followed by a single book on how to cure oneself of love (*Remedia amoris* [Remedies for love], 1 or 2 C.E.).

39. The summary here is drawn from Toohey 1996, 162–63.

40. The difference between Ovid's presentation of love and the other presentations seen so far could be explained as follows: When love, as we have seen it in chapter 2, is unconsummated, one has recourse first to persuasion. If persuasion is unsuccessful, one turns to violence. Only in some situations are neither persuasion nor violence applicable. Frustrated love may also lead to a melancholic lovesickness—anorexia and eventual death—of the sort that we take for granted in modern literature and in felt experience. In Ovid's love didactic, amatory frustration is seldom seen to extend to such a level. Ovid stops short with persuasion. So the *Ars amatoria* and the *Remedia amoris* aim to instruct lovers in the art of amatory persuasion. On all of this see Toohey 1997a.

41. See Toohey 1997a for a more full discussion of this matter.

42. That didactic poetry had taken on this ludic function for Ovid, as I have stated often elsewhere, is made most evident at *Tristia* 2.491 ff., where he writes off his amatory didactic work as mere entertainment. In this passage Ovid states that his didactic verse represents parlor games for winter. That they bear scant relationship to life and that they were understood that way is indicated when Ovid asserts (2.492), "nobody was ruined by composing them."

43. The *Ars* thus gains much of its force from its therapeutic value. "Subversive," anti-Augustan readings, it is worth observing, flatten and attempt to render Ovid's poetry purposeful. This is exactly what Augustus might have wanted—but from the right wing, as it were.

44. Ovid may have parodied this dull poem in his didactic *Ars amatoria* (so suggests Hollis 1973, 91). He may also have parodied it in the *Halieutica.*

45. The following schema of Grattius's *Cynegetica* will give some idea of its topics: (I) the huntsman's equipment (vv. 1–149): (i) nets and ropes (vv. 24–60), (ii) eulogy of the chase (vv. 1–74), (iii) the ingenious hunter Dercylus (vv. 95–110), (iv) weapons (vv. 111–26), especially spears (vv. 127–49); (II) dogs (vv. 150–496): (i) various breeds (vv. 150–212), (ii) the hunter Hagnon (vv. 213–62), (iii) mating (vv. 263–84), (iv) pups (vv. 285–300) and their feeding (vv. 301–9), (v) deleterious *luxuria* (vv. 310–25) contrasted with discipline (vv.

326–35), (vi) how to dress for the hunt (vv. 336–43), (vii) wounds, disease, and plague (vv. 344–496); (III) horses: (i) the various breeds (vv. 497–541).

46. This paragraph and the one to follow are drawn from Toohey 1996, 198–99.

47. There can be no doubt that Grattius was writing about leisure, as he saw it. His conception of hunting is not as a sustenance-producing or farming activity. It is pursued for pleasure and during free time. Yet his underlying understanding of the social significance of hunting was inherently practical. Grattius's hunting seems to have an end outside or beyond itself, that of the affirmation of the values to be associated with empire and, with this, Roman civilization and societal order, as least as Grattius understood these.

48. Referring to one "Oppian" may be misleading, for it is often claimed that there were two (Hollis 1994; Hopkinson 1994). There was the Oppian of Cilicia, the author of five books of a *Halieutica* (On fishing matters) in Greek, likely dedicated to the Roman emperor Marcus Aurelius (ruled 161–80 C.E.). There may also have been an Oppian of Syria, who has left us four books in Greek of a *Cynegetica* dedicated to the Roman emperor Caracalla (ruled 211–17 C.E.; Caracalla is reported to have paid a piece of gold for each verse of this poem).

49. This is not very far at all from Grattius's imperialistic vision of hunting.

50. Nemesianus has also left us four pastoral poems (traditionally attributed to Calpurnius Siculus) as well as twenty-eight lines from a didactic poem on fowling (looking at two birds, the *tetrax* and the snipe).

51. It may help to have some idea of the structure and contents of his poem. They run as follows: (I) proem (vv. 1–102): (i) introduction (vv. 1–14), (ii) rejection of mythological themes (vv. 15–47), (iii) Nemesianus prefers to deal with hunting (vv. 48–62), (iv) soon he will eulogize Carinus and Numerianus (vv. 63–85), (v) invocation of Diana (vv. 86–102); (II) dogs (vv. 103–239): (i) selecting dogs for breeding (vv. 102–22), (ii) selecting suitable puppies from the litter (vv. 123–50), (iii) feeding the puppies (vv. 151–76), (iv) training the pups (vv. 177–92), (v) treating growing dogs' illnesses (vv. 193–223), (vi) other breeds (vv. 224–39); (III) horses (vv. 240–98): (i) horses for hunting (vv. 240–78), (ii) raising such horses in their first year (vv. 279–98); (IV) hunting equipment: (i) nets and snares (vv. 299–320); (V) hunting (vv. 321–35), (i) hunting season (vv. 321–25; the text breaks off at v. 325).

52. This topic of watching will be addressed again in chapter 8. See also Leigh 1997.

CHAPTER 8

1. On Hostius Quadra see Citroni Marchetti 1991, 153–61; Barton 1993, 159 f.; Leitao 1998. For a very different reading see Walters 1998.

2. The murder of a master by his slaves was unusual and not often recorded. Pliny (*Epistles* 3.4) records the death of Larius Macedo in such a manner, and Tacitus (*Annals* 14.42–45) records that of Pedanius Secundus (cf. *CIL* 13.7070). I owe these references to Professor Kelly Olson.

3. Sandra Citroni Marchetti (1991, 156) reminds us that Hostius Quadra's long gaze upon himself is not unlike that of Narcissus. The parallel is of striking significance, as Narcissus's death evoked one of the first examples, I have argued in chapter 2, of depressive love melancholy. Hostius Quadra's antics almost seem to parody those of Ovid's Narcissus. I

have reproduced within this chapter a Roman version of Narcissus's gazing longingly into the reflective waters of the spring (fig. 9). This version does not downplay the sexuality (and the sexual ambivalence) of the myth. There is Narcissus's nudity, his strangely feminine groin, the phallic staff that he carries. Are we to sense that his corporeal and sexual fulfillment resides only outside himself, in that mirror? (Barton [1993, 105], citing Disalvo [1980], speaks of Narcissus, through his gaze into the mirror surface of the spring, as being lost to himself. My point is directly the reverse.)

4. On ancient mirrors and their cultural context see Frontisi-Ducroux and Vernant (1998); for a different and modern view see Gregory 1997.

5. What Tom McCarthy (1998) states of Klossowski's *Sade mon prochain* (1947) is helpful in this context, though in an obverse manner: "This interpretation holds that rationalism, although atheistic, represents no more than a secular version of monotheism because of its affirmation of the sovereignty of man. Sade 'liquidating the norms of reason,' detonates a semiotic—not to mention moral—bomb within this rationalism, both derationalizing atheism and at the same time rationalizing a monstrosity whose central sign is sodomy. Sade's goal, Klossowski tells us, is the 'disintegration of man' and Klossowski's aim, as that book's translator, Alfred Lingis points out (1991), is the extrapolation from Sade's pedagogic demonstrations of a 'programmatic Sadean logic.' Klossowski, apart from his metaphorical interest in sodomy as a symbol for the destruction of a socially sanctioned form of selfhood, is also very keen on mirrors—'as means by which selves are split, stolen, and multiplied.'" It needs to be pointed out, especially as I shall cite, in the next section of this chapter, Lacan (who was influenced by Klossowski), that I take mirrors and sodomy to create an effect that is the complete reverse. Klossowski speaks of an illusory or fragmented self; I speak of one reinforced. The continuity of the imagery, however, is startling.

6. The topic of reading deserves a chapter of its own. I have discussed aspects of this in Toohey 1994 and Toohey 1996. As has been argued by writers as diverse as Steiner (1994) and Lévi-Strauss (1961, 292: "the primary function of the invention of writing, as a means of communication, is to facilitate the enslavement of other human beings"), writing can be used to establish control and the exercise of power (see too Petrucci 1993). Svenbro (1993) makes much of the identity that can exist between speaker and text and between text and referent (cf. Steiner 1994, 100). Reading (and, with this, literacy) can represent an alienating experience (Carothers 1959; Toohey 1994; Steiner 1994, 100) perhaps because of the fissure that it so emphasizes between words and their referents, the self and the world. This fissure became particularly important in the Hellenistic period, with its stress on the ocular, rather than the auditory, aspects of reading, communication, and the interpretation of signs *(semata)* (see Bing 1988). I have argued that the alienating aspects of this form of communication are notably captured in the poetry of Nicander (Toohey 1996, 64–77). In Toohey 1994 I attempt to link this with Jason's persuasory habits. What does this have to do with Hostius Quadra? The emphasis on him in Seneca's *fabella* stresses the sense of alienation implicit in this fissure between words and their referents.

7. It will be obvious that my formulation of the discovery of self in Hostius Quadra's actions is indebted to Lacan's famous, though bizarre, idea of the emergence of the ego through an infantile "mirror stage." This useful summary of Lacan's concept (far simpler than the explanations of the great man himself) may be found in Benvenuto and Kennedy 1986, 54–55. The original article is Lacan 1977.

8. As is often asked, what if an infant never encounters a mirror? Will the infant then develop no ego? This simple objection ruins—or seems to ruin—Lacan's speculative drift. But his description of the encounter with the mirror may make a valid metaphorical point. I recently watched a repeat of one of the issues of Dr. Jonathan Miller's medical series *The Body in Question*. He interviewed a woman whose spinal nerve, the one connecting leg motion to the brain, had been severed. The woman explained to Dr. Miller that the only way she could arrange her legs was in a mirror (she had no sensation in them at all). Viewing them directly, with her own eyes, provided a distorted picture. To sense them as real and as manageable, she and Miller agreed, they had to be perceived and even acted upon as if they were other. (Is this how Hostius Quadra saw himself?) I would suggest that Miller's subject neatly challenges the romantic Lacanian notion of the illusory nature of the self. It hints, rather, that we understand ourselves through distance.

9. The conclusions that I draw, however, are un-Lacanian. The personality formed through the mirror stage in his system is ultimately fragmented, decentered, and unstable. I have suggested that it is alienated merely in the senses of being painfully conscious of itself and its separateness from the world and from others and of being painfully conscious of the fissure between perception and reality. The body becomes wholly other to the mental registering of the world.

10. The excellent book on Lucan by Leigh (1997) has much that is instructive on this topic of "viewing." (See also Barton 1993.) Leigh's reviewer Katherine Eldred (1998) suggests that his comments might be supplemented by the following references: "See, for example, J. Rose (1986) *Sexuality in the Field of Vision* (London) or S. Zizek, and R. Salecl (eds.) (1996) *Gaze and Voice and Love Objects* (Durham, London); here too Freud on perverse forms of viewing and Lacan on the gaze are crucial."

11. The following references may be of some assistance in the interpretation of the term *notitia sui* in this context: Diogenes Laertius 2.33; Plutarch *Advice to Bride and Groom*. 25, p. 141 d; Stobaeus *Florilegium* 2.31.98 and 3.1.72, concerning Demetrios of Phaleros; Galen *Protreptieus* 8, p. 10. 15 Kaibel; J. P. Postgate, "Phaedrus 3.8.14 ff. and Seneca," *Classical Review* 33 (1919): 19; Apuleius *Apologia* 14–15. I thank Emanuele Narducci for providing me with these references.

12. Think of Miller's interviewee (see n. 8). Her legs—part of her, that is—became controllable through mirror recognition.

13. A very good reproduction of this Narcissus (and one other) can be found in Guillaud and Guillaud 1990, plate 302.

14. The background is nondescript (as indeed is the technique of this whole painting). There is a forest to the right behind Narcissus. To his left rear, in the distance, is a pair of rocky crags. To his more immediate left is a large, flat-topped rock.

15. For the vagina represented, alarmingly, as a mere slash see Jacobelli 1995, plate 5.

16. Another source of confusion is this: does the javelin suggest that Narcissus is resting after hunting? Or does the garland suggest that he has just come from a party? Does this indeterminacy reflect a town-and-country opposition?

17. The ambivalence, or duality, is also mirrored by the twinned crags in the background.

18. Guillaud and Guillaud (1990, plates 278–79 [Pompeii IX 1, 7]) reproduce the remarkable painting of Thetis visiting Hephaestus and examining the arms that are being

made for her son, Achilles. Thetis is staring intently at her own image mirrored in the shield that is to become Achilles'. It is, as the Guillaud's remark, a very melancholy picture, as these arms prefigure Achilles' death. Thetis stares hard at herself in the shield mirror, puzzling at her identity, at her self. The knowledge denied to her is apparent to us. She is conniving at the death of her son. Her "mirror stage" is made known only to the viewer.

19. Ovid (*Metamorphoses* 3.348) gives some stress to the idea of self-awareness in Narcissus's case. When Narcissus was born, his parents consulted a soothsayer and inquired as to whether the boy would have a long life. The reply was yes "unless he knows himself" *[si se non noverit]*. Ovid's phrase inverts the Delphian advice "Know thyself."

20. I have not yet seen Gély-Gherida 2000.

21. Two articles that I have not yet been able to obtain but that may offer some pertinent comments on the relationship between Narcissus and Lacanian thought are Levine 1996 and Bosworth 1997.

22. Milowicki (1996) argues of Ovid's version that two influential views of the self are presented in the persons of Teiresias (who provides Narcissus's introduction, as it were) and Narcissus. The tale of Narcissus captures the desire to replicate the self (a depressive version?), while the tale of Teiresias suggests the possibilities of extending or expanding the self (a manic version?).

23. Once again I must repeat that I am describing the literary conceptualizing of these conditions. That tradition did not understand genes.

24. Nussbaum (1994, 90, 91, 101, 69) provides a very interesting understanding of anger (and hence violence). Following Aristotle, she sees in humans a gap between the emotion of anger and its acting out. She believes (101) that emotions are shaped through beliefs, not through some mindless affective drive. (It is hard to identify with her position after Rwanda, Bosnia, Albania, and the Congo—not to mention more recent events.) Nussbaum (69), following Aristotle *Eudemian Ethics* 1.3 (1214b28ff.), seems to except children and the insane from this position. (Cf. Melanie Klein's belief that what is normal in a child may be psychotic in an adult.) Nussbaum suggests (79) that grief and anger are not animal emotions; she cites to this end Lutz 1988 and Kenny 1963. (Animals do, however, feel grief—see Jamal 1998. We choose to deny them this experience, just as we might deny early Greeks or preimperial Romans boredom and melancholy. Linguistic absence points only to a discursive void, not to an inability to register the emotion.)

25. For Dido see *Aeneid* 4.300–303; for Medea, Valerius Flaccus *Argonautica* 7.300–322.

26. Solomon (2001, 257) suggests that such frustration can lead, at least in the case of the octopus, to suicide.

27. Sandbach (1975, 60) points out that a dog smells something and reacts, whereas a human being must assent. Nussbaum (1994, 247) provides an interesting discussion on the extent to which humans do not react in the animal manner. For what it is worth, I think that Nussbaum overestimates the capacity of most people for even minimal self-reflection or self-analysis. For many people, there is little between them and their emotions (however slight these may be) and their being acted out, other than the ingrained societal sanction of the superego. Many of the people I know are like this. (I include myself in this group. I have read that Montaigne claimed that he had little control over himself and his moods, adding, for good measure, that he had a poor memory; that is a comfort.)

28. Once again I would like to stress that my distinction represents a heuristic and ana-

lytic device rather than a stone-graven historical truth. History is far too open-ended and rebarbative to allow the absolute applicability of such a simple distinction.

29. See Basedow 1929, 175–79.

30. See Heliodorus *Aethiopica* 3.7–9 and Callimachus's description of Cydippe in *Aetia* fr. 75.12–20.

31. See Cannon 1942, 1957; Lévi-Strauss 1963.

32. Narcissus obviously could not negotiate this fissure. This led to his death.

33. See Richlin 1997 for a pungent analysis of these attitudes. There is also now Hallet and Skinner 1997.

34. On hysteria see Showalter 1997; Micale 1994; Gilman et al. 1993. For a more anthropological perspective on some of these hysterical conditions see Lewis 1971; La Barre 1972. Compare also Cohn 1957. (Sargant 1957, though very dated, is still instructive on some of these matters—the illustrations are marvelous. On classical matters there is Nock's 1933 classic *Conversion*).

35. For some other works on self-awareness see Lautner 1994; Syed 1997.

36. Autism and schizophrenia, in Laingian terms, read as a social protest. This is even more clear in the case of multiple personality disorder or repressed memory syndrome (cf. Ross 1994).

37. In the cases of Hostius Quadra and Narcissus it resulted in death.

38. See Barton 1993, 98 ff. on the "gaze"; 91 ff. on the "eye." On the "gaze" writ large see Barton 1993, 104 f.

39. Even the postmodern "fragmented" personality is, after all, but alienation writ large or run rampant. (Ross 1994 is interesting on applied fragmentation, as it were. I am in no position to comment on this matter other than to commend Hacking's 1995 book.) The concept of self that we see emerging in the post-Senecan world—the perception of the self as another—held sway until recently. We have since seen it argued (at least in the 1990s) that personality, rather than being reified or alienated, has become fragmented. So we see a disintegration of self. The conceptual step from the watched, alienated self to the "fragmented" personality is a simple step. (On the fragmented personality see Benvenuto and Kennedy 1986, 122. Cf. Greene 1995 for an interesting classical perspective on fragmentation; Greene uses the term *fragmentation*, however, more in the sense of conflict.)

APPENDIX

1. De Chirico often complains about his digestion (see Baldacci 1997, 53, 106). In Paris in 1911 he took a cure in an attempt to settle his severe intestinal disorder (Soby 1955, 36) while at the same time complaining of a nervous disorder that he explained as an "extreme crisis of melancholy" (Soby 1955, 34).

2. The wraith bears a striking resemblance to the figure of Death in Arnold Böcklin's *Die Toteninsel* of 1880. A reproduction of this picture can be found as plate 45 in Burger 1977.

3. Baldacci (1997, 26) suggests that this is its first appearance as a motif in de Chirico's painting.

4. Baldacci (1997, 126) links the painting to this experience.

5. The train appears again in *The Lassitude of the Infinite* (1912), reproduced later in this appendix. There the train rushes toward infinity and death. Time and death are symbolized by the motif of the tower.

6. That is provided for us in a very strange and hauntingly erotic painting by Mario Sironi, the Fascist apologist. His painting (reproduced in Braun 2000, plate V; Parks 2000, 32) was painted seven or eight years later than those of de Chirico. It is entitled *Melancholy* and depicts a nude woman, the figure of melancholy, seated in a devastated landscape. Time seems drawn into this picture, not merely through the depiction of catastrophe, but also through the egglike object (the beginning of time?) at which this sad but menacing woman stares so intently. Hers, too, is a hard, repellent, yet provocative, nudity. Eros, thus, is blended with Sironi's evocation of melancholy, time, and catastrophe. It is a terrible vision of eros. There can be little wonder that Sironi became an apologist for Mussolini. Braun (2000, 68 ff.) has written an interesting chapter entitled "Melancholy and the Modern Allegory" that aims to place Sironi's conception within the intellectual *entre-guerre* milieu.

7. Böcklin has at least three paintings entitled *Melancholia*. Reproductions of these may be found in Andree 1977 as plates 253 (1871), 338 (1879), and, most notably, 474 (1900). There is no reason to assume that de Chirico would not have known these paintings.

8. The term literally implies a journey of some form or another. This "theme of the journey" is as important in de Chirico's painting (the trains and the chips are constantly coming and going) as it is in his life (see Baldacci 1997, 128): de Chirico's illicit journey from Turin to escape the military authorities, for example, caused him much anguish (and has been linked to the vertiginous perspectives of the paintings of this era). For further references on the theme of nostalgia see the next note.

9. On the topic of nostalgia see Davis 1979; Boym 2001. Compare in addition the medical discussions of Brunnert 1984; Heuser 1994. Sultan 1999 deserves comparison.

10. The sea vista over which the Odysseus figure gazes from the heights of the oracle's room no doubt owes something to the deep valley below Apollo's temple at Delphi.

11. Note how close the figure in figures 14–15 is to those which we could describe as Calypso-like.

12. So she is also in the naturalistic version of her that de Chirico painted in *Ariadne Abandoned* in 1931–32 (reproduced as plate 9 in de Sanna 1998).

13. Braun 2000, 68 ff., on de Chirico's friend Sironi, is very helpful on the thematics of this period.

Bibliography

Abraham, Carolyn. 2001. "Do Girls Think Better than Boys?" *Globe and Mail,* November 26.

Ackerknecht, E. H. 1959. *A Short History of Psychiatry.* Trans. S. Wolff. New York: Hafner Publishing.

Adams, Francis, ed. and trans. 1844–47. *The Seven Books of Paulus Aegineta.* 3 vols. London: Sydenham Society.

Adams, Francis, ed. and trans. 1856. *The Extant Works of Aretaeus, the Cappadocian.* London: Sydenham Society.

Alford, C. Fred. 1991. *The Self in Social Theory: A Psychoanalytic Account of Its Construction in Plato, Hobbes, Locke, Rawls, and Rousseau.* New Haven: Yale University Press

Allen, Peter Lewis. 2000. *The Wages of Sin: Sex and Disease, Past and Present.* Chicago: University of Chicago Press.

Alvarez, A. 1971. *The Savage God: A Study of Suicide.* London: Weidenfeld and Nicolson.

Amigues, Suzanne. 1999. "Note sur 'l'ellebore blanc' de Dioscoride, IV, 148." *Révue de Philologie* 73:7–14.

Anderson, J. K. 1985. *Hunting in the Ancient World.* Berkeley: University of California Press.

André, J. M. 1962. *Récherches sur l'otium romain.* Paris: "Les Belles Lettres."

André, J. M. 1966. *L'otium dans la vie morale et intellectuelle romaine, des origines à l'époque augustéene.* Paris: Presses Universitaires de France.

Andree, Rolf. 1977. *Arnold Böcklin: Die Gemälde.* Basel: Friedrich Reinhardt Verlag.

Angst, Jules, and Andreas Marneros. 2001. "Bipolarity from Ancient to Modern Times: Conception, Birth, and Rebirth." *Journal of Affective Disorders* 67:3–19.

Arbesmann, R. 1958. "The *Daemonium Meridianum* and Greek Patristic Exegesis." *Traditio* 14:17–31.

Argyle, Michael. 1996. *The Social Psychology of Leisure.* Harmondsworth: Penguin Books.

Arias, Paolo Enrico. 1962. *A History of One Thousand Years of Greek Vase Painting.* Trans. B. Shefton. London: Thames and Hudson.

Arnim, Hans Friedrich August von. 1964. *Stoicorum Veterum Fragmenta.* 4 vols. Reprint, Leipzig: Teubner.

Arrowsmith, William. 1966. "Luxury and Death in the *Satyricon.*" *Arion* 5, no. 1:304–31.

Aveni, Anthony F. 1989. *Empires of Time: Calendars, Clocks, and Culture.* New York: Basic Books.

Aymard, Jacques. 1951. *Essai sur les chasses romaines des origines à la fin du siècle des Antonins (Cynegetica).* Paris: Boccard.

"A Bad Case of Lovin' You." 1997. *Sunday Telegraph*, September 14, 40.

Baehrens, E. 1914. *Poetae Latini Minores*. Vol. 5. Leipzig: Teubner.

Bail, Murray. 1980. *Homesickness*. Melbourne: Macmillan.

Bailey, Cyril. 1947. *Titi Lucreti Cari De Rerum Natura Libri Sex*. 3 vols. Oxford: Clarendon Press.

Baker, R. J. 1981. "Propertius' *Monobiblos* and Catullus 51." *Rheinisches Museum* 124:312–24.

Baker, R. J. 1989. "Well Begun, Half Done: *Otium* at Catullus 51.13 and Ennius, *Iphigenia*." *Mnemosyne* 42:492–97.

Baker, R. J. 1990. *Propertius I*. Armidale: University of New England Publishing Unit.

Baldacci, Paolo. 1997. *De Chirico: The Metaphysical Period, 1888–1919*. Boston: Little, Brown, and Company.

Balsdon, J. P. V. D. 1969. *Life and Leisure in Ancient Rome*. New York: McGraw-Hill.

Barringer, Judith M. 2001. *The Hunt in Ancient Greece*. Baltimore: Johns Hopkins University Press.

Bartley, Adam. 2000. "The Digressions and Similes of the *Halieutica* and *Cynegetica*." Ph.D. diss., University of Sydney.

Barton, Carlin A. 1993. *Sorrows of the Ancient Romans: The Gladiator and the Monster*. Princeton: Princeton University Press.

Basedow, Herbert. 1929. *The Australian Aboriginal*. Reprint, Adelaide: F. W. Preece and Sons.

Basham, A. L. 1967. *The Wonder That Was India*. 3d ed. London: Sidgwick and Jackson.

Baumeister, Roy F. 1986. *Identity: Cultural Change and the Struggle for Self*. New York: Oxford University Press.

Baur, Susan. 1988. *Hypochondria: Woeful Imaginings*. Berkeley: University of California Press.

Beagon, Mary. 1992. *Roman Nature: The Thought of Pliny the Elder*. Oxford: Clarendon Press.

Beazley, J. D. 1963. *Attic Red-Figure Vase Painters*. 3 vols. Oxford: Clarendon Press.

Beecher, Donald A., and Massimo Ciavolella, eds. and trans. 1990. *A Treatise on Lovesickness: Jacques Ferrand*. Syracuse, N.Y.: Syracuse University Press.

Benvenuto, Bice, and Roger Kennedy. 1986. *The Works of Jacques Lacan: An Introduction*. London: Free Association.

Bernstein, Haskell. 1975. "Boredom and the Ready-Made Life." *Social Research* 42:512–37.

Bettini, Maurizio. 1991. *Anthropology and Roman Culture: Kinship, Times, Images of the South*. Trans. John Van Sickle Baltimore: John Hopkins University Press.

Beye, Charles Rowan. 1982. *Epic and Romance in the "Argonautica" of Apollonius*. Carbondale and Edwardsville: Southern Illinois University Press.

Bickerman, Elias, ed. 1972. *Le culte des souverains dans l'empire romain: Sept exposés suivis de discussions*. Entretiens preparés et presidés par Willem den Boer. Vandoeuvres-Genève: Fondation Hardt.

Biersterfeldt, Hans Hinrich, and Dimitri Gutas. 1984. "The Malady of Love." *Journal of the American Oriental Society* 104:21–57.

Bing, Peter. 1988. *The Well-Read Muse: Present and Past in Callimachus and the Hellenistic Poets*. Göttingen: Vandenhoeck and Ruprecht.

Bloomfield, M. W. 1952. *The Seven Deadly Sins: An Introduction to the History of a Religious*

Concept, with Special Reference to Medieval English Literature. East Lansing: Michigan State College Press.

Bond, G. W. 1981. *Euripides: "Heracles."* Oxford: Clarendon Press.

Booth, Joan. 1997. "All in the Mind: Sickness in Catullus 76." In *The Passions in Roman Thought and Literature*, ed. Susanna Morton Braund and Christopher Gill, 150–68. Cambridge: Cambridge University Press.

Borgna, Eugenio. 1991. "L'esperienza del tempo nella malinconia." In Dolfi 1991, 33–52.

Borst, Arno. 1993. *The Ordering of Time: From Ancient Computus to the Modern Computer.* Trans. Andrew Winnard. Chicago: University of Chicago Press.

Bosworth, David. 1997. "Echo and Narcissus: The Fearful Logic of Postmodern Thought." *Georgia Review* 51:409–437.

Bouchez, Madelaine. 1973. *L'ennui: De Sénèque à Moravia.* Paris: Bordas.

Bourdieu, Pierre. 1996. *The Rules of Art: Genesis and Structure of the Literary Field.* Trans. Susan Emanuel. Stanford: Stanford University Press.

Bowersock, G. W. 1995. *Martyrdom and Rome.* Cambridge: Cambridge University Press.

Boyle, A. J., and J. P. Sullivan, trans. 1991. *Roman Poets of the Early Empire.* Harmondsworth: Penguin Books.

Boym, Svetlana. 2001. *The Future of Nostalgia.* New York: Basic Books.

Bradley, Michael. 2001. "Breathing Fresh Air." *Sydney Morning Herald*, December 10, 2001.

Braun, Emily. 2000. *Mario Sironi and Italian Modernism: Art and Politics under Fascism.* Cambridge: Cambridge University Press.

Bright, Ann. 1970. "The Originality of Robert Burton." Master's thesis, Australian National University.

Bright, David F. 1987. *The Miniature Epic in Vandal Africa.* Norman: University of Oklahoma Press.

Brough, John, trans. 1968. *Poems from the Sanskrit.* Reprint, Harmondsworth: Penguin Books.

Brown, Peter. 1988. *The Body and Society: Men, Women, and Sexual Renunciation in Early Christianity.* New York: Columbia University Press.

Bruner, Jerome. 1975. "The Importance of Play." In *Child Alive!* ed. Roger Lewin, 50–60, Garden City, NY: Anchor Press.

Brunnert, Klaus. 1984. *Nostalgie in der Geschichte der Medizin.* Düsseldorfer Arbeiten zur Geschichte der Medizin 58. Düsseldorf: Triltsch.

Büchner, Karl. 1967. *Studien zur römischen Literature.* Vol. 6. Wiesbaden: Franz Steiner.

Bull, Malcolm, ed. 1995. *Apocalypse Theory and the Ends of the World.* Oxford: Blackwell.

Bundy, E. L. 1962. *Studia Pindarica.* University of California Publications in Classical Philology 18. Berkeley: University of California Press.

Burger, Susanne, et al. 1977. *Arnold Böcklin, 1827–1901: Gemälde, Zeichnisse, Plastiken, Ausstellung zum 150. Geburtstag, 11. Juni–11. September 1977.* Basel and Stuttgart: Schwabe and Company.

Burke, Peter. 1995. "Viewpoint: The Invention Of Leisure in Early Modern Europe." *Past and Present* 146:136–50.

Burton, R. W. 1962. *Pindar's Pythian Odes: Essays in Interpretation.* Oxford: Clarendon Press.

Burton, Robert. 2001. *The Anatomy of Melancholy.* Reprint, New York: New York Review of Books Classics.

Burton, Robert. 1931. *Philosophaster.* In *"Philosophaster," with an English Translation of the Same, Together with His Other Minor Writings in Prose and Verse,* ed. and trans. Paul Jordan-Smith. Stanford: Stanford University Press.

Bussemaker, U. C., and C. Daremberg. 1851–76. *Oeuvres d'Oribase.* 6 vols. Paris.

Buxton, R. G. A. 1982. *Persuasion in Greek Tragedy: A Study of Peitho.* Cambridge: Cambridge University Press.

Cairns, Francis. 1972. *Generic Composition in Greek and Roman Poetry.* Edinburgh: Edinburgh University Press.

Cairns-Smith, A. G. 1996. *Evolving the Mind: On the Nature of Matter and the Origin of Consciousness.* Cambridge: Cambridge University Press.

Callahan, John Francis. 1948. *Four Views of Time in Ancient Philosophy.* Cambridge: Harvard University Press.

Cannon, W. 1942. "'Voodoo' Death." *American Anthropologist,* n.s., 44, 169–81.

Cannon, W. 1957. "Voodoo Death." *Psychosomatic Medicine* 19:182–90.

Carothers, J. C. 1959. "Culture, Psychiatry, and the Written Word." *Psychiatry* 22:307–20.

Carruthers, Clive Harcourt, trans. 1964. *Alicia in Terra Mirabili.* New York: St. Martin's Press.

Carson, Anne. 1986. *Eros the Bittersweet.* Princeton: Princeton University Press.

Cary, Phillip. 2000. *Augustine's Invention of the Inner Self.* New York: Oxford University Press.

Cerri, Giovanni. 2000. "L'etica di Simonide nell'*Eracle* di Euripide." In *Presenza e funzione della città di Tebe nella cultura greca,* ed. Paola Angeli Bernardini, 233–63. Pisa, Rome: Instituti Editoriali e Polygraphici Internazionali.

Chadwick, O. 1968. *John Cassian.* 2d ed. Cambridge: Cambridge University Press.

Chalk, H. H. O. 1962. "*Arete* and *Bia* in Euripides' *Herakles.*" *Journal of Hellenic Studies* 82:7–18.

Chrohns, Hjalmar. 1905. "Zur Geschichte der Liebe als 'Krankheit.'" *Archiv für Kulturgeschichte* 3:66–86.

Ciavolella, Massimo. 1970. "La tradizione dell' '*aegritudo amoris*' nel' 'Decameron.'" *Giornale Storico della Literatura Italiana* 147:496–517.

Ciavolella, Massimo. 1976. *La "malattia d'amore" dall' Antichità al Medioevo.* Rome: Bulzoni.

Citroni, M. 1989. "Marziale e la Letteratura per: Saturnali (poetica dell' intrattenimento e cronologia della publicazione dei libri)." *Illinois Classical Studies* 14:201–26.

Citroni Marchetti, Sandra. 1991. *Plinio il Vecchio e la tradizione del moralismo romano.* Biblioteca di *Materiali e Discussioni per l'Analisi dei Testi Classici* 9. Pisa: Giardini.

Clausen, Wendell V. 1987. *Virgil's "Aeneid" and the Tradition of Hellenistic Poetry.* Berkeley: University of California Press.

Clerici, Lucia Zuccoli, trans. 1996. *Cicerone: Tuscolane.* Milan: Rizzoli.

Cohn, Norman. 1957. *The Pursuit of the Millennium.* London: Secker and Warburg.

Cole, Thomas. 1991. *The Origins of Rhetoric in Ancient Greece.* Baltimore: Johns Hopkins University Press.

Collinge, N. E. 1962. "Medical Terms and Clinical Attitudes in the Tragedians." *Bulletin of the Institute for Classical Studies* 9:43–55.

Conacher, D. J. 1967. *Euripidean Drama*. Toronto: University of Toronto Press.

Conington, John. 1893. *The Satires of A. Persius Flaccus*. 3d ed. Oxford: Clarendon Press.

Conte, Gian Biagio. 1994a. *Genres and Readers: Lucretius, Love Elegy, Pliny's Encyclopedia*. Trans. Glenn W. Most. Baltimore: Johns Hopkins University Press.

Conte, Gian Biagio. 1994b. "Love without Elegy: The *Remedia Amoris* and the Logic of Genre." In Conte 1994, 35–66.

Couat, A. 1931. *Alexandrian Poetry under the First Three Ptolemies*. Trans. J. Loeb. London: William Heinemann.

Courtney, Edward, ed. 1993. *The Fragmentary Latin Poets*. Oxford: Clarendon Press.

Crump, M. Marjorie. [1931] 1997. *The Epyllion from Theocritus to Ovid*. Reprint, London: Bristol Classical Press.

Cullen, Ben. 1993. "The Darwinian Resurgence and the Cultural Virus Critique." *Cambridge Archaeological Journal* 3:179–202.

Cyrino, Monica Silveira. 1995. *In Pandora's Jar: Lovesickness in Early Greek Poetry*. Lanham: University Press of America.

Dalzell, Alexander. 1996. *The Criticism of Didactic Poetry: Essays on Lucretius, Virgil, and Ovid*. Toronto: University of Toronto Press.

Daremberg, C., and C. E. Ruelle. 1879. *Oeuvres de Rufus d'Ephèse*. Paris: L'Imprimerie Nationale.

Davidson, James. 1997. *Courtesans and Fishcakes: The Consuming Passions of Classical Athens*. New York: Harper Perennial.

Davies, Paul. 1995. *About Time: Einstein's Unfinished Revolution*. Harmondsworth: Penguin Books.

Davis, Fred. 1979. *Yearning for Yesterday: A Sociology of Nostalgia*. New York: Free Press.

Davison, Graeme. 1993. *The Unforgiving Minute: How Australia Learned to Tell the Time*. Melbourne: Oxford University Press.

de Bernières, Louis. 1991. *Señor Vivo and the Coca Lord*. London: Vintage Books.

de Grazia, Sebastian. [1962] 1994. *Of Time, Work, and Leisure*. Reprint, New York: Vintage Books.

Deleuze, Gilles, and Félix Guattari. 1977. *Anti-Oedipus: Capitalism and Schizophrenia*. Trans. Robert Hurley, Mark Seem, and Helen R. Lane. New York: Viking.

den Boer, Willem. 1968. "Rome à travers trois auteurs du quatrième siècle." *Mnemosyne* 21:254–82.

de Saint-Denis, E., ed. and trans. 1975. *Ovide: Halieutiques*. Paris: "Les belles Lettres."

De Sanna, Jole, ed. 1998. *De Chirico and the Mediterranean*. New York: Rizzoli.

Descola, Philippe. 1996. *The Spears of Twilight: Life and Death in the Amazon Jungle*. Trans. Janet Lloyd. New York: New Press.

Devereux, George. 1970. "The Nature of Sappho's Seizure in fr. 31 LP as Evidence of Her Inversion." *Classical Quarterly* 20:17–31.

Diamond, Jared. 1997. *Why Is Sex Fun? The Evolution of Human Sexuality*. New York: Basic Books.

DiBattista, Maria. 1991. *First Love: The Affections of Modern Fiction*. Chicago: University of Chicago Press.

Dickie, Matthew W. 1991. "Heliodorus and Plutarch on the Evil Eye." *Classical Philology* 86:17–29.

Dillon, John. 1994. "Sing without an Instrument: Plotinus on Suicide." *Illinois Classical Studies* 19:231–38.

D'Irsay, Stephen. 1927. "Patristic Medicine." *Annals of Medical History* 9:364–78.

Disalvo, Marilyn. 1980. "The Myth of Narcissus." *Semiotica* 30:15–25.

Dixon, Suzanne. 1991. "The Sentimental Ideal of the Roman Family." In Rawson 1991, 99–113.

Dodds, E. R. 1968. *The Greeks and the Irrational.* Berkeley: University of California Press.

Dodds, E. R. 1985. *"The Ancient Concept of Progress" and Other Essays on Greek Literature and Belief.* Oxford: Oxford University Press.

Dolfi, Anna, ed. 1991. *Malinconia: Malattia malinconia e latteratura moderna.* Rome: Bulzoni.

Donaldson, Margaret. 1978. *Children's Minds.* Glasgow: Fontana/Collins.

Douglas, Mary. 1966. *Purity and Danger: An Analysis of Concepts of Pollution and Taboo.* Harmondsworth: Penguin Books.

Dover, K. J. 1980. *Plato: "Symposium."* Oxford: Clarendon Press.

Drabkin, I. E., ed. and trans. 1950. *Caelius Aurelianus: On Acute Diseases and on Chronic Diseases.* Chicago: University of Chicago Press.

Driscoll, Jeremy. 1989. "Listlessness in *The Mirror for Monks* of Evagrius Ponticus." *Cistercian Studies* 34:206–14.

Duff, J. Wight, and Arnold M. Duff, eds. and trans. [1935] 1982. *Minor Latin Poets.* Reprint, Loeb Classical Library, London: William Heinemann.

Dupont, Florence. 1999. *The Invention of Literature: From Greek Intoxication to the Latin Book.* Trans. Janet Lloyd. Baltimore and London: John Hopkins University Press.

Durkheim, Emile. 1952. *Suicide: A Study in Sociology.* Trans. J. A. Spaulding. London: Routledge and Kegan Paul.

Dyck, A. 1989. "On the Way from Colchis to Corinth: Medea in Book 4 of the *Argonautica.*" *Hermes* 117:455–70.

Edmonds, J. M., and S. Gaselee. 1916. *"Daphnis and Chloe" by Longus, the Love Romances of Parthenius, and Other Fragments.* Loeb Classical Library. London: William Heinemann.

Edwards, M. W. 1991. *The "Iliad": A Commentary.* Vol. 5. Cambridge: Cambridge University Press.

Effe, Bernd. 1977. *Dichtung und Lehre: Untersuchungen zur Typologie des antiken Lehrgedichts.* Zetemata 69. Munich: C. H. Beck Verlagsbuchhandlung.

Eldred, Katherine O. 1998. Review of Leigh 1997. *Bryn Mawr Classical Review* 98.1.12.

Eliade, Mircea. 1954. *The Myth of the Eternal Return.* Trans. Willard R. Trask. New York: Pantheon Books.

Elias, Norbert. 1992. *Time: An Essay.* Trans. E. A. Jephcott. Oxford: Basil Blackwell.

Elkin, A. P. 1944. *Aboriginal Men of High Degree.* Sydney: Australian Publishing.

Ewald, Paul W. 2000. *Plague Time: How Stealth Infections Cause Cancers, Heart Disease, and Other Deadly Ailments.* New York: Free Press.

Faber, M. 1967. "Suicide and the *Ajax* of Sophocles." *Psychoanalytic Review* 54:441–52.

Fantham, R. E. 1975. "Sex, Status, and Survival in Hellenistic Athens: A Study of Women in New Comedy." *Phoenix* 29:44–74.

Fantham, R. E. 1982. *Seneca's "Troades."* Princeton: Princeton University Press.

Faraone, Christopher A. 1999. *Ancient Greek Love Magic.* Cambridge, Mass.: Harvard University Press.

Farquharson, A. S. L., ed. and trans. 1944. *The Meditations of the Emperor Marcus Antoninus.* Oxford: Clarendon Press.

Feeney, D. C. 1991. *The Gods in Epic: Poets and Critics of the Classical Tradition.* Oxford: Clarendon Press.

Fenichel, Otto. 1953. "The Psychology of Boredom." In *The Collected Papers of Otto Fenichel, First Series,* ed. Hannah Fenichel and David Rapaport, 292–302. New York: Norton.

Fenik, Bernard. 1968. *Typical Battle Scenes in the "Iliad": Studies in the Narrative Techniques of Homeric Battle Description. Hermes* Einzelschriften 21. Wiesbaden: Franz Steiner.

Ferrini, F. 1978. "Tragedia e patologia: Lessico ippocratico in Euripide." *Quaderni Urbinate di Cultura Classica* 29:49–62.

Fischer-Homberger, E. 1968. *Das zirkuläre Irresein.* Zurich: Juris.

Fisher, Thomas. 1993. "Nochmals zum liebeskranken Königssohn: Ein Aspekt hellenistischer Politik und Wirkungsgeschichte." In *Liebe und Leidenschaft: Historische Aspekte von Erotik und Sexualität,* ed. A. Becker and B. Effe, 123–44. Trier: Wissenschaftlicher Verlag.

Flashar, H. 1966. *Melancholie und Melancholiker in der medizinishen Theorie der Antike.* Berlin: De Gruyter.

Foucault, Michel. 1967. *Madness and Civilization: A History of Insanity in the Age of Reason.* Trans. A. M. Sheridan. London and New York: Routledge.

Foucault, Michel. 1970. *The Order of Things: An Archaeology of the Human Sciences.* Trans. A. M. Sheridan. London and New York: Routledge.

Foucault, Michel. 1972. *The Archaeology of Knowledge.* Trans. A. M. Sheridan Smith. London and New York: Routledge.

Foucault, Michel. 1973. *The Birth of the Clinic: The Archaeology of Medical Perception.* Trans. A. M. Sheridan Smith. London and New York: Routledge.

Foucault, Michel. 1977. *Discipline and Punish: The Birth of the Prison.* Trans. A. M. Sheridan Smith. Harmondsworth: Penguin Books.

Foucault, Michel. 1978. *The History of Sexuality.* Vol. 1, *An Introduction.* Trans. Robert Hurley. New York: Viking.

Foucault, Michel. 1985. *The History of Sexuality.* Vol. 3, *The Use of Pleasure.* Trans. Robert Hurley. New York: Vintage Books.

Foucault, Michel. 1986. *The History of Sexuality.* Vol. 2, *The Care of Self.* Trans. Robert Hurley. New York: Viking.

Foucault, Michel. 1987. *Mental Illness and Psychology.* Trans. A. M. Sheridan. Berkeley: University of California Press.

Fowler, Barbara Hughes, trans. 1994. *Love Lyrics of Ancient Egypt.* Chapel Hill: University of North Carolina Press.

Fraenkel, Eduard. 1935. "Naevius." *Paulys Real-Encyclopädie der classischen Alterumwissenschaft,* Supplement 6:622–40.

France, Peter. 1995. *Hermits: The Insights of Solitude.* London: Chatto and Windus.

Fränkel, H. 1968. *Noten zu den Argonautika des Apollonios.* Munich: Beck.

Fränkel, H. 1985. *Early Greek Poetry and Philosophy.* Trans. Moses Hadas and James Willis. Oxford: Blackwell.

Frontisi-Ducroux, Françoise. 1998. "Le sexe du regard." In Veyne, Lissarrague, and Frontisi-Ducroux 1998, 199–276.

Frontisi-Ducroux, Françoise, and Jean-Pierre Vernant. 1998. *Dans l'oeil du miroir.* Paris: Jacob.

Galinsky, G. Karl. 1972. *The Herakles Theme: The Adaptations of the Hero in Literature from Homer to the Twentieth Century.* Oxford: Blackwell.

Garrett, Laurie. 1994. *The Coming Plague: Newly Emerging Diseases in a World Out of Balance.* New York: Farrar, Straus, and Giroux.

Garrison, Daniel H. 1978. *Mild Frenzy: A Reading of the Hellenistic Love Epigram. Hermes* Einzelschriften 41. Wiesbaden: Franz Steiner

Garrison, Elise P. 1991. "Attitudes towards Suicide in Ancient Greece." *Transactions of the American Philological Association* 121:1–34.

Garrison, Elise P. 1995. *Groaning Tears: Ethical and Dramatic Aspects of Suicide in Greek Tragedy.* Leiden and New York: Brill.

Gärtner, H. 1970. *Rufus Ephesius: Quaestiones Medicinales.* Stuttgart: Teubner.

Gély-Gherida, Véronique. 2000. *La nostalgie du moi: Echo dans la literature europćene.* Paris: Presses Universitaires de France.

Getty, R. J. (ed.). 1940. *M. Annaei Lucani De Bello Civili Liber I.* Cambridge: Cambridge University Press.

Giedke, Adalheid. 1983. "Die Liebeskrankheit in der Geschichte der Medezin." Dissertation med., Düsseldorf.

Gildersleeve, Basil L. 1979. *The Satires of A. Persius Flaccus.* Reprint, New York: Arno Press.

Gilman, Sander, Helen King, Roy Porter, G. S. Rousseau, and Elaine Showalter, eds. 1993. *Hysteria beyond Freud.* Berkeley: University of California Press.

Golden, Kenneth. 1977. "Voodoo in Africa and the United States." *American Journal of Psychiatry* 134, no. 12:1425–27.

Golden, Mark, and Peter Toohey. 1997. *Inventing Ancient Culture: Historicism, Periodization, and the Ancient World.* London and New York: Routledge.

Goldschmidt, Victor. 1979. *Le systeme stoicien et l'idée du temps.* 4th ed. Paris: Vrins.

Goldstein, Jonathan A. 1976. *I Maccabees: A New Translation with Introduction and Commentary.* Garden City, N.Y.: Doubleday.

Goodwin, Frederick K., and Kay Redfield Jamison. 1990. *Manic-Depressive Illness.* New York: Oxford University Press.

Goody, Jack. 1987. *The Interface between the Written and the Oral.* Cambridge: Cambridge University Press.

Goody, Jack. 1997. *Representations and Contradictions: Ambivalence towards Images, Theatre, Fiction, Relics, and Sexuality.* Cambridge, Mass.: Blackwell.

Goody, Jack. 1998. *Food and Love: A Cultural History of East and West.* London: Verso.

Gow, A. S. F., ed. 1952. *Theocritus.* 2d ed. 2 vols. Cambridge: Cambridge University Press.

Gratwick, A. S.. 1983. "Ennius' *Annales.*" In *The Cambridge History of Classical Literature, Volume II P Roman Literature,* 60–76. Cambridge: Cambridge University Press.

Green, Peter, trans. 1997. *The "Argonautika" by Apollonios Rhodios.* Berkeley: University of California Press.

Green, Peter, trans. 1982. *Ovid: The Erotic Poems.* Harmondsworth: Penguin Books.

Greene, Ellen. 1995. "The Catullan Ego: Fragmentation and the Erotic Self." *American Journal of Philology* 116:77–93.

Gregory, Richard. 1997. *Mirrors in Mind*. Oxford: Spektrum.

Griesinger, W. 1845. *Die Pathologie und Therapie der psychischen Krankheiten für Ärzte und Studierende*. Stuttgart: Krabbe.

Griffin, M. T. 1976. *Seneca: A Philosopher in Politics*. Oxford: Clarendon Press.

Griffiths, John Gwyn. 1990. "Love as a Disease." In *Studies in Egyptology Presented to Miriam Lichtheim*, ed. Sarah Israelit-Groll, 1:349–64. Jerusalem: Magnes Press.

Grilli, Alberto. 1953. *Il problema della vita contemplativa nel mondo greco-romano*. Milan: Fratelli Bocca.

Grisé, Y. 1983. *Le suicide dans la Rome antique*. Montreal: Bellarmin; Paris: "Les Belles Lettres."

Gross, Nicholas P. 1985. *Amatory Persuasion in Antiquity: Studies in Theory and Practice*. Newark: University of Delaware Press.

Guillaud, Jacqueline, and Maurice Guillaud. 1990. *Frescoes in the Time of Pompeii*. Trans. Ian Robson and Alphabyte SAS. New York: Clarkson N. Potter.

Guthrie, W. K. C. 1969. *A History of Greek Philosophy*. Vol. 3. Cambridge: Cambridge University Press.

Guy, Jean-Claude, trans. 2001. *Jean Cassien: Institutions cénobitiques*. Paris: Cerf.

Hacking, Ian. 1995. *Rewriting the Soul: Multiple Personality and the Sciences of Memory*. Princeton: Princeton University Press.

Hacking, Ian. 1998. *Mad Travellers: Reflections on the Reality of Transient Mental Illness*. London: Free Association.

Hägg, Tomas. 1983. *The Novel in Antiquity*. Oxford: Blackwell.

Hallett, Judith P., and Marilyn B. Skinner, eds. 1997. *Roman Sexualities*. Princeton: Princeton University Press.

Halperin, David M. 1990. *"One Hundred Years of Homosexuality" and Other Essays on Greek Love*. New York and London: Routledge.

Hardie, P. R. 1986. *Virgil's "Aeneid": "Cosmos" and "Imperium."* Oxford: Clarendon Press.

Harkins, Paul W., trans. 1963. *Galen: On the Passions and Errors of the Soul*. Columbus: Ohio State University Press.

Harries, Hermann. 1891. *Tragici Graeci qua arte usi sint in discribenda insania*. Diss. Kiel: H. Fiencke.

Harris, William V. 1989. *Ancient Literacy*. Cambridge: Harvard University Press.

Hartigan, K. 1987. "Euripidean Madness: Heracles and Orestes." *Greece and Rome* 34:126–35.

Harvey, R. A. 1981. *A Commentary on Persius*. Leiden: Brill.

Hawley, Janet. 1997. "Dreadlocked." *Sydney Morning Herald*, May 31, 12–21.

Healy, Sean Desmond. 1984. *Boredom, Self, and Culture*. Rutherford, N.J.: Fairleigh Dickinson University Press.

Herman, Arthur. 1997. *The Idea of Decline in Western Literature*. New York: Free Press.

Heuser, Manfred, ed. 1994. *Sehnsucht*. Innsbruck: Verlag Integrative Psychiatrie.

Highet, G. 1972. *The Speeches in Vergil's "Aeneid."* Princeton: Princeton University Press.

Hirzel, R. 1908. "Der Selbstmord." *Archiv für Religionswissenschaft* 11:417–76.

Høeg, Peter. 1994. *Borderliners*. Trans. Barbara Haveland. London: Harvill Press.

Hollan, D. 1992. "Cross-Cultural Definitions of the Self." *Journal of Anthropological Research* 48:283–300.

Hollis, A. S. 1973. "The *Ars Amatoria* and *Remedia Amoris*." In *Ovid*, ed. J. W. Binns, 84–115. London: Routledge and Kegan Paul.

Hollis, A. S. 1994. "[Oppian], *Cyn.* 2, 100–158 and the Mythical Past of Apamea-on-the Orontes." *Zeitschrift für Papyrologie und Epigraphik* 102:153–66.

Hollis, A. S., ed. 1977. *Ovid: "Ars Amatoria," Book 1*. Oxford: Clarendon Press.

Hooley, D. M. 1997. *The Knotted Thong: Structures of Mimesis in Persius*. Ann Arbor: University of Michigan Press.

Hopkinson, Neil, ed. 1994. *Greek Poetry of the Imperial Period: An Anthology*. Cambridge: Cambridge University Press.

Hude, Karl. 1958. *Aretaeus*. Corpus Medicorum Graecorum II. 2d ed. Berlin: In aedibus Academiae scientiarum.

Huizinga, J. [1949] 1971. *Homo Ludens: A Study of the Play Element in Culture*. Reprint, Harmondsworth: Penguin Books.

Hull, Denison Bingham. 1964. *Hounds and Hunting in Ancient Greece*. Chicago: University of Chicago Press.

Hunter, Richard L. 1989. *Apollonius of Rhodes: "Argonautica," Book III*. Cambridge: Cambridge University Press.

Hunter, Richard L. 1993. *The "Argonautica" of Apollonius: Literary Studies*. Cambridge: Cambridge University Press.

Hurwit, Jeffrey M. 1982. "Palm Trees and the Pathetic Fallacy in Archaic Greek Pottery and Art." *Classical Journal* 77:193–99.

Hurwit, Jeffrey M. 1985. *The Art and Culture of Early Greece, 1100–480 B.C.* Ithaca: Cornell University Press.

Huxley, Aldous. 1923. *On the Margin: Notes and Essays*. London: Chatto and Windus.

Illman, John. 1991. "Maxwell Mystery: The Jumping Sailor Theory." *Sydney Morning Herald*, November 12, 1.

Ingalls, D. H., trans. 1965. *An Anthology of Sanskrit Court Poetry: Vidyakara's "Subhasitaratnakosa."* Harvard Oriental Series, vol. 44. Cambridge: Harvard University Press.

Inwood, Brad, and L. P. Gerson, trans. 1988. *Hellenistic Philosophy: Introductory Readings*. Indianapolis: Hackett.

Jackson, S. 1992. "Apollonius' Jason: Human Being in an Epic Scenario." *Greece and Rome* 39:155–62.

Jackson, S. 1997. "Apollonius of Rhodes: The Cleite and Byblis Suicides." *Studi Italiani di Filologia Classica* 15, no. 1:48–54.

Jackson, Stanley W. 1986. *Melancholia and Depression: From Hippocratic Times to Modern Times*. New Haven: Yale University Press.

Jackson, Stanley W. 1969. "Galen—on Disorders." *Journal of the History of Behavioral Science* 5:365–84.

Jacobelli, Luciana. 1995. *Le pitture erotiche delle terme suburbane di Pompei*. Rome: "L'Erma" di Bretschneider.

Jacobson, Howard. 1974. *Ovid's "Heroides."* Princeton: Princeton University Press.

Jacques, Jean-Marie. 1998. "La bile noir dans l'antiquité grecque: Medicine et littérature." *Révue des Études Anciennes* 100:217–34.

Jamal, Nadia. 1988. "Gorilla's in Mourning over Baby's Death in Zoo." *Sydney Morning Herald*, March 31, 2.

Jamison, Kay Redfield. 1993. *Touched with Fire: Manic-Depressive Illness and the Artistic Temperament.* New York: Free Press Paperbacks.

Jamison, Kay Redfield. 1999. *Night Falls Fast: Understanding Suicide.* New York: Knopf.

Jenkinson, J. R. 1980. *Persius: The Satires.* Warminster: Aris and Phillips.

Jocelyn, H. 1967. *The Tragedies of Ennius.* Cambridge: Cambridge University Press.

Jonard, Norbert. 1998. *L'ennui dans la literature européenne: Des origines à l'aube du XXe siècle.* Paris: Honoré Champion Éditeur.

Jones, W. H. S., and E. T. Withington. 1923–31. *The Works of Hippocrates.* 4 vols. Loeb Classical Library. London: William Heinemann.

Joshel, S. R. 1992. "The Body Female and the Body Politic: Livy's Lucretia and Verginia." In *Pornography and Representation in Greece and Rome,* ed. A. Richlin, 112–30. New York: Oxford University Press.

Judd, Alan. 1986. *The Noonday Devil.* London: Hutchinson.

Kaplan, Robert D. 1997. *The Ends of the Earth: A Journey at the Dawn of the Twenty-First Century.* London: Papermac.

Kaufmann, Walter, ed. and trans., with R. J. Hollingdale. 1989. *Friedrich Nietzsche: "On the Genealogy of Morals" and "Ecce Homo."* Reprint, New York: Vintage Books.

Kennedy, Paul. 1996. "Doomsterism." *New York Review of Books,* September 19, 20–22.

Kennell, Nigel. 1997. Review of Golden and Toohey 1997. *Bryn Mawr Classical Review* 97.6.13.

Kenney, E. J. 1971. *Lucretius: "De Rerum Natura," Book III.* Cambridge: Cambridge University Press.

Kenny, A. 1963. *Action, Emotion, and Will.* London: Routledge and Kegan Paul.

Kilpatrick, Ross S. 1986. *The Poetry of Friendship: Horace "Epistles."* Edmonton: University of Alberta Press.

Kitto, H. D. F. 1950. *Greek Tragedy: A Literary Study.* London: Methuen.

Klibansky, R., E. Panofsky, and F. Saxl. 1964. *Saturn and Melancholy: Studies in the History of Natural Philosophy, Religion, and Art.* London: Nelson.

Klossowski, Pierre. 1947. *Sade mon prochain.* Paris: Editions du Seuil. Translated by Alphonso Lingis under the title *Sade My Neighbor* (Evanston, Ill.: Northwestern University Press, 1991).

Klossowski, Pierre. 1997. *Roberte Ce Soir and the Revocation of the Edict of Nantes.* Trans. Austryn Wainhouse. New York: Boyars.

Knox, Peter. 1986. *Ovid's "Metamorphoses" and the Traditions of Augustan Poetry.* Cambridge Philological Society Supplementary Volume 11. Cambridge: Cambridge University Press.

Kohut, Heinz. 1971. *The Analysis of the Self: A Systematic Approach to the Psychoanalytic Treatment of Narcissistic Personality Disorders.* New York: International Universities Press.

Kohut, Heinz. 1977. *The Restoration of the Self.* New York: International Universities Press.

Kohut, Heinz. 1985. *Self Psychology and the Humanities: Reflections on a New Psychoanalytic Approach.* Ed. Charles B. Strozier. New York: Norton.

Konstan, David. 1994. *Sexual Symmetry: Love in the Ancient Novel and Related Genres.* Princeton: Princeton University Press.

Konstan, David. 1997. "Philosophy, Friendship, and Cultural History." In Golden and Toohey 1997, 66–78.

Koukopoulos, Athanasios, and Alexa Koukopoulos. 1999. "Agitated Depression as a Mixed State and the Problem of Melancholia." *Psychiatric Clinics of North America* 22, no. 3: 547–64.

Kozak, David L., and David I. Lopez. 2000. *Devil Sickness and Devil Songs: Tohono O'odham Poetics.* Washington: Smithsonian Institution Press.

Kraepelin, Emil. 1921. *Manic-Depressive Insanity and Paranoia.* Trans. R. Mary Barclay and ed. George M. Robertson. Edinburgh: Livingstone.

Kristeva, J. 1987. *Soleil noir: Dépression et mélancholie.* Paris: Gallimard.

Kudlien, F. 1967. *Der Beginn des medizinischen Denkens bei den Griechen: Von Homer bis Hippokrates.* Zurich and Stuttgart: Artemis Verlag.

Kudlien, F. 1973. "Schwärzliche Organe im frügriechischen Denken." *Medizin-Historisches Journal* 8:53–58.

Kühn, G. C., ed. 1821–33. *Claudii Galeni Opera Omnia.* 20 vols. Leipzig.

Kuhn, R. 1976. *The Demon of Noontide: Ennui in Western Literature.* Princeton: Princeton University Press.

Kurke, Leslie. 1999. "Ancient Greek Board Games." *Classical Philology* 94:247–65.

Kurtz, Donna Carol. 1975. *Athenian White Lekythoi: Patterns and Painters.* Oxford: Clarendon Press.

La Barre, Weston. 1972. *The Ghost Dance: The Origins of Religion.* New York: Delta Books.

Lacan, Jacques. 1977. "The Mirror Stage as Formative of the I." In *Écrits: A Selection*, trans. Alan Sheridan, 1–7. New York: Norton. Originally published as "Le stade du miroir comme formateur de la fonction du Je," *Révue Française du Psychanalyse* 4 (1949): 449–55.

Lachenbacher, H. 1937. "Persius und die Heilkunde." *Wiener Studien* 55:130–41.

La Penna, Antonio. 1956. "Due note sulla cultura filosophica delle epistole oraziane." *Studi Italiani de Filologia Classica* 27–28:195–201.

La Penna, Antonio. 1957. "Note sul linguaggio erotico dell' elegia latina." *Maia* 4:187–209.

La Penna, Antonio. 1995. "L'intelletuale emarginato da Orazio a Petronio." In *Da Lucrezio a Persio: Saggi, studi, note*, ed. Mario Citroni, Emanuele Narducci, and Alessandro Perutelli, 243–71. Milan: Sansoni Editore.

Lapidge, M. 1979. "Lucan's Imagery of Cosmic Dissolution." *Hermes* 107:344–70.

Lautner, Peter. 1994. "Rival Theories of Self-Awareness in Late Neo-Platonism." *Bulletin of the Institute for Classical Studies* 39:107–16.

Leeman, A. D. 1971. "Das Todeserlebnis in Denken Senecas." *Gymnasium* 78:322–33.

Lefkowitz, Mary R. 1981. "The Wandering Womb." In *Heroines and Hysterics*, 12–15. London: Duckworth.

Leibbrand, W., and A. Wettley. 1961. *Der Wahnsinn: Geschichte der abendlandischen Psychopathologie.* Freiburg: K. Alber.

Leigh, Matthew. 1997. *Lucan: Spectacle and Engagement.* Oxford: Clarendon Press.

Leitao, David D. 1998. "Senecan Catoptrics and the Passion of Hostius Quadra (Sen. *Nat.* 1)." *Materiali e Discussioni per l'Analisi dei Testi Classici* 41:127–60.

Lepenies, Wolfgang. 1992. *Melancholy and Society.* Trans. Jeremy Gaines and Doris Jones. Cambridge: Harvard University Press.

Levine, Stephen Z. 1996. "Virtual Narcissus: On the Mirror Stage with Monet, Lacan, and Me." *American Imago* 53:91–106.

Lévi-Strauss, Claude. 1961. *A World on the Wane*. Trans. John Russell. London: Hutchinson.

Lévi-Strauss, Claude. 1963. "The Sorcerer and His Magic." In *Structural Anthropology*, 167–85. London: Allen Lane, Penguin Press.

Lévy-Bruhl, Lucien. 1923. *The Primitive Mentality*. Trans. L. A. Clare. New York: Macmillan.

Lewis, A. 1967. "Melancholia: A Historical Review." In *The State of Psychiatry*, ed. A. Lewis, 71–110. London: Routledge and Kegan Paul.

Lewis, I. M. 1971. *Ecstatic Religion: An Anthropological Study of Spirit Possession and Shamanism*. Harmondsworth: Penguin Books.

Leys, Ruth. 2000. *Trauma: A Genealogy*. Chicago: University of Chicago Press.

Lichtheim, Miriam. 1976. *Ancient Egyptian Literature: A Book of Readings*. Vol. 2, *The New Kingdom*. Berkeley: University of California Press.

Lightfoot, J. L., ed. 1999. *Parthenius of Nicaea: The Poetical Fragments and the "Erôtika Pathêmata."* Oxford: Clarendon Press.

Lloyd, G. E. R., ed. 1978. *Hippocratic Writings*. Hardmondsworth: Penguin Books.

Long, A. A., and D. N. Sedley. 1987. *The Hellenistic Philosophers*. 2 vols. Cambridge: Cambridge University Press.

Longo, Oddone. 1989. *Le forme della predazione: Cacciatori e pescatori nella Grecia antica*. Naples: Liguori Editore.

Loraux, Nicole. 1987. *Tragic Ways of Killing a Woman*. Trans. Anthony Forster. Cambridge: Harvard University Press.

Lovejoy, Arthur and George Boas. [1935] 1965. *Primitivism and Related Ideas in Antiquity*. New York: Octagon Books.

Luibheid, C., and N. Russell, ed. and trans. 1982. *John Climacus: "The Ladder of Divine Ascent."* New York: Paulist Press.

Lumb, T. W., and J. Maillon. 1960. *Héliodore: Les Ethiopiques (Théagène et Chariclée)*. 2d ed. Paris: "Les Belles Lettres."

Lutz, Catherine. 1988. *Unnatural Emotions: Everyday Sentiments on a Micronesian Atoll and Their Challenge to Western Theory*. Chicago: University of Chicago Press.

Lutz, Tom. 1991. *American Nervousness, 1903: An Anecdotal History*. Ithaca: Cornell University Press.

Lyne, R. O. A. M., ed. 1978. *"Ciris": A Poem Attributed to Vergil*. Cambridge: Cambridge University Press.

MacAlister, Suzanne. 1996. *Dreams and Suicides: The Greek Novel from Antiquity to the Byzantine Empire*. London and New York: Routledge.

Macey, Samuel L. 1989. *The Dynamics of Progress: Time, Method, and Measure*. Athens: University of Georgia Press.

Maddock, Kenneth. 1974. *The Australian Aborigines: A Portrait of Their Society*. Harmondsworth: Penguin Books.

Maehler, Herwig. 1990. "Syptome der Liebe im Roman und in der griechishen Anthologie." In *Groningen Colloquia on the Novel*, ed. Heinz Hofmann, 3:1–12. Aroningen: Egbert Forsten.

Magie, David, ed. and trans. 1953. *The Scriptores Historiae Augustae*. 3 vols. Reprint, Loeb Classical Library, London: William Heinemann.

Maiuri, Bianca. 1957. *Museo Nazionale de Napoli*. Novara: Instituto Geographico de Agostini.

Marcovich, Miroslav. 1991. "Sappho fr. 31: Anxiety Attack or Love Declaration?" In *Studies in Greek Poetry*, 28–46. *Illinois Classical Studies* Supplement 1. Reprint, Atlanta: Scholars Press.

Margo, Jill. 1996. "Time and Motion Studies." *Sydney Morning Herald*, January 11, 9.

Marmorale, Enzo V. 1953. *Naevius Poeta*. Florence: La Nuova Italia Editrice.

Marneros, Andreas. 1999. *Handbuch der Unipolaren und Bipolaren Erkrankungen*. Stuttgart: Thieme.

Marneros, Andreas. 2001a. "Origin and Development of Concepts of Bipolar Mixed States." *Journal of Affective Disorders* 67:229–40.

Marneros, Andreas. 2001b. "Expanding the Group of Bipolar Disorders." *Journal of Affective Disorders* 67:39–44.

Marneros, Andreas, and Jules Angst. 2000. "Bipolar Disorders: Roots and Evolution." In *Bipolar Disorders: One Hundred Years after Manic-Depressive Insanity*. Dordrecht: Kluwer Academic Publishers.

Márquez, Gabriel García. 1988. *Love in the Time of Cholera*. Trans. Edith Grossman. Harmondsworth: Penguin Books.

Martin, Richard P. 1989. *The Language of Heroes: Speech and Performance in the "Iliad."* Ithaca: Cornell University Press.

Mascuch, Michael. 1997. *Origins of the Individualist Self: Autobiography and Self-Identity in England, 1591–1791*. Cambridge: Polity.

Mathis, J. 1974. "A Sophisticated Version of Voodoo Death." *Psychosomatic Medicine* 26:104–7.

Mattes, J. 1970. *Der Wahnsinn im griechischen Mythos und in der Dichtung bis zum Drama des fünften Jahrhunderts*. Heidelberg: C. Winter.

Mayer, Roland. 1994. *Horace: "Epistles," Book 1*. Cambridge: Cambridge University Press.

McCarthy, Tom. 1998. Review of Klossowski 1997. *Times Literary Supplement*, January 20, 21.

McGann, M. J. 1969. *Studies in Horace's First Book of "Epistles."* Brussels: Latomus.

McNeill, W. H. 1976. *Plagues and Peoples*. Harmondsworth: Penguin Books.

Micale, Mark. 1994. *Approaching Hysteria*. Princeton: Princeton University Press.

Michel, Alain. 1993. "Lucrèce, Cicéron, Horace: La serenité et l'acedia." *Studi Italiani di Filologia Classica* 11, nos. 1–2:12–35.

Miller, H. W. 1944. "Medical Terminology in Tragedy." *Transactions of the American Philological Society* 75:156–67.

Milns, R. D. 1986. "Attitudes towards Mental Illness in Antiquity." *Australian and New Zealand Journal of Psychiatry* 20:454–62.

Milowicki, Edward J. 1996. "Reflections on a Symbolic Heritage: Ovid's Narcissus." *Syllecta Classics* 7:155–66.

Milton, G. 1973. "Self-Willed Death or the Bone-Pointing Syndrome." *Lancet* 1:1435–36.

Mingazzini, Paolino. 1966. *Ceramica greca*. Milan: Fratelli Fabbri Editori.

Morel, Willy. 1975. *Fragmenta poetarum Latinorum epicorum et lyricorum praeter Ennium et Lucilium*. Stuttgart: Teubner.

Morford, Mark. 1984. *Persius*. Boston: Twayne Publishers.

Murgia, C. E. 1986. "The Date of Ovid's *Ars Amatoria*." *American Journal of Philology* 107:74–94.

Müri, W. 1953. "Melancholie und schwarze Galle." *Museum Helveticum* 10:21–38.

Myerowitz, Molly. 1985. *Ovid's Games of Love*. Detroit: Wayne State University Press.

Nagler, M. N. 1974. *Spontaneity and Tradition: A Study in the Oral Art of Homer*. Berkeley: University of California Press.

Narducci, Emanuele. 2002. *Lucano Un epica contro l'impero: Interpretazione della "Pharsalia."* Rome: Editori Laterza.

Negri, Angela Maria. 1988. "La fortuna letteraria dell' *inertia* (Hor. *Ep.* 1.11.28 and Sen. *Tranq.* 12.3)." *Paideia* 43:179–88.

Neuburger, Max. 1909. *History of Medicine*. Vol. 1. Trans. E. Playfair. London: Frowde.

Newlands, Carole E. 1995. *Playing with Time: Ovid and the Fasti*. Ithaca: Cornell University Press.

Nock, Arthur Danby. 1933. *Conversion: The Old and the New in Religion from Alexander the Great to Augustine St. Hippo*. Oxford: Oxford University Press.

Nussbaum, Martha C. 1994. *The Therapy of Desire: Theory and Practice in Hellenistic Ethics*. Princeton: Princeton University Press.

Oehler, K. 1997. *Subjektivität und Selbstbewusstsein in der Antike*. Würzburg: Königshausen and Neuman.

O'Loughlin, Michael. 1978. *The Garlands of Repose: The Literary Celebration of Civic and Retired Leisure: The Traditions of Homer and Vergil, Horace and Montaigne*. Chicago: University of Chicago Press.

Ong, Walter J. 1977. *Interfaces of the Word: Studies in the Evolution of Consciousness and Culture*. Ithaca: Cornell University Press.

Ong, Walter J. 1982. *Orality and Literacy: The Technologizing of the Word*. London: Methuen.

Padel, Ruth. 1992. *In and Out of the Mind: Greek Images of the Tragic Self*. Princeton: Princeton University Press.

Padel, Ruth. 1995. *Whom Gods Destroy: Elements of Greek and Tragic Madness*. Princeton: Princeton University Press.

Page, D. L. 1955. *Sappho and Alcaeus*. Oxford: Clarendon Press.

Paget, F. 1903. *The Spirit of Discipline: Sermons Preached by Francis Paget Together with an Introductory Essay concerning Accidie*. London: Longmans, Green.

Parks, Tim. 2000. "The Non-conformist (*Mario Sironi and Italian Modernism: Art and Politics under Fascism* by Emily Braun: Cambridge University Press)." *New York Review of Books*, September 21, 30–35.

Perkins, Judith. 1995. *The Suffering Self: Pain and Narrative Representation in the Early Christian Era*. London and New York: Routledge.

Petrucci, Armando. 1993. *Public Lettering: Script, Power, and Culture*. Trans. Linda Lappin. Chicago: University of Chicago Press.

Phillips, Graham. 1990. "Fear of Cancer Can Kill Like a Voodoo Curse." *Sunday Telegraph*, October 14, 197.

Piaget, Jean. 1929. *The Child's Conception of the World*. New York: Harcourt, Brace, and Company.

Piaget, Jean. 1954. *The Construction of Reality in the Child*. Trans. Margaret Cook. New York: Basic Books.

Pieper, Josef. 1952. *Leisure, the Basis of Culture*. Trans. A. Dru. New York: Pantheon Books.

Pigeaud, Jackie. 1981. *La maladie de l'âme: Etude sur la relation de l'âme at du corps dans la tradition medico-philosophique antique.* Paris: "Les Belles Lettres."

Pigeaud, Jackie. 1987. *Folie et cures de la folie chez les médecins de l'antiquité greco-romaine: "La manie."* Paris: "Les Belles Lettres."

Pike, D. L. 1993. "Jason's Departure: Ap. Rhod. and Heroism." *Acta Classica* 36:27–38.

Plass, Paul. 1995. *The Game of Death in Ancient Rome: Arena Sport and Political Suicide.* Wisconsin Studies in the Classics. Madison: University of Wisconsin Press.

Podlecki, A. J., ed. and trans. 1989. *Aeschylus: "Eumenides."* Warminster: Aris and Phillips.

Porter, Roy. 1987. *Mind Forged Manacles,* London: Athlone Press.

Porter, Roy, ed. 1997. *Rewriting the Self: Histories from the Renaissance to the Present.* London and New York: Routledge.

Pratt, N. T. 1983. *Seneca's Drama.* Chapel Hill: University of North Carolina Press.

Preston, Richard. 1994. *The Hot Zone.* New York: Random House.

Quinn, Kenneth. 1969. *The Catullan Revolution.* Rev. ed. Cambridge: Heffer.

Quinn, Kenneth. 1980. *Horace: The Odes.* Basingstoke: Macmillan.

Ramsey, Boniface, ed. and trans. 2000. *John Cassian: De institutis cuenobiorum et de octo principalium vitiorum remediis libri XII.* New York: Newman Press.

Rawson, Beryl. 1991. *Marriage, Divorce, and Children in Ancient Rome.* Canberra and Oxford: Clarendon Press.

Rawson, E. 1985. *Intellectual Life in the Late Roman Republic.* London: Duckworth.

Reckford, Kenneth J. 1998. "Reading the Sick Body: Decomposition and Morality in Persius' *Third Satire.*" *Arethusa* 31:337–54.

Reid, Janice. 1983. *Sorcerers and Healing Spirits.* Canberra: Australian University Press.

Richlin, Amy. 1993. *The Garden of Priapus: Sexuality and Aggression in Roman Humor.* 2d ed. New York: Oxford University Press.

Richlin, Amy. 1997. "Towards a History of Body History." In Golden and Toohey 1997, 16–35.

Richmond, J. A., ed. 1962. *The "Halieutica" Ascribed to Ovid.* London: Athlone Press.

Ridley, Matt. 1993. *The Red Queen: Sex and the Evolution of Human Nature.* New York: Viking.

Rist, John M. 1969. *Stoic Philosophy.* Cambridge: Cambridge University Press.

Robert, Jean-Noel. 1983. *Les plaisirs à Rome.* Paris: "Les Belles Lettres."

Robertson, Martin. 1992. *The Art of Vase-Painting in Classical Athens.* Cambridge: Cambridge University Press.

Rohde, Erwin. 1914. *Der griechische Roman und seine Vorläufer.* 3d ed. Leipzig: Breitkopf und Härtel.

Rose, Jacqueline. 1986. *Sexuality in the Field of Vision.* London: Verso.

Rosen, G. 1968. *Madness in Society: Chapters in the Historical Sociology of Mental Illness.* London: Routledge and Kegan Paul.

Ross, Colin. 1994. *The Osiris Complex: Case Studies in Multiple Personality Disorder.* Toronto: University of Toronto Press.

Rotman, Brian. 1996. Review of Davies 1995. *Times Literary Supplement,* July 5, 29.

Roussel, F. 1988. "Le concept de mélancholie chez Aristotle." *Révue d'Histoire des Sciences et de Leurs Applications* 41:299–330.

Rowell, Henry T. 1947. "The Original Form of Naevius' *Bellum Poenicum.*" *American Journal of Philology* 68:21–46.

Russell, D. A., and N. G. Wilson, eds. and trans. 1981. *Menander the Rhetor.* Oxford: Clarendon Press.

Rütten, Thomas. 1992. *Demokrit—lachender Philosoph und sanguinischer Melancholiker: Eine pseudohippokratische Geschichte. Mnemosyne* Supplement 118. Leiden: Brill.

Rybczynski, Witold. 1991. *Waiting for the Weekend.* New York: Viking.

Rycroft, Charles. 1997. Review of Stevens 1997. *New York Review of Books,* May 29, 36–37.

Salecl, Renata, and Slavoj Zizek, eds. 1996. *Gaze and Voice as Love Objects.* Durham: Duke University Press.

Saller, R. P., and R. D. Shaw. 1984. "Tombstones and Roman Family Relations in the Principate: Civilians, Soldiers, and Slaves." *Journal of Roman Studies* 74:124–46.

Sandbach, F. H. 1975. *The Stoics.* New York: Norton.

Sargant, William. 1957. *Battle for the Mind: The Physiology of Conversion and Brain-Washing.* London: Pan Books.

Sartre, Jean-Paul. 1966. *Being and Nothingness: An Essay in Phenomenological Ontology.* Trans. Hazel E. Barnes. 4th ed. New York: Citadel Press.

Saylor, Charles. 1990. "*Lux Extrema:* Lucan, *Pharsalia* 4.402–581." *Transactions of the American Philological Association* 120:291–300.

Schadewaldt, Hans. 1985. "Der *Morbus amatorius* aus medizinhistorischer Sicht." In *Das Ritterbild in Mittelalter und Renaissance,* 87–104. Düsseldorf: Droste.

Schein, Seth L. 1984. *The Mortal Hero: An Introduction to Homer's "Iliad."* Berkeley: University of California Press.

Schiesari, Juliana. 1992. *The Gendering of Melancholia: Feminism, Psychoanalysis, and the Symbolics of Loss in Renaissance Literature.* Ithaca: Cornell University Press.

Schnapp, Alain. 1997. *Le chasseur et la cité: Chasse et érotique en Grèce ancienne.* Paris: A. Michel.

Schneemelcher, Wilhelm, ed. 1963–66. *New Testament Apocrypha.* Trans. A. J. B. Higgins et al. and ed. R. McL. Wilson. 2 vols. Philadelphia: Westminster Press.

Schoeck, Helmut. 1969. *Envy: A Theory of Social Behaviour.* Trans. Michael Glenny and Betty Ross. New York: Harcourt, Brace, and World.

Schotes, H.-A. 1969. *Stoische Physik: Psychologie und Theologie bei Lucan.* Bonn: Rudolf Habelt Verlag.

Seidenberg, R., and E. Papathomopoulos. 1961. "Sophocles' *Ajax:* A Morality for Madness." *Psychoanalytic Quarterly* 30:404–12.

Shackleton-Bailey, D. R. 1966. *Cicero's Letters to Atticus.* Vol. 5. Cambridge: Cambridge University Press.

Shackleton-Bailey, D. R., ed. and trans. 1993. *Martial: Epigrams.* 2 vols. Loeb Classical Library. Cambridge: Harvard University Press.

Shapiro, H. A. 1994. *Myth into Art: Poet and Painter in Classical Greece.* London and New York: Routledge.

Sharrock, Alison. 1994. *Seduction and Repetition in Ovid's "Ars Amatoria" 2.* Oxford: Clarendon Press.

Sherwin-White, A. N. 1985. *The Letters of Pliny: A Historical and Social Commentary.* Reprint, Oxford: Clarendon Press.

Showalter, Elaine. 1985. *The Female Malady: Women, Madness, and English Culture, 1830–1980*. London: Virago.

Showalter, Elaine. 1997. *Hystories: Hysterical Epidemics and Modern Culture*. London: Picador.

Siegel, Rudolph E. 1968. *Galen's System of Physiology and Medicine*. Basel and New York: Karger.

Siegel, Rudolph E. 1973. *Galen on Psychology, Psychopathology, and Function and Diseases of the Nervous System: An Analysis of His Doctrines, Observations, and Experiments*. Basel and New York: Karger.

Siegel, Rudolph E., trans. 1976. *Galen: "On the Affected Parts."* Basel and New York: Karger.

Siegfried, André. 1960. *Itinéraires de contagion: Epidémies et idéologies*. Paris: Armand Colin.

Silone, Ignazio. 1948. *Fontamara*. Trans. Gwenda David and Eric Mosbacher. London: Jonathan Cape.

Simon, Bennett. 1978. *Mind and Madness in Ancient Greece: The Classical Roots of Modern Psychiatry.* Ithaca: Cornell University Press.

Skutsch, Otto. 1968. *Studia Enniana*. London: Athlone Press.

Skutsch, Otto. 1985. *The Annals of Q. Ennius*. Oxford: Clarendon Press.

Slater, Niall W. 1990. *Reading Petronius*. Baltimore: Johns Hopkins University Press.

Smith, Martin S., ed. 1975. *Petronii Arbitri Cena Trimalchionis*. Oxford: Clarendon Press.

Smith, Wesley D. 1979. *The Hippocratic Tradition*. Ithaca: Cornell University Press.

Snell, Bruno. 1953. *The Discovery of the Mind: The Greek Origins of European Thought*. Trans. T. G. Rosenmeyer. Oxford: Blackwell.

Soby, James Thrall. 1955. *Giorgio de Chirico*. New York: Museum of Modern Art.

Solomon, Andrew. 2001. *The Noonday Demon: An Atlas of Depression*. New York: Scribner.

Sommerstein, Alan H., ed. 1989. *Aeschylus: "Eumenides"*. Cambridge: Cambridge University Press.

Spacks, Patricia Meyer. 1995. *Boredom: The History of a State of Mind*. Chicago: University of Chicago Press.

Spencer, W. G., trans. 1935–38. *Celsus: "De Medicina."* 2 vols. Loeb Classical Library. London: William Heinemann.

Sperber, Dan. 1996. *Explaining Culture: A Naturalistic Approach*. Oxford: Blackwell.

Squillante, Mars. 1995. *Persio: Il linguaggio della malinconia*. Naples: M. D'Auria Editore.

Stadter, P. A. 1965. *Plutarch's Historical Methods*. Cambridge: Harvard University Press.

Stanaway, Glenn. 1992. "There's a Yawning Gap in Our Lives." *Daily Telegraph Mirror*, May 2, 3.

Stanford, W. B. 1963. *Sophocles: "Ajax."* London: Macmillan.

Starobinski, J. 1962. *History of the Treatment of Melancholy from the Earliest Times to 1900*. Basel: J. P. Geigy.

Starobinski, J. 1974. "L'épée d'Ajax." In *Trois Fureurs*, 12–71. Paris: Gallimard.

Steiner, Deborah Tarn. 1994. *The Tyrant's Writ: Myths and Images of Writing in Ancient Greece*. Princeton: Princeton University Press.

Steiner, George. 1989. *Martin Heidegger*. Reprint, with a new introduction, Chicago: University of Chicago Press.

Stephens, Susan A., and John J. Winkler, eds. and trans. 1995. *Ancient Greek Novels: The Fragments.* Princeton: Princeton University Press.

Stevens, Anthony. 1997. *Private Myths: Dreams and Dreaming.* Cambridge: Harvard University Press.

Stock, Brian. 1994. "The Self and Literary Experience in Late Antiquity and the Middle Ages." *New Literary History* 25:839–52.

Strömberg, R. 1961. "Die Bellerophontes-Erzählung in der *Illias,*" *Classica et Mediaevalia* 22:1–15.

Strzelecki, W. 1964. *Cn. Naevii Belli Punici Carmen.* Leipzig: Teubner.

Sullivan, J. P. (trans.) 1986. *Petronius: Satyricon; Seneca: Apocolocyntosis.* Penguin Books: Harmondsworth.

Sultan, Nancy. 1999. *Exile and the Poetics of Loss in the Greek Tradition.* Lanham: Rowan and Littlefield.

Summers, Walter C. 1952. *Selected Letters of Seneca.* London: Macmillan.

Svenbro, Jesper. 1993. *Phrasikleia: An Anthropology of Reading in Ancient Greece.* Trans. J. Lord. Ithaca: Cornell University Press.

Swain, Simon. 1996. *Hellenism and Empire: Language, Classicism, and Power in the Greek World, A.D. 50–250.* Oxford: Clarendon Press.

Syed, Yasmin. 1997. "Creating Roman Identity: Subjectivity and Self-Fashioning in Roman Literature, the 1995 Berkeley Conference." *Classical Antiquity* 16, no. 1:5–7.

Tan, E. S. 1977. "The Presentation of Affective Symptoms in Non-western Countries." In *Handbook of Studies on Depression,* ed. G. D. Burrows, 121–33. Amsterdam: Excepta Medica.

Tarrant, R. J., ed. 1985. *Seneca's "Thyestes."* American Philological Association Textbook Series. Atlanta: Scholars Press.

Tate, J. 1937. "Tragedy and the Black Bile." *Hermathena* 45:1–25.

Tatz, Colin. 1997. "Immortality and Black Youth Suicide." *Sydney Morning Herald,* December 20, 27.

Taylor, Charles. 1992. *Sources of the Self: The Making of the Modern Identity.* Reprint, Cambridge: Cambridge University Press.

Taylor, Steve. 1982. *Durkheim and the Study of Suicide.* London and Basingstoke: Macmillan.

Temkin, Owsei. 1971. *The Falling Sickness: A History of Epilepsy from the Greeks to the Beginnings of Modern Neurology.* 2d ed. Baltimore and London: Johns Hopkins University Press.

Temkin, Owsei. 1973. *Galenism: Rise and Decline of a Medical Philosophy.* Ithaca: Cornell University Press.

Thalmann, W. G. 1984. *Conventions of Form and Thought in Early Greek Epic Poetry.* Baltimore: Johns Hopkins University Press.

Theodoru, Z. 1993. "Subject to Emotion: Exploring Madness in *Orestes.*" *Classical Quarterly* 43:32–46.

Thiher, Allen. 1999. *Revels in Madness: Insanity in Medicine and Literature.* Ann Arbor: University of Michigan Press.

Thomas, Elizabeth Marshall. 1993. *The Hidden Life of Dogs.* Boston: Houghton Mifflin.

Thomsen, Marie-Louise. 1992. "The Evil Eye in Mesopotamia." *Journal of Near Eastern Studies* 51:19–32.

Toner, J. P. 1995. *Leisure and Ancient Rome*. Cambridge: Polity.

Toohey, Peter. 1988. "Some Ancient Notions of Boredom." *Illinois Classical Studies* 13: 151–64.

Toohey, Peter. 1990a. "Acedia in Late Classical Antiquity." *Illinois Classical Studies* 15: 339–52.

Toohey, Peter. 1990b. "Some Ancient Histories of Literary Melancholia." *Illinois Classical Studies* 15:143–63.

Toohey, Peter. 1992a. "Acedia and Eros in Apollonius Rhodius (*Arg.* 3.260–299)." *Glotta* 70:114–22.

Toohey, Peter. 1992b. "Love, Lovesickness, and Melancholy." *Illinois Classical Studies* 17, 265–86.

Toohey, Peter. 1992c. *Reading Epic: An Introduction to the Ancient Narratives*. London and New York: Routledge.

Toohey, Peter. 1994. "Epic and Rhetoric (Speech-making and Persuasion in Homer and Apollonius)", in *Persuasion: Greek Oratory and Rhetoric in Action*, ed. Ian Worthington. London and New York: Routledge.

Toohey, Peter. 1996. *Epic Lessons: An Introduction to Ancient Didactic Poetry*. London and New York: Routledge.

Toohey, Peter. 1997a. "Eros and Eloquence: Modes of Amatory Persuasion in Ovid's *Ars Amatoria*." In *Roman Eloquence: Roman Rhetoric in Society and Literature*, ed. William Dominik, 198–211. London and New York: Routledge.

Toohey, Peter. 1997b. Review of *Da Lucrezio a Persio: Saggi, studi, note*, by Antonio La Penna. *Bryn Mawr Classical Review* 97.2.28.

Toohey, Peter. 1997c. "Trimalchio's Constipation: Periodizing Madness, Eros, and Time." In Golden and Toohey 1997, 50–65.

Toohey, Peter. 1999a. "Dangerous Ways to Fall in Love: Chariton 1.1.5–10 and 6.9.4." *Maia* 50:259–75.

Toohey, Peter. 1999b. "Monsieur Dadas' Mad, Mad World." *Sydney Morning Herald*, November 6, Spectrum section, 4.

Treggiari, Susan. 1991. *Roman Marriage: Iusti Coniugales from the Time of Cicero to the Time of Ulpian*. Oxford: Clarendon Press.

Trueman, Anne. 2002. "Smile—Depression Good for Older Women." *Calgary Herald*, May 2, A7.

Trypanis, C. A. 1989. *Callimachus, "Aetia," "Iambi," "Hecale," and Other Fragments*. Reprint, Cambridge: Harvard University Press.

Ullmann, Manfred. 1978. *Islamic Medicine*. Trans. Jean Watt. Islamic Surveys 11. Edinburgh: Edinburgh University Press.

Usener, H. ed. 1966. *Epicurea*. Reprint, Stuttgart: Teubner.

Vallance, J. T. 1990. *The Lost Theory of Asclepiades of Bithynia*. Oxford: Clarendon Press.

Van der Eijk, Ph. J. 1990. "Aristoteles über Melancholie." *Mnemosyne* 41:33–72.

Van Hoof, Anton J. L. 1990. *From Autothanasia to Suicide: Self-Killing in Classical Antiquity*. London and New York: Routledge.

Van Groningen, B. A. 1960. *La composition lettéraire archaïque grecque*. 2d ed. Amsterdam: N. V. Noord-Hollandsche Uitgevers Maatschappij.

Veith, Ilza. 1965. *Hysteria: The History of a Disease*. Chicago: University of Chicago Press.

Vessereau, J., and F. Préchac, eds. 1961. *Rutilius Namatianus: Sur Son Retour.* 2d ed. Paris: "Les Belles Lettres."

Veyne, Paul. 1978. "La famille et l'amour sous le haut-empire romain." *Annales: Économies, sociétés, civilisations* 33:35–63.

Veyne, Paul. 1987. "The Roman Empire." In *A History of Private Life,* vol. 1, *From Pagan Rome to Byzantium,* ed. Philippe Ariès and George Duby and trans. Arthur Goldhammer. Cambridge: Harvard University Press.

Veyne, Paul. 1988. *Roman Erotic Elegy: Love, Poetry, and the West.* Trans. David Pellauer. Chicago: University of Chicago Press.

Veyne, Paul, F. Lissarrague, and F. Frontisi-Ducroux, eds. 1998. *Les mystères du gynécée.* Paris: Gallimard.

Vian, Francis. 1963. *Quintus de Smyrne: La Suite d'Homere, tome I, livres I–IV.* Paris: "Les Belles Lettres."

Vian, Francis. 1976. *Nonnos de Panopolis: Les Dionysiaques, tome I, chants I–II.* Paris: "Les Belles Lettres."

Vinge, Louise. 1967. *The Narcissus Theme in Western European Literature up to the Early Nineteenth Century.* Lund: Gleerups.

Volpilhac, P., ed. and trans. 1975. *Nemesien: Oeuvres.* Paris: "Les Belles Lettres."

Wack, Mary Frances. 1990. *Lovesickness in the Middle Ages: The "Viaticum" and Its Commentaries.* Philadelphia: University of Pennsylvania Press.

Waiblinger, F. P. 1977. *Senecas Naturales Quaestiones: Griechische Wissenschaft und römische Form.* Zetemata 70. Munich: Beck.

Walbank, F. W. 1957. *A Historical Commentary on Polybius.* Vol. 1. Oxford: Clarendon Press.

Wallace-Hadrill, Andrew. 1987. "Time for Augustus," in Michael Whitby, Philip Hardie, and Mary Whitby, *Homo Viator: Critical Essays for John Bramble.* Bristol: Bristol University Press.

Walsh, G. B. 1988. Review of Carson 1986. *Classical Philology* 83:301–5.

Walsh, P. G. 1961. *Livy: His Historical Aims and Methods.* Cambridge: Cambridge University Press.

Walters, Jonathan. 1998. "Making a Spectacle: Deviant Men, Invective, and Pleasure." *Arethusa* 31:355–67.

Walz, M. 1950. *Sénèque: Dialogues IV.* Paris: "Les Belles Lettres."

Warmington, E. H., ed. and trans. 1935. *Remains of Old Latin: Ennius and Caecilius.* Vol. 1. Loeb Classical Library. London: William Heinemann.

Waszink, Jan Hendrik. 1972. "Zum Anfangsstadium der römischen Literatur." *Aufstieg und Niedergang der Römischen Welt* 1, no. 2:869–927.

Watson, Patricia. 1982. "Ovid and *Cultus: Ars Amatoria* 3.113–28." *Transactions of the American Philological Association* 112:237–44.

Waugh, Evelyn. 1983. *The Essays, Articles, and Reviews of Evelyn Waugh.* Ed. D. Gallagher. London: Methuen.

Wehrli, F. 1954. *Die Schule des Aristoteles II: Aristoxenos.* Basel: Schwabe.

Wemelsfelder, F. 1985. "Animal Boredom: Is a Scientific Study of the Subjective Experiences of Animals Possible?" In *Advances in Animal Welfare Science, 1984,* ed. M. W. Fox and L. D. Mickley, 115–54. Boston: Martinus Nijhoff.

Wemelsfelder, F. 1989. "Boredom and Laboratory Animal Welfare." In *The Experimental Animal in Biomedical Research*, ed. B. E. Rollin, 243–72. Boca Raton: CRC Press.

Wenzel, S. 1967. *The Sin of Sloth: Acedia in Medieval Thought and Literature*. Chapel Hill: University of North Carolina Press.

Westra, Haijo. 2001. "Individuality, Originality, and the Literary Criticism of Medieval Latin Texts." In *Poetry and Philosophy in the Middle Ages: A Festschrift for Peter Dronke*, ed. John Marenbon, 281–92. Leiden: Brill.

Whitman, C. H. 1958. *Homer and the Heroic Tradition*. Cambridge: Harvard University Press.

Wilamowitz-Moellendorff, Ulrich von. 1959. *Euripides Herakles*. 2d ed. Berlin: Akademie-Verlag.

Wiles, David. 1997. *Tragedy in Athens: Performance Space and Theatrical Meaning*. Cambridge: Cambridge University Press.

Wilkinson, L. P. 1955. *Ovid Recalled*. Cambridge: Cambridge University Press.

Willcock, M. M. 1976. *A Companion to the "Iliad."* Chicago: University of Chicago Press.

Williams, Gordon. 1978. *Change and Decline: Roman Literature in the Early Empire*. Berkeley: University of California Press.

Williams, Heather J., ed. 1986. *The "Eclogues" and "Cynegetica" of Nemesianus*. Leiden: Brill.

Wills, G. 1967. "Sappho 31 and Catullus 51." *Greek, Roman, and Byzantine Studies* 8, 167–87.

Winkler, John J. 1990. *The Constraints of Desire: The Anthropology of Sex and Gender in Ancient Greece*. New York: Routledge.

Winnington-Ingram, R. P. 1980. *Sophocles: An Interpretation*. Cambridge: Cambridge University Press.

Worman, Nancy. 2000. "Infection in the Sentence: The Discourse of Disease in Sophocles' *Ajax*." Arethusa 31: 1–36.

Worthington, Ian, ed. 1994. *Persuasion: Greek Rhetoric in Action*. London and New York: Routledge.

Yatromanolakis, Y. 1988. "*Baskanos eros:* Love and the Evil-Eye in Heliodorus' *Aethiopica*." In *The Greek Novel, A.D. 1–1985*, ed. R. Beaton, 194–204. London: Croom Helm.

Yoshitake, S. 1994. "Disgrace, Grief, and Other Ills: Herakles' Rejection of Suicide." *Journal of Hellenic Studies* 114:135–53.

Zanker, G. 1979. "The Love Theme in Apollonius Rhodius." *Wiener Studien*, n.s., 13:52–75.

Zanker, Paul. 1988. *The Power of Images in the Age of Augustus*. Trans. H. A. Shapiro. Ann Arbor: University of Michigan Press.

Zinn, Christopher. 1995. "Death Strikes Youngsters from Islands of Paradise." *Sydney Morning Herald*, September 30, 9.

Index